1 MONTH OF
FREE
READING

at

www.ForgottenBooks.com

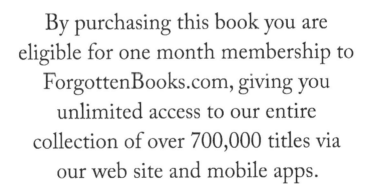

By purchasing this book you are eligible for one month membership to ForgottenBooks.com, giving you unlimited access to our entire collection of over 700,000 titles via our web site and mobile apps.

To claim your free month visit:

www.forgottenbooks.com/free581176

ISBN 978-0-484-61855-7
PIBN 10581176

ANNUAL REPORT

AND

PROCEEDINGS

OF THE

𝕭elfast 𝕹aturalists' 𝕱ield 𝕮lub,

FOR THE

Year ending 31st March, 1888. – 92

(TWENTY-FIFTH YEAR.)

SERIES II.   VOLUME III.   PART I.

𝕭elfast:
PRINTED FOR THE CLUB,
BY ALEXANDER MAYNE & BOYD, CORPORATION STREET,
PRINTERS TO QUEEN'S COLLEGE, BELFAST.

1888.

4.7.55

1 Rev. Canon Grainger. A.M. D.D. M.R.I.A., F.R.G.S.I.- 6 William Gray. M.R.I.A. 1879-81.
2 George C. Hyndman. 1864-65. 1863-64-85-87. 7 Robert Young. 1881- 82.-
3 Prof. Jas. Thompson. A.M.L.L.D. F.R.S. 1865-73. 8 Lt Genl. Smythe. F.R.S. M.R.I.A. 1882-8:
4 John Anderson. J.P. F.G.S. 1873-74. 9 Wm. H. Patterson. M.R.I.A. 1883-85.
5 Rev. Canon Mac Ilwaine. D.D. M.R.I.A. 1874-79. 10 Hugh Robinson. M.R.I.A. 1887.

·PRESIDENTS·1863·1888·

REPORT

OF THE

BELFAST NATURALISTS' FIELD CLUB,

FOR THE

Year ending 31st, March, 1888.

OUR Committee have pleasure in presenting their twenty-fifth Annual Report, and in testifying to the continued prosperity of the Club. The year which now closes compares favourably with any in its past history, whether we look at it in reference to the work done by its members, the interest which they evince in its operations, or in its financial position.

The Summer programme was, with some changes in the order of the Excursions, carried out, with the exception of that to Belvoir Park, which had from several reasons to be abandoned, the attendance on the various occasions being fully up to that of former years.

The following are the places visited :—

1. Glenarm, by the Hill Road ...   .   28th May.
2. Ardmillan and West Shore of Strangford Lough ...   25th June.

3. Portaferry and Strangford   ...   .   19th and 20th July.
4. Shane's Castle and adjoining Shores of Lough Neagh   27th August.
5. Tullamore Park for a Fungus Foray   ...   ...   17th September.

The winter Session was opened by an address from the President, Mr. Hugh Robinson, M.R.I.A., in which he gave an able review of the progress of the agencies for the Promotion of Natural Science in Belfast. The history of the Club, especially the interesting facts connected with its formation, were fully given, and your Committee have pleasure in stating that the address will be given in full in your proceedings.

The following are the communications brought forward during the Winter Session :—

1887.

15th Nov.   { Presidential Address, "A Review of the Progress of Natural Science in Belfast," by Mr. Hugh Robinson, M.R.I.A.

20th Dec.   { "On the Traps and Basalts of the Isle of Mull, and their relation to those of Antrim," by J. Starkie Gardner, Esq., F.G.S., F.L.S., of London.

„   { "Notes on Ancient Canoes recently found in Lough Mourne," by Mr. F. W. Lockwood.

1888.

24th Jan.   { "Marks of Ownership in Books," by Mr. Robert Day, F.S.A., M.R.I.A., of Cork.

28th Feb.   { "Some Notes on the Early Belfast Press, and its productions from 1700 to 1800." by Mr. R. M. Young, B.A.

„   { "Variations observed in the Growth of Mistletoe," by Mr. W. H. Phillips.

17th April.   { "Notes on Subjects brought before the late Meeting of the British Association," by Mr. Wm. Gray, M.R.I.A.

„   { "Reference to the Diatomaceous Deposits at Lough Mourne and in the Mourne Mountains," by Messrs. Wm. A. Firth, and Wm. Swanston, F.G.S.

The meetings at which the above communications were read were well attended, and the subjects are of much local interest. The communication of Mr. Gardner, in the opinion of your Committee, deserves special notice, as it brings the literature bearing on important local geological questions up to the latest date.

Your Committee, in view of the fact that the Club having now completed the first quarter Century of its existence, considered they would be acting in accordance with the wishes of the members if they would endeavour to mark the event in some special manner. After consideration it was decided to hold a Conversazione on a date as near as possible to that on which the inaugural meeting of the Club was held. The scheme was accordingly carried out on 27th March, and the Conversazione then held was pronounced a complete success, and your Committee have reason to believe that the members generally were highly gratified with the arrangements.

The Annual Report and Proceedings for the past year are now in the hands of the members, and your Committee have pleasure in directing attention to the valuable contribution by Mr. R. Ll. Praeger, B.A., B.E., which appears in it as an appendix, forming as it does an important addition to our knowledge of the Estuarine Clays and their associated beds.

Your Committee take this opportunity of again thanking Lancelot Turtle, Esq., J.P., for the very comprehensive meteorological summary and monthly weather notes with which your proceedings are again enriched, and they desire to express their appreciation of Mr. Turtle's kindness in continuing to favour the Club with his statistics.

Your Committee also avail themselves of this opportunity of thanking those noblemen and gentlemen who favoured the Club on their Excursions, and they would especially mention the kindness of Sir Edward Harland for liberty to enter Glenarm Park; to J. Warnock, Esq , and Mrs. Warnock, for their hospitality and kindness on the Excursion to Portaferry and Strangford; to Lord O'Neill, for liberty to visit the grounds of Shane's Castle ; and to the Earl of Roden, Tolly-more, for the privilege of holding the Fungus Foray in Tolly-more Park.

The Committee have pleasure in announcing that the Flora of North-East of Ireland is now almost through the Press, and will be ready for issue in a few weeks. This much needed work they are confident will supply the fullest and most accurate account of our native vegetation, and it is anticipated that it will compare favourably with similar works issued elsewhere, and will prove a stimulus to further research by local Naturalists.

Your Committee again beg to thank those kindred societies and public bodies who continue to exchange Proceedings or to present their publications to the Club. A full list of these contributions will be embodied in your Proceedings.

The following collections were submitted in competition for the Club's Prizes :—

24 microscopic slides, in competition for Prize 20, by Mr. W. A. Firth.

24 microscopic slides, in competition for Prize 21, by Mr. W. A. Firth.

24 microscopic slides, in competition for Prize 20, by Rev. John Andrew.

24 microscopic slides, in competition for Prize 21, by Rev. John Andrew.

24 microscopic slides, in competition for Prize 21, by Mr. D. M'Kee.

12 photographs, in competition for Prize 23, by Mr. Geo. Donaldson.

The following are the awards of the judges appointed to examine the above collections and report upon them.

We have carefully examined the microscopic preparations submitted in competition for Prizes 20 and 21, including 120 slides, and we have great pleasure in stating that the superior merit of each competitor's work rendered the competition very keen. We consider that Mr. Firth merits the Prize in each case ; and we recommend that a Second Prize (in No. 20) be awarded to Rev. J. Andrew ; and we highly commend the set of slides submitted by Mr. M'Kee.

W. GRAY.

J. WRIGHT.

PRIZE XXIII.—We have examined the photographs sent in by Mr. George Donaldson, and while regretting that there is no competition in this department, we have no hesitation in pronouncing the photos in every way in accordance with the conditions, and admirably adapted for the Club's albums, and have much pleasure in awarding the Prize,

WM. SWANSTON.

S. A. STEWART.

The Belfast Naturalists' Field Club in Account with the Treasurer

For the Year ending 31st March, 1888.

Dr.					Cr.			
To Balance from 1886-7	£37	17	2	By Messrs. Mayne and Boyd, Printing Annual Proceedings	£18	15	9
,, Subscriptions—238, less 15 in advance ..	55	15	0	,, Marcus Ward and Co., Zinco Blocks	3	7	6
,, Systematic Lists sold	2	7	0	,, H. Robinson, Insurance	0	11	6
,, Guides sold	0	14	6	,, *Northern Whig*, Printing	7	6	6
,, Proceedings	0	14	0	,, Delivery of Circulars	1	10	0
,, Gain on Excursions	0	8	9	,, Postages	5	0	2
,, Conversazione Tickets	5	12	0	,, Rent of Lecture Hall	5	5	0
				,, W. Darragh	3	3	0
				,, Robinson, Bros., Stationery	1	10	6
				,, Erection of Dromore Old Cross, Donation ..	1	0	0
				,, Prizes	1	15	0
				,, Cost of Conversazione	9	19	7
				,, Balance on hands	44	3	11
	£103	8	5		£103	8	5

S. A. STEWART, *Treasurer.*

WILLIAM SWANSTON, *Hon. Secretary.*

Audited and found correct.

SUMMER SESSION.

— ✠ —

The following Excursions were made during the Summer Session

On 28th May, to

GLENARM, BY THE HILL ROAD.

The first excursion of the summer season was to Glenarm, the route proposed being by the hill road and down through the glens. A numerous party left Belfast by the 8-50 train for Larne, where they were joined by a strong contingent, and they then proceeded in Mr. M'Neill's well-appointed brakes along the coast road as far as Cairncastle, the foam-capped waves of the North Channel, as they rolled before a brisk northeast breeze, or dashed in clouds of spray over the rocks, giving life and colour to the scene.

The rugged basaltic columns of Ballygally Head, and the chalk cliffs on either side, glittering in the morning sun have seldom looked finer. Several members of the Amateur Photographic Society had joined the excursion, and when a halt was called at the tiny but picturesque ruin of Cairncastle, perched amongst the waves on a rock just outside the headland, a whole battery of cameras were focussed upon it, and probably it was never so thoroughly "taken" in its history before. This and

Ballygally Castle, close by, both get in local tradition the name
of " O'Halloran's Castle ;' but this ruin on the rock has unquestionably the true claim to have been the stronghold of that
outlawed chief. Ballygally Castle, built by the Shaws in the
Scottish baronial style in 1625, and a few years ago so picturesque, has now, by the effects of rough cast, tarred felt, and
whitewash, lost most of its beauty, and except for a bit of carved
stone on door and gable here and there, is hardly now worth
the brush of the artist or the photographers camera. Leaving the
sea, the party here began to ascend the road towards the gaps between the hills, passing on their way the curious little old " Ma-
sonic Hall" of Cairncastle, which bears date 1813. Close adjoining
is the old Unitarian Meeting-house, reported to be about the
oldest Presbyterian church in Antrim ; the sundial on the front
is said to have had the original date of 1667, and also the date
of restoration, 1779. At the summit of the " new cut," between
the hills, a halt was made, and the site of some old dwellings
was examined. There are three earthworks close together,
consisting of rampart and ditch, being, in fact, true earthen
forts in miniature. The cairn of stones, known as the "headless
cross," was not visited, but a run was made over the heather
for the " priests' grave.' This is a small, square boulder, on
on which are are cut two incised crosses of an apparently ancient
type, but the stronger presumption is that this is a " mass stone,"
one of the rude altars consecrated by the Catholic clergy for use
during the time of the proscription. The scene of worship
upon the wild hillside, with the curlew and the lapwing wheeling
overhead, and the sentinels posted round to give warning of
hostile intrusion, reminds one of many scenes in the history
of the Covenanters, and affords another to the many previous
instances that opposites often meet. A few yards off are the
remains of a " giant's grave." After descending the inland slope
of the hills as far as the old Park Mill and Bridge, the bulk of
of the party left the conveyances, and carried out the programme
by following on foot the lovely glens down which flow the
Glenarm and Linford Waters, access to which, through the
kindness of Sir E. Harland, the present lessee of Glenarm

Castle, had been freely given.   The path, in many places barely discernible, descends through thickets of hazel, alder, and dwarf oak, most of them of great age, with stems and branches gnarled and twisted into a thousand fantastic forms, and now skirts the deep trout pools, now follows the brow of some miniature cliff, and now plunges through an almost impenetrable thicket.   Every here and there is a beautiful cascade, lighting up with its silver spray some dark pool, the angler's favourite resort.

In other places the ground is a mass of blue, and the air thick with the scent of wild hyacinth.   The more common local ferns uncurl their fronds everywhere, whilst some of the rarer, such as *Cystopteris fragilis*, are to be found by those who seek for them.   Too much time had been lost early in the day, and the majority of the party had as much as they could do to follow the straightest course down the glen, but half a dozen of the more active, luckily with a couple of cameras amongst them, made a dash up the sister stream to the deep, round pool, according to local repute fathomless, known as the "Bull's Eye," into which plunges one of the finest waterfalls of the country. Here, whilst two strong swimmers disported themselves in its eddies, the others were engaged with camera and pencil in snatching a hasty record of this woodland gem.

As was to be expected, these glens proved of great interest to the botanists of the party.   On the walls of Park Mill bridge was abundance of the scaly fern, *Ceterach officinarum*, and maiden hair spleenwort, *Asplenium trichomanes*.   Further down the glen, besides the masses of wild hyacinth, the marshy spots were blazing with the large yellow flowers of the marsh marigold, or Mayflower, to give it its local name.   The bird cherry, *Prunus padus*, one of our handsomest native shrubs, was here in abundance, in full blossom, lighting up the woods with its clusters of white blossoms.   By the stream grew the water avens, *Geum rivale*, and the valerian, *Valeriana officinalis*, while among the hazel thickets flourished that curious parasitic plant, the toothwort, *Iathræa squamaria*.   Numerous specimens were obtained of the very rare fungus, *Morchella esculenta*, which was previously found here by Rev. Jas. Hall, Glenarm, and Mr. R. Lloyd Praeger, a member of the club, being the first record of the occurrence of this species in Ireland. In England and on the Continent this species, better known as the Morell, is highly esteemed as a delicacy, but though numerous fine examples rewarded the search of the members, it did not form part of the refreshment of which the party afterwards partook at Glenarm. Here the whole party once more assembled, and after a hurried tea at the Antrim Arms, and a brief meeting for the election of new members, started by the coast road on their homeward route. In rounding the cliffs of the bay many house martins were observed, which have exchanged their usual resort of man's hospitable eave for what must have been their natural habitat before his advent—the under side of the projecting ledges of rock.

Passing the " madman's window " on the one side, with its pretty peephole out over the blue green sea, and the picturesque masses of landslip in the Deerpark on the other, the " haunted house," and the various other familiar sights of the coast drive were one by one noted in their turn, till Chaine's railed-in grave on the height over the harbour came in view, and the base of the round tower now being erected to his memory upon the rocks at its foot was seen. Entering Larne, dwelling houses just built or building give evidence of the rapidly increasing popularity of the town as a summer resort, and hurrying through its narrow streets the station was gained just five minutes before the train steamed up from the harbour.

On 25th June, to

ARDMILLAN, AND SHORES OF STRANGFORD LOUGH

The second excursion for the present summer was to Ardmillan and adjoining shore of Strangford Lough. Starting on vehicles from the Ulster Hall, at ten o'clock, the road is taken *via* Comber. It is soon apparent that the day promises to be one of the hottest of the very hot season, and that the dust caused by the long-continued absence of rain would deprive the journey of much of its pleasure. Some relief is gained when the main road is left ; choice bits of scenery also open up at every turn of the road, and from the summits of the many hills over which the road passes. Ardmillan has not a prosperous air about it. The contrast between its sombre, and rather dilapi-dated buildings, and the painfully white and trim farmsteads is very striking. Its subdued tints, however, prove an attraction to the photographers in the party, and soon half a dozen cameras are at work on it, much to the astonishment of the inhabitants. A further short drive and the lough shore opposite Scatrick Castle is reached. This massive square keep stands close to the water's edge, and commands a rude causeway which connects the Scatrick Island with the mainland. It, like all the other County Down castles, has played some part in history. It is recorded in " The Four Masters " that in 1470 a great army was led by The O'Neill into Clannaboy to assist MacQuillan. O'Neill on this occasion made a prisoner of Art, son of Donnell Call O'Neill, and took the castle of Sgath Deirg (Scatrick), which was delivered into the keeping of MacQuillan. The archæologists and photographers having done the ruin, which, with its shattered walls reflected in the calm waters, and with distant stretches of sea and rounded hills, formed a pretty picture, the next move is for Mahee Island, distant about a quarter of a mile by sea. Mahee Island, like Scatrick, is joined to the mainland by a causeway ; but this time boats are taken to save the longer journey by road, the causeway being at the opposite end of the island. The crossing of the narrow channel is most enjoyable. The clear quick running water of the incoming tide and the lovely views opened out being much admired. Approaching the island the visitor sees little to distinguish it trom any other of the many islands with which the west coast of Strangford is studded. Its gently-swelling hillocks are cultivated or in pasture. Its greatest elevation— about sixty feet—is however surmounted by a small ivy-mantled ruin. The base of one of the mysterious round towers and several more or less concentric grassy mounds may be seen encircling the summit of the hill. These indicate foundations of walls apparently long since removed. To the southeast of the ruined tower, traces of an oblong foundation are visible. These are supposed to be the remains of a Christian church, whose early history runs back to the days of St. Patrick. From a valuable paper, dated 1845, by the Rev. William Reeves—now the Lord Bishop of the diocese—we learn that the ancient name of the church was Nendrum, or the church of Inis Mochoi, and that John De Courcey, shortly after his invasion of Ireland in 1172, endowed it with certain lands, and by a charter attached it to the Monastery of St. Bees in Cumberland. In later times it seems to have been demolished, and its very site became a matter of doubt and conjecture. On the island there is also a ruined castle like that of Scatrick, guarding the connecting causeway. Recrossing the channel and mounting the vehicles, the return journey was made by the shore road, passing on the way the church of Tullynakill, close to its ancient graveyard and the ivy-clad walls of the older edifice. A short halt was made at Castle Espie. The now silent works, which were more than once visited by the Club when they were in full operation, testify to the amount of business that was done here. The magnificent range of kilns on the Hoffman plan, the pottery sheds, the vast quarry of rich salmon-coloured carboniferous limestone, now with about 100 feet of water in it, with the powerful engine and pumping gear, represent a vast amount of idle capital. The botany and geology of the excursion was nil, the excessive drought having scorched the vegetation, and it is also causing serious anxiety to the farming community as well as putting them already to vast trouble in conveying water, in many cases long distances, for the use of stock, &c.

PORTAFERRY AND STRANGFORD.

The third excursion of the present season was to Strangford and Portaferry. Leaving Downpatrick on cars, upon the arrival of the 10-35 train from Belfast, the party, under the guidance of the Rev. David Gordon, drove along the road skirting the Quoile. At high water the beautifully-wooded islands of this part give it a character not unlike Windermere. A halt was made at the ancient castle on the Quoile, a building of some interest which is rapidly becoming dilapidated. It is not of great size, and in its construction bears considerable resemblance to the small castle known as Castleward, and appears to be rather later in date than the larger castles of Audley's and Kilclief. It is a plain square building, having the upper floor supported on two barrel vaults, yet entire. The entrance is near one corner, and facing it on the inside is a still perfect pointed arch, from which the narrow stairs lead up in a straight flight in the thickness of the wall. It will be a great pity if this building be allowed to fall for want of a little timely care. The next place visited was the little church of Raholp, originally Rath-Colpa. This is undoubtedly one of the most ancient in the country, and may well be the original church built by St. Tassach, whom the legends report as having administered the Holy Communion to St. Patrick in his last moments. The plan of this oblong cell, for it is nothing more, is peculiar, as the door appears to have been in the south wall instead of the west gable, which is usually the case. The form of the door is, however, lost, but the east window, deeply splayed, about ten inches wide outside, and covered with a large flag on lintel, still remains, but in a critical condition. The stones of this church are laid in yellow clay instead of mortar, which may be either a transition from the dry stone walling of the oldest buildings to lime mortar, or may be a local peculiarity merely. The church also differs slightly from some of the other very early churches in having no projecting buttresses or pilasters on one or both gables. This feature is,

however, by no means universal. So long ago as 1622 ".the
Capella de Rachalpe" was returned by the Bishop of Down as
"ruynous." The church stands on a raised platform, which
may be partly of rock, the terrace of which is faced with a
number of large upright stones on the south side. In England
a church of this age would be valued as an antiquarian treasure,
and sacredly guarded. Ought it not here to be placed under
the care of the Board of Works?

From Raholp the road leads by a beautiful avenue of fine
trees to the lofty castle of Walshestown, which stands in the
grounds of R. Craig-Laurie, Esq., J.P., through whose kindness
the Club paid it a visit. Swathed in ivy from base to summit,
there is hardly a more picturesque castle ruin in the country—
if, indeed, it deserves this title—for it is in excellent order and
preservation. The view from the top, across Strangford
Lough, is particularly striking. A short distance farther
brought the party to Castleward demesne. Owing to the
recent sad affliction in Lord Bangor's family they were unable
to visit Castleward House, but were most courteously conducted
to the various spots of beauty and interest in the demesne. To
mention all in detail would be impossible ; but the wonderful
avenue of yew trees demands a word. Ranged in such perfect
order and symmetry, with their branches interlacing above,
the resemblance to a double-aisled cathedral is literally perfect,
and the effect is grand and solemn in the extreme. Had
Wordsworth been aware of them he would surely have placed
them on record, side by side, as equally worthy of note as
"those fraternal four of Borrowdale" of which he sings in
some of his noblest and most famous lines. A pair of fine
pillar stones—one upright and one fallen—on a knoll amongst
some guarded old oaks should also be recorded. The two
most interesting features to the antiquarian are Castleward and
Audley's Castle. The former is much of the same type as the
one at the Quoile, before mentioned. Audley's Castle, seated
on a rocky knoll just where the channel opens into Strangford
Lough, occupies one of the most commanding sites in the
district. It appears to be of the fourteenth century, and was

long held by the Audley family, under the Earls of Kildare. In plan it is much like Kilclief, farther down the channel, both having two square towers attached to the main square keep, in one of which is a circular stone stair leading from the door to the upper story. Between these towers a wide arch is thrown, with orifices behind it to command the entrance. It is needless to state that it is kept in excellent order by the present noble proprietor. By a beautiful drive along the shores of the various inlets, where the tide was now fast ebbing, Strangford was reached. Before crossing the ferry, by the kindness of Lord de Ros, Oldcourt was visited, which, though not of great interest, abounds in lovely views of lake and mountain. Oldcourt Chapel, which stands in the demesne, and forms the parish church of Strangford, was built, as an inscription testifies, by George, 16th Earl of Kildare, by his agent, Valentine Payne, A.D. 1629. A rapid sail across the channel brought the party to Portaferry, where a comfortable tea at M'Causland's Hotel soon put them in fresh readiness for work. A visit was first paid to the graveyard and ivy-covered bell turret that marks the site of Templecranny Church, which, it is presumed, dates from before the Reformation. Bishop Echlin, who lived at Thomastown, and died at Ardquin in 1633, is stated to be buried here. The church was appropriated by the Presbyterians in 1642, the Rev. John Drysdale, who was ordained as their first minister, suffered considerable persecution, being taken prisoner by Colonel Venables and the Cromwellians in 1650, and subsequently endured much hardship from the prelatical party in Charles II.'s reign. By kind permission of General Nugent the evening was terminated by a ramble through his delightful grounds, the sole regret being that the gathering dusk prevented full enjoyment of their beauties.

An early start was made next morning, the party proceeding on cars down the side of the channel, visiting on the way Bankmore and the bit of ruin known as " Folly Castle," from which a fine view is had of the channel, with " the routing wheel " and other whirlpools and eddies of the current, which here often runs six or seven knots an hour. A few minutes were

spent in a quarry in search of graptolites, but with only medium
success, and the party then proceeded along the scarp of a fine
raised beach, to near Ballyquintin Point, a spot very seldom,
indeed, visited by tourists. Great notice was taken of the fine
crops of wheat and other grain with which this district abounds,
and which apparently had not suffered much harm from the
recent drought. A halt was next called at the site, close to the
beach, of Templecowey old church, of which the foundation
only remains. On the east side of the graveyard were three
holy wells—the washing well, the eye well, and the drinking
well. The latter only is now noticeable, which still runs on—a
stream of deliciously cold water, acceptable after some hours of
sun and wind to all the party. On a broad rock on the margin
of the sea St. Cowey is stated by tradition to have spent most
of his time in prayer. Of course the marks of his knees are
still visible. The fort of Tara, on the highest summit of the
district, was next climbed to. · It is a very complete specimen,
with well-marked vallum and rampart ; the view from it in a
clear day is magnificent. There does not appear to be any
mention of the fort in the early records. This is not, by any
means, the only pre-Christian monument in the neighbourhood.
Not far below it is the stone circle of Keentagh. Of this eleven
stones are still to be seen forming a circle about 6oft. in
diameter. Doubtless some of the chieftians who dwelt at Tara,
or some of their battles, are here commemorated, but tradition
even is now silent. After a hasty glimpse of Quintin Castle,
a picturesque modern structure on the site of a relic of Sir John
Montgomery's, which was itself a relic of earlier times, a
hurried drive was made back through Portaferry to Ballywhite,
the hospitable residence of J. Warnock, Esq. Here a friendly
host and hostess entertained the party at lunch, at the conclusion of which a meeting was held, under the presidency of
the Rev. George Robinson, at which new members were
elected, and thanks were voted to Mr. and Mrs. Warnock and
others to whom much of the success of the excursion was due.
A climb was then made to the hill behind the house, where, as
the party gazed around upon the varied and extensive scene,

wonder was again and again expressed that visits were so rarely paid by the citizens of Belfast to these beautiful and interesting localities. Several places of interest down, at least conditionally, on the programme had to be omitted, such as Kilclief, Kirkistown, and the Abbacy, but it is hoped that in the next winter session some member will give to the club a paper on the antiquities of the district, which shall embrace all the subjects omitted perforce in this report. On the present occasion time was merciless, and many interesting themes had to be cut short to allow the party by hurried driving to reach, if it might be possible, Newtownards in time for the last train. The drive along the shore of the lough, with the sinking sun all ablaze in the waters, cannot now be dwelt on, but the memory of the two days about Strangford, Portaferry, and the Ards will long remain in the minds of some members of the Naturalists' Field Club. Perhaps the best testimony to their enjoyment is to be found in the fact that several of them elected to remain and see a little more of Portaferry and its vicinity before returning.

On 27th August, to

SHANE'S CASTLE AND SHORES OF LOUGH NEAGH.

The fourth excursion was to Shane's Castle. The morning being favourable a good number of members and their friends were conveyed to Antrim by rail, where their numbers were further augmented by the addition of several local members. Under the guidance of Rev. W. S. Smith, the party proceeded by road for a short distance, the extensive grounds were entered by a side gate, for which permission had been kindly granted. The first point touched was the mouth of the Six-mile River, a picturesque piece of water. The photographers of the party were soon busy with their cameras, and doubtless many pleasing pictures of the sedge-bordered margins of the stream were obtained. The archæologists meanwhile were

eagerly scanning the heaps of sand and gravel, the results of
dredging being actively carried on to deepen the channel.
Though several good stone weapons had been discovered by the
men engaged in the work, none of the members of the party
were rewarded in their search by anything more valuable than
a few rude flints, doubtfully of human origin. After some time
spent here, the way to the castle is taken by the shore of the
lough. The water being low a good stretch of sand was
exposed, and the walk here, or among the natural timber that
skirts the shores higher up, was very enjoyable, and to the
botanists most profitable. The castle being reached in scattered
sections, soon its subterranean chambers and other points of
interest are visited, the members subsequently re-assembling
under the shelter of the castle walls, when the business meeting
of the day is held. A number of the interesting plants known
to grow on the shores of Lough Neagh were found during the
day, but the flora of the lough is fairly well-known, and on the
present occasion no additional plants were secured. Those who
desire further information regarding the botanical features of
the district, should peruse the extremely interesting work, by
Rev. W. S. Smith, entitled " *Gossip about Lough Neagh*." In
this little book there is concentrated, and presented in small
compass, what is known of the Flora and Fauna, as well as the
physical features, and folk-lore relating to Britain's greatest
lake. While referring to Lough Neagh's flora, it may be
mentioned that on the shore close to Antrim, there are found
several plants, whose habitat is usually on the sea coast.
Geologists know that the sea, at no very remote time—
geologically speaking—filled Lough Neagh, and this is further
illustrated by the teachings of botanical science. The excursion
was considered a thoroughly satisfactory one, though the
photographers present, earnestly wished for less wind, to enable
them to prosecute their fascinating branch more satisfactorily
among the fine woodland subjects which present themselves at
almost every turn. After visiting the ancient graveyard
adjoining the castle, the party leisurely wended their way
through the grounds to Antrim, and were soon speeding homeward by rail, arriving in due time.

On 17th September, to

TOLLYMORE PARK FOR A FUNGUS FORAY.

The society concluded its summer session by a most successful excursion to Tollymore Park. About forty members left
by the County Down Railway, at 10-35 a.m., and on arrival at
the other terminus at Newcastle, they took cars to the gate of the
picturesque grounds of Bryansford, entrance to which had been
kindly granted to the club. The chief feature in the day's
programme was the examination of the ground for *Fungi*.
Before entering the gate the party was met by a fellow-member,
Rev. H. W. Lett, M.A., T.C.D., author of a valuable list
of the *Fungi* of the North of Ireland, recently published in the
club's proceedings. A meeting was called, and the day's
programme announced. A prize was offered for the best
collection of *Fungi* made during the day, collections to be
submitted before leaving the grounds. It was evident, however, that *Fungi* would not claim the attention of the entire
party, the presence of no less than eight cameras indicated that
the beauties of the woods and stream would be pretty well
done ; all, no matter what the special pursuit, were in high
anticipation, the weather being most favourable for outdoor work. On reaching the rocky stream course, the members
scattered in various directions in search of the rare or beautiful.
Many ferns were observed showing departures from the normal
forms; this was especially noticeable in the *Blechnum*, bifur-
cating, and other varieties being not uncommon ; one very fine
specimen showing serration on most of its fronds, was observed.
The season was too advanced for flowering plants, but the
search for *Fungi* was vigorously pursued, under the guidance
of Mr. Lett, into the dark and secluded parts of the wood,
while the brighter, picturesque pieces were sure to be ranged
by one or more cameras from various vantage points. Slowly
converging as the day advanced, the party met as arranged at
the Barbacan gate, where the collections were spread on the
grass, and the scrutiny of the species made. After careful

examination the judge awarded the prize to Mrs. Ferguson, whose collection numbered fifty-six species; other members followed with forty and thirty-seven respectively. These results, when compared with former forays, indicate an un-favourable season for the growth of these lowly plants ; possibly the excessively dry summer may in some measure be responsible for it. It is remarkable also that no species of unusual rarity had been observed, and as the woods had been frequently searched by Mr. Lett, previous to his completing his list, it is needless to say that nothing was added to it. The Secretary read a letter from a member—a prominent medical gentleman—requesting that any specimens of the large puff ball (*Lycoperdon giganteum*) that might be found would be reserved for him, as a former gift of a giant specimen, some two years past, had been instrumental in his hands of alleviating much suffering. It was regretted that this species was remarkable for its absence on the present foray, and it would be interesting to ascertain if this holds good this season in other localities.

The President (Mr. Hugh Robinson, M.R.I.A.), before the close of the meeting, drew attention to the fact that in March next the club will have completed the twenty-fifth year of its history, and he was happy to be able to say that several of the members who enjoyed the present excursion had also taken part in its initiatory meetings, and its first organised field meeting which was held in Islandmagee, in 1863.

The photographers having fired off their last plates, and having packed up, the road is taken at an easy pace for New-castle, and not the least enjoyable portion of the day's pro-gramme was spent round the well-provided tea tables in Lawrence's refreshment-rooms. Few places can boast of such suitable accommodation and hearty attendance as is there obtainable, and but one opinion was expressed—that with such varied natural attractions and such an establishment, and with perhaps a little acceleration of train service, Newcastle should take the foremost place in Ulster with health-seekers and holiday-makers. The train journey was relieved of part of its monotony by the exhibition by one of the members of a magnificent specimen of larva or caterpillar of *Bombyx cecropia*, a species of silk moth found in America and elsewhere. The species is easily reared, and it feeds on apple, willow, or hawthorn leaves. It spins a large cocoon, and the mature insect is one of the most handsome and largest of moths,

WINTER SESSION.

NOTE.—The authors of the various Papers, of which abstracts are here appended, are alone responsible for the views expressed in them.

OPENING ADDRESS.

THE twenty-fifth Winter Session of the Club was held in the Museum, on 15th November, when the President (Mr. Hugh Robinson, M.R.I.A.), gave the following opening address on the subject "A Review of the Progress of Natural Science in Belfast."

In considering what might be a suitable subject upon which to address you at the beginning of another Winter Session, it has occurred to me, that as our Club has now reached a special point in its existence, having almost attained to a quarter of a Century's career, and ere another Presidential Address will be delivered to you, the twenty-fifth anniversary of its establishment will be past and gone ; it may not be inappropriate to bring before you a short history of the origin and early progress of the Club. Seeing, as I do, before me several of its original members, I feel that to them at least such a subject will not be uninteresting, calling up, as it must do, pleasant recollections of early associations, and of difficulties overcome. To the younger members I hope the subject may have an equal interest, as to many of them the details of the formation of the Club, and the causes which led to its origin, are to a considerable extent unknown.

Before commencing to the subject proper, we may for a short time consider what had previously been done for the advancement of the study of Natural Science in Belfast. Prior to the present century we have, so far as I am aware, no records on the subject, nor can we consider from the extent of Belfast at that time, that much effort had been spent in that direction. We find, however, that the century was but young when a special effort was made, not only to advance the cause of ordinary education, but also to specially further the study of the various branches of Physical and Natural Science. I allude to the establishment of the Belfast Academical Institution in the year 1807. As many changes have taken place since its establishment, the circumstances of its origin are but little known to the present generation. From the published report of a Committee, submitted and adopted at a meeting of the friends of the intended Institution, held in the Exchange Rooms, on 22nd September, 1807, under the presidency of Edward May, jun., Esq., Sovereign of Belfast, it appears that the Institution was to combine not only a primary, or school department, and a higher or collegiate department, with, amongst others, Professors of Natural Philosophy, Chemistry, Botany, and Agriculture, but in addition (I quote from the report) " That the benefits of the College may be more extensively diffused, it is expedient, that in addition to the private lectures to be attended by the students, a public course of popular lectures shall be delivered on those subjects which are most conducive to the improvement of the Agriculture, Arts, and Manufactures of the country. A Library and Museum shall be attached to the College for the use of students and subscribers. The Museum shall be set apart for the reception and exhibition of Natural Curiosities, specimens of Fossils, Models of useful Instruments, Machines, Engines, and other articles of a similar nature."

In the subsequent deliberations of the Committee appointed
at the public meeting, we find that a more extensive staff of
Professors was spoken of, and a Chair of Irish Language and
Antiquities was considered requisite, while to that of Chemistry
the subject of Mineralogy was added.

A considerable sum of money was collected, and plans (which
still exist) were drawn up by Sir John Soane. These plans
were so arranged that a portion of the buildings might be
erected, and subsequent additions made from time to time, as
was found necessary. The buildings as they now exist form only
the central wing of the original design, the intention being to
complete them by an elaborate frontage extending along what
is now known as College Square East.

While preparations were being made for the building, the
ardent enthusiasm of those whose tastes were in unison with
our own, exhibited itself, and suggestions were made as to the
advisability of obtaining temporary premises pending the
erection of the Institution. In May, 1809, Mr. Templeton,
whose fame as a naturalist reaches down to our own day,
brought before the Managers a paper, in which, after alluding
to the delay which must necessarily occur before the Institution
could be brought to a state of efficiency, urged them to devote
special attention to scientific subjects in order that that department might keep pace with others. He advocated the appointment of a committee, in whose hands should be placed an
annual sum for expenditure, and that they should in the first
place be directed to form a Botanic Garden. To use his own
words—" Without this, one prominent part of our plan must
fail, and we can scarcely hope to gain some of the most powerful men in Ireland, without this necessary appendage to every
seat of learning." Secondly, he advocated the formation of a
Museum, which he considered would receive contributions from
sailors, fishermen, and others, and form the receptacle of many
curious objects scattered throughout the country. Lastly, he
suggested the formation of a Natural History Library to aid in
the correct naming and classification of the specimens. In the
September following a Committee was appointed to arrange for

the Botanic Garden, and authorised to expend such a sum for the ground as they might consider advisable, and as the funds would admit. An annual sum of £50 was also voted for the purchase of apparatus, specimens, books, &c. From this time onward frequent entries appear of donations to the Museum, and a document, which unfortunately is not dated, but bears evidence of its issue about this time, was" prepared, giving detailed directions as to "the means of preserving Natural History specimens, and the transmission of seeds and plants.

The preamble of the circular is as follows :—

"From the most savage state of man, to the most civilized, a knowledge of nature has been" indispensibly necessary. The Savage, by studying the habits and instinct of Animals, was enabled either to combat them with success, or render them subservient to his will. The civilized man extending his views, not only derives from this knowledge, security, food, and clothing, but even turns it to the gratification of his luxuries.

"Enlightened men of every nation, ranking a knowledge of the productions of nature among the most important objects of pursuit, have therefore endeavoured to facilitate this study, by preserving specimens, and making collections of Animals, Vegetables, and Fossils, in places adapted for their exhibition, wherein the Student might acquire a knowledge of their structure, and going abroad among the fields and woods, cultivate and extend those rudiments acquired in the Museum, or Botanic Garden; enjoying by these means, that pleasure which the possession of knowledge always bestows, and be enabled ultimately to confer lasting benefits on his country. At the present time, when the value of this species of knowledge is so well known, and cultivated with so much ardour, the *Conductors* of *The Belfast Academical Institution* have accordingly turned their attention to the forming of a Museum, and Botanic Garden ; aware that without these necessary appendages to every extensive seat of learning, their scheme must be incomplete. From the attention of many friends to the *Institution*, in sending a great variety of rare Fossils, Minerals, and other Natural and Artificial Curiosities, the Managers are led to believe, that if the exertions of its numerous friends could be directed to the most easy methods of collecting and preserving specimens, they would soon be able to exhibit a useful collection to the student ; and under this impression, they hope that the publication of the following methods of preserving Beasts, Birds, Fishes, and Insects, and transmitting Seeds and Plants, may be the means of facilitating the endeavours of those interested in the success of the Institution. And thus the same laudable spirit of emulation which has already characterised the promoters of *The Belfast Academical Institution*, may again still appear conspicuous."

Unfortunately the subscriptions to the Institution, large as they were, did not admit, as has been already stated, of the original project being carried out in its entirety. Much, however, was done in the advancement of science by the delivery of public lectures. As instances of this it may be stated that a course of such lectures was delivered by Dr. Ure, of Anderson's University, of Glasgow, during the Summer Sessions of 1814 and 1815, and that Dr. Knight gave a similar course in 1821, his lectures being delivered tri-weekly, at 8 p.m. In 1822 and 1823 Dr. James L. Drummond, who had been appointed Professor of Anatomy and Physiology in 1818, volunteered to deliver series of lectures upon Natural History subjects. A pamphlet issued in 1818, entitled "An Account of the System of Education in the Belfast Academical Institution," gives some interesting particulars regarding the public lectures, and it states that they are equally accessible and intelligible to both sexes, thus showing that our admission of lady members had a precedent many years before. In referring to the classes, a statement is made that it was intended to commence a Botanical Class, during the next year, and that in it, each student would investigate plants for himself, under the eye of the Professor, and that special attention would be directed to the indigenous botany of this part of Ireland, to practical results, and to the structure and physiology of vegetables in general. These public lectures were delivered regularly for many years, and it appears from a Parliamentary return issued in 1827, that the proprietors of the White Linen Hall had paid to the Institution a sum of £100 per annum for several years on condition that public lectures on Chemistry should be delivered to artisan students ; and that the Mechanics' Institute, which some of you may remember being located in Queen Street, paid an annual sum to entitle its members to attend the courses of lectures on various subjects. The return referred to states that 400 members of the Institute had attended the introductory lectures, but that as the membership of the Institute itself had fallen off, the attendance at the lectures had correspondingly decreased.

The records of the Institution show that in 1832 an application was made to the Managers by a number of pupils for permission to establish a Natural History Society. The permission was given, and the first meeting held on 29th April in that year. The Society had a successful career for many years, but as its records are not available, I cannot say when it ceased to exist. As a practical outcome of the attention given in the Institution to those subjects which come within our own province, it is interesting to note that essays upon them were frequently submitted by the students of the Collegiate department for the sessional class prizes. A few of these essays still exist in the archives of the Institution, unfortunately, in most instances, without the author's names. Amongst them may be noted " A History of the Ancient and Present State of the Town of Newry," statistical accounts of the parishes of Carrickfergus; Billy, Co. Antrim ; Aghamullan, Co. Monaghan ; and Aghadowey; and also "A Statistical of Lough Neagh." Several of these are illustrated by maps and drawings, the work of the authors, and each makes particular reference to the antiquities, minerals, petrifications, and to the Flora of the localities treated upon. In connection with this subject it is interesting to note that "Benn's History of Belfast" first appeared as a class essay, while Mr. Benn was a pupil at the Institution, he having been awarded a sessional prize for it in 1821.

The establishment of the Medical School in a complete form in 1835, and the appointment of a complete staff of Professors, placed the subjects of Botany, Comparative Anatomy, and Natural History upon a more solid basis, and the appointment to these Chairs of Dr. James L. Drummond, who had already done so much service with regard to these subjects, ensured thorough attention being devoted to them. The recognition of this school by the different licensing bodies, gave to it, notwithstanding the withdrawal of the Parliamentary grant which the Institution had enjoyed for many years, a successful career ; in fact, until the transfer of the school to the Queen's College in 1849. Several of the Institution Professors were appointed to Chairs in the Queen's, of whom Professor Hodges is the only one retaining his position.

The opening of the Queen's College, and the transfer to it of the Collegiate department of the Institution, rendered it unnecessary for the latter to maintain the delivery of lectures so far as the students were concerned, and the establishment of the Natural History Society gave facilities for the maintenance of the public lectures which the Institution had originated. In the school department, however, the Rev. Isaiah Steen, whom many of you may recollect, carried on a system of lectures on Physical and Natural Science. Since his death a similar work has been done by Dr. Henry Burden, and latterly by Mr. Robert Barklie. As an old pupil of the Institution, I have referred at some length to the work accomplished by it, but it should be noticed that the study of Natural Science which was so much furthered in it by Dr. Drummond and others, had in the Belfast Academy, a similar advocate in the person of Mr. James Bryce, whose valuable paper upon the geology of our district, read before the British Association at the Belfast meeting in 1852, and whose many contributions to the Geological Society placed him high in the ranks of authorities upon that subject. During Mr. Bryce's long connection with the Academy, he did much to foster a taste for Natural History amongst his pupils, not only by his lectures, but by his Saturday rambles with them, and I am sure that many of them look back with pleasure to his efforts in that direction. I find from a paper read before the Natural History and Philosophical Society in 1840, by the late Mr. Robert Patterson, that Mr. Bryce was the first to place Natural History in the rank of a branch of ordinary education, he having introduced it into his Geographical Class in the Academy, and having established a Natural History Society among his pupils. In the Institution, the same subject became a branch of education in the English department, under the Rev. William Hamilton, and a similar society had, at the time at which Mr. Patterson wrote, held its meetings for some years under the guidance of Rev. Isaiah Steen, who had latterly been joined in the management of it by Mr. Hamilton.*

Note.—Since the above was written, a most valuable " History of the Belfast

The next organisation, in point of time, to which reference may be made, is the Natural History and Philosophical Society.

The origin and history of this Society formed the subject of the Presidential Address delivered by Mr. R. Lloyd Patterson, to its members on 1st November, 1881, which was the fiftieth anniversary of the opening of its Museum. Mr. Patterson's comprehensive address covered the ground so completely that nothing worthy of note can be added to it. But in the case of a Society whose objects are so similar to our own, and whose Museum was the first erected in Ireland by voluntary subscription, any historical sketch of scientific progress in Belfast would be incomplete without reference to it. From the address to which I refer I take mainly the following particulars. It appears that at a meeting, held in the house of Dr. Drummond, on 5th June, 1821, he and seven other gentlemen, viz., Messrs. William M'Clure, jun., George C. Hyndman, James Grimshaw, jun., Francis Archer, James M'Adam, jun., Robert Patterson, jun., and Robert Simms, jun., resolved to form themselves into the Belfast Natural History Society. Dr. Drummond was elected President ; rules were adopted, and thenceforward meetings were held once a fortnight in Dr. Drummond's house until October, 1822. At that date accommodation was found for the Society in the Academical Institution, until in the following year rooms were taken in the Commercial Buildings, where the meetings continned to be held until the erection of the Museum in which we now are, and in which rooms the nucleus of the present collections was formed. The progress of the Society was such that the members began to experience inconvenience, both from the smallness of the meeting-room and the crowded state of their Museum. This inconvenience increased until they

---

Library and Society for Promoting Knowledge," has been published by our esteemed fellow-member, Mr. John Anderson, J.P., F.G.S. From this work I learn that much was done by that Society, in its earlier years, to advance the study of Natural Science. Soon after its establishment in 1788, a geological collection was formed, and in 1793 Mr. John Templeton was appointed to superintend the Botanical part of the Institution, and to take charge of Dickson's collection of dried plants " until he can get them properly secured in their places,"

were compelled to seek more commodious accommodation, and failing to find it, resolved upon erecting a building for themselves.

This project was decided upon early in 1829, when the membership had increased from eight persons in 1821, to sixty-nine in 1829. A prospectus and subscription list was issued in the February of that year, bearing the names of Dr. Drummond, as President, and Mr. G. C. Hyndman, as Secretary. In the month of May following, a Committee was appointed to conclude a bargain for the ground upon which the Museum is now erected. In October, another Committee was appointed to make arrangements for the proposed building, and in the January following advertisements appeared for estimates.

It is interesting to note that Mr. Thomas Jackson, one of the firm of architects engaged upon the work, is still living amongst us. The foundation stone was laid on 4th May, 1830, by the then Marquis of Donegall, who used for the purpose the silver trowel employed by him at a similar ceremony at the Academical Institution some years before, and also at several other public buildings. The opening of the Museum took place on 1st November, 1831, some eighteen months after the laying of the foundation stone; a rate of progress which compares favourably with the time occupied in the erection of some of our more recent public buildings.

At this time the membership had still further increased to ninety-one, and out of a total sum of £2,000 required, rather over £1,400 had been subscribed. From a circular issued on 1st January, 1834, it appears that at a General Meeting, held on 19th September, 1833, it was stated that the debt was £727, arrangements were made with a view of getting rid of this, and at a meeting held on 19th December following, the Treasurer made the announcement that the debt had been entirely wiped out.

The large room of the Museum was, however, not completely finished, and in order to complete it, and to properly accommodate the attendance at the public meetings, and to provide for the delivery of courses of lectures on various branches, which the circular states was then in contemplation, additional subscriptions were sought. From Mr. Patterson's address I find that at intervals from 1838 till 1843, various Fine Art Exhibitions were held in the upper room, the Society showing then, as it has ever done since, its desire to afford accommodation to other bodies, and so to aid in the advancement of scientific, literary, and artistic knowledge. In 1852 a further addition was made to the Museum by the erection of the "Thompson Room," as a memorial of the late William Thompson, one of the earliest members of the Society, and one of the most indefatigable and celebrated of our local Naturalists. I may state in passing that this room now contains a fitting memorial of one of the originators of the Society, in the shape of the geological collection of the late James M'Adam, which was during the past year presented to the Museum by his brother, Mr. Robert M'Adam.   From various causes a debt occurred about the year 1852, but courses of public lectures delivered by Messrs. Robert Patterson, Richard Davidson, M.P., George C. Hyndman, Dr. Andrews, Mr. James M'Adam, and Dr. Wyville Thomson, materially reduced it, and by a continued increase in the membership of the Society, the Council's Report submitted in May 1866 intimated that the Society was then free of debt. The more recent history of the Society is known to most of you, but I must not omit to refer to its action in recent years with regard to public lectures. By its aid the Belfast public have had year by year the opportunity of hearing at a nominal charge the interesting utterances of some of the most eminent scientists of our day.

The opening of the Queen's College in 1849 forms the next point to which reference may be made. So far as the teaching within its walls is concerned, but little is necessary to be said, as the high scientific attainments of those who have occupied its Chairs, and the distinguished position taken by its graduates in all professions, and I may say in all lands, are matters known to us all. Since the opening of the College its professorial staff have not been those who confined their work to their class-rooms, or who felt that their students were the only persons to

whom information might be imparted. The records of the
Natural History Society, and our own, amply testify to the
contrary, as some of the most valuable papers brought forward
from time to time were those of the College professors. Nor
were the services of these gentlemen confined to contributions
to societies established for the study of scientific subjects, for
the references I have already made to public lectures delivered,
show that they have been ever ready to aid in that direction.

The great Exhibition of 1851 called attention to the educational facilities of our own country as compared with others,
and with a view to extend them, and to advance scientific and
artistic knowledge throughout the country, in order that our
manufactures might successfully compete with those of other
nations, we find the Government Department of Science and
Art established in 1852. It was not, however, until 1859 or
1860 that the operations of the Department were extended to
Belfast. It was, I believe, in the Winter of the former, or
Spring of the latter year that a course of most interesting
lectures on Geology were delivered in the Music Hall by
Professor J. Beete Jukes, then engaged upon the Geological
Survey of Ireland.

This course was arranged for by the "Committee of Lectures,
Dublin Castle," the local arrangements being looked after by
a Belfast committee, who, if I mistake not, were the prime
movers in the matter. The course was concluded by a field
excursion to the Cave Hill, conducted by Professor Jukes, and
attended by some 300 or 400 persons. Soon after, the Depart
ment held an examination in the subjects of Geology and
Mineralogy, the place of examination being what was then
known as the Gallery of Art, at the corner of Donegall Place
and Castle Street, and which now forms part of Messrs. Anderson and M'Auley's premises. The interest awakened by
Professor Jukes' lectures was maintained by the preparation
for the examinations, and the subsequent award of valuable
prizes to the successful candidates. In the following year a
course was delivered by Professor Hodges, also under the
Dublin Committee, and a similar examination was held at its
close.

In the Winter of 1861 the functions of the " Committee of Lectures," which seems to have been an organising body, were taken up by a local committee, and arrangements made for the establishment of classes on a more permanent basis. The Committee consisted of Messrs. Samuel Coey, James Darbishire, John Herdman, James Cuming, M.D., Herbert Darbishire, Robert Patterson, Thomas Sinclair, jun., James Hind, William Bottomley, Robert M'Adam, James Hamilton, Charles Duffin, Thomas Andrews, M.D., Wyville Thomson, LL.D., J. J. Murphy, and A. F. Herdman, the two latter gentlemen acting, if I recollect aright, as secretaries. From this list we find that the majority, if not the whole of this Committee, were members of the Natural History Society; and a newspaper paragraph some few years later refers to the classes which have been conducted under the auspices of that Society. I think we may assign to it, therefore, the credit of thus aiding the popularisation of the study of Natural Science. The Committee were fortunate in obtaining the services, as teacher, of Mr. Ralph Tate, F.G.S. (now Professor at Adelaide, South Australia), and in a short time his classes in Geology and Mineralogy were in full operation, not only in Belfast, but also in Lisburn and Carrickfergus. It is worthy of note, in order to show the subsequent extension of the Science and Art system, that during Mr. Tate's first year in Belfast, there were in the subjects taught by him only eleven classes throughout the Kingdom. His classes in Geology were most successful, all the candidates passed the examination ; and out of the thirteen first-class prizes awarded in the Kingdom, eleven fell to the lot of his pupils ; while out of the eight medals, or honorary awards in lieu of medals, six were gained by them. In the following Winter, 1862-63, the scope of Mr. Tate's classes was extended, and the subjects of Vegetable Physiology and Systematic Botany, Animal Physiology and Zoology, were taken up, in addition to the subjects taught during his first year, and with a very marked amount of success. The next year saw a further development of the scheme in the opening of classes in Chemistry by our fellow and corresponding member, Dr. J. S. Holden, now of Sudbury, then Mr. J. S. Holden. These classes were held in the old Anatomical department of the Academical Institution. It is unnecessary to refer further to the development which ensued of the various Science Classes in Belfast and its neighbourhood, and which have been so ably and successfully conducted by Mr. Robert Barklie and others of our members.

The practical outcome of the introduction of Science Classes in Belfast, was that Mr. Tate's marked ability in imparting instruction, and the novelty and fascination of attending his field lectures, soon gathered around him a band of earnest, active workers, who imbibed from him that thorough investigative love of nature, which was so characteristic of him ; and amongst whom are to be found those to whom our Club owes its origin. Having now to some extent reviewed the work accomplished by other organisations, we come to the subject in which we are most interested, that of the origin of the Belfast Naturalists' Field Club.

In the month of January, 1863, a letter appeared in the columns of the *Northern Whig*, as follows :—

" FIELD NATURALISTS' CLUBS."

"Sir,—An earnest desire to awaken the Naturalists of this town, especially the young ones, to the want of a ' Field Naturalists' Club,' in this our Northern Athens, and which I sincerely hope will not continue long, has induced me to trouble you with this letter. Field Naturalists' Clubs are formed for the furtherance of Natural History by means of excursions in the Summer to some well-known provincial locality rich in Nature's beauties and wonders, there to observe, collect, and admire. The locality selected for an excursion is generally rich in the subject or branch of Natural History, for which the object of the excursions is intended, and the members are always accompanied by some of the local eminent Naturalists, who lecture to them on the subject of the day's excursion. Prizes are also awarded to the party who succeeds in collecting and arranging the largest variety of specimens in the day's excursion, and season prizes for the best collection in every branch at the end of the season. Throughout the Winter, meetings are held in the lecture room. Clubs of this kind are now quite common in England, the most prosperous being in Manchester and Liverpool, each having from between 600 to 700 members; and one of the chief causes, as stated in the report, of their great rise and popularity, is the admission of lady members, whose presence doubles the enjoyment both of rural rambles and scientific investigation. We have a Natural History and Philosophical Society, which supplies a want for our older and more enlightened

Naturalists, but the papers and topics read and discussed are in most cases too abstruse and scientific for the young Naturalist to comprehend or appreciate, and also the subscription is beyond his means. Therefore what is wanted is a Society which will elucidate Natural History in a popular and pleasing manner to the young Naturalist, and the subscription of which will come within the bounds of his pocket—say five shillings—which is the subscription generally established in all the English Clubs.

The study of nature must always refresh the enquiring mind, and every branch of Natural History, whether it be the study of plants, insects, or that of birds and animals, shells, minerals, fossils, &c., has in this district wide fields for the zealous student to explore. Now that nature is just awakening from her Winter sleep, it is therefore a very suitable time to commence to study her. I hope, therefore, that the formation of such a Society will at once be taken up, and also that the eminent Naturalists of our present Society will come forward and further its promotion.

I remain, your obedient Servant,

W. T. C.

Belfast, January 26, 1863."

The author was a young gentleman, who though unconnected with any of our local Societies, or with the Science Classes to which I have referred, had for some time devoted his attention to the entomology of the district. In the course of a few days the following letters appeared in reply to that which I have just read :—

"Sir—I was much pleased on reading your paper of the 27th inst. with the excellent suggestions thrown out by your correspondent, 'W. T. C.,' respecting the formation of a Field Naturalists' Club in Belfast.

I would gladly join such a Club, and have no doubt that a large number of young people would consider it a great privilege to be connected with it, as it would be calculated to improve and expand the mind, while the excursions would improve the health and strengthen the constitution, enabling the members to attend to their other avocations with clearer heads and lighter hearts.

Many in Belfast may not be aware of the classes that have been open for the last two years in the Museum here, under the "Department of Science and Art," comprising Botany, Natural History, Geology, Mineralogy, &c. Examinations are held in these classes in April or May, and prizes and medals are awarded by the Government to the successful competitors. It is also usual for these classes to have frequent excursions to places of scientific interest for the purpose of making collections of specimens in the different branches they are connected with. I think it would be a great advantage to those who wish to join the 'Club' to join the above classes, the subscription to which is a mere trifle, as by doing so they would get some knowledge of the different sciences before the weather would be suitable for either botanical or other excursions; and as these classes are not held during the Summer months, I would suggest that all the class members should join the 'Club,' and continue their excursions at stated periods during the time the classes are closed. By this means a knowledge of the natural objects and rare forms of the district might be obtained, which it would be very difficult for a single person to gain without the assistance of his brother Naturalists.

Hoping that some of our eminent men of science and influence will take up the subject, and for the sake of those less learned than themselves, set about it in earnest, and not cease till they get formed a 'Field Naturalists' Club'; and if once formed there is little danger of the youths of Belfast being last in the race for fame.

I remain, sir, yours respectfully,

A Young Geologist.

"Sir—I am glad to see your correspondent 'W. T. C.' calling attention to the want in our town of a Field Naturalists' Club. Belfast surely contains as many ardent students of Natural Science as would maintain efficiently a Club conducted on the plan proposed by your correspondent. Since the formation of the railway lines which radiate from our town, we have easy access to a district second to no other in the United Kingdom for the study of the various branches of Natural Science. The Geologist has choice of many formations of palæozoic, and of secondary rocks rich in fossil remains of the fauna of former epochs. The Conchologist has a magnificent sea coast to explore, and the beautiful diversity of mountain and valley scenery which we possess makes it a delightful occupation to be engaged in making a collection of examples of the flora of our country. We have in Belfast many gentlemen whose scientific attainments reflect honour on our town, and I do hope that some of these gentlemen may be induced to countenance such a Club as your correspondent has sketched. Under their guidance it would be a great success, and would impart a lasting stimulus in our locality to pursuits whose value cannot be over estimated.

I happen to know that several other parties with whom I am acquainted are anxious for the establishment of some organisation to conduct scientific excursions.

I am, your obedient Servant,

S. A. S.'

One of these was the first newspaper communication of a youth just entered upon his apprenticeship, the other the more matured production of one some few years his senior. Both of the writers are still members of the Club, and have, by the favour of their fellow-members, occupied seats upon its Committee from the foundation of the Club until the present day. I may add that in the present year's Committee two more of the original members may be found. None of the three letters I have quoted were fully signed by the writers. The result, however, was that the gentleman who first broached the subject, forwarded to the editor of the *Whig*, for transmission to the writers of the subsequent letters, a request that they would meet him to consider how the project might be carried out. Thus began the courteous and kindly help which the *Whig* has ever since afforded to the Club, and in which it has been paralleled by its fellow journal the *News-Letter*, indeed, I may say by all the Belfast press.

The authors of the three letters met at the house of Mr. W. T. Chew. who had first suggested the formation of the Club, and it was resolved by them to request the aid of Mr. Tate, who had, prior to his coming to Belfast, some experience of the working of similar Clubs in England. He entered into the matter heartily, and drew up the following document :—

1. "Names of Guarantors to form a Society to be called the 'Belfast Naturalists' Field Club,' for the practical study of Natural History, in all its branches, by

(*a*) Holding at least six field meetings in the year.

(*b*) By fortnightly (or otherwise) evening meetings for the reading of papers by members ; as far as possible such papers to treat of the Natural History and Archæology of the district ; further, that these meetings be discontinued during the Summer months.

2. That the officers of the Club be a President, Vice-President, Treasurer, Secretary, and twelve of a Committee.

3. That some gentleman eminent in Natural Science be requested to fill the Presidential Chair (otherwise such gentlemen be requested to become patrons of the Club).

4. That a system of prizes be instituted for local collections and papers.

5. That the subscription be from 2s. 6d. to 5s. per annum, payable in advance (such subscription to be dependant upon the probable expenses of the Club).

6. As soon as a sufficient number of members be found, that a deputation wait upon such eminent gentlemen as may be suggested to become President, &c., or Patrons of the Club.

Further, that an evening be fixed for a public meeting to inaugurate the opening of the Society."

This document was brought before the members of Mr. Tate's classes, and was largely signed by them. Efforts were also made to obtain the signatures of other persons interested in such matters, and in a short time a sufficient number of names were obtained to warrant a public meeting being held. After the lapse of so many years it may be interesting to note the signatures, which were as follows :—Ralph Tate, F.G.S., S. A. Stewart, Hugh Robinson, James Taggart, Samuel Symington, George Donaldson, Daniel M'Kee, Robert M'Kee, Abraham Wilson, W. M'L. Smith, Robert Smith, Robert M. C. Stevenson, William M'Millan, Hugh Morrison, Isaac Waugh, John Anderson, Richard Ross, M.D., William Brown, James W. Jamison, Thomas O'Brien, W. F. C. S. Corry, R. Smeethe, Hugh Small, P. Linehan, John Begley, John M. Greer, Thomas Mathews, Robert Young, W. A. Robinson, W. H. Patterson, W. H. Phillips, Alexander Hunter, George C. Hyndman, Robert Douglas, John S. Holden, D. S. M'Millan, John Darragh, John Love, W. T. Chew, W. E. Parkinson, John Cameron, John A. Taylor, William Campbell, James W. Valentine, David E. Patterson, J. W. Forrester, John Hartley, Hugh Savage, David M. Murphy, A. F. Herdman, John Grainger, George A. Reid, J. A. M'Donald.

In addition to these the names of some sixteen ladies appear. Of the 53 gentlemen on the list of guarantors, the names of 18 still appear upon our list of members, while 11 others are still living, but are not now connected with the Club. It would certainly appear from this that membership of a field club is not detrimental to longevity. Perhaps the most interesting fact connected with this list is that on it are to be found the names of two out of eight gentlemen who had originated the Natural History Society some forty-one years before, and who, having maintained their connection with it during that lengthened period, now came forward to aid in the formation of the younger Society. The gentlemen to whom I refer were the late Mr. Robert Patterson, F.R.S., and the late Mr. George C. Hyndman. In the month of March, 1863, a public meeting of those interested in the formation of the Field Club was held in the room down stairs, which then formed the Library of the Museum, the chair being, if I recollect aright, occupied by Dr. Samuel Browne. The meeting was large and enthusiastic, and a considerable number of members whose names do not appear on the list I have read, were enrolled. I believe I am correct in stating that Mr. William Gray, who has already occupied the Presidential chair, and who for so many years efficiently acted as Secretary, was one of them.

At this meeting rules were adopted, a Committee and officers appointed, and excursions arranged for ; the first Secretaries being Messrs. Ralph Tate and W. T. Chew ; the Treasurer, the late Mr. A. F. Herdman ; and the Chairman, my predecesor, Rev. Canon Grainger, then Mr. John Grainger. The programme of the first year's excursions and other early particulars of the Club are unfortunately out of print, and I have been unable to see a copy. The Report for the following year, 1864-65, a tiny pamphlet of some eight pages, however. gives as an appendix, a short account of the previous year's field work, and from it we learn that much was done, the first excursion being to Islandmagee and the shores of Larne Lough. During the Summer the Committee entered upon negotiations with the Natural History Society with the view of obtaining accommodation for the Winter meetings. It might have been supposed that the older Society would either look upon the younger one as a competing rival in the same field, or on the other hand as being of so small importance as to deserve little consideration at its hands. No such view was taken, for we find from the Society's report for the year that the right hand of fellowship was at once extended to us, as the following extract will show :— " This new Club, in whose welfare your Council feels much interest, expressed a desire to be affiliated in some way with the Natural History and Philosophical Society." After detailing the arrangements made, the report goes on to say :—" The Council trust that the Club will have a prosperous career, and that the ranks of the Museum Society will, from year to year, be reinforced by accessions from the young men who are thus showing their interest in Natural History by grouping themselves into a Society for its practical investigation." A further proof of the Society's interest in the Club is to be found in the names of its members who joined the Club at its formation, amongst whom in addition to the two gentlemen whose names I have already quoted, were Professors Wyville Thomson and James Thompson, Messrs. John Anderson, J. J. Murphy, A. O'D. Taylor, and Robert Young.

From that date the favourable conditions afforded to the Club have, with some slight modifications, been continued, and it is to this fact that much of the success of the Club is due. The first Winter meeting was held on 5th November, 1863, the subject for the evening being " The aims and progress of the Society," the author being appropriately Mr. W. T. Chew, whose letter, to which I have already alluded, led to the Club's formation.

In the following Spring the Club lost the services of both of its first Secretaries, Mr. Chew leaving for London, to occupy a new business position there, and Mr. Tate to enter upon the Assistant Secretaryship of the Geological Society. Mr. Tate's leaving was made the occasion of the presentation to him of an address from his former pupils and other friends, one sentence of which may appropriately be quoted: " As persons desirous of acquiring a knowledge of Natural History, we take a lively interest in every effort made to facilitate its study, especially in our own neighbourhood, and therefore cannot allow the present appropriate occasion to pass without alluding to your exertions for the establishment of the Belfast Naturalists' Field Club, the existence of which, we have reason to know is largely owing to your agency."

Mr. Tate's connection with the Geological Society was not of long duration, for we soon find him engaged in a more remunerative occupation in making a Geological and Mining Survey of Nicaragua ; and soon after he received an appoint- ment worthy of his abilities, as Professor of Natural History in the University of Adelaide. As his old pupils look back to the days when he first led their footsteps into the mystic paths of science, they may well apply to him the words of Oliver Wendell Holmes in his " Farewell to A assiz" :

> " May he find with his apostles,
> That the land is full of fossils.
> That the waters swarm with fishes,
> Shaped according to his wishes,
> New birds around him singing,
> New insects, never stinging.
>
>   *   *   *   ˜
>
> God bless the great Professor,
> And the land his proud possessor,
> Bless them now and evermore."

In 1864 we find the Secretaryship devolving upon one of your former Presidents, Mr. W. H. Patterson, with Mr. C. H. Brett as his colleague, while the removal of Mr. Grainger to Dublin, to pursue his theological studies, led to the appointment of Mr. George C. Hyndman, thus honouring, as far as we could, one who had been so long actively engaged in scientific work, and at the same time honouring ourselves by his occupancy of that position. The following year again saw a change in the Secretaryship, Messrs. William Hooker Ferguson and William Gray assuming its duties, while Professor James Thompson entered upon the Chairmanship, and at the close of the Session our first conversazione was held. These meetings, which have for so long formed a distinctive feature of our organisation, were not long in finding imitators, and our members have frequently been called upon to aid in the arrangement and carrying out of similar meetings on behalf of various local objects. The Club's report for 1866-67 shows a considerable advance upon its predecessors, extending to some 56 pages as compared with the first issued—a mere pamphlet of 12 pages, covering two years' work. Mr. Ferguson's Secretaryship terminated in 1869, in which year I became Mr. Gray's colleague. The Winter Session of 1869-70 inaugurated an important change in the Club's method of working, as during it the system of holding our meetings jointly with the Natural History Society began. The similarity of object contemplated by both Societies led those interested in their mutual prosperity to suggest a combined action between the two associations. It was not proposed to merge the individual existence of either, but to recognise practically a community of interests and aims by the joint meetings. Coincident with this arrangement was the undertaking on the part of certain members of the Field Club, the re-arrangement of the local collections in the Museum, which was completed some years after. The joint meetings to which I have referred began with an address by Dr. Wyville Thomson, "On the aims of Natural History Societies and the uses of Local Museums," and continued for some two years. It was found, however, that the identity of each Society was becoming imperilled, and after mature deliberation by the managing bodies of both, it was decided to revert to the former plan of separate meetings, arrangements being made by regular alternations to avoid any possible clashing. The same friendly feelings continue to exist, while each Society is free to pursue its own particular path. In 1869 we find Mr. Greer Malcomson assuming the office of Treasurer, which he held for many years with much advantage to the Club. In this year an important change was made in our rules, to the effect that the members should elect annually a President and Vice-President, in lieu of the former arrangement by which the Committee elected a Chairman from their own number. The first to receive the title of President was Professor James Thompson, who had for several years conducted our meetings under the old title.

The Report for 1869-70 evidences another new departure, as with it was issued the first of our "Appendices," that by Professor Tate, entitled "A List of Irish Liassic Fossils." These Appendices contain a series of most valuable papers, and the recent issue of them in a collected form as the first volume of "Systematic Lists of the Fauna, Flora, and Antiquities of Ireland," is a work of which any Society might feel proud.

Some three years later another change in our rules was made, empowering the Committee to exchange the publications of the Club with other Societies of a similar nature. It was found that, as year by year the Annual Reports of the Club became more voluminous, increased applications for them were made. A system was adopted by which our Reports were regularly forwarded to the leading Societies, as soon as issued, and a glance at any of our recent publications will show how extensive the system has become. Not only are exchanges maintained throughout Britain, but also in the United States—largely due to the facilities afforded by the Smithsonian Institution—and in addition with many of the Colonial and Continental Societies.

The commencement of the second decade of the Club's existence was considered as appropriate to adopt the title of " Annual Report and Proceedings" for our publications, instead of the former title only. The first year of that period is marked specially in our history, by the fact that we sent a deputation to the Bradford Meeting of the British Association, in order to obtain such information as would enable the Club to render effective assistance in preparation for the meeting which had been arranged to be held in Belfast in the following year. From that date until the present we have annually appointed a delegate to the Association's meetings, and have been formally recognised as one of its corresponding Societies. I think I am correct in stating that at the recent Manchester meeting we were the only Irish Society so represented.

In our Report for 1873-74 the project of the publication of a guide book for the use of the members of the Association and others, was first mooted. Though the time for its preparation was but limited, the work was undertaken, and the publication of our " Guide to Belfast and Adjacent Counties " successfully accomplished. It is gratifying to find that the example which we first set has been followed in other places, notably at the meetings at Glasgow, Bristol, &c.

During the Belfast meeting, the Club, aided by a grant from the local Committee, brought together and exhibited in the Ulster Minor Hall a large collection of Irish antiquities, which were of much interest to those who visited our town at that time. The year 1875 records Mr. Gray's resignation of the office of Secretary, which he had held for the long period of ten years, during which his energetic services tended much to the prosperity of the Club. It also records the accession to office of his able successor, your present senior Secretary, Mr. William Swanston.

As I have now reviewed some of the leading events of the early history of our Club—the first ever established in Ireland— up to a point to which most of my hearers' knowledge extends, it is unnecessary to trouble you with further details.

As we look back to the Club's early days many of us can call up recollections of companions found with interests and pursuits identical with our own, friendships formed which have been steadfastly maintained through fair weather and foul, ever since; and though at times we may have differed in our conclusions, the earnest desire after truth and knowledge taught us that we were far from possessing any monopoly of either, and so caused us to respect the opinions of others. True, our discussions have been earnest, and may have even assumed a " mammoth " form, but each of our members have been actuated by the same spirit as that expressed by Bret Harte's " Truthful James " :

> " Now, I hold it is not decent for a scientific gent
> To say another is an ass—at least to all intent :
> Nor should the individual, who happens to be meant,
> Reply by heaving rocks at him, to any great extent."

I would have liked, had time permitted, to have made some reference to the wonderful strides with which science has progressed since we first met as a Club, but a mere casual review of such matters would more than occupy the time of an entire meeting. I cannot, however, conclude my remarks without some references to the changes which have occurred during our quarter century's existence. Faces long familiar to us have disappeared. Some of our early members have transferred their abilities to other localities, amongst whom are Professor Tate, to whom I have already referred. Professor James Thompson, for several years our President, still occupies his Chair in Glasgow University—a colleague of his eminent brother, Sir William—worthy sons of a worthy father, and of whom as natives of our northern province we may well be proud. Professor Macloskie, at Princeton, pursues the investigations which he began in his native isle. Sir William MacCormac and Dr. J. Sinclair Holden, are actively engaged in

the duties of their profession.   But others of our early members
have passed away from us for ever—George C. Hyndman, our
second Chairman, eminent as a conchologist, and one of the
originators and earliest supporters of our Club.   Robert Patterson, who at the early age of nineteen was one of the founders
of the Natural History Society, who maintained his connection
with it until his death, and who was also one of our original
members.   Few, if any of our local Naturalists did more to
advance the study of Natural History as a branch of ordinary
school education than he did.   As a witness of which we have
his " Zoology for Schools," first issued in 1846, and which was
the pioneer of the many works of like nature which other
authors have given to the world.   Though he is gone his
name remains with us, his sons maintaining their active
membership, one of whom was a former holder of the Presidential chair, and now we have a later generation represented
amongst us by his grandsons.   Rev. Canon MacIlwaine, kind,
genial, and accomplished, and who for years was a familiar
figure at our excursions, has disappeared from amongst us also.
So, too, has Dr. James Moore, skilful as a surgeon, accomplished
as an artist, adept as an antiquarian, and who by his long and
active connection with the Society for the Prevention of
Cruelty to Animals, showed himself a true Naturalist in his
regard for them.   From our list of members we miss the name
of Sir Charles Wyville Thomson, another of our earliest
members, and who on his removal to Edinburgh University
was placed upon our honorary list.   The magnificent work
accomplished by him in the *Challenger* and similar expeditions
will long rank him amongst the foremost men of our age, and
we cannot but feel the honour it was to have him enrolled in
our membership.   Another on our honorary list who has
passed away is Mr. James Bryce, F.G.S., to whom I have
already referred, and whom, though he did not take an active
part in our work, having resided in Glasgow for many years
before our Club was formed, we looked upon as one of ourselves,
on account of the work he had done while in Belfast, and as a
member of a family long and favourably known in connection

with education in it. Those of whom I have already spoken, had most of them, reached beyond the allotted span of life, and had attained to high honours in science and position. Amongst our younger men blanks too are to be found. William M'Laren Smith, one of a family of father and three sons who sat side by side at many of our meetings, after a successful career at the Queen's College, obtained a Professorship in one of the colleges of our Indian Empire, and found an early grave in that far off land. Thomas Hughes Corry, who even in his boyhood exhibited that taste for Natural History, which afterwards became his life work, perished in the very pursuit of his favourite study. More recently Dr. Samuel Malcomson, one of our most devoted students of microscopical science, was called from our midst.

But as we look back, we find that as gaps have been made in our ranks, fresh recruits step forward to take their places, and so our club marches bravely on, ever advancing, and long may it do so. May we each one try to do our part in investigating truth for its own sake, in imparting to others, so far as lies in our power, the knowledge which we ourselves have gained, and above all in looking from nature's works upward to the Great First Cause, to whom they all owe their origin. With the recollections fresh in my memory of the labours of those whose names I have quoted to you, and calling up before me those of the many eminent men of science whose deaths have been recorded since our Society's existence began, I cannot better conclude than in the words of Sir J. William Dawson, in his address at the Birmingham meeting of the British Association : " These men have left behind them ineffaceable monuments of their work, in which they still survive, and we rejoice to hope that though dead to us, they live in that great company of the great and good of all ages who have entered into that unseen universe where all that is high, and holy, and beautiful, must go on accumulating till the restitution of all things. Let us follow their example and carry on their work as God may give us power and opportunity, gathering in the precious stores of knowledge, in the belief that all truth is immortal, and must go on for ever, bestowing blessings on mankind."

Mr. William Gray, on rising, apologised for doing so, as he was aware it was not the custom for one of the audience to speak to the Presidential Address, and he promised he would not in the present case depart from that honoured custom ; but he could not refrain from congratulating the members on the admirable, exhaustive, and instructive address to which they had just had the pleasure of listening, and he would ask liberty to move a resolution to the effect that it be embodied in full in the Club's Proceedings.

Canon Grainger spoke of the pleasure he had derived from living over again perhaps the pleasantest part of his life while following the President in his admirable discourse.

The resolution, having been put to the meeting, was passed by acclamation.

Mr. G. Donaldson, one of the original members of the Club, while testifying to the carefulness, and accuracy even in details, with which the early years of the Club's history had been brought before them, presumed it was his natural modesty that had prevented the President from acknowledging himself the author of one of the three important letters which he had read, and from which the Club had sprung.

The second meeting of the Session was held in the Museum, on 20th December, when two communications were brought forward. The first was by J. Starkie Gardner, Esq., F.G.S., F.L.S., &c., of London. Owing to the unavoidable absence of the President—Mr. Hugh Robinson, M.R.I.A.—the chair was, on the motion of Mr. Lockwood, seconded by Mr. G. Donaldson, taken by Mr. Wm. Gray, M.R.I.A. The Chairman, after thanking the meeting for the honour they had conferred upon him, said that he greatly regretted that the author of the first paper had been prevented from coming over to read it in person. Mr. Gardner had previously favoured the Club with a valuable contribution

to our local geology ; his reputation as an original and pains-
taking worker, and writer, was well known ; and as he had for
many years directed his attention to the basaltic rocks and the
associated floras of Antrim and Mull, we were always sure to
hear some new facts and discoveries on the age and origin of
this wonderful but puzzling series of rocks. In his absence this
evening they had an admirable substitute in their senior hon.
Secretary (Mr. Swanston), whom he would now call upon to
read the paper. Mr. Swanston, before commencing, pointed
out on a large geological map the areas of basalts referred to by
the author, and also drew attention to the sequence of all the
beds, recognised by geologists, above the chalk, as it was with
some of them that the paper specially dealt.

The reading of the paper, which was followed with great
interest, was then proceeded with. The following is an
abstract of it :—

" The Trap Formation which covers so large a part of Ulster,
and with which members of the Club must be especially
familiar, is believed to have originally had an enormous
extension in a northerly direction. In examining the traps of
the Inner Hebrides, of the Faroes, and of Iceland, we are indeed
forced to the conclusion that they are but fragments of a
formation, once probably dry land, but now sunk beneath the
waves. . . . The extensive tract of basalt, one edge of
which hangs frowning over Belfast, does not yield in interest
to those outside the limits of Ireland. Standing on Fair Head,
when the air is extremely clear, we are just able to discern
another of the fragments of our trap formation, its position
being fixed by the far peaks of Mull, round whose flanks its
level sheets are piled to a height of 1,200 feet. Around Belfast
we have in all probability the very southernmost original
termination of the series. In Mull we have a portion of their
original eastern boundary. But while in Ireland the flows
seemed to have passed over a merely undulating country, in
Scotland the molten lavas surged against mountain tracts
around which they were piled in vain endeavours to submerge
them, until their summits came to stand out like islets in a

petrified ocean." Having pictured the character of the surface upon which these flows were erupted in Antrim and in Scotland, the author proceeds to describe the beds themselves, dwelling at considerable length upon the immense time necessary for their accumulation. Regarding their age . . . "they have been regarded as of Miocene age for many years, but nothing in the progress of geology has been more surprising than the way in which this belief has become rooted, when we consider the kind of evidence upon which it is based. Of the many writers accustomed to refer to the age of the Traps as one of the ascertained landmarks in geology scarcely any troubled to investigate it. I have detailed it, however, in the pages of the Quarterly Journal of the Geological Society for last May, and we trust the question is in a fair way of being set at rest. Within 100 feet of the base of the basalts in Mull occurs the Ardtun flora, a rich assemblage of plants, not one of which is known in any European rocks of Miocene age. By known Miocene age, I mean whose age has been determined on other data than plants. They even bear no resemblance whatever to such, but they do bear a resemblance to those of Sezame, believed to be the oldest Eocene plants in France. Next in age seems to come the Glenarm and Ballypallady beds, with a peculiar group of nettles known when fossil as Maclintockii. Now this group has only been met with fossil in one bed of known age—the Heersian—a formation of Thanet, or oldest English Eocene age, bearing the same relation to the Sezame flora, as that of Ardtun does to that of Glenarm. Lastly, the Lough Neagh beds have yielded plants about which I would like to say something if time permitted ; though the only plants I have yet determined from it are of middle or lower Eocene species, but we cannot yet make out their relation to the traps. We agree, however, that it is much newer than the horizon at Glenarm, and it might provisionally be placed as high up as the Oligocene. The origin of these vast lava flows is an interesting problem. I myself firmly believe they are due to what are called fissure eruptions, and that the lavas welled up through long cracks, or parallel series of cracks, running in the same direction as the axis of the formations."

The author, after giving some remarkable evidence on the flexibility of the earth's crust, and its sensitiveness to such outflows as producing subsidence, concluded by pointing out the importance of members of the Club setting themselves to examine these trap formations, with a view of ascertaining if there be any rythmic succession in the character of the rocks composing them, and thus, if possible, obtaining an insight into the inner working and physical history of that hitherto unwitnessed, but awful visitation—a fissure eruption.

The second paper read was by Mr. F. W. Lockwood descriptive of various ancient canoes found recently in Loughmourne, and presented by the Water Commissioners to the Museum, as well as some found during the recent dry summer in the County Fermanagh.

Of those in the Museum from Loughmourne, one is a mere fragment, being the spoon-shaped end of an oak canoe. The second is a complete " cot," or flat-bottomed boat, 13 feet long, 2 feet 6 inches wide, and 9 inches deep. It has five holes neatly bored, running longitudinally along the centre of the bottom. These, it is suggested, were to receive the wooden pins of a keel. The third is a regular rowing boat, rather over 13 feet long, 2 feet 9 inches wide, and 9 inches deep, and must have been very shallow and crank. Before it shrank in drying it must have been wider, as is shown by the loose seat or "thwart" now remaining. Like all the others, it was "dug out" of a solid oak trunk. A projecting piece was left in each side of the gunwale, with two holes to take pins, through two similar holes in the end of the seats, of which there are two. Similar projections were left, with a large hole in each, to receive a single large thole-pin (not two, as in use now). Raised crescent-shaped pieces were also left in the bottom of the boat for the rowers' heels to press against. There are two rows of four or five holes bored right through the bottom, in a straight line across from side to side, the purpose of which cannot easily be explained. These boats are well worth an inspection by present disciples of the oar.

Mr. Lockwood also described a number of canoes found in

the County Fermanagh last summer, from particulars furnished by Thomas Plunkett, Esq., M.R.I.A., of Enniskillen.

The first, found by Mr. J. A. Pomeroy at St. Angelo, is a canoe 43 feet 10 inches long, 2 feet 4 inches wide, and 12 inches deep, hollowed out of a single oak trunk. (Such trees are now very rare.) The ends were spoon-shaped (whaleboat like), and at the stern a seat was left with two depressions on its surface, evidently to afford greater purchase to the steersman whilst using his paddle. There are no traces of seats for the other rowers.

The second was found in Upper Lough Erne, between Derryadd and Derrylea, by Mr. Morrison, who sent word to Mr. Plunkett. It is nearly 32 feet long, 4 feet wide, and 3 feet deep, and must, therefore, have been formed out of an oak tree, with a stem 16 feet in circumference, by over 30 feet high. Truly a noble specimen. There was a raised triangular piece on each gunwale, with a notch at one side, into and against which the seat was apparently pressed. The bottom had been patched with a piece of oak 4 feet long and 6 inches wide, neatly inlaid, flush with the surface, and secured with wood pins.

A third, very like the flat boat in the Museum, was found in the Claddagh River by Mr. James Willis, of Moneen, 22½ feet long, 3 feet wide by 2 feet deep. The square end had holes for securing by a thong or rope.

A somewhat similar one was found by Mrs. Jones' steward at Lisgoole Abbey.

Colonel Irvine has also found at Goblush Point, in Lower Lough Erne, a canoe 55 feet long by 2 feet 3 inches wide. It is understood to have been too much decayed to admit of preservation. This is to be regretted, as its extreme length renders it of peculiar interest.

The third meeting of the Winter Session was held on 24th January, at the Museum, College Square North—the President of the Club, Hugh Robinson, Esq., M.R.I.A., in the chair—

when a paper was read by Robert Day, Esq., of Cork, F.S.A.,
M.R.I.A., &c., upon " Marks of Ownership in Books." The
lecturer stated that his subject might be equally well described
as on " Book Plates." He found many people hardly knew of
the existence of book plates, or what they were, although of
extreme interest to collectors. The books in early times were
of great value, and were often secured against theft or other
loss by chains or similar safeguards. Afterwards their owners
inserted plates upon the inside of the covers as a proof of
ownership, frequently inscribing their names upon the shield
of their coat of arms, with appropriate mottoes. The lecturer
traced a succession, in the main chronological, from the
heraldic book plates of the Elizabethan age (though they were
earlier in use on the Continent), and described several different
types of plates. There were the allegorical of the Jacobean
age, or end of the seventeenth century, of which an example
was given of Minerva instructing a class of students in a library.
These were merged with the Chippendale plates, in which the
ornament was of the type designed by the Brothers Chippendale, about the middle of the eighteenth century, and many of
the designs were copied exactly for their book of designs for
furniture. A beautiful example of these was shown, in the
same manner as many others were, by enlarged lantern
transparencies from photographs. Towards the end of the
century this type gave way to the landscape type, of which the
Bewicks produced many fine specimens ; several examples of
these were shown with the lantern. Mr. Day mentioned a
number of book-plates in his possession, interesting as having
belonged to famous men. Amongst these were plates of Lord
Nelson, Charles Dickens, and one of Napoleon Bonaparte,
affixed during his exile at St. Helena. Another interesting
class of book-plates are those containing cautionary hints to
book borrowers and book pilferers. The lecturer quoted some
very amusing instances of these. He then referred to the
principal engravers of book-plates in Ireland, including Thompson, of Belfast, and related several anecdotes of some of them.
In conclusion, he said he had touched but the fringe of the

subject, and that it contained a mine of wealth for those who were disposed to pursue it, and he referred to the interesting side light that was thrown upon it by the study of heraldry. A vote of thanks was moved by Mr. Joseph Wright, F.G.S., and seconded by Mr. Robert Young, C.E., M.R.I.A., &c.; and an animated discussion was continued by Mr. W. H. Patterson, M.R.I.A., Mr. John Vinycomb, Mr. W. Gray, M.R.I.A., and others. The lantern transparencies were very skilfully exhibited by Mr. W. Nicholl.

The fourth meeting of the Session was held in the Museum, College Square, on 28th February—the President, Mr. Hugh Robinson, M.R.I.A., in the chair. Two distinct communications were brought forward. The first was by Mr. Robert M. Young, B.A., entitled, "Some Notes on the Early Belfast Press and its Productions." The lecture was prefaced with a short account of the history of printing in Ireland from its introduction in 1551, when a Book of Common Prayer was printed in Dublin. Mention was made of the presses set up in Kilkenny and Waterford in 1641 by Rinnaini, and of the later productions of the Dublin printers. A copy of the extremely rare Book of Common Prayer issued by authority of Charles II. in 1666, and printed in a Gothic letter by John Crook, Dublin, was shown, Dr. Madden being cited as the authority for its rarity, he having seen only one copy of the book in his lifetime, and that in the library of Earl Charlemont, long since dispersed. The introduction of the printing press in Belfast for publishing proclamations of King William's army in 1690 was dwelt upon, followed as it was shortly after by the arrival of two printers from Scotland—Patrick Neill and James Blow—who were induced to settle in the town by the Sovereign, William Crawford. As the reader intimated that he would eschew all theological and polemical works in his description of the early productions of the local Press, several of the more generally known works, such as "Presbyterian Loyalty Displayed," printed in 1713, were passed over, the first volume fully dilated upon being the very rare "Experienced Hunts-man," written by Arthur Stringer, himself huntsman to Lord Kilultagh, published by James Blow in 1714. A copy of this work has been recently presented to the Linen Hall Library, by the late Henry Bradshaw, librarian of Cambridge University. Reference was here made to the unwearied exertions of John Anderson, Esq., J.P., F.G.S., hon. Secretary of Linen Hall Library, in getting up the valuable catalogue of Belfast printed books, which has thrown much light on a subject hitherto most imperfectly known. A sketch of James Blow's life was given with an extract from a contemporary journal of a funeral notice, in which his many virtues were fully recorded. Some of his books were shown to the audience to illustrate his practice of putting his autograph and the name of his customer in a printed form for the purpose. James Magee, the printer at the "Bible and Crown," Bridge Street, was next treated of, and an extract given from "A Tour in Ireland, 1776," to show the superiority of his books, of which copies were also exhibited. By the kindness of the Misses Mackey, daughters of the late Alexander Mackey, jun., whose father acquired the *Belfast News-Letter* at the end of last century, several copies of early *Belfast News-Letters* were shown, including the complete set for 1770, which has been presented by them to the Museum. The original founder of the paper, Francis Joy, as was pointed out by the lecturer, was a remarkable man. He introduced paper-making so far back as 1748 in the neighbourhood of Belfast. A list was given of all the printers of Belfast from 1700 to 1800, as well as an analysis of the different works printed by them, and given in the Anderson catalogue already referred to. Some remarks were made on the advanced ideas of education then prevalent, quotations being given from David Manson's Dictionary of 1762, with a view to show his far-sighted views on this subject. It was remarked that the muse of poetry was not much cultivated by the public of that period. "Marriott's Fables for the Use of the Ladies," 1771, was quoted as the first original work composed in the locality. Judging by the various text-books on law issued from the local

Press, much legal knowledge was essential to the merchants of the period. Extracts were given from one of these works, " The Young Clerk's *Vade Mecum,*" 1765, including a warrant not much used at present; which runs thus—" Warrant for not coming to church, to &c., County of——to wit. Whereas, oath has been made before me, one of his Majesty's justices of the peace for the county aforesaid, that A. B , of——did not upon the Lord's Day last past resort to any church, chapel, or other usual place appointed for common prayers, and there hear Divine service according to the form of the statute in that case made and provided. These are, therefore, to request you to bring the said A.B. before me or some of his Majesty's justices of the peace to answer the premises given, &c." Other books were then described, including dramatic works and the reprints of the poets, such as Pope, Goldsmith, Burns, &c. It was noted that the early editions of Burns were very scarce, as they were much defaced, and, indeed, destroyed by the thumbing undergone in the country houses where they circulated largely. Six titles of tracts printed on the state of the linen trade in the last century were given, and the hope was expressed that this branch would receive further elucidation. It was shown that but two works in the Irish language were produced, the first an Irish Catechism, in 1722, the other the *Gaelic Magazine,* printed in 1795, and edited by Miss Brooks, one of whose spirited renderings was quoted, a translation of an elegy on Carolan. The art aspects of the Belfast Press were then treated of. It was shown that the early printing, with, perhaps, the exception of the beautiful little ' Psalms of David in meter, 1700," now preserved in the First Presbyterian Church (Rev. A. Gordon), was of a moderate character, no embellishments of an artistic kind being used till the year 1738, when the first woodcut is observed in a reprint of the *London Magazine.* This woodcut is a poor reproduction of the copper plate which figures in the original edition. The first book published in Belfast illustrated with woodcuts was exhibited. It is entitled, " The most pleasing and delightful History of Reynard the Fox and Reynardine his son," printed by Daniel

Blow, in 1763. It was mentioned that Mr. Quaritch had informed Mr. Lavens Ewart that for a similar volume, belonging to the latter gentleman, entitled " Valentine and Orson," the cuts were probably obtained from London. Through the kindness of Mr. Govan, of the *Northern Whig*, and Mr. Boyd, of Messrs. Alex. Mayne & Boyd, a large number of illustrations —woodcuts—were shown, some of which were undoubtedly executed in Belfast. Many of these dated from the commencement of this century or a little earlier, and represented rude renderings of coats of arms, titles to ballads, broadsheets, and advertisements. Some of the original wood blocks were also shown. The lecture was concluded by a brief description of some of the leading local printers of the early part of the century, special mention being made of the fine work executed by A. Mackey, jun., in the beautiful History of Belfast, 1823, and illustrated by the well-known local engraver, John Thompson, whose merits as an artist deserve wider recognition.

The second communication of the evening was by Mr. W. H. Phillips, on " Variations observed in the growth of the Mistletoe." Mr. Phillips was perhaps the earliest, as he has also been the most successful, grower of Mistletoe in the neighbourhood. Growing it, as he does, within easy reach, he has enjoyed special opportunities of studying its habits. After a brief but interesting review of the position the plant occupies in the natural system, the traditions and legends associated with it, the lecturer exhibited specimens from his garden in Holywood in flower and fruit, and with various modifications of foliage. An examination of specimens and the election of members concluded a most interesting evening.

CONVERSAZIONE

On 27th March, the members of the Club celebrated its twenty-fifth anniversary (the Club having been founded in March, 1863) by a Conversazione, in the Museum, College Square North. An unusually large number of members and their friends were present on this occasion. Tea was served in the lower rooms from 7-30 o'clock till 8-30 by the lady members, after which the president, Hugh Robinson, Esq., M.R.I.A., took the chair, and made a brief statement. He said it became his duty to offer them all, on behalf of the committee, a hearty welcome. They were assembled under special circumstances, to commemorate the twenty-fifth anniversary of the formation of the Club. It was to him a source of very great pleasure to look back upon a quarter of a century's unbroken official connection with the Club, and to see present so many of its original members, and of those who in its earlier years were associated in establishing the Club upon a permanent basis. He was sure many could look back with similar feelings, and upon fast friendships formed and maintained by its agency. It would be out of place for him to occupy much time on that occasion, but he might express the hope that in the years which were to come the same friendly feelings and spirit of co-operation which had existed in the past, might continue ; and while they might without egotism congratulate themselves upon the work the Club had already accomplished, they might hope, with increased knowledge and efficiency gained, to show a still better record in the future.

After several new members had been elected, the guests turned their attention to the various objects of interest lent for exhibition. The subject of " Old Belfast " had been selected for special illustration, and a number of drawings, engravings, and maps were lent by various members. Amongst these were a set of water-colour drawings by the late Andrew Nicholl, R.H.A. ; some lent by the nephew of the artist, Mr. W. Nicholl, and some by Alderman L. M. Ewart, J.P. Mr. Ewart also lent engravings of the old Long Bridge, and of the Paper Mill Bridge, and an oil painting of the old paper mill and bridge ; also an oil painting of the launch of the first steamer built in Belfast. A fine water-colour of the launch of the Circassian, by Stannus, showing another stage in the history of Belfast industry was lent by Mr. Hall. Amongst other mementoes of Old Belfast was the date stone

(1696) of the Long Bridge, from the Museum collection, and one of the wooden water pipes that supplied the old fonn-tain in Fountain Street. Mr. Ewart lent several old maps of Belfast and the adjacent counties, and Mr. J. Stelfox a map of Belfast and the Lough, showing a scheme of military and naval evolutions planned by the Volunteers in 1781. A number of graphic sketches of coast and river scenery in the vicinity were contributed by Mr. George Trobridge. Mr. W. Swanston, F.G.S., lent some landscapes by Stannus, and a series of framed engravings of O'Neill's Irish crosses. Amongst other artistic contributions were a fine series of drawings of the bills and feet of birds executed by Mr. C. Bennington, and lent by Mr. F. Wrathall. Of exhibits illustrating the natural history and archæological work of members of the Club, there were a large variety. Mr. C. Bulla showed a collection of flint and other implements. Mr. W. Gray, M.R.I.A., showed a set of flint implements, and also the various stages and methods of mak-ing gun flints, &c. He also showed a case illustrating the pro-fusion of the lower forms of marine life. Mr. D. M'Kee showed a fine collection of Cretaceous fossils. Mr. S. F. Milligan, M.R.I.A., showed a number of bronze weapons, a bronze rivetted pot, and other utensils, and a finely illuminated Roman missal, probably of the fourteenth century. Mr. J. Hamilton exhibited the eggs, larvæ, and imago of an American moth, *Bombyx cecropia*, hatched, reared, and brought to perfection in this country. He also showed the curious nest of the tarantula spider, and several other curiosities lent by Captain Barkeley. Professor Everett, D.C.L., F.R.S., kindly lent a number of scientific appliances, which were exhibited in operation by Mr. Pinkerton, and were the source of much interest during the evening. At nine o'clock Mr. W. Nicholl and Mr. R. Welch exhibited a number of lantern transparencies illustrating Old Belfast, as well as other subjects.

The microscopes were not so fully represented as on former occasions. Mr. J. J. Andrew, L.D.S., &c., exhibited a "rock-ing microtome," for cutting sections, and in the microscope, sections of the pistil of the white lily, cut by this beautiful machine. Mr. Joseph Wright, F.G.S., showed Foraminifera, including specimens of *Lagena acuticosta*, dredged last year off the southwest coast of Ireland, and also off Dublin Bay, but not previously known to British waters. Mr. Stewart, F.B.S.E., and Mr. Gray, M.R.I.A., also showed a variety of microscopic subjects.

The Club's sketch book, mainly of antiquities, the portrait album, and its photographic albums, were all on view. Of the latter there are now four volumes, mainly the work of members, illustrating the scenery, antiquities, and geology of the North of Ireland. Mr. G. Donaldson also showed some frames of fine local photographs, and Mr. W. Gray a number of albums and photographs of the Suez Canal, Red Sea, &c., &c.

There were also on view a number of volumes of Indian sketches from the Museum collection.

Mr. Jerdan Nichols showed some fine specimens of pendulograph writing. A very interesting feature was a case lent by Mr. Sheals containing two live specimens of the Egyptian jerboa, and a pretty little flying squirrel. Their movements attracted much attention.

A number of ornaments for the decoration of the room were kindly lent by Mr. W. Gibson and Mr. S. D. Neill. Messrs. L. M. Ewart and W. Valentine, J.P., generously contributed cut flowers and plants in pots.

The success of the Conversazione proves that the Field Club has in no degree diminished in public interest during the twenty-five years of its existence. We may hope that another quarter of a century will see it celebrating its jubilee under still more prosperous circumstances.

On 17th April, the fifth meeting was held in the Museum, when two communications were brought forward. The first was by Mr. Wm. Gray, M.R.I.A., entitled, " Notes on Subjects brought before the late Meeting of the British Association." Mr. Gray gave a concise account of all the papers read before the Association, in so far as they treated upon subjects which came within the range of the Club's aims, referring more fully to the work of the Corresponding Societies Committee, on which he had been appointed a delegate to represent the Club.

The next communication was by Messrs. W. A. Firth and Wm. Swanston, F.G.S. It was entitled, "References to the Diatomaceous Deposits at Lough Mourne, and in the Mourne Mountains." Mr. Firth stated that on becoming interested in the study of Diatomaceæ some years ago, he was attracted by our local deposits, as represented in dealers' catalogues. Toomebridge and Stoneyford deposits were easily localised, and samples obtained, but Mourne Mountains was a puzzle, and until very recently he was under the impression that it was really the same as the Lough Mourne deposit, wrongly named. On making inquiries during the past few weeks, F. Kitton, Esq., F.R.M.S., informed him that he had an old slide in his possession, labelled " Mourne Mountains," the forms on which were small and insignificant, and a hope was expressed by that gentleman that during the coming season samples of the deposit might be obtained, if it were not entirely removed or covered.

Loughmourne deposit—As you are well aware, this deposit is found in Loughmourne, near Carrickfergus. To show the confusion which has arisen, Mr. Firth stated that a correspondent of his, a Liverpool gentleman, had made searches year after year at Lough Mourne, Co. Donegal, when on annual visits to Irish property, and was much surprised when a sample was sent him from our locality. For a long time it seemed as if this deposit was a thing of the past, through being covered with water, but in 1882, when the lough was drained, it was found, as stated by Rev. W. Smith in *The Annals and Magazine of Natural History*, 1850. · Samples were taken from the N.E. and S.E. shores, the former being remarkably rich in fine bold forms, and contained 48 species, the S.E. material being quite as rich, but the forms smaller, and the number of species fewer. The reader had no doubt but that all the species observed in the deposits might be found living in the lough. During the past season he had collected material in a ditch on

Colin Mountain, which contained 44 species, and was remarkably like the Loughmourne deposit in many respects.

The following is a list of species from Loughmourne :—

Surirella biseriata	Stauroneis anceps
,, linearis	,, Phœniceuteron
nobilis	Navicula (?) bacillans
,, splendida	,, elliptica
,, turgida	,, firma
Campylodiscus costatus	,, gibberula
Cocconema cistula	,, pusilla
,, cymbiforme	Pinnularia gibba
,, lanceolata	,, interrupta
Cymatopleura elliptica	,, major
,, solea	,, (?) nodosa
Cymbella cuspidata	,, staurœniformis
,, Ehrenbergii	,, tabellaria
Amphora oralis	,, viridis
Cyclotella operculata	,, radiosa
Epithemia alpestris	Cocconeis placentula
,, aigus	Gomphonema acuminatum
gibba	Himantidium gracile
,, granulata	Odontidium (?)
,, Hyndmanii	,, Harrisonii
,, turgida	Orthosira arenaria
,, zebra	,, orchilacea
Pleurosigma attenuatum	Nitzschia (?) palea
,, . Spencerii	

Mr. Swanston followed by reading the original record of the discovery of Diatomaceous earth in the Mourne Mountains, as published in the *Magazine of Natural History*, Vol. III., new series. 1839, p. 353. The article was contributed by James L. Drummond, M.D., Professor of Anatomy in the Royal Belfast Institution, and President of the Belfast Natural History Society. From it we learn that Wm. Thompson, Esq., when residing at Newcastle, Co. Down, sent the author specimens of a light, white, earthy substance, which had been found in the neighbourhood, and which proved to be rich in diatoms—in fact, a deposit of fossil diatomaceæ. Other specimens were obtained from Dr. Hunter, of Bryansford (near Newcastle), which proved on examination to be similar, Dr. Hunter's examples were obtained from Lough Islandreavey, a few miles from Bryansford, and the fossil deposit was found underlying about a foot of boggy soil, in the bed of the lough, on the water being lowered by the Bann Company.

It was stated by a member that this deposit was not now accessible, as the lough referred to was used at the present time as a reservoir, and the sides had been pitched with stones, thus preventing the original margins being examined, except in the event of the lough being again drained

ANNUAL MEETING.

THE twenty-fifth Annual Meeting was held in the Museum, College Square North, on Tuesday evening, 24th April—the President (Mr. Hugh Robinson, M.R.I.A.) in the chair. The business of the evening, as announced by circular, was to hear the Secretaries' and Treasurer's Reports for the past year, to hear the awards of the judges appointed to examine the collections submitted in competition for the Club's prizes, and to elect officers for the ensuing year.

The President having called for the Report, it was read by Mr. W. Swanston, the senior hon. secretary, and will be found in full in the early pages of this part of the pro· ceedings.

The Treasurer (Mr. S. A. Stewart), on being called on for a Statement of Accounts, said that the Club's funds were in a very satisfactory condition, showing at the close of the year a larger balance in hands than they had at its commencement, notwithstanding many subscriptions have yet to be collected. Among the items of expenditure was a contribution toward the erection and preservation of the ancient cross of Dromore, which, it was stated, had now been restored and erected on a suitable site near the cathedral.

The election of president and officers for the next year was then proceeded with. Mr. William Gray, in referring to the admirable manner in which Mr. Robinson had discharged the duties of President for the past year, moved that he be re-elected to that office. The motion having been seconded by Mr. John Donaldson, it was put to the meeting by the proposer and passed unanimously. Mr. Robinson, after acknowledging the confidence the members had placed in him, thanked them for the honour they had again done him in re-electing him for the ensuing year. Mr. Joseph Wright, F.G.S., was, on the motion of Mr. R. Ll. Praeger, seconded by Mr. D. M'Kee, re-elected to the office of Vice-President. The Treasurer and Hon. Secretaries also retained their offices for another term, and the Committee was, with some changes, elected. The remainder of the evening was spent in hearing suggestions as to places suitable for excursions, and the best modes of visiting them, and in discussing changes that may be considered necessary in the prize list. The examination of the micro-slides and the photographs which received the prizes, and the election of new members—among whom Mr. Eliott, the Librarian of the new Free Library, was heartily welcomed—brought the meeting to a close.

It is with extreme regret that we are unable this year to furnish the Meteorological Summary and Weather Notes as formerly.

The death of Lancelot Turtle, Esq., J.P., to whose kindness we were indebted for these valuable records, took place at his residence, at Aghalee, in November, 1888.

The Committee take this opportunity of expressing their sorrow at the loss the Club has sustained of a valuable assistant, whose annual contributions to the Club's Proceedings were looked forward to with much pleasure, and were highly appreciated by the members.

RULES

OF THE

Belfast Naturalists' Field Club.

I.

That the Society be called "THE BELFAST NATURALISTS' FIELD CLUB."

II.

That the objects of the Society be the practical study of Natural Science and Archæology in Ireland.

III.

That the Club shall consist of Ordinary, Corresponding, and Honorary Members. The Ordinary Members to pay annually a subscription of Five Shillings, and that Candidates for such Membership shall be proposed and seconded at any meeting of the Club, by Members present, and elected by a majority of the votes of the Members present.

IV.

That the Honorary and Corresponding Members shall consist of persons of eminence in Natural Science, or who shall have done some special service to the Club, and whose usual residence is not less than twenty miles from Belfast. That such Members may be nominated by any Member of the Club, and on being approved of by the Committee, may be elected at any subsequent meeting of the Club by a majority of the votes of the Members present. That Corresponding Members be expected to communicate a paper once within every two years.

V.

That the Officers of the Club be annually elected, and consist of a President, Vice-President, Treasurer, Two Secretaries, and Ten Members, who form the Committee. Five to form a quorum. No Member of Committee to be eligible for re-election who has not attended at least one-fourth of the Committee Meetings during his year of office. That the office of President or that of Vice-President, shall not be held by the same person for more than two years in succession.

VI.

That the Members of the Club shall hold at least Six Field Meetings during the year, in the most interesting localities, for investigating the Natural History and Archæology of Ireland. That the place of meeting be fixed by the Committee, and that five days' notice of each excursion be communicated to Members by the Secretaries.

VII.

That Meetings be held Fortnightly or Monthly, at the discretion of the Committee, for the purpose of reading papers ; such papers, as far as possible, to treat of the Natural History and Archæology of the district. These meetings to be held during the months from November to April inclusive.

VIII.

That the Committee shall, if they find it advisable, offer for competition Prizes for the best collection of scientific objects of the district; and the Committee may order the purchase of maps, or other scientific apparatus, and may carry on geological and archæological researches or excavations, if deemed advisable, provided that the entire amount expended under this rule does not exceed the sum of £10 in any one year.

IX.

That the Annual Meeting be held during the month of April, when the Report of the Committee for the past year, and the Treasurer's Financial Statement shall be presented, the Committee and Officers elected, Bye-laws made and altered, and any proposed alteration in the general laws, of which a fortnight's notice shall have been given, in writing, to the Secretary or Secretaries, considered and decided upon. The Secretaries to give the Members due notice of such intended alteration.

X.

That, on the written requisition of Twenty-five Members, delivered to the Secretaries, an Extraordinary General Meeting may be called, to consider and decide upon the subjects mentioned in such written requisition.

XI.

That the Committee be empowered to exchange publications and reports, and to extend the privilege of attending the Meetings and Excursions of the Belfast Naturalists' Field Club to members of kindred Societies, on similar privileges being accorded to its Members by such other societies.

The following Rules for the Conducting of the Excursions have been arranged by the Committee.

I. The Excursion to be open to all Members, each one to have the privilege of introducing two friends.

II. A Chairman to be elected as at ordinary meetings.

III. One of the Secretaries to act as conductor, or, in the absence of both, a member to be elected for that purpose.

IV. No change to be made in the programme, or extra expense incurred, except by the consent of the majority of the members present.

V. No fees, gratuities, or other expenses to be paid except through the conductor.

VI. Every member or visitor to have the accommodation assigned by the conductor. When accommodation is limited, consideration will be given to priority of application.

VII. Accommodation cannot be promised unless tickets are obtained before the time mentioned in the special circular.

VIII. Those who attend an excursion, without previous notice, will be liable to extra charge, if extra cost be incurred thereby.

IX. No intoxicating liquors to be provided at the expense of the Club.

BELFAST NATURALISTS' FIELD CLUB.

TWENTY-SIXTH YEAR.

THE Committee offer the following Prizes to be competed for during the Session ending March 31st, 1889 :—

			£	s	d
I. Best Herbarium of Flowering Plants, representing not less than 250 species ...			£1	0	0
II. Best Herbarium of Flowering Plants, representing not less than 150 species ...			0	10	0
III. Best Collection of Mosses			0	10	0
IV.	„	Lichens	0	10	0
V.		Seaweeds	0	10	0
VI.		Ferns, Equiseta, and Lyco-pods	0	10	0
VII.		Tertiary and Post Tertiary Fossils	0	10	0
VIII.		Cretaceous Fossils ...	0	10	0
IX.	„	Liassic do. ...	0	10	0
X.		Permian and Carboniferous Fossils	0	10	0
XI.	..	Older Palæozoic do. ...	0	10	0
XII.		Marine Shells	0	10	0
XIII.	..	Land and Freshwater Shells	0	10	0

XIV.	Best Collection of Lepidoptera	...	...	£0	10	0
XV.	.. .. Hymenoptera	...	...	0	10	0
XVI.	Coleoptera	...	...	0	10	0
XVII.	Crustacea and Echino-					
	dermata	...	...	0	10	0

XVIII. Best Collection of Fungi ; names of species not necessary. Collectors may send (post-paid, from time to time during the season) their specimens to Rev. H. W. Lett, M.A., T.C.D., Aghaderg Glebe, Loughbrickland, who will record them to their credit   ... 0 10 0

XIX. Best Collection of Fossil Sponges 0 10 0

XX. Best Collection of 24 Microscopic Slides, illustrating some special branch of Natural History 0 10 0

XXI. Best Collection of 24 Microscopic Slides, showing general excellence 0 10 0

XXII. Best Set of 6 Field Sketches appertaining to Geology, Archæology, or Zoology   .. 0 10 0

XXIII. Best Set of 12 Photographs, illustrative of Irish Archæology. This Prize is open to Members of the Ulster Amateur Photo-graphic Society 0 10 0

SPECIAL PRIZES.

XXIV. The President offers a Prize of £1 1s. for the Best Set of three or more Original Sketches, to be placed in the Album of the Club. These may be executed in pen and ink or water colour, and must illustrate one or more ancient monuments somewhere in Ireland. In determining the relative merits of the sketches, accuracy in representing the subjects and their details will have chief place. This Prize is open to the Members of the Ramblers' Sketching Club, and to the Students of the School of Art

XXV. Mr. William Swanston, F.G.S., offers a Prize of 10s. 6d. for Six Photographs from Nature, illustrative of Geology, contributed to the Club's Album

---

CONDITIONS.

No competitor to obtain more than two Prizes in any year.

No competitor to be awarded the same Prize twice within three years.

A member to whom Prize No. 1 has been awarded shall be ineligible to compete for Prize No. 2, unless the plants are additions to those in previous collection.

In every case where three or more persons compete for a Prize, a second one, of half its value, will be awarded if the conditions are otherwise complied with.

All collections to be made personally during the Session in Ireland, except those for Prize 21, which need not necessarily be Irish, nor Competitors' own collecting. Each species to be correctly named, and locality stated. The Flowering Plants to be collected when in Flower, and classified according to the Natural System. The Microscopic Slides to be Competitors' own preparation and mounting. The Sketches and Photographs to be Competitors' own work, executed during the Session; and those sets for which Prizes are awarded, to become the property of the Club.

No Prizes will be awarded except to such Collections as shall, in the opinion of the Judges, possess positive merit.

The Prizes to be in books, or suitable scientific objects, at the desire of the successful competitor.

NOTICE.

---◇---

EXCHANGES OF PROCEEDINGS.

---◇---

Amiens—Societe Linneenne du Nord de la France.
Bulletins Nos. 175 to 186.

Belfast—Library and Society for Promoting Knowledge.
History of, by John Anderson, F.G.S, 1888.

   ,,   Natural History and Philosophical Society
Proceedings, 1887-88.

Berwickshire Naturalists' Field Club.
Proceedings. Vol. XI., No. 2.

Bristol Naturalists' Society.
Annual Report, 1888.

Cardiff Naturalists' Society.
Transactions. Vol. XIX., Parts 1 and 2, and Vol. XX., Part 1.

Cornwall—Royal Institution of,
Journal. Vol. IX., Parts 1, 2, 3.

Costa Rica—Muse Nacional.
Anals. Tomo I., 1887.

Dublin Naturalists' Field Club.
Report, 1888.

Dublin Royal Irish Academy,
>   Proceedings. Series II., Vol. II., No. 8; Series III., Vol.
>   I., No. 1.
>   Transactions. Vol. XXIX., Parts 1 and 2.
>   Cunningham Memoirs, No. 4.
>   List of Papers, 1786 to to 1886.

„   Royal Geological Society of Ireland.
>   Journal. New Series, Vol. VII., Part 2.

Edinburgh Botanical Society.
>   Transactions and Proceedings. Vol. XVII. Part 1.

„   Geological Society.
>   Transactions. Vol. V., Part IV.

Frankfurt—Monatliche Mittheilungen, aus dem Gesammt-
gebliete der Naturwissenschaften.
>   Nos. 7 to 12, 1887-88; Nos. 1 to 6, 1888-89.

Frankfurt—Societatum Litteræ.
>   Jarg. 1887-19.

Glasgow Natural History Society.
>   Proceedings and Transactions. New Series, Vol. II., Part 1.

Hertfordshire Natural History Society and Field Club.
>   Transactions. Vol. IV., Parts 8 and 9; Vol. V., Parts 1, 2, 3.

Leeds Philosophical and Literary Society.
>   Annual Report, 1887-88.

Liverpool Geological Society.
>   Proceedings, 1887-88.

„   Naturalists' Field Club.
>   Proceedings, 1887.

London—British Association for the Advancement of Science.
>   Report of Manchester Meeting, 1887.

„   Geologists' Association.
>   Proceedings. Vol. IX., No. 8; Vol. X., Nos. 1 to 8.

Manchester Microscopical Society.
>   Transactions and Annual Report, 1887.
>   Scientific Students' Association.
>   Report and Proceedings, 1887.
>   Field Naturalists' and Archæologists' Society.
>   Report and Proceedings, 1887.

New Brunswick Natural History Society.
Bulletin, No. VII.

Plymouth Institution.
Annual Report and Transactions. Vol. X., Part 1.

Toronto—Canadian Institute.
Proceedings. Vol. V., Fasciculus 2 ; Vol. VI., Fasciculus 1.
Annual Report, 1886-87.

U.S.A.—California Academy of Sciences.
Bulletin. Vol. II., No. 8.

,   Minnesota Geological and Natural History Survey.
Fifteenth Annual Report, 1886 ; Bulletin, Nos. 2, 3, 4.

,,   Meriden Scientific Association.
Transactions. Vol. II.

,,   New York—American Museum of Natural History.
Annual Report, 1887-88.

         Academy of Sciences.
Transactions. Vols. VI., VII., Nos. 1 to 8.

         ,   Lyceum of Natural History.
Proceedings from January 1873, to June, 1874 ;
Annals Vols. X., and XI.

,   Philadelphia—Academy of Science.
Proceedings. Parts 1, 2, 3 ; Part 2, 1888.

,,   Raleigh—Elisha Mitchell Scientific Society.
Journal, 1887-88.

,,   Salem—American Association for Advancement of
Science.
Proceedings of Thirty-sixth Meeting, 1887.
Essex Institute Bulletin, Vol. XIX., Parts 1 and 2.
Guide to Salem, published by Henry P. Ives.

,,   Trenton—Natural History Society.
Journal, No. 3.

..   Washington Smithsonian Institution.
Annual Report. Part 2, 1885.
The American Microscopical Journal, 2 parts.

Warwickshire Naturalists' and Archæologists' Field Club.
Proceedings, 1887.

Wiltshire Archæological and Natural History Society.
Flowering Plants of Wilts, by Rev. T. A. Preston, M.A.

BELFAST NATURALISTS' FIELD CLUB

TWENTY-SIXTH YEAR, 1888-89.

LIST OF OFFICERS AND MEMBERS.

PRESIDENT:

HUGH ROBINSON, M.R.I.A.

VICE-PRESIDENT:

JOSEPH WRIGHT, F.G.S.

TREASURER:

S. A. STEWART, F.B.S.Edin.,
THE MUSEUM.

SECRETARIES:

WM. SWANSTON, F.G.S.,   F. W. LOCKWOOD,
50 KING STREET.   EAGLE CHAMBERS, ROYAL AVENUE

COMMITTEE:

JOHN J. ANDREW, L.D.S.,   WM. GRAY, M.R.I.A.
R.C.S., Eng.

CHARLES BULLA.   JOHN HAMILTON.

GEORGE DONALDSON.   DANIEL M'KEE.

JOHN DONALDSON.   R. Ll. PRAEGER, B.A., B.E.

W. A. FIRTH.   JOHN VINYCOMB.

Members.

Any Changes in the Addresses of Members should be notified to the Secretaries.

Edward Allworthy, Langford Villa.
John Anderson, J.P., F.G.S., Hill-
brook, Holywood.
Robert Anderson, Meadowlands.
Rev. John Andrew, Belgravia, Lis-
burn Road
John J. Andrew, L.D.S., R.C.S.,
Eng., Belgravia, Lisburn Road.
Mrs. Andrews, Seaview, Shore Rd.

James M. Barkley, Queen's Square.
Robert Barklie, Wilmont Terrace
James Barr, Sandringham.
William Batt, Sorrento, Windsor.
Miss Emma Beck, Old Lodge Road.
Geo. R. Begley, Wolfhill Lodge,
Ligoniel.
James Best, Great Victoria Street.
Francis J. Bigger, Airdrie, Antrim
Road.
Edward Bingham, Ponsonby Av.
Mrs. Blair, Camberwell Terrace.
E. Blair, Camberwell Terrace.
Edward Braddell, St. Ives, Malone
Park.
Wm. Thomas Brand, M.B., Florida
Manor, Killinchy.
Hugh B. Brandon, Atlantic Avenue.
Chas. H. Brett, Gretton Villa South.
John Thorley Brindley, Ulsterville
Terrace.
Rev. John Bristow, St. James'
Parsonage.
John Brown, Edenderry House, Co.
Down.
Miss Rowena Brown, Edenderry
House.
Thomas Brown, Donegall Street.
James A. Browne, Wilmont Terrace.
John Browne, J.P., Ravenhill House.
John Browne, M.R.I.A., Drapers-
field, Cookstown.
W. J. Browne, M.R.I.A., Highfield,
Omagh.
W. W. Brydon, Silverstream, Green-
island.
Charles Bulla, Brougham Street.

H. Burden, M.D., M.R.I.A., Alfred
Street.
J. R. Burnett, Martello, Holywood.

Wm. Campbell, Allworthy Avenue.
Ernest Carr, Cliftonville
Miss Carruthers, Claremont Street.
E. T. Church, Donegall Place.
J. C. Clarke, Antrim Road.
Jas. Cleland, Tobarmhuire, Crossgar.
William Clibborn, Windsor Terrace.
Stanley B. Coates, L.R.C.P., Edin.,
Shaftesbury Square.
James Coey, Victoria Street.
W. F. C. S. Corry, Chatsworth.
Rev. W. Cotter, D.D., Riversdale
Terrace, Balmoral.
George B. Coulter, Helen's Bay.
Mrs. Coulter, Helen's Bay.
James Creeth, Riversdale Terrace,
Balmoral.
Robert Culbert, Distillery Street.
Samuel Cunningham, Glencairn.
Francis Curley, Dunedin, Antrim
Road.
Mrs. Curley, Dunedin, Antrim Road.
William Curry, Botanic Avenue.

Marquis of Dufferin (Hon. Mem.)
John Henry Davies, Glenmore
Cottage.
Henry Davis, Holywood.
Robert Day, F.S.A., Cork.
Wakefield H. Dixon, J.P., Dunowen.
Geo. Donaldson, Bloomfield Avenue.
John Donaldson, Eglinton Street.
W. J. Dunlop, Bryson Street.

David Elliott, Albert Bridge Road.
Geo. H. Elliott, Lorne Villas, South
Parade.
George Elliott, Royal Avenue.
Lavens M. Ewart, J.P., Glenbank.

John Fagan, F.R.C.S., J.P., Glen-
gall Place.

Godfrey W. Ferguson, Murray's
Terrace.
J. H. Ferguson, Belgrave, Knock.
Joseph Firth, Whiterock.
W. A. Firth, Springfield Road.
Thomas J. G. Fleming, F.G.S.,
Limavady.
T. M. H. Flynn, Sunnyside, Bess-
brook.

J. Starkie Gardner, F.G.S., Damer
Terrace, Chelsea (Hon. Mem.)
R. M. Gilmore, Garden Vale, Ath-
lone.
William J. Gilmore, Camberwell
Villas.
George J. Glen, Hartington Street.
William Godwin, Queen Street.
Rev. David Gordon, Downpatrick.
James Goskar, Carlisle Circus.
James Gourley, J.P., Derryboy,
Killyleagh.
Rev. Canon Grainger, D.D.,M.R.I.A.,
Broughshane.
Robert Graham, Brookview Terrace.
William Gray, M.R.I.A., Mount-
charles.
Miss Gray, Mountcharles.
Mrs. Arabella Greer, Seville Lodge,
Strandtown.
Geo. Greer, Esq., J.P., Woodville,
Lurgan.
Edward Gregg, Claremont Street.
Rev. S. Griffiths, Ponsonby Avenue.
Mrs. Griffiths, Ponsonby Avenue.

John Hamilton, Mount Street.
Rev. Thos. Hamilton, D.D., Brook-
vale House.
Richard Hanna, Charleville Street.
Mann Harbison, Ravenhill Terrace.
Rev. Canon Hartrick, The Rectory,
Ballynure.
Sir James Haslett, J.P., Princess
Gardens.
Thos. Hassen, Strangemore House
Rev. Canon Hayes, Dromore.
W. D. Hazelton, Cliftonville.
F. A. Heron, Cultra.
J. S. Holden, M.D., F.G.S., Sud-
bury, Suffolk (Cor. Mem.)
John Horner, Cliftonville.
Alexander Hunter, Northern Bank.
W. J. Hurst, J.P., Drumaness,
Lisburn.

James Imrie, Fitzroy Avenue.

H. Jamison, Duncairn Terrace.
W. J. Johnston, J.P., Dunesk,
Stranmillis.
Prof. T. Rupert Jones, F.R.S.,
Chelsea, London (Hon. Mem.)

John Kane, LL.B., Chichester Street.
W. Kennedy, Crescent Terrace.
Archibald Kent, Newington Street.
Wm. Kernahan, Wellington Park.
George Kidd, Lisnatore, Dunmurry.
F. Kirkpatrick, Ann Street.
W. J. Knowles, M.R.I.A., Bally-
mena.
Robert A. Kyle, Richmond.

W. W. Lamb, Salisbury Avenue.
Prof. Charles Lapworth, F.G.S.,
Mason College, Birmingham
(Hon. Mem.)
F. R. Lepper, Carnalea.
Rev. H. W. Lett, M.A., T.C.D.,
Aghaderg Glebe, Loughbrick-
land.
Fredk. W. Lockwood, Wellington
Park terrace.
James Logan, Donegall Street.
Joseph Lowe, Pim Street.
W. B. Lowson, Chichester Park.
H. W. Luther, M.D., Chlorine
House.

John Mackenzie, Myrtlefield.
Henry Magee, Eglantine Avenue.
Rev. J. J. Major, Belvoir Hall,
Ballymacarrett.
Greer Malcomson, Granville Ter.
Harold Malcolmson, Holywood
Jas. Malcomson, Rosemount, Knock.
Mrs. Malcomson, Rosemount, Knock.
John Marsh, Glenlyon, Holywood.
Mrs. Marsh, Glenlyon, Holywood.
Joseph C. Marsh, Castleton Terrace.
Rev. James Martin, Eglintoun,
Antrim Road.
J. M'Clelland Martin, Oceanic Av.
Mrs. Martin, Eglintoun, Antrim Rd.
James Meneely, Donegall Pass.
Seaton Forrest Milligan, M.R.I.A.,
Royal Terrace.
Dr. Moran, Bangor.
Thomas Morrison, Great George's
Street.

R. Joynt Morrison, Limestone Rd.
David Morrow, Church Hill, Holy-
    wood.
Geo. Morrow, North Queen Street.
John Morton, Clifton Park Avenue
Mrs. George E. Murray, Botanic
    Avenue.
James Murdoch, Denmark Street.
Joseph John Murphy, Osborne Park.
J. R. Musgrave, J.P., Drumglass,
    Malone.
John M'Alister, Fitzwilliam Street.
Thomas M'Alister, Carlisle Street.
Joseph M'Chesney, Holywood.
Francis P. M'Clean, Huntly Villas.
H. M'Cleery, Clifton Park Avenue.
James M'Clenahan, Tennent Street.
Rev. Ed. M'Clure, M.A., M.R.I.A.,
    Onslow Place, South Kensing-
    ton, London (Cor. Mem.)
John M'Clure, Donlure, Bloomfield.
Sir Thomas M'Clure, Bart., Belmont.
W. J. M'Clure, Elizabeth Street.
Jas. M'Connell, Caledonia Terrace.
F. W M'Cullough, Stoneyford.
W. F. MacElheran, Botanic Av.
Miss M'Gaw, Wellington Park Ter.
John H. MacIlwaine, Brandon
    Villa.
Mrs. MacIlwaine, Brandon Villa.
Daniel M'Kee, Adela Place.
W. S. M'Kee, Fleetwood Street.
Alexander MacLaine, J.P., Queen's
    Elms.
Miss Annie M'Liesh, The Mount,
    Mountpottinger.
John M'Liesh, The Mount, Mount-
    pottinger.
John M'Liesh, Jun., The Mount,
    Mountpottinger.
Robert M'Liesh, The Mount, Mount-
    pottinger.
William MacMillan, Enniscorthy.
John M'Stay, College Square East.

Lucien Nepveu, Claremont Street.
W. Courtney Nesbitt, Kinnaird
    Terrace.
William Nicholl, Donegall Square
    North.
H. J. Nicholson, Ardsallagh, Windsor.
Jerdan Nichols, Meadowbank Street.

Henry O'Neill, M.D., College Square
    East.

Jas. O'Neill, M.A., College Square
    East.
A. T. Osborne, Rosetta Terrace,
    Ballynafeigh.
Graham L. Owens, Henry Street.

W. J. Pasley, Carrickfergus.
D. C. Patterson, Holywood.
Robert Lloyd Patterson, J.P., F.L.S.,
    Croft House, Holywood.
Wm. H. Patterson, M.R.I.A., Gar-
    ranard, Strandtown.
Frank Peel, Annesley Street.
W. H. Phillips, Lemonfield, Holy-
    wood.
Mrs. Sara T. Pickop, The Rectory,
    Hatcliffe, Lincolnshire.
E. W. Pim, Elmwood Terrace.
John Pim, J.P., Bonaven, Antrim
    Road.
Joshua Pim, Slieve-na-Failthe,
    Whiteabbey.
Thomas W. Pim, The Lodge, Strand-
    town.
R. Lloyd Praeger, B.A., B.E., The
    Croft, Holywood.

Joseph Bradley, Prospect Hill, Lis-
    burn.
John H. Rea, M.D., Shaftesbury
    Square.
D. Redmond, Antrim.
Robert Reid, King Street.
Richard Ridings, Hampton Terrace.
Rev. George Robinson, M.A., Beech
    Hill House, Armagh.
Hugh Robinson, M.R.I.A., Helen's
    View, Antrim Road.
Jas. R. Robinson, George's Terrace.
W. A. Robinson, J.P., Crofton,
    Holywood.
Richard Ross, M.D., Wellington
    Place.
W. A. Ross, Craigavad.
John Ryan, Cork.
Robt. A. Russell, Colinview Terrace.

James Shanks, Ballyfounder, Porta-
    ferry.
Edward Smith, Chichester Terrace.
Rev. W. S. Smith, The Manse,
    Antrim.
Rev. Canon Smythe, M.A., Coole
    Glebe, Carnmoney.
Wilson Smyth, Virginia Street.

Adam Speers, B.Sc., Holywood.
A. C. Stannus, Holywood.
Sir N. A. Staples, Bart., Lissan (Life Member).
Jas. Stelfox, Oakleigh, Ormeau Park.
John B. Stephens, Martello Terrace, Holywood.
John Stevenson, Coolavin.
J. M'N. Stevenson, Carrickfergus.
S. A. Stewart, Springfield Road.
W. A. Story, Methodist College.
W. Swanston, F.G.S., Cliftonville Avenue.
Mrs. Swanston, Cliftonville Avenue.
Richard Glascott Symes, M.A., F.G.S., Portrush.
Saml. Symington, Ballyoran House.

Alex. Tate, C.E., Longwood House.
Prof. RalphTate, F.G.S., F.L.S., Adelaide, South Australia (Hon. Member).
Mrs. Thomas, Lower Crescent.
S. G. Thomas, Limestone Road.
George Thomson, Falls Road.
Mrs. H Thompson, Crosshill, Windsor
Prof. Jas. Thomson, L.L.D., F.R.S. Hon. Member).
John Todd, Clonavon.
W. A. Todd, Elgin Terrace.
W. A. Traill, M.A.I., Portrush.
W. J. Trelford, Vicinage Park.
James Turner, Mountain Bush.
James G. Turtle, Cambridge Terrace.

John Vinycomb, Holywood.

Rev. Chas. Herbert Waddell, Glengormley.
W. F. Wakeman, M.R.I.A., Dublin (Cor. Mem.)
Robert Walker, Brookhill Avenue.
T. R. Walkington, Edenvale.
George G. Ward, Eversleigh, Strandtown.
Isaac W. Ward Salisbury Terrace.
Joseph Ward, Salisbury Terrace.
Thomas Watson, Shipquay Gate, Londonderry.
Isaac Waugh, Clifton Park Avenue.
Robert J. Welch, Lonsdale Street.
Louis Werner, B.A., Thorndale Terrace.
Walter L. Wheeler, Lennoxvale.
Robt. Whitfield, Kenbella Avenue.
Wm. Whitla, M.D., J.P., College Square North.
Jas. Wilson, Oldforge, Dunmurry.
Jas. Wilson, Ballybundon, Killinchy
James F. Wilson, Ventry Street.
Rev. R. Workman, M.A., Rubane, Glastry.
Thomas Workman, J.P., Craigdarragh.
Frederick A. Wrathall, Lisburn.
Joseph Wright, F.G.S., York Street.
Mrs. Wright, York Street.
W. C. Wright, Lauriston.
S. O. Wylie, Melbourne, Australia.
Wm. Wylie, Mountpleasant.

Robert Young, C.E., Rathvarna.

ANNUAL REPORT

AND

PROCEEDINGS

OF THE

Belfast Naturalists' Field Club

FOR THE

Year ending the 31st March, 1889.

(TWENTY-SIXTH YEAR)

SERIES II.   VOLUME III,   PART II.

Belfast:

PRINTED FOR THE CLUB,

BY ALEXANDER MAYNE & BOYD, CORPORATION STREET,
PRINTERS TO QUEEN'S COLLEGE, BELFAST.

1889.

REPORT

OF THE

BELFAST NATURALISTS' FIELD CLUB,

FOR THE

Year ending 31st March, 1889.

HE year which now closes is one in which the Club's position has been fully maintained in all its departments of work. The membership remains about the same as at the close of the preceding year.

The summer programme proved a very attractive one, and it was with one exception carried out, embracing seven field meetings as follow :—

1. Dromore	...	...	...	May 26th.
2. Stoneyford	...	...	...	June 23rd.
3. Greenore and Carlingford	. .	...	...	July 7th.
4. Drogheda and the Boyne	...	...	...	July 26th & 27th.
5. Cave Hill	...	...	...	August 4th.
6. Ballycastle	...	...	...	August 18th.
7. Belvoir Park	...	...	...	September 8th.

The excursion to Drogheda and the Boyne was a departure from the ordinary custom, in that it was jointly undertaken with the Dublin Naturalists' Field Club. The result was an exceedingly instructive and interesting meeting, and it proved a source of pleasant and profitable interchange of thought with the members of the Dublin Society.

The excursion to Belvoir Park was perhaps the most largely attended of any in the Club's history.

The Winter Session was opened by a Social Meeting in November, and in addition six Ordinary Meetings were held, one of which, devoted to the microscope and its manipulation, was more than usually appreciated, and it proved a good opportunity for estimating the advances made in this highly popular field of work.

The attendance of members at both the Summer and Winter Meetings was above the average of past years.

The following are the particulars of the various Winter Meetings :—

6th Nov.   I.— Social Meeting.
20th Nov.   II.—Presidential Address.
18th Dec.   III.—" A Deep Sea Dredging Expedition," by R. L. Praeger, B.A., B.E.
29th Jan.   IV. { " Photography as an Aid to the Club's Work," by W. Swanston, F.G.S.
26th Feb.   V.—Microscopic Evening.
26th Mar.   VI. { "Vestiges of Early Man in Antrim and Down, " by William Gray, M.R.I.A.
9th April   VII. { " Notes on Desmids found in the North of Ireland," by Rev. H. W. Lett, M.A., T.C.D.
                     { " Notes on the Seven Churches of Glendalough," by F. W. Lockwood.

A most important event of the year was undoubtedly the issue under the Club's auspices of " The Flora of the North-East of Ireland," by S. A. Stewart, F.B.S. Edin., and the late T. H. Corry, M A., F.L.S., M.R.I.A., &c., a publication which your Committee look upon with pride as the original work of two members of the Club, and which, they consider, reflects much credit upon the authors. The careful and thorough manner in which it was carried through the press by Mr. Stewart, upon whom, under most melancholy circumstances, fell the entire work of editing, is deserving of high praise.

The volume of Proceedings for the past year, which has been recently issued, is a more than usually important one, the Presidential address, given in full, being a valuable record of the progress of science during the period that has elapsed since the establishment of the Club.

Besides this address and the usual reports of the excursions and summaries of the papers read, there is a valuable appendix on the Marine Shells of the North of Ireland, by Robert Lloyd Praeger, B.A., B.E., the result of a great amount of patient work and research in bringing together into a connected form all that is published and known of this important branch of local natural history, information which until the present time was scattered in many different publications difficult of access, and often obscured by a multiplicity of synonyms.

It is with deep regret that your Committee record the loss the Club has sustained during the past year by the death of Launcelot Turtle, Esq., J.P., to whom the Club have for many years been indebted for the valuable meteorological tables and weather notes which enriched your proceedings. Your Committee, anxious to continue the publication of these important tables, ask the aid of observers in this department.

Your Committee have also to record the loss of one of the past Presidents of the Club, Lieutenant-General Smythe, R.A., F.R.S., M.R.I.A., &c., a gentleman who took a lively interest in the Club's operations, especially in the department of Irish archæology. The death of Mr. George O'Brien also removed from your ranks one of the earliest members, who for many years assisted by his counsel on the Committee, and otherwise in advancing the Club's interests.

Your Committee avail themselves of this opportunity of thanking all who have in any way assisted the Club in carrying out its aims during the past year, and they would especially mention the Belfast Water Commissioners and their engineering staff at Stoneyford, for the manner in which the Club were conducted over the works in operation there; also Lord Deramore for kindly granting permission to enter the extensive grounds of Belvoir Park.

Your Committee continue to exchange your published proceedings for those of kindred societies, and they beg to express their thanks to the United States Government for the valuable publications received from time to time from various state scientific departments.

The following is the report of the Judges appointed to examine the collections sent in by members in competition for the Club's Prizes :—

We have carefully examined the several collections submitted in competition for the Club's Prizes, and regret that they are not so numerous as on former occasions.

We award No. 9 Prize, for Liassic Fossils, to Mr. Daniel M'Kee, whose collection contains a few very good specimens ; we think, however, that they have not been mounted as carefully as would be desired.

We regret that we cannot award Mr. M'Kee Prize 20 for his collection of Microscopical Slides, which is excellent in many respects, but does not strictly conform to the terms of competition.

We have no hesitation in awarding Mr. J. J. Andrew Prize No. 21 for Microscopic Slides showing general excellence. His collection contains some very difficult subjects, and all are carefully prepared and beautifully mounted.

WILLIAM GRAY
JOSEPH WRIGHT.

Dr. THE TREASURER IN ACCOUNT WITH THE BELFAST NATURALISTS' FIELD CLUB, Cr.

FOR THE YEAR ENDING 31st MARCH, 1889.

	£	s.	d.		£	s.	d.
To Balance from 1887-8 ...	44	3	11	By Expenses of Social Meeting ...	4	16	3
,, Subscriptions—231, less 10 paid in advance ...	55	5	0	,, Mayne and Boyd, Printing and Binding "Flora" ...	73	4	3
,, Gain on Excursions ...	0	1	11	,, Index for Volume of Proceedings ...	1	16	0
,, Tickets for Social Meeting ...	0	19	0	,, Printing Annual Proceedings ...	25	6	3
,, R. W. Corry, Esq., towards cost of "Flora" ...	35	0	0	,, R. Welch, Collotype Photos. for do. ...	5	0	0
,, Sales of the "Guide to Belfast" ...	4	0	6	,, S. A. Stewart, expenses re "Flora" ...	5	0	0
,, ,, "Flora—N.E. Ireland" ...	7	15	8	,, M. Ward & Co., Scrap Album ...	0	10	6
,, Interest on Bank Account ...	0	17	7	,, ,, Writing names on Photos.	0	5	0
				,, Stationery, Printing, and Advertising ...	13	0	9
				,, Delivery of Circulars ...	1	10	0
				,, Postages ...	5	9	2
				,, Rent of Lecture Hall ...	5	5	0
				,, W. Darragh ...	3	3	0
				,, Insurance of Books ...	0	11	6
				,, Prizes awarded ...	1	0	0
				,, Balance in hand ...	2	5	11
	£148	3	7		£148	3	7
To Balance ...	£2	5	11				

Audited and found correct

WILLIAM SWANSTON, *Hon. Secretary.*

S. A. STEWART, *Treasurer.*

SUMMER SESSION.

The following Excursions were made during the Summer Session :—

On May 26th, to

DROMORE AND THE VICINITY.

The party, reaching Dromore about noon, proceeded first to the old Bishop's Palace, which has some historical interest, as having been the residence for many years of Dr. Percy, Protestant Bishop of the diocese, the author of " The Reliques of English Poetry." It was here several of his ballads were written, including the well-known " O ! Nannie, wilt thou gang wi' me ?" After the consolidation of the Irish sees the property was sold, and, on the recent death of the proprietor, was converted into a Jesuit seminary. The Rev. J. Colgan, the principal, most courteously showed the party over the house. Great as is the change since the days of the literary bishop, the house is still dedicated to the advancement of letters, and the leafy murmur of the lofty trees that surround it is as conducive as ever to academic musings. In a corner of the grounds is " the Mass Forth," an ancient fort, with a very deep and perfect ditch and lofty rampart. It derives its local name from having been used by the Catholic clergy for the celebra-

tion of the Mass during the days of the proscription. From
thence the route was taken towards Gilhall, but a halt was
made by the way at another very fine double fort, close to the
banks of the Lagan. Through the kindness of Mr. George
Brush, J.P., the party then visited the demesne of Gilhall, the
woods of which were just bursting into leaf, and the ground
was thickly carpeted with wild hyacinth. The marshy and
wooded ground by the riverside is well suited for a variety of
native plants, but the season was not yet sufficiently advanced for
successful botanising. The Giant Bellflower (*Campanula latifolia*) has been introduced to the grounds, and grows there in
great abundance. It was seen on the present occasion in plenty
by the Lagan side, but not yet in flower.

On returning to Dromore, a visit was paid to the Cathedral,
where lie the remains of Jeremy Taylor and of Mr. Stott, a
bleacher of literary repute, whom Byron has rather unfairly
pilloried in his *English Bards and Scotch Reviewers*, under
the epithet of " Grovelling Stott," the adjective being presumably intended for his standing as a poet rather than his character as a man. The remains of the ancient cross, recently set
up adjoining the Cathedral, were then visited, and focussed by
the cameras of the party. The cross, which has been very
neatly and appropriately restored, bears the following inscription :—" The ancient historical cross of Dromore, erected and
restored after many years of neglect, by public subscription, to
which the Board of Works were contributors, under the auspices of the Town Commissioners of Dromore.—1887." It may
be stated that the Belfast Naturalists' Field Club were amongst
the contributors to its re-erection. An adjournment was then
made to Malloch's Hotel, where tea was partaken of. Afterwards a meeting was held—Alexander Tate, Esq., C.E., in the
chair—when several new members were elected. The excursion was finished up by a visit to the great fort, with triple
ramparts, just outside the town. The central fort is very high,
being on the summit of a hill which has been scarped out to
form ditches and ramparts. At the foot of the hill, beside the

river, is a large square enclosure, with earthen ramparts. The fort is one of the finest and most conspicuous in the county.

On June 23rd, to

STONEYFORD.

An extra excursion was made on 23rd June to Stoneyford, to examine the new works in progress there for the Belfast Water Commissioners. Although the special circular announcing the excursion gave but very short notice to members, a large party assembled at the Linen Hall at two o'clock, and, mounted on brakes and cars, rattled at a rapid pace through the town. The day is hot and sultry, and in the streets rather oppressive ; but when the Borough Cemetery is passed, and the road, rising by degrees, runs through green fields over which a gentle breeze is blowing, a decided sense of relief and pleasure is experienced. The eye wanders from the dull yellow cloud which overhangs the busy, noisy town, to where the richly-wooded Lagan valley lies sleeping in the afternoon sun, and beyond, where over the undulating extent of County Down the peaks of the Mourne Mountains rise through the summer haze. The road winds steadily upward along the slopes of the Black Mountain ; Colin Glen is crossed, and, rounding the fir crowned Colin Mountain, Castle Robin, the first halting-place, is reached. Here the party is met by an advanced guard from Stoneyford, consisting of a detachment of the engineering staff of the Water Commissioners.

Castle Robin is now but a fragmentary ruin, hung with clinging ivy, and tenanted by chattering sparrows. Its erection is ascribed to Roger Norton, an officer in the army of the Earl of Essex. Its name appears to have been derived from the rath close to which it stands, and which in old days was called Lis-ne-robin. Both rath and castle have now to bear the trying ordeal of being the target for a whole battery of cameras, after which the vehicles are once more mounted, and crossing now into a broad valley behind the ridge of hills, a short run brings the party to Stoneyford. Here they are met by the courteous and energetic manager of the works, Mr. Lattimore, who is ably supported by several of the engineering staff, and the party proceed to examine the site of the great future reservoir. A broad, flat valley, flanked on either side by low hills, and narrowed suddenly near its lower end, affords an excellent opportunity for the construction of an artificial lake of large extent, and across the valley a huge embankment over a mile long is now steadily rising. It being Saturday afternoon, no work is at present in progress ; but the network of tram-lines, the rows of tip-waggons, and piles of wheel-barrows, and great heaps of stone, clay, and " puddle" show the extent of the works, and the number of the army of men who on Monday morning will recommence their weekly labours. A low, swelling hill in front of the dam has half disappeared beneath the attack of pick and shovel, and its steep escarpment affords the geologists an excellent opportunity of observing over a considerable area a section of the boulder clay of which it is composed. Below a couple of feet of fine yellowish clay, which is all carefully preserved for making " puddle," there is a band, some six feet in thickness, of blackish boulder clay, which overlies a thick bed of typical boulder clay of the usual red colour, full of fragments and blocks of rock of a variety of descriptions, trap and chalk predominating. A member points out that many of the smaller pieces of chalk have been completely dissolved away, and that in the cavities thus left in the tough clay calcareous incrustations often occur, apparently the result of precipitation of the calcium carbonate held in solution by percolating water. Some small fragments of the well-known silicified wood of Antrim are found in the Boulder Clay, and on the bank near at hand some fine pieces of the same material, found in the excavations, are inspected. Nodules of iron-stone, derived from the basaltic formation of Antrim, are present in abundance, some of them yielding very perfect impressions of leaves and twigs belonging to the rich Tertiary flora which the

valuable papers of Mr. J. Starkie Gardner, F.G.S., contributed
to the Club's Proceedings, have made familiar to us.

But now the Secretary's shrill whistle sounds the recall, and
the scattered party assemble near the manager's cheerful house,
where a hearty vote of thanks is passed to Mr. Lattimore and
the engineering staff for their attention and courtesy, and to
Mrs. Lattimore and her amiable daughters for their hospitable
treatment of the lady members of the party. Then taking the
road once more, Castle Robin is repassed, and, turning down
the hill, a new route is taken *via* Derriaghy, and at about eight
o'clock Belfast is once more reached.

On 7th July, to

GREENORE AND CARLINGFORD.

The third excursion of the season was to Greenore and Carlingford. Starting at seven o'clock, the party of about a dozen
was augmented to upwards of twenty ere the journey was
finished. After an hour spent at Greenore, which was devoted
to a rather hurriedly-taken refreshment and a stroll along the
beach, where the botanists were repaid by some rare plants, the
road was taken to Carlingford, skirting some low ground with
pools rich in aquatic species. The excursion was mainly, however, an archæological one, Carlingford and neighbourhood
being famous for castellated remains ; and perhaps never in its
history were its ancient buildings so well "done" as on this
occasion. The party mustered in its numbers no less than five
photographers, with cameras of as many shapes and sizes, bent
upon illustrating the place in a manner more complete than
ever before attempted. The ruined abbey to the south of the
town was first visited. It dates from the fourteenth century,
and its erection is ascribed to Richard De Burgh, Earl of Ulster.
Its ruin took place in the seventeenth century. It now forms
a picturesque pile, and what remains of it seems to be taken
care of, and further decay prevented. Entering the town we

pass under the ancient Tholsel, which has lost its antique character by an improved roof. In the street a castellated buiding with quaint window tracings attracts attention, and there is another further on of larger dimensions. Both are evidently dwellings of the Elizabethan age. King John's Castle should, perhaps, have been named first, for certainly it is the most conspicuous and important feature in the town. Its history, too, has been an eventful one. It was occupied as early as A D. 1210, and it played a most important part in the changeful history of the place between that early date and its final ruin early in the seventeenth century. The modern town is a clean, tidy, crooked little place, the inhabitants much given to whitewashing, and altogether it wears a cheerful, contented air, which the London and North-Western Railway, passing its doors, has not altered in the least degree from its quiet old ways. The surroundings from any point of view are simply charming. The sheltered lough, across which the well-wooded Rostrevor mountains, backed by the more distant Mourne range, form an outlook few places possess ; while Slieve Foy, with its dark serrated ridge rising immediately behind the town, makes a fitting background to the bright houses and ancient castles, nestling along the shore. Viewing the sights, botany, and photography soon sped away the best part of the day. Several of the party had scaled the mountain ; but the approach of train time assembled all on the railway platform well pleased with the trip. A few good plants were secured by the botanists. The Horned Poppy (*Glaucium flavum*) was found near Greenore, the Columbine was found at the base of the mountain, the Beech Fern among the crags higher up, while the Red Valerian (*Centranthus ruber*) has seized on every piece of old wall or suitable rock exposure, and with its huge tufts of crimson flowers has lighted up their otherwise grey tints. The photographers were happy. A total of about fifty plates were exposed, which will no doubt be brought into requisition during the winter session. Leaving Carlingford by train, a short halt was made at Newry, where, after a welcome tea at the Athenæum, the business meeting of the day was held. After the formal business had been transacted, the hon. secretary called attention to the fact that the long-looked-for *Flora of the North-East of Ireland*, by Messrs. Stewart and Corry, was now completed and in his hands, and he was pleased to say that it was a work that the members should be proud of, as he considered the authors had conferred a lasting honour on the Club by allowing it to be brought out under their auspices. Mr. Harbison (the chairman) spoke in strong terms of praise on the manner in which Mr. S. A Stewart, under the sad circumstances of the death of his colleague, had carried the work to completion, and he was sure the members generally would possess themselves of a book of such great local importance. The return journey left the party at 9 p m. in town again, after a long but very pleasant and profitable day.

On 26th and 27th July, to

DROGHEDA AND THE BOYNE.

The fourth excursion of the session was the " long excursion" of the year, and brought the Club to the banks of the historic Boyne Water. They had previously challenged the younger Field Club of Dublin to meet them on the Boyne, and accordingly a representative party from each Club met at Drogheda on the arrival of the early trains from Dublin and Belfast, and immediately proceeded by train to Kells. The Rev. Canon Grainger, D.D., M.R.I.A., was elected Chairman for the excursion. Many circumstances combined to compel the party to direct their attention almost exclusively to archæological matters, chiefly because of the extraordinary number, variety, and importance of the antiquarian remains to be found in the district. Kells and its neighbourhood could furnish interesting occupation for as many days as the party had hours to spend. The town itself, which is most beautifully situated, is a creditable example of an Irish inland town—orderly, clean, and well built, its stately buildings illustrating the superior quality of the local carboniferous limestone as a building material, and its neat thatched cottages, hedgerows, and flower plots forming picturesque subjects for the rambling artist, but beyond all, its rich assemblage of antiquarian remains associated with the ancient glory and romantic history of Ireland as well as with the piety, heroism, and devotion of its most gifted sons. Here St. Columba founded a monastery in 550 A.D., and the saint's house, a stone-roofed building, still exists. This was probably a chapel or an oratory as well as a residence. The chapel is arched over, and above it there are the remains of three cells, in one of which is a flat stone which is considered as the saint's penitential bed. St. Columba was an active missionary, and founded many monasteries besides that of Kells, including those of Derry, Tory Island, Drum Cliff, Lambay, Dublin, Swords, and Raphoe. He was an industrious scribe, and to him we owe the well-known volume in Trinity College long known as the Book of Kells. St. Columba died in 597 A.D., when almost in the act of copying a psalter, which he left to be finished by his nephew. The united parties then visited the round tower and three ancient crosses in the churchyard. The round tower is above 100 feet high, nearly perfect, and forms a most picturesque and prominent feature, rising from the plantation that bounds the graveyard next the public street. Within a few yards of the tower there are the remains of three elaborately sculptured crosses, and a fourth, the "Great Cross of Kells," stands in the main street. The arms and shaft are cut out of one stone that must have been 13 feet by 6 feet. What remains of the sculpture work is still sharp and distinct, and the crosses themselves are remarkably perfect when we remember how often Kells was the battle ground between contending native chieftains, the Dublin Danes and the forces under Edward Bruce, who burnt the town in 1315.

After visiting the ancient wells and other remains of antiquity, the entire party adjourned to the Headfort Arms Hotel, where Mr. Wolff provided a most excellent and well-served dinner, which renewed the waning energies of the party, and enabled them to start afresh for Navan by the afternoon train. Arriving at Navan, the party moved off for Donaghmore Round Tower. Some remained to see the tower and its surroundings, and the more enthusiastic pressed on to Tara, where every desirable point was identified. Donaghmore Round Tower is one of the most remarkable in Ireland, and one of the few that are decorated with unquestionable Christian devices. Antrim has a cross cut on the lintel over its square door, but Donaghmore has a figure of the crucifixion on the keystone of its arched doorway. Leaving Donaghmore, the party visited Dunmore Castle, beautifully situated on the banks of the Boyne. Returning to Navan, several places of interest in the town were visited, and the party met again at the station in time for the last train to Drogheda, where a comfortable tea awaited them at the White Horse Hotel.

Early next morning the Cameranians were again on the warpath, and several excellent views were taken before breakfast, including the Boyne Viaduct and St. Lawrence's Gate, one of the finest examples of the kind in Ireland. Sharp at eight o'clock the conductor's whistle hurried the party to breakfast, and at nine gave the signal for the vehicles to start on the day's trip. Rain fell thick and heavy, and continued without interruption the entire day. The first halt was made at Monasterboice, where there are the remains of two churches, three crosses, and a very fine example of the Irish round tower, the principal cross being one of the most elaborately-carved and best preserved examples of Celtic art in Ireland. The second cross is twenty-seven feet high, in good condition, which unfortunately cannot be said of the third. From Monasterboice a rapid drive brought the party to Mellifont Abbey, which was founded by St. Malachi in 1142, and was the first monastery in Ireland conducted under the discipline of the Cistercians. From Mellifont through King William's Glen the party drove to Slane, visiting the remains of Slane Abbey, Tober Patrick, and other ruins, and thence passed on through the ancient Royal

Cemetery of Brugh na Boinne, extending from Slane to
Netterville, along the north bank of the Boyne. Of the many
tumuli included in this cemetery, only the three great mounds
of Knowth, New Grange, and Dowth were examined, and of
these the underground chambers were thoroughly explored,
even by the lady members of the party. A partially successful
attempt was made by a Belfast amateur to photograph the
subterranean chamber of New Grange by a magnesium flash
light. Leaving the ancient Royal Cemetery now forming the
undulating, grand, and picturesque scenery by the windings of
the Boyne, the party reached the Boyne Obelisk, but the falling
rain and limited time prevented them from tracing the various
features of the great battlefield of 1690 ; so, hurrying on to
Drogheda, they partook of a hasty dinner, and left by the last
train for Belfast.

On 4th August, to the

CAVE HILL.

A special field meeting was held on this date, the object
being to examine some of the geological phenomena so well
displayed in the limestone quarries at Whitewell, and to
become better acquainted with the Flora of the Cave Hill.
Undeterred by the thick, close rain, and reinforced by an
English contingent, the party proceeded by steam tram. The
wet weather, however, considerably reduced the attendance and
prevented the full programme being carried out. The extensive quarries at Whitewell cut deep into the hillside, and afford
a rare opportunity for studying the stupendous operations of
nature in past ages. As explained by the leader on the present
occasion, the sections here indicate the following order of
events :—1st. Greensand deposit, which forms the floor of the
quarry, and is seen only at the entrance ; a coarse sandy marine
deposit of dark-green colour, which has been formed near a
shore, or at any rate in water of only moderate depth. It was
the home of an interesting fauna. Such shells as *Exogyra*,

Pecten, Lima, Terebratula, and *Rhynchonella* are abundant.
These sandstones pass up into (2nd) hard white limestone of the
chalk formation. This is, as a rock, unique in the British
Islands, notwithstanding the fact that it is chemically the
equivalent of the English chalk, aud only differs geologically
by being slightly younger. This limestone, or hard chalk, was
formed in a deeper sea, the most characteristic fossils found in
it being its belemnites, conico-cylindric bodies which were the
internal axes of ancient cuttlefish. The formation of the flints,
so abundantly arranged in layers in our chalk rocks, has been
the subject of much discussion ; that they originated in sponges
which flourished in the ancient cretaceous seas seems, however,
most probable. That the chalk itself was built up by innumerable aggregations of the shells of animals of microscopic dimensions can be demonstrated by a lens of moderate power applied
to a sufficiently thin slice of rock. 3rd. The elevation of the
ancient sea-bottom, its consolidation into the hard rock we now
find, and its subsequent long-continued erosion, which is
nowhere better seen than in the Whitewell quarries. The once
level sea-bottom has been worn into an irregular surface, having
in places deep hollows or pockets now filled up with loose flints
that have resisted the force of decomposition which wore away
the chalk rock. A section at the northern end is peculiarly
instructive—a confused mass of angular blocks of limestone lies
up against a vertical cliff of the same rock. This is evidently
the effect of ancient erosion, as the basaltic lava has been poured
out equally over the limestone *debris* and the limestone in
place, the interpretation being that this limestone *debris* is the
talus or undercliff of an escarpment which existed in early tertiary
times. 4th. The eroded surface of the chalk, then covered
with heaps of loose flints, was overflowed by lava welling up
from the innumerable crevices which we now find filled with
trap rock, and which are known to geologists as dykes. There
were, no doubt, several of these outflows, and the once plastic,
but now indurated mass, forms the massive rock known as
whinstone. In the absence of the secretaries no formal meeting

was held, and the election of new members was not proceeded with. Though several rare plants occur on the hill, the ascent was abandoned on account of the continued downpour. A small consolation was afforded by the testimony of a witness present to the effect that Orkney and the Hebrides have enjoyed a remarkably dry season, being in fact threatened with a water famine, and also that there has been a strangely dry summer at Valentia.

On 18th August, to

BALLYCASTLE.

A numerous party assembled on the platform of the Northern Counties Railway, and took the early train *en route* for Ballycastle. A fast run brought them to Ballymoney, where carriages were changed, and proceeding at a more leisurely rate along the narrow-gauge line, passing Dervock, and Armoy, with its round tower and ancient crosses, the summit level is reached, and the train glides at a faster pace around the western base of Knocklayd, and draws up at the platform at Ballycastle. After a short halt at the Antrim Arms Hotel, a start is made, and the party proceed to the shore. And here they feel, indeed, the delight of escaping for a few hours from the smoke and dust of the city to such a spot as this. Beneath a cloudless sky, the blue waters of the Atlantic are raised into a thousand dancing wavelets by the crisp, fresh, northerly breeze, and break with a continuous murmur on the long, white stretch of shining sand. Straight opposite, across the sunny channel, rise the white and black cliffs and heathery hills of Rathlin Island. Eastward, the grand promontory of Benmore, or Fair Head, stands out into the sea with rugged boldness, while to the westward the snow-white rocks of Kinbane project into the azure waters.

A short walk brings the party to the ruined abbey of Bonamargy, or *Bunn-na-Mairge*, which figures perhaps more than any other edifice in North Antrim in the ancient historical records. From the beginning of the sixteenth century it was used as a Franciscan Priory, but its original foundation probably dates from a much earlier period. Here was the favourite burial-place of the great Clan-Donnell, and many a brave MacDonnell chieftain has his last resting-place within these mouldering walls. After a space, devoted to examining the ruined abbey—more interesting on account of historical associations than of architectural features—a move is made to where, on a hill overlooking the sea on the other side of the stream, stand the ruins of Dunanynie Castle, which vies with the abbey on the river bank below, in historical importance. For many years it was the residence of the MacDonnell chiefs, and here the great Sorley Boy MacDonnell was born, and here he came in 1585 to spend in peace the closing years of his long and eventful life. But the MacDonnells would appear to have been comparatively modern tenants of the castle, as mention is made of this fortress in manuscripts of much earlier date. A few moss-grown walls, crowned with ferns and grasses, are all that now remain of what was in old times a stronghold of much importance.

The road is now taken for Kinbane, but a section of the party, charmed with the varied prospect of land and sea, and with the heathery pastures, laden with the perfumes of a hundred flowers, linger behind, and only the more energetic members reach the shining promontory of hard white chalk which, seamed and scarred with the war of the elements, boldly withstands the incessant wash of the Atlantic waves. Here another ruined castle, picturesquely perched on the narrow headland, claims the attention of the archæologists, while the botanists rejoice in the profusion of maritime species which abound among the rocks. But the slanting rays of the sun now warn the party that their time is getting short, so the road is taken for Ballycastle, and soon the scattered forces unite to make a combined and vigorous attack on the ample repast provided by Mr. Hunter. Here notes are exchanged among those who have chosen different routes. The photographers, who are in force to-day, congratulate each other. Bonamargy, Dunanynie, and Kinbane have successively occupied their attention, not to mention pretty pieces of landscape and cliff scenery : and one energetic photographer, backed by a small contingent, has penetrated westward as far as Carrick-a-Rede, and " done " the celebrated swinging bridge there. After a formal business meeting, at which some new members are elected, the party make for the railway station, and as at nine o'clock the train rolls under the lofty arch of York Street Terminus, the members feel that a delightful day's outing has come to a close.

On 8th September, to
BELVOIR PARK.

A beautifully fine afternoon, and the prospect of a pleasant ramble through the well-timbered grounds of Belvoir Park, conduced to a very large muster of members and their friends —the largest, indeed, in the records of the club. But the well-kept grounds of Lord Deramore's demesne, with its trim walks and shrubberies, are not the kind of place best adapted for Field Club work, so although an enjoyable hour or two was spent, little of a scientific nature could be effected. A visit was made to the site of the old Dredagh Church, of which no trace now remains, although the graveyard which surrounded it is still in use. The old oak, over thirty feet in girth, from which Lord Deramore derives his title, was also visited, and after a short formal meeting the party retraced their steps, and broke up.

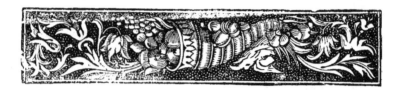

WINTER SESSION.

Note.—The authors of the various Papers, of which abstracts are here appended, are alone responsible for the views expressed in them.

SOCIAL MEETING.

THE twenty-sixth Winter Session was inaugurated on the evening of the 6th November, by a social meeting in the Museum, College Square North.   Tea was served in the lower room by the lady members.

Shortly after eight o'clock, the chair was taken by the President—Hugh Robinson, Esq., M.R.I.A.—who said that about six months ago the Club celebrated the completion of its twenty-five years of existence by a conversazione, held in the same room in which the Club had been started a quarter of a century before.   Although technically the twenty-sixth year began with the first excursion last May, yet they might look upon this social meeting as in some sort the commencement of their second quarter of a century.   He hoped that at the end of that term their jubilee celebration would find them in as flourishing a condition as they were now, and that many of the present members would be spared to take part in that anniversary. He then called attention to the principal objects which had been lent for exhibition.

Mr. W. Swanston, F.G.S., the senior secretary, made a few remarks upon the table of specimens illustrating the *Crustacea.* It has been usual, he said, on our opening meetings to select some special subject for illustration. We have had lime, silica, echinoderms recent and fossil, as well as other groups. This year we have selected the class *Crustacea.* This special subject had been suggested to us by the visit to our shores of a very distinguished stranger, *Lithodes Maia,* who was found aimlessly wandering about the Holywood banks last summer. This gentleman, the Northern Stone-crab, of whom there is no previous record (except a doubtful one in the Dublin Museum) of any of his name having been met with on Irish soil, was carried to our valued fellow-member, Mr. John Marsh. This stranger's relatives are mostly connected with warmer latitudes, but he himself hails from colder shores. He has, however been recorded as having before this visited the Isle of Man and the coast of Ayrshire. The family of *Crustacea* generally find their largest development in the tropic and sub-tropic seas, as was well indicated by the enormous claw of a species of crab from China, exhibited by Mr. S. F. Milligan, M.R.I.A. This claw alone must have contained several pounds more meat than the whole body of one of those degenerate crustaceans that find their way to our markets. The place of the *Crustacea* in the order of nature is rather a lowly one, coming next below the spiders and the great insect family generally. The *Cirrhipeda,* or barnacle shells, are the lowest order of the family. The *Entomostraca,* a microscopic group, come next, and the *Malacotrica,* containing the well-known crabs, are the highest. This last is the most important, and is subdivided into two sections—first, the stalk-eyed, or those with their eyes on good supports, a convenient arrangement, enabling them to see well about them ; and, second, the sessile-eyed, those whose eyes appear like black spots. On the table were specimens from the Museum and private collections illustrating these various groups.

Mr. Joseph Wright, F.G.S., next referred to the class of *Ostracoda*, and to the late Dr. Malcomson's researches in connection therewith.

The Rev. H. W. Lett, M.A., then drew attention to a table of specimens of the fungus *Agaricus nebularis*, exhibited by Mr. J. H. Davies, of Glenmore. These were found in a wood at that place, where they had been growing for some years. This species forms the " fairy rings," and the ring at Glenmore, which in 1885 was only twenty-one feet in diameter, has by the growth of the last three years reached a diameter of thirty feet. The species is edible, and at the close of the meeting several members took home some of the specimens to put the rev. member's statements to the proof.

Mr. C. Bulla drew attention to some collections of Silurian fossils from Pomeroy, and Cretaceous fossils from the special zone at Kilcorig.

Mr. John Hamilton commented on two specimens of Pallas's Sand-grouse recently shot in the vicinity. The presence of individuals of this species (natives of Siberia) in the North of Ireland during the past season has several times been the occasion of comment and correspondence in the public Press.

After the election of a number of new members, the formal meeting broke up, and the members devoted themselves to a study of the various objects of interest lent for the occasion.

A very conspicuous exhibit was a set of skins from Lapland, including a magnificent one of a polar bear, lent by Mr. John Marsh, who also showed some ancient silver ornaments and bowls recently brought from Norway.

A number of members showed their microscopes at work, as usual. Messrs. Wright, F.G.S., and R. Welch showed *Foraminifera*. Mr. J. J. Andrew, L.D.S., showed a micro-camera, and its method of working. Mr. D. M'Kee, Mr. John Donaldson, and Mr. George Donaldson also exhibited microscopes.

Mr. D. M'Kee showed, besides a variety of old coins, a gold

one of William III. A.D. 1698, several Elizabethan coins, a book published in 1851, by Dr. Harvey, discoverer of the circulation of the blood ; and a copy of the Ion Basilike, 1648. He also exhibited a sun dial containing a table of the equation of time, for changing the solar time as shown by the dial into mean time to the nearest minute.

The photographic members of the Club exhibited a number of frames of photos taken during recent excursions—one especially, illustrating the antiquities of the Boyne, visited last July.   The chief of these were by Messrs. W. Swanston, F.G.S., George Donaldson, John Donaldson, and Robert Welch.

The Club's albums have also been enhanced during the year by contributions from the members above-named, and with the portrait and sketch albums, and other books of the Club, were on the tables.

Mr. Isaac Ward showed a splendidly illustrated book of recent astronomical research, published by Harvard University, which shows what wonderful strides American astronomers, aided by the clear air of the Rocky Mountains, are making in the observational branches of the science.

Messrs. Wright, Firth, and Swanston lent a number of oil and water-colour drawings and engravings, and Mr. F. W. Lockwood showed two large drawings of St. Saviour's priory and cathedral and round tower, Glendalough, County Wicklow.

OPENING ADDRESS.

The first business meeting of the Winter Session was held in the Museum, College Square North, on the evening of November 20th, when the President—Mr. Hugh Robinson, M.R.I.A.—delivered the following inaugural address :—

When I had the honour of addressing you at the opening of our last session, the time at my disposal only permitted of my giving you some account of the various institutions which had aided in the progress of the study of Natural Science in Belfast, the circumstances which led to the establishment of our Club in the year 1863, and some particulars regarding the principal events of the earlier years of its history. I had purposed on that occasion to make some reference to the general progress of scientific inquiry during the quarter century which has elapsed since the Club began its work, and with your permission I shall now do so. The title of our Society, and its objects, as defined in our constitution —viz., the practical study of Natural Science and Archæology in Ireland—would, at the first appearance, rather limit the scope of the subject under consideration. I shall, however, take a broader view, and consider that in order to fulfil that object it is absolutely necessary that our studies should extend far beyond our own country, and that we should be acquainted with the working of those mighty forces in nature which in ages past have exerted their action here, but whose full powers are now only to be realised in distant lands. It is somewhat difficult to lay down a hard-and-fast boundary line between what may be termed Natural Science and Physical Science, as the action of the physical forces exert such a paramount influence upon the fauna and flora of any district. I therefore think it is quite within the scope of the subject I have selected for this evening's address, to refer, not only to the advance in knowledge of natural science, strictly speaking, but also to the similar progress in physical science, and the application of some of its more recent discoveries to the development of our home comforts, our facilities for travel, and consequent opening up of unexplored or undeveloped regions, and so furthering our commerce, and enabling us to avail ourselves of the natural products of distant countries. No matter what our special hobbies may be, these are matters which concern us all, and I shall therefore in the first place refer to them.

In the facilities for transport, both by land and sea, marked progress has been made during the past twenty-five years. It does not require a very great stretch of some of our memories to go back a few years further, when vessels in the timber trade, after discharging in Prince's Dock, had rough bunks fitted up for the conveyance of passengers to American ports. Passengers had to provide their own bedding and cooking utensils, and perhaps wait for days on the sailing of the vessel. Now we have the passage accomplished in as many days as it sometimes took weeks before, and passengers may book through from distant inland towns, and calculate upon leaving our ports almost as punctually as for a railway journey of a few miles. Year by year has witnessed the increase in the size and safety of our ocean steamers, and the substitution of screw propellers for paddles. The use of steel in construction, and the increased adoption of the principle of water-tight compartments, transverse and longitudinal, have tended to this increased safety, as it is found that iron casing breaks if struck, while steel only bends. Instances are are also on record of vessels coming into port with water flowing in and out of the front compartments, without in any way endangering the safety of the ship, or delaying its voyage. The use of double expansion engines has led to a considerable saving of waste power, and in two new steamers of the White Star line, triple expansion engines, which were first used in 1874, have been adopted, thus, by extra cylinders, using the steam three times. It is believed that increased speed will be gained at less cost. Substantial advances have been made in other directions in connection with our mercantile marine, notably in the matter of lighthouse illumination, the adoption of sirens and similar apparatus in foggy weather, and the system of meteorological observations and weather forecasts.

Vast engineering works have been accomplished in order to reduce distance. The Suez Canal has been completed, the Panama is in progress, while at home we have the Manchester Ship Canal in active preparation. In railway engineering, our Club has seen the completion of the Mont Cenis and St. Gothard Tunnels, while in Britain the Mersey and Severn Tunnels are also in use. The Canadian Pacific Railway was opened some two years ago, enabling a traveller to reach Port

Moody, in British Columbia, the western terminus of the line, within a fortnight of leaving Liverpool. The importance of this line as a means of communication with Eastern Asia cannot be over-estimated. Apparently, by it and a quick service of steamers from Vancouver to Yokohama, and by the Suez Canal and overland route, it will be quite possible to carry out Jules Verne's idea of "round the world in eighty days." Throughout the world almost, railway extension progresses, penetrating even into Lapland, the first train upon the Lulea Ofolen line having passed the Arctic circle in October of last year, while in Burmah two lines have been opened within the past three years. Others are projected in Siam, which, when completed, will make Moulmein a port both for Siamese and Chinese trade. In 1886, the Trans-Caspian Railway was opened so far as Merv, and the complete line to Samarcand was to have been opened in May last, thus enabling the journey from Michaelovsk on the Caspian to Samarcand to be completed in a day and a half.

In somewhat minor matters, but more immediately concerning ourselves, we have had, in the period under review, the substitution of steel for iron in rails and tires, the general adoption of the block system, and also that of continuous brakes, the taking up of water *en route* from tanks between the metals, and the introduction of drawing-room, dining, and sleeping cars. The various improvements in railway travelling, while tending to increased speed, have not been accompanied with diminished safety, but quite the reverse, for the average number of persons killed annually, from causes beyond their own control, has been reduced from 35 in the quinquennial period ending in 1878, to 16 in that ending in 1887. One outcome of the undertaking of vast engineering works such as those to which I have referred, has been the development of special machinery for their execution. In the Mont Cenis Tunnel, compressed air was used as the motive power in the drilling machinery, and, having done its duty in that way, served a further use in ventilating the workings. The same power was used in sinking the caissons for the Forth Bridge, but when the boulder clay was reached, its tenacious nature required special appliances—spades with hydraulic rams in the hollow handles. With the roof of the chamber to thrust against, it was only necessary to place the spade in position, turn a tap, and the cutting edge was thrust with a force of tons into the clay. In the construction of the Manchester Canal a giant navvy is at work, excavating daily a mass of earth 50 feet wide, 23 feet deep, and 20 feet long. In the general application of mechanical science, we have had the introduction and general adoption of gas engines, and the extended use of hydraulic motors, showing a considerable economic advantage in comparison with steam, in cases where the amount of power is small, or required only at intervals. While progress has been made in the arts of peace, those of war have also advanced. Some thirty years ago steam had been adopted as the motive power in our warships, and armour-plated vessels were taking the place of our wooden walls, the first ironclad ship built for our Government having been ordered in 1859. The introduction of such vessels as the Merrimac and Monitor in the American Civil War was another step, and we have seen the gradual development of armour plates supposed to be invulnerable, and of heavy ordnance to prove that they were not so, till in recent years we find that a tiny torpedo boat or a submarine mine is capable of effecting more destruction than the one can prevent, or the other accomplish.

In no department of science has progress been so marked as in electrical research and its applications. In our Club's early days we had, I believe, only one telegraph office in Belfast, and the rate was 3s. 6d. for twenty words. Now we have telegraph business transacted at almost every post office in the kingdom, and at the sixpenny rate we send messages upon the veriest trifles. The increase in the number of telegrams sent last year, as compared with the number sent in 1869 or 1870, is about 850 per cent., while the annual revenue has increased from £550,000 to £2,000,000. Mr. W. H. Preece, in his address to the Mechani-

cal Section of the British Association, at the present year's
meeting, gave some interesting particulars regarding the development of multiplex telegraphy. He stated that while Cooke
& Wheatstone's instrument required five wires, and transmitted
four words per minute, now one wire transmits six messages at
ten times the speed. In 1875, it was thought wonderful to
transmit to Ireland 80 words per minute ; but in Belfast, Mr.
Preece timed messages coming in at the rate of 461 words per
minute. I believe that this record was exceeded on the occasion
of the Marquis of Hartington's first visit here. To give a further instance of the vast increase in telegraphy, Mr. Preece
stated that on the occasion of Mr. Gladstone's introduction of
his Home Rule Bill, in April, 1886, no less than 1,500,000
words were transmitted from the Central Telegraph Office in
London in one night.

In connection with the subject of Press telegrams, it is interesting to note, incidentally, the progress made in the issue of
our daily papers. The adoption of the rotary press, the use of
stereotype plates, the printing from a continuous roll of paper,
and the possession of a private wire, enable a paper to go to
press at a much later hour than before, and still be in time for
the early morning trains. On the occasion of the visit of the
Marquis of Hartington, to which I have already referred, a full
report of his speech—in fact, I believe, the full text—was transmitted to the London papers ; while in the second edition of
our local dailies, ready upon our breakfast tables, we had, alongside the complete report of the meeting, the opinions of the
London Press upon it.

Rapid and enormous as the increase of telegraphing has
been, that of telephoning has been still more marked. It was
only at the Plymouth meeting of the British Association, in
1877, that the telephone was first shown at work in Britain,
and now every town of importance has its exchange. In the
earlier years of its use, it was considered that this means of
communication was only available for short distances. This
has not, however, been found to be the case, and by the adop-

tion of copper wires, which possess a greater amount of conductivity than iron, and, I believe, bronze, which possesses it still more, distant towns, some so far apart as 600 miles, are brought within speaking distance. If ten years show such rapid progress, what may be the result of the next ten's research. The peculiar law of electrical induction, by which a current sent through a wire creates a sympathetic current in another parallel to it, was one of the difficulties to be contended with in telephoning, but which has been overcome. It has been practically taken advantage of on the Lehigh Valley Railway in America, for the transmission of messages to and from trains in motion. The conducting wire is placed upon short poles some ten or twelve feet from the track. The inductive receiver consists of the metal roof of the carriage, or, where no metal roof exists, of a wire extending along the eave of the car. By a combination of the "buzzer" arrangement and a telephone, messages in the Morse character can be received and transmitted while the train travels at the rate of sixty miles an hour.

In the transmission of power by electricity, we have in our own neighbourhood the first electric tramway laid in Britain : that between the Giant's Causeway and Portrush, opened in 1883, and in which, by means of a dynamo, the energy of the water power of the Bush River is developed into an electromotive force. Lines have also been laid at Ryde, Blackpool, and Brighton, while in our own district we have the important line from Newry to Bessbrook. The invention of accumulators, in which electricity can be stored and transmitted, has been utilised for the propulsion of omnibuses, tricycles, launches, and other means of conveyance.

In electro-metallurgy, dynamos have largely taken the place of batteries for electro-plating, and we now find that they are not only used for the deposition of the precious metals, and for the duplication in copper of finely engraved plates, but other metals are similarly treated. Nickel plating has become a large industry, and is used to give a rust-proof covering to our car and harness mountings, to our cycle fittings, and to our table cutlery and surgical instruments. The electro-deposition of tin takes the place of ordinary dipping when special articles warrant the extra work. Even our Jubilee coins have been produced by electrical action, as the dies for them were modelled in plaster, intaglios formed by the electro-deposition of copper, and these again strengthened by the deposition of a layer of iron one-tenth of an inch thick. In the purification of copper, immense quantities of that metal are at Swansea and Widnes obtained by electro-deposition. The principle of electrolysis, upon which electro-metallurgy depends, has recently been experimented upon in many directions—as in the purification of sewage, and that of drinking water, and in the maturing of wines and spirits. Quite recently, it was stated that at the offices of a London journal in the interests of the confectionery trade, the first specimens of sugar said to have been refined by electric action were on exhibition. In our own district, experiments have recently been conducted with a view to its utilisation in bleaching processes.

With the adoption of electric lighting in our railway stations, steamships, and factories, and the introduction of electric bells in our dwelling-houses, you are all familiar. Everywhere we look around us we see the evidences of the utilisation of electrical energy. Our fire alarms are sounded by it ; divers work beneath the sea by its light ; submarine mining and destruction of ships and harbours can be accomplished by its aid ; hidden rocks which impede navigation are got rid of by its power ; the same apparatus which forms a portable gas lighter has been applied instead of a percussion lock to rifles ; our doctors examine our throats by its light, and use a platinum wire heated by its means instead of a knife ; tiny incandescent lights, controlled by a pocket battery, sparkle instead of diamonds on the head-dresses of ladies, and by a similar one at the tip of his baton, a conductor directs his band when darkness sets in. Even the familiar postman's knock is being superseded, for letter-boxes have been constructed in which the raising of the flap by the insertion of letters completes the circuit and rings a bell. The tampering with our safes, doors, and windows, and the increase of temperature in our shops and warehouses by fires breaking out, are indicated in a similar way. Telegraphs have been perfected by which portraits of criminals can be accurately transmitted, and when caught, and the extreme sentence of the law passed upon them, the penalty can be carried out by this wonderful power.

In chemistry, the past twenty-five years has been marked by a similar advance in knowledge. Not only has the system of nomenclature been changed, but the number of distinct elementary bodies has been increased to seventy (not including the twenty, or more, new elements said to have been discovered by Krüss and Nilsen in certain rare Scandinavian minerals) Spectrum analysis has given to us a knowledge of the chemical. constitution of the sun and stars. The investigations which have recently been laid before the Royal Institution by Mr. Crookes, with reference to the examination of bodies under electric discharges *in vacuo* would point to the possibility of decomposing some of the elementary substances and resolving them into more simple forms, as he states there is reason to suspect that Yttrium has been formed by the combination of six simpler substances, caused by varying states of electricity and heat to shape themselves into that element. Within the last year M. Moissan has succeeded, after three years' incessant labour, in the isolation of Fluorine, a substance which burns hard crystalline Silicon like tinder, sets fire to organic matter, and forms fluorides by incandescence with many other elements.

The direction in which chemical research has had, perhaps, its greatest development, so far as commercial enterprise is concerned, has been in the utilisation of the coal tar products. It was in the year 1856 that Mr. W. H. Perkins, while carrying on investigations as to the probability of artificially preparing quinine, discovered the substance from which the colour mauve is produced. Soon after, about the year 1859, came the discovery, by a French chemist, of the brilliant red colour Fuchsine, or Magenta and Solferino, as some of its shades

were termed, from the battles fought about the time of its discovery. These were, I think, the only aniline colours in existence when our Club was formed. Since then we have had the
discovery of Hoffman's violet, the aniline green, and Nicholson's golden yellow hue, Phosphine, the latter obtained from a
residuum or bye-product in the manufacture of magenta.
Again, when carbolic acid, obtained by the distillation of tar, is
treated with nitric acid, picric acid is obtained, which in solution imparts a bright, pure yellow dye. Strange to say, this
yellow colouring matter, when treated with cyanide of potas-
sium, gives a rich purple dye, identical with the famous Tyrian
purple. With every varying change of fashion, new shades of
colour are introduced from coal tar products, and at such
cheap rates as the natural and original sources cannot possibly
compete with.

One of the peculiarities of some of these colouring matters is
their extreme diffusibility. It is stated that one ten-millionth
of a grain of magenta will give its colour to a drop of water.
Not only do we find these substances used for dyeing and
printing textile fabrics, but they enter into the composition of
our printing and writing inks, and give the colour for rubber
stamp pigments, while the diffusibility of the purples and reds
enables us to multiply copies of writing by the various cento-
graph and hectograph processes. The most interesting feature,
however, from a natural history point of View, in connection
with these coal tar products, has been the synthetic production
of Alizarine, which is identical with the colouring matter
obtained from the madder root. In the earlier days of
chemistry, it was considered that while the chemist, having
determined upon the constituents of an inorganic body, could
in many instances form it in his laboratory, the formation of
organic substances was quite beyond his power, and that they
could only be produced in the living bodies of animals or
plants, requiring a vital force for their construction. So far
back as 1828, Wöhler succeeded in producing Urea synthetically, and some seventeen years after, Kolbe accomplished the

preparation of acetic acid from its elements. Since then numerous other discoveries have been made in synthetic organic
chemistry. That of Alizarine is the one which has had the
greatest effect upon our arts and manufactures, having revolutionised the trade of Turkey red dyeing, and having seriously
interfered with the cultivation of madder. It has been stated
that the same works and machinery can with these modern
dyes turn out 50 to 70 per cent. more printed calico than could
have been done in the old madder dyeing days. Unfortunately, the production of Alizarine is restricted by the quantity
of anthracene procurable from coal tar. It is found that from
the distillation of two thousand tons of coal tar, only one ton of
anthracene is obtained, and from this substance, by a complex
treatment, Alizarine is produced. Indigo has also been formed
synthetically, but I believe that as yet the process has not been
accomplished with the commercial success which has attended
the production of Alizarine. When we consider the complex
processes by which these substances are formed in the laboratory, and their formation by vital force in plants, we may, to
use Dr. Schunk's words, say—"We stand confounded at the
simplicity of the apparatus employed by the plant, and are
obliged to confess we have no conception of the means whereby
the end is attained." Synthetic organic chemistry has resulted
in the production of numerous compounds, and an alkaloid
hitherto found in hemlock has been so prepared, and we may
reasonably hope that the artificial manufacture of such alka-
loids as quinine will be accomplished. In 1883, Knorr, of
Erlangen, obtained from aniline a new alkaloid named Anti-
pyrine, which has proved a potent remedy for sea-sickness.

Recent investigations with coal tar derivatives have resulted
in the formation of that peculiar substance, saccharine, possessing 250 times the sweetening power of sugar. This is now
manufactured in Germany on a commercial basis, and we are
led to believe that it may usefully take its place as a substitute
for sugar in certain diseases where the use of that substance in
food is attended with injurious results, as Saccharine is not fer-

mentable, and cannot be assimilated. Quite recently its use has been condemned in France, on the ground that it is not only indigestible itself, but also retards the digestion of other substances with which it is mixed. It has been insinuated that this condemnation is an interested one, as the production of beet sugar is a large industry in France. A few weeks ago I noticed in one of the Dublin papers a column advertisement, in which were a large number of testimonials from competent men in favour of the merits of saccharine.

Among other products of coal tar distillation, we have nitro-benzol, or, as it is commonly called, Essence of Myrbane, used as a substitute for oil of bitter almonds in perfuming soap and flavouring confectionery. We have also perfumes resembling those of the Tonquin bean, and of the Woodruff, while much of the scent sold as " new-mown hay" really comes from our gas works. The greater part of the trade in the production of aniline colours is a German industry ; but it is to our country-man Perkins, that the honour of the discovery of the first of them belongs.

The wonderful petroleum industry, which has so largely developed during the last quarter century, while coming under the head of chemistry, has also a bearing upon geological science. As the demand for burning oils increased, we had first, in America, the adoption of pipe lines for the conveyance of the crude oil to the coast, where, after refining, it is exported under the name of refined petroleum. The more recent deve-lopment of the trade has led to the construction of vessels for the conveyance of the oil in bulk, and we may soon look for the establishment of large storage tanks at our leading sea-ports, into which the oil may be discharged on the arrival of such vessels, and only requiring the use of barrels for distri-bution to interior towns. Even that will not be necessary, for in the States, railway and street tank waggons convey it directly to the tanks of the retailers. Petroleum has been used for firing the boilers of Russian locomotives, and it has recently been reported to the Government of that country that it can be solidified by the addition of from one to three per cent. of soap, forming a mass like compact tallow—hard to ignite, but burning without smoke, giving great heat, and leaving only about two per cent. of a hard, black residuum. The oil deposits of Upper Burmah are considered to be as rich as those of America, and we may possibly look to it as a further source of supply. An industry akin to that of petroleum, and which has been largely developed of late years, is the Scotch paraffin trade, in which burning oils and other substances are obtained by the distillation and treatment of coal shale. This branch of trade began by the distillation of the Boghead Mineral Coal, by Young, and thus Britain has again the honour of being first in the field. The production of oil from shale is one of the many instances in which substances formerly looked upon as waste have been utilised. In addition to the light burning and heavier lubricating oils obtained from the crude petroleum, we have also the white, semi-transparent substance known as paraffin wax, which has so largely taken the place of tallow in the manufacture of candles, and which has proved an effective insulator in electricity, and is employed in conjunction with cotton in covering bell wires. Another product is vaseline, which from its healing properties forms a valuable medicinal ointment, and has been much used instead of animal fats in the production of perfumes from flowers, possessing as it does in a marked degree the power of absorbing their odours from them. Another direction in which chemical science has progressed is that of the discovery and manufacture of the various explosives, and their adoption to blasting and mining purposes.

The art of photography may well be included in any review of the recent advance of chemical knowledge. I shall not refer specially to it in the presence of so many of our members who have made that interesting art a study. I may, however, refer to the introduction of the dry plate processes, the pneumatic shutters, and other apparatus by which instantaneous photographs may be taken ; the improvements which have been effected in order to enable tourists to take and bring home with them a series of views of places visited—for example, the Eastman bromide paper, and the Vesgara gelatine films, as substitutes for the less portable and more brittle glass plates ; the platino and Woodbury types, aud others of a like nature ; photo-lithography, photo-zincography, and the various means by which process blocks are made for book and newspaper illustrations. Now-a-days, we cannot tell when our features are being reproduced by this art. The individual who appears to be intently examining the interior of his hat, may, through what seems to be a ventilator in its crown, be quietly focussing a camera concealed there; while an equally innocent-looking mortal, whose opera glass is turned towards us, may be taking a "snap shot"; or when an old acquaintance meets us, and as we talk keeps his distance (focussing distance, I mean), our attention is caught by a somewhat abnormal vest button, rather out of keeping with the rest of the set, and we afterwards find that it is the only visible portion of his cherished bosom friend, in the shape of a detective camera, and that its presence has deceived us into the idea that our friend is somewhat stouter than when we last saw him. It has recently been stated that it is quite possible for some notability to address a forenoon audience, have his portrait taken unknown to himself, a process block formed therefrom, and the speaker's likeness appear alongside the report of his address in the afternoon papers.

We now come to the consideration of the progress of Natural Science since the date of the formation of our Club. The question which has undoubtedly engrossed most of the attention of scientists since that time has been that of Evolution. The theory is one which had been at different times promulgated in various forms, but it was only when Charles Darwin published his "Origin of Species," in 1859, that it became one of the main questions of scientific research and argument. While Darwin was engaged in the researches which led to the publication of this work, Alfred Russell Wallace had been independently working out a similar theory, but it has been admitted that Darwin has the prior claim. At the meetings of the British Association, at Oxford in 1859, Manchester in 1860, and Cambridge in 1861, this theory was the question of the hour. Our Club was formed at the time when the arguments *pro* and *con.* waxed fast and furious, and as year by year since the matter has been investigated, the strong feelings on either side have toned down ; deductions based upon insufficient premises have been abandoned, and investigators have settled down to the even tenor of their ways. While we may hesitate to give our adhesion to many of the propositions laid down, we cannot deny the fact that the promulgation of this theory has led to a vast increase in the spirit of inquiry, and that the study of natural science received a greater impulse than ever it received before. One of the directions in which that spirit of inquiry was manifested was the theory of spontaneous generation. The researches of Tyndall have shown that the air we breathe teems with micro-organisms, and that vegetable infusions, if exposed to the air, will after a certain time show such forms, derived from it ; but if their vitality is destroyed by heat, and the air excluded, no living forms appear ; or if the air is admitted, but passed through a tube heated sufficiently to destroy the germs, no reproduction of the organisms takes place ; and that life only comes from pre-existing life. Tyndall's researches, conducted first in London, were afterwards repeated in the higher Alps, and it was found that the colder air of that region had the same effect upon the non-development of these germs that its exclusion in London had. In an interesting paper by Dr. Frankland, in the *Nine-teenth Century* for August, 1887, some interesting particulars are given regarding the widespread diffusion of these organisms in the air. In a journey from Norwich to London, it was found soon after leaving the former place that in a third-class carriage with four passengers, one window being open, 395 organisms were falling on the square foot per minute, while half-way between Cambridge and London the number was 3,120. In a barn where flail threshing was going on, Dr. Frankland found the number to be 8,000. Confirming Tyn-

dall's Alpine investigations, he found that the higher we go
above the level of the sea, or the further from busy towns and
crowded streets, the more free from these microbes do we find
the air.   Thus, at St. Paul's Cathedral, the Golden Gallery
yielded 11, the Stone Gallery 34, and the churchyard 70.
Some fifty years ago, Schwann demonstrated that fermentation
and putrefaction were due to micro-organisms.   Henle argued
that contagious diseases had a similar origin.   The real progress in this study dates from 1860, when Pasteur, having
established Schwann's theory of fermentation, took up that of
Henle regarding living contagia.   The researches of Pasteur,
Koch, Klebs, and others, have been the means of determining
the special cause of many diseases both in plants and animals.
Thus, *Bacillus tuberculosis* is found in the breath and tissues
of those afflicted with consumption ; *Bacillus subtilis* in
splenic fever, which is so fatal to cattle, and which is also com-
municable to man, in whom it is known as the wool-sorter's
disease, while Koch has discovered the *Comma bacillus* in
cholera ; and in typhoid fever, scarlatina, erysipelas, and other
diseases, special *bacilli* have been found.   The general current
of recent investigations would seem to prove that micro-
organisms are widely diffused, that when they meet with a
suitable soil they develop and multiply, and that the diseases
are not so much due to the organisms themselves as to the
effect of certain poisonous chemical compounds which are
formed during the life of the organism, for the diseases can be
communicated by these poisons in entire absence of the germs.
Sir Henry Roscoe expresses the opinion that it is by chemical
rather than by biological investigation that the cause of diseases
will be discovered, and the power of removing them obtained.
The main feature of Pasteur's researches has been in the development, exterior to the body, of these organisms.   It has been
found that in the case of *Bacillus subtilis* so developed, if kept
at a heightened temperature, it loses its virulence, and becomes
incapable of producing the poisonous compound.   Animals
inoculated with it in this form sustain no mischievous results,

and become proof against the attacks of the virulent type of the disease. Dr. Gamaleia, of Odessa, in his researches on the cholera vibrion, has found that the ordinary forms, as discovered by Koch, are so little virulent that it is almost impossible to communicate disease by inoculation with them. He has, therefore, in the first instance developed the virus by introducing it into a pigeon after it has passed through a guinea pig. It then kills pigeons by producing cholera, and after a few passages it acquires an increased virulence. This passage virus is developed in a nutritive broth, which is heated to kill all the microbes it contains. It is found that this sterilised broth produces death, with choleraic symptoms, but when the fatal dose is divided, and the period of inoculation extended over from three to five days, the animals experimented upon do not die from the inoculation, but become proof against cholera.

We may look forward with interest to the further investigation of this subject, in which Dr. Gamaleia has offered to repeat his experiments before the French Academy of Science during the present month, I believe. Pasteur's treatment of hydrophobia is accomplished on somewhat different lines. In it, the spinal cords of rabbits which have died of the disease are dried for a certain number of days, and diffused in a sterilised broth which is hypodermically injected into the patient on successive days, the number of days during which the cord has been dried being decreased gradually for each injection. It is maintained that by this treatment hydrophobia can be communicated to healthy animals, or, by a modification of it as a preventative measure, inoculation rendered the animals proof against the disease, and that in the case of man, when inoculation is accomplished after infection, the mortality is materially reduced. One of the developments of the study of micro-organisms has been the adoption of the antiseptic treatment of wounds, to which, when air gets access, it brings with it innumerable germs, which produce putrefying action. Lister found that dilute carbolic acid killed the germs without injuriously affecting the wound. Its use has now become general, and in a recent paper by our eminent townsman, Sir Wm. MacCormac, it was stated that the present system of antiseptic surgery had in recent warfare reduced the mortality to a mere tithe of what it was in the Crimea.

The increased interest in the various branches of natural history during the past quarter century has led to Government aid being extended to the investigation of them, as in the case of the " Lightning," " Porcupine," and " Challenger " Expeditions. The results of these expeditions have been far beyond the most sanguine expectations, revealing to us much information regarding the abysmal depths of the ocean, their structure and deposits, and showing to us that the depths in which it was at one time supposed life did not exist, teem with forms specially adapted to the conditions in which they exist. One of the recently issued volumes on the zoology of the " Challenger " Expedition is devoted to an account of the deep sea fishes. In them we find some interesting instances of these adaptations. In several forms, such as *Opostomias* and *Astronethes*, large glandular, phosphorescent organs are found underneath the eyes, and which appear to be under the control of the fish, and capable of projecting a beam of light or shutting it off, as suits the owner's purpose. In others, there are found tentacles with phosphorescent spots at their ends, which may possibly be used as lures in these deep, dark depths. Another question which has been brought to the front by these deep sea dredging operations is that of the formation of coral reefs. The theory with which we were familiar in our early days was that of Darwin, published in 1842, in his great work upon " Coral Islands," in which the formation of Barrier Reefs and Atolls was accounted for by subsidence. Doubts have been thrown upon the accuracy of this theory by Alexander and Louis Agassiz, Geikie, and Murray of the " Challenger," while Dana still maintains the subsidence theory. The matter has in the past year been a subject of discussion, in various journals, between the Duke of Argyle, Huxley, and others.

Upon the study of Geology much light has been **thrown** by

the published results of these voyages, while in other directions much attention has been given to the determination of the ages of our eruptive rocks, and the phenomena of metamorphism. In the elucidation of the latter, microscopic examination has proved a valuable aid, while synthetical chemistry has shown that some of our minerals may be artificially formed. We may anticipate that further investigations in that direction will enable us to determine the means by which they have been formed in the conditions under which we find them. While micro-geology and lithology have progressed, palæontology in its various branches has similarly advanced.

The establishment of the Biological Laboratories at Naples and Plymouth, and I think at St. Andrew's also, have already produced good results, and as such facilities for study are in-creased we may look forward to valuable information being gained with regard to the life history of our food fishes, and the harvest of the sea may be made more productive.

Naturalists' investigations have proved that birds are in many instances not the enemies, but the friends of the farmer, and while they may take toll from him occasionally, they render good service for it. Our legislators have been led to look upon the matter in this light, hence we have the Wild Birds' Preser-vation Act, a thing also undreamt of when our Club first met. Birds are an important factor in keeping down the ravages of insects, which in certain seasons inflict an amount of damage which cannot be estimated. The appointment of Miss Ormerod as consulting entomologist to the Royal Agricultural Society of England shows that this subject of injurious insects is being taken up thoroughly, and if her warnings and directions to farmers regarding the stamping out of these pests were attended to, considerable gain would result. One somewhat peculiar instance of injury being done is by the carrion beetle develop-ing vegetarian habits. Naturally a gross flesh-eater, it has acquired a taste for mangold, and has during the past summer wrought considerable havoc in that crop in Somersetshire.

The Hessian Fly, about which such alarm was created in

1886, is an old enemy. From a paper by the late Robert Patterson, F.R.S., published in 1840, I find that exactly one hundred years ago there was a similar alarm lest it should be imported from America, and that the Privy Council sat day by day debating how to ward off the calamity. Fortunately, on its appearance here this insect brought all his known enemies with him, and Miss Ormerod has hatched out specimens of the whole seven parasites which infest him. It is interesting to note that they are all Russian, and though heretofore we did not know the country of which he was a native, we now find it by the company he keeps.

There are many other matters to which I would like to have called your attention, but I have already trespassed too far upon your time, and must apologise for the somewhat inordinate length of this address, and for having introduced into it many topics which do not appear to be quite cognate to the objects of our Club. I think, however, that their connection is not quite so remote as it might seem to be. The progress of mechanical science has given us largely increased facilities for travel, and has tended to open up unexplored and undeveloped countries, to which British civilisation and commerce may be extended, and as that extension proceeds, the opportunities afforded for the investigation of the physical configuration, geological structure, and natural products of these countries, and of comparing them with those of our own, become greater ; while, on the other hand, the researches of naturalists who have gone off as pioneers to these far off lands have shown the commercial advantages to be gained by their being opened up to British trade. Central Africa has been made known to us by the travels of Livingstone and Stanley. The Congo, one of the largest water-ways of the world, has been investigated, showing a reach of navigable water 1,068 miles long, from Leopoldsville to Stanley Falls. The great affluents already explored give a total of 6,000 miles of water-way accessible from the former place, and this may possibly be increased by further exploration,

In the far north, British enterprise has opened up a new water-way from the Arctic Ocean to Central Asia. Captain Wiggins for many years held the opinion that the Gulf Stream flowed eastward, along the coast of Lapland, towards Nova Zembla, and that this force, combined with the volume of the rivers Obi and Yenisei, drove the ice to the north of the Kara Sea, leaving the route through the Kara Straits open in the summer months. This opinion he proved to be correct in 1874, by sailing through these straits to the mouths of the Obi and Yenisei. In 1876 he ascended the latter river for a thousand miles, and three years later he landed a cargo at the mouth of the Obi. Last year, leaving Newcastle-on-Tyne on 5th August, on 9th October following for the first time a British sea-going steamer landed her cargo in the very heart of Siberia, at Yeniseisk, 2,000 miles from the mouth of the Yenisei, and only a few miles from the Chinese frontier. Now the Phœnix Company of merchant adventurers purpose establishing a fleet to communicate with the mouth of the Yenisei, where cargoes would be transhipped to another fleet trading upon the river, and the cargoes brought down by it taken on board, thus dividing the journey, and allowing the return voyage to be made before winter sets in. By this route Central Asia can be supplied with European commodities, and the vast mineral wealth of Siberia brought into the market.

The extension in the application of electrical science, girding, as it now does, the globe with a series of submarine cables and land lines, gives us information, within a few hours of their occurrence, of those mighty outbursts of volcanic activity which so seriously alter in many instances the configuration of our earth. Chemical science, again, by patient investigation in the laboratory, revolutionises entirely an extensive branch of trade, determines the economic value and properties of newly discovered natural products, and aids us in the determination of the conditions under which the mineral components of our rocks have been formed. In fact, all branches of natural and physical science are intimately interwoven, and I hold that the in-

vestigation of every one of those natural laws by which our
world is held in being, or which has contributed to its adapta-
tion for man, and the study of the development and utilisation
of those laws, is quite within our province, and cannot but give
to us an extended reverence for the wisdom and power of Him
by whom these laws were set in force, and at whose word the
" heavens and earth rose out of chaos."

The second meeting of the session was held in the Museum,
College Square North, on 18th December—the President (Mr.
Hugh Robinson, M.R.I.A.) in the chair—when a paper was
read by Mr. Robert Lloyd Praeger, B.E., B.A.—subject : " A
Deep Sea Dredging Expedition." The meeting was well attended by members and visitors. The reader commenced his
paper with an account of the aims and objects of the expedition
of which he was about to speak. The Royal Irish Academy,
desiring information respecting the marine fauna of the South-
West of Ireland, appointed a committee who were to explore
these waters, and report on the results of their dredgings. Professor A. C. Haddon, of the Royal College of Science, Dublin,
and Mr. Joseph Wright, F.G.S., of Belfast, were heads of the
scientific staff, while the general management was entrusted to
Rev. W. S. Green, M.A., of Carrigaline, County Cork. Under
these auspices three expeditions were despatched—in 1885, 1886,
and 1888. Having briefly described the events of the two former, Mr. Praeger came on to speak of the present year's trip,
and before entering on the narrative of the cruise, he described
the apparatus and equipments which are used in deep-sea
sounding and dredging, with special reference to the machines
which were employed on the present occasion. The difficulties
which attend the correct ascertaining of depths, and the obtaining of specimens of the sea-bottom and of the animals that live
thereon, in the deep waters of the ocean, have only been completely overcome during the last few years, and this is largely
due to the introduction of fine steel wire in the sounding machine

and steel wire rope for dredging purposes, in place of the hempen cords and ropes that had previously been employed in these observations. Owing to the much smaller diameter of the wire, and its smooth surface, it is far less influenced by the retarding action of friction as it passes through the water, while, on account of its superior weight, it sinks readily, and by its employment for sounding purposes the depth can be accurately ascertained even in several miles deep of ocean. A new form of sounder, wherewith a sample of the sea-bottom is secured and brought to the surface, enclosed in a cylinder of gun-metal, was described, and the machine exhibited. It was made in Belfast, from a design by Mr. William Swanston, of this city, and was used with success on the expedition. Samples of the fine wire used for ascertaining the depths, and of the steel wire rope used for dredging, were also shown. The lecturer then described the various forms of dredges and trawls, and explained how they are employed for the capture of the wonderful variety of animals that live on the ocean floor. Proceeding then to the narrative of their trip, Mr. Praeger stated that the party consisted of the Rev. W. S. Green, M.A.; John Day, Cork ; Dr. C. B. Ball, F.R.C.S.I.; J. Hewitt Poole, C.E., and W. de V. Kane, of Dublin ; and Joseph Wright, F.G.S., and the reader, of Belfast. Leaving Queenstown at four a.m. on May 27th, on board the Clyde Shipping Company's powerful steamer Flying Falcon, a delightful day was passed in running down the romantic coast of County Cork, under a cloudless sky, with the Atlantic as calm as a millpond. Some trawling was done in Long Island Sound and Bantry Bay *en route*, and at six o'clock in the evening they entered the picturesque harbour of Berehaven, and cast anchor for the night. The next day, being Sunday, was spent quietly in harbour, and the reader gave a short account of a ramble along the rocky seacoast, and described the rich flora of that district, exhibiting at the same time dried specimens of some of the rarer and more striking plants. A start was made for the deep water at eight o'clock that evening, and, steaming westward all night, a sounding was taken at four o'clock next morning, about sixty miles from land, which gave 345 fathoms. The beam trawl was immediately sent down, and, on being brought to the surface at 7·30, was found to contain a large number of rare and beautiful specimens. Among the Echinoids, or sea-urchins, *Dorocidaris* and *Spatangus* were conspicuous, and the beautiful starfish *Brissinga* was present in abundance; the net also contained a fine example of the large univalve shell, *Cassidaria Tyrrhena*, which was first obtained as a British species on the previous cruise of the Lord Bandon. Steaming westward again, when the log registered 19 knots, another sounding was taken, and the machine recorded the great depth of 1,020 fathoms, and the sounder came up with the interior of the gun-metal tube filled with *Globigerina* ooze. The Agassiz trawl was then unshipped and sent to the bottom, with 1,270 fathoms of steel rope attached; and when this great length of rope was at last reeled in, and the trawl got on board, it yielded some very extraordinary forms. During the night a gale was encountered, and all steam was made for Valentia, but as morning advanced the storm subsided, and the boat's head was again turned westward, and at midday, in a very heavy sea, the Agassiz trawl brought up a magnificent assortment of deep-sea animals from 750 fathoms. There were great *Holothuriæ* or sea-slugs, red, purple, and green; beautiful corals, numerous sea-urchins, with long, slender spines; a great variety of splendid *Asteroidea*, or star fishes, two of which will constitute an entirely new genus; and many other most interesting specimens. Photographs and drawings of these rare animals were displayed on the walls of the lecture-room.

By the time these deep-sea treasures had been safely bottled away, it was blowing so hard that it was deemed necessary to run for shelter, and ere Berehaven was reached, heavy seas had swept the decks, smashing the starboard paddlebox, and wrecking the cook's galley. Next day the gale continued, and the Flying Falcon remained at anchor opposite Castletown, while the crew busied themselves in repairing damages, and the scientists in overhauling their tackle, and carefully labelling and preserving the treasures secured on the previous day. On Thursday the weather continued boisterous, and a very high sea was running outside, but some successful trawling was done in Berehaven and Bantry Bay, and in the afternoon, as the wind was falling and the barometer continued to rise, another attempt was made to reach deep water, but when the steamer had reached a point ten miles west of the Bull Rock, stress of weather again necessitated return to land. The following day a flying visit was paid to Baltimore, and then a south-easterly course was taken, and some trawling done with good results on the fifty fathom line ; and here the lecturer gave a graphic account of a narrow escape from collision with a White Star liner, which came down on them while enveloped in a thick fog, and was very near sending them to the bottom. The night was spent in the pretty harbour of Glandore, and on Saturday, after some successful dredging south of Galley Head, in wind and pouring rain, the steamer's course was set for Queenstown, which was reached at three o'clock. The lecturer concluded by giving a more detailed account of some of the rarer forms obtained during the cruise, referring especially to the *Foraminifera* which occured, to exemplify which a number of large diagrams, artistically executed by Mr. Joseph Wright, F.G.S., were displayed on the walls. The paper was further illustrated by samples of the dredging ropes and sounding wire, by examples of some of the Echinoids obtained, and by a large chart showing the courses of the steamer on the present, and also on the two previous expeditions, while the dredge and deep-sea sounder were also exhibited, and their use and mode of working explained. At the close of the paper Professor Everett, M.A., F.R.S., &c., spoke in praise of the admirable manner in which Mr. Praeger had brought the subject before the meeting. Mr. Joseph Wright, F.G.S., gave some further information regarding the *Foraminifera* which he had obtained in the dredgings, and after several other members had spoken, the audience gathered round the tables to examine the various interesting objects there displayed.

The third meeting of the winter session was held on January 29th—the Vice-president, Mr. Joseph Wright, F.G.S., in the chair—when a communication was brought forward by Mr. William Swanston, F.G.S., entitled, "Photography, as an aid to the Club's Work." The reader, on being called upon, proceeded as follows:—

Twenty-six years ago the founders of our club framed an admirable set of rules for its guidance, which have remained to the present time with scarce any alteration to govern its management. The first gave the society its name, the second defined its aim. They are—1st. That the society be called the Belfast Naturalists' Field Club. 2nd. That the objects of the society be the practical study of natural science and archæology in Ulster—afterwards extended to all Ireland.

Though holding an official position in the club it will not, I am sure, be considered egotistical on my part if I state that, in my opinion, the club is, to some extent, succeeding in fulfilling its mission. Doubtless, the numbers who really work and who contribute to the club's proceedings is small in proportion to those who merely sympathise with its doings, but this is so, and ever will be, in similar societies. It is not just, however, to measure the usefulness of the club in advancing our know-ledge of natural science or archæology by the number of its published papers, or by the thickness of its annual proceedings ; the reports of our meetings and excursions have a wide-spread circulation through the local Press, and they are, let us hope, in some degree educating, not only those who are members nominally, but the outside public as well. Looking back, one is inclined to say that there is perhaps not so much field work done by our younger members now as there was in the early days of the club, but still the work goes quietly on, and our recent publications, I think, satisfactorily prove that we are not retrograding. Much more, however, remains to be done under both departments of our work than has yet been attempted, and I have no hesitation in saying that as an organisation we are in a good position for doing it. What I feel is most wanted is not so much workers, as a more complete development of our organisation, and the better utilisation of the energy and skill within our borders. In natural science this might take the form of a more systematic recording of natural facts, and by workers as far as possible avoiding paths of research that are perhaps already well trodden, or which are being well investigated by others. This failing or weakness is not confined to our club alone, but it seems to have crept into all kindred societies, and strong efforts are being made by many of them to systematise their resources. A grand example of this is set us by the British Association in their efforts to make the work done by provincial societies, such as ours, available to the scientific world at large. What is termed a corresponding society committee was formed for tabulating all scientific papers read in the smaller societies, and publishing their titles and other particulars in their voluminous reports. This committee also suggests subjects in which they ask the aid of provincial societies. For example, they ask workers to take the temperature of the waters of lakes and rivers, collect records regarding erratic blocks, sea-coast erosion, life history of plants, and pre-historic remains. The secretary of this comprehensive committee also requests photographs of ancient monuments and other remains, also photographs of geological sections, with, of course, short explanatory notes in both cases. It is in this latter direction that I would endeavour to direct your attention this evening. Photography is a comparatively new art-science, and the more recent introduction of dry plates has so simplified it, and made, it easily available for field use, that it has suddenly sprung into prominence, and taken a firm hold on the public taste. As one of the popular and fascinating pursuits, archæology, where truthfulness in delineating every detail is such an essential, is especially a field in which photography can render aid. Our district—

which, be it remembered, is all Ireland—is particularly rich
in monuments of its early inhabitants—monuments, too, with
a character and richness almost impossible to delineate with
pencil or brush, but for which the camera seems specially
designed. It is to be regretted that many of these monuments
are slowly but surely passing to decay. Our Government, in
taking charge of many of our most remarkable and conspicuous
monuments, and preserving them from destruction at the public
cost, establishes thereby the principle that it is right to act
as conservators for future students. As a club we can, I fear,
do little in this direction, but we can, at least, place on record
the state in which they exist in our time. Those remains
under the protecting care of the Government may safely be
left to those appointed to look after them, but it is only one
in a hundred of the many remains scattered over the country
that is thus protected. The wayside pillar stone, the stone
circle or the cromlech on the lone hillside, the raths and forts,
castles, and abbeys of the valleys and uplands, are in many
cases left to the tender mercies of the surrounding people.
Superstition has saved many ; the solidity of others has evidently been their protection, while it is painfully evident that
many of our ruined castles, abbeys, and churches have suffered
much from the rapacity of those needing the material of
which they are built, and by the apathy of those who should
have interested themselves in their preservation. If one were
to judge by a review of our summer programmes, the conclusion might be arrived at that fashion governed our club as
well as our social life. Some seasons have the botanical, others
the geological feature strongly pronounced in them ; while
marine research at other times seized upon the fancy. Last
year's programme, like others that have preceded it, was
decidedly an archæological one, four out of its six excursions
having been arranged to allow the members the opportunity
of examining the many antiquities within reach. Dromore,
with its rath, its cathedral, and its ancient cross ; Drogheda
and the Boyne alone offered a programme the richest in

antiquities ever placed before the members—monuments of surpassing interest, mounds, churches, crosses, castles, and round towers forming a collection which, with a panorama of wonderful scenery, gave a variety which it would be difficult to equal in a two days' excursion elsewhere in the British Isles. Again, Ballycastle and Carlingford, two other excursions, always attractive for their scenery, are equally so to lovers of the past. Is it any wonder, then, that those members who have added photography to their many other pursuits, availed themselves of these attractive programmes and formed a feature with camera and apparatus, rather novel, we must confess, and at first sight apparently an innovation at field club excursions? It is this new element, or I might almost call it, new section of the club's members, which is, perhaps, most in need of reorganisation. At present there is no place for them; they do not fit into any department properly. True, the club has a series of photo albums, and offers annually prizes for photos to fill these; but there is a lack of system in even this. The same popular subjects are frequently repeated, to the almost entire exclusion of the study and search after the detail, which often tell more of the past story of the object represented than the most artistically rendered picture would do. I might be pardoned for suggesting that we take a lesson out of the action of the British Association, to which I have already referred, and commit these albums to a sub committee, which might direct and regulate the intense energy of our photographic members. Lists might be issued periodically of the objects already represented in the albums, and help might be given in also noting such as are desired. The results should also be printed in some of the approved permanent processes of photo-printing, and more often made accessible to the members than once a year, as is pretty much the case at present; the pictures should also be supplemented by short descriptive notes published in our proceedings from time to time. Many of the English societies largely employ photography in their work, and it is well known that it has become a recognised branch or department in all imperial, colonial, and even private scientific research. Pleading guilty to exposing a few plates during the past season, some of them, indeed, on the club's excursions, and several fellow members having with great trouble and patience prepared lantern slides from most of them, it was suggested to me that they should be shown on the screen, with a short historical commentary on the subject as they pass before you. For myself I might say that I was not on the club's excursion to the Boyne, as it was arranged for a date of which I could not avail myself, but taking advantage of an opportunity in June I visited the locality in company with Mr. Stewart. The negatives then obtained have been supplemented by others taken by members, To these again others which fall in with them have been added. and thus the scheme which originally intended the illustration of the Boyne views has grown till it embraces the entire past season's work, as well as some of former years, together with examples of how geology, botany, and zoology may be illustrated. It is to be hoped that copies of most of the pictures will, before long, find a place in the club's albums. At this point the lights in the room were lowered, and a series of 120 views were, in succession, thrown on a large screen by lime-light, many of which elicited applause by the brilliant manner in which they were shown. The reader supplemented the views with concise notes on their most striking features or historical associations. The pictures illustrative of geology and botany especially elicited approbation. Three magnificent astronomical photographs were also exhibited ; they were taken by Mr. S. W. Barnham, who was well known in Chicago as an amateur photographer before he recently accepted the post of one of the astronomers at the Lick Observatory on Mount Hamilton, in California. These photographs were sent by him to Mr. J. W. Ward, a member of the club, who had them prepared for lantern illustration. They represent the moon in three aspects, and were taken by his immense telescope in the Lick Observatory. A thirty-three-inch photo lens was inserted in the telescope, making an image $5\frac{1}{4}$ inches in diameter, of which the prints were the full size.

The meeting concluded by several of the members expressing their high appreciation of the views, the running commentary upon them, and the suggestions as to the desirability of preserving records of them in the club's albums.

The fourth meeting of the winter session was held in the Museum, on 28th February, when the evening was devoted to the illustration of various departments of research by the microscope. The circular inviting members engaged in microscopic work to bring their instruments, and exhibit and explain the scientific objects in which they were specially interested, was liberally responded to, and the tables in the lecture room were fully occupied, while a large turn-out of non-microscopic members and their friends, who followed with deep interest the demonstrations on many branches of science given by the exhibitors, completed the success of the meeting.

Mr. D. M'Kee, and Mr. George Glen showed a number of sections of rocks, minerals and precious stones. Mr. Joseph Wright, F.G.S., exhibited *Foraminifera* taken in recent deep-sea dredgings off the south-west of Ireland, several of the species being new to science, and many of extreme rarity. Mr. R. Welch devoted himself to the important branch of photo-micography, and Mr. Geo. Donaldson to the exhibition of a number of live objects. Messrs. J. Ward and W. A. Firth chose the interesting group of the *Diatomaceæ* for demonstration ; Mr. Elliott showed a variety of histological subjects, and Mr. J. J. Andrew, L.D.S., R.C.S., sections of teeth, recent and fossil. The wonderful profusion of minute organisms that abound in brackish water, with their never-ending activity and apparently aimless hurryings to and fro, always form objects of attraction and interest, and these were shown to advantage by Mr. John Donaldson in samples of water from Victoria Park. So great was the store of material, that it was late ere the members left the brilliantly-lighted tables, surfeited with the wealth and variety of the wonderful lesser world that the microscope reveals.

A beautiful set of photographs of sea-birds and their nests and haunts, the work of Mr. Green, of Berwick-on-Tweed, hung on the walls of the room, was the subject of much admiration ; they were exhibited by Mr. R. Welch. A photograph of a number of Pallas' Sand-grouse was exhibited by Mr. John Hamilton. The election of several new members brought a pleasant and highly instructive evening to a close.

The fifth meeting of the session was held on 26th March, with Mr. Hugh Robinson, M.R.I.A. (President), in the chair, when a lecture was delivered by Mr. William Gray, M.R.I.A., entitled "Vestiges of Early Man in Antrim and Down." After an apology from the lecturer for scanty preparation of the subject, owing to the urgency of professional duties, he said he should treat the subject broadly, without reference to dates or figures, more particularly as much of it being previous to written historical records, it would have to be dealt with by means of comparison and analogy. It would not be necessary to go into Darwinian theories as to whether or no early man was a development from an ape-like progenitor. It would be sufficient to say that there was now a very general agreement between all scientific authorities, that man dated back from a very much earlier period than was at one time held to be the case, and that, whilst some held that he was, though of great antiquity, yet still only post-glacial in origin, others placed him further back, and ascribed to him an inter-glacial, or even a pre-glacial existence. Before going further, the lecturer then went on at some length into an astronomical and geological explanation of the glacial epoch, and illustrated his remarks by a series of beautiful limelight views of various glacial phenomena, such as scenes from the Alps, of glaciers, snow fields, moraines, polished rock surfaces, and boulders, as well as types of various extinct animals of the glacial and post-glacial periods. He then referred to the various traces of early man in North-east Ireland, describing the sand dunes such as those at the mouth of the Bann, Ballintoy, and Newcastle. He next referred to caves and their inhabitants, showing in each case, as he proceeded, many beautiful views in the lantern to illustrate his statements. The interesting class of pillar stones and holed stones were next reviewed, and examples shown. Cromlechs, and the analogous structures known as kistvaens, were then described with numerous examples. The relation to these of stone circles was dwelt upon.   Crannoges, or artificial islands, were referred to. The lecturer said it had been his intention to have followed up the subject by discussing the round towers, and other early monuments of a more advanced nature, but would have to leave them to another occasion.

The Chairman, and Messrs. Wright and Lockwood spoke in high terms of the lecture, and hoped the subject would be continued upon the first opportunity.

The election of several new members then took place, and it was announced that owing to the visit of Sir William Thomson the next meeting would be held a week earlier than the date on the programme.

————————

The sixth meeting of the winter session was held in the Museum, College Square North, on 9th April—the Vice-President (Mr. Joseph Wright, F.G.S.) in the chair—when three distinct communications were brought forward.

The first was by Rev. H. W. Lett, M.A., T.C.D., entitled " Notes on some Desmids found in the North of Ireland." The lecturer stated that there was no popular name for the plants known as fresh-water *Algæ*, as there is the word " sea-weeds " to describe those which are marine. However, in Ulster the country people use the word " glit " to describe the green threads and slimy coating of objects in and under fresh water. These are the microscopic plants known as fresh water *Algæ*. They are formed everywhere where water collects in large or small quantities—in lake, river, pond, canal, or ditch, as well as in the tiniest tricklet by the wayside path, and even on the face of damp walls and slippery surfaces of mountain rocks. One great family of these *Algæ* is the Diatoms, which are aquatic plants, consisting of a single cell, the colouring matter of which is uniformly of a pale golden brown when living. Their peculiar characteristic is their skeleton, which is a pair of plates of indestructible silex, and when the plant dies the tiny frame remains, so that in some places they form immense beds many feet thick composed of myriads of Diatoms. The Desmids are another group of single-celled *Algæ*. They consist of a transparent envelope enclosing a bright green colouring matter, the forms and arrangement of which are very varied, and form the basis of the genera and species into which they are divided. Besides these two, there is another great tribe of fresh-water *Algæ*, including very different forms, some of which, in their thread-like fronds, much resemble their relatives of the sea, while others grow on damp soils and clays, or swim freely, or even spin round in the water. One species, which grows in pools, often spreads over the entire surface of the water, and can be lifted out and dried, when the thick felted mass is not unlike a blanket of faded green baize. Of these a fair number have been recorded as occuring in the North of Ireland, from gatherings made during recent botanical excursions, in all, so far, three hundred and eight species ; but this is very far short of what might be found in the district if observers would collect, examine, and name their finds. This, it is to be hoped, will be done, so as to enable a list of all the fresh-water *Algæ* occuring in the North of Ireland to be published by the Club, and thus fill a long-standing gap in the natural history of the neighbourhood. The work is one in which all possessed of a microscope can participate, as the material requires no tedious preparation before examination, but can be put on a glass slip on the stage, just as it is taken from the water ; and, moreover, some of the species can always be found all the year round. Observers will do well to make drawings and measurements of the various species, and to note the season and place of collection. The Diatoms, Desmids, and the other fresh-water *Algæ*, all of which are known in the North of Ireland by the popular name of "glit" are but lowly objects, but the great naturalist Ray has observed—"God is said to be *maximus in minimus*. We even esteem it a more difficult matter to frame a small watch than a large clock, and no man blames him who spent his whole time in the consideration of the nature and works of a bee, or thinks his subject was too narrow. Let us, then, not esteem anything contemptible or inconsiderable, or below our notice-taking ; for this is to derogate from the wisdom and art of the Creator, and to confess ourselves unworthy of those endowments of knowledge and understanding which He has bestowed on us. What the All wise did not disdain to create cannot be unworthy of notice ; and if in the minute Desmids and Diatoms so long concealed from the unassisted eye, we have at length been enabled to recognise objects as carefully arranged as the bulky elephant or the majestic oak, and as happily adapted to their position in nature, possessing, too, an economy whose laws are no less constant and regular, shall we not gladly examine this fresh evidence of an almighty hand as distinctly impressed on these as on the rest of His creation ? To Him no law is high, no law too great nor small. He fills, He bounds, connects, and equals all." The difference between the three great divisions into which cryptogamic botanists separate fresh-water *Algæ* was explained by the aid of diagrams of the most characteristic species of each. At the close a list was exhibited of those from Mr. Lett's own gatherings, which had been examined and named by Messrs. William West and G. S. West, of Bradford, and Mr. William Joshua, of Cirencester ; and the members of the Club were invited to collect and examine "glit" from the bogs and pools and ponds and rivers of the district, and assist in compiling a list of the fresh-water *Algæ* of Ulster, which it is proposed to contribute to the proceedings of the Club.

The second communication was by Mr. F. W. Lockwood,
being some notes on the "Seven Churches" of Glendalough,
County Wicklow.   The paper was illustrated by a set of
beautiful sketches by Mr. J. P. Addey, a Dublin artist, lately
a resident in the valley.   The writer observed that the title
"Seven" Churches was a misnomer, there being in reality
nine—viz : five in the central group beside the tower and
great cross, two lower down the valley, and two on the shore
of the upper lake.   Attention was called to the stone-roofed
church with the small round tower built on the roof, known
as St. Kevin's kitchen ; and it was pointed out that Trinity
Church, as shown by a drawing of Beranger's made more than
one hundred years ago, had also a similar tower built on part
of the stone roof, which has now entirely disappeared except part
of the springing stones at the base.   We have, therefore,
records of three or four such structures in Dublin and Wicklow, of which the lower tower of St. Kevin's "kitchen" only
remains.   St. Kieran's Church had its foundations cleared
away from a heap of rubbish by the Board of Works when
they took charge of these monuments. — The Rheefert Church,
surrounded by the rude crosses that mark the "tombs of the
kings" beside the upper lake, is most romantically situated,
and the Church of Teampull-na-Skellig, or Church of the Rock,
at the foot of lofty cliffs, accessible only by a boat, is even
more so.   The monastery, which lies lower down the valley,
contains some of the richest and most elaborate Romanesque
work in Ireland.   Glendalough is now very accessible by
excursion trains from Dublin, and the beauty and attractive-
ness of the place can hardly be exaggerated.

The Chairman (Mr. Joseph Wright, F.G.S.) next brought
before the meeting some results of observations that he had
made into the growth of *Foraminifera.*   He remarked as a
peculiarity, that he had been frequently struck with the remarkable coincidence that where the primordial chamber was of
small size, the following chambers rapidly increase in size, and
in species whose primordial chamber was relatively larger,

the subsequent development of chambers of less increasing proportions was the rule. This was illustrated by a series of diagrams and views of remarkable foraminal growth, thrown on the screen by lantern and limelight.

Canon Grainger begged leave to read a letter received by him from Rev. H. B. Carter, D.D., Cookstown, of the occurence of a seal on the North Antrim coast, near Ballintoy. The species seemed to be *Phoca vitulina*. It was killed by the fishermen of the neighbourhood.

The examination of the admirable series of drawings and diagrams, illustrations of the various papers, and the election of members concluded the evening.

ANNUAL MEETING.

The twenty-sixth annual meeting of the club was held in the Museum, College square North, on Monday evening, 29th April, the President (Mr. Hugh Robinson, M.R.I.A.) in the chair.

The President opened the business of the evening by calling for the Secretaries' report.

Mr. Wm. Swanston, F.G.S., Senior Hon. Secretary, then read the report, which, with the statement of accounts, appears in full in the earlier pages of this part of the Proceedings.

The Treasurer (Mr. S. A. Stewart) was then called upon, and from the statement presented by him it transpired that the Club was in a sound financial position.

Mr. R. Lloyd Praeger, B.E., in moving the adoption of the report and statement of accounts, said that it was most satis-factory to know that the twenty-seventh year of the Club's existence found it in a flourishing and prosperous condition, providing pleasant recreation for its members in the shape of summer excursions and winter lectures, and at the same time steadily fulfilling the objects for which it had been set on foot—the practical study of natural science and archæology in Ireland. He would draw particular attention to what, in the report which they had just heard, has been rightly styled the most important event in the Club's history of the past year—the publication of Messrs. Stewart and Corry's " Flora of the North East of Ireland." This work, the result of many years' patient investigation by members of the Naturalists' Field Club, notably by Mr. S. A. Stewart, is one of which any scientific society may well feel proud. Owing to the untimely death of Mr. Corry, the laborious work of compiling, editing, and revising the great amount of matter which the book contains, fell entirely on the senior editor, who has performed his task with a thoroughness and zeal which are worthy of the highest commendation. The book has been most favourably reviewed by the scientific Press, and is one whose appearance will be welcomed by all those who are interested in the science of botany, while to Irish botanists it will be simply invaluable.

Rev. C. H. Waddell, M.A., seconded the motion, and the report and financial statement were adopted.

The next business was the election of officers for the ensuing year. Mr. William Gray, M.R.I.A., was elected President, and Mr. John Vinycomb, Vice-president. The Treasurer and Hon. Secretaries were re-elected, and the Committee, with some slight changes, resumed office.

Mr. Hugh Robinson (outgoing President), before leaving the chair, thanked the members for the kindness and courtesy they had extended to him during his term of office, and expressed the pleasure he felt in vacating office in favour of Mr. William Gray, an old and tried friend of the Club.

Mr. Gray, who was received with applause, thanked the members for the honour they had again conferred upon him by electing him as President for a second term after a lapse of some years, an honour which, he believed, had not previously been conferred on any other member of the Club. The first Presidential duty he would be called upon to perform was a very pleasant one. He had been asked to undertake it on behalf

of the members, and that was to assist in presenting an address
and portrait to their outgoing President. He would now call
on Mr. W. Swanston, Senior Secretary.

Mr. Swanston then read the address, after which Mr. Robinson read his reply, which, with the address, will be found below.

The portrait was unveiled, amid applause, by Mr. John
Anderson, J.P., F.G.S., one of the original members of the
Club, who spoke of his early acquaintance with Mr. Robinson,
and his high appreciation of his scientific attainments and
sterling qualities, and also testified to the great pleasure which
it gave him to be the medium of presenting to Mr. Robinson,
on behalf of his fellow-members of the Naturalists' Field Club,
that well deserved mark of esteem. He expressed the hope
that Mr. Robinson might be long spared to favour the Club
with the benefit of his experience and counsel.

The portrait, which was executed by Mr. Ernest Taylor,
of Belfast, was an admirable likeness, and the address was
illuminated in most artistic style by Messrs. Marcus Ward & Co.

Some formal business having been transacted, the proceedings concluded.

ADDRESS TO HUGH ROBINSON, ESQ., M.R.I.A.

Dear Sir,—The close of your term of office as President of the Belfast Naturalists'
Field Club marks, in the opinion of your fellow-members, a time in your connection
with it which it would be ungrateful on their part to allow to pass without recognition.

Twenty-six years have now elapsed since you met in consultation with four others
imbued like yourself with an unaffected love of nature, and a desire to study with
scientific method, and as nature can only be really studied—in the field. The outcome of this meeting was the establishment of the Belfast Naturalists' Field Club, a
society organised mainly for the purpose of promoting a better knowledge of the flora
and fauna and antiquities of the country. Since 1863 these objects have never been
overlooked, and no year has elapsed without some marked advance in this direction.

During all this period you have been officially connected with the Club, and we
feel that much of its success may be attributed to your zeal for its interests. In 1869
you were chosen to be one of its Honorary Secretaries, which position you held till
1880. Largely owing to your untiring energy in this capacity, accompanied by organising
powers of a high order, the Club was established on a firm basis, and became the

means of accomplishing much original work, which has secured for it a foremost place among kindred societies throughout the kingdom.

In 1885 you were elected to the office of Vice-President, and in 1887 to that of President, positions which you filled with much honour to yourself and satisfaction to the members.

In accordance with the rules of the Club, you this evening vacate the office of President, and in recognition of your long and valued official career, the members avail themselves of the opportunity of asking your kind acceptance of this Address and accompanying Portrait as testifying in some degree to their appreciation of your services, so long and so willingly rendered ; and they also express the hope that they may long enjoy the advantages of your counsel and co-operation.

We are, dear Sir, Your Sincere Friends,

Signed on behalf of the members,

WILLIAM GRAY, President,

JOHN VINYCOMB, Vice-President.

WILLIAM SWANSTON,
F. W. LOCKWOOD, } Honorary Secretaries.

S. A. STEWART, Treasurer.

JOHN J. ANDREW,
GEORGE DONALDSON,
JOHN DONALDSON,
WILLIAM A. FIRTH,
JOHN HAMILTON,
DANIEL M'KEE,
R. LLOYD PRAEGER,
ROBERT J. WELCH,
JOSEPH WRIGHT, } Committee.

The Museum, 29th April, 1889.

REPLY.

Mr. President, Ladies, and Gentlemen,—It is with feelings of much pleasure and gratitude that I accept your Address and Presentation, and tender to you my sincere thanks for the kindness which prompted you to recognise in this manner my connection with the Club, and for the very flattering terms in which you refer to it.

The intimation that the arrangement to confer this honour upon me had been completed, and the request that I should give sittings to Mr. Ernest E. Taylor for the Portrait which accompanies the Address, came upon me most unexpectedly, as I was not conscious of having done anything to merit such a mark of your esteem. Any services which I have been able to render to the Club have not been the result of individual efforts on my part, but simply those of one of an earnest, active staff of office-bearers, each cordially co-operating for the advancement of the Club's interests and for the promotion of the objects for which it was founded. To their united efforts, much more than to mine, belongs the credit of placing the Club in the position it now occupies.

I fully reciprocate the desire expressed in your address that my official connection with the Club may long continue, and I can only hope that in future years I may be able to show that I appreciate as I should do the honour you now bestow upon me. The recollections of the many pleasant hours spent in connection with the Club, and the fast and enduring friendships formed by its agency, must ever remain green in my memory.   The tangible expressions of your sentiments with regard to me must tend to deepen these recollections and make more firm these friendships, and on this account the Address and Portrait will ever be looked upon by me as being amongst the most valued of my possessions.

I remain, Ladies and Gentlemen, yours very truly,

HUGH ROBINSON.

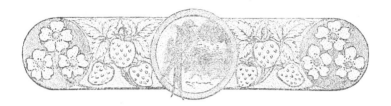

RULES

OF THE

𝕭𝖊𝖑𝖋𝖆𝖘𝖙 𝕹𝖆𝖙𝖚𝖗𝖆𝖑𝖎𝖘𝖙𝖘' 𝕱𝖎𝖊𝖑𝖉 𝕮𝖑𝖚𝖇.

———✠———

I.

That the Society be called "THE BELFAST NATURALISTS' FIELD CLUB."

II.

That the objects of the Society be the practical study of Natural Science and Archæology in Ireland.

III.

That the Club shall consist of Ordinary, Corresponding, and Honorary Members. The Ordinary Members to pay annually a subscription of Five Shillings, and that candidates for such Membership shall be proposed and seconded at any Meeting of the Club, by Members present, and elected by a majority of the Votes of the Members present.

IV.

That the Honorary and Corresponding Members shall consist of persons of eminence in Natural Science, or who shall have done some special service to the Club; and whose usual residence is not less than twenty miles from Belfast. That such Members may be nominated by any Member of the Club, and on being approved of by the Committee, may be elected at any subsequent Meeting of the Club by a majority of the votes of the Members present. That Corresponding Members be expected to communicate a Paper once within every two years.

V.

That the Officers of the Club be annually elected, and consist of a President, Vice-President, Treasurer, and two Secretaries, and Ten Members, who form the Committee. Five to form a quorum. No member of Committee to be

eligible for re-election who has not attended at least one-fourth of the Committee Meetings during his year of office. That the office of President, or that of Vice-President, shall not be held by the same person for more than two years in succession.

VI.

That the Members of the Club shall hold at least Six Field Meetings during the year, in the most interesting localities, for investigating the Natural History and Archæology of Ireland. That the place of meeting be fixed by the Committee, and that five days' notice of each Excursion be communicated to Members by the Secretaries.

VII.

That Meetings be held Fortnightly or Monthly, at the discretion of the Committee, for the purpose of reading papers ; such papers, as far as possible, to treat of the Natural History and Archæology of the district. . These Meetings to be held during the months from November to April inclusive.

VIII.

That the Committee shall, if they find it advisable, offer for competition Prizes for the best collections of scientific objects of the district ; and the Committee may order the purchase of maps, or other scientific apparatus, and may carry on geological and archæological searches or excavations, if deemed advisable, provided that the entire amount expended under this rule does not exceed the sum of £10 in any one year.

IX.

That the Annual Meeting be held during the month of April, when the Report of the Committee for the past year, and the Treasurer's Financial Statement shall be presented, the Committee and Officers elected, Bye-laws made and altered, and any proposed alteration in the general laws, of which a fortnight's notice shall have been given, in writing, to the Secretary or Secretaries, considered and decided upon. The Secretaries to give the Members due notice of such intended alteration.

X.

That, on the written requisition of twenty-five Members, delivered to the Secretaries, an Extraordinary General Meeting may be called, to consider and decide upon the subjects mentioned in such written requisition.

XI.

That the Committee be empowered to exchange publications and reports, and to extend the privilege of attending the Meetings and Excursions of the Belfast Naturalists' Field Club to members of kindred societies, on similar privileges being accorded to its Members by such other societies.

*The following Rules for the Conducting of the Excursions have,
been arranged by the Committee.*

1. The Excursion to be open to all members; each one to have the privilege of introducing two friends.

II. A Chairman to be elected as at ordinary meetings.

III. One of the Secretaries to act as conductor, or in the absence of both, a member to be elected for that purpose.

IV. No change to be made in the programme, or extra expenses incurred, except by the consent of the majority of the members present.

V. No fees, gratuities, or other expenses to be paid except through the conductor.

VI. Every member or visitor to have the accommodation assigned by the conductor. Where accommodation is limited, consideration will be given to priority of application.

VII. Accommodation cannot be promised unless tickets are obtained before the time mentioned in the special circular.

VIII. Those who attend an excursion, without previous notice, will be liable to extra charge, if extra cost be incurred thereby.

IX. No intoxicating liquors to be provided at the expense of the Club.

BELFAST NATURALISTS' FIELD CLUB.

——o——

TWENTY-SEVENTH YEAR.

——o——

THE Committee offer the following Prizes to be competed for during the Session ending March 31st, 1890 :—

I. Best Herbarium of Flowering Plants, representing not less than 250 species, .. £1 0 0

II. Best Herbarium of Flowering Plants, representing not less than 150 species, ... 0 10

III. Best Collection of Mosses, ... 0 10

IV. .. .. Lichens, ... 0 10 0

V. „ „ Seaweeds, ... 0 10

VI. Ferns, Equiseta, and Lycopods, 0 10

VII. Tertiary and Post Tertiary Fossils, ... 0 10 0

VIII. „ „ Cretaceous Fossils, ... 0 10 0

IX. „ „ Liassic Fossils, ... 0 10 0

X. Permian and Carboniferous Fossils, ... 10

XI. Older Palæozoic Fossils, ... 10 0

XII. : Marine Shells, ... 10

XIII. „ „ Land and Freshwater Shells, 10

XIV. Lepidoptera, ... 0 10 0

XV. Hymenoptera, ... 10 0

XVI. Coleoptera, ... 10 0

XVII. Best Collection of Crustacea and Echinodermata,   0   10   0

XVIII. Best Collection of Fungi; names of species not necessary. Collectors may send (post-paid, from time to time during the season) their specimens to Rev. H. W. Lett, M.A., T.C.D., Aghaderg Glebe, Loughbrickland, who will record them to their credit, ...   0   10   0

XIX. Best Collection of Fossil Sponges, ...   0   10   0

XX. Best Collection of 24 Microscopic Slides, illustrating some special branch of Natural History, ...   0   10   0

XXI. Best Collection of 24 Microscopic Slides, shewing general excellence, ...   0   10   0

XXII. Best set of 6 Field Sketches appertaining to Geology, Archæology, or Zoology,   ...   0   10   0

XXIII. Best set of 12 Photographs, illustrative of Irish Archæology, ...   0   10   0

SPECIAL PRIZES.

XXIV. The President offers a Prize of £1 1s for the Best Set of three or more Original Sketches, to be placed in the Album of the Club. These may be executed in pen and ink, or water colour, and must illustrate one or more ancient monuments somewhere in Ireland. In determining the relative merits of the sketches, accuracy in representing the subjects and their details will have chief place. This Prize is open to the Members of the Ramblers' Sketching Club, and to the Students of the School of Art.

XXV. Mr. William Swanston, F.G.S., offers a Prize of 10s. 6d. for Six Photographs from Nature, illustrative of Geology, contributed to the Club's Album.

CONDITIONS.

No Competitor to obtain more than two Prizes in any year.

No Competitor to be awarded the same Prize twice within three years.

A member to whom Prize No. 1 has been awarded shall be ineligible to compete for Prize No. 2, unless the plants are additions to those in previous collection.

In every case where three or more persons compete for a Prize, a second one, of half its value, will be awarded if the conditions are otherwise complied with.

All collections to be made personally during the Session in Ireland, except those for Prize 21, which need not necessarily be Irish, nor Competitors' own collecting. The species to be correctly named, and locality stated, and a list must accompany each collection. The Flowering Plants to be collected when in flower, and classified according to the Natural System. The Microscopic Slides to be Competitors' own preparation and mounting. The Sketches and Photographs to be Competitors' own work, executed during the Session; and those sets for which Prizes are awarded, to become the property of the Club.

No Prizes will be awarded except to such Collections as shall, in the opinion of the Judges, possess positive merit.

The Prizes to be in books, or suitable scientific objects, at the desire of the successful competitor.

NOTICE.

———◇———

EXCHANGES OF PROCEEDINGS.

———◇———

Amiens—Societé Linnéenne du Nord de la France.
  Bulletin Tome IX., Nos. 187 to 210.

Belfast Natural History and Philosophical Society.
  Report and Proceedings, 1888-89.

Berwickshire Naturalists' Club.
  Proceedings. Vol. XII., No. 1.

Bristol Naturalists' Society.
  Proceedings. Vol. IV., Part 1.

Cardiff Naturalists' Society.
  Report and Transactions. Vol. XX., Part 2.

Cornwall—Royal Institution of,
  Journal. Vol. IX., Part 4.

Dublin—Royal Irish Academy.
  Transactions. Vol. XXIX., Parts 3 to 11.

Dumfries and Galloway Nat. Hist. and Antiquarian Society.
  Transactions, 1886-87.

Eastbourne Natural History Society.
  Transactions. Vol. II., Part 5.

Edinburgh Botanical Society.
  Transactions and Proceedings. Vol. XVII., Part 2.

Frankfurt—Monatliche—Mitthielungen aus dem Gesammtge-
bliete der Naturwissenschaften.
  Nos. 10 to 12, 1888-89 ; Nos. 1 to 8, 1889-90.
  Societatum Litteræ.
  2 Jarg. 11 and 12 ; 3 Jarg. 1 to 9.

Genoa Societa di Letture.
  Giornale.   Anno. II., Fasc. 11 & 12.

Glasgow—Geological Society.
  Transactions.   Vol. VII., Part 2.

Hertfordshire Natural History Society and Field Club.
  Transactions.   Vol. V., Parts 4 and 5.

Leeds Philosophical and Literary Society.
  Annual Report, 1888-89.

Liverpool Naturalists' Field Club.
            Proceedings, 1888.
     „   Geological Society.
            Proceedings. Vol. VI., Part 1.

London—British Association for the Advancement of Science.
  Report, 1888, Bath Meeting.
     „   Geologists' Association.
          Proceedings.   Vol. X., Part 9 ; Vol. XI., Parts 1 to 4.

Manchester Field Naturalists' and Archæologists' Society.
  Report and Proceedings, 1888.

            Microscopical Society.
            Transactions, 1888.

            Scientific Students' Association.
            Report and Transactions, 1888.

New Brunswick Natural History Society.
  Bulletin.—No. VIII.

Penzance Natural History and Antiquarian Society.
  Report and Transactions, 1888-89.

Plymouth Institution.
  Annual Report and Transactions.   Vol. X., Part 2.

Toronto—Canadian Institute.
  Annual Report, 1887-88.   Proceedings.   Vol. VI., Fasc. 2.

U.S.A.—American Association for the Advancement of Science.
Proceedings of Twenty-seventh Meeting, 1889.

,, Boston Society of Natural History.
Proceedings. Vol. XXIII., Parts 3 and 4.

,, California Academy of Sciences.
Proceedings. Vol. I., Parts 1 and 2.

,, Essex Institute.
Bulletin. Vol. XIX., Nos. 1 to 12.

,, New York Academy of Sciences.
Transactions. Vol. VIII., Nos. 1 to 4.

,, New York—American Museum of Natural History.
Bulletin. Vol. II., No. 2.

,, Philadelphia Academy of Natural Sciences.
Proceedings. Part 3, 1888 ; Part 1, 1889.

,, Raleigh—Elisha Mitchell Scientific Society.
Journal, 1888-89.

,, St. Louis Academy of Sciences.
Transactions. Vol. V., Nos. 1 and 2.

,, St. Paul's—Geological and Natural History Survey of Minnesota.
Sixteenth Annual Report, 1887.

,, Trenton—Natural History Society.
Journal. Vol. II., No. 1.

,, Washington Smithsonian Institution.
Annual Report for year ending 1886.

Received from the Author.

On the discovery of Palæolithic Implements in the neighbourhood of Kennet, Cambs., by A. G. Wright, Esq.

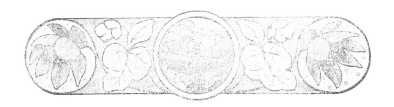

BELFAST NATURALISTS' FIELD CLUB

—— —:— ——

TWENTY-SEVENTH YEAR, 1889-90.

—— —:— ——

LIST OF OFFICERS AND MEMBERS.

—— —:— ——

PRESIDENT :
WILLIAM GRAY, M.R.I.A.

VICE-PRESIDENT :
JOHN VINYCOMB.

TREASURER :
S. A. STEWART, F.B.S., Edin.

SECRETARIES :

WM. SWANSTON, F.G.S.,
80, KING STREET.

F. W. LOCKWOOD,
WARING STREET.

COMMITTEE :

JOHN J. ANDREW, L.D.S., R.C.S., Eng.	DANIEL M'KEE.
GEORGE DONALDSON	R. Ll. PRAEGER, B.E., B.A.
JOHN DONALDSON.	HUGH ROBINSON, M.R.I.A.
W. A. FIRTH.	ROBERT J. WELCH.
JOHN HAMILTON.	JOSEPH WRIGHT, F.G.S.

Members.

Any changes in the Addresses of Members should be notified to the Secretaries.

Edward Allworthy, Mosaphir, Cave Hill Road.
John Anderson, J.P., F.G.S., East Hillbrook, Holywood.
Robert Anderson, Meadowlands.
J. J. Andrew, L.D.S., R.C.S.Eng., Belgravia, Lisburn Road.
Mrs. Andrews, Seaview, Shore Road

James M. Barkley, Holywood.
Robert Barklie, Wilmont Terrace.
James Barr, Beechleigh.
William Batt, Sorrento, Windsor.
Miss Emma Beck, Old Lodge Road.
George R. Begley, Wolfhill Lodge, Ligoniel.
James Best, Great Victoria Street.
F. J. Bigger, Ardrie, Antrim Road.
Edward Bingham, Ponsonby Avenue
Mrs. Blair, Camberwell Terrace.
E. Blair, Camberwell Terrace.
J. H. Boyd, Eblana Street.
Edward Braddell, St. Ives, Malone.
Wm. Thomas Brand, M.B., Florida Manor, Killinchy.
Hugh B. Brandon, Atlantic Avenue.
Chas. H. Brett, Gretton Villa South
John Thorley Brindley, Ulsterville Avenue.
Rev. John Bristow, St. James's Parsonage.
John Brown, Bellair, Windsor Av.
Robert Brown, Donoughmore.
Thomas Brown, Donegall Street.
James A. Browne, Wilmont Place.
John Browne, J.P., Ravenhill House.
John Browne, M.R.I.A., Drapersfield, Cookstown.
W. J. Browne, M.R.I.A., Highfield, Omagh.
W. W. Brydon, Silverstream, Greenisland.
Chas Bulla, Wellington Park Terrace
Henry Burden, M.D., M.R.I.A., Alfred Street.
J. R. Burnett, Martello, Holywood.

Wm. Campbell, Allworthy Avenue.
Ernest Carr, Botanic Avenue.

Miss Carruthers, Claremont Street.
E. T. Church, Donegall Place.
William Clibborn, Windsor Terrace.
Stanley B. Coates, L.R.C.P. Edin., Shaftesbury Square.
James Coey, Victoria Street.
Wm. F. C. S. Corry, Chatsworth.
Rev. W. Cotter, D.D., Riversdale Terrace. Balmoral.
George B. Coulter, Helen's Bay.
Mrs. Coulter, Helen's Bay.
James Creeth, Riversdale Terrace, Balmoral.
Robert Culbert, Distillery Street.
Samuel Cunningham, Glencairn.
Francis Curley, Dunedin.
Mrs. Curley, Dunedin.
William Curry, Botanic Avenue.

Marquis of Dufferin and Ava.
J. H. Davies, Glenmore Cottage, Lisburn.
Henry Davis, Holywood.
Robt. Day, J.P., F.S.A., M.R.I.A., Cork.
Wakefield H. Dixon, Dunowen.
George Donaldson, Bloomfield.
John Donaldson, Eglinton Street.
W. J. Donnan, Holywood.
W. J. Dunlop, Bryson Street.

David Elliott, Albert Bridge Road.
George Elliott, Royal Avenue.
George H. Elliott, Lorne Villas, South Parade.
Lavens M. Ewart, J.P., Glenbank.

Godfrey W. Ferguson, Murray's Terrace.
J. H. Ferguson, Belgrave, Knock.
Joseph Firth, Whiterock.
Wm. A. Firth, Glenview Terrace, Springfield Road.
Thomas J. G. Fleming, F.G.S., Limavady
T. M. H Flynn, Sunnyside, Bessbrook.

J. Starkie Gardner, F.G.S., Damer Terrace, Chelsea. (Hon. Mem.)

J. G. Gifford, Holywood.
R. M. Gilmore, Garden Vale Terrace, Athlone.
W. J. Gilmore, Camberwell Villas.
George J. Glen, Hartington Street.
William Godwin, Queen Street.
Rev. David Gordon, Downpatrick.
James Goskar, Carlisle Circus.
James Gourley, J.P., Derryboy, Killyleagh.
Rev.Canon Grainger, D.D.,M.R.I.A. Broughshane
Robert Graham, Brookview Terrace.
Wm. Gray, M.R.I.A., Mountcharles.
Miss Gray, Mountcharles.
George Greer, J.P., Woodville, Lurgan.
Edward Gregg, Donegall Pass.

John Hamilton, Mount Street.
Richard Hanna, Charleville Street.
Mann Harbison, Ravenhill Terrace.
Rev. Canon Hartrick, The Rectory, Ballynure.
Sir James Haslett, J.P., Princess Gardens.
Thos. Hassan, Strangemore House.
W. D. Hazelton, Cliftonville.
F. A. Heron, Cultra.
J. S. Holden, M.D., F.G.S., Sudbury, Suffolk (Cor. Mem.).
John Horner, Clonard Foundry.
Alexander Hunter, Northern Bank.
W. J. Hurst, J.P., Drumaness, Ballynahinch.
James Imrie, Fitzroy Avenue.

H. Jamison, Duncairn Terrace.
Hugh Smith Jefferson, Rosnakill, Strandtown.
James F. Johnston, Holywood.
Wm. J. Johnston, J.P., Dunesk, Stranmillis
Prof. T. Rupert Jones, F.R.S., Chelsea, London (Hon. Mem.).

John Kane, LL.B , Chichester Street.
Archibald Kent, Newington Street.
Wm. Kernahan, Wellington Park.
George Kidd, Lisnatore, Dunmurry.
F. Kirkpatrick, Ann Street.
Wm. J. Knowles, M.R.I.A., Ballymena
Robert A. Kyle, Richmond.

W. W. Lamb, Salisbury Avenue.
Prof. Charles Lapworth, F.G.S., Mason College, Birmingham (Hon. Mem.)
F. R. Lepper, Carnalea.
Rev. H. W. Lett. M.A., T.C.D., Aghaderg Glebe, Loughbrickland.
Frederick W. Lockwood, Wellington Park Terrace.
James Logan, Donegall Street.
Joseph Lowe, Essex Street.
W. B. Lowson, Chichester Park.
H. W. Luther,M.D., Chlorine House.

John Mackenzie, C.E., Myrtlefield.
Henry Magee, Eglantine Avenue.
William A. Mahaffy, Dublin Road.
Rev. J. J. Major, Belvoir Hall, Ballymacarrett.
Harold Malcolmson, Holywood.
Greer Malcomson, Granville Terrace.
Jas. Malcomson, Rosemount, Knock.
Mrs. Malcomson, Rosemount, Knock.
John Marsh, Glenlyon, Holywood.
Mrs. Marsh, Glenlyon, Holywood.
Joseph C. Marsh, Castleton Terrace.
Rev. James Martin, Eglintoun, Antrim Road.
Mrs. Martin, Eglintoun, Antrim Road.
J. M'Clelland Martin, Oceanic Avenue
James Meneely, Donegall Pass.
Henry Merrick, Great Victoria Street.
Seaton Forrest Milligan, M.R.I.A., Royal Terrace.
R. Joynt Morrison, Limestone Road.
Thomas Morrison, Great George's Street.
David Morrow, Church Hill, Holywood.
John Morton, Clifton Park Avenue.
James Murdoch, Denmark Street.
Joseph John Murphy, Osborne Park.
Mrs Agnes Murray, Ulster Terrace.
J. R. Musgrave, J.P., Drumglass House, Malone.

Thomas M'Alister, Eglinton Street.
Joseph M'Chesney, Holywood.
Francis P. M'Clean, Huntly Villas.
H. M'Cleery, Clifton Park Avenue.

Rev. Ed. M'Clure, M.A , M.R.I.A.,
Onslow Place, South Kensington, London (Cor. Mem.).
John M'Clure. Donlure, Bloomfield.
Sir Thomas M'Clure, Bart., Belmont
Wm. J. M'Clure. Elizabeth Street.
Jas. M'Connell, Caledonia Terrace.
F. W. M'Cullough, C.E., Chichester Street.
W. F. MacElheran, Botanic Avenue.
Miss M'Gaw, Wellington Park Terrace.
J. H. MacIlwaine, Brandon Villa.
Mrs. MacIlwaine, Brandon Villa.
Daniel M'Kee, Adela Place.
W. S. M'Kee, Fleetwood Street.
Alexander MacLaine, J.P., Queen's Elms.
Miss Annie M'Liesh, The Mount, Mountpottinger.
John M'Leish, The Mount.
John M'Leish, Jun., The Mount.
Robert M'Leish, The Mount.
William MacMillan, Enniscorthy.
Jas. M'Mordie, Belgravia Avenue.
John M'Stay, College Square East.

Lucien Nepveu, Claremont Street.
W. Courtney Nesbitt, Kinnaird Terrace.
Wm. Nicholl, Donegall Square North.
Jerdan Nichols, Meadowbank Street.
H. J. Nicholson, Windsor Gardens.
Mrs. Nicholson, Windsor Gardens.

Henry O'Neill, M.D., College Square East.
James O'Neill, M.A., College Square East.
A. T. Osborne, Rosetta Terrace.

W. J. Pasley, Carrickfergus.
David C. Patterson, Holywood.
Robert Lloyd Patterson, J.P., F.L.S., Croft House, Holywood.
Robert Patterson, Windsor Park Terrace, Lisburn Road.
William H. Patterson, M R.I.A., Garranard, Strandtown.
James J. Phillips, Arthur Street
William H. Phillips, Lemonfield, Holywood.

E. W. Pim, Elmwood Terrace.
John Pim, J.P., Bonaven, Antrim Road.
Joshua Pim, Slieve-na-Failthe, Whiteabbey.
Thomas W. Pim, The Lodge, Strandtown.
E. A. Praeger, The Croft, Holywood.
R. Lloyd Praeger, B.A., B.E., The Croft, Holywood.

Joseph Radley, Prospect Hill, Lisburn.
John H. Rea, M.D., Shaftesbury Square.
D. Redmond, Antrim.
Right Rev. Dr. Reeves, Bishop of Down and Connor and Dromore, Conway House, Dunmurry.
Robert Reid, King Street.
Richard Ridings, Hampton Terrace.
Rev. George Robinson, M.A., Beech Hill House, Armagh.
George Robinson, Woodview, Holywood.
Hugh Robinson, M.R.I.A., Helen's View, Antrim Road.
Jas. R. Robinson, George's Terrace.
William A. Robinson, J.P., Culloden, Cultra.
Richard Ross, M.D., Wellington Place.
Wm. A. Ross, Iva-Craig, Craigavad.
John Russell, C.E., The Eyries, Newcastle
Robt A. Russell, Colinview Terrace.
Jno. Ryan, Myrtle Hill Terrace, Cork.

James Shanks, Ballyfounder, Portaferry.
Chas. Sheldon, M.A., B.Sc., D. Lit., Royal Academical Institution.
Edward Smith, Chichester Terrace.
Rev. W. S. Smith, The Manse, Antrim.
Rev. Canon Smythe, M.A., Coole Glebe, Carnmoney.
Wilson Smyth, Virginia Street.
Adam Speers, B.Sc., Holywood.
A. C. Stannus, Holywood.
Sir N. A. Staples, Bart., Lissan, (Life Mem.).

Jas. Stelfox, Oakleigh, Ormeau Park.
John Stevenson, Coolavin.
J. M'N. Stevenson. Carrickfergus.
S. A. Stewart, Springfield Road.
William Swanston, F.G.S., Clifton-
    ville Avenue.
Mrs. Swanston, Cliftonville Avenue.
Richard Glascott Symes, M.A.,
    F G.S., Portrush.
Samuel Symington, Ballyoran House.

Alex. Tate, C.E , Longwood House.
Prof. Ralph Tate, F.G.S., F.L S ,
    Adelaide, South Australia,
    (Hon. Mem).
H. F. Thomas, Lower Crescent.
S. G. Thomas, Limestone Road.
Mrs. H. Thompson, Crosshill, Wind-
    sor.
George Thomson, Falls Road.
Prof. James Thomson, LLD.,F.R.S..
    Florentine Gardens, Glasgow,
    (Hon. Mem).
John Todd, Clonaven.
W. A. Todd, Elgin Terrace.
W. A. Traill, B.E..M.A.I., Portrush.
W. J. Trelford, Vicinage Park.
James Turner, Mountain Bush.
Jas. G. Turtle, Cambridge Terrace.

John Vinycomb, Holywood.

Rev. C. Herbert Waddell, M.A.,
    Whitewell.

Miss Wardell, Cave Hill Road.
W. F. Wakeman, M.R.I.A., Dublin
    (Cor. Mem.).
Thos. R. Walkington. Edenvale.
George G. Ward, Eversleigh,
    Strandtown.
Isaac W. Ward, Salisbury Terrace.
Thomas Watson, Shipquay Gate,
    Londonderry.
Charles W. Watts, F.I.C., Holborn
    Terrace.
Isaac Waugh, Clifton Park Avenue.
Robert J. Welch, Lonsdale Street.
Walter L. Wheeler, Lennoxvale
Wm. Whitla, M.D., J.P., College
    Square North.
Jas Wilson, Oldforge. Dunmurry.
Jas. Wilson. Ballybundon. Killinchy.
James F. Wilson, Greenville Terrace.
Berkley D. Wise, C.E., Northern
    Counties Railway.
Rev. Robert Workman, M.A., Ru-
    bane, Glastry.
Thomas Workman, J.P., Craigdar-
    ragh.
W. C. Wright, Lauriston, Derrie-
    volgie Avenue.
Joseph Wright, F.G.S., Alfred
    Street.
Mrs. Wright, Alfred Street.
William Wylie, Mount-pleasant.

Robert Young, C.E., Rathvarna.

ANNUAL REPORT

AND

PROCEEDINGS

OF THE

Belfast Naturalists' Field Club

FOR THE

Year ending the 31st March, 1890.

(Twenty-Seventh Year.)

SERIES II.　　VOLUME III.　　PART III.

Belfast:
PRINTED FOR THE CLUB,
BY ALEXANDER MAYNE & BOYD, CORPORATION STREET,
PRINTERS TO QUEEN'S COLLEGE, BELFAST.

1890.

REPORT

OF THE

BELFAST NATURALISTS' FIELD CLUB,

FOR THE

Year ending 31st March, 1890.

N presenting their twenty-seventh Annual Report, your Committee have pleasure in recording the continued prosperity of the Club, the number of members on the roll being about the same as at the close of last year.   The year now completed has been marked by a fair amount of devotion to those pursuits for which the Club was originally established.

The Summer programme was carried out, and excursions were made to the following places, viz :—

1. Scrabo Hill, Newtownards, and Movilla   ...   ..   25th May.
2. Glenariffe via Ballymena   ...   .   15th June.
3. Carnmoney and Whiteabbey   ...   .   6th July.

4. Kilkeel, Greencastle, and Mourne Mountains	...				24th & 25th July.
5. Loughinisland	..	...	...	...	17th August.
6. Tynan and Caledon	...	...	...	...	7th September.

The attendance at most of these excursions was quite up to the average, and several of the districts had never before been visited by the Field Club as an organised body.

The Committee have, as usual, to acknowledge the kindness of various gentlemen in granting access to their grounds, and are especially indebted to Sir J. C. Stronge, Bart., for admission to Tynan Abbey, and to Mr. Robert Hassard, J.P., for permission to pass through the grounds of Parkmore.

An application having been made to the Club by Messrs. William Gray, M.R.I.A., and R. Lloyd Praeger, B.E., who have received grants from the Royal Irish Academy to investigate the flint implement beds and Estuarine Clay deposits of the North of Ireland, offering out of these grants a sum of £5, provided the Club would contribute a similar sum, to be devoted to a further examination of the Larne gravels and underlying beds, your Committee voted this sum under the powers given by Rule VIII., and appointed Messrs. Wright, Stewart, and the Honorary Secretaries to assist Messrs. Gray and Praeger in the work. The investigation took place on May 27th and subsequent days, and a full report of the results was read by Mr. Praeger at a meeting of the Club on the 19th November, and is incorporated in the Proceedings of the current year.

The following communications were brought forward during the Winter Session :—

19th Nov.
{ Introductory Remarks by the President, William Gray, M.R.I.A.
Report of the Committee appointed to investigate the Gravels and underlying Beds at Larne, by R. Lloyd Praeger, B.E.
Notice of the occurrence of the Stock Dove in the County of Antrim, by R. Lloyd Praeger, B.E.

17th Dec.
{ "Some Notes on Plant Life," by Rev. C. Herbert Waddell, M.A.
"On the Cells of Mosses," by Rev. H. W. Lett, M.A., T.C.D.

	"A Contribution to the Post-tertiary Fauna of Ulster," by R. Lloyd Praeger, B.E.
28th Jan.	"Three Days on Rathlin Island, with Notes on its Flora and Fauna," R. Lloyd Praeger, B.E.
19th Feb.	"A Gossip about British Ferns and their Varieties, with Notices of local Finds," by W. H. Phillips.

In addition to these Lecture Evenings, an Opening Social Meeting was held in the Museum on November 13th, which was largely attended, and a microscopic evening was held on March 26th, when an instructive hour was spent in the manipulation of the microscope, and in a survey of the lesser world which it reveals.

Your Committee take this opportunity of calling the attention of the members of the Club to the circular recently issued under the auspices of the Belfast Natural History and Philosophical Society, by Messrs. Robert Patterson and R. Lloyd Praeger, on the proposed " Vertebrate Fauna of Ulster," and of inviting their co-operation in promoting the valuable objects to which it is directed.

It is with profound regret that your Committee have to record the decease, upon the 11th April, of their fellow-member and late President, Mr. Hugh Robinson, M.R.I.A. Their feelings may perhaps be best expressed in the words of a re-solution passed by them upon the next day, and which they here subjoin :—" It is with deep sorrow that the Committee of the Belfast Naturalists' Field Club have to record the death of their esteemed colleague, Hugh Robinson, M.R.I.A., one of the founders of the Club. Whilst they acknowledge his untiring services for many years as Hon. Secretary, and his subsequent cordial interest in the Club's work during his terms of office as Vice-President and President, they feel that their loss is far more than that of a mere colleague, however able ; it is of a tried and sincere friend. They tender to Mrs. Robinson and the other members of his family their deep sympathy in this painful bereavement."

It is scarcely needful to remind the earlier members of the Club, but those who have joined in more recent years may be interested to learn the great services rendered by Mr. Robinson in the founding of the Club and the earlier administration of its affairs. Mr. Robinson has himself—but with a modesty in which his own share is almost entirely suppressed—in a recent number of our Proceedings narrated its history ; and if in those days the success of the Club was largely due to the ubiquitous energy of our President, Mr. Gray, it was in an equal degree the result of the business habits and assiduous attention to necessary details of his colleague, whose untimely loss we have now to deplore.

Your Committee again have to thank a number of kindred societies and public bodies for the interchange of copies of their Proceedings and other publications. By these means a valuable collection of works continues to be added to the Club's property.

Your Committee are glad to state that arrangements have been made for the continuation of the Annual Meteorological Reports which formerly embellished their Proceedings, and which have been discontinued since 1887, owing to the death of Mr. Lancelot Turtle, who for many years supplied an annual summary. They tender their thanks to the Council of Queen's College, Belfast, for kind permission to use the valuable meteorological records kept at that institution, and they expect that the next number of Proceedings will contain not only a meteorological summary of the current season, but the arrears of the last two years.

It is to be regretted that the Competition for the prizes offered by the Club has this year been almost totally neglected by the members, only one collection having been sent in, and the Committee trust that more attention will be given during the ensuing season to this most valuable branch of the Club's work.

The following is the report of the judges on the collection mentioned:—

"Mr. W. D. Donnan has sent in a series of flowering plants in competition for Prize II. This collection represents 254 species, correctly named and beautifully mounted, and complies in all respects with the conditions. We consider it highly creditable to the collector, and have great pleasure in awarding this prize to Mr. Donnan."

S. A. STEWART.
W. GRAY.
R. LLOYD PRAEGER.

Dr. THE TREASURER IN ACCOUNT WITH THE BELFAST NATURALISTS' FIELD CLUB,

FOR THE YEAR ENDING 31st MARCH, 1890.

	£	s	d			£	s	d
To Balance from 1888-9 ...	2	5	11	By Expenses of Social Meeting ...		4	11	
" Subscriptions —219, less 5 paid in advance ...	53	10	0	" Mayne & Boyd, Printing Annual Proceedings		11		
" Tickets for Social Meeting ...	0	11	0	" Stationery, Printing, and Advertising ...		9	1	
" Sales of the Guide to Belfast ...	0	4	6	" Grant in aid of Larne Gravels Exploration		5		
" " Proceedings ...	0	2	6	" Postages ...		5		
" " Flora N.E. Ireland ...	4	17	0	" Delivery of Circulars ...		1	1	
" Interest on Bank Account ...	0	9	9	" Rent of Lecture Hall ...		5		
				" W. Darragh ...		3		
				" Loss on Excursions ...		1		
				" Insurance of Books ...		0	1	
				" Prize awarded ...		0	1	
				" Balance in hand ...		14		
	£62	0	8			£62		
To Balance ...	£14	0	5					

Audited and found correct.

WILLIAM SWANSTON, *Hon. Secretary.*

S. A. STEWART, *Treasurer.*

SUMMER SESSION.

———◇———

The following Excursions were made during the Summer Session :—

On May 25th, to

SCRABO HILL AND MOVILLA.

The first excursion of the season was made on the 25th inst., to Scrabo Hill, near Newtownards, when a party on outdoor science bent left the Ulster Hall in a four-horse brake, and, quickly leaving the smoky city behind them, were soon following the fresh green roads of the County Down. Passing the tumulus that gives name to Dundonald, they left the main road to Newtownards, and proceeded by the older and more hilly one that leads to the back of Scrabo Hill. Leaving this again by a sharp turn to the right, they passed the once well-known " Cargo's quarry," now a deserted heap of grass-grown *debris*, and about a mile further on reached the Glebe quarry, from whence the stone used in Robinson & Cleaver's new building was taken. Nearly all the quarrying about Scrabo Hill is done under difficulties. The chief obstacle here consists of the bank of stiff boulder clay, over forty feet thick, that covers the sandstone, a mass of unproductive material to be removed before the stone can be got at. To the geologists of the party, how-

ever, the clay was itself a feature of interest, being more than
usually full of ice-polished stones, from the massive boulder of
basalt weighing several tons, to the small hand specimen of
Antrim chalk that recorded plainly the direction in which the
ice-movement must have travelled.   Passing round by Killy-
nether House, the party made their way to the top of the hill,
and most of them to the summit of the tower, the view from
which nearly, if not quite, equals that from the adjacent Helen's
Tower, celebrated in Laureate's verse.   The clearness of the
day allowed full justice to the panorama, which embraced
Cantyre, the rugged summits of Arran, Ailsa Craig, the long
stretch of the Scottish coast backed by the Ayrshire mountains,
Galloway, the Isle of Man, and the whole extent of the County
Down, with the broad, level sands of Strangford Lough.   The
scene to the geologist is particularly interesting.   The undulations of rock of lower Silurian age, which forms almost the
entire of the county, may be looked upon as a floor, upon the
upturned and contorted strata of which are scattered patches
of more recent formations that must have covered the silurian
beds for ages, until a vast process of denudation has swept away
the newer to bring the older once more to light.   The oldest of
these perhaps is the little patch of Carboniferous limestone at
Castle Espie, and the still smaller patch of Carboniferous shale
and limestone at Cultra.   There is the narrow strip, only seen
at low water, of the Permian or magnesian limestone also at
Cultra, and there is this outlier of Triassic sandstone that forms
the bulk of Scrabo Hill, which in itself is capped by the vastly
more recent outlier of basalt from the great volcanic plateau of
Antrim.   As we have seen again, the flanks of the hill are
buried beneath a considerable thickness of the Boulder Clay,
which lies as a recent covering upon all the formations alike,
and whose parent ice had no inconsiderable share in moulding
the features of the country as we now know it.   The sandstones
of Scrabo are generally supposed to belong to the lower Triassic
beds—the Bunter-sandstein of Germany.   The grounds for this

belief are that they are apparently a continuation of the lower triassic bed of sandstone that underlies Belfast; that they are, like nearly all the trias sandstones, devoid of fossils, and that they appear to lie above the Carboniferous fragment of Castle Espie. A geologist of some standing in the party ventured to question this general conclusion upon grounds which may be briefly stated—viz., that the absence of fossils is of course in in itself a purely negative piece of evidence ; that as the beds are not continuous from the Antrim side of the lough and there are numerous "faults" in the district, they may be of other age besides Triassic—either Carboniferous or Permian—so long as they are later than the Silurian ; that in their hardness, colour, and general texture they more resemble the Carboniferous than the softer and redder sandstones of the valley of the Lagan. On the whole, however, most geologists will probably unite in the conclusion that the officers of the Survey have followed the weight of the evidence in placing these sandstones at the bottom of the triassic rather than in the older formation. Descending the hill, the large quarries on the Newtownards side were next visited. These are at present only partially worked, though some of them yield excellent stone. The most interesting feature is the dykes by which they are pierced. In one case the once molten lava has forced itself between the beds of the stone, now showing of course as a horizontal bifurcated dyke. Through this, the result of a volcanic outlet of a later period, is to be seen a large dyke penetrating the earlier dykes and the sandstone, impartially shattering and altering the texture of both for some distance on either side. From the edge of the quarry one looks out across the railway upon the latest of the geologic changes, and one in which man has had a share—the reclamation which has converted a strip of lough into fertile fields, laid out in regular parallelograms, the name of the "Scrabo Isles" alone surviving as a relic of the former tide-covered stretch of mud and sand. The botanists of the party did not find much to reward their search. A member exhibited some fine specimens of a very rare fern, the variety *acutum* of the Black Spleenwort (*Asplenium Adiantum-nigrum*), obtained in the vicinity of the hill. This is one of the only two localities in which it has been found in the North of Ireland, the other being the steep basaltic cliff of Benevenagh, in County Derry. The Greater Celandine (*Chelidonium majus*), and the Pennywort (*Cotyledon umbilicus*), with its succulent leaves, were also observed. Passing through New-townards, a visit was paid to the graveyard and ruined church of Movilla. Newtownards was, as its name implies, the Newtown, or " Villa Novo," that sprung up round the Castle planted by De Courcy on the shore of the lough, but Movilla had been a native Irish centre of religion and learning from the earliest Christian times, having been founded by St. Finnian in A.D. 540. The name " Magh-bile," plain of the ancient tree, suggests indeed that it was a sacred place in pre-Christian times, which from other indications is also believed to have been the case of Holywood, Knock, Downpatrick, and many other early Christian sites. The Abbey of Movilla was at the height of its importance in the seventh and eighth centuries, and was then one of the greatest schools in Ireland. After its sack by the Danes in 823 it probably never recovered its early importance, and Dr. O'Laverty suggests that it was in the next century it was partially united with Bangor. Nearly all the buildings have now disappeared except the two gables and part of the side wall of the choir. The windows still show some remains of late Gothic tracery. The most interesting feature is, however, the set of crosses now built into the side wall. One of these, with the inscription " Or do Dertrend"—a prayer for Dertrend—is supposed to be of the eleventh century, or even earlier ; but research has failed to discover who Dertrend was. The other crosses, all of which were horizontal slabs, are curious, several, from the swords and daggers, forming the tokens of the warrior, and others, with a shears or scissors by the side, presumably the token of some lady of high degree.

Tea at Newtownards and the election of new members brought the day's work to a pleasant close.

On June 15th, to

GLENARIFF.

Upwards of forty members left the Northern Counties terminus by the 9·5 a.m. train, bound for Glenariff, and, after a quick run, were at Ballymena transferred to the carriages of the Ballymena and Cushendall branch. This line is a narrow-gauge one, and the passenger cars on it are a departure from those on our ordinary systems, the plan of the tramway cars having been adopted. They are of unusual length, seating between thirty and forty on each side, and from their being well supplied with windows, and the occupants seated sociably *vis-à-vis*, they are well adapted for excursions, affording as they do good opportunities for viewing the district through which they run. The country between Ballymena and Parkmore—the northern terminus of this newly-opened branch—is for the most part agricultural, but as we advance northward and gain a higher elevation, the open moorland is reached. Openings in the hill-sides, with patches of rich-coloured iron ore, and all the machinery and accompaniments of mining, indicate the use for which this line and its many branches were originally constructed. Parkmore offers at first sight little to attract visitors. The View is certainly an extended one, but it is bounded on almost every side by rounded heath-clad hills. One exception is a wooded valley to the right of the line. In this direction lies Glenariff. Under the guidance of the President of the club, Mr. William Gray, M.R.I.A., the upper reaches of the glen are entered—permission having been specially granted to the club. Here the Glenariff water finds its way in a comparatively open course through a plantation of young firs, but soon its descent becomes more rapid, and its work of cutting a chasm for itself more marked. Presently a waterfall—the first of many—deepens the glen, along the steep sides of which a path has been cut. It is found difficult in such places to keep the large party together, various pursuits leading the members in different directions. The botanists, delighted with the variety and luxuriance of the vegetation, peer into the dark recesses in search of the less conspicuous plants. Others, with net in hand, are bent on making captures in the insect world, while the photographers of the party, with their array of cameras of all sizes, have sufficient scope for all their available plates, and enough to occupy their attention in choosing the best views and finding their ways to them ; warm work under such circumstances this highly popular department seems to be. Still proceeding downward, other picturesque waterfalls are reached, one of which, with a double bound plunging into a dark chasm, is only seen at its best by the more active of the party, who venture down to the bottom of the rocky stream bed. Eventually the greater number of the party find their way in small detachments to the " meeting of the waters," where the Glenariff and the Inver streams join. Near this point is another fine cascade. Both stream courses are richly wooded, and the view from the higher ground, looking over the many-tinted foliage and down the wide valley, with its steep and rugged sides, is very fine. There are several fine falls on the Inver water, and on the northern side of the glen are others, where side streams join, but they must be left for another day. All were loud in their praises of the beauty of the scene, while several who had "done" all the attractions in the Isle of Man were strong in their assertions that the best glen in that highly-advertised holiday resort will not bear comparison to Glenariff.

The botanists of the party had perhaps most to show for the day's work. The locality was long since known for the rich flora to be found there, as is seen by the notes of the late Mr. Templeton. About the latter end of the last century the father of local botany was in the habit of visiting this rocky glen, and he frequently quotes the name Glenarve as the station for some rare wild-flower or fern. The most striking feature in the botany of this spot is, without doubt, the great luxuriance of its vegetation. None of the glens in the Mourne Mountains, though so far to the south, can compare in this respect with Glenariff. Hawkweeds are abundant on the damp rocks, and three species,

none of which are common, were met with on this occasion—
namely, *Hieracium cæsium*, *H. iricum*, and *H. vulgatum·*
The rarer of our two Cow-wheats, *Melampyrum sylvaticum*,
was found in abundance, while the Northern Bedstraw, *Galium
boreale*, and Wintergreen, *Pyrola minor*, were plentiful. The
Bird's-nest Orchis, *Neottia nidus-avis*, was met with, as also
the Fragrant Orchis, *Gymnadenia conopsea*, and the Green
Orchis, *Habenaria viridis*. The large Sundew, *Drosera
anglica*, grows in a bog close to the station, and wild Garlic,
Allium ursinum, is quite a feature in the glen. The little
Selaginella, *S. spinosa*, grows on the wet rocks, as also the
Beech Fern, *Polypodium phegopteris*. Many of the commoner
ferns were in great force. A visit to this spot at a later season
would, doubtless, reveal still other rarities. Assembling again
in the comfortable railway carriage, a hurried meeting is held—
the President presiding—when a new member is elected, and a
vote of thanks proposed by Rev. Canon Grainger, D.D., and
seconded by Mr. Mann Harbison, is carried by acclamation to
Mr. Robert Hassard, J.P., for granting the club the very great
privilege of passing through the grounds of Parkmore, and thus
enjoying a most delightful day in what is undoubtedly the finest
of the many beautiful glens of Antrim. On the return journey,
when passing through Glenravel, a fine view is obtained of
Slemish Mountain, rising abruptly from the valley of the Braid-
water. Again changing carriages at Ballymena, the run home
is accomplished in good time.

On July 6th, to

CARNMONEY AND WHITEABBEY.

The third excursion of the season was taken on 6th July, to
Carnmoney and Whiteabbey. A start was made from Glengormley about three o'clock, the party making their way first
to Carnmoney Church, where they examined the beautiful Irish
cross erected by their ex-President, the late General Smythe,

F.R.S., in his family burying-place. The ancient graveyard, with the holy well of spring water in its centre, and the prettily-decorated modern church, also claimed their attention. They then proceeded to the fine quarry, many of the basaltic columns of which almost rival those of the Causeway in regularity. Here they are not perpendicular, however, but inclined at an angle of 40 deg. with the horizon, their ends only appearing in the quarry face. Professor Hull and other geologists have suggested that this portion of Carnmoney Hill formed one of the "volcanic necks" of the great plutonic outburst of the North of Ireland, Slemish, the rock of Dunluce Castle, and others also being similar. The members here secured a good quantity of the chalcedony for which this quarry is famous. The more active of the party climbed to the fort on the hill above, which, though not large, is very perfect, with a high rampart and deep ditch. From the quarry the route was taken beneath the richly-wooded escarpment of Carnmoney Hill to the remains of the Abbey Church from which Whiteabbey derives its name. The little church, whose inside dimensions are about thirty-six feet by eighteen or nineteen feet, has its four walls still standing, with three lancet windows in the east gable, all richly draped with ivy, and closely shadowed by several old trees, the whole forming a strikingly interesting and picturesque group, the merits of which the photographic members of the party were prompt to recognise. The advent of a somewhat robust bull upon the scene caused a hasty adjournment, and the party dispersed, not all to re-assemble until they met at the old Whitehouse near Macedon Point, the "little pyle" of one of the old chronicles. Before leaving, however, the photographers of the party attempted to get an "instantaneous" of John Bull and several members of his bovine harem. Of the old Whitehouse there are still standing the walls and gables, with three circular towers, the old kitchen fireplace, and the oak beams that supported the floor, and the tradition is still cherished that this was one of the lodging-places of King William of "glorious, pious, and immortal" memory.

Close by, through the courtesy of Mr. James Thompson, J.P., the party were directed to a curious specimen of the English elm, which has forked out about a foot above the sward, and, after growing in two trunks for a height of fifteen or twenty feet, re-unites and becomes apparently a single stem above that height.   One of the party who climbed the tree reported that a line of junction could still be traced, although from the ground the stem appeared single.   A brief meeting was held at Whitehouse station for the election of new members, the advancing tide having prevented an inspection of the sandstone beds and trap dykes at Macedon Point.

On July 24th and 25th, to

KILKEEL AND THE MOURNE MOUNTAINS.

The fourth excursion of the season was taken on July 24th and 25th, to Kilkeel and the Mourne Mountains.   The unsettled weather of the previous week damped the ardour of some, but a fair number turned up at the County Down Station, and were soon speeding along the railway for Newcastle. Arrived there, the prospect of a fourteen miles drive along the coast road, swept by rain and driving mist from the sea, required a little courage to face, but naturalists have faith and hope, and they were soon upon the road.   Newcastle, with its lodging-houses and hotels, its half dilapidated harbour, where a pier should be receiving steamboats and tourists from the Isle of Man, is left behind.   We go on past " Maggie's Leap" and " Armor's Hole "; past " Donard's Cave," which tradition says runs straight into the heart of the mountain, and where the saint from which it derives its name is still said to dwell.   Then we pass the picturesque " Bloody Bridge," with its ivy-covered arches without a parapet, and overlooking it the ruined walls of St. Mary's Church, with its tiny chancel arch, probably of the 10th century, void of ornament, through which a beautiful glimpse can be had out seaward.   The road passes many a

romantic little gorge and glen down which the mountain streams
have cut their way to the shore, and the coast itself is full of
interest to the geologist, from the number of basaltic and other
volcanic dykes, some of which are in their turn cut across by
other dykes of a later date.   The most noticeable feature from
the road, however, is the thick beds of moraine matter, full
chiefly of granite fragments from the hills immediately above.
As the party nears Kilkeel the rain gets lighter, and by the time
a few minutes have been devoted to some light refreshment in
the Royal Hotel the clouds have broken, the sun has burst out,
and we are revelling in a glorious July afternoon.   Kilkeel
presents an aspect of bustle, for it is market day.   We proceed
along the road to Rostrevor, past several old earthen forts, one
called the " Mass Forth," reminding us of the nearly forgotten
days of the Catholic proscription.   Near by is the present large
and handsome Catholic Church, and just beyond the corner of
the grave-yard are the remains of a very fine "giant's grave"
or kistvaen, about forty feet long.   The covering stones of the
chamber, have, however, disappeared.   On returning to the
hotel a substantial tea is done justice to, and the *char-à-banc*
once more mounted *en route* for Greencastle.   As we drive
along the sandy spit on which the great castle stands, the London and North-Western Railway Company's ferry steamer is
passed lying with steam up at the little pier ; but we have no
time for a trip to Greenore or Carlingford, so passing the coastguard station we climb the green artificial mound that terminates the point.   This is " Knock Tinnel," doubtless a great·
burial mound of some forgotten chieftain ; but, as its name
purports, better known by tradition as the " Knock Tinoil," or
the hill of the assembly, from the summit of which edicts were
promulgated, and on which the chief stood or sat when his
followers swore allegiance to him.   In a field close by stand
the west gable and belfry of Greencastle Church.   The door
was at the northern side, and there is no trace of a chancel.   It
is the usual old Irish type of a single oblong nave without
aisles.   It groups picturesquely with the great castle behind

upon its rocky knoll. Greencastle, with its huge square or oblong keep and its massive outworks, was, next to Dundrum, the most important Anglo-Norman structure in Down. It dates from the reign of King Henry II., or of John at the latest, though much altered and no doubt strengthened in later reigns, for it is recorded that in 1343 (three years before Crècy) the " felons of Ulster" stormed and dilapidated its walls. It was speedily restored, and in 1403 the joint governor of it and Carlingford had his salary raised from £25 to £40 a year on condition of spending a certain amount yearly in strengthening and keeping it in order. Again in 1495 it was enacted that none but Englishmen should be governors. It stands on the summit of a knoll of rock. Below are gloomy vaults, above a great hall forty feet by twenty, and the stone gutter of the roof formed a broad ledge where the warders walked behind the parapets. Abutting on the main keep can be traced the kitchen, guardrooms, and other structures, all now much dilapidated. Little, doubtless, cared the members of the old Anglo-Norman garrison for scenery, but the view before them was a noble one. Northward, and beyond the rich alluvial plain, stand all the finest peaks of the Mourne Mountains, southward stretches the sea, while westward rise the rocky serrated edges of Carlingford Mountains, the quaint old town with its reminiscences of Dane and Norman at its foot, and beyond the beautiful lough winding past the wooded Killowen Point to Warrenpoint and Rostrevor. As we look a storm cloud comes driving from the westward, and from underneath it burst the last rays of the setting sun, and the whole lough is presently filled with a golden haze of sunlit rain, producing an effect such as only a Turner could paint or a Ruskin describe. The shower passes as quickly as it came, and on our way back we visit the noble earthen fort of Dunnaval. This has been cut out of the top of a great esker or gravel mound, in a commanding position midway between Greencastle and Kilkeel, the massive walls of the castle being modern in comparison with these time-worn earthworks. A stroll in the twilight to the beach and little harbour of Kilkeel finished the day's work.

On Thursday the party were early afoot, visiting first the cromlech which stands in a ditch of a field just outside the town, off the Newcastle Road. After securing photographs of this, another visit was paid to the harbour, in which schooners and fishing smacks can lie in perfect security, but the entrance is somewhat narrow and difficult of access during an easterly gale. After breakfast a visit was made to the ruins of Kilkeel old church and graveyard, just opposite the hotel. Kilkeel (*the narrow church*) was described in 1622 as being then ruinous, but was repaired and altered considerably, and used as the parish church till 1815, when the present Protestant church was built upon another site. The old church stands inside an earthen fort, and whether the custom dates from heathen times or no, corpses before interment were carried three times round the ramparts. The Rev. J. O'Laverty in his "Down and Connor" mentions an instance of this having been done so lately as twelve years ago. There is a rude granite cross of great age in the graveyard, resembling many of those in Dublin and Wicklow.

A start was now made for Slieve Bingian, whose rocky summit stands out most conspicuous amongst the granite peaks of *Beanne Boirchy*, as the Mourne Mountains were originally called. As we cross the bridge over the Kilkeel River, the vast extent of the glacial drift through which the stream cuts its way is to be noted. Seen from the harbour's mouth, it is even more conspicuous, where the sea has cut into the low cliffs of granite *debris* that stretch for several miles, and which tell a tale of the enormous amount of denudation that must have gone on amongst the mountains. On leaving the car, Slieve Bingian, which is about the same height (2,449 feet) as Errigal, in Donegal, and reminds one of it, rises before us, and the road or track passes amongst thickly scattered boulders of granite, from which it is cheering to hear the clink of the mason's hammer, for many of these stones are being worked up into curbs and setts, and are carted down and shipped at Annalong. As we rise we skirt round a small pointed hill, Moolieve, 1,090 feet high, with rocky top, an outlier of Slieve Bingian, and as we come in view of its north-western side find it to be one of the most striking specimens of ice-polished rock surface to be found in Ulster. The granite rock shoulders of the larger mountains are similarly rounded. Up we go, stepping from ledge to ledge, but the climbing, though steep, is nowhere difficult, though profusion of bilberries just now ripe offer an excuse for the climber to proceed leisurely. He has time also to note upon the damper spots the two insectivorous plants of our northern clime—*Pinguicula* or Butterwort and *Drosera rotundifolia* or Sun-dew, with its tiny red, hairy leaves, each hair tipped with a seductive dew to close upon and entrap the unwary insect that alights on it. But we are at last upon the summit, and it seems incredible that Slieve Bingian is not more heard of and more often visited. The masses of weather-beaten granite that form the top, the " Castles of Bingian," rise tower beyond tower, of more than the height and appear-ance of genuine built castles ; battlement, pinnacle, bartisan, and broad buttressed wall, all complete as though Conway or Carnarvon had been piled upon the summit of this wild moun-tain. The peculiar weathering of the granite into what might easily be mistaken for horizontal courses of masonry adds to the illusion, and from the rocky base the slope plunges at once into a valley more than a thousand feet deep on either side. The scene around is indescribable. From one side of our rocky bastion we look into the " Happy Valley," a glen traversed only by the shepherd and the turf cutter, through which the upper waters of the Kilkeel River find their way. In the opposite direction lies the valley of the Annalong River, which finds and sometimes loses its way amongst the intricacies of granite cliffs, which might be worth exploring some day. Towering above this glen rise the precipitous sides of Slieve Lamagan and Cove Mountain, as rocky and wild as the wildest part of Emer-dale, yet who ever hears or tells of them ? Closing the head of this valley north-eastward is Slieve Donard, which from this side appears almost a perfect cone, and towers above everything else. Then just visible beyond the others is Slieve Bearnagh, which proudly

" Lifts to heaven
Her diadem of towers,"

piled by the hand, not of man, but of nature. But Slieve Bearnagh, like Lord Nelson, deserves, and shall one day have, "a gazette all to herself."

As one looks abroad from this quoin of vantage upon the sea of mountains the old controversy is revived between the Elevationists and the Denudationists, and the question is naturally asked—Were these heights shot up by the force of subterranean fires from below, or do their summits represent the original surface-level of the strata which has been slowly carved out by the unceasing action of running water, frost, and sand ? As we look southward over the gravel banks that line the Kilkeel River we may incline to the latter view, and agree that, though the forces of an earlier period may have been more potent, they were yet the same in kind, though not necessarily in degree, that operate at present. There was a time when those hills were more rugged and the valleys deeper than they are now. During the height of the great ice age, had we stood here, what should we have seen ? Far away in the western horizon, where now rise the hills that divide Derry from Tyrone, we should have seen, had the perpetual fog and cloud permitted us, the glistening summit of a vast dome of hardened snow, such as now covers Greenland, and which is supposed to have stretched out on all sides till it met the great snow field of Scotland, whose edge curved in a line round the outer Hebrides, and the lesser one of the North of England and the Cumberland mountains. The officers of the Geological Survey assure us that all the ice-marks here point to a glaciation from the west-north-west, breasting against and flowing round the Mourne Mountains ; and what would then have been their lee side, about Annalong, is piled thick with glacial *debris*. Our own eyes have informed us that the ice wave reached to the rocks at our feet, and went clean over the polished hummock of Moolieve that we have before described, and which is ground smooth on every side but the south-east. The three or four little lakes of these hills all lie too on the south-east side of high precipices, just where in this hypothesis they ought to. They are probably, like most of these mountain tarns, in part, " rock basins"—that is, ground out by glacier ice, and partly dammed up by boulder clay and moraine matter. As a relic of a later phase, when the ice sheet receding left only small local glaciers, are the moraines that stretch across the mouth of the Happy Valley, and of the Annalong and Newcastle valleys in their upper part, and many a perched boulder, some of great size, tells a similar tale. Two members, with the expenditure of a little trouble, got a camera to the top, and on the ascent and at the summit took several views, only regretting that their stock was not enough to take double the number they had material for. The Mourne district is yet almost unworked by the photographer, and also, with the exception of the late Dr. James Moore, is almost a virgin field for the brush of the artist. When the Belfast " Ramblers" are inclined to go further afield than the banks of the Lagan, a noble field awaits them here. Meanwhile, the botanists of the party have discovered some mountain plants among the granite crags. The Cow-berry (*Vaccinium vitis-idœa*), with its round evergreen leaves, lines the crevices of the rocks, and with it the Dwarf Willow (*Salix herbacea*), and the Crow-berry (*Empetrum nigrum*) ; all three plants have their home among the barren rocks and wind-swept summits of lofty mountains ; but with them we find some of our best-known woodland plants, which are here far above their usual station—the common Wood Violet (*Viola sylvatica*), the Lady Fern (*Athyrium Filix-fœmina*), and the Common Poly-pody (*Polypodium vulgare*). But the north wind now blows keen, and time is flying, and a descent must with all speed be made to the car, and the party are once more *en route* for New-castle. Tea at Mr. Lawrence's, at the station, and a hasty meeting for election of new members, and the appointment of a delegate to the meeting of the British Association at Newcastle, brought the day's work to an agreeable close.

On August, 17th to

LOUGHINISLAND.

The fifth Club excursion for the year was to Ballynahinch, Loughinisland, and Clough. The 10-50 a.m. train conveyed a party of twenty-four members and friends, who were in no way daunted by the torrential rains of the preceding evening or by the still threatening aspect of the morning. At Ballynahinch half-a-dozen well-equipped cars were in readiness, and the road leading southward through a richly cultivated district is taken ; a halt is called at the northern end of Loughinisland to visit a cromlech, after which the party soon spread, attracted by the waters of the upper end of the lough, in which flourish both the white and yellow Water-lily and other less conspicuous but interesting plants. Adjoining the western shore of the lough, on what was undoubtedly once an island, but now connected by a causeway to the land, is an assemblage of ruined buildings surrounded by an ancient graveyard. The island, according to Reeves, is about an English acre in extent, and contains the ruins of three churches. The largest is called the old parish church ; the second, or middle one, is exceedingly ancient, and was probably disused when the other, which is also very ancient, was built ; the third and lowest down is called M'Cartan's Chapel. Over the door are the letters " P. M. C." (Phelim M'Cartan), and the date 1639. Continuing the drive, Clough is reached, and the ancient rath, surrounded by a deep fosse, is visited This rath is surmounted by the remains of a small but solidly-built castle, an unusual accompaniment of these earth-works, and probably the work of a much later period than the rath. The return journey is through Seaforde and by the Spa, where another halt is made. The President (Mr. William Gray, M.R I.A.) here intimated that he had many years ago noticed some remarkable markings in rocks a short distance off, and he considered the Club should visit them. Accordingly the way is led through some fields, and after clearing away some bramble and moss from a rock exposure the surface is laid bare, and certainly the markings brought to view are most unusual in character. A close examination proves them to be natural, but they might easily be mistaken for the rude stone inscriptions of ancient man, and it is quite possible that similar markings may ere now have figured in the note-books of enthusiastic antiquaries. The markings in this case occur on an exposed protrusion of basalt, or probably portion of a large basaltic dyke, and are doubtless due to the weathering of the soft coatings of nodules of rock foreign to the basalt. The light suiting admirably, a photograph of a portion is taken to assist in further reference to them. After tea in Ballynahinch a visit is paid to a castle some distance north of the town. This, as is usual with such structures, is on high ground, and from its remains it seems to have been a place of considerable importance. The botany of the district had not been lost sight of. To those in quest of lacustrine plants Loughinisland offers attractions that are irresistible. A lake with gravelly bottom and shallow, reedy margins, more or less sheltered by trees— such are the conditions here. In such a place one may look with confidence for some of the rarer plants, and will not be disappointed. The Great Reed-grass (*Phragmites communis*) grows here in immense luxuriance, and the Reedmace (*Typha latifolia*), popularly known as Blackheads, flourishes abundantly. The Great Water Docken (*Rumex hydrolapathum*) occurs more sparingly. These are amongst the giants of our water plants, but peer close into the water in certain places and it will be seen that nature has not by any means been exhausted. Unnoticed by the ordinary observer, tiny plants grow on the lake floor, and these minims usually have the greatest charm for the naturalist. Several *Charas* flourish in Loughinisland, and in some parts the little round leaves of the Waterwort (*Elatine hexandra*) form a green carpet down under the water, where the plant flowers and ripens its seed without ever being in contact with the atmosphere. A Bur-reed (*Sparganium simplex*) and many other of the more common water plants were also seen. At Clough some plants that prefer rocks, or stone and mortar, were observed. The Black Spleenwort (*Asplenium Adiantum-nigrum*) and the Wall-rue fern grow on the walls of the old castle ; the latter grows most luxuriantly and abundantly on walls near Clough. The Maidenhair Spleenwort (*A. trichomanes*) and the Scaly Hart's-tongue (*Ceterach officinarum*) were seen on the walls in the neighbourhood, but more sparingly. Belfast was reached about 8.30 p.m., after a most enjoyable and instructive excursion.

On September 7th, to

TYNAN AND CALEDON.

The last field meeting for the season took place on September 7th, Tynan Abbey being the locality visited. Rather a smaller party than usual responded to the circular, and left by the 8-45 train. On arrival at Tynan they at once proceeded to the village, in which is an ancient cross of large size, which has evidently been taken good care of. Time, however, has almost obliterated the carvings with which it was once embellished ; on one of the panels figures representing the temptation can still be traced, but the other subjects represented are too much weathered to allow of their being interpreted. Shortly after leaving the village the richly-wooded grounds of Tynan Abbey are entered, the party being conducted to the house—an imposing building of comparatively modern date. Its situation is very fine, surrounded as it is by exceptionally well-grown timber, and overlooking a small lake. On one of the terraces adjoining is an ancient stone cross, one of three within the grounds. Sir J. Calvert Stronge, Bart.—the proprietor of the estate—informed the members that they were erected in their present positions many years since, having been removed from Glenarb, County Tyrone, where they were at the time being destroyed and used for building purposes. The second cross visited has quite a romanti c situation on a small island enshrouded by trees ; and the third, which, on the side of the main avenue, is erected over an arch and well, is sheltered by venerable hawthorns.

The evidence of the ill-usage they are said to have at one time received is borne out by the fact that many missing parts seem to have been supplied at the time of their erection. These three crosses, which may be said to be of small size, are some-what similar in character. The ornamentation is simple, con-sisting for the most part of sunk mouldings running parallel with the outer margins of the stone. The photographers of the party "took" these crosses from various points, and no doubt they will in due time be represented in the Club's albums. The lakes, woods, and slow streams that abound in the district visited promise well for the botanical collector, but, the season being now far advanced, not many rare plants were met with. The tiny and scarce Trefoil (*Trifolium filiforme*) was seen at Tynan, and in woods at the same place *Arctium nemorosum*, a rather rare Burdock. A rare Sedge (*Carex paludosa*) is plenti-ful by streams and by the margin of the lake. The Greater Celandine grows on some hedge banks, and the small, silky form of Lady's Mantle (*Alchemilla vulgaris* var. *minor*) was found sparingly. A rare fern, the Marsh Fern, grows by the side of a little lake near Caledon, and the rector, Rev. Mr. Armstrong, kindly indicated the spot, but time did not permit the party to reach it. The ground so hurriedly passed over on the present occasion is a promising district for sylvan and aquatic plants, and the botanist visiting it at an earlier season, and in less haste, would doubtless be well rewarded. Leaving the grounds, the road is taken to Caledon, where tea is served in the Caledon Arms Hotel, after which the business meeting of the day is held, and a vote of thanks is unanimously accorded to Sir J. Calvert Stronge, Bart., for his kindness not only in granting the Club liberty to examine his extensive grounds, but in greatly en-hancing the pleasure and interest of the excursion by accom-panying the party for the greater part of the day.

WINTER SESSION.

Note.—The authors of the various Papers, of which abstracts are here appended, are alone responsible for the views expressed in them.

SOCIAL MEETING.

THE Winter Session of the Club was opened on November 13th, by a social evening in the Museum, College Square North. According to the practice of recent years, the lady members dispensed tea and other refreshments in the lower room with their accustomed grace and skill, after which a brief business meeting was held in the lecture-room, the chair being taken by Mr. W. Gray, M.R.I.A., the President of the Club. In the course of his remarks he referred to his recent visit to Newcastle-on-Tyne, where he attended the meeting of the British Association as Delegate from the Club, and in that capacity was placed on several of the Committees. To the work of these he referred, stating that the Geological Committee were anxious to encourage the recording by photography of geological phenomena, and solicited the co-operation of photographers, professional or amateur, for this purpose. The Biographical Committee, of which Mr. Gray was also a member, he stated, had under consideration the reckless destruction of native wild plants, especially ferns, many species of which, particularly about our large towns, have practically ceased to exist. He recommended the members of the Club to devote their attention to this subject.

The President then called on Mr. Vinycomb to describe a finely carved oak bedboard exhibited by Mr. Seaton F. Milligan, M.R.I.A. The bed, of which it formed a part, was recently sold by an old family in the County of Cavan. Mr. Vinycomb pointed out that the coat of arms carved on the bedboard were those of the Tudor dynasty. He described the arms and supporters of the various English sovereigns, and pointed out that with all but certainty this bed must have belonged to Queen Elizabeth, and on her death may have been bequeathed, as was customary in those days, to some connection, and brought to Ireland early in the seventeenth century.

Mr. John Hamilton then drew attention to some " weather prophets "—two little green frogs in a glass case, natives of the South of France, which in dry weather lie low in the moss and grass, but on the approach of rain climb up the stems. They seemed able to climb about the sides of the glass jar with the greatest ease.

Mr. Joseph Wright, F.G.S., then made a few remarks upon the table of fossil fish, which formed a special subject of the evening's exhibition, and traced the changes in structural character from the earliest ganoid fishes of the Upper Silurian period to the vertebrate and scaled fish of recent times.

Mr. Robert Welch referred to a few photos recently taken of eggs and nests of wild birds, chiefly in Rathlin Island.

Next came the election of new members, among whom the name of the most Reverend the Lord Bishop of Down, Connor, and Dromore, so widely known as a distinguished archæologist, and already so intimately connected with the Club, was received with loud applause. The company then scattered about the rooms to examine the various objects lent for exhibition.

In the centre of the lecture-room was the table of fossil fish, which included some magnificent specimens from the Cretaceous rocks of North America, lent by Mr. Joseph Wright, and also a large and varied collection of teeth and hard bony palates of fishes that browse upon coral, lent by Mr. C. Bulla, and some nearly unique specimens sent by Mr. Parker, of Oldham, who has devoted himself for the past thirty years to the study of fossil fish. Mr. D. M'Kee on a separate table also exhibited a large collection of fish remains. A number of bronze weapons, and several very curious ancient bronze cauldrons recently found, were exhibited by Mr. Seaton F. Milligan, in addition to the carved Elizabethan bedboard before described.

The President (Mr. Gray) lent a case of extremely fine specimens of Zeolites and other minerals from the trap rocks of Antrim. He also showed an aquarium, with a number of specimens of the *Hydra*, and gave a personal explanation of them during the evening with the microscope. Other microscopes were exhibited by Mr. Joseph Wright, F.G.S., who had a large set of *Foraminifera* recently dredged from a depth of 1,000 fathoms off the south-west coast of Ireland. Mr. John Donaldson showed a microscope with revolving plate, extremely useful for purposes of study. Messrs. Elliott, I. W. Ward, and R. Welch also exhibited microscopes.

An interesting series of photographs taken by Messrs. Swanston and John Donaldson during their summer trip to Norway were well worth study, especially for the forms of glaciers. Mr. George Donaldson showed an album of photos, chiefly archæological, taken during recent excursions of the club. The President lent a splendid collection of Californian photographs. A set of water-colour sketches of the "Seven Churches" and the Valley of Glendalough, County Wicklow, were exhibited by Mr. J. P. Addy. A number of pictures by Callow, the two Nicholls, and Burgess, kindly lent by Mr. Robert Reid and Mr. W. Nicholl, decorated the walls.

The first regular meeting of the winter session was held in the Museum, College Square North, on Tuesday evening, November 19th.

The President (Mr. William Gray, M.R.I.A.), opened the proceedings. He said : — In taking a rapid survey of the events that have transpired around us since I addressed you in 1880—events that were the direct outcome of that address—I think we cannot fail to see that our speculations have not been altogether visionary, that our deliberations had a direct practical result, and that to-day we are in the enjoyment of public advantages, the direct outcome ot our Club's thought and action. In my address of November, 1880, I held out the hope that a proper fernery and aquarium would be formed in the Royal Botanic Gardens. Unfortunately my project had to give way to the directors' more popular scheme for providing what is now known as the Exhibition Hall. Since then nothing has been done to provide an aquarium ; indeed, the small tanks formerly maintained have been abandoned, and what is equally to be regretted, the whole botanical collection, the pride and glory of the original promoters, has been entirely rooted out. During the past year a fernery has been formed in the Botanic Gardens, on the site of my original project. I would be glad to find it more educational in its character, and to see more attention given to our native ferns. It is, however, a step in the right direction, and 1 hope the directors will see their way to aid in making the love of flowers more popular, by favouring us occasionaly with a worthy exhibition of flowers in bloom. Another outcome of the address of 1880 is the adoption of the Public Libraries' Act, and the establishment of a central municipal institution, embracing a Public Library, an Art Gallery, and a Museum. This project, I submit, must be considered a most important event in the history of Belfast, and is the direct outcome of our deliberations here. The first formal action was taken at a meeting called on my requisition, and held on April 11th, 1881, at Messrs. Campbell's establishment, then in Donegall Place, resulting in a deputation to the Town Council on May 1st, 1881, praying that legal steps be taken to ascertain the wishes of the rate-payers as to the adoption of the Public Libraries' Act. The prayer of this memorial, ably supported by the several members of the deputation, was rejected by a resolution of the Council, adopted on July 1st, 1881, and signed by the late Sir John Savage. We renewed our action in April, 1882, again appearing before the Council on June 1st, and on July 1st the Town Council yielded to the influential deputation that supported the memorial, and agreed to take the ratepayers' opinion by vote. This was done in October of the same year, and on December 1st, 1882, the successful result was formally declared at the monthly meeting of the Council. Prompt and efficient action was taken on this decision of the Council, and the following letter was sent me :—

. " TOWN HALL, BELFAST,

6th December, **1882.**

" PUBLIC LIBRARY.

" Dear Sir,

"I am instructed by the Library Committee to inform you that they have had the subject of the building of a Library under consideration, and that they will be glad to receive any suggestions from the Deputation who waited on the Council some time ago respecting same.—Yours faithfully,

"SAMUEL BLACK, Town Clerk.

"WM. GRAY, ESQ., M.R.I.A., Mount Charles."

Just at this juncture I had promised the Club a paper on "The Public Libraries' Acts, and the possible consequences of their adoption in Belfast;" and therefore I considered it advisable to hold over our reply to Mr. Black's letter until after my lecture. My paper was read on December 19th, 1882, and on December 21st our Promoters' Committee met at the Chamber of Commerce, and formulated a set of suggestions to be sub-mitted to the Library Committee, which was done on January 11th, 1883. Our suggestions were received by the Council with the polite intimation that they would be " considered,". and at the May meeting of Council they were published in the form of an appendix to the report of the Library Committee,

·which contained some free comments on them. The mover,
referring to our recommendation for a Composite Committee
said it was the duty of the Council alone to put up the building,
and "*when this duty was discharged, they could open the doors
and have a large Committee for the carrying out of the work
when it was once commenced on a sound foundation.*" This
was stated by the Council in 1883, or six years ago. The large
or Composite Committee has not yet been formed. We must,
therefore, assume that it is because in the opinion of the
Council the scheme is not yet "*commenced on a sound foundation,*" an opinion in which the generality of the ratepayers
may have their misgivings. For myself, I think we have made
a reasonably good start. The suggestions recommended that
the Town Council's scheme under the Act

"should be framed with the view of making the proposed institution *Educational* in
character, utilising the experience of other towns, and avoiding all unnecessary expense
and all temporary experiments. What is to be the permanent Municipal Institution
should be commenced at once, and all expenditure from the beginning should be
devoted towards the ultimate realisation of a central educational institution that will be
really worthy of the wealth, intelligence, and commercial importance of the capital of
Ulster." And that "the required building should include provision for at least a
Newsroom, a Lending Library, a Reference Library, a Museum, an Art Gallery. A
Public Hall or Exhibition Room capable of accommodating about 1,000 people, and a
suitable Lecture-room to seat 500, should be added as funds will permit."

The suggestions met with the general approval of the local
press, which emphasised the recommendation that the institution
should be *Educational* in its character. Fifteen days after we
presented our suggestions, designs were called for, and the
Town Surveyor's conditions informed architects that the
buildings should comprise " A large General Library and
Reading room in one, a Lending Department, a Select Library,
a Picture Gallery, a Ladies' Reading-room, an additional
Picture Gallery or Lecture-room, with the usual offices, &c."
Unfortunately there was no Museum referred to, and the
Lecture-room was not provided in the selected plan. As soon
as the plans were exhibited their deficiencies were clearly and
fully pointed out, but no steps were taken to meet the objections,

and the building was put in hand, progressing deliberately until the foundation stone was laid on June 18th, 1884, by his Excellency the Earl Spencer, K.G., &c. The omission of a Museum has been all along seriously commented upon, because it was considered one of the most essential points in the scheme of the promoters *as a necessary condition towards obtaining any valuable aid from South Kensington.* Upon this ground the necessity for a Museum was most forcibly advocated by the Joint Committee from the SCHOOL OF ART, UNITED TRADES' COUNCIL, and our NATURALISTS' FIELD CLUB, who waited on the Library Committee, 3rd December, 1883.

With an expression of regret that local building materials were not used in the superstructure, I must pass over the long time occupied by the erection of the building, from the laying of the foundation stone on 18th June, 1884, up to the 13th October, 1888, when the Lending Library was formally opened by His Excellency Lord Londonderry, Lord Lieutenant of Ireland.

In preparation for that event, the Mayor called a meeting of citizens to consult as to the best means of furnishing the Art Gallery, and a committee was formed with the result that by their aid a very interesting and instructive loan collection of art objects was brought together in a few weeks, which became a source of intellectual recreation to the thousands who visited the gallery during the short time it remained open. The complete success of this undertaking demonstrated the value of a composite committee, and should be an inducement to the Town Council to adopt such a committee for the entire management of the Library and all that is possible under the Libraries Act. This management has been adopted with great advantage in all the best regulated Public Libraries throughout the Kingdom.

Since the end of last year, when the Loan Exhibition was closed, I had a correspondence with the Library Committee, and advocated the necessity of obtaining a loan from South Kensington, so as to occupy the rooms vacated by the late local exhihition. The monthly reports of the Library Committee will show the progress made in this direction, which involved the necessity of having a Museum under the Public Libraries Act.

At the January meeting, the report only referred to improving the light and ventilation of the reading-room.

At the February meeting, a Councillor asked a question about the promised South Kensington loan. An Alderman answered that their Committee *were in communication* with South Kensington, and the authorities there were to place at the disposal of our Library Committee, a collection of objects in two departments, namely, Plaster Modelling and Ironwork, and that further particulars would be given next month.

This was encouraging, but the March and April meetings passed without any further reference to the matter.

At the May meeting, it was stated that a formal application had been made to South Kensington, and in the discussion thereon, it was stated that up to that date *no formal application was made*, so that all the promises previously given were without foundation.

I visited South Kensington early in May, and confirmed this fact, and ascertained that the authorities were most anxious to assist Belfast, and were prepared to deal liberally with the City, but that State aid was only given to localities willing to help themselves, and that collections for extended periods of exhibition could only be given to " permanent Museums or Schools of Science and Art, and to Museums established under the Public Libraries Acts, or under Municipal Authority." Here then we have the official confirmation of what I have been contending for so long, namely :—That in order to obtain the great advantages offered by the State, we must have a museum under the Public Libraries Act.

At the Council meeting on 1st June, no reference was made to the matter. At the last Library Committee meeting a few days before the July Council meeting, a letter was read from me, and in reply I was told by the Town Clerk that the Committee's report on 1st July would refer to the Museum. The report did not refer to it, and in reply to a question from one of the Council, the Town Clerk explained that a reference to the Museum was accidentally omitted from the report. I again pressed the matter upon the attention of the Library Committee, and at the August meeting the report of the Library Committee contained the following paragraph :—

"Your Committee have to report that they have for some time past been in communication with the Directors of South Kensington Museum, with a view of obtaining from them a loan collection for Exhibition in the Free Library. Two members of Council and the Town Clerk, who were lately in London on other business of the Corporation, had an interview with Sir P. Cunliffe-Owen, Director, and Mr. Cundall, Inspector, and your Committee are glad to be able to report that arrangements have been made for a loan collection, to be sent to Belfast in November next, and allowed to remain on Exhibition for six months. Your Committee have undertaken to supplement it with local exhibits, and feel assured that parties having such will lend them for Exhibition."

At this meeting the Mayor made the very important announcement—"That it was a rule of the Science and Art Department, that the inhabitants must make some effort themselves before it grants any loan."

The monthly meetings of the Town Council for September and October passed without any reference to the exhibition.

The Library Committee's report read at the November meeting of Council stated, that final arrangements were made for a loan from South Kensington, and the Chairman expected that the *Museum* would be opened in a month or six weeks. I had a communication from the Committee intimating that "it is not probable the exhibition can be open much before the beginning of the year."

But the Chairman's remarks were valuable as being the first intimation that the Council had yielded to pressure and authority. As all my recommendations for a Town Museum, published by the local press or placed directly before the Town Council, had been ineffective, I was most anxious to obtain from the Town Council an official acknowledgement of their intention to have a Town Museum formed. I therefore wrote again, and had the satisfaction of receiving from the

Town Clerk under date 15th November, 1889, the following reply :—

"That Mr. William Gray be informed in answer to his letter of this date, that it is intended to have a Museum in connection with the Library, and that a number of purchases have been made, with the assistance of the authorities of South Kensington Museum, who have also kindly promised a further collection on loan when the Committee are ready to receive them."

So that because the Town Council has wisely yielded to a long sustained pressure, and resolved to establish a Town Museum, we obtain at once the advantages offered by the State, namely :—We get a GRANT TOWARDS THE PURCHASE of Works of Art, I believe a grant of £500, to supplement a local expenditure of £500, giving us a permanent collection of Works of Art, of the value of £1,000, and in addition a liberal loan of examples of applied Art, which is to *remain for six months* and will be renewed at the end of that term, thereby commencing a permanent Museum capable of extension with time, and one that must be free to the public.

Already a thousand pounds worth of Works of Art have been purchased and are being packed for Belfast, and a contribution from South Kensington is ready to be forwarded. If we but "wait a little longer" we will have a permanent Museum opened for Belfast.

This is the direct outcome of our efforts, and a most significant proof that mere spectators or amateur scientists can sometimes accomplish something practical.

NOTE.—It may be interesting to compare the letter from the late Edward Benn, with the letter referred to above from the Town Clerk, under date 15th November, 1889. Mr. Benn's letter is dated 17th August, 1873, and referred to a movement I then commenced for the promotion of a Town Museum.

GLENRAVEL, BALLYMENA,
17th August, 1873.

MY DEAR SIR,
I thought to have heard from you before this about the Museum. I now write to say that I will give £1,000 towards this object, and hope that something will be done that will be a credit to the Town. When you have secured a site let me know, and I will give my view of the matter.

Yours faithfully,
EDWARD BENN.

Mr. Gray, Mountcharles, Belfast.

The President then called on Mr. R. Lloyd Praeger to read
the report of the Larne Gravels Committee, which was the
next item in the business of the evening. It is here published
in extenso.

REPORT OF A COMMITTEE OF INVESTIGATION ON THE GRAVELS AND ASSOCIATED BEDS OF THE CURRAN, AT LARNE, CO. ANTRIM.

(*Compiled by R. Lloyd Praeger, B.E.*)

I.—ORIGIN AND OBJECTS OF THE INVESTIGATION.

In the Proceedings of the Belfast Naturalists' Field Club, for
1886-7 (Series II., Vol. II., p. 519), there appears the report of
a committee " appointed to investigate the Larne Gravels, and
determine the position in them of the Flint Flakes and Cores
for which they are noted." In this report the general features
of the Curran and of the beds in question, and also the different
views held by local archæologists, regarding the distribution in
the gravels of the worked flints, are fully and accurately set
forth, and need not be further dwelt on here. The Gravels
were at that time carefully scrutinised down to a depth of about
twelve feet by a number of competent observers, and this
scrutiny showed that flakes and cores were in abundance on the
surface and for a few feet downwards, and became fewer as the
depth increased. Lower than seven feet no flakes were found,
with the exception of one well-formed example, which suggested
the idea that it might have accidentally fallen from a higher
zone. The conclusions of the committee referred to are that
the Gravels form a stratified deposit resting on the Estuarine
Clay, and that man manufactured the flint flakes subsequent to
the accumulation of the gravel beds in their present position.
It was, however, generally felt that a more extended examination of the lower bed of coarse gravel, where the single flake
above-mentioned was obtained, was desirable, and might yield
interesting results.

At a committee meeting of the Club, held in the Museum, on 5th April, 1889, a letter was read signed by W. Gray, M.R.I.A., and R. Lloyd Praeger, B.E., in which the writers stated that being at present engaged in investigations of the Post-tertiary deposits of the North of Ireland, the former as regards the flint implements found in connection with these beds, and the latter as regards the fossils which they yield, they now proposed that the Field Club should co-operate with them in making a complete and exhaustive examination of the Gravels and underlying beds at Larne. In this way they hoped to settle definitely the questions of the geological age of the deposits, and the position in them of the worked flints ; a full report of the proceedings, accompanied by figured sections and lists of the fossils obtained, to be brought before the Club and embodied in their Proceedings. A resolution was passed approving the suggestion, and appointing Messrs. S. A. Stewart, F.B.S.E., Joseph Wright, F.G.S., and William Swanston, F.G.S., a committee to co-operate with the above-named. This committee was authorized to expend a sum of £5, a like amount being advanced by Messrs. Gray and Praeger.

II.—NARRATIVE OF THE INVESTIGATION.

The spot selected for the investigation was at the place marked A on the map accompanying the above-mentioned re- port. This is on the southern side of the railway, 1,200 feet from the edge of the quay in front of the southern terminus, the exact spot being 75 feet North by West (magnetic), of the eastern corner of the houses called "The Strand" in Fleet Street ; here the escarpment of gravel is at its highest. The debris that lay along the base of the bank was carefully cleared away, leaving a clean and almost perpendicular face of gravel 15'-6" in height. On the turf on the top of the bank above this cleared face a space 9 feet long by 5 feet broad was marked out, and a cutting of this area was carried down the whole depth of the section exposed, the material being taken out in horizontal layers and cast down on the cleared ground below, by three workmen stationed above, where it was spread out and carefully examined, and then cast back by three other men posted at the foot of the bank, the flints and shells from each zone being labelled and put away in numbered bags. In the ground at the foot of the cleared face a trench 6 feet long by 3 feet wide was sunk to a depth of 6 feet, in order to prove the underlying strata and correlate the beds ; all the material from this excavation was also closely scrutinized. At a convenient spot 30 feet north of the cleared face a trial pit 6 feet square was sunk through the beds underlying the gravels as far as the funds at the disposal of the committee would permit, and samples of the clays and sands here found, as well as of the different beds of gravel above, were secured and brought away for microscopic examination. Altogether some 32 cubic yards, or 41 tons, of the gravels were subjected to a rigid scrutiny, as well as some 5 cubic yards of the underlying clays, &c., so the committee can claim that their examination of the beds over the area selected has been tolerably complete ; and, altogether 140 worked flints from the various zones were labelled and brought away to illustrate this report, and for the present may; be seen in the Museum of the Belfast Natural History and Philosophical Society, whence they will be transferred to the Museum of the Royal Irish Academy, in Dublin.

The investigation was begun on May 27th. Mr. Gray, Rev. Canon Grainger, D.D., M.R.I.A. ; Mr. Stewart, and Mr. Praeger superintended the commencement of operations, and the latter two remained in Larne during the period occupied by the work, which was seven days. The services of three workmen had been kindly granted by Mr. B. D. Wise, Chief Engineer of the Northern Counties Railway, and three more were obtained from a local contractor, and with this staff the work proceeded rapidly and satisfactorily. The day was spent in the examination of the upper bed of gravel, and in the evening a depth of 8'-9" (the surface of the bed of fine sand subsequently mentioned) had been attained, and work was suspended.

Next day three men were started to clear the ground for the trial pit, a short distance from the gravel escarpment, while the other three excavated a trench, at the foot of the cleared face, to determine the nature of the underlying strata, it having been resolved to reserve the examination of the lower bed of gravel for the following day (Saturday), when it was expected that others interested in the work might attend. During the afternoon Mr. Gray was present, and assisted the investigation.

On the 29th inst., the sinking of the trial pit through stiff Estuarine Clay was continued. In the afternoon the trench at the base of the cleared face had attained a depth of 5'-6" below the level of the ground, at which depth the Estuarine Clay was struck. No further excavation here being desired, as the clay was being thoroughly examined in the trial pit, and Mr. Gray having arrived, the exploration of the lower bed of coarse gravel was commenced, the mode of excavation and examination being that already detailed. At a depth of 13 feet work was suspended for the day. Rev. Canon Grainger and Mr. W. H. Patterson, M.R.I.A., arrived as the day's work was concluding, and examined the sections, and the flakes, &c., which had been found.

On Monday, July 1st, the sinking of the trial pit through the beds below the Estuarine Clay was continued, but in the evening a stratum of coarse gravel was reached, so charged with water as to flood the excavations and endanger the stability of the banks, and it was determined not to attempt any deeper sinking here, as it would entail heavy expense in staying and pumping. On 2nd inst., the scrutiny of the lower gravel, which had been stopped at 13 feet, was continued, Mr. Joseph Wright, F.G.S., being present, in addition to Messrs. Stewart and Praeger.

The following morning the examination of the lower gravel was concluded, and some time was spent in inspecting sections of the gravels exposed at other points on the Curran, the points of resemblance or difference to the typical section chosen for detailed examination being noted. The dip of the various beds was taken, and levels were run to a fixed bench-mark, that the heights of the beds might be referred to the datum of the Ordnance Survey. This concluded the field work of the investigation.

III.—GEOLOGICAL AND PALÆONTOLOGICAL FEATURES OF THE BEDS.

Beds A and B.—The first bed in descending order, or upper gravel, the surface of which is 35 feet above Ordnance Survey Datum, or 22 feet above high water mark, consists of 6 feet of coarse gravel, composed of pebbles up to 6 inches diameter, chiefly of trap and chalk, with a matrix of yellow sand ; the uppermost 1'-6" has been disturbed by cultivation, and consists of brown, gravelly soil. This bed is regularly stratified and has a dip of about 8° South-east. Fossils are not uncommon, though less frequent than in the underlying beds ; they consist chiefly of littoral shells which still abound in the adjoining waters, but are in an extremely fragile state, owing to the disintegrating effect of the percolating water. A full list of the species observed in this and the succeeding strata is appended.

Bed C.—Below this gravel bed come several alternating bands of fine gravel and sand, attaining a depth, at the point examined, of 3'-6". Shells of littoral species are frequent, and several bivalves were found (*Tapes decussatus, Ostrea edulis, Lucina borealis*), with the pairs of valves still in the natural position. The basal zone is a band 9" thick, of fine brownish sand, which is persistent over the whole length of section exposed (200 feet), having a uniform dip of 2° South-east; it yields abundance of *Littorina litorea, L. obtusata*, and similar shells.

Bed D.—Underlying the sandy zones is another bed of coarse gravel, 8'-6" in thickness, resembling in general appearance and characteristics the upper gravel. The dip, however, is in a different direction, and at a high angle, showing a steep slope (1 in 3) along the face, and the same at right angles to this direction, which combined, give a dip of 25° West. Fossils are numerous, *Littorinæ* being again the prevalent species, but

many others occur, their names being given below. The lower
2'-6" of this bed was below the level of the ground at the base
of the escarpment, and was examined by means of the trench
already mentioned. In places near the base of this bed the
matrix was observed to be red and clayey, but very soft, and
apparently the result of infiltration.

Bed E.—Next in descending order came a band 2'-6" deep of
black clayey gravel, in which much water was encountered.
Except for the clayey matrix, it did not differ materially from
the overlying gravel, and the fossils obtained were similar.

Bed F.—Below this was 1'-0" of black, coarse sand, stained
with iron in places, this being the transition bed between the
gravels and the Estuarine Clay. *Tapes aureus* and *Cardium
exiguum* now became characteristic species.

Bed G.—Underlying the sand was typical Estuarine Clay—
tough homogeneous blue clay, with well-preserved littoral shells,
and abundance of Grass Wrack (*Zostera marina*). It was
observed to correspond exactly with the clay exposed at the old
pottery (see previous report), and like it, merged downwards
into black sand. A large sample (30 lbs.) of this interesting bed
was brought away for more minute examination.

Bed H.—Next came a stratum 2'-0" in thickness of fine
blackish sand, much resembling the clay, both in colour and in
the shells which it yielded, and not separated from it by any
sharp line of demarcation. *Littorina obtusata* and *Trochus
cinerareus*, which prevail throughout the series, were present
in this zone in great profusion.

Bed I.—Below the black sand a deposit of considerable
interest was discovered, consisting of coarse, blackish gravel,
containing large, rounded boulders of up to 2 feet diameter,
covered with *Spirorbis* and Corallines so fresh looking, that
when cleaned, the stones might easily have been supposed to
have just been brought from some neighbouring beach. Shells
were abundant, and in a far better state of preservation
than those in the gravels above. *Littorina obtusata* again pre-
dominated, occurring in great abundance. On account of the

quantity of water encountered here, further sinking was impracticable, and the excavation was stopped at a total depth of 29 feet below the surface of the gravels, without the base of Boulder Clay being reached.

At the section exposed a short distance to the northward, by the side of the road running from Larne to the Harbour, and near the large stone building used as a grain store, an examination of the beds showed that the Boulder Clay, which contains the characteristic polished and grooved pebbles, rises up at one spot to within 2 feet of the surface, the gravels resting directly on it. It dips rapidly southward and eastward, and runs down under the section previously examined. This bank of Boulder Clay is of small extent, as at the old pottery, about 200 yards further north, the gravels are again seen resting on the Estuarine Clay. Behind the store just mentioned a good section of the gravels is exposed, some 12 feet in height ; the base is sandy and rests on Boulder Clay. At a depth of 9 feet below the surface a sandy layer was observed full of the littoral bivalve *Tapes pullastra*. The pairs of valves were in all cases in juxtaposition, and the plane of the valves perpendicular, showing that they lived on the spot where they are now found.

IV.—DISTRIBUTION AND CHARACTER OF THE WORKED FLINTS.

The uppermost zone of gravelly soil yielded flakes in the greatest profusion, at least 10 to every cubic foot, and it was observed that they were most abundant in a pebbly layer in the lower part of this bed, at a depth of 1'-0" to 1'-6" below the surface. The flakes are all of a rude type, with little appearance of secondary chipping, the edges blunt, and the surface much oxidized ; undoubted cores are rare, and no scrapers or other implements were here discovered. In the succeeding 4'-6" of gravel much fewer flakes were found, and their number was observed to rapidly diminish as the depth below the surface increased, and they ceased altogether at a depth of between 4 and 5 feet. In character the flakes found in this upper gravel

were identical with those from the surface layer.   In the sandy
and gravelly zones lettered C, flakes are very rare, only two
being found by the committee.   Next in order is the lower
gravel D, and as this bed was considered to require special examination, it was divided into four zones (lettered D1, D2, D3,
and D4, in descending order), which were consecutively examined, the flints from each zone being kept separate.   It was
found that flakes occur sparingly all through this bed, from top
to bottom ; a few cores were also obtained, and one fine example
of a rude celt (at a depth of 11 feet from the surface).   It was
noted that the flints were fresher and less oxidised than those
of the upper gravel, and the edges sharper.   In the next bed, E,
which consists of black clayey gravel, and which could not be
so thoroughly examined on account of water coming in, one
fine flake was obtained (19 feet below surface) ; it was remarked
that it bore no trace of oxidation, and that its edges were as
sharp as if it had been just struck off.

Underlying this bed came the Estuarine Clay and associated
strata, in which no flakes were discovered ; but it is worthy of
mention that in the lowest bed of gravel, at a depth of 28 feet
below the surface, several flint chips were obtained bearing a
considerable resemblance to flakes.

Table showing Distribution of Worked Flints.

Bed.	Thick-ness of bed.	Material.	No. of worked flints found.	No. per cubic ft. of material examined.
Bed A.	1-6	Gravelly soil.	Great quantity.	At least 10.
,, B.	4-6	Coarse gravel.	Quantity diminishing	10 diminishing to 0.
,, C.	3-6	Sandy layers.	2	·013
,, D1.	2-1½		30	·31
,, 2.	2-1½		33	·34
,, 3.	2-1½	Coarse Gravel.	36	·37
,, 4.	2-1½		3	·08
,, E.	2-6	Coarse clayey gravel	2	·04

V.—CONCLUSIONS OF THE COMMITTEE.

The Curran Gravels form a stratified deposit extending over a considerable area, and possessing at each point the same characters. They consist of beds of gravel and sand which rest unconformably on one another, the whole series resting on the Estuarine Clay, which in turn rests on the Boulder Clay. In places where the surface of the Boulder Clay has had a greater elevation during the Estuarine Clay period, the latter has not been deposited, and the gravels lie directly on the former. The gravels were probably thrown down by powerful currents as a bar across the entrance of Larne Lough ; the shells which they contain lived on the spot where they are now found. The character of the fauna in the whole depth of strata, and its similarity throughout, point to the conclusion that no marked climatic changes occurred during the period of deposition, the temperature of the sea being about the same as at present. There is no trace of ice action in any of the beds examined, and the character of the fauna of even the lowest bed of the series shows that it was deposited subsequent to any glacial period. The worked flints which the gravels contain consist almost entirely of rude flakes, and occur chiefly on the surface of the deposit. They decrease rapidly in quantity through the upper bed of gravel, and are nearly absent from the sandy layers ; and in the lower gravel they occur sparingly throughout the bed down to a depth of 20 feet below the surface, where the Estuarine Clay series begins.

Tabulated List of Mollusca observed in the Gravels and Underlying Beds.

NOTE.—The fossils of the gravel beds A to D having been already investigated by *Hull, †Grainger, and others, no exhaustive examination of these zones was considered necessary, but the lists given below indicate the character of their fauna. More attention was given to beds G, H, and J, as these are not easily accessible, and as their fossils have not previously been catalogued. Beds E and F being subordinate zones, were not separately examined.

SPECIES.	Gravels.			Bed G. (Est. Clay.)	Bed H. (Black Sand.)	Bed I. (Blk. Gravel.)	REMARKS.
	Bed B.	Bed C.	Bed D.				
Anomia ephippium	...	...	..	vr	vr	vr	Small.
Ostrea edulis	..	...	r	f	vr	...	
Pecten varius	...	...	..	r	...	...	
—— maximus	...	...	vr	...	..	...	One large valve.
Mytilus edulis	...	...	..	r	...	...	
Crenella decussata	...	..	...	...	f	..	Seven fine examples.
Nucula nucleus	...	..	..	vr	...	...	Only one valve found.
Montacuta bidentata	...	..	...	...	..	vr	
Lucina borealis	...	r	..	...	f	r	
Axinus flexuosus	...	...	..	vr	...	.-	One specimen.
Cyamium minutum	...	...	...	vc	f	r	Abundant in the clay.
Cardium exiguum	...	...	...	c	f	f	
—— edule	...	...	r	f	f	r	Rare but general.
Cyprina Islandica	..	..	..	vr	...	...	One fragment.
Venus lincta	...	..	...	...	vr	...	
—— ovata	...	...	...	...	r	...	
—— gallina	...	...	..	...	vr	..	
Tapes aureus	..	...	...	f	f	..	Of large size.
—— virgineus	..	...	...	vr	vr	...	
—— pullastra	...	...	f	vr	r	r	
—— decussatus	...	r	...	r	...	...	
Tellina Balthica	...	...	...	f	r	...	
—— tenuis	...	...	...	...	vr	..	
Mactra subtruncata	...	..	...	vr	..	...	One young specimen.

* British Association Report, 1872.   † British Association Report, 1874.

TABLE—Continued.

SPECIES.	Bed B.	Bed C.	Bed D.	Bed G. (*Est. Clay.*)	Bed H. (*Black Sand.*)	Bed I. (*Blk Gravel.*)	REMARKS.
	Gravels.						
Scrobicularia alba	...	...	...	..	vr	r	*S. piperata* occurs in some abundance in the clay at the old pottery.
Solen ensis	...	...	...	f	f	...	
Thracia papyracea	..	...	...	vr	r	...	Two single valves.
Corbula gibba	..	...	...	f	c	...	
Patella vulgata	...	...	...	f	f	c	Of depressed shape.
Helcion pellucidum	..	..	...	vr	...	..	
—————— v. lævis	...	...	...	vr	vr	...	
Tectura virginea	...	...	...	..	..	f	
Fissurella Græca	..	..	...	..	...	vr	One very young example.
Cyclostrema nitens	...	...	...	vr	...	...	
Trochus cinerareus	...	f	f	c	vc	c	Throughout the beds.
—— umbilicatus	...	...	...	vr	..	vr	
—— zizyphinus	...	vr	...	...	...	...	One large example.
Phasianella pulla	...	...	...	f	...	...	
Lacuna divaricata	...	...	...	vr	r	r	
—— puteolus	...	..	..	r	r	c	
Littorina obtusata	..	f	r	c	vc	c	Generally abundant.
—— rudis	...	...	r	r	r	f	
—— litorea	...	f	..	c	f	f	
Rissoa inconspicua	...	..	...	vr	..	vr	In the upper beds, *Rissoæ* and other small shells do not occur, having been destroyed by the action of percolating water.
—— membranacea	..	...	...	c	f	f	
—————— v. elata	..	...	..	f	...	...	
—— violacea	..	...	...	vr	...	...	
—— striata	...	...	..	vc	r	c	
—————— v. arctica	...	...	..	c	...	..	
Hydrobia ulvæ	...	...	..	c	f	f	
Skenea planorbis	..	..	...	vc	r	f	
Cœcum glabrum	...	...	...	vr	...	...	One specimen.
Turritella terebra	...	vr	...	...	...	...	
Cerithium reticulatum	...	...	...	vr	..	...	Remarkable for its rarity.
Purpura lapillus	...	..	r	vr	r	r	
Buccinum undatum	...	...	r	...	r	...	
Murex erinaceus	...	...	...	vr	...	...	One example.
Nassa reticulata	...	...	...	vr	vr	...	
—— pygmæa	...	..	...	vr	...	...	
Pleurotoma rufa	..	...	...	..	r	..	
Utriculus obtusus	...	...	...	f	f	vr	
Acera bullata	..	...	...	r	...	...	
Limnæa palustris	..	...	...	vr	..		One example.
Cancer ——	...	...	...	c	...		Claws chiefly—undeterminable.
Balanus ——	...	...	...	...	...	vr	
Spirorbis ——	..	...	...	f	...	f	
Corylus avellana	..	...	...	...	..	r	A few hazel nuts in the lowest bed.

The Report was illustrated by large diagrams, and photographs taken during the excavations, and by samples of all the beds mentioned, collections of fossils, and over one hundred flint implements from the Gravels.

Mr. Gray, the President of the Club, opened a very interesting discussion upon the report, stating that he had strongly advocated the necessity for this careful and systematic investigation of the Gravels, and was delighted to have the opportunity of joining in a work that had been so thorough and satisfactory, although the results tended to confirm the opinions of the officers of the Geological Survey and other Irish and English investigators, rather than his own. He (the President) had maintained that the worked flints were found only on the surface or at a moderate depth below it, and were not found in the stratified marine deposits of which the accumulation of gravel is made up. He was now prepared to give up this idea, and to admit the fact that the worked flints are found more or less throughout the several marine deposits resting upon the Estuarine Clay, and that this conclusion, taken together with the fact that worked flints are dredged from the harbour near Greencastle, presents phenomena that call for further elucidation.

The discussion was continued by Rev. Canon Grainger, D.D., M.R.I.A., Messrs. Joseph Wright, F.G.S., W. H. Patterson, M.R.I.A., R. M. Young, B.A., F. W. Lockwood, Mann Harbison, George Donaldson, S. A. Stewart, F.B.S.E., and R. Lloyd Praeger, B.E., B.A. General satisfaction was expressed at the results of the investigation, and at the thoroughness with which it had been carried out.

EXPLANATION OF PLATES.

Plate I. shows a diagramatic section, drawn to scale, of all the beds exposed during the investigation. The figures at top and bottom of the left hand margin show the level of these points reduced to Ordnance Survey Datum.

Plate II. is a collotype print of a photograph taken during the investigation by Mr. W. Gray, the point selected being a few yards S.W. of the trial section. This shows the natural appearance of Beds A., B., C , and D. ; the unconformability of the two last-named zones, and the steep dip of Bed D., may be noted. The section shown is 15 feet in height.

SECTION

OF THE BEDS ON THE CURRAN AT LARNE.

35.00 9.22

GRAVELLY SOIL............................ 1·6″ A

COARSE GRAVEL .... 4·6″ B

SANDY LAYERS............................ 2·9″ ⎫
                                            ⎬ C
FINE SAND............................ 9″ ⎭

COARSE GRAVEL .... 8·6″ D

BLACK MUDDY GRAVEL ...... 2·6″ E

BLACK SAND ...... 1·0″ F

H.W.M. 13.00

ESTUARINE-CLAY 3·0″ G

BLACK SAND 2·0″ H

COARSE BLACK GRAVEL ⎫
2·6″, Base not reached ⎭ I

6·00

L.W.M

PLATE II.

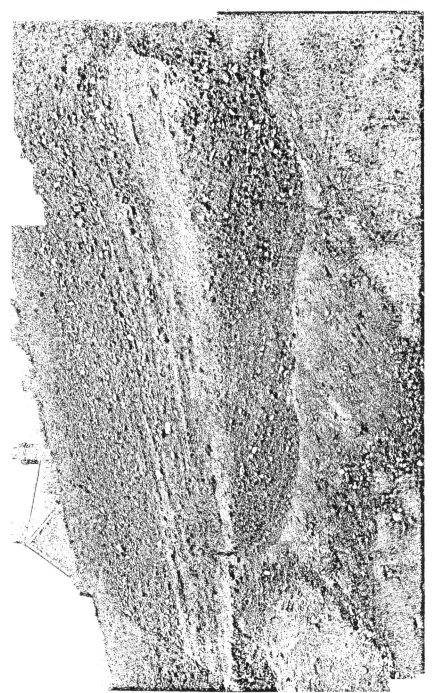

THE GRAVEL ESCARPMENT AT THE CURRAN, LARNE

The third communication was on the recent occurrence of the Stock Dove in the County of Antrim, and was also brought forward by Mr. Praeger. He said that in consequence of a letter in one of the local papers reporting the breeding of the Stock Dove (*Columba œnas*) near the town of Antrim, in May last, he was requested by the committee to examine into the matter and to report to them concerning it, which he had now much pleasure in doing. The nest in question was found in the deer-park of Viscount Massereene by the Rev. J. Gordon Holmes, Vicar of Antrim, who, in response to enquiries, kindly sent one of the eggs for identification, accompanied by a detailed description of the nest. These were forwarded to Mr. J. E. Harting, of London, who pronounced them to be undoubtedly those of the Stock Dove. The nest which Mr. Holmes found was situated in a hole among the roots of a large elm which formed a tangled mass on the edge of a steep bank; it consisted of a few twigs and roots, and contained two fresh eggs.

The Stock Dove was first found in Ireland by Mr. Thomas Darragh, of Belfast, in 1875, when two birds were shot near Dundonald, Co. Down. The next year another specimen was obtained in Co. Down, and in the following spring this species was found nesting near Dundonald by Mr. Darragh, and in Ravensdale Park, Co. Louth, by Lord Clermont.

It had now been authentically discovered breeding in Co. Antrim, and its further spread in Ireland would be watched with interest.

Irish specimens of the Stock Dove, and of its congeners, the Rock Dove and the Ring Dove or Wood Pigeon, were exhibited.

The election of several new members brought the evening's proceedings to a close.

The third meeting of the Winter Session was held in the Museum, College Square North, on Tuesday evening, 17th December—the President (Mr. William Gray, M.R.I.A.) in the chair—when two communications were brought forward. The first was by Rev. C. Herbert Waddell, M.A., entitled "Some Notes on Plant Life." The lecturer stated that it would be impossible in a single lecture to give anything like a complete account of plant life. All he could do would be to give an outline of some of the most interesting parts of the economy of plants. Some of the lowest forms of plants and animals were then described and illustrated by coloured diagrams, and it was shown that the two kingdoms are divided by a faint and uncertain line at this region. The question was asked, What are all plants and animals, what is man himself made of ? In reply, it was pointed out that all living organisms are built up of a colourless viscid substance called protoplasm. *Amœba*, one of the lowest animals, consisted of a structureless mass of protoplasm. Amœban life was certainly very simple and primitive. The animal could move in any direction, and seize a diatom or other prey with that part of its body which happened to be nearest, not taking the trouble to turn round. Protoplasm was the substance which built up the bodies of all plants and animals. Like a builder, it has been given the wonderful property of being able to gather, select, and prepare the complex materials of which the marvellous human body, the mighty oak, and the humble wayside flower respectively consist. As a rule, protoplasm occurred in plants in little masses called cells, surrounded by cell walls formed of cellulose. These grouped together formed a tissue. Inside the cell was the nucleus, embedded in the protoplasm. In a similar way man built his structures—houses, ships, &c.—of many compartments. This kind of construction united a sparing use of material with strength and lightness, and afforded easy means of intercommunication. According to the new theory, the "continuity of protoplasm," all the cells were connected one with another by minute pores opening through the cell wall, but this had not been proved as yet. Mr. Waddell then explained the reason of the flow of sap, and other vital processes in the plant, and, in a drawing of a common desmid (*Closterium lunula*), explained a curious motion of the cell contents called *Cyclosis*. It is interesting to watch this process under the microscope, and it can be easily observed in the cells of the American weed, stinging hairs of nettles, &c. In the desmid a little group of granules keep up a slow but continuous motion round and round, but what this motion is for, no one knows. The structure and use of leaves in the life of a plant were then explained and illustrated by a section of the common Liverwort, showing the pores or *Stomata* which were found in great numbers on the surfaces of leaves. Their green colour arose from the grains of chlorophyll contained in their cells. These green parts were not only ornamental, but were also the most useful and hard-working parts of the whole organism. Leaves correspond more or less to lungs; for the chlorophyll has in sunlight the power of assimilating carbon from the atmosphere ; and when it is remembered that there is only ·04 per cent. of carbon dioxide in the air, and that half a plant's weight is made up of carbon, the enormous work they do is apparent. Chlorophyll was truly a wonderful substance, and did a mighty work in nature. These little grains were the manufactories of the plant, mills to grind its corn, teeth to masticate it, stomachs to digest it. All of us were dependent upon them for our daily food, for every particle of food that we ate had at some time or other passed through these mills, and been prepared for our use. These chlorophyll mills in the leaf only worked by means of light. Fungi, which were not manufacturing plants, could live in the dark. All other green plants were hard workers, and the power they used to drive their were mills sunlight. With the first rays of the rising sun the mills commenced to work, and went on continuously until sunset. Then they had rest, and other parts of the plant took up other divisions of labour— growth and cell division were greatest during darkness—and thus was caused an alternation of rest and work. It had been proposed to make plants work night and day under electric light, and thus ripen peaches and strawberries, but such long hours of work would be sure to wear out their constitutions. The chlorophyll was hard at work all summer gathering in and laying up supplies against hard times in storehouses, in bud, or tuber, or bulb, or stem. With the autumn deciduous plants left off work. The green chlorophyll passed away in the beautiful tints of autumn leaves. Then they withered and died. This had long been foreseen and provided for by the great Architect of nature. By a beautiful and simple contrivance a little wedge of differently constituted tissue had been growing across the base of the leaf stalk, and thus formed a joint, beginning at the outside and making its way across. Then a slight touch of wind or frost was sufficient to break the remaining connection, and the leaf fell. Plant life was a most interesting part of biology, and much was to be gained in its study; but it was full of mysteries. Protoplasm—In this the life of the plant was centred, but how little did we know about it! The life seemed to be there: what the life was we could not tell. As Tennyson says—

> Little flower—but if I could understand
> What you are, root and all, and all in all,
> I should know what God and man is.

The second communication was by Rev. H. W. Lett, M.A., T.C.D., " On the Cells of Mosses." Mr. Lett described mosses as, of all tribes of plants, the best adapted for studying how vegetable cells come into existence, increase in size, multiply and reach maturity, because mosses are in most stages of their growth of a semi-transparent nature, and can be found at any time of the year, and almost everywhere. The growth of a moss was briefly traced from a spore up to the complete fruit-bearing plant, and it was shown how cell walls, protoplasm, cell sap, chlorophyll, tissues, &c., can be studied by their aid. A vast field of interesting work is also contained in comparing the cells of mosses, which are very various, long, linear, square, hexagonal, rhomboidal, sinuous, &c. The preparation of specimens of the cells of these plant for examination under the microscope was alluded to as affording a field for experiments in order to obtain a perfectly satisfactory and trustworthy medium for mounting them as microscopic objects, so as to have the cells as nearly as possible in the same state as they were when the plant was growing.

At the conclusion, Mr. Lett mentioned having found during the summer of 1889 the following mosses in the County Antrim :—*Sphagnum rigidum*, and *S. molle*, which have hitherto been collected in only one other Irish locality, near Hilltown, in the County Down, where he found them a few years ago. He also announced meeting in last June with *Sphagnum Austini* in Glenariff, County Antrim. This is an extremely rare moss, having as yet been discovered in only two British localities—the Hebrides and Westmoreland. An interesting discussion and the election of new members brought the meeting to a close.

The fourth meeting of the Winter Session was held in the Museum, College Square North, on Tuesday evening, January 28th—the President (Mr. William Gray, M.R.I.A.) in the chair—when two communications were brought forward by Mr. R. Lloyd Praeger, B.E. The first paper was on a somewhat technical subject, the title being " A Contribution to the Post-tertiary Fauna of Ulster." The reader stated that having been recently engaged in an examination of the Estuarine Clays of the North of Ireland, he now ventured to bring before the Club a few notes of shells observed by him in these beds, which have not previously been recorded therefrom. The Estuarine Clays, he explained, form a series of marine deposits, consisting mostly of tough homogeneous blue clay, attaining a considerable thickness in places ; they usually rest on submerged peat, post-glacial sands, or Boulder Clay, and are often overlaid by raised beaches, which have accumulated to a depth of ten to twenty feet in some spots, since the deposition of the clay beds. The Estuarine Clays yield a rich and varied molluscan fauna, characteristic of the littoral and laminarian.

zones, and differing somewhat from that now inhabiting the adjacent waters.

The Belfast clay forms a thick deposit of large area in the Lagan estuary, and has been examined successively by Thompson[1], Hyndman[2], Grainger[3], Stewart[4], and the writer[5]. The bed at Magheramorne, on Larne Lough, is singularly rich in shells, a list of which appears in Stewart's paper, mentioned below ; in addition to these, the writer has examined Estuarine Clays occurring at Eglinton and Limavady Junction, on Lough Foyle, at the mouth of the Bann, and at Larne, Kilroot, Holywood, Kircubbin, Downpatrick, Newcastle, Greenore, and Dundalk.

The following species of *Mollusca* are additions to the fauna of the North of Ireland Estuarine Clays :—

Lima Loscombii, G. B. Sowerby. A single valve of this species occurred among a large number of examples of its congener *L. hians*, at Magheramorne.

Crenella decussata, Montagu. This rare and beautiful little northern shell occurs sparingly at Magheramorne and Larne.

Nucula sulcata, Bronn. A single valve in the Downpatrick bed. Does not now inhabit the North of Ireland.

Nucula nitida, G. B. Sowerby. Eglinton, sparingly.

Pentunculus glycymeris, Linné. Frequent at Magheramorne.

Kellia suborbicularis, Montagu. Magheramorne, rare.

Gastrana fragilis, Linné. A valve of unusual dimensions ($2\cdot1 \times 1\cdot5$), at Downpatrick. Not previously noticed in the North of Ireland, either recent or fossil.

Mactra solida, Linné. Magheramorne, very rare. The varieties *truncata* and *elliptica* have been previously recorded from the Belfast bed.

---

[1] Belfast Museum Collection. [2] British Association Report, 1857. [3] Natural History Review, Vol. vi, for 1859. [4] Annual Report, Belfast Naturalists' Field Club, 1870-1: Appendix. [5] Proceedings, Belfast N.F. Club, 1886-7: Appendix.

Thracia distorta, Montagu. Several valves at Magheramorne. They are of remarkable size ('9 × 1'2), these dimensions being half as large again as those given by Jeffreys.

Trochus helicinus, Fabricius. Not uncommon in the Maghera-morne deposit.

Trochus millegranus, Philippi. Several small examples at Downpatrick.

Phasianella pulla, Linné. This pretty shell is frequent in the clays at Larne, Magheramorne, and Downpatrick.

Rissoa reticulata, Montagu. Magheramorne, not common.

Rissoa albella, Lovén, var. *Sarsii*. A single specimen at Magheramorne.

Rissoa parva, Da Costa. Magheramorne bed, rare. Though extremely abundant at the present day, it has not been hitherto noticed in the Estuarine Clays, where its place is taken by *R. violacea*. The typical form appears to be very rare everywhere as a fossil.

Rissoa costata, Adams. Kircubbin, frequent.

Skenea planorbis, Fabricius. In the clays at Limavady Junction, Magheramorne, Larne, Downpatrick, and New-castle ; abundant in some of these beds.

Odostomia nitidissima, Montagu. Two examples of this tiny and exquisite shell were found at Eglinton. Jeffreys says that it has never been found fossil.

Several other *Odostomiæ* have been found, which are believed to be additional species ; but these are not recorded till they have been examined and confirmed by an authority.

Utriculus truncatulus, Bruguière. In the Downpatrick bed, very rare.

Utriculus obtusus, Montagu, var. *Lajonkaireana*. Sparingly at Limavady Junction, where the typical form was very common, along with *U. mammillatus*. A curious monstrosity of *U. obtusus* also occurred, having a slender tapered spire as long as the mouth.

In connection with this subject, the subjoined note of recent shells was added :—

Tapes decussatus and *Scrobicularia piperata.* These two species, which are so abundant in, and characteristic of our Estuarine Clays, were considered to be now extinct on the North of Ireland shores, and this opinion has been recently endorsed by the writer[1]. Mr. Wm. Swanston, F.G.S., has since informed him that he obtained the latter in a fresh state on the strand near Horn Head, in Donegal ; and they have both been taken by the writer (the former alive, the latter recently dead), at Fort Stewart, Lough Swilly, during the past summer.

Gastrana fragilis. This shell is noted above as having been found fossil at Downpatrick. A number of fresh single valves were obtained on the Lough Swilly shore along with the two last-named species ; and Rev. Canon Grainger, M.R.I.A., has since informed the writer that he has also taken it there. It without doubt lives in that locality.

The second paper was entitled " Three Days on Rathlin Island: with Notes on its Flora and Fauna." A large map of the island hung on the wall, and on the table were collections of the local birds and birds' eggs, plants, and antiquities, to which constant reference was made, and during the course of the lecture lantern views, artistically executed by Mr. Welch from photographs taken by him on the island, were successfully exhibited by Mr. George Donaldson. The reader first described the position and physical features of Rathlin, which lies off the North Antrim coast, separated from the mainland by a deep and turbulent sound, through which the tides run with tremendous force, so that except during calm weather the passage is effected with difficulty. The island is almost completely surrounded by high, inaccessible cliffs, but at the

---

[1] Proc. B.N.F.C., 1886-7: Appendix, and "Marine Shells of the North of Ireland," in Proc. B.N.F.C., 1887-8 : Appendix.

southern extremity the ground becomes lower. The greater part of the surface consists of rocky heath, with frequent marshes and lakes. The flora and fauna of an area thus isolated might, he said, be expected to possess interest for the naturalist, and in this respect Rathlin has claimed a fair amount of attention from local scientists. At the beginning of the present century, Mr. John Templeton examined the flora of the island; in 1836 Dr. David Moore paid it a visit; and in the following year an elaborate paper dealing with the zoology, botany, and geology, as well as with the scenery, history, agriculture, and statistics of the island, appears in the Transactions of the Royal Irish Academy, from the pen of Dr. James Drummond Marshall. Miss Gage, sister of the courteous and kindly owner of Rathlin, prepared a list of its flora for the Botanical Society of Edinburgh in 1850, and Mr. Gage himself has for many years made the birds of his little kingdom his especial study. In 1884, Mr. S. A. Stewart, a leading member of the Naturalists' Field Club, contribu"ed a most valuable paper to the Proceedings of the Royal Irish Academy, in which the flora of the island is fully and accurately described. Mr. Praeger next touched on the scenery of the island, with special reference to the magnificent sea cliffs, which form such a conspicuous feature. It is at the north-west extremity that these cliffs attain their greatest elevation, and there the huge wall, from 300 to 450 feet in height, rises sheer out of the water, carved by the ocean into vast amphitheatres and bold headlands, with occasional detached rock-pillars of great height standing in fantastic shapes, like giant sentinels guarding that savage coast. Amid these craggy fastnesses the seabirds have their home, and hither as spring advances come thousands of guillemots, razorbills, puffins, kittiwakes, and black-backed gulls, to bring forth their young on the lofty ledges of the cliffs. The kestrels yell from the adjoining rocks; the hooded crow and chough flit along the shore; cormorants sit motionless by the water's edge; an occasional raven soars majestically around the topmost crags. In the marshes above coot, waterhen, and dabchick push their noiseless way among the reeds; teal and wild duck have their nests among the high watergrass ; overhead, the lapwing utter their melancholy musical note, and the brown snipe, wheeling in wide, rapid circles, produces that weird, bleating sound which still puzzles naturalists to explain. On the flower-bespangled heaths the rocks re-echo the cheerful chatter of wheatear, pipit, and stonechat; the yellowhammer sings his short, sweet song ; the linnet pours forth his livelier lay, and, above all, the skylarks soar heavenward, filling the whole air with music. Having touched on the geology of Rathlin, the reader came on to speak of a visit which Mr. Robert Patterson, Mr. Welch, and he paid to the island in the spring of last year. Leaving Ballycastle early one May morning under a cloudless sky, with the white cliffs of Rathlin flashing back the morning sunlight, a light southerly breeze wafted them across the Channel into Church Bay, whence they made sail down to the west end of the island. Once round Bull Point, the heavy surge of the Atlantic swell was encountered, and the oars were got out. Now they approached the great bird colonies, and the rock-ledges were lined with razorbills and guillemots standing in close packed rows, while in the water a constant commotion was kept up by the numbers of the same birds that dived or fluttered away before the approach of the boat. Doonmore, or the Great Stack, a huge rock pillar that raises its perpendicular sides and dome-shaped top to a height of some 200 feet above the sea, now appeared in view. What a sight its top presented ! So thickly packed were the guillemots that there did not appear to be standing-room for another bird : it was a living mass of bird-life. As the rock was neared, air and water alike became alive with birds. Doonmore being inaccessible to all but the most experienced climbers—the last time it was scaled being some ten years ago—a landing was effected on Stack-na-cally, from the summit of which a magnificent view of the cliffs and sea-birds was obtained. Then they rowed on below gigantic cliffs. The air around was simply blackened by the innumerable birds that rose in tumult as the boat advanced, yet apparently without diminishing the thousands that crowded every niche and ledge of the great basaltic wall. Like volleys of black and white cannon-balls, the guillemots and razorbills rushed past, dashing into the foaming water, or sailing swiftly for a hundred yards and wheeling back to their perches again ; while like snowflakes the pretty kittiwakes floated on outspread sunny wings, and, above all, the black-backed gulls sat on the loftiest cliffs, shouting and laughing in half a dozen discordant tones; and the whole air was filled with a musical din that was quite indescribable. Thus they proceeded, enveloped in a cloud of birds, till high on the cliff above their heads they saw the mysterious "Sun Rock," a most peculiar example of radiating columnar structure, which forms an interesting and striking object. There the ground swell became so heavy, and the risk of accident so great, that the skipper ordered a retreat, which, however, was not made until a second landing had been with difficulty effected, and some instantaneous photographs secured of the birds and their nests, and of the magnificent cliffs and rock pillars, which were most artistically displayed by Mr. George Donaldson by limelight on a large screen. The return was effected without mishap, and as night was falling the boat landed its passengers in Church Bay. On the following morning an early start was made on foot for the north-west end of the island. The wind rapidly increased in force as the day advanced, and by the time the party reached the shelter of the bay in which the Great Stack stands, a furious gale was blowing. The channel was white with roaring waves, and the dim outline of the mainland was scarcely discernible through the thick mist of driving spray that intervened. According to arrangement, a party was to have sailed across from Ballycastle and joined them at the Stacks, but it was only too evident that no boat could cross the wild waste of waters that stretched between the island and the Antrim shore. So the day was spent in exploring along the base of the cliffs, disturbed only by furious gusts that raged and roared among the rocks. The following day turned out very wet, with pelting rain and wind and thick mist, but the party were out all day along the northern cliffs ; and in the evening, just as they were setting sail for Ballycastle, the clouds broke, the fog lifted, and before a fresh easterly breeze they covered the seven and a half miles of water in fifty five minutes, and once more stepped ashore at Ballycastle. In conclusion, the reader briefly summarised the zoological and botanical notes taken during their three days' visit. Of birds, they had observed 47 species on the island, one of which, the Sedge Warbler, is an addition to Mr. Gage's very complete list of 132 Rathlin birds. Of the 318 species of Flowering Plants and higher Cryptogams recorded in Mr. Stewart's list as growing on the island, they noted 228, and obtained 29 additional species, as follows :—*Brassica campestris, Raphanus Raphanistrum, Drosera rotundifolia, Honkeneja reploides, Cerastium tetrandrum, Alchemilla arvensis, Rubus Idæus, Pyrus Aucuparia, Sempervivum tectorum,† Carum Carui,† Scandix Pecten-Veneris, Myrrhis odorata,† Aster Tripolium, Fraxinus excelsior,† Veronica scutellata,* V. serpyllifolia, Beta maritima,* Ulmus montana,† Salix viminalis,† Populus tremula, Alnus glutinosa,† Scilla verna,* Luzula sylvatica, Scirpus cæspitosus, Carex præcox, Equisetum arvense, E. maximum, Lastrea dilatata, Botrichium Lunaria.* Of these, the species marked (†) are to be considered introduced plants ; those bearing an asterisk were previously recorded in Miss Gage's list, but were not found by Mr. Stewart.

Mr. Welch's photographs, exhibited by limelight, were much admired, as was a beautiful series of guillemots' eggs, showing the great variation of colour to which the eggs of this bird are subject. At the close of the papers a discussion ensued, in which Messrs. Hamilton, Welch, John Marsh, Lockwood, the President, and others took part.

The fifth meeting of the Winter Session was held in the Museum on February 19th—the President (Mr. William Gray, M.R.I.A) in the chair—when a paper was read by Mr. W. H.

Phillips, entititled " A Gossip about British Ferns and their Varieties, with notices of local finds ; with illustrations." The Chairman, in his introductory remarks, referred to the long-continued and earnest way in which Mr. Phillips had worked at this most attractive department of botany, and the well-recognised position which, as a result, he now occupied of being one of the foremost British authorities on that subject.

Mr. Phillips, on being called upon, said—In the Proceedings of the Club for 1885-86 appears an appendix, entitled " The Ferns of Ulster," by W. H. Phillips and R. Lloyd Praeger. In this list an attempt has been made to put in a permanent form as much information as was possible to be obtained of all the species of British ferns that had been found in Ulster, their localities, and first finders. Besides this we gave lists of all the varieties which had been found by ourselves and others, as far we could get information. As compared with any similar lists published elsewhere, it shows a good record of work done in this province, but unfortunately by a very few people, our own names occurring conspicuously, not from our wish to monopolise everything, but from the absence of other workers in this field of botany, the few varieties found by others being more the result of accident than the reward of careful search. Out of the 46 species of ferns indigenous to Great Britain and Ireland, Ireland yields 32 species and the province of Ulster 31. The varieties we record number over 150, of which *Polystichum angulare* is credited with 55, and *Athyrium* with 30. It occurred to me that a paper on these varieties, with illustrations of local finds, would be of interest to the Club. In compiling this list we were struck with the almost complete absence of any records of finds by *bona fide* working men. In Ireland working men do not take any interest in ferns, either as hunters or cultivators. With them all kinds are alike—brackens. The working men in England are largely members of geological and botanical societies. Many of them have been both finders and cultivators of ferns. Many of the best forms have been the results of their hunting when on holiday excursions.

Ferns, Lycopods, and *Equiseta* have come down to us from a
period of the world's history when probably flowering plants
had not commenced to appear, that first essential of floral
existence, bright sunshine, being obscured by a dense and constant veil of cloudy moisture floating in an atmosphere of
tropical temperature. That period of the pre-Adamite age in
which ferns commenced to grow corresponds with the third
day's work of the Mosaic account of the creation. After the
muds had ceased to flow and the limestone rocks by upheaval
appeared above the waters, the warm, moist, carbonic atmosphere thrown off by the fresh lime muds produced such a
rapid growth of vegetation that the whole land became quickly
clothed with ferns and magnificent trees. Amongst the buried
forests of the Mountain Limestone 500 varieties of this vegetation, tree-ferns, and species of pines are found hardened to
stone. Ferns are there seen in astonishing variety and of
very different sizes. Some, resembling the common bracken of
the woods, grew into trees of large dimensions, bending with
flowing fronds; others remained lowly, like the ferns that
flourish in our vales to-day. Gradually these ancient forests
sank beneath the floods of sea water, and, settling into the sand
and mud of the sea bottom, have been transformed by time,
heat, and pressure into the black shining coal seams, which now
reveal their history to our curious eyes. Francis estimates the
recent ferns of Great Britain at forty-one species, and as the
flowering plants of the country do not fall short of 1,400
species, the ferns bear the rather small proportion of 1 to 35 ;
whereas of the British Coal Measures flora, in which we do not
reckon quite 300 species of plants, about 120 were ferns. Three-
sevenths of the entire Carboniferous flora of Great Britain
belonged to this familiar class, and for about 50 species more
we can discover no nearer analogues than those which connect
them with the fern allies ; and if with the British Coal Measures
we include those of the continent of America we shall find the
proportion in favour of the ferns still greater. The number of
Carboniferous plants hitherto described amounts to about 500,
and of these 250, or one half of the whole, are ferns.

It will thus follow that, in rightly estimating the economic value of ferns, we must not, as is usually done, consider it nil, but place to their credit the great advantages which the world has derived from coal, without which it would have been well nigh impossible to carry on the vast manufactories which now exist, our steam and gas engines, our locomotives by sea and land. What wonderful products are derived from coal; and from the tar residuum of gas-making there are several hundred different substances extracted—sulphate of ammonia, oils, the wonderful aniline dyes, of all the hues of the rainbow, and the latest product saccharine, the sweetest substance yet discovered. Ferns are mentioned by the older botanists, and their nomenclature handed down to us, but little had been done in the way of cultivation or finding new forms until about 45 years ago. To those who have taken up the study of our native ferns, and have thus been enabled to form a just opinion of the wealth of beautiful forms into which our few British species have sported, either under natural conditions or in cultivation, it is a matter of surprise that popularly they should be so little known and so rarely cultivated, as the popular taste is largely created by those who cater for it, the proper display of a good thing being generally the needful preliminary to the demand for it. To nurserymen generally must be imputed much of the blame attached to the neglect of these beautiful plants, well-grown specimens of which are very seldom displayed for sale, though exotic ferns with less pretentions to beauty are grown with the greatest care and shown by thousands. An idea seems to prevail that British ferns are common, and only fit for stop-gaps in out-of-the-way corners where nothing else would grow. This ignorance has been in no small degree shared apparently by popular writers on the subject, since in all but two or three works the varieties are relegated to an entirely subordinate position, while in some they are not even alluded to. What should we think of a rose-book or series of rose-books professing by their titles to exhaust the subject, while confining themselves exclusively to wild roses, and never even distantly alluding to the glorious array of Marechal Neil, Gloire de Dijon, and the hundreds of rivals of the queen of flowers? Yet this is precisely what has been done in ferns. The time has happily passed when all botanists were content to regard the varieties of ferns as only monstrosities—mere garden varieties. It has long been recognised that, with very few exceptions, all the more marked forms have been found growing wild, nature being solely responsible for them. It is also beginning to be recognised that varieties do not appear at haphazard, but in conformity with certain fixed laws of development or deviation to which all species are more or less subject. The varieties of ferns cannot, therefore, be dismissed without attention, even if the extreme beauty of many of them did not render this impossible. He must, indeed, be wanting in some quality of sense or in knowledge who can regard all the varieties of the British ferns as only degradations. Can it be maintained that many of them are not in every sense higher developments, possessing, with all the symmetry of the normal form, greater delicacy of division and of texture, more freshness and variety of colour, more grace of habit, often larger size, and at times an intricacy of detail or of structure which interests the mind not less than it attracts the eye?

The late Colonel Jones, of Clifton, that *facile princeps* of fern-hunters and raisers, in a paper read before the Bristol Naturalists' Society, 1888, after enumerating the ferns found in the neighbourhood of Bristol and Somersetshire, says :—" It was in the lower parts of the Quantock district that the late Mr. Elworthy, many years ago, made those remarkable finds in *Polystichum angulare* which helped to give a greatly increased interest to the study of British ferns ; and subsequently Mr. G. B. Wollaston, Rev. C. Padley, Dr. Wills, and Colonel Jones found many fine and distinct varieties in the same district. Nor may it be without interest to bear in mind that it was in this same district which formed Mr. Elworthy's happy hunting ground, that Mr. Perceval made his remarkable discovery of Devonian corals, not less beautiful than geologically interesting. It would show that the affinity between this part of Somerset and South Devon, where so many of the finer forms of *Polystichum angulare* have been found, is not merely superficial. Nor may it be unworthy of notice that that energetic discoverer, Mr. W. H. Phillips of Belfast, has proved by his researches that a certain marked botanical affinity exists between the South-West of England and Ireland, the North more particularly. There are certain marked forms of *Polystichum angulare* of which single plants had been found in the West of England, and which, after very exhaustive researches, having never been found in any other part of England, had long been classed among the forms peculiar to the South-West. Yet after all this had been comfortably settled, Mr. Phillips turns up with his inconvenient discoveries and unsettles everything. If there were two ferns which had earned the character of having been entirely unique those ferns were *Polystichum angulare rotundatum*, of Elworthy, a Somerset form ; and *Polystichum angulare acrocladon*, found by Mr. Mapplebeck in South Devon. Mr. Phillips produces unmistakable counterparts of both. Another most rare and marked form, *Polystichum angulare brachiato-cristatum*, which long experience had seemed to have conclusively proved to be peculiar to the South of England, Mr. Phillips finds in the North of Ireland. It was the same with another rare and beautiful form, *Polystichum angulare setoso-cuneatum*, of which only two plants had ever before been found, one by Mr. Moly, the other by Mr. Wollaston, and both in the South-West of England. Also the extreme form of *Polystichum angulare grandiceps*, two plants of which, apparently identical, had been found by different people in other parts of Ireland, and was found more than once by Mr. Moly in Devon. The grand form of *Polystichum angulare polydactylum*, found by the late Rev. Charles Padley in the Vale of Avoca, was long considered a unique plant, until found by Colonel Jones in the South of England. To these may be added the *Polystichum angulare divisilobum* Phillips, on which Mr. G. B. Wollaston, the greatest authority on *Polystichums*, has passed his judgment, calling it 'a gem of the first water;' and the *Polystichum angulare divisilobum Crawfordiæ*, found some years ago by a labourer at Crawfordsburn. These most exquisite forms had only hitherto been found in Devonshire." He concludes in these words :—" Nature herself having in this as in many other ways linked Ireland to us so closely in every branch of natural history, shall we not all breathe a prayer—more than that, resolve—that nothing shall ever sever the connection ? " Shortly before Colonel Jones's death, in a letter to me about some of my fern finds, he says :—" I have always regarded the ferns in question as a distinct credit to you and to Ireland ; and goodness me ! when I think of it, where would British ferns be in case of a severance of Ireland from us ? I do not think that this side of the subject has ever received the attention it deserves." Within the last two years the collection at Kew has been immensely enriched by gifts and bequests representing many thousands of the finest forms. To what may not such a collection as this be expected to grow, containing all that is most beautiful, rare, and strange amongst the varieties of British ferns ? Nor should such a collection fail to excite a special interest in this country as being illustrative of, and at the same time a record of, a branch of botany exclusively British, and likely to remain so. For whatever discoveries in other parts of the world may be in store for the future, it is at present the fact that in no country of any considerable size has the natural tendency of ferns to vary been developed to anything like the same extent as in the British Isles.

However great our taste and fancy for ferns may be, we can never realise the enjoyment to be derived from them unless we are successful in cultivating them. The love of ferns does not merely consist in admiring them in a state of maturity when presented to the eye, but in gathering them from their native haunts and bringing them under cultivation, in administering to their wants, and anxiously watching them as they slowly unfurl their fronds. The common hedgerow, the old wall, the rocks by the sea, the wooded glen, the wild moor, and the stream provide for us the kingdom of ferns, whose peculiar habits form a pleasant study for our hours of recreation. The fern lover who has any leisure at command is almost sure, sooner or later, to become a fern hunter, and to be successful a familiar knowledge of all the normal ferns is necessary, so that at a glance he can recognise them, and then an education of the eye by constant, careful examination of the plants which come in his way, that should there be any abnormality in the fronds over which his eye travels, it may at once be detected. It may not be out of place here to add a word in justice to the true hunter of varieties, who is too often confounded in the minds of the thoughtless with those ruthless destroyers of species who, year by year, throw back the fern line farther from our cities. How sad to see the quantities of ferns in our markets each week with all the roots cut off to make them look smart. I never see these without the thought that death in a few days must be the result. How often in glens do we find ferns rooted up by thoughtless persons and lying thrown away. When a fern has been dug out, and not required, it should be planted again. The true hunter of varieties is, on the contrary, the preserver of rare forms, and but for him many a beautiful thing which is now a delight to many hundreds would have perished entirely. As a rule the finer organisms, if left to themselves, have scarce a chance of permanent survival in the hard struggle that is ever going on. The fecundity of ferns is enormous. Mr. Druery has calculated that a fully developed frond of *Polypodium vulgare* bears no fewer than 200,000,000 spores.

The lecturer then called attention to some of the more marked groups into which the varieties are divided, explaining the characters by reference to a magnificent display of dried specimens, mounted, and hung on the walls, numbering several hundreds, and made up principally of local finds ; and attention was drawn to several forms lately found. A most beautiful collection of ferns sent by Mr. O'Kelly, nurseryman, of Bally-vaughan, County Clare, was exhibited. These were all his own finds in County Clare. There were nine most strange and beautiful forms of *Ceterach officinarum*. One in particular is deserving of special notice, *multifido-cristatum*, a perfect gem. Until lately no varieties of this species had been found. Mr. O'Kelly is the first and only finder. All who wish for really good varieties should write for these ; no collection can be complete without them. A large number of freshly cut fronds of exquisite beauty and variety were shown round, and afterwards distributed among the audience, who seemed to highly appreciate them.

The election of members, and the announcement by the Secretary that the next evening would be devoted to the microscope, terminated the meeting.

The sixth meeting of the Winter Session was held in the Museum on Wednesday evening, March 26th. The chair was taken by Mr. William Gray, M.R.I.A., President of the Club. This being a "microscope evening," there was no regular paper read, but the President gave a brief account of a stone sepulchre recently found near the Giant's Ring, to supplement the communication on the subject which appeared in the Press that morning. The chamber was altogether about nine feet in diameter, nearly circular, having a central stone-roofed division with three or four compartments radiating from it, in one of which was a quantity of calcined bones. It is much to be regretted that the haste of the proprietor to proceed with his farming operations, and to utilise the materials for building purposes, prevented an adequate photograph being taken of this interesting structure. The microscopes were by this time ready for work, and the members passed an interesting hour in the investigation of the wonders and beauties of nature. Amongst other objects were specimens of *Hydrozoa* and *Polyzoa* gathered the same morning from fishermen's nets on the north coast ; *Infusoria*, alive and in rapid motion ; *Foraminifera*, including several rare species from recent dredgings ; marine specimens to illustrate methods of mounting ; frog-spawn freshly gathered, in which were included many freshly-hatched tad-poles of the mature age of a few minutes, &c., &c. Amongst the exhibitors were Messrs. William Gray, M.R.I.A.; Alexander Tate, C.E., M.R.I.A. ; John Donaldson, J. J. Andrew, L.D.S. ; G. Elliot, R. Welch, and others. The election of some new members brought the meeting to a close.

ANNUAL MEETING.

The twenty-seventh annual meeting of the club was held in the Museum, College Square North, on Wednesday evening, 16th April, the President (Mr. W. Gray, M.R.I.A.) in the chair.

The President opened the business of the evening by calling for the Secretaries' report, which, with the statement of accounts, appears in full in the earlier pages of this part of the Proceedings.

The Treasurer (Mr. S. A. Stewart, F.B.S.E.) who was next called on, gave a satisfactory account of the Club's finances for the past year.

On the motion of Rev. C. Herbert Waddell, M.A., seconded by Mr. H. S. Jefferson, the report and statement of accounts were received and ordered to be printed.

The next business was the election of Office-bearers for the ensuing year. Mr. W. Gray, M.R.I.A, was re-elected President, and Mr. John Vinycomb, Vice-President. Mr. S. A. Stewart resumed office as Treasurer. Mr. W. Swanston, F.G.S., Senior Hon. Secretary, having tendered his resignation, his colleague, Mr. F. W. Lockwood, assumed the Senior Secretaryship ; and Mr. R. Lloyd Praeger, B.E., was elected to fill the vacancy thus created.

Mr. Lockwood spoke in suitable terms of the great services rendered to the Club by Mr. Swanston during his long period of office, and moved— " That the members of the Belfast

Naturalists' Field Club take the present opportunity of expressing their regret that Mr. William Swanston, F.G.S., finds himself unable longer to give them his valuable services as Honorary Secretary. During the fifteen years he has held this office he has been distinguished by an assiduous attention to his duties, he has been uniformly courteous to all, and has ever been on the watch for opportunities of increasing the Club's usefulness. The members now tender to him their heartiest thanks for all the valuable services he has rendered to the Club during so many years."

The motion was ably seconded by Mr. Joseph Wright, F.G.S., who spoke of Mr. Swanston's unflagging zeal and wide scientific attainments.

The resolution was put to the meeting by the President, and was carried amid hearty applause.

Mr. Swanston having suitably replied,

The election of the Committee was proceeded with, after which

The President called for any suggestions as to improving or extending the work of the Club.

Mr. R. Lloyd Praeger, B.E., in a speech of some length, advocated the systematising of the photographic work of the Club. He pointed out the great value of photography in scientific work when properly and methodically undertaken, and suggested that the energy of the photographic section of the Club's members should be devoted to the systematic illustration of local archæology. He moved—"That a committee be appointed, consisting of Mr. W. Swanston and Mr. George Donaldson, with Mr. John Donaldson as secretary and the President as *ex-officio* chairman, with power to add to their number, to commence the systematic registration and photographing of the antiquities of the North of Ireland, and that they present a yearly report to the Club showing the progress made."

An animated discussion ensued, which was taken part in by the President and Messrs. W. Swanston, Joseph Wright, R. Welch, J. Hamilton, and others.

The motion was seconded by Mr. Swanston, and, on being put to the meeting, was carried.

Mr. S. A. Stewart here drew attention to a rare local plant that had been just forwarded to him. This was the small hoary scorpion-grass (*Myosotis collina*), which was found near Portstewart, in County Derry, within the last few days, by Miss Davies, of Glenmore, Lisburn. The plant occurs very sparingly in Down and Antrim, and has not previously been recorded from Derry.

Suggestions were then received as to suitable localities for excursions during the coming summer season, after which

The proceedings terminated.

RULES
OF THE
Belfast Naturalists' Field Club.

I.

That the Society be called "THE BELFAST NATURALISTS' FIELD CLUB."

II.

That the objects of the Society be the practical study of Natural Science and Archæology in Ireland.

III.

That the Club shall consist of Ordinary, Corresponding, and Honorary Members. The Ordinary Members to pay annually a subscription of Five Shillings, and that candidates for such Membership shall be proposed and seconded at any Meeting of the Club, by Members present, and elected by a majority of the votes of the Members present.

IV.

That the Honorary and Corresponding Members shall consist of persons of eminence in natural science, or who shall have done some special service to the Club; and whose usual residence is not less than twenty miles from Belfast. That such Members may be nominated by any Member of the Club, and on being approved of by the Committee, may be elected at any subsequent Meeting of the Club by a majority of the votes of the Members present. That Corresponding Members be expected to communicate a Paper once within every two years.

V.

That the Officers of the Club be annually elected, and consist of a President, Vice-President, Treasurer, and two Secretaries, and Ten Members, who form the Committee. Five to form a quorum. No member of Committee to be

eligible for re-election who has not attended at least one-fourth of the Committee Meetings during his year of office. That the office of President, or that of Vice-President, shall not be held by the same person for more than two years in succession.

VI.

That the Members of the Club shall hold at least six Field Meetings during the year, in the most interesting localities, for investigating the Natural History and Archæology of Ireland. That the place of meeting be fixed by the Committee, and that five days' notice of each Excursion be communicated to Members by the Secretaries.

VII.

That Meetings be held Fortnightly or Monthly, at the discretion of the Committee, for the purpose of reading papers; such papers, as far as possible, to treat of the Natural History and Archæology of the district. These Meetings to be held during the months from November to April inclusive.

VIII.

That the Committee shall, if they find it advisable, offer for competition Prizes for the best collections of scientific objects of the district ; and the Committee may order the purchase of maps, or other scientific apparatus, and may carry on geological and archæological searches or excavations, if deemed advisable, provided that the entire amount expended under this rule does not exceed the sum of £10 in any one year.

IX.

That the Annual Meeting be held during the month of April, when the Report of the Committee for the past year, and the Treasurer's Financial Statement shall be presented, the Committee and Officers selected, Bye-laws made and altered, and any proposed alteration in the general laws, of which a fortnight's notice shall have been given, in writing, to the Secretary or Secretaries, considered and decided upon. The Secretaries to give the Members due notice of such intended alteration.

X.

That, on the written requisition of twenty-five Members, delivered to the Secretaries, an Extraordinary General Meeting may be called, to consider and decide upon the subjects mentioned in such written requisition.

XI.

That the Committee be empowered to exchange publications and reports and to extend the privilege of attending the Meetings and Excursions of the Belfast Naturalists' Field Club to members of kindred societies, on similar privileges being accorded to its Members by such other societies.

The following Rules for the Conducting of the Excursions have been arranged by the Committee.

I. The Excursion to be open to all members ; each one to have the privilege of introducing two friends.

II. A Chairman to be elected as at ordinary meetings.

III. One of the Secretaries to act as conductor, or in the absence of both, a member to be elected for that purpose.

IV. No change to be made in the programme, or extra expense incurred, except by the consent of the majority of the members present.

V. No fees, gratuities, or other expenses to be paid except through the conductor.

VI. Every member or visitor to have the accommodation assigned by the conductor. Where accommodation is limited, consideration will be given to priority of application.

VII. Accommodation cannot be promised unless tickets are obtained before the time mentioned in the special circular.

VIII. Those who attend an excursion, without previous notice, will be liable to extra charge, if extra cost be incurred thereby.

IX. No intoxicating liquors to be provided at the expense of the Club.

BELFAST NATURALISTS' FIELD CLUB.

TWENTY-EIGHTH YEAR.

The Committee offer the following Prizes to be competed for during the Session ending March 31st, 1891 :—

			£	s.	d.
I.	Best Herbarium of Flowering Plants, representing not less than 250 species,	...	£1	0	0
II.	Best Herbarium of Flowering Plants, representing not less than 150 species,	...	0	10	0
III.	Best Collection of Mosses, ...	...	0	10	0
IV.	,, Lichens, ...	...	0	10	0
V.	,, ,, Seaweeds, ...	...	0	10	0
VI.	,, Ferns, Equiseta, and Lycopods,		0	10	0
VII.	.. :: Tertiary and Post-tertiary Fossils, ...	...	0	10	0
VIII.	,, ,, Cretaceous Fossils,...	...	0	10	0
IX.	,, ,, Liassic Fossils, ..	...	0	10	0
X.	Permian and Carboniferous Fossils, ...	...	0	10	0
XI.	.. Older Palæozoic Fossils,	...	0	10	0
XII.	,, ,, Marine Shells, ...	...	0	10	0
XIII.	Land and Freshwater Shells,		0	10	0
XIV.	.. Lepidoptera, ...	...	0	10	0
XV.	,, .. Hymenoptera, ...	...	0	10	0
XVI.	.. .. Coleoptera, ...	...	0	10	0

XVII. Best Collection of Crustacea and Echinodermata, 0 10 0

XVIII. Best Collection of Fungi ; names of species not necessary. ·Collectors may send (post-paid, from time to time during the season) their specimens to Rev. H. W. Lett, M.A., T.C.D., Aghaderg Glebe, Loughbrickland, who will record them to their credit, ... 0 10 0

XIX. Best Collection of Fossil Sponges, ... 0 10 0

XX. Best Collection of 24 Microscopic Slides, illustrating some special branch of Natural History, ... 0 10 0

XXI. Best Collection of 24 Microscopic Slides, shewing general excellence, ... 0 10 0

XXII. Best set of 6 Field Sketches appertaining to Geology, Archæology, or Zoology,   ... 0 10 0

XXIII. Best set of 12 Photographs, illustrative of Irish Archæology,   ...   ---   ... 0 10 0

SPECIAL PRIZES.

XXIV. The President offers a Prize of £1 1s for the Best Set of three or more Original Sketches, to be placed in the Album of the Club. These may be executed in pen and ink, or water colour, and must illustrate one or more ancient monuments somewhere in Ireland. In determining the relative merits of the sketches, accuracy in representing the subjects and their details will have chief place. This Prize is open to the Members of the Ramblers' Sketching Club, and to the Students of the School of Art.

XXV. Mr. William Swanston, F.G S., offers a Prize of 10s. 6d. for Six Photographs from Nature, illustrative of Geology, contributed to the Club's Album.

XXVI. Mr. Francis Joseph Bigger, Solicitor, Belfast, offers a
Prize of £1 1s for the best set of Twelve Photographs
(not less than cabinet size) of Ecclesiastical Structures
mentioned in Reeves' *Ecclesiastical Antiquities of Down
and Connor*, contributed to the Club's Album.   The set
of Photographs taking this Prize cannot be admitted
in competition for Prize XXIII.

CONDITIONS.

No Competitor to obtain more than two Prizes in any year.

No Competitor to be awarded the same Prize twice within three
years.

A member to whom Prize I. has been awarded shall be ineligible to compete for Prize II., unless the plants are additions
to those in previous collection.

In every case where three or more persons compete for a Prize, a
second one, of half its value, will be awarded if the conditions are
otherwise complied with.

All collections to be made personally during the Session in Ireland, except those for Prize XXI., which need not necessarily be Irish,
nor Competitors' own collecting.   The species to be correctly named,
and locality stated, and a list must accompany each collection. The
Flowering Plants to be collected when in flower, and classified according to the Natural System.   The Microscopic Slides to be Competitors' own preparation and mounting.   The Sketches and Photographs to be Competitors' own work, executed during the Session ;
and those sets for which Prizes are awarded, to become the property
of the Club.

No Prizes will be awarded except to such Collections as shall, in
the opinion of the Judges, possess positive merit.

The Prizes to be in books, or suitable scientific objects, at the desire of the successful competitor.

ɳ O T I ᏟᏋ.

---◇---

EXCHANGES OF PROCEEDINGS.

---◇---

Amiens—Societé Linnéenne du Nord de la France.
Memoirs, 1886-88.

Berwickshire Naturalists' Club.
Proceedings, Vol. XII., Part II.

Cardiff Naturalists' Society.
Report and Transactions, Vol. XXI., Part I.

Dublin Science and Art Museum.
List of Irish Birds, by A. G. More, F.L.S., &c.

„   Royal Irish Academy.
Proceedings, Series III., Vol. I., No. 2.
Transactions, Vol. XXIX., Parts XII. and XIII.

Eastbourne Natural History Society.
Transactions, Part III., Vol. II., New Series.

Edinburgh—Botanical Society
Transactions and Proceedings, Vol. XVII., Part III.

Frankfurt—Monatliche Mitthielungen, aus dem Gesammt-
gebliete der Naturwissenschaften.
Nos. 9, 10, 11, 1889-90.

Societatum Litteræ.
Nos. 10, 11, 12, 1889-90.

Hertfordshire Natural History Society and Field Club.
Transactions, Vol. V., Parts 6 and 7.

Liverpool Geological Association.
Journal, Vol. IX., 1888-89.

Shanghai—China.
Catalogue of the Chinese Imperial Maritime Customs Collection at the
United States International Exhibition at Philadelphia, 1886.

Toronto—Canadian Institute.
Annual Report, 1888-89.
Proceedings, Series III., Vol. VII., Fas. I.

U.S.A.—Milwaukee Public Museum.
Annual Report, Seventh.

„   New York Academy of Sciences.
Transactions, Vol. VIII., Nos. 5, 6, 7, 8.

„   Philadelphia Academy of Natural Sciences.
Proceedings, Part II., 1889.

„   Salem—Essex Institute.
Charter and Bye-Laws, 1889.
Do.   Bulletin, Vol. XX., Nos. 1 to 12, Vol. XXI., Nos.
1 to 6.

From Joseph Smith, Junr., Warrington.
Ten detached papers on scientific subjects.

BELFAST NATURALISTS' FIELD CLUB.

TWENTY-EIGHTH YEAR, 1890-91.

LIST OF OFFICERS AND MEMBERS.

PRESIDENT:
WILLIAM GRAY, M.R.I.A.

VICE-PRESIDENT:
JOHN VINYCOMB.

TREASURER:	LIBRARIAN:
S. A. STEWART, F.B.S. Edin.	WILLIAM SWANSTON, F.G.S.

SECRETARIES:

F. W. LOCKWOOD, WARING STREET.	R. LLOYD PRAEGER, B.E., HOLYWOOD.

COMMITTEE:

JOHN J. ANDREW, L.D.S., R.C.S., Eng.	DANIEL M'KEE.
GEORGE DONALDSON.	WILLIAM SWANSTON, F.G.S.
JOHN DONALDSON.	REV. C. HERBT. WADDELL, M.A.
W. A. FIRTH.	ROBERT J. WELCH.
JOHN HAMILTON.	JOSEPH WRIGHT, F.G.S.

Members.

Any changes in the Addresses of Members should be notified to the Secretaries.

Edward Allworthy, Mosaphir, Cave Hill Road.
John Anderson, J.P., F.G.S., East Hillbrook, Holywood.
Robert Anderson, Meadowlands.
J. J. Andrew, L.D.S., R.C.S. Eng., Belgravia, Lisburn Road.
Mrs. Andrews, Seaview, Shore Road.

James M. Barkley, Holywood.
Robert Barklie, Wilmont Terrace.
James Barr, Beechleigh.
William Batt, Sorrento, Windsor.
Miss Emma Beck, Old Lodge Road.
George R. Begley, Wolfhill Lodge, Ligoniel.
James Best, Great Victoria Street.
F. J. Bigger, Ardrie, Antrim Road.
Edward Bingham, Ponsonby Avenue.
Mrs. Blair, Camberwell Terrace.
E. Blair, Camberwell Terrace.
J. H. Boyd, Eblana Street.
Edward Braddell, St. Ives, Malone.
Hugh B. Brandon, Atlantic Avenue.
Chas. H. Brett, Gretton Villa South.
John Thorley Brindley, Ulsterville Avenue.
Rev. John Bristow, St. James's Parsonage.
John Brown, Belair, Windsor Av.
Robert Brown, Donoughmore.
Thomas Brown, Donegall Street.
John Browne, J.P., Ravenhill House.
John Browne, M.R.I.A., Drapersfield, Cookstown.
W. J. Browne, M.R.I.A., Highfield, Omagh.
W. W. Brydon, Silverstream, Greenisland.
Chas. Bulla, Wellington Park Terrace.
Henry Burden, M.D., M.R.I.A., Alfred Street.
J. R. Burnett, Rostellan, Malone Road.

Wm. Campbell, Allworthy Avenue.
Ernest Carr, Botanic Avenue.
Miss Carruthers, Claremont Street.
E. T. Church, Donegall Place.

Stanley B. Coates, L.R.C.P., Edin., Shaftesbury Square.
James Coey, Victoria street.
Wm. F. C. S. Corry, Chatsworth.
Rev. W. Cotter, D.D., Riversdale Terrace, Balmoral.
George B. Coulter, Helen's Bay.
Mrs. Coulter, Helen's Bay.
James Creeth, Riversdale Terrace, Balmoral.
Robert Culbert, Distillery street.
Samuel Cunningham, Glencairn.
Francis Curley, Dunedin.
Mrs. Curley, Dunedin.
William Curry, Botanic Avenue.

Marquis of Dufferin and Ava, Clandeboye (Hon. Mem.)
J. H. Davies, Glenmore Cottage, Lisburn.
Henry Davis, Holywood.
Robt. Day, J.P., F.S.A., M.R.I.A., Cork.
Wakefield H. Dixon, Dunowen.
George Donaldson, Bloomfield.
John Donaldson, Thorndale Terrace.
W. D. Donnan, Holywood.
W. J. Dunlop, Bryson street.

David Elliott, Albert Bridge Road.
George Elliott, Royal Avenue.
George H. Elliott, Lorne Villas, South Parade.
Lavens M. Ewart, J.P., Glenbank.

Godfrey W. Ferguson, Murray's Terrace.
J. H. Ferguson, Belgrave, Knock.
Joseph Firth, Whiterock.
Wm. A. Firth, Glenview Terrace, Springfield Road.
Thomas J. G. Fleming, F.G.S., Limavady.
T. M. H. Flynn, Sunnyside, Bessbrook.

J. Starkie Gardner, F.G.S., Damer Terrace, Chelsea (Hon. Mem.)

R. M. Gilmore, GardenVale Terrace, Athlone.
W. J. Gilmore, Camberwell Villas.
George J. Glen, Hartington Street.
William Godwin, Queen Street.
Rev. David Gordon, Downpatrick.
James Goskar, Carlisle Circus.
James Gourley, J.P., Derryboy, Killyleagh.
Rev.CanonGrainger,D.D.,M.R.I.A., Broughshane.
Robert Graham, Brookview Terrace.
Wm. Gray, M.R.I.A.,Mountcharles.
Miss Gray, Mountcharles.
George Greer, J.P., Woodville, Lurgan.
Edward Gregg, Donegall Pass.

John Hamilton, Mount Street.
Richard Hanna, Charleville Street.
Mann Harbison, Ravenhill Terrace.
Rev. Canon Hartrick, The Rectory, Ballynure.
Sir James Haslett, J.P., Princess Gardens.
Thos. Hassan, Strangemore House.
W. D. Hazleton, Cliftonville.
F. A. Heron, Cultra.
J. S. Holden, M.D., F.G.S., Sudbury, Suffolk (Cor. Mem.).
John Horner, Clonard Foundry.
Alexander Hunter, Northern Bank.
W. J. Hurst, J.P., Drumaness, Ballynahinch.
James Imrie, Fitzroy Avenue.

Hugh Smith Jefferson, Rosnakill, Strandtown.
James F. Johnston, Holywood.
Wm. J. Johnston, J.P., Dunesk, Stranmillis.
Prof. T. Rupert Jones, F.R.S., Chelsea, London (Hon. Mem.).

John Kane, LL.B.
Archibald Kent, Newington Street.
Wm. Kernahan, Wellington Park.
George Kidd, Lisnatore, Dunmurry.
F. Kirkpatrick, Ann Street.
Wm. J. Knowles, M.R.I.A., Ballymena.
Robert A. Kyle, Richmond.
W. W. Lamb, Salisbury Avenue.

Prof. Charles Lapworth, F.G.S., Mason College, Birmingham (Hon. Mem.).
F. R. Lepper, Carnalea.
Rev. H. W. Lett, M.A., T.C.D., Aghaderg Glebe, Loughbrickland.
Prof. E. A. Letts, Ph.D., F.C.S., Craigavad.
Frederick W. Lockwood, Wellington Park Terrace.
James Logan, Donegall Street.
Joseph Lowe, Essex Street.
W. B. Lowson, Chichester Park.
H.W. Luther,M.D.,Chlorine House.

John Mackenzie, C.E., Myrtlefield.
Henry Magee, Eglantine Avenue.
Rev. J. J. Major, Belvoir Hall, Ballymacarrett.
Harold Malcolmson, Holywood.
Greer Malcomson,GranvilleTerrace.
Jas. Malcomson, Rosemount,Knock.
Mrs.Malcomson, Rosemount,Knock.
John Marsh, Glenlyon, Holywood.
Mrs. Marsh, Glenlyon, Holywood.
Joseph C. Marsh, Castleton Terrace.
J. M'Clelland Martin, Oceanic Avenue.
Henry Merrick, Great Victoria Street.
Seaton Forrest Milligan, M.R.I.A., Royal.Terrace.
R. Joynt Morrison, Limestone Road.
Thomas Morrison, Great George's Street.
David Morrow, Church Hill, Holywood.
John Morton, Clifton Park Avenue.
James Murdoch, Denmark Street.
Joseph John Murphy,OsbornePark.
Mrs. Agnes Murray, Ulster Terrace.
J. R. Musgrave, J.P., Drumglass House, Malone.

Thomas M'Alister, Eglinton Street.
Joseph M'Chesney, Holywood.
Francis P. M'Clean, Huntly Villas.
H. M'Cleery, Clifton Park Avenue.
Rev. Ed. M'Clure, M.A., M.R.I.A., Onslow Place, South Kensington, London (Cor. Mem.).
John M'Clure, Donlure, Bloomfield.

Sir Thomas M'Clure, Bart,Belmont.
Wm. J. M'Clure, Elizabeth Street.
Jas. M'Connell, Caledonia Terrace.
F. W. M'Cullough, C.E., Chichester
  Street.
W. F. MacElheran, Botanic Avenue.
Miss M'Gaw, Wellington Park
  Terrace.
J. H. MacIlwaine, Brandon Villa.
Mrs. MacIlwaine, Brandon Villa.
Daniel M'Kee, Adela Place.
W. S. M'Kee, Fleetwood Street.
Alexander MacLaine, J.P , Queen's
  Elms.
John M'Liesh, The Mount,
  Mountpottinger.
John M'Liesh, Jun., The Mount.
Robert M'Liesh, The Mount.
William MacMillan, Enniscorthy.
Jas. M'Mordie, Belgravia Avenue.
John M'Stay, College Square East.

Lucien Nepveu, Claremont Street.
W. Courtney Nesbitt, Kinnaird
  Terrace.
Wm. Nicholl, Donegall Square
  North.
Jerdan Nichols,Meadowbank Street.
H. J. Nicholson, Windsor Gardens.
Mrs. Nicholson, Windsor Gardens.

Henry O'Neill,M.D.,College Square
  East.
James O'Neill,M.A.,College Square
  East.
H. Lamont Orr, Clanbrassil Terrace.
A. T. Osborne, Eglantine Avenue.

David C. Patterson, Holywood.
Robert LloydPatterson,J.P.,F.L.S.,
  Croft House, Holywood.
Robert Patterson, Windsor Park
  Terrace, Lisburn Road.
William H. Patterson, M.R.I.A.,
  Garranard, Strandtown.
Herbert Pearce, Fitzroy Avenue.
James J. Phillips, 61,Royal Avenue.
William H. Phillips, Lemonfield,
  Holywood.
E. W. Pim, Elmwood Terrace.
John Pim, J.P., Bonaven, Antrim
  Road.

Joshua Pim, Slieve-na-Failthe,
  Whiteabbey.
Thomas W. Pim, The Lodge,
  Strandtown.
E. A. Praeger, Woodburn, Holy-
  wood.
R. Lloyd Praeger, B.A., B.E.,
  Holywood.

Joseph Radley, Prospect Hill, Lis-
  burn.
John H. Rea, M.D., Shaftesbury
  Square.
D. Redmond, Antrim.
Right Rev. Dr. Reeves, Bishop of
  Down and Connor and Dromore,
  Conway House. Dunmurry.
Robert Reid, King Street.
Richard Ridings, Hampton Terrace.
Rev. George Robinson, M.A., Beech
  Hill House, Armagh.
George Robinson, Woodview, Holy-
  wood.
Hugh Robinson, M.R.I.A., Helen's
  View, Antrim Road.
Jas. R. Robinson, George's Terrace.
William A. Robinson,J.P.,Culloden,
  Cultra.
Richard Ross, M.D., Wellington
  Place.
Wm. A. Ross, Iva-Craig, Craigavad.
John Russell, C.E., The Eyries,
  Newcastle.
Robt. A. Russell,Colinview Terrace.
John Ryan, Myrtle Hill Terrace,
  Cork.

James Shanks,Ballyfounder, Porta-
  ferry.
Chas. Sheldon, M.A., B.Sc., D.Lit.,
  Royal Academical Institution.
Edward Smith, Chichester Terrace.
Rev. W. S. Smith, The Manse,
  Antrim.
Rev. Canon Smythe, M.A., Coole
  Glebe, Carnmoney.
Wilson Smyth, Virginia Street.
Adam Speers, B.Sc., Holywood.
A. C. Stannus, Holywood.
Sir N. A. Staples, Bart., Lissan,
  (Life Mem.).
Jas. Stelfox, Oakleigh, Ormeau Park.
John Stevenson, Coolavin.
J. M'N. Stevenson, Carrickfergus.

S. A. Stewart, Springfield road.
William Swanston, F.G.S., Cliftonville Avenue.
Mrs. Swanston, Cliftonville Avenue.
Richard Glascott Symes, M.A., F.G.S., Portrush.
Samuel Symington, BallyoranHouse.

Alex. Tate, C.E., Longwood.
Prof. Ralph Tate, F.G.S., F.L.S., Adelaide, South Australia, (Hon. Mem.).
H. F. Thomas, Lower Crescent.
S. G. Thomas, Limestone Road.
Mrs. H. Thompson, Crosshill, Windsor.
George Thomson, Falls Road.
Prof. James Thomson, LL.D., F.R.S., Florentine Gardens, Glasgow, (Hon. Mem.).
John Todd, Clonaven.
W. A. Todd, Elgin Terrace.
W. A. Traill, B.E., M.A.I., Portrush.
W. J. Trelford, Vicinage Park.
James Turner, Mountain Bush.
Jas. G. Turtle, Cambridge Terrace.

John Vinycomb, Holywood.

Rev. C. Herbert Waddell, M.A., Whitewell.
Miss Wardell, Cavehill Road.

W. F. Wakeman, M.R.I.A., Dublin (Cor. Mem.)
Thos. R. Walkington, Edenvale.
George G. Ward, Eversleigh, Strandtown.
Isaac W. Ward, Salisbury Terrace.
Thomas Watson, Shipquay Gate, Londonderry.
Charles W. Watts, F.I.C., Holborn Terrace.
Isaac Waugh, Clifton Park Avenue.
Robert J. Welch, Lonsdale Street.
Walter L. Wheeler, Lennoxvale.
Wm. Whitla, M.D., J.P., College Square North.
James Wilson, Oldforge, Dunmurry.
Jas. Wilson, Ballybundon, Killinchy.
James F. Wilson, Greenville Terrace.
Berkley D. Wise, C.E., Northern Counties Railway.
Rev. Robert Workman, M.A., Rubane, Glastry.
Thomas Workman, J.P., Craigdarragh.
W. C. Wright, Lauriston, Derrievolgie Avenue.
Joseph Wright, F.G.S., Alfred Street.
Mrs. Wright, Alfred Street.
William Wylie, Mountpleasant.

Robert Young, C.E., Rathvarna.

ANNUAL REPORT AND PROCEEDINGS

OF THE

BELFAST

NATURALISTS'

FIELD CLUB

For the Year ending the 31st March, 1891.

(TWENTY-EIGHTH YEAR)

SERIES II.

VOLUME III.

PART IV.

1890-91.

Belfast :

PRINTED FOR THE CLUB,

BY ALEXANDER MAYNE & BOYD, 2 CORPORATION STREET,
PRINTERS TO QUEEN'S COLLEGE, BELFAST.

1891.

REPORT

OF THE

BELFAST NATURALISTS' FIELD CLUB,

FOR THE

Year ending 31st March, 1891.

N submitting their twenty-eighth Annual Report, your Committee have satisfaction in recording a year of marked activity and steady progress. The membership of the Club, which at the beginning of the year stood at 251, now numbers 281, 28 names having been withdrawn from the list through death or resignation, and 58 new members having been elected.

The Summer programme was a successful one, and was carried out in every particular. Excepting only the first day of the long excursion, the Club was on each occasion favoured with magnificent weather, in spite of a generally unfavourable season. On two excursions of the year the party numbered over sixty. The field meetings were as follow :— '

1. Kilroot and Whitehead	24th May.
2. Killinchy and Strangford Lough	14th June.
3. Magheramorne and Islandmagee	5th July.
4. Cushendall and district	30th & 31st July.
5. Cave Hill	16th August.
6. Glenarm	6th September.

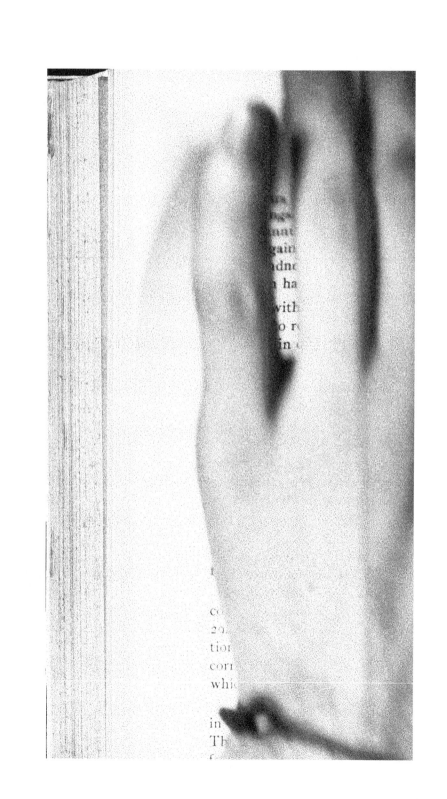

is greatly diminished by thir being unmounted and
, and that several of ther are erroneously named.
ere is an undesirable and unnecessary repetition of
nest species, as in the case f *Hypnum cupressiforme*,
presented by no less tha fourteen separate speci-
task of examining the cdection is thus rendered
t and less instructive, and he objects contemplated
in these competitions a not so fully attained as

Best collection of Ferns, quiseta, and Lycopods.—
nnan is a competitor, wh a series of 32 specimens.
represents 21 species of Ferns, 7 of Equiseta, and
s. It thus includes to-thirds of the vascular
which are native in Irehd, and we consider it to
ze offered for these plant

In competition for th prize Miss Sydney M.
ubmits a number of foss, representing 24 species.
mens were obtained from he Chalk and Greensand
County of Antrim, and clude the greater part of
characteristic fossils of t Irish Cretaceous strata.
mpson has complied with ll the conditions of the
on, and we consider that er collection merits the
ich is now awarded to her.

ze 11. Miss Thompson has sit in a collection in com-
for this prize also, which corists mainly of Graptolites
e Silurian schists of County Dwn. There are specimens
much-disputed *Oldhamia* fror the Wicklow Cambrian
and 14 species of Graptolites. Taking into account the
r and difficulty involved in daining such a series, we
der the collection highly credible to the collector, and
no hesitation in awarding th prize to Miss Sydney
pson.

rize 16. For this competition Rv. S. A. Brenan, B.A., has a
s of Beetles which we consider derving of the prize. The
mens number nearly 400, and roresent 182 species, which

The Committee beg to thankfully acknowledge the kind permission of the Countess of Shaftesbury to visit the Deerpark, and of Robert Armstrong, Esq., to pass through the grounds of Thronemount, on the occasion of the excursion to Cave Hill; and the valuable assistance of Mr. B. D. Wise, A.M.I.C.E., a member of the Club, to the geologists at Whitehead.

The Winter Session opened on November 1st with a Social Meeting, the attendance at which was above the average of some years past. An exhibition illustrative of the art of chromo-lithography was made the specialité of the evening, and through the courtesy of three well-known local firms, to whom the best thanks of the Committee are due, a very interesting and instructive exhibition was brought together. In addition to an evening devoted to the microscope, to be presently referred to, five ordinary meetings were held, at which thirteen different communications were brought forward. The dates and particulars of the Winter meetings, all of which were well attended, are given below.

1st Nov.	Social Meeting.
19th Nov.	Opening Address by the President. "A Notice of some ancient Grave-slabs found near Dundonald," W. H. Patterson, M.R.I.A. "On Foraminifera which construct their Tests of Sponge-spicules," Joseph Wright, F.G.S.
16th Dec.	"The Primrose and its Allies," W. D. Donnan. "Some new or rare North of Ireland Plants," R. Lloyd Praeger, B.E. "Strange Pets I have had," W. H. Phillips, F.R.H.S.
20th Jan.	Proposal to transfer the books which the Club has received as exchanges or otherwise to the Belfast Free Public Library; the Secretaries. Suggestion to form a Joint Microscopical Section of the Club and Natural History and Philosophical Society; the Secretaries. "Four Days in Arran," F. W. Lockwood.
17th Feb.	"A Chat about Lichens," Henry Davis. 'The Birds of the Bog Meadows," Robert Patterson.
17th March	Microscopical Evening.
14th April	"Notes on some rare Mosses and Hepatics found in Ulster," Rev H. W. Lett, M.A. "The Gold Antiquities of Ireland," C. Winston Dugan, M.A.

The question of the furthering of the science of microscopy by the Club's agency having been brought before the Committee, was referred to a general meeting, at which it was decided to form a special Section of the Club for the prosecution and encouragement of microscopical work. This Section, which has its own Chairman and Committee of Management, held its Inaugural Meeting on March 17th, when twenty members attended with their instruments, and illustrated nearly as many different branches of microscopical research, to the satisfaction of a company of some two hundred members and their friends.

The Committee trust that the new Section will receive the support of all members who are interested in this important department of the Club's work. Application for membership of the Section, which does not involve any additional fee, should be made to the Secretary of the Section, Mr. H. M'Cleery, 82 Cliftonpark Avenue, Belfast.

By a resolution passed at last Annual Meeting, a special committee was appointed for the purpose of systematising the photographic work of the Club. The report of this committee will be laid before the meeting.

The means available for the cataloguing and storing of the Club's books and exchanges having been considered by the Committee, an application was made to a general meeting of the Club for power to approach the management of the Belfast Free Public Library with a view of ascertaining whether certain privileges of consultation would be granted to members, should the Club hand over to the Library their entire collection of books. This sanction was duly obtained, and overtures were made to the Library Committee, but your Committee regret that the terms proposed on behalf of the Library were not such as they considered themselves justified in accepting.

The Committee have pleasure in being this year again in a position to publish in the Proceedings a meteorological summary, such as was for many years contributed by the kindness of the late Mr. Lancelot Turtle, J.P. Abstracts for the last three years will appear with the forthcoming number of the Proceedings. These will carry on the record continuously from the last annual summary supplied by Mr. Turtle. The Committee again thank the Council of Queen's College, Belfast, whose kindness in granting access to the records kept in that institution has enabled these abstracts to be prepared.

It is with great satisfaction that your Committee are this year able to record a large increase in the number of collections submitted in competition for the prizes offered by the Club and by private members, eight collections having been sent in to the Secretaries by the date specified. The advantages to be derived from a participation in this important branch of the Club's work, both by the habits of close and accurate observation and neatness of manipulation which it induces, and by the assistance which it renders towards a systematic knowledge of the natural history and archæology of our district, cannot be too strongly impressed on members.

The following is the report of the judges appointed to examine the collections submitted, and to award the prizes :—

" We have examined the collections sent in in competition for the prizes, and have to report as follows :—

Prize 1. Best collection of Flowering Plants.—The only competitor is Mr. W. D. Donnan, whose collection represents 294 species and eight varieties. These plants, which are additional to 254 sent in last year, are well selected as specimens, correctly classified and named, and well worthy of the prize, which is now awarded to Mr. Donnan.

Prize 3. Rev. S. A. Brenan, B.A., has collected and sent in a large quantity of mosses, representing nearly 100 species. This collection includes several of the rarer species not heretofore recorded from the North of Antrim, and shows a commendable amount of zeal and energy. On these grounds we consider Mr. Brenan's plants deserving of the prize offered by the Club, and we accordingly award it to him. While making this award, it is necessary to observe that the value of these specimens is greatly diminished by their being unmounted and unclassified, and that several of them are erroneously named. Further, there is an undesirable and unnecessary repetition of the commonest species, as in the case of *Hypnum cupressiforme,* which is represented by no less than fourteen separate specimens. The task of examining the collection is thus rendered more difficult and less instructive, and the objects contemplated by the Club in these competitions are not so fully attained as should be.

Prize 6. Best collection of Ferns, Equiseta, and Lycopods.— Mr. W. D. Donnan is a competitor, with a series of 32 specimens. This collection represents 21 species of Ferns, 7 of Equiseta, and 4 of Lycopods. It thus includes two-thirds of the vascular cryptogams which are native in Ireland, and we consider it to merit the prize offered for these plants.

Prize 8. In competition for this prize Miss Sydney M. Thompson submits a number of fossils, representing 24 species. These specimens were obtained from the Chalk and Greensand rocks of the County of Antrim, and include the greater part of the most characteristic fossils of the Irish Cretaceous strata. Miss Thompson has complied with all the conditions of the competition, and we consider that her collection merits the prize, which is now awarded to her.

Prize 11. Miss Thompson has sent in a collection in competition for this prize also, which consists mainly of Graptolites from the Silurian schists of County Down. There are specimens of the much-disputed *Oldhamia* from the Wicklow Cambrian rocks, and 14 species of Graptolites. Taking into account the labour and difficulty involved in obtaining such a series, we consider the collection highly creditable to the collector, and have no hesitation in awarding the prize to Miss Sydney Thompson.

Prize 16. For this competition Rev. S. A. Brenan, B.A., has a series of Beetles which we consider deserving of the prize. The specimens number nearly 400, and represent 182 species, which may be accounted a good amount of work for one season. It is to be regretted that Mr. Brenan was unfortunately prevented, by circumstances beyond his control, from making such a scientific arrangement and classification of these specimens as would display them to the greatest advantage, and more fully meet the requirements of the Club.

Prize 20. Mr. William Hanna, B.A., submits a series of microscopic slides in competition for this prize, consisting of a series of sections illustrating the development of the chick. They are very complete, and highly illustrative of a subject not hitherto undertaken by any member of the Club. The slides as such are excellent in every respect, displaying a scientific knowledge and manipulative skill that is highly creditable to the collector, who beyond question merits the prize offered.

Prize 23. Miss A. H. Tate competes for this prize with twelve photographs illustrative of Irish archæology. This set includes several local remains not hitherto illustrated, and we have much pleasure in awarding the prize to Miss Tate.

(Signed),   { WILLIAM GRAY.
                 { WILLIAM SWANSTON.
                 { S. A. STEWART."

An application was lately received from the Royal Meteorological Society requesting the assistance of the Club in the department of phenological observations. The Committee are glad to state that no difficulty was experienced in providing from among the Club's members the requisite number of observers in the Counties of Down and Antrim, and they take this opportunity of thanking those members for their willing aid.

The attention of members is again called to the work which is being carried on by the Belfast Natural History and Philosophical Society in regard to the compilation of a work on the vertebrate fauna of Ulster, and they trust that all assistance wil be given, and all occurrences of rare birds, fishes, &c., immediately communicated to the Secretaries of the Fauna Committee, Belfast Museum, College Square North.

In conclusion, your Committee have again to return their thanks to those kindred societies and public bodies who have favoured the Club with an interchange of their Proceedings and other publications during the past year.

		£	s	d
To Balance from last Account	...	£14	0	5
,, Subscriptions	...	66	10	0
,, Tickets for Social Meeting	...	1	12	0
,, Gain on Excursions	...	0	16	3
,, Sales of the Guide to Belfast	...	0	6	6
,, ,, Proceedings	...	0	13	6
,, ,, Flora N.E. Ireland	...	0	4	6
		£84	3	2
To Balance ...	...	£4	3	0

				£	s	d
By Expenses of Social Meeting	...	...		£6		1
,, Printing Annual Proceedings	...	...		23		1
,, Stationery, Printing, and Advertising	...			16		1
,, Book Case	...	...		2		
,, Meteorological Summary, 3 years	...			3		
,, Rent of Lecture Hall	...	...		8		
,, Commission collecting Subscriptions	...			3		1
,, Prizes Awarded	...	...		4		1
,, General Expenses :—						
Postages	...	£7	3	3		
Insurance	...	0	16	6		
Delivery Circulars	...	1	10	0		
Incidental	...	2	7	6	11	1
,, Balance in Hand	...				4	
					£84	

Audited and found correct.

R. LLOYD PRAE

SUMMER SESSION.

———◆———

The following Excursions were made during the Summer Session :—

On May 24th, to

KILROOT AND WHITEHEAD.

The first excursion was made on Saturday, May 24th, Kilroot and Whitehead being the district visited. Leaving Belfast by the 9.50 train, the party was joined by local contingents at several stations *en route*, so that nearly forty members and their friends mustered on the platform at Kilroot. Arrived there, a move was made first to the gravel beds, a short distance west of the station, long known for the flint implements which they yield. The deposit, which consists of stratified gravel, composed mainly of local rocks, and containing marine shells, is now nearly worked out, having been utilized for railway ballast; but a number of rude flint flakes were collected. The secretaries here announced that two books would be offered as prizes for collections made during the day—one for the best collection of flowering plants, the other for the best collection of rocks, minerals, and fossils. The members were not slow to enter into eager competition for the prizes, and as the party proceeded along the railway towards Whitehead every hedge-bank and copse were carefully explored for botanical specimens, the ladies of the party proving themselves especially active and observant. A member of the Club, Mr. B. D. Wise, M.Inst.C.E., chief engineer of the Northern Counties Railway, having kindly placed at the disposal of the Club a lorry manned by stalwart navvies, it was speedily loaded with cameras, vasculums, and geological hammers, and proceeded down the line in front of the party. At one point a detour was made in order to pay a visit to the site of the old church from which the district *Kilroot* derives its name, and which is associated for a brief period with the early days of the great Dean Swift. This is a very ancient ecclesiastical foundation. O'Laverty, in his valuable history of the diocese, gives it as the " Ceall-Ruaidh " where St. Ailbé (whose death is recorded A.D. 527) landed with a small band of disciples, after having " sailed in a great calm over the sea in a most wretched boat." In acknowledgment of their merciful preservation he directed his companion, St. Colman, to build here a church, and, when the latter objected, on the plea of scarcity of water, St. Ailbé blessed a stone, and a small spring of water trickled out, " which," said he, "though small, will never fail, and will continue till the end of the world." The tiny stream still forms a well for the adjoining farmhouse, and overflows into a pretty duck-pond. Of the first ancient cell or oratory no trace now remains ; and of the church or churches which must have succeeded it, the foundations are buried under the long grass of the graveyard, though a rude stone font still stands in its centre. Abutting on a corner of the graveyard are the picturesque ivy-covered ruins of "Brice's" or " Bruce's " house, surrounded with tall trees, which now form the

"Copse where once the garden smiled,
And still where many a garden flower grows wild."

Amongst these the sweet-scented verbena, not often seen except under glass, was observed growing luxuriantly to a height of eight or ten feet. This mansion house is reported to have been once the residence of the bishops of Connor. Re-suming their walk along the railway, the party soon reached the commencement of the great bank of New Red Sandstone which extends along the shore till it is cut off by the basaltic rocks of Whitehead. These Keuper Marls, as the upper divi-sion of the New Red Sandstone is called, here form a steeply sloping bank of bright red hue, traversed by irregular seams of gypsum and selenite. Now the hammers and picks were got to work, and a number of fine specimens obtained. The sulphate of lime occurs here in various forms—in transparent blocks formed of thin lamellæ, which can easily be split asunder, which form suitable examples for experiments in polarization of light ; in lustrous masses of fibrous texture, to which form most of the larger specimens belong ; and in white granular masses composed of numbers of small transparent crystals loosely bound together. Proceeding slowly along this interesting escarpment, a halt was called just beyond where the railway emerges from a deep cutting through a projecting spur of red marl, flanked by a trap dyke, and opens into the pretty bay on the southern side of Whitehead. Here, the Secretary's whistle having called the party together, the formal meeting of the day was held, the only business transacted being the pleasant formality of electing a number of new members. A short descriptive address was then given by the President of the Club (Mr. William Gray, M.R.I.A.) on the geology of the neighbour-hood. In the course of his remarks he pointed out that the geological features displayed in the immediate vicinity of where they now were, illustrated admirably the structure of the greater part of Antrim and the adjoining counties. Looking southward from Whitehead over the undulating hills of County Down to where rose the distant blue peaks of the Mourne Mountains was, as it were, looking backward into remote geological time, and the record which it has left is displayed in the series of rocks that extend from point to point. The granite represents the fundamental rock—the base on which the whole series of stratified rocks has been laid down. Lying against the flanks of the Mourne range, and stretching out over Down and Armagh, we have a vast accumulation of Silurian rocks, containing in some places abundant remains of a strange and very ancient fauna, as described in Mr. Swanston's exhaustive and very interesting paper dealing with that subject. Immensely newer than the Silurians are the lowest beds exposed in this part of the County Antrim—the Triassic rocks which crop out along the slopes that flank the base of nearly all our Antrim escarpments, and which consist of red sandstones, clays, and marls, containing beds of rocksalt and gypsum. The upper strata of the Triassic rocks pass gradually into the Lower Lias beds, where the latter occur, but we miss the great series of Jurassic rocks, such as the Bath and Portland Oolites. The Cretaceous rocks, Chalk and Greensand, rest upon the Lower Lias, or on the New Red, where the Lias is absent. The Chalk constitutes the white cliffs that are so familiar to us all round the Antrim coast, and which so enhance the beauty of our district. It is made up almost entirely of the shells of microscopic animals, and was deposited as soft mud at the bottom of an ancient sea. Then, above all, is the Tertiary formation, represented by the exceptional series of basaltic rocks, which have been forced up by internal forces from profound depths below, and have spread in the form of great sheets of lava over the ancient surface. It will therefore be seen that the geology of County Antrim includes five main formations, which occur in the following descending order—Trap, Chalk, Greensand, Lias, and New Red Sandstone. The sequence may be diagrammatically represented by one's open hand, a space being left between the second and third fingers. The thumb indicates the exceptional trap rocks. The four fingers represent the stratified deposits, Chalk, Greensand, Lias, and New Red Sandstone. The parting between the second and third fingers represents the absent series of Oolitic or Jurassic rocks.

Meanwhile the photographers of the party, regardless of the fascinations of geology, were preparing for a royal salute from a whole battery of cameras; and a pretty study they had to beguile them away. A clear blue lagoon of still water lay in front, crossed by a bridge of several spans, supported on columns of white chalk. On the further side stood a row of whitewashed cottages, nestling at the foot of a steep bank, which, covered with a blaze of yellow whins, rose to a height of several hundred feet, terminating in the precipitous escarpment of Whitehead. But the abrupt appearance of an unceremonious goods train, which came flying round a sharp curve in the rear, effected a sudden interruption in the proceedings, and produced some striking examples of instantaneous work on the part of some knights of the camera who had incautiously pitched their tents between the metals. The shore at this point, where the sea was eating into the bank of soft marl, offered a fine section of the beds—a cliff over fifty feet high, with an irregular network of veins of selenite—while on the beach, at its base, huge blocks of the same mineral were lying about. This place also furnished the curious phenomenon of a raised beach, full of recent marine shells, apparently underlying a considerable depth of Triassic rocks. Needless to say, a landslip, such as frequently occurs here, accounted for the anomaly. After a short inspection of the outcrop of Greensand at the base of the Chalk, the party passed through the tunnel which pierces the head, and visited the large quarry near by, which displays excellent examples of columnar basaltic structure. Then an adjournment was made to the prettily-situated refreshment rooms beyond the railway station, where, after a hearty tea, the examination of the botanical and geological collections was gone into, Messrs. Stewart and Praeger acting as judges. For the botanical prize there was keen competition, Miss Donaldson being first with a collection of sixty-three species, and Mrs. Wise a good second with fifty-nine, while two other ladies followed closely with fifty-seven and fifty-one species respectively. The geological prize was awarded to Mr. M'Kee, whose collection included ten species of fossils from the Chalk, Greensand, and Lias, besides a number of rock specimens. Among the plants the best species found were the purple willow (*Salix purpurea*) and one of the interesting group of the *Characeæ* (*Nitella opaca*). A rare butterfly, the Little Blue (*Polyommatus alsus*), was obtained on the slopes near Whitehead, and also the chrysalis of the Burnet moth. The prizes having been awarded, the road was taken for the railway station, and the party reached Belfast at 7.30.

On June 14th, to

KILLINCHY AND STRANGFORD LOUGH.

The second excursion was made on June 14th to Killinchy and Strangford Lough, and again the Club were favoured with magnificent weather. The morning, indeed, was somewhat gloomy, but, trusting to the indication of a high and steady barometer, an unexpectedly numerous party assembled at the Ulster Hall at ten o'clock, and were soon rattling through the town in three well-appointed brakes, bound for the shores of Strangford Lough. Nor did the weather disappoint those who, overlooking its somewhat fickle disposition, had put their trust in it ; by the time Dundonald was reached the party were revelling in the bright sunshine of a perfect June day. Passing through Comber, no halt was made till Balloo Crossroads, near Killinchy, were reached, at which point the party dismounted to visit a fine old earthen fort, or rath, which stands by the side of the Saintfield road. It is still in a tolerable state of preservation ; the fosse which surrounds it is of considerable depth, and a portion of the breastwork which surmounted the steep earthen wall and protected the interior is still intact. Resuming the journey, the main road was forsaken near Moorball, and a bye road led down towards the lough, which now appeared in front, affording exquisite glimpses of grassy islands, and bays and lagoons of intensest blue. Beyond lay the long fertile stretch of the Ards peninsula, over which the blue mountains of Wigtonshire and the Isle of Man were distinctly visible. A lane winding by the water's edge led to Ringhaddy Castle, standing in

picturesque decay on the inner extremity of what was formerly
an island, though now joined to the mainland by a substantial
causeway. The photographers were now in their element, and
for a time focussing and exposing were the order of the day.
Crowning the hill, which rises immediately behind the castle,
are the remains of Ringhaddy Church—a simple nave, the
crumbling walls of which are crowned with polypody and
spleenwort. The east window appears to have been of comparatively large size. Surrounding the site of the church two
faint circles of earthwork may be traced, which, however, are
probably of comparatively modern date, and may have formed
the boundary of an old churchyard in proximity to the building.
The secretary's whistle now called the party together on the
wooded margin of the lough, where two large boats lay ready
on the calm water. The embarkation being effected, the brown
lug-sails were hoisted, and before a gentle easterly breeze the
boats glided out on the calm blue waters of Strangford Lough,
and shaped their course northward among the islands. Such
was the clearness of the water that the forests of *Zostera* and
Chorda which grew on the bottom, tenanted by their marine
inhabitants, could be minutely examined from the boat's side
as they passed by in succession, interspersed with barren gravelly
patches, and deeper tracts where the bottom was not visible.
Gliding smoothly onward, Roe Island and Trasnagh Island
were passed on the right hand, and Darragh Island and Conly
Island on the left, and rounding Sketrick Island the boats ran
before the wind up a narrow winding channel, and soon their
keels grated on the shingle at Ballydoran. A short walk brought
the party to Sketrick Castle, visited by the Club on one of their
excursions three years ago, but which can well afford a second
visit. A massive square keep rises on the shore of the island,
guarding the narrow causeway which forms the sole connection
with the mainland. A huge piece has fallen, leaving a wide
gothic arch in the front wall of the castle, but it still stands, a
grim reminder of past troublous times. Advancing on it by a
winding road, the Club made a rapid reconnoitre of the position,

but, instead of steel-clad warriors pacing the massive battlements with clanking stride, the only visible enemy consisted of two parsons, reposing in luxurious ease on the summit of the mossy wall. A field battery of quick-firing cameras was speedily brought into action, and under cover of their well-directed fire a storming party crossed the causeway, and soon the mystic emblems of the Field Club were seen on the topmost pinnacle of the tower. The party now proceded on foot past Whiterock towards Killinchy, and, being met on the way by the machines, they drove through Killinchy village to Ballygowan, the bog on each side of the road being brightened with extensive patches of snow-white cotton grass, and tall spikes of purple foxglove. On the way from Whiterock several of our less common plants were noted. In Killinchy village the chervil (*Chaerophyllum anthriscus*) grew in some abundance, and in fields near the same place the shepherd's needle (*Scandix pecten-Veneris*) and the toothed corn salad (*Valerianella dentata*) were found growing in profusion. At Ballygowan an important part of the day's duties was effected in the shape of tea, which was provided on substantial lines by Mrs. Magee, after which the business meeting of the day was held—the Vice-President (Mr. John Vinycomb) in the chair, when a number of new members were elected. Then the brakes were once more mounted, and punctually at 8.30 Belfast was reached, after a highly successful and enjoyable day.

On July 5th, to

MAGHERAMORNE AND ISLANDMAGEE.

The third excursion of the season was taken on Saturday, the 5th July, to Magheramorne and Islandmagee. Notwithstanding the unpropitious weather of the previous week, a good-sized party mustered at the Northern Counties Railway, and were rewarded by seeing the clouds of the morning rapidly dispersed before a brisk north wind, which covered the wavelets of Larne Lough with caps of white foam. The members of the party first took their steps to the large quarry close to Magheramorne station, whence limestone is shipped to Glasgow and other British ports.   The white Chalk with flints is here quarried in two levels, making altogether a thickness of considerably over a hundred feet.   Its surface, as seen in the upper quarry, is very uneven, having evidently formed at one time an ancient land surface, the hollows of which are now filled with rolled flints, covered with a layer of volcanic basalt, as usual in the district.   The basalt, in turn, has its coating of the glacial epoch, but in this case the ordinary yellow Boulder Clay is only about four or five feet thick, and between it and the basalt is a partially stratified bed of brown gravel, apparently an interglacial deposit local in its character.   The Boulder Clay, gravel, and basalt all thin out rapidly to the northward, and have evidently been subjected to a powerful denuding agency coming from that direction.   After witnessing from a safe distance the firing of several "shots," the party returned to the shore, and crossed in a capacious ferryboat to the opposite side. The route was then taken along the flat beach towards Barney's Point.   The numerous boulders, relics of the ice age, made walking in some places a little difficult, but the fringe of stranded *Zostera marina* which marked the extreme limit of the highest spring tides formed a strip of soft carpet easy to the feet.   The pursuit of some moth or butterfly, or speculation upon some wave- or ice-borne lump of quartz or conglomerate, passed the time till the point was reached, a place well known amongst local geologists as one of the best outcrops of the Lias.   The tide was unfortunately too high to allow access to the more fossiliferous beds, but a careful search amongst the gravel of the upper part of the beach was rewarded by a number of characteristic fossils, including several small, but nearly perfect ammonites, and the fragments of many of a large size.   An examination of the sand at high-water mark showed also many minute shells, spines of echinoderms, &c., of Liassic age.   Striking inland from here, the party returned towards Larne by the road, which skirts a narrow deep valley that bisects the island, and which during a period of greater submergence would have turned it into two or three instead of one island as at present. The " Druids' altar," a fine cromlech, with a capstone that weighs about five tons, resting upon four other stones, was passed, and some members also visited the iron ore quarry near by, which is no longer worked. The swell rolling in from the open sea made the passage over the ferry a somewhat lively affair, though of short duration. An American liner lay at the quay taking in iron ore, and the new cross-channel steamer Princess Victoria had her steam up ready for starting, whilst the travelling crane was busy at the shipment of boxes of salmon for the English markets, of which during the season it seems upwards of thirty tons are shipped daily. Then came the rush of passengers from the Belfast train, in five minutes all were aboard, and the Princess Victoria was steaming full speed out into the Channel. The party of naturalists made their way to the King's Arms, and after the much needed refreshment of tea adjourned to the old graveyard of the Inver Church. The original building has been replaced by the present comparatively modern structure, but some of the stones in the graveyard bear the date of over two centuries back, 1633 showing on one of them.

On July 30th and 31st, to

CUSHENDALL AND NEIGHBOURHOOD.

The two-day excursion of the present season was held on July 30th and 31st, Cushendall and district being the locality selected by the Committee out of a large number of interesting spots proposed by members at the last annual meeting. On all three previous excursions of the present session the Club were favoured with magnificent weather, in spite of a generally unfavourable season, and it was only to be expected that such good fortune could not last for ever. Wednesday morning looked unsettled, and a comparatively small number of members and friends sallied forth. Among these one-half were ladies, who, to their credit be it said, cheerfully faced the probability of a downpour of rain among the Antrim mountains in the noble cause of science, and subsequently endured rain, wind, and mud with a calm indifference worthy of true naturalists. Leaving Belfast by the 9.5 train, a strong contingent joined the party at Ballymena, where the narrow-gauge railway was taken. The morning had brightened, and a brilliant gleam of sunshine made the hopes of the party rise in spite of falling aneroids; but as the railway, steadily ascending, allowed views of the more distant hills, an ominous greyness spread across the western sky, and by the time Parkmore was reached rain was falling heavily. Nothing daunted, cloaks and waterproofs were donned, and mounting a well-appointed waggonette, provided by Mr. M'Neill, of Larne, Glenariff was soon reached. No longer in its condition of pristine wilderness, this lovely glen can now be traversed from end to end without difficulty. Without in any way interfering with or destroying the natural beauties of the place, paths have, thanks to the energy of the Northern Counties Railway Company, been constructed along the steep, and in places precipitous sides of the glen, and the beautiful waterfalls and rich luxuriance of verdure can be seen and admired by those who have not that natural propensity for climbing that was previously indispensable. Down in this deep ravine the rain fell more quietly, and interfered but little with the enjoyment of the party. The cascades, swollen by heavy showers on the mountains, were roaring in wild confusion of brown foam among their rocky chasms, and were seldom seen to greater advantage, and the rich vegetation, at all times of the most charming green, was rendered still more vivid by the rain drops that shimmered on every leaf. The luxuriance and variety of the fern world was a point of special comment. Three of our rarer species were noted—the beech fern (*Polypodium phegopteris*), bladder fern (*Cystopteris fragilis*), and sweet-scented mountain fern (*Lastrea montana*). When the glen had been thoroughly explored the party proceeded by road

down the wide vale of Glenariff towards the sea. The high
hills and rugged cliffs on either side looked strangely huge and
gaunt in the grey mist, and this effect, with the great masses
of cloud which hung around the mountains, gave an additional
grandeur, if not beauty, to the scene ; and the numerous
waterfalls that come down the cliffs, in dry weather mere
trickling streamlets, were now transformed into roaring cascades
that bounded into the valley in huge leaps of over a hundred
feet at a time. A halt was called at a quarry by the roadside,
where some good examples of Iceland spar, of a pale amber
colour, were obtained from the white Chalk, some of them
showing to advantage the characteristic double refraction.
When Waterfoot was reached the waggonette was again
mounted, and the party rattled quickly into Cushendall, where
Mr. Delargy and his efficient staff showed true Irish hospitality
in their treatment of the half-drowned travellers ; and when in
a few minutes the party were seated in dry garments at a most
excellent repast, the drenching of the morning was almost
forgotten. Shortly after six the rain ceased, and presently the
sun struggled through the heavy masses of vapour, and lit up
hills and valleys with mellow golden light. No time was lost
in getting again out of doors, and while one section started off
to visit Ossian's grave, high on the hillside above Cushendall,
others spent the remaining hours of daylight in a botanical
ramble along the shore. The bee nettle (*Galeopsis versicolor*)
and fools' parsley (*Æthusa cynapium*) were found not far from
the village, while the rocks at Redbay Castle yielded the sweet-
scented orchis (*Gymnadenia conopsea*), the hemp agrimony
(*Eupatorium cannabinum*), and wild poplar (*Populus tremula*) ;
and the sandy flat at Waterfoot abundance of sea holly
(*Eryngium maritimum*), salt-wort (*Salsola Kali*), and rest-
harrow (*Ononis arvensis*). The archæologists returned delighted
with their walk to Ossian's grave, a rude stone monument on
the south side of Glenaan, and about two miles north-west of
Cushendall. From this interesting memorial of early times a
magnificent prospect of the surrounding hills and vales opens

out, an example of the common practice in primitive times of considering the physical features of the landscape in relation to sites for sepulchral monuments. The opportunity was taken to visit the cottagers in the glen and on the mountain slope, when the folk-lore of the locality was freely recited, with graphic tales of giants and fairies. The sites and ruins of two cromlechs were also inspected, and the party were sorry to hear of the destruction of ancient structures within the memory of some of the "ould people." Assembling once again at the hotel, an examination of the specimens, geological and botanical, brought to a conclusion the day's work, which, despite the rain, was voted to have been highly enjoyable.

Next morning the sun had not long risen in a cloudless sky before some energetic members sallied forth for a swim in the clear waters of the bay. Punctually at seven o'clock the secretary's whistle called the party together, and met with a prompt response, and the route was taken to the seashore south of Limerick Port, a spot noted for the occurrence of jasper. The whole neighbourhood around Cushendall is of high geological interest, and it was a matter of regret to many of the party that the time at their disposal for geological exploration was so limited. To the southward may be seen splendid sections of the trappean plateau of Antrim, and the highly fossiliferous formations that underlie it. The flat elevated table-lands which extend inward from Lurigethan and Garron Point, bounded by steep escarpments along which the level sheets of dark volcanic rock may be traced for miles, are eminently characteristic of the basaltic formation, and suggestive of the manner in which it has been formed. Buried below the superincumbent mass, and thus protected from the ravages of time, lie the Chalk, Greensand, and Lias, full of the remains of the strange fauna which inhabited the ancient seas in which these rocks were deposited. Below the Lias come the thick beds of the New Red Sandstone. Looking northward from Cushendall, however, all is different. The prevailing rock is mica slate, which extends over a large area in highly foliated and contorted beds—a formation which takes its place at the very base of the great series of stratified rocks. Resting on these ancient rocks an interesting patch of conglomerates and sandstones of Old Red Sandstone age extends in an oblong form from Retreat Castle to Cushendun, at which latter place it forms the rock in which the ocean has hollowed out the caves that are so widely known. On the south side of Cushendall, extending in a wedge-shaped tract from Glenballyemon to the sea, occurs a mass of intrusive porphyry, and it is in this igneous rock, in the form of thin and irregular veins, that the jasper mentioned above is met with. The rock is extremely hard, and it put to the test the hammers and picks of the party, who made a vigorous onslaught on the stubborn material, and were rewarded with some fine specimens of bright red jasper. After a hearty breakfast, the machines were mounted, and a start was made for Cushendun. The first halt was made at Glendun Viaduct, whence a lovely view was obtained both up and down this fine glen. Turning seaward now, a visit was paid to the " Altar in the Wood," where, in the absence of a chapel, mass was formerly held, and which was found prettily decorated with moss and ferns. The next point of interest was the caves of Cushendun, which were thoroughly explored and photographed from various points of view. The picturesque appearance of these arches and grottoes in the high cliff of coarse conglomerate must be seen to be appreciated; they form an object of at the same time artistic and geological interest. Again getting under weigh, a heavy shower was encountered, but after the experience of the previous day the party were quite waterproof, and treated the rain with but scant ceremony. Cushendall was again reached at one o'clock, where a hearty dinner was provided, and then bidding adieu to their hospitable host the coast road was taken *en route* for Larne. On Garron Point a half hour was spent in examining the outcrop of Liassic beds, and several species of fossils were obtained, the best being a vertebra of an *Ichthyosaurus*. Rounding Garron Point, and passing Garron Tower and Drumnasole, one of our loveliest wild flowers, the grass of

Parnassus (*Parnassia palustris*), was collected by the roadside, where in one spot it grew in profusion. At Carnlough the party were transferred to another machine, and again proceeded, with little to break the pleasant monotony of the journey. The sky had cleared and the wind had died away, and it was now a lovely summer afternoon, and the Antrim coast, always beautiful, was looking its best. Across the placid waters of the Irish Sea rose the blue hills of Cantire, and further southward the island of Sanda and the rugged peaks of Arran and the conical mass of Ailsa Craig. Northward, point beyond point, stretched the Antrim coast ; southward, the low, fertile land of Islandmagee bounded the view. Inland rose ridges of heathery hills, gilded by brilliant sunshine, and in front the sea lay as if asleep, undisturbed by even a ripple, and rivalling in its brilliant blue the sky above it. Near Ballygalley Castle a halt was made for the purpose of calling on an elderly lady who resides on the seashore in a cabin of her own construction. A massive block of rock forms one wall, and shelters from the north ; a bank of earth forms the back, and all is covered with a thick sheet of seaweed, through which the smoke of a small fire comes as though it was in process of being burnt for kelp. The old dame was found seated inside the very small doorway, contentedly preparing her supper of shell-fish, while a single hen, her only companion, as contentedly roosted beside her. She did not resent the sudden invasion of her dwelling, but in the most friendly manner told her experience of the struggle for existence. She gathered food on the beach, some of which she sold to enable her to purchase a " drap o' tay," and her hen supplied eggs when she wasn't moulting. A reaping hook, hanging on the wall, was significantly pointed out as the protection of the household.

Larne was reached punctually at seven, and the party sat down to tea at the King's Arms Hotel, after which the formal meeting of the excursion was held, the chair being taken by the President of the Club, Mr. William Gray, M.R.I.A. The first business was the election of some new members, after which came the appointment of a delegate to the forthcoming meeting of the British Association. On the motion of Mr. John Vinycomb, Vice-President, seconded by Mr. R. Lloyd Praeger, Mr. Gray was asked to continue to represent the Club, as in former years. The President thanked the meeting for again electing him as their representative, and said he would do all in his power to further the interests of their Society. He congratulated the members on the success of the present excursion, which had been most enjoyable, in spite of most unfavourable weather, and specially commended the ladies of the party for the way they had borne themselves under circumstances of no little discomfort and inconvenience. Mr. Howat, member of the Geological Society of Glasgow, spoke of the great pleasure he had derived from the present excursion, of the energy with which the Club devoted themselves to the objects which brought them together, and of the good-fellowship which existed among them, which they freely extended to members of kindred societies. Mrs. Henry Thompson, on behalf of the ladies of the party, thanked the President for the compliment he had paid them, and assured him that whatever little inconvenience they had experienced was quite forgotten in the great pleasure they had derived from the excursion. The party then bent their steps towards the railway station, and arrived in Belfast at 9.35, well satisfied with their two days among the Glens of Antrim.

On August 16th, to

CAVE HILL.

The fifth excursion was made on August 16th to the Cave Hill, a spot well known to Belfast folk, yet ever attractive to the lover of fresh pure air and charming scenery, and ever interesting to the naturalist. Favoured with their usual good fortune in regard to weather, a splendid afternoon tempted many of the members and their friends out of doors, and a party numbering no fewer than sixty assembled at the gate of

Thronemount on the arrival of the 2.30 steam tram. Through the kindness of their courteous proprietor, the extensive grounds of Mr. Armstrong were thrown open, and, passing through them, the party soon reached the base of the steep rough ground that stretches along the foot of the cliffs. There the secretary announced that a prize, consisting of a botanist's lens, would be given for the best collection of flowering plants made during the afternoon, and an excellent and very close competition was the result. Some stiff climbing now ensued, and some awkward fences barred the way ; but, accustomed to surmount difficulties, even barbed wire could not turn the naturalists from their course, and the rough undercliff, bespangled with flowers, was soon gained. The glory of primrose and wild hyacinth was now long since past, and the flowers that succeeded them were gone likewise, but there still remained a brave show of autumn flowers. The heather and ling were at their best, and the ground was covered with the blue flowers of the scabious, while bedstraw and harebell lent their colours to the picture. On the cliffs which towered above, the purple splashes of heather were diversified with yellow stars of hawkweed, which bespangled the dark basaltic rock. Below the caves a half-hour's halt was called, which was spent by many of the party in ascending to the summit of MacArt's Fort, while others were content to spend the time in pleasant idleness, leisurely contemplating the beautiful and extensive prospect of land and sea that lay in front. The day was unusually fine and clear, and the green and golden fields on the Scotch side could be plainly distinguished. The view to the south-east, offering a pleasing alternation of land and water, was especially fine. Beyond the foreground of the Antrim shore and Belfast Lough lay the fertile slopes of County Down, with the blue waters of Strangford Lough behind, on whose further shore stretched the low hills of the Ards. Further still lay the Irish Channel, and beyond all the distant hills of the Isle of Man formed a fitting background to the picture. Meanwhile some enterprising members had discovered a mysterious, but by no means

ornamental inscription, high up on the rocks, which excited
some little discussion among the antiquarians of the party. To
decipher it was a task of some difficulty, but, as usual, scientific
perseverance triumphed, and it was found that it was in the
English language, and consisted of a eulogistic reference to the
goods of a certain enterprising hatter in North Street.

Commencing now the descent, the grounds of the Deerpark
were entered, and, through copses of hazel and fir, the party
proceeded past the Castle and through the picturesque grounds
of the Countess of Shaftesbury, and made their way along the
Antrim Road to Ardrie, where, on the hospitable invitation
of Mrs. Bigger, the entire party were entertained at a most
substantial and sumptuous tea, to which, after their exertions
of the afternoon, the members did full justice. At the conclusion of the repast the business meeting of the day was held.
Mr. John Vinycomb, Vice-President of the Club, who occupied
the chair, said his duties were very short and very pleasant.
He moved a vote of thanks to Mr. Armstrong, for kind
permission to pass through the grounds of Thronemount; to
the Countess of Shaftesbury, for the privilege of passing
through the Deerpark ; and especially to their hostess, Mrs.
Bigger, for her kindness and hospitality. The motion was
seconded by Mr. Mann Harbison, and supported, on behalf of
the visitors, by Mr. F. A. Porter, and carried amid applause.
After the election of some new members, the examination of
the botanical collections sent in for the prize was undertaken,
Messrs. S. A. Stewart and R. Lloyd Praeger acting as judges.
The competition was very keen, no fewer than seventeen
collections being entered, and it resulted in a double tie,
Messrs. Richard Hanna and Harold Malcolmson being equal
first, with 75 species each, and Miss Mary Phillips and Miss
Hamilton equal second, with 61 species. On account of the
closeness of the competition, the judges awarded four prizes,
two first and two second; and the Chairman expressed his
pleasure at the amount of observation and enthusiasm shown by
the many competitors. The best plants collected were the red

broom-rape (*Orobanche rubra*) and three hawkweeds (*Hieracium boreale, H. anglicum,* and *H. stenolepis*), of which the latter has not been previously recorded from Ireland. The party shortly afterwards separated.

On September 6th, to

GLENARM.

Queen's weather is well known and almost proverbial, and during our last two summers of cloud and rain has been often sighed for in vain; but Field Club weather promises, among a smaller circle, to obtain a reputation even more enviable. Of the seven days, ranging from May to September, announced in the Club's summer programme as the dates of their excursions, six have turned out as fine as that which on Saturday last delighted the hearts of townspeople and farmers alike, and caused those whom business or pleasure had brought out into the country to feel that to be allowed to live, to feel the fresh, cool breeze and watch the brilliant sunlight, was alone a privilege great and gracious. So thought the party of naturalists who on Saturday morning took an early train to Larne, and, on geological discovery intent, drove through the town and out along the coast road. Halting at Waterloo, a profitable hour was spent in examining the interesting variety of secondary rocks there exposed. Below the mass of white Chalk which overhangs the road occur reddish beds of impure limestone, the numerous fossils of which show that they form the upper portion of the Greensand formation. On the shore below, an extensive series of Liassic rocks crop out. They dip northward at a somewhat high angle, so that by walking south-ward along the shore between tide-marks the whole series, some two hundred feet in thickness, may be examined from top to bottom. Geological picks and chisels being brought into play, a number of characteristic fossils were obtained, and others, washed out of the softer zones, were picked up on the beach.

Again mounting, the party drove to Ballygalley Head, a fine mass of intrusive trap that stands boldly out into the channel. Its seaward face shows huge columns tilted at a slight angle, while on each side the trap is flanked by the Chalk through which it has forced its way. Here the botanists of the party put in a claim to share the honours of the day, and exhibited as their trophies the field chamomile (*Matricaria Chamomilla*), a rare plant, perhaps introduced with American seed, which appears to be spreading in Antrim ; a rare thistle, *Onopordon Acanthium*, not native in Ireland ; several rare mosses from the bare rocks on the summit of the headland ; and an uncommon rose (*Rosa mollis*) found at Waterloo. Climbing up the steep hillside, the party were soon reposing on the short green turf on the hilltop, an object of admiration to a number of rabbits and a fine herd of inquisitive cattle. The warm sunshine and drowsy hum of insect life, with the faint murmur of the water lapping the rocks three hundred feet below, had a soothing, if not a lazy effect, and some time was spent in leisurely admiring the extensive and beautiful view that stretched both northward and southward, and in letting the eye wander along the blue extent of distant Scottish shore till it lost itself among the dim purple peaks of Arran. But the secretary's shrill whistle soon sounded the advance, and descending the steep slope, the party proceeded to a spot by the wayside about a mile north of Ballygalley Castle, where an interesting glacial deposit occurs. It consists of coarse gravel, and underlies some thirty feet of upper boulder clay, and has yielded a number of Arctic shells. Near this it was that a mammoth's tooth was found some years ago, the geological origin of which excited discussion at more than one of the Club meetings. On the present occasion the gravel bed was almost hidden by a quantity of boulder clay that had fallen from above, and some fragments of shells were all that rewarded the labours of the party. Once again proceeding, no halt was made till within a mile of Glenarm, where an extensive quarry in the Chalk excited attention, furnishing, as it did, a magnificent section of this formation, over a hundred feet in height, the horizontal bands of flints being especially well shown. While the greater part of the party drove on into Glenarm, some preferred remaining here to examine the beds of Lias and Greensand near at hand. The Lias here does not crop out as a solid rock as at Waterloo, but occurs in its more usual form of plastic blue clays, which, undermined by percolating water, continually slide down on the road below. On the surface of these clays, washed out by recent rains, a large number of fossils were obtained— *Ammonites Johnstoni*, *Cardium Rhœticum*, *Cardinia ovalis*, *C. Deshayesii*, *Pentacrinus Bryareus*, *Ammonites planorbis*, *Astarte Guexii*, and others—the first three of which, with *Gryphœa incurva* and *Lima gigantea*, were also obtained at Waterloo. Another Ammonite, of which two fragments were obtained near Glenarm, would appear to belong to *A. laqueolus* Schlöenbach, a species which has not hitherto been recorded from Irish Liassic strata. A few Greensand fossils were also secured, including *Pecten equicostatus* and *Terebratula carnea*. The party having again rejoined, the return journey was commenced, and Larne was reached a few minutes after seven, where a substantial tea was provided by Mr. M'Neill at the King's Arms Hotel. At the conclusion of the repast a short business meeting was held—Mr. Mann Harbison in the chair. The announcement that the rainfall during the month of August had been abnormally small—little more than one-half of the average August rainfall for the last twenty years—was received with some surprise and a little ironical laughter. The party then made their way to the railway station, and in spite of somewhat limited accommodation provided by the railway company on the last train from Larne, they all safely reached Belfast a few minutes before ten.

WINTER SESSION.

NOTE.—The authors of the various Papers, of which abstracts are here appended, are alone responsible for the views expressed in them.

SOCIAL MEETING.

THE Winter Session of the Club was inaugurated on Saturday evening, November 1st, by a social meeting in the Museum, College Square North. Tea was served in the lower rooms from six to seven o'clock, when a number of lady members dispensed the necessary refreshments with skill and despatch. At seven o'clock the business of the evening was opened by the President of the Club (Mr. William Gray, M.R.I.A.), who said it was his pleasing duty, in the name of the Club, to bid a cordial welcome to the many visitors present that evening, and in his own name, as President, to congratulate the members on the largeness of the present meeting, and on the high interest of the objects on exhibition, which showed that the vitality and energy of their Society was in no degree diminished. He would draw special attention to the exhibition illustrative of the art of chromo-lithography—an art in which our city excels, and has a world-wide reputation for beauty of design and excellence of workmanship in this important branch of printing. This exhibition was the result of the combination of three important local firms, who had all most generously responded to the invitation of the secretaries to give an exhibition explanatory of this special department.

Mr. F. W. Lockwood, Senior Secretary, then briefly drew attention to various objects on exhibition which were not mentioned in the list of exhibits in the programme.

Mr. R. Lloyd Praeger, B.E., Junior Secretary, at the invitation of the President, made some remarks on a fine series of British ferns and their varieties which hung on the walls, and also explained the various processes illustrated by the large number of chromo-lithographs and lithographic stones which were on exhibition.

The company then scattered, and devoted themselves to the examination of the objects that crowded the tables and walls of the lecture hall and library.

Conspicuous at the lower end of the room hung an immense lithographic reproduction of Edward Bisson's famous picture "La Cigale," which was one of the pictures of the year at the last Paris Salon exhibition—the figure of a beautiful minstrel girl standing in the falling snow, clasping her guitar. This work, which is executed in monochrome, is one of the latest productions of Messrs. David Allen & Sons, and is undoubtedly one of the finest pieces of lithographic work on a large scale ever produced. Facing it at the opposite end of the room was another very fine specimen of chromo-lithography—a large reproduction of the well-known picture, "Home from the Soudan," the work of Messrs. Marcus Ward & Co. The delicacy and variety of colouring here displayed excited general admiration. Messrs. M'Caw, Stevenson, & Orr supplied some excellent examples of finer chromo-lithographic work, shewing the original sketch, the photographically-reduced key, and all the consecutive printings up to the finished picture, with printed explanations of each process, which they had kindly specially prepared for this meeting. Messrs. Marcus Ward & Co. also exhibited a series of thirteen sheets showing the separate printings of a chromo-lithograph, the combination of which produces the effect desired. Messrs. David Allen & Sons showed two sets—one of five, and one of seven large lithographic stones, prepared for printing the different colours of two highly-finished pictures. The original drawings from which the stones were prepared, and the finished chromo-lithographs printed from them, were also exhibited, as were a number of very bold water-colour drawings, from which chromo-lithographs, several of them well known, have been made.

Flanking the lithograpic exhibition on either hand hung a fine series of dried and mounted specimens of British ferns, shown by Mr. W. H. Phillips and Mr. R. Lloyd Praeger. They displayed to advantage the wonderful variability to which this race of plants is subject. A large number of fronds of the more striking varieties, freshly cut, were also exhibited, and the permission given to members and visitors to select from them any they wished was largely taken advantage of. As usual, microscopic work was a prominent feature of the evening, although the wealth of other exhibits on the tables hardly gave the microscopists a fair chance of displaying their treasures. Mr. W. S. M'Kee showed living specimens of *Rotifera* and *Polyzoa*. Their exquisite structure and graceful movements were objects of much admiring comment. Mr. J. J. Andrew showed a number of living freshwater organisms, and Mr. John Donaldson did the same with marine life. The beautiful group of the *Foraminifera* found an able exponent in Mr. Joseph Wright, F.G.S., and Mr. William Swanston, F.G.S., was equally successful in *Echinodermata*. The beauties of rock sections and precious stones, under both direct and polarised light, were well exhibited by Mr. Daniel M'Kee. Mr. William Gray, M.R.I.A., showed some fine slides of sections of coal plants, prepared by Mr. James Lomax, of Radcliffe. Mr. James Stelfox, in addition to many interesting objects of his own, showed some slides of living growths of the yeast plant and other *micro-fungi*, kindly prepared for the meeting by Mr. Allan P. Swan. Mr. H. M'Cleery and Mr. A. Fulton, jun., illustrated the bee and its structure. Mr. George Elliott showed dental sections, and Mr. J. Murdock general objects.

In the department of archæology, Mr. W. J. Knowles, M.R.I.A., of Ballymena, contributed a fine series of flint arrow-heads, scrapers, knives, and celts, obtained mostly from the sand-dunes of the North of Ireland. On an adjoining table, Mr. S. F. Milligan showed a number of similar and other implements, and the President of the Club had also an interesting contribution in this department. A magnificent Irish gold fibula was exhibited by Mr. C. W. Dugan, M.A., H. M. Inspector of Schools, and also a large piece of the well-known silicified wood of Lough Neagh, bearing what closely resembled axe-marks, the origin of which excited some discussion. Mr. Dugan also showed a collection of ancient Chinese coins, and of Japanese carved and inlaid swordguards, which formed one of the finest exhibits in the room. Some valuable examples of inlaid Japanese swords, and enamelled vases and plaques, were kindly lent by Mr. R. M. Young, B.A.

Fresh-water aquaria, exhibited by Messrs. R. Welch, J. Hamilton, and J. J. Andrew, L.D.S., full of life of all kinds, attracted a constant crowd during the evening. Among groups of water-plants artistically arranged, myriads of water-beetles of various species, frogs and newts, water-scorpions, and fresh-water shrimps were disporting themselves. On the surface of one of the aquaria the whole four British species of duck-weed were exhibited growing together. Mr. John Hamilton exhibited a living chameleon from Alexandria, whose slow, deliberate movements and curious colour-changes evoked considerable amusement. He also showed a fine specimen of the death's-head moth, captured last month on board a vessel in the Bay of Biscay.

Mr. John Vinycomb contributed a selection from his large collection of ancient seals ; a number of water-colour drawings, the work of Messrs. Ernest Hanford, A. Lytle, H. F. Thomas, and J. Vinycomb, which hung on the walls, added greatly to the embellishments of the lecture room. An interesting series of photographs by Mr. George Donaldson, taken on the Club excursions of the present year, recalled to many the pleasant trips of the summer session. Among other photographs exhibited were a series illustrating the antiquities of Donegal and Fermanagh, by Mr. R. Welch, and photographs of bird life by Mr. Green, of Berwick-on-Tweed, lent by Mr. Robert Patterson. Mr. W. D. Donnan had on exhibition a collection of Irish flowering plants, for which he obtained a Club's prize last year. The Club's portrait, photograph, and sketch albums, which were on view in the library, also attracted attention.

During the evening two lantern exhibitions were given in the upper room by Mr. John Donaldson. The subjects illustrated included the ancient dovecots of Herefordshire, from a fine series of photographs by Mr. Alfred Watkins ; the antiquities of Donegal and Fermanagh, by Mr. R. Welch ; photographs of wild flowers, by Mr. Wm. Swanston ; carboniferous plants, by Mr. James Lomax ; and the cromlechs of County Dublin, by photographs by Mr. Thomas Mason. A number of living fresh-water animals, in their native element, thrown on the screen by means of an ingenious apparatus, devised by the President, caused great amusement. The various movements of gigantic-looking shrimps, beetles, and fishes, as the swam about, or dashed wildly across the field of view, were followed with the deepest interest.

At 8.30 a short business meeting was called. The President said it was not usual to thank their own members for the assistance that was always most willingly granted ; but, on behalf of the Club, he desired to tender their most sincere thanks to those ladies and gentlemen, not members of the Club, who had in many ways contributed so materially to the success of the present meeting. He wished especially to mention the names of Mr. C. W. Dugan, of Lurgan ; Mr. Allan P. Swan, of Bushmills ; and the three firms whose combined exhibition had made chromo-lithography the specialité of the evening. He would now call for any nomination of new members. A long list of proposed members was then read out by the secretaries, with their proposers and seconders, and the chairman having put them formally to the meeting, they were declared duly elected.

This concluded the business of the evening, but until a late hour the company remained, interested in the variety of exhibits that crowded the rooms.

The second meeting of the Winter Session was held on Wednesday evening, November 19th, when the President (Mr. William Gray, M.R.I.A.) opened the meeting with some remarks on the work of the British Association for the Advancement of Science in connection with societies such as our local Field Club. He said that, with a view of securing the co-operation of provincial societies, the British Association has made arrangements by which all qualified societies may become identified with the Association and be acknowledged as " corresponding societies." Our Field Club has been a corresponding society of the Association for many years, and as such has yearly sent up a delegate to represent the Club at the meeting of the Association. One committee of the Association is known as the " Corresponding Societies Committee," and in its annual report publishes a list of all papers, lectures, or other communications published by the corresponding societies during the past year, provided that such papers deal with subjects coming within the scope of one or other of the sections of the Association. At every annual meeting of the Association one or more conferences are held between the Corresponding Societies Committee and the delegates representing the provincial societies throughout the three kingdoms, the object being to consider how far the work of the various societies can be rendered helpful in promoting the purposes of the Association, and to discuss all suggestions for the systematising of methods of investigation, and the securing of greater uniformity in the modes of tabulating and publishing results. In order to understand how far the members of our society may be able to co-operate with the British Association, it may be well to glance at the constitution of the latter. The work of the Association is divided into eight sections, each identified by a letter from A to H. The sections are as follows :—A, Mathematical and Physical Science ; B, Chemical Science ; C, Geology ; D, Biology ; E, Geography ; F, Economic Science and Statistics ; G, Mechanical Science ; H, Anthropology. Each section has its own committee of management, and, in addition, there are special committees appointed to investigate special subjects ; it is with these special committees that the corresponding societies can most usefully co-operate. Mr. Gray then dealt with the work of a number of the special committees, pointing out the way in which our Naturalists' Field Club may usefully co-operate with them. Under section C—Geology—he referred to the Underground Waters Committee, appointed to investigate the circulation of underground waters, and their quality and quantity, questions of the deepest importance in towns and districts where wells are habitually used, and particularly in Belfast, where costly wells are often sunk for trade purposes. The work of the Erratic Boulders Committee, the Seacoast Erosion Committee, and the Geological Photographs Committee was dealt with as affording fields in which the Club may render valuable aid to the Association. Mr. Gray stated that the photographs of geological subjects, sent from Belfast to the Leeds meeting, were highly appreciated. In the section of Biology the work of the Committee on Freshwater Fauna and Flora, and of the Committee on the Disappearance of Native Plants, may well fall within the scope of our Society ; and in the Anthropological Section a wide field is open to us in the way of assisting the work of the Prehistoric Remains Committee by systematically cataloguing and mapping the ancient monuments in which our district is so rich. Mr. Gray here exhibited the 1-inch scale Ordnance Maps of Counties Antrim and Down, on which all the ancient monuments which he knew of had been marked by a recognised system of symbols ; these maps had been shown at the last meeting of the British Association, and were received and approved. In conclusion, Mr. Gray referred to the value of a division of labour, and to a proposed Microscopical Section of the Field Club, and suggested the possibility of a section of the Natural History and Philosophical Society for astronomical work, and that the latter should endeavour to make some use of the instruments and astronomical apparatus so long devoted to the geometrical creations of spiders in the otherwise unused observatory at the Queen's College. Now that so much had been done, and well done, to popularise university education, the utilizing of the Queen's College observatory for the benefit of the public would be an appropriate and acceptable outcome.

Mr. W. H. Patterson, M.R.I.A., next made some remarks on some ancient grave slabs near Dundonald, of which he exhibited drawings. He said that the three monumental slabs under notice are preserved in the townland of Greengraves, the first at the farm of Mrs. Kennedy, the second and third at Mr. Hugh Ferguson's farm. The slabs are of Anglo-Norman type, and belong to the thirteenth or fourteenth century. No. 1 is a fragment, the head being broken off. The only sculpture upon it is a long, straight Norman sword, formed by incised lines. The stone is 3ft. 8in. long, and over a foot wide, tapering to the lower end. No. 2 slab is broken in two, but the parts are in excellent preservation ; the total length is 5ft.; the edges are bevelled. The design consists of a handsome floriated cross, carved in relief within a sunk circular panel. Two incised lines form the cross stem, which terminates in a Calvary or series of steps at the narrow lower end of the slab. Alongside the stem the emblem of the shears has been formed by incised lines ; this emblem is supposed to indicate the monument of a female. Slab No. 3 resembles No. 2 in general design, but is remarkable on account of its exceedingly small size, being only 1ft. 11in. long, 9in. wide at one end, and 7in. at the other. The floriated cross differs in design from that of No. 2, but it has the incised stem and Calvary, and also the shears. As to how the slabs came here, the Rev. James O'Laverty states (Hist. Ac. Down and Connor, Vol. II., p. 141, 1880) that the one at Mrs. Kennedy's was brought here from Killarn some fifty years ago. The slabs at Mr. Ferguson's (Nos. 2 and 3) came to light, the reader was informed by Mr. Ferguson, jun., some six or eight years ago, when some old farm buildings were taken down at a short distance from the present house. In Mr. Munce's farm, in the townland of Killarn, and in a field called the "chapel field," close to where these slabs are now, there was an ancient church, and it is probable that these slabs were taken from the cemetery surrounding this church, to be used as hearth stones, or for some other domestic purpose. About a mile distant from this place stood the ancient church of Ballyoran, in a place now called the "chapel field," in Rockfield demesne. This church, under the name of Wauerantone, was valued in the Pope Nicholas taxation at six marks. An inquisition in the year 1334 found that William de Burgo possessed these lands. This, then, brings the Anglo-Normans into the district at the same period when these grave slabs were formed, and it is very probable that these monuments were those of members of De Burgo's family, or of some of his warlike retainers, whom he planted on these lands to maintain them for him. Therefore probably No. 1 is the monument of a knight, No. 2 of a lady, and No. 3 that of a little girl.

It may be observed that when the slab at Mrs. Kennedy's was examined by the Rev. J. O'Laverty some years prior to the publication of his work, it was in a much more perfect condition than it is at present ; he describes it as having a floriated cross, and a rubbing, which is preserved, shows the cross and sword.

Mr. Joseph Wright, F.G.S., drew attention to a series of diagrams illustrating the shells of a most interesting section of the microscopic order of the *Foraminifera*. In this section the animals built up their tiny and exquisite shells of the spicules of sponges. In most of the species these spicules are of irregular size, and often fragmentary, but in one species, of which a drawing was exhibited, the spicules of which the entire shell is made up are of exactly uniform shape and size, and there is a possibility that these spicules are not derived from sponges at all, but are the production of the *Foraminifer*, in which case this species offers a most interesting and important link between the families of the sponges and the *Foraminifera*.

The third meeting of the Winter Session was held on Tuesday evening, 16th December, the President (Mr. William Gray, M.R.I.A.) in the chair, when three communications were brought forward.

The first item on the programme was a paper by Mr. W. D. Donnan, his subject being "The Primrose and its Allies." The reader first referred to the abundance of the common primrose, the beauty of its flowers, and the pleasant associations of the spring season which its sulphur-coloured petals always recall. The botanical position which the order *Primulaceæ*, to which the primrose belongs, occupies, was pointed out, coming as it does under the sub-division *Gamopetalæ* of Dicotyledonous plants, and its affinities to other orders were explained. A description was then given of the component parts of a flower of a typical member of the order under consideration, showing how a specimen might be referred to it. The different British plants belonging to the *Primulaceæ* were next reviewed. Of the genus *Primula*, besides the primrose, there are four species —the cowslip, oxlip, and two smaller species with mealy leaves, which inhabit the heaths and mountains of the North. Reference was made to the peculiar dimorphism displayed by the flowers of all the species of *Primula*, and which causes the so-called "male" and "female" flowers of the primrose. The sow-bread (*Cyclamen hederifolium*) is a doubtfully native species, whose most interesting characteristic is its curious power of burying its seeds in the earth when they approach maturity. The genus *Lysimachia*, or loose-strife, furnishes four British

species, of which three may be called common, the best known being the moneywort or herb-twopence (*L. nummularia*), so called from its opposite pairs of round coin-shaped leaves. The chickweed winter-green (*Trientalis europæa*) is a small alpine plant ; the chaffweed (*Centunculus minimus*) a tiny, inconspicuous species, found in damp, sandy ground ; and the sea milkwort (*Glaux maritima*) a common little flower, growing abundantly in salt marshes and on seashores. The well-known scarlet pimpernel or shepherd's weather-glass (*Anagallis arvensis*) is one of our prettiest wild flowers, whose beauty is perhaps outshone by that of its smaller relative, the lovely little bog pimpernel (*A. tenella*). The brookweed (*Samolus Valerandi*) is a plant remarkable for its wide distribution, being found in many parts of Europe, Africa, America, and in New South Wales. The last British species is the water violet (*Hottonia palustris*), a beautiful aquatic plant, of which the tall, slender flower-stem, encircled with whorls of delicate pink blossoms, alone rises above the surface of the water. The *Primulaceæ* is a highly interesting and attractive order of plants, and is especially so from the fact that our favourite wild flower, the common primrose, is a typical member of the group.

The second communication consisted of some remarks by Mr. R. Lloyd Praeger, B.E., on some new or rare North of Ireland plants, of which he exhibited specimens.

The following is an abstract of the remarks on the more interesting species :—

Elatine hydropiper, Linn. A tiny aquatic plant which is very rare not only in Ireland, but throughout Britain. Recorded over fifty years ago from the Lough Neagh terminus of the Lagan Canal, and in the canal at Newry, but not recently seen. Found in 1886, and again last summer, by Rev. H. W. Lett, in Loughbrickland, Co. Down.

Rhamnus frangula, Linn. Recorded from several stations in the North-east of Ireland, but not seen in the district for some thirty years. Re-discovered by Prof. Cunningham,

M.D., growing in bushy places near the River Main in Shane's Castle Park, June, 1890.

Prunus cerasus, Linn.   Recorded from shores of Lough Neagh by Templeton nearly a century ago, and from two stations in Co. Derry by Dr. Moore some 50 years back, but not recently seen in the district.   Mr. Praeger now records it from near Crawfordsburn, Co. Down, 1882 ; and from Annalong and near Clandeboye demesne, Co. Down, 1890.

Hieracium stenolepis, Lind.   First mentioned as a British plant by Mr. Hanbury in the *Journal of Botany* for June, 1888, and first recognised as Irish by Mr. Hanbury in 1889, from specimens gathered on the Cave Hill, near Belfast, in 1886, by Mr. Praeger.   Mr. S. A. Stewart has since worked out the local distribution of the species, and finds it plentiful on the basaltic cliffs of the Cave Hill, Knockagh, and Sallagh Braes, and more abundant in those stations than *H. murorum*, to which it is closely allied.   *H. stenolepis* is conspicuously absent from the Mourne range.

Lobelia Dortmanna, Linn.   Abundant in a lakelet on summit of Binnagee, near Carnlough, Co. Antrim, at an elevation of 1100 feet, R. Lloyd Praeger, 1890.   Only previous Antrim record was the shores of Lough Neagh, at a much lower elevation.

Hottonia palustris, Linn.   The original, and, excepting Down-patrick, the only Irish station for this beautiful plant, would appear to be " marshy ditches on the right side of the road at Everogue bridge near Downpatrick," (*Templeton MS.*), where it was found by Richard Kennedy about 1816. More recently it was discovered on the lands of Inch, and near the Quoile railway bridge, both close to Downpatrick, and it would appear to have been assumed that this was Kennedy's station.   Everogue's Bridge, however, is the old name for the village of Crossgar, five miles N.N.W. of Downpatrick, and here the plant still grows abundantly where described by Templeton, in ditches on the right (or west) side of the road at the bridge. The stream which drains these ditches flows into the River Quoile, and thus, probably, the plant has spread to its Downpatrick station, which is on the banks of the latter stream.

Anagallis arvensis, Linn., var. β., *A. cærulea*, Schreb. This very rare blue-flowered variety of the scarlet pimpernel was found a few months ago by Mr. J. J. Andrew on a bank not far from the gate of the Belfast Botanic Gardens.

Orchis pyramidalis, Linn. Grows sparingly on limestone rubbish at Magheragall quarries, near Lisburn, Co. Antrim (R. Lloyd Praeger, 1888), where Mr. Stewart considers it certainly native. An addition to the flora of District 12 of *Cybele Hibernica*, since the single plant found at Magilligan by Dr. Moore, and the two found at Ballyholme, Co. Down, by Mr. Stewart were undoubtedly casuals.

Chara contraria, Kuetzing. Margins of brackish pools, Limavady Junction, Co. Derry, R. Lloyd Praeger and W. D. Donnan, 1889. New to Ulster.

A number of other species, a few of them new to Ireland, and others new to County Down, which have been found among the Mourne Mountains by Messrs. Stewart and Praeger, were also shown. These will form part of a report which will be presented to the Royal Irish Academy, and are therefore omitted here.

The third communication was by Mr. W. H. Phillips, F.R.H.S., M.R.S.A. Ireland, the subject of his paper being "Strange Pets I have had." The paper commenced by a reference to the love most people have for pets, and to the pleasure experienced in examining their habits and modes of life, and how the world has been benefited by the labours of naturalists whose field of work never extended beyond their own home, and the contrast supplied by some others whose only aim is the destruction of every bird, beast, and fish which comes within reach, which they call sport. Fortunately the proclaiming of the country has effected a change in the former indiscriminate slaughter of birds on St. Stephen's Day, as guns cannot now be carried without licence. The pets which the lecturer had kept had been very various—dogs, cats, white mice, piebald rats, Guinea pigs, rabbits, snakes, toads, frogs, newts, monkeys, seagulls, spiders, hedgehogs, lizards, tree-frogs, and birds of various kinds. The present paper dealt chiefly with the reptile class—toads, frogs, and newts. The erroneous belief in the venom of the toad was shown by reference to ancient writers, and to the witches' cauldron in *Macbeth*, into which a toad was first put. A short description was given of the anatomy of the toad and frog, which are both without ribs, and have instead several muscles by which air is pumped into the lungs ; but, as the heart has only one ventricle, the blood is only partially aërated, and is therefore cold. The tongue performs a leading part in the capture of the prey ; it is soft and fleshy, and fastened to the front interior edge of the jaw. In a state of repose its free extremity lies in the back part of the mouth, and is covered with a tenacious, viscous secretion, so that when it touches the prey, the latter so firmly adheres to it, that it is carried back with the tongue into the mouth. There it is in most cases compressed, involved again in a glutinous saliva, and almost instantly submitted to the act of swallowing. The motion of throwing out and returning the tongue is so rapid that the eye can scarcely detect it. Then followed a description of a scene with wasps and toads, and also an amusing description of two toads swallowing the same worm at different ends, at the same time. The supposed longevity of toads, and the stories of their being found in the heart of trees and rocks, will not bear investigation, Dr. Buckland's experiments showing that they will not live long when enclosed without food and air. There is no doubt that toads can exist a considerable time without food, but when they can get it they are voracious gormandisers, and devour almost every insect pest. This renders them most useful to the farmer and gardener, for at night, when noxious insects and slugs come out to feed on the fruits and crops, the toad also comes out to prey on them, and quietly renders a great service by the steady and thorough-going manner in which it clears the plants of every creature that moves. Toads and frogs are very prolific, laying as many as 9,000 eggs each, but in every stage they form the food of numerous enemies, and when eventually they leave the water and take to the land, they become the food of almost every species of wild-fowl. It is estimated that not one in one thousand of the young frogs ever reach their winter quarters—like too many of ourselves, they have bills to meet for which they are quite unprepared ; these are always drawn at sight, and have to be accepted and paid without any days of grace. Frogs, in the course of their career, have a dual existence. In the tadpole state they belong entirely to the water ; advanced to the position of froghood, they are equally at home in the pond or the meadow. There is much about the tadpole that is interesting. Look at his figure. How round ; what an image of easygoing softness! Which is his head? Which is his capacious stomach? The little being which issues from the frog's egg is provided in the first instance with a long, fleshy tail, which he repudiates in after life (which Lord Montboddo held that we ourselves have done), and a small horny beak. Beyond the operation of eating, he does not lead a life of great activity. He, however, makes up for this quiesence when his metamorphosis is accomplished. There never was change more complete. Even the magic of the Treasury Bench does not effect a greater, for the tadpoles which swarm towards that haven of bliss generally remain tadpoles till the end of the chapter. As a tadpole he was a vegetarian, but now, being a frog, he knows better. Animal food is what he goes in for now, and, that there may be no mistake about it, he swallows everything whole—not, as some suppose, from sheer voracity, but on account of the quickness and impatience of his nature, which cannot afford to wait. He has no time to be fastidious about cookery, but makes the most of his opportunity ; an example which, if always followed by mankind, might not be altogether amiss. Frogs and toads have wonderful voices. The *Hyla*, for instance, indulges in a shrill treble ; the *Rana typhonica*, or hurricane frog, has a fine baritone voice, which he exercises in rapid passages on the approach of tropical storms ; and the bull frog has a bass which may be heard for miles. There is the clamorous frog of North America, a noisy fellow in all probability, always annexing his neighbour's property. To give full expression to his vocal exercises, which the envious call clamour, is as much the nature of the frog, as to develop the muscular capabilities of his finely developed limbs. The frog can also do something with his voice besides sing. The *Rana temporaria* possesses the ability of making a noise by night, like that of an angry man. Very likely he is angry ; no snails for supper, perhaps, or his bed not quite damp enough. Water newts and their habits were described, and the superstitions connected with their supposed going down the throats of animals and men, and the paper closed with some reference to snakes.

The election of some new members brought the meeting to a close.

The fourth meeting of the Winter Session was held on Tuesday evening, January 20th, the chair being taken by the President. The first business of the evening was the consideration of a proposal by the Committee that the library of the Club should be handed over *in toto* to the Belfast Free Public Library. Mr. F. W. Lockwood, Senior Secretary, in bringing the matter forward, said that the Club had received from time to time, as donations or in exchange for their Annual Proceedings, a number of scientific works and Proceedings of scientific societies, some of these, such as the splendid books on Canadian geology, presented to the Club by the Marquis of Dufferin, being of high value. The Club having no rooms of their own, difficulties had arisen as to the proper displaying and cataloguing of these works ; and, taking into consideration also the fact that they were at present accessible only to the comparatively limited circle of the Club's members, the Committee now asked the meeting for power to approach the Public Library Committee, with a view of ascertaining whether that body would be willing to grant certain special privileges of consultation to members of that Club, should the Club present to the Public Library the whole of the books before-mentioned. Mr. Lockwood moved that the proposal to transfer the Club's books to the Free Public Library, subject to the conditions set forth in a draft letter, which he read, be approved. The President opened a discussion on the suggestion, strongly advocating the proposed transfer, which, he said, would confer benefit both on the Club and on the Public Library. Mr. W. Swanston, F.G.S., Librarian to the Club, further explained the circumstances at present attending the Club's property, and seconded Mr. Lockwood's resolution. Mr. Alexander Tate, C.E., while favouring the proposed transfer, cautioned the Club against acting too hastily in the matter ; property given away could not be regained. Messrs. Joseph Wright, F.G.S.; W. Nicholl, G. H. Elliot, and H. M'Cleery having also spoken, the motion authorising the Committee to proceed in the matter was put to the meeting, and was carried *nem. con.*

The next business was the consideration of a suggestion to form a joint section of the Field Club and Natural History and Philosophical Society, for the prosecution and encouragement of microscopical work. The subject was introduced by Mr. R. Lloyd Praeger, B.E., Junior Secretary, who stated that the suggestion made through the local Press some time ago to form a microscopical society in Belfast had led to a promise by the President and Secretaries that the question of furthering microscopical work by the Club's agency should be brought before the Committee. This had been duly done ; and, a suggestion having been made that the Belfast Natural History and Philosophical Society might co-operate with the Club in the formation of a joint section devoted to microscopical work, a joint sub-committee representing both societies was appointed, and had now presented their report, which approved the formation of a joint section on the basis of a draft constitution which they submitted. Having arrived at this stage, the Committee now laid the whole matter before the Club, in order that the microscopical members might decide for themselves what form of section, if any, should be adopted. Mr. Praeger then read the provisional code of rules recommended by the joint sub-committee. Mr. J. Brown, as the originator of the suggestion for a joint section of the two societies, stated his reasons for believing that joint action might in this case be advantageous, and he moved that a joint section of the societies named be formed for the prosecution of microscopical work. Mr. Joseph Wright, F.G.S., spoke in favour of the joint scheme, and seconded the resolution. The President, while thoroughly approving the idea of a microscopical section, thought that a combination of the societies would only be a multiplication of organisations, unnecessary and unwise, and he moved as an amendment that a section of the Club be formed for the special study and practice of microscopical work, and that five members be appointed to make such arrangements as they may consider necessary, subject to the approval of the Committee. The amendment was seconded by Mr. R. Welch. An interesting and somewhat lengthy discussion on the two proposals ensued, which was taken part in by Messrs. Alexander Tate, C.E.; J. Donaldson, H. M'Cleery, F. W. Lockwood, Rev. J. Kirk Pike; Messrs. John Hamilton, Joseph Wright, W. Nicholl, and R. Lloyd Praeger. Ultimately the amendment was put to the meeting, and was carried by twelve votes to ten. On the motion of the President, Messrs. Joseph Wright, F.G.S.; J. Donaldson, Alexander Tate, C.E.; W. A. Firth, and H. M'Cleery were appointed a Committee to make the necessary arrangements, Mr. M'Cleery to act as convener.

Mr. F. W. Lockwood read a short paper upon "Four Days in Arran." He stated Arran could be reached in a few hours from here at the cost of only a few shillings. Although outside of Ireland, yet being in sight from our hilltops it was legitimately within the sphere of the Field Club's operations. The terrace which lies a few feet above the beach, and marks a recent sea level, and which runs nearly all round the island, was described. The chief road on the island is formed on this terrace, and is as full of interest and beauty as the coast road of Antrim. There are only two or three roads crossing the interior of the island. All else is moor and mountain. Some interesting antiquities at the mouth of Glen Sannox were described, and a sketch was shown of a head, probably on the door jamb of an eleventh or twelfth century Celtic Church ; it is now built into the sidewall of an old graveyard. Glen Sannox is one of the wildest and grandest spots in Scotland outside of Skye. It bears many striking marks of glacial action. Loch Ranza, on the north-west of the island, is a charming spot, full of historic interest. It was here Bruce met his companions before his famous descent upon the Carrick shore. There is a ruined castle on the beach, and one may still in imagination recall the scenes so well depicted in Scott's *Lord of the Isles*. There are several interesting features near the road which runs along the west coast. The striking series of mounds that resemble some great fortification, that lie near the mouths of Glen Catacol and Glen Rosa, were described ; these probably formed the delta at the mouth of the valleys, deposited when the land level was lower than at present, and which, as the land rose, have been cut out by the shifting bed of the stream into their present shape. A sketch was shown of a pillar stone, 18 feet in height, the tallest in Scotland, which, with its fallen companion, stands near the road. An account was given also of the effect produced by the westerly gales and sea spray upon the birch woods along the coast. The trees grow only 10 feet high, and their tops are at that level matted together, and the branches intertwisted into a compact canopy almost proof against the passage of light and rain. Arran is infinitely better worth seeing than the Isle of Man, and the members of the Club were strongly urged to take the first opportunity of paying it a visit.

After a brief discussion on the paper, the election of new members brought the proceedings to a close.

The fifth meeting of the Winter Session was held on Tuesday evening, February 17th, the President in the chair, when two papers were read. The first was by Mr. Henry Davis, his subject being "A Chat about Lichens." The reader stated that he was led to take up the study of lichens some time ago, on account of the interesting objects that parts of these plants offer for the microscope. He did not think that this subject had been brought before the Club by any of its members, and he wished to draw their attention to these interesting plants. They give patches of colour to quaint bits of the landscape, and are on that account dear to artists and lovers of the beautiful in nature. They abound almost everywhere, growing in shrubby tufts, in long beard-like filaments, in powdery patches, and dark stains, and on all sorts of materials —on trees, rocks, moss, earth, and even on other lichens. Lichens take their sustenance from the atmosphere, and merely attach themselves to the materials on which they are found. The Rev. W. A. Leighton, a celebrated lichenologist, says that "these plants grow in perfection only in pure air, and their abundance in a fully-developed and fruiting state is a sure and certain indication of the purity of the atmosphere and salubrity of the climate." The older botanists held that lichens were a distinct order of flowerless plants, but some of the later authorities believe that they are only unicellular *Algæ*, on which a fungus grows in a parasitic state. Mr. Davis pointed out by the aid of a diagram how the *thallus* of a lichen is built up, it being composed of three layers, namely—the first or cortical layer, consisting of closely packed cells which form the outer bark, as it were, of the *thallus ;* the second, or gonidal, in which the green cells lie prisoners ; and the third, or medullary layer, with its *hyphæ* intertwined in a felty mass. He also showed where the spores lay *perdu* in their *theca*, and stated that if a thin section of an *apothecium* be made, or if a bit be rubbed down in a drop of water, the spores make beautiful objects for the microscope. Lichens are classed by the general appearance of their *thalli*, by the colour, shape, &c., of their *apothecia*, and by the number, shape, and colour of their spores. There are about two thousand species and varieties of these plants already known in Great Britain, Ireland, and the Channel Islands. The reader concluded his paper by referring to the use of lichens for domestic and medicinal purposes, their geographical distribution, and their distribution in altitude. The paper was illustrated and explained by specimens of lichens collected about Holywood, and some which the reader had got from England and Wales ; and a few very fine plants were shown by Mr. R. Lloyd Praeger. A discussion followed, chiefly with regard to the supposed dual nature of lichens, in which the President, Messrs. J. J. Murphy, George Donaldson, and others took part.

The President then called on Mr. Robert Patterson for his paper on "The Birds of the Bog Meadows." Mr. Patterson began by describing the position and extent of the Bog Meadows, and said that on Saturdays and Sundays they are overrun with men, boys, and dogs engaged in ratting ; on other days the birds are left to themselves. He had been out on the meadows at all times and seasons, and what he proposed to bring under the Club's notice was the observations he had made, extending over several years. Even in the limited time at his disposal he had observed upwards of sixty different species of birds on the Bog Meadows, and further search would probably reveal more. The birds are as follow :—Missel-thrush, song-thrush, redwing, fieldfare, blackbird, stone-chat, whin-chat, robin, whitethroat, golden-crested wren, willow-wren, wood-wren, sedge-warbler, grasshopper-warbler, hedge-sparrow, great tit, blue tit, wren, pied wagtail, grey wagtail, meadow-pipit, swallow, martin, sand-martin, greenfinch, house-sparrow, chaffinch, bullfinch, linnet, twite, lesser redpoll, yellow-hammer, reed-bunting, starling, magpie, jackdaw, rook, skylark, swift, kingfisher, cuckoo, barn owl, long-eared owl, merlin, kestrel, sparrow-hawk, heron, bernacle goose, mute swan, wild duck, teal, wigeon, corncrake, water-rail, lapwing, woodcock, snipe, jack-snipe, redshank, curlew, and black-headed gull. Of these sixty-one birds, twenty

have been found breeding in the meadows. The remarkable
increase of the missel-thrush was commented on, this now
common bird being unknown in Ireland until about the year
1800. Mr. Patterson gave extracts from his notebook, showing
the increase and diminution of these birds according to the
season, and next proceeded to speak of the fieldfare, which, he
said, builds in large colonies in Northern Europe. The whin-
chat, a rare and local summer visitor, has been observed in the
meadows, and the chief differences between it and the stone-
chat were pointed out. Interesting details about the migration
of the golden-crested wren were given, the great migration
waves of 1882, 1883, and 1884 being mentioned. The most
uncommon bird Mr. Patterson has observed on the meadows is
the very rare wood-wren (only obtained in Ireland three or four
times), and the original entry in his notebook was read. He
pointed out the differences between the three warblers, and how
they may be known apart. The grasshopper-warbler was heard
for the first time on the meadows last year by the junior
secretary of the Club, to whom the reader was indebted for the
information. Of the two wagtails, the grey is resident, the pied
partially migratory. Interesting details about the sand-martins
were given, these useful birds having been turned out of their
nests by sparrows and starlings, and having now deserted their
former breeding place. A pair of bullfinches bred in 1887, and
the other buntings were described as common. The starling is
an interesting bird in Belfast, owing to its marvellous increase
of late years, extracts from the late Mr. Thompson's book
showing that about thirty years ago this bird was very uncommon in the neighbourhood; yet recently a flock of not
less than 10,000 to 12,000 starlings has been seen in a district
of Belfast, and the increase is still going on. Jackdaws and
rooks were next noticed, and a small rookery in the meadows
described. Mr. Patterson described the difference both in
structure and habits between swifts and swallows, and stated
that the swift, although so common here, is rare in the
West of Ireland. He gave in detail his notes on a kingfisher

observed on five occasions on the meadows. Both the barn-owl and the long-eared owl have been found, the latter being much more common in the North of Ireland than the former. Of the birds of prey, the little merlin has once been shot on the meadows, and the kestrel and sparrow-hawk are frequent. The reader commented on the senseless destruction of the kestrel by ignorant gamekeepers, this bird living principally upon mice, and being, therefore, of great service to farmers. He described one occasion when he saw a sparrow-hawk pursue and kill a pipit a few feet from where he was, and then proceeded to speak of the differences between falcons and hawks. A falcon has long wings, short thighs and *tarsi*, comparatively robust toes, with powerful claws, and always has a dark eye. A hawk has short wings, long thighs, and slender *tarsi* and toes, and invariably has a coloured eye, usually yellow or orange. Wild geese are sometimes met with on the meadows, and have been observed, Mr. Thompson being quoted in corroboration ; while the mute or tame swan is occasionally seen. Wild duck, teal, and wigeon frequent the meadows when flooded in winter, and afford excellent sport to many sportsmen who wait for the evening flight. Mr. Patterson next gave extracts from his notebook illustrative of the habits of the lapwing, or green plover, the flocks of these birds showing a regular tendency to increase towards the end of January, for which he gave the reason. Snipe are frequent on the meadows, and many are shot every year. Of the waders, curlew and redshank occur—the former is frequently seen, large flocks being often heard passing at night. The black-headed gull is often to be seen inland, and is of great service to farmers, as it devours large quantities of grubs and worms. In winter it loses the black head. Mr. Patterson concluded by saying that he hoped he had shown it was not necessary to go very far from home to observe the wonders of bird life.

The paper elicited a number of questions about the birds mentioned, and some additional facts about bird life in the neighbourhood of Belfast. Mr. John Hamilton stated that the

ring-ouzel had been seen on the Black Mountain not far from
the meadows. Mr. Alexander Tate, C.E., spoke of the increase
of the starling, of its partial migration, and of the friendliness
existing between starlings and rooks. Mr. George Donaldson
also bore testimony to the former rarity of starlings, stating that
a nest built in his house between thirty and forty years ago had
to be guarded with jealous care against the persistent efforts
made by youthful collectors to obtain the young birds from it.
Mr. F. D. Ward, M.R.I.A., gave an interesting instance of the
boldness of the sparrow-hawk when in pursuit of its prey, a fine
bird having dashed itself against a plate-glass window of the
Royal Ulster Works in Dublin Road not many years ago,
killing itself instantly. Mr. F. W. Lockwood, the President,
and others having spoken, Mr. Patterson replied to the questions
that had been asked.

The sixth meeting of the Winter Session was held on Tuesday, March 17th, when the evening was devoted to an exhibition of microscopical objects and appliances. This was the
inaugural meeting of the new section of the Club recently
formed for the practical study and encouragement of the science
of microscopy. The meeting was opened at 7.30 by the
President, who testified to the great pleasure it gave him to
preside on this interesting occasion. He reminded members
that this was the first annual general meeting of the new section,
and that its other meetings would be for those only who
enrolled themselves members of the microscopical section, which
they could do without any additional fee. He was sure there
were many present who would be glad to pay the small annual
subscription that entitled them to membership of the Club for
the privilege of obtaining the advantages of the microscopical
section alone. He would now call on the Chairman of the new
section. Mr. Alexander Tate, C.E., chairman of the microscopical section, briefly explained the aims and objects for which

the section was established. There had been a want of system in the microscopical work carried on in Belfast, a want of that union among workers that so much encourages and fosters scientific research, and especially a want of a central body to whom all beginners in this interesting branch of study could come for information and assistance. To fill these wants the new section had been established, and he thought its power as an educational institution was shown by the wide range of subjects on exhibition that night, and the interesting demonstrations that were about to be given of the preparation and mounting of all kinds of microscopical objects. The meeting was then declared open, and the company scattered themselves around the tables, on which fully twenty microscopes were ranged, illustrating nearly as many different branches of research. Special prominence was given to demonstrations of the modes of preparing slides of various objects and materials. Mr. Joseph Wright, F.G.S., explained the means adopted for the examination of the interesting group of the *Foraminifera*. By his side stood a bag of sandy mud, obtained from the sea bottom off the South-West of Ireland on one of the dredging expeditions recently sent out by the Royal Irish Academy. He showed how by drying the material, throwing it into water, and skimming off and straining all that floated on the surface, the *Foraminifera* were separated from the mud that encompassed them, and thousands of their tiny and exquisite shells secured for examination. Mr. Adam Speers, B.Sc., demonstrated the mode of cutting sections of vegetable tissues with a razor, and shewed a number of such sections to advantage. In close proximity, Mr. William Hanna, B.A., exhibited a ribbon-sectioning microtome, with which he cut a block of paraffin into a long ribbon, one-four thousandth part of an inch in thickness, with ease and despatch. The President had one of the most interesting exhibitions in the room, consisting of a demonstration of the compound structure of the eyes of insects. A watch hung at the back of the table, and viewed by aid of the microscope through the eye of various insects, was seen to be multiplied many hundred times. Messrs. James Stelfox and W. S. M'Kee illustrated pond life, and the variety and beauty of the tiny organisms that frequent fresh water were displayed by them to great advantage, as testified by the constant crowd that surrounded their table. In the department of geology Messrs. Daniel M'Kee and George J. Glen showed sections of precious stones, and the manner in which they are prepared ; Mr. William Swanston, F.G.S., showed a variety of geological subjects ; and Mr. John Donaldson illustrated the crystallisation of salts. Animal tissues were well shown by Mr. William Chancellor, B.A. ; Mr. J. C. Rowan displayed histological subjects ; Mr. George Elliott, micro-organisms and pathological sections ; Mr.W. D. Donnan, lower forms of animal and vegetable life ; and Mr. I. W. Ward illustrated insects. In cryptogamic botany, sections and spores of lichens were shown by Mr. Henry Davis, and rare diatoms by Mr. W. A. Firth. Mr. Alexander Tate, C.E., had an interesting collection of miscellaneous objects, and Mr. Robert Welch gave an excellent exhibition of the method of micro-photography. At nine o'clock a short business meeting was called, and a large number of nominations followed the President's request that the names of any proposed new members of the Club should then be submitted to the meeting. A few formal announcements by the Secretaries concluded the formal business of the evening, but it was long after that the company departed, well pleased with the opening meeting of the microscopical section.

The seventh meeting of the Winter Session was held on Tuesday evening, April 14th, the President in the chair, when two communications were brought forward.

The first paper was entitled "Notes on some rare Hepatics and Mosses found in Ulster," and, in the absence of the writer, Rev. H. W. Lett, M.A., was brought forward by Mr. R. Lloyd Praeger, junior secretary. No abstract of this communication has been furnished by the author.

The second paper was entitled "The Gold Antiquities of Ireland," and was brought forward by the writer, Mr. C. Winston Dugan, M.A., H.M. Inspector of Schools. Mr. Dugan, in introducing his subject, said that every people, civilised and uncivilised, have, as it were, by a kind of instinct, a deep interest in their own history ; their records and traditions form a sort of national inheritance which nothing else can replace. Why should not every Irishman feel a pride and interest in the history of his country ? Why should he not do everything in his power to bring to light and to preserve all the materials which serve to illustrate and build up that history, and then strive to emulate and better what is past ? The question arises : What authority have we in the Present to relate what has occurred in the intangible Past ? How can we arrive at the truth of early history ? Clearly the answer is threefold—1, by that which is spoken ; 2, by that which is written ; and 3, by that which is left, as memorials of the time, in works upon tangible things. It was with the third of these three sources of history that the present paper had to deal, and with only one section of that source, which might be divided into the following heads :—Language, buildings, weapons, utensils, and ornaments. The last of these heads—ornaments—was what the reader proposed to consider that evening, and his remarks would be confined to such ornaments only as were made of gold. All authorities agree in stating that the ancient inhabitants of Ireland must have been very familiar with gold, and well accustomed to its use. Native gold has been found in geological deposits in many parts of Ireland. Until lately the gold mines of Wicklow were the most productive in the British Isles, and, besides this, there are six other known gold-producing localities —Antrim, Derry, Tyrone, Kildare, Dublin, and Wexford. It is probable, however, that many of the earlier auriferous deposits have been worked out, or are now unknown. It is a fact that no country in Europe possesses so much manufactured gold belonging to early ages as Ireland. In the museum of the Royal Irish Academy alone there are nearly four hundred specimens of Irish gold antiques. The gold antiquities in the British Museum illustrative of British history are, without exception, Irish. The museum of Trinity College, Dublin, contains many fine examples, and there are several large private collections. But there is no doubt that much greater quantities of gold ornaments than are now known as existing have been lost for ever. A number of quotations from various early Irish writers were next given to show how constantly gold and golden ornaments are mentioned by the ancient chroniclers, and what abundance of the precious metal must formerly have been in use. The principal antiquities of gold that remain to us may be classed under ten heads, as follow :—1. Crowns—A magnificent gold ornament resembling in shape a helmet or skullcap, found in County Tipperary in 1692, and now in the Royal Irish Academy collection, which has been called a crown for want of a better name, was described, and a drawing exhibited. This specimen is unique, but a somewhat similar gold cap is described by Vallancey in 1783. 2. Minds of *lunulæ*—These elegant ornaments may be described as flat crescent-shaped plates of gold, with a small plate at each extremity ; they have been discovered on frequent occasions ; and their surface is frequently enriched with minute and elaborate designs. Mr. Dugan showed a fine example from his own collection, found in boggy land in West Mayo, and exhibited drawings of some of the finest of the fifteen *lunulæ* in the Royal Irish Academy collection. 3. Diadems — These gorgeous and elaborate ornaments have also been frequently found, and are undoubtedly the most magnificent specimens of gold work to be found in the world. Like the *lunulæ*, they were probably head ornaments, and their great antiquity is shown by the fact that they are not mentioned among any of the known annals. 4. Gorgets—These were probably collars of gold, such as Malachi " won from the proud invader." Some of them exhibit the peculiar herringbone ornamentation characteristic of Celtic work. 5. Necklaces of gold and amber were not uncommon in Ireland, and must have constituted unique and splendid ornaments. The amber probably came from the Baltic shores. 6. Ear-rings or *unasca*—The ancient Irish ear-rings are not unlike those used in modern days. 7. *Armillæ*—Armlets and bracelets would appear to have been extensively used. They usually consist of rings of gold not quite closed, and the early annals state that royal princes bestowed rings of gold on poets, philosophers, and warriors, and that tribute was frequently paid in similar ornaments. 8. *Fibulæ* —There has been some difference of opinion as to the use of these peculiarly-shaped gold ornaments, but the theory that they were used as fasteners for cloaks, &c., would appear to be the most reasonable one. The *fibulæ* vary greatly in size, weighing from seven ounces up to the extraordinary weight of thirty-three ounces. 9. Torques must be considered as a distinctive and common form of decoration among the ancient Irish, but we know that they were similarly used by the Egyptians, Persians, Gauls, &c. They in shape consist of twisted bands, and according to their size were worn on the finger, in the hair, round the neck or waist. In the celebrated statue " The Dying Gladiator" there is a torque round the neck, as also in the exquisite bronze statue of Mercury in the British Museum. 10. Ring Money—It is probable that many of the circular ornaments already described were used as a sort of money, but there are certain small gold rings whose size would preclude their use for anything else, unless indeed for portions of chains. Mr. Dugan then entered into evidences which point to a very early Oriental connection with Ireland, and to a subsequent long period of social and artistic darkness. But Ireland rose again like a phœnix, and from the fourth to the eighth centuries of the Christian era was the light of Europe. Reference was next made to the composition of the gold ornaments, which varies from eighteen to twenty-one carats fine. The alloy consists of silver and a little copper, probably identical with that of the native ore from which they have been manufactured. After recapitulating the evidence to show that the Irish gold ornaments were manufactured in Ireland, and out of Irish gold, the reader said that in researches like these at least, in the study and contemplation of our ancient history and civilisation, all our countrymen may join, and all may unite in a labour of love and of duty in rescuing from oblivion the existing memorials of a long-lost and unique artistic age. But in this work we must constantly bear the truth in mind, nor allow any cloud of prejudice to obscure our reason or warp our judgment. Historical truth stands on a lofty pedestal, and if we would see her we must purify ourselves by work and by love. Researches, antiquarian and historical, made in the light of this purified love, must needs consolidate, instead of weaken, the bonds between nations, between Celt and Saxon, and mayhap heal the scars that rend them asunder. To quote Sir Edward Arnold's beautiful words in the "Light of Asia"—

> Love, which is sunlight of peace,
> Age by age to increase,
> Till anger and hate are dead,
> And sorrow and death shall cease.

A discussion on the paper ensued, in which Mr. Seaton F. Milligan, M.R.I.A., Mr. F. W. Lockwood, and the President took part, and Mr. Dugan was warmly thanked for his excellent communication. The election of a number of new members, and some announcements by the Secretaries brought the meeting to a conclusion.

ANNUAL MEETING.

The twenty-eighth annual meeting of the Club was held in the Belfast Museum, on Wednesday evening, 29th April, the chair being taken by the President.

The first business was to receive the Secretaries' report, which was read by Mr. F. W. Lockwood, Senior Secretary, and which, with the statement of accounts, appears in full in the earlier pages of this part of the Proceedings.

The President next called for the annual statement of

accounts, which, in the unavoidable absence of the Treasurer, was read by Mr. R. Lloyd Praeger, M.R.I.A., Junior Secretary, and showed that the Club was in a sound financial condition.

On the motion of Mr. Joseph Wright, F.G.S., seconded by Mr. Alexander Tate, C.E., the report and statement of accounts were adopted.

The report of the Photographic Committee was next submitted, which ran as follows :—The Photographic Committee beg to report that they have met six times since last annual meeting, at which they were appointed. Early in the year they issued a special circular calling the attention of members to the formation of this section, and requesting their co-operation. Since then the Committee have been engaged in collecting lists of all photographic negatives of antiquities, &c., at present in the possession of members, and it is hoped that members will favour the Committee with permanent prints of all such negatives as are considered suitable for the new albums which the Committee purpose providing. In these, the photographs will be systematically arranged according to class, and they will, it is hoped, in time become a sort of illustrative catalogue of the antiquities, &c., of at least the North of Ireland. Any members possessing negatives, who have not yet sent in a list of such to the Committee, are requested to do so without delay. The Committee trust that during the coming summer members will lose no opportunity of securing photographs of all ancient monuments, rock sections, &c., which they may have an opportunity of visiting, and of furnishing to the Committee a permanent print (platinotype if possible) of all such negatives obtained. Each photograph should be accompanied by a filled schedule of particulars. Printed schedules specially prepared for this purpose may be obtained from the Secretaries on application.

On the motion of Mr. John Hamilton, seconded by Mr. Robert Patterson, the report was received.

The election of office-bearers for the coming year was then proceeded with.

On the motion of Mr. Wm. Swanston, F.G.S., seconded by Mr. Daniel M'Kee, Mr. John Vinycomb, F.R.S.A.I., was elected President for the ensuing year.

The retiring President, rising, said that his duties had now ended. He thanked the members for their courtesy and assistance during his term of office, and had great pleasure and confidence in resigning his post to an old and tried member of the Club like Mr. Vinycomb.

Mr. Vinycomb, in taking the chair amid applause, thanked the meeting for the honour they had done him in selecting him to fill the office of President.

Mr. Wm. Swanston, F.G.S., was then elected Vice-President; Mr. W. H. Phillips, F.R.H.S., Treasurer ; and Messrs. R. Lloyd Praeger, B.E., M.R.I.A., and Francis Joseph Bigger, Secretaries.

Mr. Wm. Gray, M.R.I.A., moved, and Mr. Geo. Donaldson seconded, a vote of thanks to Mr. F. W. Lockwood for his valuable services as Secretary during the period of the past eleven years, to which

Mr. Lockwood suitably replied.

The Committee, with some slight changes, were re-elected, and the receiving of suggestions for places to be visited on the summer excursions, an exhibition of a rare bird—an albino twite or mountain finch—captured near Ballymena, and an examination of the prize collections, brought the proceedings to a close.

METEOROLOGICAL SUMMARIES
for 1888, 1889, and 1890.

In November, 1888, the death of Mr. LANCELOT TURTLE, J.P., of Aghalee, brought to a termination the valuable meteorological summaries which for many years he had annually contributed to the Proceedings of the Club, and which were much appreciated by the members.

We have pleasure in now being in a position to supply this deficiency. Through the kindness of the Council of Queen's College, Belfast, access has been granted to the records kept at that institution, and we publish with this number meteorological summaries for the three years that have elapsed since the appearance of the last of Mr. Turtle's reports. The nature of the information in the following pages will be found to vary somewhat from that supplied by Mr. Turtle. This is the result of differences in the nature of the observations taken, but while some records formerly published do not now appear, additional information on other points is, on the other hand, now included in the summaries.

The station at which the records are made is situated in the Lagan Valley, at an elevation of about sixty feet above mean sea level. The Belfast hills, which attain a maximum elevation of 1,567 feet, lie to the west and north, stretching in a N.E. and S.W. line, and passing within three miles of the Obsèrvatory. Southward and eastward stretch the low undulating lands of Co. Down. Lough Neagh is situated some 14 miles to the westward. Belfast Lough approaches to within two miles on the N.E., and the open sea lies some 16 miles east of the observing station.

REVIEW OF THE WEATHER FOR 1888.

Meteorological Observations taken at Queen's College, Belfast, at 9 a.m. each day.
Latitude, 54° 35′ N.; Longitude, 5° 56′ W.

	BAROMETER 70 Feet above Sea Level.—Actual Readings.									SELF-REGISTERING THERMOMETERS in shade, in stand outside window, 21 feet above ground.										HYGROMETER	
	Highest of the Month			Lowest of the Month			Mean		Range	Highest of the Month		Lowest of the Month		Mean Maximum	Date	Mean Minimum	Mean of two preceding	Monthly Range			Mean of dry Bulb	Mean of wet Bulb
	Inches	Att. Ther.	Date	Inches	Att. Ther.	Date	Inches	Att. Ther.	Inches	Deg. F.	Date	Deg. F.	Date	Deg. F.	Date	Deg. F.	Deg. F.	Deg. F.				
	30·630	47·0	13	29·100	38·0	2	30·125	43·1	1·530	55·0	26	24·0	28	46·2	28	36·9	41·6	31·0			42·7	40·9
	30·500	42·0	28	29·460	40·0	11	30·041	40·8	1·040	52·0	6	19·5	14	43·6	14	33·7	38·6	32·5			37·9	35·1
	30·370	38·0	21	28·700	40·0	28	29·546	40·6	1·670	54·0	10	26·0	17	44·9	17	32·9	38·9	28·0			40·2	38·1
	30·230	42·0	7	29·400	52·0	17	29·868	47·2	·830	59·0	29	28·0	8	51·9	8	38·1	45·0	31·0			45·7	33·5
	30·500	60·0	23	29·010	50·0	1	29·958	52·8	1·490	69·0	21	34·8	13	59·9	13	39·6	49·7	34·2			52·8	48·3
	30·260	61·8	19	29·500	62·0	28	29·943	56·7	·760	80·0	26	41·0	17	64·6	17	47·4	56·0	39·0			55·6	51·1
	30·100	58·0	12	29·400	62·0	23	29·740	59·4	·700	68·0	13	42·0	7	60·2	7	49·5	54·8	26·0			57·0	54·0
	30·200	58·0	17	29·400	61·0	24	29·887	61·5	·800	69·0	25	42·0	2	65·1	2	50·5	57·8	27·0			58·3	54·8
ber	30·460	55·0	8	29·720	55·0	30	30·130	55·7	·740	65·0	3	39·0	9	61·0	9	47·8	54·4	26·0			53·2	51·8
ber	30·400	48·0	22	29·260	45·0	2	29·961	50·0	1·140	64·0	29	36·0	21	54·7	21	42·6	48·6	28·0			49·0	46·8
er	29·970	48·0	6	29·126	40·0	27	29·626	48·5	·844	56·0	15	32·0	27	51·7	27	41·7	46·7	24·0			46·8	44·3
er	30·380	43·8	16	29·120	46·5	23	29·800	48·0	1·260	58·0	4	26·0	31	48·6	31	35·6	42·1	32·0			42·2	41·4
	364·000	601·6		351·196	591·5		358·625		12·804	749·0		390·3		652·3		496·3	573·7	358·7			581·4	540·1
s..	30·333	50·1		29·266	49·3		29·885		1·067	62·4		32·5		54·4		41·4	47·8	29·9			48·5	45·0

REVIEW OF THE WEATHER FOR 1888.—*Continued.*

1888.	WIND. Direction and Amount of Wind, as indicated by Casella's Self-Recording Anemometer.															RAINFALL. Gauge—Diameter of Receiver, 11in.; height of top above ground, 7ft. 11in.; height above sea level, 60ft.				
	Average Daily Direction.									Daily Amount.						Total Depth.	Greatest fall in one day.		No. of days on which .01 or more fell.
	N.	N.E.	E.	S.E.	S.	S.W.	W.	N.W.	Var.	Greatest in one day.		Least in one day.		Mean Daily Am'nt.					
	Days	Days	Days	Days	Days	Days	Days	Days	Days	Miles.	Date.	Miles.	Date.	Miles.		Inches.	Inches.	Date.	Days
January......	1	2	6	5	5	6	2	1	3	582	25th	40	12th	138		1·789	·503	3rd	11
February......	6	9				2	9		2	395	19th	65	15th	206		·273	·184	2nd	7
March.........	5	3	7	2	1	2	3	5	3	565	15th	60	24th	207		3·272	·800	11th	18
April.........	3	6	2	4	1	4	4	4	2	460	15th	64	6th	233		1·285	·244	18th	15
May..........	2	3	4	3	1	2	5	6	5	616	2nd	74	9th	196		2·847	1·333	29th	10
June..........	5	7	4	3	2	1	3	1	4	340	11th	68	27th	163		3·783	1·025	27th	14
July..........	4	4	3	5	2	3	4	2	4	380	10th	35	13th	145		4·326	·802	27th	21
August.......	2	2		3	3	8	6	2	2	305	19th	37	1st	143		3·827	·843	21st	18
September...	2	1	8	2	1	4	6	2	3	353	1st	23	22nd	122		1·434	·364	1st	10
October......	2		2	1	5	6	4	8	2	360	4th	25	9th	161		1·118	·205	27th	14
November....	2	5	7		7	6		1	1	512	20th	115	13th	324		6·326	1·533	12th	25
December....	1		1	3	7	9	6	4		380	21st	70	30th	150		2·650	·365	2nd	16
Totals......	35	42	44	37	35	53	52	36	31	5248		676		2193		32·830			179
Means										437		56		183					

REVIEW OF THE WEATHER FOR 1889.

Meteorological Observations taken at Queen's College, Belfast, at 9 a.m. each day.
Latitude, 54° 35' N.; Longitude, 5° 56' W.

	BAROMETER. 70 Feet above Sea Level.—Actual Readings.									SELF-REGISTERING THERMOMETERS in shade, in stand outside window, 21 feet above ground.								HYGROMETER.	
	Highest of the Month			Lowest of the Month			Mean		Range	Highest of the Month		Lowest of the Month		Mean Maximum	Mean Minimum	Mean of two preceding	Monthly Range	Mean of dry Bulb	Mean of wet Bulb
	Inches.	Att. Ther.	Date	Inches.	Att. Ther.	Date	Inches.	Att. Ther.	Inches.	Deg. F.	Date	Deg. F.	Date	Deg. F.	Deg. F.	Deg. F.	Deg. F.		
	30·550	44·0	22	29·100	45·0	9	30·037	45·5	1·450	55·0	19	24·0	2	46·3	34·9	40·6	31·0	41·2	39·9
	30·400	48·0	19	29·360	43·0	14	29·899	43·8	1·040	55·0	1	25·0	10	46·7	34·8	40·7	30·0	40·2	38·3
	30·500	51·0	15	29·000	45·0	20	29·923	48·4	1·500	57·0	25	26·0	4	48·9	39·9	44·4	31·0	42·7	40·4
	30·080	50·0	18	29·166	48·5	4	29·702	47·6	·914	59·0	20	34·0	15	51·8	40·1	45·9	25·0	46·1	42·5
	30·100	64·0	21	29·450	62·0	29	29·722	57·7	·650	72·0	22	41·0	2	62·3	46·0	54·2	31·0	56·0	52·0
	30·470	61·0	5	29·660	54·0	5	30·058	63·0	·810	76·0	27	40·8	8	68·8	49·0	58·9	35·2	60·7	55·3
	30·500	64·0	1	29·500	58·0	25	29·928	61·6	1·000	74·0	7	45·0	24	66·7	50·9	58·8	29·0	59·1	54·7
	30·110	58·0	31	29·250	57·0	21	29·750	60·5	·860	69·0	10	41·0	25	65·1	50·1	57·6	28·0	60·1	55·2
er	30·392	60·5	15	29·366	52·0	20	29·990	57·4	1·026	69·0	10	38·0	25	62·5	47·1	54·8	31·0	56·6	52·9
er	30·220	48·0	26	29·110	48·0	8	29·630	49·0	1·110	58·0	5	33·0	14	53·8	41·2	47·5	25·0	49·3	47·3
er	30·532	47·0	17	29·226	52·0	1	30·116	48·5	1·306	57·0	8	30·0	17	51·5	40·2	45·8	27·0	45·7	43·7
er	30·600	45·0	5	29·510	45·0	10	29·995	42·3	1·090	55·0	18	30·0	14	47·6	36·3	41·9	25·0	41·4	40·3
	364·454	640·5		351·698	609·5		358·750		12·756	756·0		407·8		672·0	510·5	591·1	348·2	599·1	562·5
	30·871	53·4		29·308	50·8		29·895		1·063	63·0		33·9		56·0	42·5	49·3	29·0	49·9	46·9

Review of the Weather for 1889.—Continued.

WIND.

Direction and Amount of Wind, as indicated by Casella's Self-Recording Anemometer.

RAINFALL.

Gauge.—Diameter of Receiver, 11in.; height of top above ground, 7ft. 1in.; height above sea level, 6oft.

1889.	Average Daily Direction.									Daily Amount.					Total Depth.	Greatest fall in one day.		No. of days on which .01 or more fell.
	N.	N.E.	E.	S.E.	S.	S.W.	W.	N.W.	Var.	Greatest in one day		Least in one day		Mean Daily Am'nt		Greatest fall		
	Days	Days	Days	Days	Days	Days	Days	Days	Days	Miles.	Date.	Miles.	Date.	Miles.	Inches.	Inches.	Date.	Days
January......	1	1	2	1	4	9	9	3	2	327	15th	58	6th	157	2·577	·800	8th	15
February.....	5	2	1	3		3	5	5	4	512	3rd	56	25th	234	2·768	·528	6th	19
March........	3	4	1	4	1	4	6	7	3	522	25th	45	2nd	169	2·639	·813	19th	19
April........	5	1	8	3	1	4	2	1	2	425	1st	98	17th	222	2·646	·694	8th	16
May..........		2	4	6	8	2	4	2	4	408	2nd	35	18th	136	1·675	·368	12th	11
June	4	2	6	6	2	1	3	2	3	452	1st	75	17th	133	·308	·220	2nd	5
July.........	5		4	5	1	6	5	5	3	462	26th	60	20th	131	2·553	·648	10th	15
August.......	3	1	2		1	1	7	10	2	285	28th	60	31st	169	6·399	1·342	21st	23
September...	3		4	4	7	4	2	7	1	475	19th	35	4th	175	2·351	·670	18th	12
October......	3	6	7	1			4	3	3	514	7th	22	16th	194	3·854	·604	6th	22
November....	3			4	1	12	10	4		507	1st	18	17th	142	1·206	·315	24th	12
December...					6	11	7	2	1	345	18th	50	4th	181	2·223	·428	6th	19
Totals......	35	19	39	37	32	59	65	51	28	5234		612		2043	31·199			188
Means.......										436		51		170·2				

REVIEW OF THE WEATHER FOR 1890.

Meteorological Observations taken at Queen's College, Belfast, at 9 a.m. each day.
Latitude, 54° 35′ N.; Longitude, 5° 56′ W.

	BAROMETER 70 Feet above Sea Level.—Actual Readings.									SELF-REGISTERING THERMOMETERS in shade, in stand outside window, 21 feet above ground.								HYGROMETER	
	Highest of the Month.			Lowest of the Month.			Mean.		Range.	Highest of the Month.		Lowest of the Month.		Mean Maximum.	Mean Minimum.	Mean of two preceding.	Monthly Range.	Mean of dry Bulb.	Mean of wet Bulb.
	Inches.	Att. Ther.	Date	Inches.	Att. Ther.	Date	Inches.	Att. Ther.	Inches.	Deg. F.	Date	Deg. F.	Date	Deg. F.	Deg. F.	Deg. F.	Deg. F.		
	30·322	48·0	31	28·830	40·0	23	29·967	44·4	1·492	55·0	12	30·0	23	49·1	34·3	41·7	25·0	42·4	40·9
	30·700	48·0	23	29·510	43·0	16	30·264	45·8	1·190	54·0	1	31·0	14	46·9	36·0	41·4	23·0	42·4	38·5
	30·550	39·0	3	29·172	47·0	3	29·718	47·4	1·378	58·0	13	28·0	3	51·1	37·0	44·0	30·0	44·9	42·4
	30·260	47·0	1	29·400	49·0	25	29·780	48·9	·860	59·0	5	30·0	12	43·4	38·6	41·0	29·0	47·1	44·0
	30·170	60·0	28	29·430	57·0	17	29·814	57·2	·740	71·0	25	39·0	14	61·2	45·2	53·2	32·0	54·4	50·0
	30·350	57·5	7	29·100	60·0	30	29·900	61·0	1·250	71·0	15	37·0	1	61·3	49·4	55·4	34·0	60·5	54·6
	30·180	63·5	21	29·510	58·0	8	29·894	60·6	·670	70·8	15	42·0	12	65·6	50·1	57·8	28·8	60·1	54·8
	30·180	62·0	7	29·250	50·6	26	29·849	60·6	·930	74·0	5	41·0	30	65·5	49·0	57·2	33·0	59·5	54·3
	30·450	62·0	6	29·340	60·0	21	30·047	60·8	1·110	70·0	8	42·0	1	62·8	51·5	57·1	28·0	60·8	56·5
	30·490	54·0	22	29·590	49·0	31	30·000	53·0	·900	65·0	6	34·0	27	58·0	43·9	50·9	31·0	51·7	48·3
	30·320	52·0	20	29·110	45·0	4	29·800	42·8	1·210	58·0	20	26·0	27	50·8	37·8	44·3	32·0	43·9	42·3
	30·426	40·0	26	29·230	43·0	19	29·980	42·7	1·196	54·0	2	23·0	21	44·2	34·1	39·1	31·0	38·8	37·3
	364·898	633·0		351·472	609·6		359·012		12·926	759·8		403·0		659·9	506·9	583·1	356·8	606·5	563·9
	30·366	52·7		29·289	50·8		29·918		1·077	63·3		38·6		54·9	42·2	48·6	29·7	50·5	46·9

REVIEW OF THE WEATHER FOR 1890.—Continued.

WIND.

Direction and Amount of Wind, as indicated by Casella's Self-Recording Anemometer.

1890.	Average Daily Direction.									Daily Amount.				
	N.	N.E.	E.	S.E.	S.	S.W.	W.	N.W.	Var.	Greatest in one day.		Least in one day.		Mean Daily Am'nt.
	Days	Days	Days	Days	Days	Days	Days	Days	Days	Miles.	Date.	Miles.	Date.	Miles.
January....	1	2	4	12	4	12	12	2	3	650	18th	135	23rd	289
February...	3	1	2	4	1	2	2	4	2	340	11th	35	23rd	143
March......	1	6	5	4	1	5	11	1		575	6th	67	28th	236
April........	6	2	8	4	1	4	3	1	2	542	22nd	25	3rd	203
May.........	1	5	2	8	3	3	5	1	3	369	25th	107	2nd	193
June.........	1	2	1	1	2	3	8	4	1	475	3rd	74	14th	213
July.........	5	1	4			3	8	8	3	410	22nd	105	16th	217
August......	5	1	2	2	6	1	9	7	1	310	15th	68	6th	164
September...		1		3	1	3	8	5	1	492	20th	80	12th	207
October.....	2				5	6	10	10	4	532	16th	94	22nd	229
November...	1	3	7	3	1	9	3	2		612	6th	75	26th	211
December...	3	11		3			2	2	2	502	30th	25	19th	171
Totals......	29	35	35	40	25	51	82	46	22	5809		890		2476
Means.. ...										484		74		206

RAINFALL.

Gauge—Diameter of Receiver, 11in.; height of top above ground, 7ft 11in.; height above sea level, 6oft

1890.	Total Depth.	Greatest fall in one day.		No. of days on which ·01 or more fell.
	Inches.	Inches.	Date.	Days.
January....	3·148	·634	9th	24
February...	1·356	·338	17th	9
March......	2·519	1·052	15th	15
April........	1·228	·206	9th	16
May.........	1·619	·456	29th	14
June.........	2·779	·570	28th	21
July.........	1·968	·323	30th	18
August......	2·589	·628	10th	18
September...	3·311	·895	20th	15
October.....	2·245	·469	15th	14
November...	7·763	1·723	6th	23
December...	2·053	·595	2nd	14
Totals......	32·578			201
Means.. ...				

RULES

OF THE

Belfast Naturalists' Field Club.

I.

That the Society be called "THE BELFAST NATURALISTS' FIELD CLUB."

II.

That the objects of the Society be the practical study of Natural Science and Archæology in Ireland.

III.

That the Club shall consist of Ordinary, Corresponding, and Honorary Members. The Ordinary Members to pay annually a subscription of Five Shillings, and that candidates for such Membership shall be proposed and seconded at any Meeting of the Club, by Members present, and elected by a majority of the votes of the Members present.

IV.

That the Honorary and Corresponding Members shall consist of persons of eminence in Natural Science, or who shall have done some special service to the Club; and whose usual residence is not less than twenty miles from Belfast. That such Members may be nominated by any Member of the Club, and on being approved of by the Committee, may be elected at any subsequent Meeting of the Club by a majority of the votes of the Members present. That Corresponding Members be expected to communicate a Paper once within every two years.

V.

That the Officers of the Club be annually elected, and consist of a President, Vice-President, Treasurer, and two Secretaries, and Ten Members, who form the Committee. Five to form a quorum. No member of Committee to be

eligible for re-election who has not attended at least one-fourth of the Committee Meetings during his year of office. That the office of President, or that of Vice-President, shall not be held by the same person for more than two years in succession.

VI.

That the Members of the Club shall hold at least Six Field Meetings during the year, in the most interesting localities, for investigating the Natural History and Archæology of Ireland. That the place of meeting be fixed by the Committee, and that five days' notice of each Excursion be communicated to Members by the Secretaries.

VII.

That Meetings be held Fortnightly or Monthly, at the discretion of the Committee, for the purpose of reading papers; such papers, as far as possible, to treat of the Natural History and Archæology of the district. These Meetings to be held during the months from November to April inclusive.

VIII.

That the Committee shall, if they find it advisable, offer for competition Prizes for the best collections of scientific objects of the district; and the Committee may order the purchase of maps, or other scientific apparatus, and may carry on geological and archæological searches or excavations, if deemed advisable, provided that the entire amount expended under this rule does not exceed the sum of £10 in any one year.

IX.

That the Annual Meeting be held during the month of April, when the Report of the Committee for the past year, and the Treasurer's Financial Statement shall be presented, the Committee and Officers elected, Bye-laws made and altered, and any proposed alteration in the general laws, of which a fortnight's notice shall have been given, in writing, to the Secretary or Secretaries, considered and decided upon. The Secretaries to give the Members due notice of such intended alteration.

X.

That, on the written requisition of twenty-five Members, delivered to the Secretaries, an Extraordinary General Meeting may be called, to consider and decide upon the subjects mentioned in such written requisition.

XI.

That the Committee be empowered to exchange publications and reports, and to extend the privilege of attending the Meetings and Excursions of the Belfast Naturalists' Field Club to members of kindred societies, on similar privileges being accorded to its members by such other societies.

The following Rules for the Conducting of the Excursions have been arranged by the Committee.

————∘∘⟐∘∘————

I. The Excursion to be open to all members; each one to have the privilege of introducing two friends.

II. A Chairman to be elected as at ordinary meetings.

III. One of the Secretaries to act as conductor, or in the absence of both, a member to be elected for that purpose.

IV. No change to be made in the programme, or extra expense incurred, except by the consent of the majority of the members present.

V. No fees, gratuities, or other expenses to be paid except through the conductor.

VI. Every member or visitor to have the accommodation assigned by the conductor. Where accommodation is limited, consideration will be given to priority of application.

VII. Accommodation cannot be promised unless tickets are obtained before the time mentioned in the special circular.

VIII. Those who attend an excursion, without previous notice, will be liable to extra charge, if extra cost be incurred thereby.

IX. No intoxicating liquors to be provided at the expense of the Club.

BELFAST NATURALISTS' FIELD CLUB.

——o——

TWENTY-NINTH YEAR.

——o——

THE Committee offer the following Prizes to be competed for during the Session ending March 31st, 1892 :—

I.	Best Herbarium of Flowering Plants, representing not less than 250 species,		...£1	0	0
II.	Best Herbarium of Flowering Plants, representing not less than 150 species,		... 0	10	0
III.	Best Collection of Mosses,	...	.. 0	10	0
IV.	,,	Lichens,	... 0	10	0
V.	,,	Seaweeds, ...	... 0	10	0
VI.	,,	Ferns, Equiseta, and Lycopods, ...	... 0	10	0
VII.	,,	Tertiary and Post-tertiary Fossils, ..	... 0	10	0
VIII.	,, ,,	Cretaceous Fossils,	... 0	10	0
IX.	,,	Liassic Fossils, ...	... 0	10	0
X.	,,	Permian and Carboniferous Fossils, ...	... 0	10	0
XI.	,,	Older Palæozoic Fossils, ...	0	10	0
XII.	,, ,,	Marine Shells, ...	.. 0	10	0
XIII.	,, ,,	Land and Freshwater Shells,	0	10	0
XIV.	,, ,,	Lepidoptera, ...	... 0	10	0

XV. Best Collection of Hymenoptera, ... £0 10 0

XVI. „ „ Coleoptera, ... 0 10 0

XVII. „ „ Crustacea and Echinodermata, ... 0 10 0

XVIII. Best Collection of Fungi; names of species
not necessary. Collectors may send (post-
paid, from time to time during the season)
their specimens to Rev. H. W. Lett, M.A.,
T.C.D., Aghaderg Glebe, Loughbrickland,
who will record them to their credit, ... 0 10 0

XIX. Best Collection of Fossil Sponges, ... 0 10 0

XX. Best Collection of 24 Microscopic Slides,
illustrating some special branch of Natural
History, ... 0 10 0

XXI. Best Collection of 24 Microscopic Slides,
shewing general excellence, ... 0 10 0

XXII. Best set of 6 Field Sketches appertaining to
Geology, Archæology, or Zoology, ... 0 10 0

XXIII. Best set of 12 Photographs, illustrative of
Irish Archæology, ... 0 10 0

SPECIAL PRIZES.

XXIV. The President offers a Prize of £1 1s. for the Best Set
of three or more Original Sketches, to be placed in
the Album of the Club. These may be executed in
pen and ink, or water colour, and must illustrate
one or more ancient monuments somewhere in
Ireland. In determining the relative merits of the
sketches, accuracy in representing the subjects and
their details will have chief place. This Prize is
open to the Members of the Belfast Art Society,
and to the Students of the School of Art.

XXV. Mr. William Swanston, F.G.S., offers a Prize of 10s. 6d. for Six Photographs from Nature, illustrative of Geology, contributed to the Club's Album.

XXVI. Mr. Francis Joseph Bigger, Solicitor, Belfast, offers a Prize of £1 1s. for the best Set of Twelve Photographs (not less than cabinet size) of Ecclesiastical Structures mentioned in Reeves' *Ecclesiastical Antiquities of Down and Connor*, contributed to the Club's Album. The set of Photographs taking this Prize cannot be admitted in competition for Prize XXIII.

XXVII. The Secretaries of the Ulster Fauna Committee offer a Prize of 10s. for the best Collection of Bats, Rodents, Insectivora, and Carnivora (names of species not necessary) collected in Ulster during the year. Specimens to be sent in a fresh state to the Museum, Belfast.

CONDITIONS.

No Competitor to obtain more than two Prizes in any year.

No Competitor to be awarded the same Prize twice within three years.

A member to whom Prize I. has been awarded shall be ineligible to compete for Prize II., unless the plants are additions to those in previous collection.

In every case where three or more Persons compete for a Prize, a second one, of half its value, will be awarded if the conditions are otherwise complied with.

All collections to be made personally during the Session in Ireland, except those for Prize XXI., which need not necessarily be Irish, nor Competitors' own collecting. The species to be classified according to a recognised system, to be correctly named, and localities stated, and a list to accompany each collection. The Flowering Plants to be collected when in flower, and classified according to the Natural System. The Microscopic Slides to be Competitors' own preparation and mounting. The Sketches and Photographs to be Competitors' own work, executed during the Session ; and those sets for which Prizes are awarded, to become the property of the Club.

No Prizes will be awarded except to such Collections as shall, in the opinion of the Judges, possess positive merit.

The Prizes to be in books, or suitable scientific objects, at the desire of the successful competitor.

NOTICE.

——⊕——

EXCHANGES OF PROCEEDINGS.

——⊕——

Amiens—Societé Linnéenne du Nord de la France.
  Bulletin, Tomes IX., and X.

Belfast—Linen Hall Library.
  Catalogue of early Belfast Printed Books, new and enlarged edition, 1890.

Brighton & Sussex— Natural History & Philosophical Society of.
  Abstracts of Papers, &c., 1888 to 1890.

Bristol—Naturalists' Society.
  Proceedings, Vol. VI., Part II.

Cardiff—Naturalists' Society.
  Report and Transactions, Vol. XXI., Part II., Vol. XXII., Part I.

Cornwall—Royal Institution of.
  Journal, Vol. X., Parts I. and II.

Costa Rica— Antiquities of Costa Rica.

Devizes—The Wiltshire Archæological and Natural History
        Magazine.
  Vol. XXV., No. 72.

Dublin—Royal Irish Academy.
        Transactions, Vol. XXIX., Part XIII.
        Cunningham Memoirs, Nos. V. and VI.

    „   Naturalists' Field Club.
        Reports, 1889 and 1890.

Dumfries and Galloway—Natural History and Antiquarian Society.
Transactions and Journal, Sessions 1887-88, 1888-89, 1889-90.

Edinburgh—Geological Society.
Transactions, Vol VI., Parts I. and II.

Frankfurt—Monatliche Mitthielungen, aus dem Gesammt-gebliete der Naturwissenschaften.
Nos. 1 to 9, 1890-91.

„ Societatum Litteræ.
Nos. 1 to 8, 1890-91.

Glasgow—Philosophical Society of.
Proceedings, Vols. XX. and XXI.

„ Natural History Society of.
Proceedings and Transactions, Vol. II., Part I., Vol. III., Part I.

Halifax—Nova Scotian Institute of Natural Science.
Proceedings and Transactions, Vol. VII., Part III.

Hertfordshire—Natural History Society and Field Club.
Transactions, Vol. V., Parts 8 and 9, Vol. VI., Parts 1, 2, 3.

Holmsdale—Natural History Club.
Proceedings, 1888-89.

Huddersfield—Naturalists' Society.
Monthly Circulars, 1889-90.

Leeds—Philosophical and Literary Society.
Annual Report, 1889-90.

Liverpool—Geological Society.
Proceedings, 1889-90.

„ Geological Association.
Transactions, Vol. X.

London—British Association for the Advancement of Science.
Report, 1889.

„ Geologists' Association.
Proceedings, Vol. XI., Nos. 6 to 8.

Manchester—Field Naturalists' and Archæologists' Society.
Report and Proceedings, 1889.

Scientific Students' Association.
Report and Proceedings, 1890.

Manchester—Microscopical Society.
Transactions, 1889.

Marlborough College—Natural History Society.
Reports, Nos. 38 and 39.

Norfolk and Norwich—Naturalists' Society.
Transactions, Vol. IV., Part IV.

Oldham—Microscopical Society and Field Club.
Journal, 1889.

Penzance—Natural History and Antiquarian Society.
Report and Transactions, 1889-90.

Plymouth—Institution.
Report and Transactions, Vol. X., Part III.

St. John's—Natural History Society of New Brunswick.
Bulletin, No. IX.

Stockport—Society of Naturalists.
Report, 1887-88.

Toronto—Canadian Institute.
Proceedings, Vol. VII., Fas. 2
Transactions, Vol. I., Part I.

U.S.A.—Boston Society of Natural History.
Proceedings, Vol. XIV., Parts I. to IV.

„ California—Academy of Sciences.
Proceedings, Vol. II., 1889.
Occasional Papers, I. and II.

„ Milwaukee Public Museum.
Annual Report (Seventh).

„ Minnesota Geological and Natural History Survey.
Report, 1888.
Bulletins, Nos. 1 to 5.
„ Geological Survey.
Parts I. and II.

„ New York—American Museum of Natural History.
Bulletin, Vol. II., Parts 3 & 4, & Vol. III., Part I.
„ Academy of Sciences.
Transactions, Vol. IX., Nos. 1 to 8.

„ Philadelphia—Academy of Natural Sciences.
Proceedings, 1888, Parts II. and III., and 1890, Parts I. & II.

U.S.A.—Raleigh, N.C.—Elisha Mitchell Scientific Society.
       Journal, Vol. IV., Part II., and Vol. V., Parts I. and II.

,,   Rochester—Academy of Sciences.
       Transactions, Vol. 1.

,,   Salem—American Association for the Advancement of Science.
       Proceedings of 28th Meeting, 1889.

,,   Washington—Smithsonian Institution.
       Report, 1886, Part II., Report, 1887·88.

       United States National Museum.
       Report, 1887-88.

,,   Wisconsin—Natural History Society.
       Occasional Papers, Vol. 1.

BELFAST NATURALISTS' FIELD CLUB.

TWENTY-NINTH YEAR, 1891-92.

LIST OF OFFICERS AND MEMBERS.

PRESIDENT:

JOHN VINYCOMB, F.R.S.A.I.

VICE-PRESIDENT:

WILLIAM SWANSTON, F.G.S.

TREASURER:	LIBRARIAN
W. H. PHILLIPS, F.R.H.S.,	WILLIAM SWANSTON, F.G.S.,
8 CHICHESTER STREET.	QUEEN STREET.

SECRETARIES:

R. LLOYD PRAEGER, B.E., M.R.I.A.,	FRANCIS JOSEPH BIGGER,
HOLYWOOD.	REA'S BUILDINGS, BELFAST.

COMMITTEE:

JOHN J. ANDREW, L.D.S., R.C.S., Eng.	F. W. LOCKWOOD.
GEORGE DONALDSON.	DANIEL M'KEE.
JOHN DONALDSON.	S. A. STEWART, F.B.S. Edin.
WILLIAM GRAY, M.R.I.A.	ROBERT J. WELCH.
JOHN HAMILTON.	JOSEPH WRIGHT, F.G.S.

Members.

Any changes in the Addresses of Members should be notified to the Secretaries.

John J. Adams, M.D., Ashville, Antrim.
Hugh Allen, Donegall Street.
Edward Allworthy, Mosaphir.
Alex. H. Anderson, Osborne House, Balmoral.
John Anderson, J.P., F.G.S., East Hillbrook, Holywood.
J. J. Andrew, L.D.S., R.C.S. Eng., Belgravia.
Mary K. Andrews, College Gardens.
W. G. Andrews, Dunluce Street.

James M. Barkley, Larne.
Robert Barklie, M.R.I.A., Working Men's Institute.
James Barr, Beechleigh, Windsor Park.
John Barr, Belmont Park.
William Batt, Sorrento, Windsor.
Emma Beck, Old Lodge Road.
George R. Begley, Wolfhill Lodge.
James Best, Clarence Place.
Francis Joseph Bigger, Ardrie, Antrim Road.
Edward Bingham, Ponsonby Avenue
E. Blair, Camberwell Terrace.
Mrs. Blair, Camberwell Terrace.
J. H. Boyd, Eblana Street.
Edward Braddell, St. Ives, Malone Park.
Hugh B. Brandon, Atlantic Avenue.
Rev. Samuel Arthur Brennan, B.A., Knocknacarry.
Chas. H. Brett, Gretton Villa South.
Rev. John Bristow, St. James's Parsonage.
John Brown, Belair,Windsor Avenue.
Thomas Brown, Donegall Street.
Edward M. Browne, Pembroke Road, Dublin.
John Browne, J.P., Ravenhill.
John Browne, M.R.I.A.. Drapersfield, Cookstown.
W. J. Browne, M.A., M.R.I.A., Highfield, Omagh.
Chas. Bulla,Wellington Park Terrace
Henry Burden, M.D., M.R.I.A., Alfred Street.

John R. Burnett, Rostellan, Malone Road.

William Calwell, M.D., College Square North.
George Montgomery Capper, Botanic Avenue.
John Malcomson Capper, Botanic Av.
Miss Carruthers, Claremont Street.
William Chancellor, B.A., Cromwell House, Cromwell Road.
E. T. Church, Donegall Place.
James A. Cleland, Wellington Park.
Stanley B. Coates, L.R.C.P. Edin., Shaftesbury Square.
James Coey, Victoria Street.
James Colbeck, Shaw's Bridge.
Arthur J. Collins, Belgravia Avenue
W. F. C. S. Corry, Chatsworth, Malone Road.
Rev. W. Cotter, D.D., Riversdale Terrace, Balmoral.
Gerald Coulson, College St. South.
J. P. Coulson, University Street.
George B. Coulter, Helen's Bay.
Mrs. Coulter, Helen's Bay.
James Creeth, Riversdale Terrace, Balmoral.
David Crozier, Mill Street.
Robert Culbert, Distillery Street.
Samuel Cunningham, Glencairn.
Francis Curley, Dunedin, Antrim Rd.
Mrs. Curley, Dunedin, Antrim Rd.
William Curry, Botanic Avenue.

Marquis of Dufferin and Ava, Clandeboye (Hon. Mem.).
John Henry Davies, Glenmore Cottage, Lisburn.
Henry Davis, Holywood.
Robt. Day, J.P., F.S.A., M.R.I.A. Cork.
Wakefield H. Dixon, Dunowen.
George Donaldson, Bloomfield.
John Donaldson, Thorndale Terrace.
William D. Donnan, Ardmore Terrace, Holywood.
W. J. Dunlop, Bryson Street.

David Elliott, Albert Bridge Road.
George Elliott, Royal Avenue.
George H. Elliott, Holywood.
Lavens M. Ewart, J.P., M.R.I.A.,
  Glenbank House.

Godfrey W. Ferguson, Murray's
  Terrace.
J. H. Ferguson, Belgrave, Knock.
Joseph Firth, Whiterock.
Wm. A. Firth, Glenview Terrace,
  Springfield Road.
T. M. H. Flynn, Sunnyside, Bess-
  brook.

Peter Galloway, University Street.
J. Starkie Gardner, F.G.S., Damer
  Terrace, Chelsea (Hon. Mem.).
Henry Gibson, Glencairn
John Gilliland, Prospect Street.
R. M. Gilmore, Upper Salt Hill,
  Galway.
W. J. Gilmore, Camberwell Villas.
George J. Glen, Hartington Street.
William Godwin, Queen Street.
Rev. David Gordon, Downpatrick.
James J. Goskar, Carlisle Circus.
James Gourley, J.P., Derryboy,
  Killyleagh.
Robert Gracey, Minerva House,
  Brookfield Avenue.
Rev. Canon Grainger, D.D., M.R.I.A.,
  Broughshane.
Wm. Gray, M.R.I.A., Mountcharles.
Miss Gray, Mountcharles.
Mrs. Greer, Dulce Domo, Strandtown.
George Greer, J.P., Woodville,
  Lurgan.

James H. Hamilton, Eden Terrace,
  Shankhill Road.
John Hamilton, Mount Street.
Thomas Hamilton, Queen Street.
Ernest Hanford, Melrose Terrace.
Richard Hanna, Charleville Street.
William Hanna, B.A , Lisanore Villa.
Mann Harbison, Ravenhill Terrace.
W. D. Harris, St. Mary's Terrace.
Rev. Canon Hartrick, M.A., The
  Rectory, Ballynure.
Sir James Haslett, J.P., Princess
  Gardens.
Thomas Hassan, Strangemore House
F. A. Heron, Cultra.

J. S. Holden, M.D., F.G.S., Sudbury,
  Suffolk (Cor. Mem.).
Alexander Hunter, Northern Bank.
James Hyndman, Holywood.

James Imrie, Rugby Road.

John Jacques, Parkview Terrace.
Hugh Smith Jefferson, Rosnakill,
  Strandtown.
James F. Johnston, Holywood.
Wm. J. Johnston, J.P., Dunesk,
  Stranmillis.
Prof. T. Rupert Jones, F.R.S.,
  Chelsea, London (Hon. Mem.).

David Keay, 22 College Green.
Archibald Kent, Newington Street.
Wm. Kernahan, Wellington Park.
George Kidd, Lisnatore, Dunmurry.
F. Kirkpatrick, Ann Street.
Wm. J. Knowles, M.R.I.A., Bally-
  mena.
Robert A. Kyle, Cliftonville.

Wm. W. Lamb, Salisbury Avenue.
Prof. Charles Lapworth, F.G.S.,
  Mason College, Birmingham
  (Hon. Mem.)
Samuel Leighton, Cooke Terrace.
F. R. Leppor, Elsinore, Crawfords-
  burn.
James Leslie, Somerset Terrace.
Rev. H. W. Lett, M.A., T.C.D.,
  Aghaderg Glebe, Loughbrick-
  land,
Prof. E. A. Letts, Ph.D., F.C.S.,
  Avonmore, Craigavad.
Frederick W. Lockwood, Wellington
  Park Terrace.
James Logan, Donegall Street.
W. B. Lowson, Chichester Park.
H. W. Luther, M.D., Chlorine House

Miss Macdonald, Model School, Falls
  Road.
John Mackenzie, C.E., Myrtlefield.
Rev. J. J. Major, Belvoir Hall.
Greer Malcomson, Granville Gardens
Harold Malcomson, Holywood.
James Malcomson, Cairnburn,
  Strandtown.
Mrs. Malcomson, Cairnburn.
John Marsh, Glenlyon, Holywood.

Mrs. Marsh, Glenlyon, Holywood.
Joseph C. Marsh, Castleton Terrace.
J. M'Clelland Martin, Oceanic Avenue.
A. C. Mathers, M.D., Coleraine.
Seaton Forrest Milligan, M.R.I.A., Royal Terrace.
John Moore, Shaftesbury Square.
C. E. Morgan, Martello, Caledonia Street.
R. Joynt Morrison, Limestone Road.
Thomas Morrison, Great George's Street.
David Morrow, Church Hill, Holywood.
John Morton, Clifton Park Avenue.
William Moss, Camberwell Terrace.
Henry Mull, Glendore, Crawfordsburn.
James Murdoch, Denmark Street.
Joseph John Murphy, Osborne Park
J. R. Musgrave, J.P., Drumglass House, Malone.

Thomas M'Alister, Eglinton Street.
Joseph M'Chesney, Holywood.
Francis P. M'Clean, Huntly Villas.
H. M'Cleery, Clifton Park Avenue.
William M'Cleery, General Post Office.
Rev. Ed. M'Clure, M.A., M.R.I.A., Onslow Place, South Kensington (Cor. Mem.).
Sir Thomas M'Clure, Bart., Belmont
Wm. J. M'Clure, Elizabeth Street.
James M'Connell, Caledonia Terrace
John M'Cullough, Martello Terrace, Holywood.
W. F. MacElheran, College Gardens.
Miss M'Gaw, Wellington Park Terrace.
John H. MacIlwaine, Brandon Villa, Strandtown.
Mrs. MacIlwaine, Brandon Villa, Strandtown.
Daniel M'Kee, Adela Place.
W. S. M'Kee, Fleetwood Street.
Alexander MacLaine, J.P., Queen's Elms.
John M'Leish, Ballyhackamore.
John M'Leish, Jun., Ballyhackamore
Robert M'Leish, Ballyhackamore.
William MacMillan, Enniscorthy.
Jas. M'Mordie, Belgravia Avenue.

W. D. M'Murtry, Helen's View.

Lucien Nepveu, Courtney Terrace.
W. Courtney Nesbitt, Kinnaird Terrace.
Wm. Nicholl, Donegall Square North.
Jerdan Nichols, Meadowbank Street.
H. J. Nicholson, Windsor Gardens

Henry O'Neill, M.D., College Square East.
James O'Neill, M.A., College Square East.
H. Lamont Orr
A. T. Osborne, Eglantine Avenue.
John S. Owens, St. James Street.

David C. Patterson, Clanbrassil Terrace, Holywood.
Robert Lloyd Patterson, J.P., F.L S., Croft House, Holywood.
Robert Patterson, M.B.O.U., Windsor Park Terrace, Lisburn Road.
William H. Patterson, M.R.I.A., Garranard, Strandtown.
Thomas Paul, Redcot, Knock.
H. W. Payne, Beechcroft, Holywood.
Herbert Pearce, Fitzroy Avenue.
James J. Phillips, 61, Royal Avenue
William H. Phillips, F.R.H.S., Lemonfield, Holywood.
Rev. J. Kirk Pike, Rosetta Terrace.
John Pim, J.P., Bonaven, Antrim Road.
John William Pim, Moyallen.
Joshua Pim, Slieve-na-Failthe, Whiteabbey.
Thomas W. Pim, The Lodge, Strandtown.
James Pinion, University Road.
F. A. Porter, Queen's Square.
William Porter.
E. A. Praeger, Holywood.
Robert Lloyd Praeger, B.A., B.E., M.R.I.A., Holywood.

Joseph Radley, Prospect Hill, Lisburn.
David Redmond, Kilkeel.
Right Rev.Wm. Reeves, D.D., LL.D., Bishop of Down and Connor and Dromore, Conway House, Dunmurry.

Robert Reid, King Street.
Richard Ridings, Hampton Terrace.
Rev. George Robinson, M.A., Beech
Hill House, Armagh.
George Robinson, Woodview, Holy-
wood.
Jas. R. Robinson, George's Terrace.
William A. Robinson, J.P., Culloden,
Cultra.
Richard Ross, M.D., Wellington
Place.
Wm. A Ross, Iva-Craig, Craigavad.
J. C. Rowan, Eglantine Avenue.
John Russell, C.E., The Eyries,
Newcastle.
Robt. A. Russell, Colinview Terrace
John Ryan, Myrtle Hill Terrace,
Cork.

James Shanks, Ballyfounder, Porta-
ferry.
Chas. Sheldon, M.A., B.Sc., D.Lit.,
Royal Academical Institution.
Joseph Skillen, Springfield Road.
Henry Smith, C.E., Eastern Villa,
Newcastle.
Rev. W. S. Smith, The Manse,
Antrim.
Wilson Smyth, Virginia Street.
Rev. Canon Smythe, M.A., Coole
Glebe, Carnmoney.
Adam Speers, B.Sc., Holywood.
A. C. Stannus, Holywood.
Sir N. A. Staples, Bart., Lissan
(Life Mem).
Jas. Stelfox, Oakleigh, Ormeau Park
John Stevenson, Coolavin.
J. M'N. Stevenson, Carrickfergus.
S. A. Stewart, F.B.S. Edin., Spring-
field Road.
William Swanston, F.G.S., Clifton-
ville Avenue.
Mrs. Swanston, Cliftonville Avenue.
Samuel Symington, Ballyoran House.

Alex. Tate, C.E., Longwood,
Whitehouse.
Prof. Ralph Tate, F.G.S., F L.S.,
Adelaide, South Australia (Hon.
Mem.).
Ernest E. Taylor, Melrose Terrace.
S. G. Thomas, Limestone Road.
John Todd, Clonaven,

Mrs. Henry Thompson, Crosshill,
Windsor.
George Thomson, Broadway Factory.
Prof. James Thomson, LL.D., F.R.S.,
Florentine Gardens, Glasgow
(Hon. Mem.).
W. A. Todd, Elgin Terrace.
Percy T. Tolputt, Carlisle Street.
W A. Traill, B.E., M.A.I.,Portrush.
W. J. Trelford, Vicinage Park.
James Turner, Mountain Bush.
Jas. C. Turtle, Cambridge Terrace.

John Vinycomb, F.R.S.A.I., Holywood.

Rev. C. Herbert Waddell, M.A.,
The Rectory, Saintfield.
W. F. Wakeman, M.R.I.A., Dublin
(Cor. Mem.)
Thomas R. Walker, Rugby Road.
Thos. R. Walkington, Edenvale.
George G. Ward, Eversleigh, Strand-
town.
Isaac W. Ward, Salisbury Terrace.
Miss Wardell, Cavehill Road.
Thomas Watson, Shipquay Gate,
Londonderry.
Charles W. Watts, F.I.C., Holborn
Terrace.
Isaac Waugh, Clifton Park Avenue.
Robert J. Welch, Lonsdale Street.
Prof. Whitla, M.D., J.P., College
Square North.
James Wilson, Oldforge, Dunmurry.
Jas. Wilson, Ballybundon, Killinchy,
James F. Wilson, Greenville Terrace
Alexander G. Wilson, Stranmillis.
Walter H. Wilson, Stranmillis.
Berkley D. Wise, C.E., Waterside,
Greenisland.
Rev. Robert Workman, M.A.,
Rubane, Glastry.
Thomas Workman, J.P., Craig-
darragh.
Joseph Wright, F.G.S., Alfred
Street.
Mrs. Wright, Alfred Street.
W. C. Wright, Lauriston, Derrie-
volgie Avenue.
William Wylie, Mountpleasant.

Robert Young, C.E., Rathvarna.

ANNUAL REPORT AND PROCEEDINGS

OF THE

BELFAST
NATURALISTS'
FIELD CLUB

For the Year ending the 31st March, 1892.

(TWENTY-NINTH YEAR).

SERIES II.

VOLUME III.

PART V.

1891-92.

𝔅elfast:

PRINTED FOR THE CLUB
BY ALEXANDER MAYNE & BOYD, 2 CORPORATION STREET,
PRINTERS TO QUEEN'S COLLEGE, BELFAST.

1892.

REPORT.

Your Committee beg to submit their twenty-ninth Annual Report, and have pleasure in recording an augmented energy and vitality in all departments of the Club's work. The membership of the Society, which last year showed a considerable increase, is still rapidly rising. During the year now closed 71 new members were elected, while 31 names have to be erased from the list owing to death or resignation, making the present membership 323, which is the largest ever attained since the foundation of the Club, 29 years ago.

The summer programme proved a highly attractive one, and was carried out in all particulars, and the members had the good fortune to enjoy beautiful weather on almost every occasion. The attendance at the various excursions was good, averaging fifty members and friends on each field day. The localities visited were as follows :—

1. Armagh	...	...	..	..	23rd May.
2. Downpatrick..	..	...	..		13th June.
3. Killyleagh	...	...	...	...	4th July.
4. Enniskillen and Lough Erne		...	...		29th, 30th, & 31st July.
5. Cultra (extra excursion)		...	...		7th August.
6. Woodburn and Duncrue		...	...		15th August.
7. Templepatrick and Dunagore		...	..		5th September.

Your Committee have again to thank a number of noblemen and gentlemen for kind permission to pass through their grounds, and for assisting the work of the Club in a number of other ways. They would specially mention the courtesy of the Lord Primate and the Rev. Dean Chadwick at Armagh, Colonel Hamilton at Killyleagh, the Earl of Erne at Crom Castle, the local representatives of the Salt Union (Limited), and the Belfast Water Commissioners at Woodburn, and Lord Templetown at Templepatrick. They have also to acknowledge the generous hospitality of Mr. James Heron, J.P., at Killyleagh, and Captain Archdall, D.L., at Castle Archdall, on the occasion of the Club's visits to these places; and to Mr. Thomas Plunkett, J.P., M.R.I.A., the best thanks of the Club are due for his valuable assistance at the three day excursion to Lough Erne. A number of country members of the Club also merit recognition of assistance given to the Secretaries in making arrangements of excursions to their respective districts.

The Winter Session was opened on October 20th with a social meeting in the Belfast Museum, at which the attendance of members and visitors numbered 360, being the largest recorded for many years. In connection with this meeting your Committee would return thanks to Messrs. Wm. Ewart & Sons (Limited), for their interesting display illustrative of the linen industry on that occasion. Five ordinary winter meetings were held, at which there was an average attendance of 100 members and visitors, being a decided increase on the winter attendances of some years past. The subjects brought before the Club on these occasions were as follow :—

17th Nov.   1. Presidential Address.
            2. "On the cross of Donaghmore, County Down"—Rev. H. W. Lett, M.A.
            3. "A Notice of the ancient Celtic shrine recently obtained by Mr. Thomas Plunkett in Lough Erne"—Francis Joseph Bigger, junior secretary.

15th Dec.   1. "Falconry"—Arthur J. Collins.
            2. "Remarks on a fossiliferous Eocene ironstone nodule from the Boulder Clay at Stoneyford"—William Swanston, F.G.S.

19th Jan.   "The Beetles of the Belfast District"—Rev. W. F. Johnson, M.A., F.E.S.

16th Feb.   1. "The late Mr. John Templeton's work among the birds of the district, and some MS. notes of his recently discovered"—Rev. C. H. Waddell, M.A.
            2. "On the occurrence of flint flakes in the Glacial gravels of Ballyrudder, County Antrim"—W. J. Knowles, M.R.I.A.
            3. "On a large jar or amphora (probably Roman or Grecian) recently obtained by sponge divers in the Bay of Ekanjik, near Rhodes" —Francis Joseph Bigger, junior secretary.

4. " On the skull of an Irish elk, recently found in dock excavations at Belfast "—R. Lloyd Praeger, B.E., M.R.I.A., senior secretary.

15th March.   Microscopical Evening.

The formation towards the end of last year of a special Section of the Club for the prosecution of microscopical study supplied a want that had long been felt by those engaged in that department of our work. The Section has held a number of meetings during the past year, and, although the summer excursions were not as well attended as they deserved to be, the attendance at the winter meetings was quite satisfactory, and the Microscopical Section may be considered an accomplished success. The annual report of the Section will be found in the present number of the Proceedings.

The special committee appointed for the purpose of collecting and arranging photographs taken by members of antiquarian and natural history objects continues its labours, and up to the present some 200 photographs have been got together, which will be classified and mounted in suitable albums.

Your Committee regret to have to record the loss by death of several well-known members of the Society. In April, 1891, Daniel M'Kee, an original member of the Club, and a member of Committee for the last ten years, passed away. Later in the year the Club sustained a serious loss in the death of Rev. Canon J. Grainger, D.D., M.R.I.A., who held the position of Chairman of Committee during the first year of the Club's existence, and from 1885 to 1887 the analogous office of President, and who always took a warm and active interest in the progress of the Club. Still more recently an irreparable loss to Irish archæological and historical research has been sustained by the loss of our fellow-member, Right Rev. Wm. Reeves, D.D., Bishop of Down and Connor and Dromore.

The judges appointed by the Committee to examine the various collections submitted in competition for the Club's prizes report as follows :—

Prize 10. Miss Sydney M. Thompson submits a set of fossils

collected at Ballycastle, Cultra, and Armagh, and numbering about 36 species, including some fine samples of fish teeth, and being fairly representative of the fauna of the Carboniferous rocks of our district. We accordingly award the prize to Miss Thompson.

Prize 16. We have examined a series of specimens of *Coleoptera* sent by Rev. W. F. Johnson in competition for this prize. This is one of the best possible collections, being named, arranged, and displayed in the most perfect manner. The specimens number about 750, representing 290 species, no less than 59 being the only Irish records. We cannot speak too highly of the skill exhibited by Mr. Johnson, and we have great pleasure in awarding him the prize.

Prize 21. We have examined two sets of microscopic slides submitted in competition for this prize. One set, by one of our lady members, is of very considerable merit, illustrating our local *Foraminifera.* The other is a varied assortment, mainly insect preparations, mounted in balsam with neatness and skill ; each specimen has been properly named and clearly displayed. We have no hesitation in awarding the prize to the author, Mr. H. M‘Cleery.

Prize 22. In competition for this prize, Miss Sydney M. Thompson sends six water-colour sketches of geological subjects, including dykes and erratic blocks. Miss Thompson's drawings form a very useful record, and we award her the prize.

Prize 25. Another lady member competes for this prize, submitting six excellent photos showing quarry and river sections, illustrative of our Northern geology, for which we award the prize to the artist, Miss A. H. Tate.

WILLIAM GRAY.
SAMUEL A. STEWART.

Prize 27. The Secretaries of the Ulster Fauna Committee report as follows :—

We regret that only one member has competed for this prize. Mr. Arthur J. Collins has sent in from time to time during the year two *Cheiroptera* (common bat, long-eared bat), five

Rodentia (brown rat, common mouse, long-tailed field mouse, hare, rabbit), two *Insectivora* (hedgehog, lesser shrew), and one carnivore (stoat).   All of them were collected in Ulster, and, as the conditions have been complied with, we award the prize to Mr. Collins.   At the same time, the collection is by no means as representative as it might have been ; for instance, of the eight Irish bats, only two were collected.   We would be glad to see larger collections sent in another year.

ROBERT PATTERSON.
R. LLOYD PRAEGER.

The present is a suitable time for specially drawing the attention of members to the recent publication of the first number of a new magazine devoted to Irish natural history and geology — *The Irish Naturalist*—the production of which cannot fail to have an important stimulating effect on the study of natural science in this country.   Your Committee have appointed the new magazine the official organ of the Club, and they strongly urge members to assist the new venture by becoming subscribers, and, as far as possible, contributors. Your Committee have, as usual, to return thanks to a number of scientific societies and public bodies for the interchange of their Proceedings during the past year.

R. LLOYD PRAEGER, } *Secretaries.*
FRANCIS JOSEPH BIGGER,$

TREASURER IN ACCOUNT WITH THE BELFAST NATURALISTS' FIELD CLUB   Cr.

FOR THE YEAR ENDING 31ST MARCH, 1892.

			£	s.	d.
...nce from last Account	...	...	£4	3	0
...scriptions	...	...	75	5	0
...kets for Social Meeting	...	...	2	9	0
...es of the Guide to Belfast	...	...	2	11	9
,, Proceedings	...	...	0	2	0
,, Systematic Lists	...	...	0	6	0
,, Flora N.E. Ireland	...	...	0	4	6
			£85	1	3

		£ s. d.	£	s.	d.
By Expenses of Social Meeting	...		£5	17	2
,, Printing Annual Proceedings	...		15	4	0
,, Stationery, Printing	...		17	16	1
,, Meteorological Summary	...		1	0	0
,, Rent of Lecture Hall	...		6	6	0
,, Commission Collecting Subscriptions	...		3	6	0
,, Prizes Awarded	...		2	10	0
,, Loss on Excursions	...		0	17	5
,, Restoration of Donaghmore Cross	...		2	0	0
,, Expenses of Photographic Committee	...		3	15	5
,, Expenses of Microscopical Section	...		1	12	0
,, GENERAL EXPENSES :—					
Postages	...	£9 7 7			
Insurance	...	0 17 6			
Delivery Circulars	...	1 0 0			
Incidentals	...	1 10 11	12	16	0
,, Balance in hand	...		12	1	2
			£85	1	3

orrec

R. LLOYD PRAEGER Hon. Secretary.

W. H. PHILLIPS, Treasurer.

PROCEEDINGS,

SUMMER SESSION.

ARMAGH.

The first excursion of the Summer Session was held on Saturday, May 23rd, Armagh being the place chosen. A party of twenty-five left the Great Northern Railway by the ten o'clock train, reaching Armagh at 11-30, where a wagonette was in attendance, and a start was made through the city for the Palace, the residence of the Primate, where the fine old Abbey in the grounds was inspected and photographed by several lady and gentlemen amateurs. These ruins are part of the ancient Cill-na-Fearta, and were formerly very extensive. At present some fine arches and a door still remain, while scattered around are old mossy tombstones, not, however, of a very ancient date. The beauty and picturesqueness of the ruins were much admired. The party then inspected the gardens, and drove through the demesne to Corr's quarries, where the geologists, who were in great force, held high revelry for over an hour. This quarry, as well as the Navan quarry, which was afterwards visited, affords a wealth of fish remains. The Carboniferous Limestone here rests on the Lower Silurian strata, and is divided into upper and lower limestone, with an intervening "calp," then sandstone. It is in the lower beds of limestone that the fish remains are found, and consist of about 150 species, divided amongst six groups—viz., *Hybodus, Orodus, Petalodus, Cochliodus, Psammodus,* and *Copodus.* Several members obtained fine specimens of these fossil teeth and spines, also some beautiful shells. Some photographs of sections were also taken for the Club's album. These remains are sufficient to warrant the palæontologist in assuming that the huge sharks of warmer climes do not rival in size the departed monsters of the Armagh quarries. Some very perfect specimens of coral were obtained by nearly all the members of the Club. Those present were very thankful for the able assistance of their co-member Mr. C. Bulla, and the studious paper which he read. After the treasures of the quarries had been ransacked, the wagonette was again filled (with members and specimens), and a start was made for Emania, the palace of the kings of Uladh (Ulster). The circumvallations of Emania surround about twelve acres, and a smaller fort (the survivor of two) remains upon the centre. At the present time the entrenchment around one side is nearly perfect, but the other side has almost disappeared under the influence of an enterprising farmer. Seeing that this royal residence has a written history of six centuries, ending A.D. 300, surely it is of sufficient importance to be conserved by the Government, and thus prevented from the total destruction which will undoubtedly take place in a few years unless those in authority step in and preserve what the late Sir Samuel Ferguson described as the most historical remains north of the Alps. Thirty-five kings, all of the Irian race, reigned successively within the halls of Emania, and of these twenty-four became ardrigh (supreme kings). King Connor MacNessa and the Knights of the Red Branch long held revelry within the palace, and many are the stories recounted of their deeds of valour and daring courage, and some also of their works of charity. The classical writings of the late Sir Samuel Ferguson, particularly *Congal*, beautifully describe this portion of our country's history. Upon the destruction of Emania by the Clan Colla, A.D. 332, the Royal residence was removed first to Rath-Celtchar (Downpatrick), then to Rath-Mor of Maghline, near Dunadry. After the scene of these departed glories had been duly contemplated, the party returned to Armagh, where the beautiful Roman Catholic Cathedral was much admired, and the details of architecture carefully inspected. It was observed, however, that this building is not built in the canonical position, as the chancel does not face the east. Doubtless the natural features of the ground may account for this anomaly. Through

the kindness of the Dean, the ancient Cathedral of St.. Patrick
was subsequently shown to the party, and its various interesting
monuments and relics of the past thoroughly appreciated and
admired. Its graceful simplicity and beauty are truly admirable,
but its present aspect was rather disappointing to those who
expected the fabric would have borne more evidences of its
illustrious past. The history of this Cathedral is truly a
chequered one. Founded by St. Patrick, A.D. 445, upon the
Royal foot of Rath-Daire, it was sacked and destroyed many
times by the Danes and others, and finally burned to the ground
by Sir Phelim O'Neill in the wars of 1642. The original cill
or church erected by St. Patrick was known as the Damhliacc-
Mor, or the great stone church, and had a clochteac, or round
tower, attached. At present the base of the old town cross and
part of the shaft are deposited opposite the western door, whilst
the remainder of the shaft and one of the arms lie in the crypt.
The citizens of Armagh should at once undertake the re-erection
of this very valuable and most important antiquity, and not be
so far behind other towns, which have restored their town
crosses when they were not nearly so perfect or so beautiful.
Armagh will surely not be beaten by Dromore in this respect.
After a short visit to the Library, the Club adjourned to the
Museum, where the objects exhibited, including a fine collection
of shells, were examined, and a short business meeting was held,
with Mr. Alex. Tate, C.E., in the chair. After the election
of eight new members, resolutions of thanks for benefits conferred
were returned to his Grace the Lord Primate, the Very Rev.
Dean Chadwick, Rev. George Robinson, Rev. W. F. Johnson,
Rev. John Elliot, and the Armagh Natural History Society and
its courteous secretary. Several members had the privilege of
examining the extensive collection of *Lepidoptera*, *Hymenoptera*,
and *Coleoptera* belonging to the Rev. W. F. Johnson. After a
sumptuous and enjoyable tea in the Beresford Arms, the Club
returned to Belfast by the 7-30 train, after a very pleasant day's
excursion, only faintly marred by the slight showers that fell at
intervals.

DOWNPATRICK.

A party of forty members and their friends assembled at the
County Down terminus shortly after nine o'clock on June 13th,
and were soon speeding towards Downpatrick in one of the
splendid new composite carriages which the enterprising railway
company have lately added to their rolling stock, and which was
obligingly reserved by Mr. Smith, the courteous station-master
at Belfast. Arrived at Downpatrick, the party immediately
mounted the cars which were in waiting, and drove off towards
Struell, which was reached before midday. Here the well-known
wells of St. Patrick engaged their attention, long resorted to by
pious pilgrims for the cure of the ills that flesh is heir to. The
word Struell, or Sruthair, signifies a stream. A rivulet flowing
down a pretty valley with rocky hillocks on either hand is
diverted, and passes through a number of wells, which are protected by being enclosed in cells, well built and roofed with stone
from the neighbourhood. Passing from the well called Tobar-
Patric, the water flows through four other wells, called respectively the Body Well, the Limb Well, the Eye Well, and the
Well of Life. The Body Well, or Well of Sins, is sufficiently
large to admit of bathing, and spacious dressing-rooms are added.
These wells were long patronised by the rural population,
but the buildings are of no great age—only a few hundred
years—and the adjoining ruined chapel is quite modern ; the
place has now an air of decay and disuse.

Remounting the vehicles, the party drove on to Ballyalton,
and while a larger section elected to ascend the hill of Slieve-
na-griddle, the others contented themselves with an inspection
of the stone circle close at hand, and there awaited their more
energetic companions. Those who ascended the hill were well
repaid for their labour. Although little over 400 feet in height,
the summit conveys the impression of a much greater elevation,
on account of its isolated position and the low level of the surrounding country. The view obtained by the party from the
ruined cromleac on the highest point of the hill was most

beautiful and extensive. The clouds of the morning had now cleared away, and bright sunshine with a mild balmy wind had succeeded, while a summer haze still hung on the more distant points, and obscured the coasts of Scotland and the Isle of Man. Strangford Lough with its myriad islands and broad lagoon-like surface lay before the eye, the winding estuary of the Quoile stretching to the left, and the long narrow entrance of the lough to the right. Further south stretched the Irish Sea, while to the west and north lay the beautiful and varied surface of County Down, flanked on the one hand by the majestic domes of the Mourne Mountains, and on the other by the distant hill of Scrabo. Descending the hill, the party reunited at the stone circle of Ballyalton. This interesting relic now consists of eight stones on end, forming part of a circle of about forty-three feet diameter, with an avenue of stones thirty-two feet long and four feet wide leading up to it. It is situated on a slight eminence on the farm of Mr. John Clelland, who, it is hoped, will carefully preserve this interesting monument. The bushes of thorn which grow among the upright stones are supposed to be under the special protection of the fairies, whose favourite haunts appear still to be these prehistoric monuments, for a resident informed the party that when some years ago an individual dared to take some cuttings of these fairy thorns, the plates that night danced on the dresser in his kitchen !

The next halting-place was on the edge of Lough Money, and a number of members, intent on botanical pursuits, made their way along the picturesque shore of the lake, the waters of which yielded a rich store of aquatic plants, including water-lilies and water-crowfoots, and several species of the interesting crypto-gamic group of the *Characeæ*. A short detour was made near the northern end of the lough, for the purpose of visiting a perfect cromleac which stood in a field of corn close to a bye-road. It consists of a large slab, over 9 feet by 5 feet, resting on two upright and parallel stones of about the same size. This fine monument, as well as the stone circle of Ballyalton, is described and figured in the publications of the Club.

A drive of a couple of miles brought the party to the ruined church of Rathcolpa, now Raholp, which is one of the very oldest ecclesiastical buildings in Ulster. This edifice was erected by Saint Patrick, and it was the abbot of this church who administered to the saint the last sacrament. The building is of small size and of very primitive construction, yellow clay being used in the joints instead of mortar. The eastern window is splayed on the inside, and measures $4\frac{1}{2}$ feet high by 10 inches wide. Some effort should be made to conserve this highly important Christian edifice and to prevent its further destruction by the growth of the bushes which infest it, and the action of the wind and weather. Leaving Raholp, the return journey was commenced, and driving back by the Strangford Road, the party crossed the Quoile, to visit the beautifully-situated ruins of Inch Abbey.

The Abbey of Inch, or Inis-Cumscraid (signifying the Island of Cumscraid (Cooscry), who was one of the sons of Connor MacNessa, and succeeded his father as King of Ulster in the first century) is a very ancient ecclesiastical foundation, and has had a chequered history, having been plundered by the Danes in the year 1001, and rebuilt by John de Courcy in 1180, and called after him Inis-Courcy. At present the ruins, with the exception of the choir and east window, have almost disappeared, but what remains shows the former extent and beauty of the abbey, and with a little trouble a great deal could be done towards restoring fallen portions, and saving the existing remains from sharing a similar fate. In spite of the masses of hoary ivy that cling around the walls, the beautiful proportions of the altar windows may still be traced. Will not the generous and enlightened lord of the soil come forward to rescue these lovely ruins from the destruction that certainly awaits them should they remain much longer in their present neglected condition ? With but little expense the ruins of Inch could be made as charming and interesting a spot as Grey Abbey, so widely known and highly appreciated by visitors and antiquarians.

Returning from Inch along the beautiful wooded banks of

the Quoile, Downpatrick was reached at five o'clock, when a hearty and excellent tea was provided at Denvir's Hotel. At the conclusion of the repast, a business meeting of the Club was held, the President, Mr. John Vinycomb, F.R.S.A.I., taking the chair. The President spoke of the enjoyment they had had on the present trip, and returned the thanks of the Club to Rev. David Gordon for his courtesy and assistance to the party during the day. He also spoke of the loss the Club had recently sustained in the death of their esteemed fellow-member, Mr. Daniel M'Kee, an original member of the Club, and whose face, until a few weeks ago, had been so familiar to members at their summer and winter meetings. The nomination of new members was then taken up, and five names were submitted to the meeting, and duly elected. Mr. William Gray, M.R.I.A., said he desired to draw the attention of that meeting to the present condition of the grave of Ireland's patron saint, St. Patrick, in the graveyard by the cathedral of Downpatrick. Its neglected condition was a national disgrace, and he considered this a most suitable opportunity for drawing the attention of the Club to the matter, and of suggesting that steps should be taken to communicate with other scientific bodies, as well as with the public at large, with the object of erecting a national monument on the tomb of St. Patrick. Mr. Gray's remarks were supported and supplemented by Messrs. James Gourley, J.P.; Edward Allworthy, W. H. Patterson, M.R.I.A.; Alexander Tate, C.E.; the President, and Rev. D. Gordon. The matter was finally referred to the committee, the senior secretary promising that every effort would be made to remove this slur on the Irish nation, and to attain the commendable object advocated by the speakers. A prize had been offered in the earlier part of the day for the best collection of flowering plants made during the excursion, and on the nomination of the President, Messrs. S. A. Stewart, F.B.S.E., and R. Lloyd Praeger, M.R.I.A., were appointed judges to examine the collections and award the prizes. Seven collections were sent in, most of them showing a large amount of assiduous search, and the winner was declared to be Mrs. Leslie, whose collection included no less than 117 species. An hour was spent in visiting the cathedral, the huge dun, and the dilapidated grave of St. Patrick, and the party returned to Belfast by the 7-10 train, well pleased with their visit to Downpatrick and neighbourhood.

KILLYLEAGH.

Assembling at the County Down Railway terminus shortly after nine o'clock on Saturday, July 4th, rail was taken to Crossgar, where a number of brakes and cars were in readiness, and a rapid drive brought the party to the picturesque little seaside town of Killyleagh. Ever on the alert for rare specimens, the botanists of the party scored two points ere the first halt was made, their finds being the trailing dog-rose (*Rosa arvensis*) and the great water-dock (*Rumex hydrolapathum*), both rare species in our district. Arrived at Killyleagh the first object to claim attention was the ruined church of Killowen, which, surrounded by a graveyard overgrown with grass and weeds in true local style, stands among tall trees a short distance from the main road. Of the building, which is of considerable antiquity, only the eastern gable remains standing. Some time having been spent in clearing the east window of the mass of dead ivy that encumbered it and obscured the mouldings, several photographs were obtained of this relic, and two rare grasses (*Bromus sterilis* and *Trisetum flavescens*) were discovered among the ruins. The party then proceeded to Killyleagh Castle, where by the kind permission of Colonel Hamilton, the extensive and beautiful gardens and grounds were thrown open to the visitors, and were much admired, special comment being excited by the magnificent size of the ancient yew-trees that ornament the lawns. The Castle itself, an imposing pile, is mostly modern, though the two large circular towers on either side of the entrance are of early date. Fragments of walls and numerous pieces of carved stone-work scattered through the gardens attest the former extent of the Castle.

Proceeding through the town, a pause was made at the site of the house where Sir Hans Sloane was born, whose extensive natural history collections formed the nucleus of the now enormous establishment of the British Museum. The house was rebuilt some ten years ago; and of the original dwelling only the keystone remains, built into the lintel over the present door-way—a block of Castle-Espie limestone, bearing the inscription " 1637. G. S., M. W." The photographers having obtained a permanent memento of this interesting relic, the party next proceeded to the quay, where two fine sailing boats lay ready, and, the embarkation being effected, a light south-easterly breeze bore them out upon the calm surface of Strangford Lough, and a course was shaped northward towards Dunnaneile Island. This island is conspicuous among the myriad islets of Strangford Lough for the huge mound that occupies a large part of its surface. This rath, which is apparently partly natural and partly artificial, is of large dimensions, but in its present condition rather shapeless. Here, according to tradition, the kings of Ulster kept the hostages obtained by their valour and might from other nations—a safe prison surely, if somewhat bleak and inhospitable. Certain it is that the island was inhabited in early times, as shown by the layer of blackish earth, charged with fragments of bones and shells, exposed on the face of the steep bank, some forty feet above high water mark, where the sea has eaten into the side of the mound. The bones obtained were too fragmentary to admit of an opinion being formed as to whether they were human or not; the shells were of species still abundant in the lough, and which might have been used as food, or bait for fishing lines. While some members examined these traces of human occupation, others busied themselves collecting moths, insects, seaweeds, and terrestrial plants. Of the latter, fine specimens of one species which is rare locally, the sea-beet (*Beta maritima*), were obtained. It was the ornithologists, however, that carried off the honours on the island. A red-breasted merganser, a fine bird of the duck family, had been observed flying from the island as the party approached, and the circumstance led to a close search among the rank grass and weeds, which resulted in the discovery of no fewer than six mergansers' nests, lined with grass and feathers, and most of them containing the complement of seven or eight large yellowish eggs. Not only were the nests discovered, but one of the birds was caught ere it could leave the nest, and in spite of its energetic protests and expostulations had to undergo the scrutiny and comments of the majority of the party. However, preservation and not destruction being the watchword of the Club, neither bird nor eggs were harmed. Some dotterel were observed along the pebbly margin of the lough, where they undoubtedly had their nests, and a few terns were flying around, stragglers from the islands further northward, where they breed in large numbers. The geologists also found food for reflection on the stony beach, where it was observed that a large percentage of the pebbles were composed of reddish Carboniferous Limestone, such as only occurs *in situ* in the district at Castle-Espie, near Comber, some ten miles to the northward. These numerous fragments are derived from the Boulder Clay, and show the direction in which the great ice currents set during the bygone period of arctic conditions known as the Glacial Epoch. Many of the limestone pebbles were riddled with the tunnels of a boring shell (*Saxicava rugosa*), of which some examples were obtained. Other marine trophies found were specimens of a fine sea urchin (*Echinus sphœra*), and the formidable jaw of a large fishing-frog or sea-devil (*Lophius piscatorius*). An interesting and profitable hour having been spent on the island, which to the uninitiated would appear a mere barren, weed-covered wilderness, the secretary's whistle called the party together, and, re-embarking, a pleasant and rapid sail brought the party back to Killyleagh, where the vehicles were once more mounted, and, passing through the beautiful and thriving village of Shrigley, Clay Lake (Lough Claith, the Lough of the Hurdles) was soon reached.

Here the party was met by Mr. James Heron, J.P., who had two boats in readiness, and while a large detachment proceeded by water under Mr. Heron's guidance to visit the remains of a crannog, or ancient lake dwelling, in the centre of the lower lake, the remainder proceeded by road to inspect a caiseal, or old stone fort, which stands on an eminence overlooking the upper lake. The wall of the caiseal is some six feet thick, and six to eight feet high, and is dry-built of comparatively small stones, but apparently only a small portion even of the existing wall is original work ; the circular enclosure, in which the thrifty tenant was cultivating a fine crop of vetches, measures about eighty feet in diameter. Some photographs were here obtained, showing the caiseal in the foreground, with the beautifully diversified surface of Clay Lake behind. The waters of the lake offered a tempting hunting-ground for the botanists of the party, who made a rapid dash along the margin, and secured a number of good plants, including the flowering rush (*Butomus umbellatus*), of which, however, leaves only were obtained ; the rest-harrow (*Ononis arvensis*), water-fennel (*Ranunculus tricophyllus*), horse-bane (*Œnanthe phellandrium*), shepherd's needle (*Scandix Pecten-Veneris*), toothed corn-salad (*Valerianella dentata*), and a rather rare spurge (*Euphorbia exigua*).

The party were next conducted to Tullyvery House, where they were most sumptuously entertained by Mr. and Mrs. Heron, and had the pleasure of meeting a large number of the local gentry. At the conclusion of the repast, a short business meeting of the Club was held, according to the usual custom. In the unavoidable absence of the President of the Club, the chair was taken by Mr. Alexander Tate, C.E., chairman of the Microscopical Section. The election of new members was first taken up, and several ladies and gentlemen were elected members. The Chairman said his only other duty was to accord, on behalf of the Club, their most hearty thanks to those who had contributed in many ways towards the success of what he thought had been one of the most enjoyable excursions at which he had been present ; to Colonel Hamilton, D.L., for permission to visit Killyleagh Castle ; to several local members, whose kind assistance had been of much service ; and most of all, to their host and hostess, for their liberal hospitality and great kindness. He asked the meeting to accord their thanks to them by acclamation, which was done with much heartiness. Mr. Heron having said a few suitable words in reply, the party dispersed for a stroll through the extensive grounds, after which the vehicles were once more mounted, and the return journey was made to Crossgar, in time to catch the evening train to Belfast, and the members arrived in town at 8 30.

ENNISKILLEN AND LOUGH ERNE.

The long excursion of the Club took place on Wednesday, Thursday, and Friday, July 29, 30, and 31. Enniskillen and Lough Erne were the places chosen, and happy, indeed, was the choice, as three days were spent by the members in scenes of unsurpassed loveliness, and in visiting places teeming with historical and mythological associations. Over three dozen members and their friends assembled at 8-45 at the Great Northern Railway, and took their departure in a carriage specially reserved by the courteous manager of the line. After a pleasant run, Clones was reached, and a stoppage of half an hour was fully taken advantage of by the members in inspecting the fine fort which enhances the summit of a hill overlooking the town. Surrounding the central dun are three concentric raths, all in good preservation. The site and appearance mark it out as being a considerable stronghold in the good old times when might was right. It was erected by a pagan chief called Eos, hence the name Clones—viz., Cluain, a meadow, and Eos, the chief's name—the meadow of Eos. Close by, in the centre of the large market square, overlooked by the graceful spire of the parish church, stands the old town cross, well preserved, and with the exception of a stone in the shaft, it appears quite perfect, but its beautiful sculptured figures and Celtic ornament are now smoothed by the hand of time, and the grey lichen speaks of the many centuries of evidence that it has borne to the faith of our people. Near at hand in an overcrowded and dreadfully neglected graveyard, that could not by any possible stretch of imagination be called "God's Acre," stands one of "the round towers of other days," only the conical roof being wanted to make it a most perfect and interesting specimen of Celtic architecture. The style of the masonry employed in its construction certainly places this clochteac amongst the earliest erected, probably the eighth century, but the whole beauty of the place is spoiled by the rubbish and rank growth of nettles that entirely cover the graves in the adjoining cemetery. The well-meaning clergy and laity of Clones should surely remedy this eyesore at their very doors.

Half an hour more in the train brought the party to Newtownbutler, where cars had been provided to carry the baggage and a few members of the Club to Crom Castle, a distance of three miles, the walk to which was fully enjoyed after the long seat in the train, and was a pleasant relaxation to all parties. The delightful shades of Crom were soon reached, and the grandeur of the modern castle fully admired ; the situation is perfect, overlooking as it does the rich meadows and winding loughs of the Maguires' country, whilst all around is a most extensive growth of oak, ash, and beech. Through the usual courtesy of the Earl of Erne the grounds and gardens were fully open to the members. The favourite haunt, however, was the old castle, beautiful in its ruins, on the edge of the lough, surrounded by undulating terraces and ancient yew trees, under whose branches hundreds of knightly warriors might stand with ease. Here the Club was met by Mr. Thomas Plunkett, M.R.I.A , of Enniskillen, for whose care and kindness during the excursion all the members were very grateful. The old towers and walls, though now covered with green, had successfully held aloft the banner of William of Orange in the troublesome times of the Revolution, and Colonel Crichton, the ancestor of the present noble lord, rendered a good account of himself and his castle to the new king he had chosen to serve. Old Crom sustained its reputation upon the visit of the Club, for it was assailed at every angle by photographers and sketchers, yet never yielded an inch, but maintained its own with an equanimity that was marvellous.

After a couple of hours spent at Crom in lunching and other profitable employments, the good s.s. "Belturbet" was boarded at a little jetty, consisting of a few stones and two planks, and a start was made down the upper lough for Enniskillen. The sun had unfortunately ceased to shine, and a cold wind had arisen, which rendered wraps very desirable. Our skipper lost no time, and there was plenty of talent on board in the shape of three Sligo fiddlers and a large party of local young men and maidens, who turned the small forecastle into a dancing saloon, where an Irish jig was performed to perfection by some true-hearted sons of old Ireland, so that with the gaiety on board and the pleasing landscape, varied at every turn by wooded islands and branching loughs, the cold wind was scarcely felt in the enjoyment of the novelty of the situation. Belleisle and Clean-Inis were soon observed, and about six o'clock the two towers of the old castle of the Maguires, lords of Fermanagh, were passed, and Enniskillen reached, when there was no delay in getting into the Imperial and Royal Hotels, where good dinners were made doubly enjoyable by the appetites rendered sharp by the first day's sail on the pleasant waters of Lough Erne.

The party was early astir on Thursday morning, and many an anxious glance was cast up to the clouds to foretell the weather if possible. The fondest hopes were, however, more than realised by the perfect day that was enjoyed. The "Belturbet" was specially chartered for a day's steaming on the lower lake, and at nine o'clock all were on board and a start made for the Holy Island of Devenish (Dabhinis), whilst a flood of sunshine lighted up the good old town of Enniskillen, revealing the beauties of the

stately tower of the parish church, and the graceful modelling
of Cole's monument on the Fort Hill.   The towers of the old
castle at Portora, long the stronghold of the Maguires, were
admired ; but alas ! for the changes of time, the crumbling walls
only now speak of the troops of kernes and gallowglasses who
once surrounded this spot ever ready to serve their chieftain
either in peace or war.

An old, picturesque flat-bottomed cot, embedded amongst the
reeds at Devenish, made an excellent landing-place, and the
party were soon scattered about inspecting the ruins of this
sacred spot.   The round tower, cross, and abbey, from an
artist's standpoint, make a perfect picture ; but the antiquarians
of the party were not satisfied until every minute detail of
architecture was carefully examined, and in many cases photographed or sketched, thus forming a lasting record for the Club's
albums.   The beautiful cross lately conserved by the Board of
Works, under the guidance of Mr. Plunkett, was the centre of
an animated discussion on the question lately raised by Mr.
Wakeman and others as to whether the head of the cross was
originally a piece of tracery from a window of the abbey or a
memorial erected to a departed abbot or chieftain.   After a
most careful examination of the cross by the chief archæologists
of the Club, it was unanimously agreed that the cross as at
present erected serves its original purpose, and the beautiful
carvings on the terminals of the arms and other appearances
conclusively prove that the whole is an excellent specimen of a
mediæval memorial cross.   The priory church and dwelling
were examined, and a rubbing of a grave-slab bearing the date
1449 was made by the President.   The arches supporting the
tower are very fine, and the corbels and capitals are peculiarly
Celtic.

Some fine old stones bearing interlacing ornament were
observed built into the walls of the priory, and of these rubbings
were also made.   The clochteac then attracted attention.   Its
imposing size and beauty, and the skilful chiselling of its
masonry, clearly place it in a premier place amongst our

national round towers. Its height is eighty-four feet, and the unique band of carved heads and Celtic ornament around the base of the conical roof make it interesting in the extreme. As time was short, only a hurried visit could be paid to the adjoining cill of St. Molaise and his grave, the stone coffin from which was lately raised, and is now preserved in the ruined church. Many very fine incised crosses and some armorial bearings were observed and copied, and altogether it was with difficulty the secretary was able to coax, by whistle, the stragglers to return to the boat from the many interesting memorials of the past.

Steam was now got up for Castle Archdall, and a rapid run past the most lovely of islands and deeply-wooded demesnes brought to sight the stately residence of Captain Archdall, and here a short stay was made, and an interesting outcrop of sandstone upon the shore was inspected by the geologists. Afterwards the glorious view from the summit of the castle was fully admired, and the many interesting objects in the hall and drawing-room were pointed out by the owner, including some beautiful oil paintings of local scenery by his daughter, Mrs. Manwarring, and refreshments were dispensed in the dining-room. After all the party had been photographed at the entrance hall the party re-embarked, and after giving three hearty cheers for Captain Archdall for his kindness, way was made for the abbey on White Island, picking up on the way a small party of the Club who had gone in a rowing boat to visit the historical ruins of old Castle Archdall. The ruins of the old abbey on White Abbey were found to be well worth a visit. Two curious carved figures built into the walls are perfectly unique, and are evidently of a much earlier date than the church. We hope these ruins will be carefully preserved by their present worthy owner. A quick run was now made across the broadest portion of this lough of islands in a delightful breeze, past the Gull Rock, which is a breeding place for the black-headed gull, common tern, and wild duck, nests of which had been previously photographed by an ornithologist of the Club. A landing was made, by means of a plank from the deck of the steamer,.on the strand close to old Tulla Castle, a most picturesque ruin of the Scotch baronial style, overlooking the lough, and formerly occupied by the Hume family. This castle was burned and the inhabitants massacred in the wars of 1641. A short walk through the fields afforded the botanists ample time to indulge in their pursuit, and some large sweet-scented orchids and other plants were collected here, and also upon the islands where landings had been previously made. The green net of an entomologist did good work both here and in the woods of Castle Archdall.

Wagonettes and cars were then mounted, and the road taken for Carrick Lake, close by Knockmore, whose beetling cliffs, burrowed by huge caves, invited investigation, but time did not permit. The drive up the rocky gorge afforded the geologists an opportunity of picking up some specimens of fossils, partially weathered out in the stone ditches and exposed sections, but the delight afforded to many could not be exceeded when the secretary discovered the first abode of the royal fern (*Osmunda regalis*), and no time was lost in securing specimens by all the party. Although many were taken, the supply seemed inexhaustible, as the growth was a most luxuriant one. The sunset and increasing appetites bade a speedy return to Enniskillen, which was soon accomplished, time not permitting the party to visit Boho or the interesting old castle at Monea. A pleasant reunion for dinner at eight, succeeded by some music, brought the day to a close.

On the third morning of the excursion many of the party were up at six o'clock, and visited the new public gardens known as the Fort Hill, where the fine column and statue to the Peninsular hero, General Cole, have been erected. This park has been laid out and planted in the most graceful manner, and all the natural advantages of the ground have been fully appreciated. The enterprising way in which this benefit has been conferred upon Enniskillen reflects the greatest credit upon its author, Mr. Plunkett, the present chairman of the

Town Commissioners. After an ascent to the giddy heights of
the Cole column and a ramble round the town, breakfast was
taken, and a start was made at nine o'clock for the Marble Arch.
The weather was most beautiful, and the views of mountain,
lough, and wood were unsurpassed for extent and variety. The
vehicles were left at the foot of the glen, whilst the party
walked about a mile by the side of a mountain torrent, over-
hung with luxuriant foliage, and covered with ferns, whilst here
and there the lower Carboniferous Sandstone jutted out in sharp
and unmistakable lines. After all the known expressions of
wonder and delight had been exhausted in admiration of the
Marble Arch, a happy thought seized the secretary to hold the
Club meeting in a rocky cavern on the edge of a ravine. After
a few pleasant remarks from the President, (Mr. John Vinycomb,
F.R.S.A.), Mr. W. H. Patterson, M.R.I.A., moved, and Mr. F.
A. Heron seconded, a resolution that the best thanks of the
Club be given to Mr. Thomas Plunkett, M.R.I.A., for his
kindness and attention to the Club. Mr. Plunkett having
expressed the pleasure the visit of the Club had afforded him,
Mr. F. A. Porter moved, and Mr. H. C. Marshall seconded, a
resolution of thanks to the Earl of Erne and Captain Archdall
for their courtesy and hospitality. Seven new members having
been elected, the meeting was closed with cheers for Mr.
Plunkett. And now all was interest and excitement, for the
huge cave was to be visited, and all sorts of weird effects produced by the burning of torches and magnesium wire to show
with the light of day the practically unexplored depths of this
vaulted cavern. After ascending and descending many huge
walls of rock a level floor was reached, and traversed for over
100 yards, when the sound of rushing water was heard, and an
underground river glittered in the light of the torches held
aloft. Ghastly effects were produced by the floating of candles
on pieces of wood down the river into the bowels of the earth.
It is to be hoped that the good people of Enniskillen may not
hear more of these wandering lights. So enjoyable did the
caves and the glen appear to be that no time was found for

visiting the souterrian, close at hand, nor the ancient cill of
St. Lasser. The machines were mounted, and the return made
past the stately groves of Florencecourt to Enniskillen, where
dinner was ready, and a special carriage prepared to take the
Club home by the train reaching Belfast at nine o'clock.

CULTRA.

A special excursion was made to Cultra on Friday, August 7th,
for the purpose of examining the outcrop of Carboniferous and
Permian rocks on the seashore at Cultra. The excavations for
the foundation of a sea-wall, which is at present in course of
construction, furnished a suitable opportunity for the inspection
of these interesting deposits, the fossils of which have been
catalogued by Mr. Joseph Wright, F.G.S., in the Ninth Annual
Report (1871-2) of this Society.

A party of about thirty left Belfast by the 4-30 p.m. train,
and spent several hours in an examination of the beds, and in
procuring rock-specimens and fossils, for the best collection of
which, made during the afternoon, a prize had been offered by
the secretary.

Subsequently the members were entertained to tea by the
President at his residence. Mr. S. A. Stewart, F.B.S.E., having
been appointed judge, reported that three collections had been
submitted in competition for the geological prize, and declared
Miss S. M. Thompson the winner, her collection including three
species of fossils and seven rocks. A hearty vote of thanks was
passed to the President and Mrs. Vinycomb for their kindness
and hospitality, after which the party separated.

DUNCRUE AND WOODBURN.

Saturday, 15th August, was spent by the members in an
examination of the salt mines of Duncrue, near Carrickfergus,

and while some, on pleasure bent, saw in this excursion only an afternoon of novelty not unmixed with excitement, the majority perceived and appreciated the valuable practical lesson in geology which a visit to the underground regions of the mine presents. Favoured with a bright sunny day, to which a couple of short showers only lent piquancy, a party numbering no less than eighty assembled at Carrickfergus railway station on arrival of the midday train from Belfast, and took the road for Duncrue. A member of the Club resident in Carrickfergus pointed out to the party a remnant of the ancient embattled wall of the town, which stands on the northern side of the Albert Road—an interesting relic, of the existence of which most of the members were not aware. This fragment appears to be in a line with the much larger portion of the old wall, which may be seen a few hundred yards further eastward, and the fine old North Gate stands about midway between. The walls of the town were built in 1608, with the assistance of the Deputy-Governor (Sir Arthur Chichester), who furnished on behalf of His Majesty James I. one hundred men to assist in the work, the Corporation of Carrickfergus on their part engaging to find "a hundred good, able, and sufficient men " "to arme, muster, and keepe in readiness for the defence " of the town.

Passing out into the open country, road was taken for the salt mines, where the party were met by Mr. Pennall, one of the courteous officials of the mine, and without delay the work of lowering the large party, four at a time, to the bottom of the shaft, a depth of 750 feet, was commenced. The time thus spent afforded those waiting their turn to descend an opportunity of examining the character of the rock-salt recently brought to the surface, and of learning something of the history of the mine. The deposit of salt was first discovered in the year 1850, when borings were being carried on in the hope of finding coal below the New Red Sandstone. When a depth of between 1,000 and 1,500 feet had been reached without result, the search for coal was wisely abandoned, and mines were opened for the extraction of the salt. The original mine has now been in disuse for some years, but several others have replaced it, and quite recently some new shafts have been sunk in the neighbourhood of Eden, a couple of miles to the eastward, in each of which salt has been discovered. The mineral occurs in beds of considerable thickness near the base of the Keuper marls, which form the upper division of the Triassic or New Red Sandstone series. In the original boring the salt was first struck at a depth of 500 feet, and from a depth of 522 feet downwards pure salt was passed through for 88 feet, and at a still greater depth salt was again encountered. In the mine which the Field Club had the pleasure of exploring the salt is brought from a depth of 750 feet, and the workings are some twenty to thirty feet in height. The mine is like a huge natural cavern, massive square pillars of salt being left at intervals to support the roof. The mineral is of glistening appearance and brownish colour, the latter being due to a small quantity—amounting to 10 per cent.—of earthy impurity ; but specimens are occasionally obtained of perfect purity and transparency, and showing the characteristic cubic crystallisation.

The large party was safely landed at the bottom of the shaft, with no inconvenience except a curious sensation and singing noise in the ears, due to the pressure of 750 additional feet of atmosphere. As each detachment stepped out of the cage they found themselves in a large and dimly lighted cavern, in which candles glimmered and twinkled in various directions. A regular constellation of candles at one point guided them to where the majority of the party were busily employed in examining the mode of quarrying rock salt, and in obtaining hand specimens as mementoes of their visit. When all had satisfied their natural curiosity or geological cravings, the secretary's whistle echoing through the dim vaults called the party together, and by the light of powerful red and blue lights, which illuminated the huge columns and glistening roof of salt, a short business meeting was held.

The President, in a few words, expressed his pleasure in being present on that highly interesting occasion, and called for any nomination of new members, and, in response, six names were duly proposed and seconded, and formally passed by the meeting. Rev. W. S. Smith, of Antrim, in a happy speech, moved that the best thanks of the meeting be given to the Salt Union (Limited) and Mr. Miscampbell, manager of the mine, and Mr. Pennall, works manager, for their kind permission to pay that interesting visit, and for their courtesy and attention to the party. The motion was seconded by Mr. J. M'N. Stevenson, and carried amid applause. After some further words from several members, the party separated, and the ascent of the shaft was safely accomplished.

Road was next taken for Woodburn Glen, and by kind permission of the Belfast Water Commissioners, a pleasant hour was spent in examining the beauties of the glen, and in admiring the fine view that is obtained from the bank of the reservoir immediately above it. When the party were thoroughly rested, the return walk was commenced, and Carrickfergus was reached sufficiently early to permit of a ramble through the ancient town before train time. Assembling once again at the railway station at 6-30, the return journey to Belfast was made in good time, and the party separated, having spent a highly enjoyable and instructive day.

TEMPLEPATRICK AND DUNAGORE.

The final excursion for this season was held on Saturday, September 5th, under atmospheric conditions not at all in keeping with the weather usually enjoyed by the Club. The party left the Free Library at ten o'clock in wagonettes for Templepatrick, Rathmore, and Dunagore. Passing along the beautiful slopes of Ben-Madighan (Cave Hill), the fine views of lough and hill were much enjoyed, and the fort at Duneanach, overlooking the beautiful Church of Carnmoney, was observed with interest. Passing through Glengormley (the dark blue glen), the old coach road to Templepatrick was soon reached ;

driving close to a fine standing stone, whilst on the hill opposite could be seen the small fort at Biggerstown, surrounded by the beautiful hills of Collinward and Buachaill (pronounced Bohill —the hill of the standing stone). Time did not permit of an examination of the old font in Moylusk graveyard, nor the curious old " resurrection " lamp that still stands sentinel—a grim reminder of the times when the friends of the " rude fore-fathers of the hamlet " had to keep watch over their dead to prevent desecration by the body-snatchers. Here are interred many of the patriots of 1798, including Luke Hope, the editor of the *Rushlight*, and his famous father, James Hope, the leader of the "Spartan Band" at the battle of Antrim, whose chronicles occupy many pages in Dr. Madden's *United Irishmen*. A short halt enabled the party to Visit the Rough Fort, the symmetry of which is now much spoiled. This is to be doubly regretted, as it was not only an ancient stronghold, but was the rallying point for a large contingent of Presbyterian insurgents at the outbreak of hostilities in 1798, and from its heights floated the Irish flag, which afterwards led the column, singing the " Marseillaise " and other revolutionary songs, to Antrim.

The huge pagan monument of Carn Greine next attracted attention, and its antiquity was guessed at, whilst some of the more practical measured the large top stones, which number ten, and approximated their weight at from four to eight tons each. Many theories have been put forth as to its origin and use, but the former is lost in the mists of the past, and the latter has only a little light thrown upon it by the name of *Carn Greine*, which means the grave of Greine, who was a princess. Close by, adjoining a modern farmhouse, was the old Church and the graveyard of Carn Greine, which was used so recently as 1830. The wagonettes being mounted, the old Clubhouse at Rough-fort was passed, where many important conclaves were held in the troublous times, and which was used for a circulating library amongst the yeomen of the district when the century was young, thus showing that literature had a charm for the people before free education was talked about. Perhaps the neighbouring schoolhouse, being one of the first established by Erasmus Smith, deserves some of the credit for this commendable spirit. Near at hand, in the side of a field, the murdered body of the informer Newell, whose fate has not yet been fully written, was thrown into a hole which is still pointed out. One who knew him well wrote of him :—

> He duped his friends, betrayed his native land,
> Deceived e'en those whose bribes were yet in hand.

Killmakee (Cill-mac-aedh, the Church of the son of Hugh) being reached, a curious structure, resembling both a stone circle and a cairn, was examined. It consists of 40 large boulder stones, laid in a circle over 70 feet in diameter, the interior being filled with loose stones and earth and planted with trees. After a short time spent at this very perfect and interesting example of the architecture of primitive man, a short drive brought the party to the Royal residence of Rath-Mora of Moylinne, thus completing the Club's visits this season to the three Royal residences in our district in their historical sequence —viz., Emania, Dun-da-leth-glas, (Downpatrick), and Rath-Mora of Moylinne, so called, according to the annals of Tigearnach, from Mora, wife of Breasal, King of Ulster, A.D. 161. It was inhabited by the Princes of Dalaradia.

Edward, brother of Robert Bruce, King of Scotland, landed at Olderfleet, Larne, on the 25th May, 1315, with a fleet of 300 sail and 6000 Scots, and had in his train a great number of the nobility of Scotland. Bruce waged war in Ireland for three years, and was slain at Faughart, near Dundalk, on the 28th May, 1318. During this time he won eighteen battles, and " he burnt the towns of Downedealgan (Dundalk), Athfirdia (Ardee), and Rath-Mora, and harried and spoyled all Ulster." Since that date Rath-Mora has not been used as a residence. Some members of the Club partly explored the cave on the western side of the rath, but the place was so filled up with loose stones and earth that the passage was stopped at a distance of about thirty feet from the entrance. The impromptu cavemen were afterwards refreshed with sweetmilk and oatcake by Mr. Campbell, the kindly farmer who now tills the former residence of princes. The hill was now ascended to Dunagore, and the beautiful little Church visited, close to whose walls a simple tablet records the fact that Sir Samuel Ferguson, the sweet singer of Ulster, sleeps beneath, in the spot he had long thought of even when residing at a distance, and when he had choice of a grander sepulchre, for in his ode on Westminster Abbey he sings :—

> Yet hold not lightly home, nor yet
> The graves on Dunagore forgot ;
> Nor grudge the stone-gilt stall to change
> For humble bench of Gorman's Grange.

The people of Belfast have never properly estimated the ability and worth of Sir Samuel Ferguson, who was born and educated in their midst, and who dearly loved every hill and valley of " Sweet Dalaradia."   His love for Ireland was true, and in the political excitement of 1845 his muse burst forth in the strong Scottish vernacular of his Northern home, when he wrote :—

> Lord, for ae day o' service done her,
> Lord, for ane hour's sunlight upon her,
> Here, fortune take warld's wealth and honour—
>   You're no my debtor.
> Let me but rive ae link asunder
>   O' Erin's fetter.
>
> Let me but help to shape the sentence
> Will put the pith o' independence
> O' self-respect in self-acquaintance
>   And manly pride,
> Intil auld Ebor Scots descendants
>   Take a' beside.
>
> Let me but help to get the truth
> Set fast in ilka brother's mouth,
> Whatever accent, north or south,
>   His tongue may use ;
> And then ambition, riches, youth —
>   Take which you choose.

Some good rubbings were taken of the two or three fine sculptured stones in the graveyard, and the peculiar old vault that did duty in the times when medical students had some difficulty in procuring "subjects" was carefully examined. The moat or dun was then visited, and the view from its summit much admired. This dun is partly natural, and partly artificial, and is extensively burrowed with souterrains. On the hill behind can still be traced the trenches thrown up by the United Irishmen in 1798, to which they retreated after their defeat at Antrim, but subsequently laid down their arms upon a general amnesty being granted by the authorities to all except the leaders. A speedy drive soon brought the party to Temple-patrick and to tea, after which the general meeting was held— Mr. Alex. Tate, C.E., in the chair. It was moved and seconded that the best thanks of the Club be given to those who had granted permission to visit the various objects of interest on their properties. Three new members were elected, and the secretary read the list of attendances at the different excursions for the season, which were much larger than those of any recent year. It was also announced that the present roll of membership is the largest ever attained by the Club. After a few flattering remarks by some of the members in regard to the way in which the Honorary Secretaries had conducted matters, the meeting ended ; and shortly afterwards the good horses brought the party quickly home.

WINTER SESSION.

NOTE.—The authors of the various Papers, of which abstracts are here appended, are alone responsible for the views expressed in them.

SOCIAL MEETING.

THE Winter Session was opened with a Social Meeting on Tuesday, October 20th, at which the attendance of members and visitors numbered 360, being a considerable increase on the attendance at last Social Meeting. After tea had been dispensed in the lower room by a number of lady members, the President of the Club (Mr. John Vinycomb, F.R.S.A.) took the chair, and made a brief opening statement. He referred to the summer excursions of the past season, which had been one of the most enjoyable and successful series that had been held for many years, and at which the attendance of members and visitors had shown a considerable increase. The membership of the Club, he was happy to say, was also rapidly on the increase, having risen by nearly thirty per cent. since the beginning of the preceding year, the present membership being over 320, being the largest roll of members of any provincial scientific society in Ireland. Having referred in general terms to the exhibits which covered the walls and tables of the lecture hall and library, he called upon some of the exhibitors for a further explanation of the objects. Mr. Alexander Tate, C.E., chairman of the Microscopical Section, stated that his section was represented by seven microscopes, each under the direction of a member, and illustrating a variety of subjects, including pond life, marine life, insects, echinodermata, seaweeds, and geological objects. Mr. R. Lloyd Praeger, B.E., M.R.I.A., senior secretary, in the absence of Mr. L. M. Ewart, J.P., called attention to the fine display illustrative of the linen industry, which occupied one end of the lecture hall, and which was kindly shown by Messrs. William Ewart & Sons. He also directed attention to the collections of natural history and geological objects, for which prizes had been awarded at the last Annual Meeting of the Club, and which were now on view, showing a highly commendable amount of energy, zeal, and neatness of manipulation on the part of the competitors. He regretted to have to announce that the beautiful Celtic shrine recently found in Lough Erne, which was to have been on exhibition, had not arrived in time for the meeting, and also that the unfavourable state of the weather would prevent the successful working of an astronomical telescope on the roof of the Museum, which had been kindly undertaken by the secretary of the Ulster Astronomical Society.

The company then scattered themselves through the rooms, engaged in an examination of the various exhibits. Prominent on the walls of the lecture hall hung a magnificent set of archæological photographs, executed in the platinotype process on full photographic plates, and illustrating to the number of 130 the ancient castles, abbeys, churches, round towers, cromleacs, stone circles, caiseals, forts, and crosses of the North of Ireland. This splendid series is the work of Mr. Robert Welch, and is a gift from him to the Club, and forms the neuclus of the systematic collection of antiquarian and other photographs, which a special committee is engaged in bringing together. Prominent among Mr. Welch's photographs was a series illustrating the Irish antiquities in the large and valuable collection of their past President, Rev. Canon Grainger, M.R.I.A., recently presented to the city, and part of which had been opened that day for public inspection at the Free Library. Two large frames of photographs, mostly taken on the excursions of the summer session, were exhibited by Mr. George Donaldson, and were much admired, his view of the interior of Armagh Cathedral being indeed a triumph of the photograhic art. A number of other members, including Miss

A. H. Tate and Messrs. William Gray, M.R.I.A. ; A. Tate, C.E.|; D. C. Beggs, W. Hanna, B.A. ; James Leslie, and R. Welch also showed series of photographs taken on the trips of last summer, and reminding members of pleasant drives through country lanes, or walks over heathery hilltops, or boating expeditions on sea, lake, and river, and of many other incidents of the summer programme. Among the other exhibits in the photographic department was a set of geological photographs by Miss M. K. Andrews, some very fine enlargements by Mr. William Gray, and a most interesting set of photographs of astronomical objects and apparatus, taken at the Lick Observatory in California, and shown by Mr. Isaac Ward. Displayed on a long table across the end of the lecture hall was a series illustrating the various processes in the manufacture of linen, obligingly supplied by Messrs. W. Ewart & Sons, Ltd. At one end of the table was a box of flaxseed and a bundle of flax, at the other finished linen goods from the coarsest sailcloth to a handkerchief of marvellously fine cambric, and displayed on the space between were specimens showing every successive process, illustrated also by some of the machinery by means of which the process is carried out. The exhibition was a highly effective one, and was a source of much interest during the evening. The President of the Club contributed a series of early bookplates, and also a series of modern ones of his own design, many of the latter being familiar to readers not only in Belfast, but in many places both at home and abroad. Hanging on the walls opposite to the photographic exhibition were two fine series of dried plants, one of flowering plants, the other of cryptogams, being portions of the prize collections of Mr. W. D. Donnan. The other prize collections on exhibition were Palæozoic fossils and Cretaceous fossils, by Miss Sydney M. Thompson ; archæological photographs, by Miss A. H. Tate ; beetles, by Rev. S. A. Brenan, B.A. ; and a series of microscopic slides, showing great excellence of manipulation, by Mr. Wm. Hanna, B.A. Mr. John H. Davies exhibited specimens of a rare moth, *Nonagria typhœ*, which he had recently obtained in the neighbourhood of Moira. The larvæ of this moth burrow in the stems of the *Typha* or reed-mace, and some of these were exhibited, showing the ravages of the animal. A choice selection of microscopical objects examined through a good instrument always proves an attraction, and on this occasion the representatives of the Microscopical Section of the Club had a busy time of it, and were indefatigable in their efforts to minister to the curiosity or scientific zeal of their many guests. Meanwhile a lantern exhibition was in progress in the upper room of the Museum, under the direction of Mr. John Donaldson, and an interesting and, in many cases, amusing series of views were thrown on the screen. Here the summer excursions were again to the fore. A number of instantaneous views not only of scenery, but of the members themselves, were exhibited, much to the surprise of some of the latter, who had little imagined, as they strolled about in quest of a rare flower or moth, or pondered on some antiquarian fragment, that they were being quietly " kodaked " by their friends of the camera. Some good views of Irish antiquities were shown, and of forest trees also ; and a number of photographs of trained cats, dressed in quaint costumes, excited much laughter and applause. At nine o'clock the President again took the chair, and a short business meeting was held. On behalf of the Club, the President returned thanks to those ladies and gentlemen whose efforts had made the meeting a most gratifying success. He specially mentioned Mr. Lavens M. Ewart, J.P., and the ladies who had presided at the tea tables. A special vote of thanks was passed to Mr. Welch, on the motion of Mr. F. J. Bigger, junior secretary, seconded by Mr. Robert Young, C.E., for his magnificent gift of photographs for the Club's albums. The election of new members was then proceeded with. Eighteen ladies and gentlemen were duly nominated, and, their names having been put to the meeting, they were declared elected. This concluded the formal business of the evening, and a second lantern display was given, after which the exhibits again claimed attention, and the meeting gradually dispersed.

The second meeting of the Winter Session was held on November 17th, when Mr. John Vinycomb, F.R.S.A., delivered his presidential address, which is here given *in extenso:*

The President said—The pursuit of knowledge, in some of its various forms, and the pleasure of intercourse with minds similarly directed, form the main links which bind the members of this Society together, and while we meet and take pleasure in meeting each other on common ground, with a general toleration of each other's strong points, it will be readily understood that, while our aims and aspirations all tend in the same direction, our ways are naturally divergent. I have often thought that the title of the Society of which I have the honour to be President does not fully indicate the wide scope of subjects which its rules permit, and so it is found that, while some course the flowery meads in entymological or botanical pursuits, others, with a different bias are on the look out for objects of antiquarian interest, or, with hammer in hand, strive to unlock the secrets of the rocks. So true it is that the scientific lover of nature

> Finds tongues in trees, books in the running brooks,
> Sermons in stones, and good in every thing.

In the domains of natural history, archæology, and kindred subjects, the fields are wide, and call for investigation, and a rich store yet awaits the patient student. You will not be surprised, therefore, if I depart a little from the usual course in this, my opening address, and take up a subject which, at first sight, seems to lie far afield, and to have little connection with the operations of a Naturalists' Field Club. I crave the indulgence of the many friends with whom I have so long associated in this Society while I lightly sketch out some of the leading features of that universal symbolism which has existed in ancient and modern times. The subject, however, is so wide that I can only barely touch the fringe of it. I am induced to take up this somewhat neglected subject because to me it has the greatest interest, and because I feel that some knowledge of the science is indispensable to all who would read aright the literature and the art of past times as expressed in its monuments.

In the scant leisure of busy lives the study of some particular branch of natural science, archæology, or kindred subject has the greatest charm for thoughful minds, in that for the time being it lures the attention from the cares and worries and the events of everyday life ; and more than this, it is a delightful relaxation to an active mind, and lays the foundation of enduring pleasures of a refined and elevating kind. Such study may be likened in the words of the Psalmist to "the green vales of the desert where water springs," the kind resting-places in "life's dreary round," the oasis in which toil may be relaxed, and the weary spirit may recover its tone and resume its strength and its hopes. " Blessed are they who going through the vale of misery use it for a well, and the pools are filled with water."

From the earliest ages of the world's history, arbitrary signs and symbols have been used to represent ideas, or persons, or abstract qualities. The figurative language of the East, so generally employed by Hebrew writers, full of grand and beautiful imagery, strikes deep into the heart and conscience. Not only do we find constant reference in the Scriptures to the natural qualities of men and animals, and to many terrestrial and celestial objects, by way of simile and illustration, but throughout the entire East such has invariably been the practice at all times. In the ancient Book of Job (who, according to Hales, was contemporary with Nahor, the grandfather of Abraham) the swiftness of time was symbolised by a weaver's shuttle, and the hypocrite's hope by a spider's web. The knowledge of the Deity is described as being " high as the heavens, deeper than hell, longer than the earth, broader than the sea." Man is symbolised as a flower of the field, prosperity by a lighted candle, and adversity by a candle extinguished. The dying Jacob, when blessing his children, used a series of significant emblems to express the character and fortunes of their respective descendants, which were treasured up in their memories and used as the insignia of the tribes in their advance into and occupation of the Promised Land. Expressive symbols, however, are coeval with the creation of the first man, of which the Divine covenant itself is an example ; for the trees of life and knowledge were emblematical of life and happiness or misery and death ; the rainbow, of God's covenant with Noah as a perpetual memento of His promise ; the serpent, a fit emblem of guile and subtlety, as the dove is of innocence and peace.

Our Lord, in His parables, clothes His moral teachings in the form of vivid metaphor and searching paradox. Many of the expressions used in the Sacred Writings are clear, expressive ideas, typifying in words under the similitude of a figure, what to a greater or less extent can also be depicted in art. Francis Quarles quaintly tells us—" An emblem is but a simple parable; let not the tender eye check to see the allusion to our Blessed Saviour figured in these types. In Holy Scripture He is some-times called a sower, sometimes a fisher, sometimes a physician ; and why not presented to the eye as well as to the ear ? Before the knowledge of letters God was known by hieroglyphics ; and, indeed, what are the heavens, the earth, nay, every creature, but hieroglyphics and emblems of His glory ? "

Sir Samuel Ferguson, in his " Notes on Ornamentation," appended to a work by him, says, regarding these early symbols —" We are contemplating the infancy of art, and find it to contain many attributes which form all the charm of childhood ; that courage which proceeds from perfect trust and all ignorance of cause for fear ; that confidence which gives freedom of ex-pression to the happiest natural faculties. Beyond this, art was, in its earlier manifestations, the hieroglyphic language of the human soul. Men found in the material images that nature gave a vestment for their deepest thoughts and feelings. The globe and the circle embodied their conceptions of the universe and heaven. The Rock and the Lamb and the Pelican tearing her breast open to feed her young with her blood were to them images of Christ. Man in his savage state, when only following the instincts of his nature, converses in figures. Indeed, the farther back we go into history, the nearer we attain to the primitive state of man, the more picturesque his language becomes, and the more entirely all spiritual truths are represented by material signs. It seems as if, when first the necessity arose for expressing metaphysical and abstract ideas, and bringing them into form, men were compelled to make choice of words whose literal signification presented a greater or less analogy with these new ideas, and as if it had always been natural for men to feel that a correspondence between visible things and human thoughts does exist. So that symbolism would seem to be a natural impulse of the human mind, and has been ever used by man in his unfettered state, as in his hours of deepest thought and faith. It is found not only in the language and art of all primitive ages, but lives still in our poetry, Scriptures, and the most sacred forms of our religion ; and, so far as symbolism is the setting forth of a material sign, it will still be found in all the highest efforts of art. Painting, in its noblest form, is no mimetic art, but the effort to express in the visible and material forms of creation the internal beauty that gleams through all ; while the effort to perceive, assimilate, and interpret the poetry of life that lies hidden in and emanates from all visible nature, may still be found the sacred office of the poet and the artist."

A recent writer, after tracing the origin and connection between hieroglyphic or pictorial alphabets, and all writing by letters or phonetic signs, states :—" It will be seen that the progress from hieroglyphic to phonetic writing is one of conventionality. The earliest sign was like its object as a picture, the perfected letter is like nothing on earth ; the one appealed to the senses with the intellect, the other calls upon the intellect alone. Such is the progress towards letters or literature, or the exchange of thought in written language. There may be an analogous advance of the rude original picture, which may become less and less conventional, and more and more like what it stands for in the mind, until strong resemblance is attained, and realistic art is established. But letters and realistic art arise together in the infancy of human expression.

Again, it is the infancy, or rather, let us say, the imperfection of man's power of expressing the thought within him, which is the chief cause of the use of symbolism everywhere. It is employed alike in speaking, writing, and painting. All who are accustomed to teaching can tell us the value of a simile, especially in elementary instruction. They well know what number of trite comparisons and cut-and-dried illustrations they are obliged to keep by them as stock-in-trade. It is remarked, again, how great use is made by savage orators of trope and figure, and civilised people, who are unaccustomed to express themselves, or are uneducated, or happen to be dealing with matters they do not perfectly understand, are always having recourse to similes if they have the ingenuity to frame them. In short, symbolism is one great means of expressing imperfect thought or incomplete conception. It is virtually an appeal from one mind to another for assistance or fellowship ; the speaker confesses himself unable to unwind a length of thread, and tries to throw the ball over to his friend, that he may unravel some more. This gives us a definition of symbolism, the attempt to suggest higher, wider, deeper, or more complicated ideas by the use of those which are simpler and more familiar."

The term "symbol" is from the Greek *sun ballo*, to put or cast together, and originally meant the corresponding part of a tally, ticket, or coin cut in twain. The person who presented the piece which fitted showed a " symbol " of his right to what he claimed.

It is not my intention to do more than touch upon the ancient use of symbols, but I cannot refrain from mentioning some employed by the ancient Egyptians, a species of hieroglyphic writing. Phre or Phrah (our Pharaoh) meant the sun, and was the title of the Egyptian monarch, the hieroglyph for which was a point within a circle. It was also an emblem of God, because His centre is everywhere, and His circumference is immeasurable. The serpent signified wisdom, and turned in a circle it denoted eternity. The symbol of the life to come was a cross and a

circle, called the *crux ansata*, or the cross with a handle ;
sometimes life was denoted by a lamp, and sometimes by zigzag
lines denoting water, because that element is essential to animal
and vegetable existence, a figure which has come down to us as
a zodiacal sign, ≈ Aquarius, the water-bearer. Hieroglyphic
characters bore considerable resemblance to the object intended
to be described. The sun, for instance, could not be more
strikingly represented than by a circle, nor the waning moon
than by a half-circle. Chemistry indeed perseveres in using this
species of symbolic designation, for by the former it denoted
gold, by the latter silver. In ancient Egypt the same hieroglyph, in ancient Greece the same word, was synonymous for
writing and painting ; and words are but symbols of our ideas,
expressed by the medium of sound. In the remote past, as in
the middle ages, and during the slow advance of knowledge and
culture generally, almost to the present time, the only language
understood of all people was that transmitted through the traditions of the past expressed and typified by figures as by colours.

Pythagoras, the philosopher, seems to have introduced a
system of hieroglyphics or symbols, which are contained in his
esoteric doctrines, and were of two classes—the one, a visible
emblem, as an emblem or geometrical figure ; the other, a pithy
sentence, combining many ideas or sparks of truth for those
who are able to enkindle them. The use of animal hieroglyphics
among the followers of Pythagoras was very extensive in its
application and symbolic meaning. According to this system,
the ox was an emblem of patient industry ; the elephant, of
fidelity, justice, and piety ; the bull, of ferocity ; the horse, of
fame and swiftness ; the dog, of fidelity, friendship, memory,
and gratitude ; the lamb, of innocence ; the ram, of boldness,
profanity, or slander ; the ass, of docility ; the camel, of strength
and abstinence ; the mule, of sterility ; and so on. An anchor
represented magnanimity and fortitude. " These," said Pythagoras, " no tempest can shake ; virtue alone is firm ; everything
else is unstable." Fortitude was also symbolised by a rock
amidst the waves of the sea. A bridle was symbolical of wisdom,

because as a horse cannot be governed without a bridle, so also are riches without wisdom unmanageable and pernicious ; the pomegranate, of populousness ; the ivy, antiquity ; ears of corn, fertility ; the palm branch was a token of joy, and used as an emblem to express the conviction that trouble had been exchanged for prosperity. A crown symbolised the laws, and therefore the phrase " Pluck not a crown " meant offend not the laws, which are the crown of a nation. Anger was represented by fire, and contention by a sword ; a lamp burning, from its united qualities of brightness and purity, was an emblem of philosophy.

In the sculptures, coins, gems, and other subjects of ancient art that have come down to us, we have abundant evidence of the constant use of typical forms to express ideas suited to the general understanding; and from contemporaneous literature we know how thoroughly each device must have been understood and appreciated by a quick-witted people. In the later, as well as the earlier times, the thoughtful sought and found semblances in all things. Philo, a celebrated philosopher among the Platonists, relates that the Christians who lived in Alexandria in his time used to employ themselves in this holy exercise, and that they seemed to regard the law as having a body and soul represented by the letter and spirit.

Mythological emblems, and emblems of early faiths, and particularly Christian symbolism, open too wide a field, and one too rich in precious memories, to enter on at the present time. I therefore only mention this great branch of symbolic art, that I may not be accused of altogether ignoring it. For the same reason the symbolism of colours, and also of floral emblems, I must pass over, as well as some other branches of the subject.

THE IMPRESS OR DEVICE.

Long ago it was the custom for persons in the higher ranks to choose an impress or device as a personal mark, peculiarly their own, as their fancy might dictate. Generally it was a sort of playful reference to the name or the emblem of some quality

which they admired or possessed, or having some special
significance relating to the person or circumstances of the time.
Frequently the device was associated with a motto or legend,
as such a short pithy sentence was termed, which elucidated the
idea contained in it, or else gave to it a peculiar shade of
meaning. These devices or emblems were embroidered upon
garments and hangings, and depicted in various ways for
personal adornment, and for many other purposes, yet not subject to rigid and pedantic heraldic laws, being altogether
more free in their uses and interpretations. Many of the
devices of noble and illustrious families which have become
hereditary as household badges or crests were originally of this
nature. Our Plantagenet kings took their name from the
circumstance of Geoffrey, Earl of Anjou, husband of the
Empress Matilda or Maud, wearing a plume of blossoming
broom (*planta genista*) in his head-gear. Who does not know
the dreadful story of the wars of the rival houses of York and
Lancaster, when the red and white roses become the badges of
faction, and the best blood of England flowed in lavish streams
in fratricidal strife. Many other emblems that have become
historical in our literature will be recognised by the careful
reader, but unless he is well read in the works of the early
emblem-writers he will miss much that is weighty and significant. To take only a single instance : Shakspere makes the
victorious Richard exclaim,

> "Now is the winter of our discontent
> Made glorious summer by this sun of York ;
> And all the clouds, that lower'd upon our house,
> In the deep bosom of the ocean buried."

To the ordinary reader this may sound only a prettily turned
phrase, but there is much more than meets the eye, as in numberless instances in Shakspere and other writers of his age, in
which happy allusions, understood at the time, are now obscure.
To know that the "sun in splendour" was the badge of the
House of York at once gives the key to the bright imagery in
which the immortal bard enwrapped his ideal, and played upon
the double sense.

Sir William Stirling Maxwell, in his introduction to "The Chief Victories of the Emperor Charles V.," says, "The noble gentlemen of Europe. . . . declared their inward pretensions, purposes, and enterprises, not by speech or any apparent manner, but shadowed under a certain veil of forms and figures," and "it was the fashion for men of all degrees to clothe in symbolic shape their sympathies or antipathies, their sorrows, joys, or affections, or the hopes and ambitions of their lives." Gentle and simple, following the example of sovereigns, each adopted an impress or device, with its appropriate legend. Such inventions were held in high esteem, and took firm root in these countries, exercising the ingenuity of the bravest and wisest in devising them. That the fashion of expressing their thoughts in emblems must have been very prevalent appears from frequent references from our older poets. Chaucer's "Prioress" had

> " A broche of gold ful shene,
> On which was ywritten a crounéd A,
> And after, *Amor vincit omnia*."

"Emblem books," as they were termed by English writers, have never been numerous, and seldom original, the field being occupied by the writers of Italy, France, and Germany. A revival of interest was given to this most attractive branch of symbolic or emblematic art by the publication, a few years ago, of an excellent work on the subject, "Historic Devices, Badges, War Cries, &c.," by Mrs. Bury Palliser. It is an admirable exposition of the subject, and full of interest to the student of history. A copy is here on the table, also a copy of Alciati's "Emblems," published 1589 ; "Imagines Mortis," Holbein's "Dance of Death," 1573 ; Valeriani's "Hieroglyphica of the Ancient Egyptians," including Horapolla's works ; *facsimile* reprint "The Mirror of Majesty," 1618 ; "Whitney's Choice of Emblems," edited by Henry Green, 1870 ; "Shakspere and the Emblem Writers," Henry Green, 1870 ; and other works treating of the subject.

COINS AND MEDALS.

Coins and medals furnish most valuable historical evidence, and present perfect examples of emblems and symbolic representations. We find, to use heraldic language, that the owl is the crest of Athens, and appears upon all her coins ; a pegasus, of Corinth ; a wolf's head, that of Argus ; and a tortoise, the badge of the Peloponnesus. A glance through Dr. Smith's larger "Classical Dictionary," Humphrey's "Coin Collector's Manual," or the fine series of ancient coins in the Free Library will show the immense use made of symbolism in the coinage of ancient Greece and Rome ; not one figure in the whole series of monetary types but has its appropriate meaning, and would be readily understood by the communities using it. Modern coinage more frequently adopts the national heraldry of the State, with the portrait of the reigning sovereign. The whole history of Louis XIV. and that of his great adversary William III. are represented in the splendid series of medals that were struck to commemorate the leading events of their reigns, and, although outrageously untrue to nature and reality by the adoption of the Roman costumes and classic symbols, they serve as records of remarkable occurences. Many of our later war medals also err in having modern heroes and events depicted as if of 2,000 years ago, a species of anachronism analogous to that of the Dutch painter of representing Scriptural personages dressed in the costumes of his own time, and in scenery essentially Dutch.

HERALDRY.

Heraldry throughout employs the language of emblems. It is, says an eminent writer, the picture history of families, of tribes, of nations, of princes, and of emperors. Many a legend and many a strange fancy may be mixed up with it which demand almost the credulity of simple childhood in order to obtain our credence ; yet in the literature of chivalry and honours, there are enshrined abundant records of the glory that belonged to mighty names. About the time of the Crusades, the miscellaneous gatherings from various countries, each under its separate leaders, found the necessity of having distinctive signs or emblems emblazoned upon their persons, by which they might be recognised. Tasso, Ariosto, and other poets contemporary with the different periods of the Crusades have told us of the splendid banners and armorial ensigns borne by the nobles who participated in those expeditions. Every soldier of the Cross bore the sacred emblem upon his person, each country adopting a different form or colour by which they might be distinguished one from the other. The leaders, however, each bore in addition special ensigns which, once adopted, became hereditary in his family, and the glory of his descendants.

It was during this period that heraldry as a science may be said to have taken its rise, though devices and emblems on armour and on military banners and standards may be traced long before that period. Thus Sir Bernard Burke—no mean authority—states heraldry to be no more than an organisation of the emblems and devices which had previously existed beyond the memory of man. After the date of the Norman Conquest (1066) heraldry made rapid progress in England, and the high estimation in which it was held is attested by its union with other arts, especially with painting and sculpture. Thus was heraldry connected with the lasting monuments of architecture, and became " the handmaid of history." The assumption of devices on coat armour and the crest or cognisance on the helmet were in reality a necessity, caused by the mode of warfare practised in the middle ages. The defensive armour of the period completely concealed the person. King James is stated to have remarked "that it was an excellent invention, for it not only saved the life of the wearer, but hindered him from doing harm to anybody else." Mounted on his horse, the baron or knight, armed *cap-a-pie*, could not be known to those about him, hence the adoption of distinctive bearings upon coat armour. In the thick of the *melée* the waving pennon and dancing crest of the leader formed the rallying point for his friends and followers. His motto, or *cri de guerre*, ringing through the air above the noise and din of battle, was the inspiriting sound shouted from many lusty throats, urging each other on to victory.

A recent writer says that "heraldry is the last remnant of ancient symbolism, and a legitimate branch of the Christian art ; the griffins and unicorns, fesses and chevrons, the very tinctures are all symbolical ; each has its mystic meaning singly or in combination, and thus every old coat-of-arms preaches a lesson of chivalric honour and Christian principle to all who inherit it." Arms were assumed or granted to commemorate some notable or heroic deed performed in the service of the Sovereign or the State, in the battle-field or in the defence of a fortress ; in later times in reward of some signal service, warlike or statesmanlike. All orders of the nobility, the greater and lesser gentry, eagerly sought these coveted distinctions, which were afterwards enrolled by officers appointed by the State. The right to wear coat armour was guarded by most stringent rules ; and only the well-born, or those who could prove their descent for at least four generations of reputable ancestors, could hope to be considered "gentlemen of coat armour." The rise of the great middle class in these countries has to a great extent revolutionised the antique notion of pure blood, and to be "the ancestor" very many would consider greater glory than to be the descendant of the longest line of titled mediocrities. Ignorance should not exist in this enlightened age with reference to a subject so intimately connected with the history of our country. Are not the lion of England, the red cross banner of St. George, the white and red roses, the shamrock of Ireland, and Scotia's barbed thistle of interest to all? Do not the plays of Shakspere, the words of Scott and other eminent writers abound in heraldic allusions, while to the student of history an acquaintance with the subject of heraldry is a necessity, for, as Victor Hugo remarks, "The whole history of the second half of the middle ages is written in blazon."

But the great purpose for which heraldry was called into being—the display of personal insignia by the leaders of armies

—no longer exists. National and regimental emblems alone are now used in modern warfare. The science of military emblems, however, which heraldry really was in the beginning, soon became of general application to all who were in any way entitled to bear coat armour. But it is not alone in its warlike aspect that heraldry may have a use and convey a meaning. "Peace hath her victories no less renowned than war," and her triumphs and aspirations are as capable of being depicted by signs which preach a lesson, as those pertaining exclusively to battles and bloodsheds ; her emblems, drawn from other sources, grace the escutcheons of our noblest citizens, and fitly symbolise their successes, and many persons who profess to despise heraldry are not infrequently the first to adopt its principles to record their achievements in the arts of peace.

SIGNBOARDS.

The custom of old inns and hostelries, and also places of business and public resort, bearing signboards with heraldic or allusive devices of some kind, is a relic of the good old barbarous times, when reading and writing were the accomplishments of the few. A bunch of grapes at a house door, an optician's spectacles, or a gold beater's arm and hammer, represent the business done within symbolically, and are understood at a glance by the most unlettered. From very early times this was the only way such places were distinguished. Many of these old signs remain to the present day, and will be in the recollection of everyone ; and, as houses in London streets were not numbered till 1764, every house or place of business was known by its sign—a lamb, an eagle, a wolf, a vat, a bale of wool, &c., &c. In Gay's "Trivia" he says :—

> If drawn by business to a street unknown,
> Let the sworn porter point thee through the town ;
> Be sure observe the signs, for signs remain
> Like faithful landmarks to the walking train.

English literature abounds with references to scenes enacted at places historically known by the sign ; as the "Tabard Inn," renowned by Chaucer as the rendezvous of the Canterbury Pilgrims 500 years ago ; "The Mermaid," frequented by Raleigh, Shakspere, and the great wits of the time, well known from a quotation from a letter of Beaumont to Ben Jonson, beginning :—"What things have we seen done at the Mermayde." It was no uncommon thing for publicans and others to adopt the heads of popular heroes—a class of subject, however, particularly liable to transmutation by the accession of some later favourite, as the "Duke's Head," which in the time of Blenheim implied the hero Marlborough, was changed to his Royal Highness the Duke of York, or his Grace of Wellington. The heads of Homer, Horace, Cicero, Milton, Shakspere, &c., were also taken by booksellers. The heads of Æsculapius, his "serpent and staff," or his "cock" were appropriate for professors of the healing art ; these, as well as the head of Galen, or the phœnix rising from the flames, are still found decorating our modern druggists. Sir Thomas Gresham, founder of the Royal Exchange, in 1560, was appointed ambassador at the Court of the Duke of Parma, Regent of the Netherlands, and received thereon from Elizabeth the honour of knighthood, which was a real honour in those days. Notwithstanding this promotion, he continued business as a merchant, and kept his shop open in Lombard Street, with a great grasshopper—his family crest—over his door as a sign.

I may just call your attention for a moment to a modern instance, a lingering relic, of this good old custom near our own doors. As you pass up and down High Street you cannot fail to perceive a great golden canister over the door of an eminent townsman, whose name, like his tea, is a household word in our mouths. It speaks of the days when tea caddies were prevalent, when the precious young Hyson, the cheering Congou, the bold Souchong, and the Mandarin varieties of black and green were supposed to be imprisoned in splendid receptacles of this kind in the shops of the tea merchants. The well-known shape of the canister in this case symbolised the contents. "Assam," "Ceylon," "Sirocco," "Lipton," &c., are the catch words now used to conjure with, instead of the old forms of symbols.

As a lingering relic of the old custom of exhibiting trade symbols, we still meet the barber's pole and brass chafing-dish dangling from it, the striped and twisted colours representing the bandaged limb, telling of the days when barbers were also surgeons. In the East, even in far-away Japan, at the present day we find the well-known sign of "the bush" outside a saké shop the same as that used in England in the old times, which gave rise to the proverb "Good wine needs no bush." The "bush" was a tavern sign in ancient Rome, which gave rise to the proverb *vino vendibile suspensa hedera non opus est*, and from which our sign of the "bush" is derived. The Greeks and Romans appeared to have used symbolic signboards. Thus Aristotle says (*Problematum* x. 14)—"As with things drawn above the shops, which, though they are small, appear to have breadth and depth." And Athenæus, "He hung the well-known sign in the front of his house." From the many similar references it would seem that the custom was very prevalent. The incorporated companies and trade guilds of London and many of the provincial towns had each their coat-of-arms and trade devices, which their members exhibited as signs of their trade and profession.

Are we in want and possess valuables? The well-known sign of "Mine uncle," the three golden balls of the pawnbroker, invite us to be relieved of our distresses. It is interesting to know that this famous sign is derived from the shield of the Medici family, and was the arms of Lombardy, which nation introduced over Europe the system of lending money on the security of articles of value.

IN CONCLUSION

Let me hope that the slight introductory sketch of some of the main features of the symbolic art may induce at least some of those present to continue its study as expressed in the language, the literature, and the art of all the ages past.

The next communication was by Rev. H. W. Lett, M.A., on St. MacErc's Cross, Donaghmore, Co. Down. Mr. Lett said :— The ancient Celtic cross, which is the subject of this paper, is situated in the churchyard of Donaghmore, in the County of Down, five miles north of Newry, and seven miles south of Banbridge, not far from the Four-mile House on the leading road between these towns.

The Church of Donaghmore was founded about the middle of the fifth century by St. MacErc, who became its first Bishop. He was a brother of St. Mochay, of Nendrum, and died A.D. 497. Another brother was St. Columban Mulinn, of Derrykeighan, in Dalriada ; their mother being Bronagh, daughter of Milcho, with whom St. Patrick had been a captive near Slemish in the Braid Valley.

The cross stands twenty-five feet to the south of the chancel of the present parish church. The material is a coarse County Down granite. It consists of three stones, a base, a shaft, and a collared head. Until its recent restoration by the Rev. J. Davidson Cowan, chiefly through the assistance of the Club, it was in a sad condition. The head was displaced and partly buried at the head of a grave close by, and the shaft, though resting on its base, was broken across about the middle.

The parts have been carefully set together with cement, and a stout iron dowel put into the broken shaft. This was done under the personal superintendance of Mr. Cowan and myself.

The total height of the cross is ten feet six inches. The base stone measures where it rest on the mouth of the cave three feet from north to south, and two feet ten inches from east to west. It rises by three steps of five inches rise and two inches tread to the height of seventeen inches, and has no traces of carving or inscriptions.

The shaft is five feet six inches high, by eighteen inches wide one way and fourteen inches wide the other way. The angles are rounded into a corner-staff three inches in diameter, the spaces between on all the four faces being similar, and filled in with figures or interlaced patterns carved in high relief. The

WEST FACE.　　　　　　　EAST FACE.

condition of these, considering the coarse nature of the stone, and the many centuries that it has been exposed to the weather, is wonderfully clear and sharp. For seven inches from the base the shaft is one inch wider than in the main portion, and it is not sunk, there being simply an interlaced pattern cut on it.

The west face of the shaft is entirely filled with figures representing events in early Bible History. Commencing from the bottom, there are Adam and Eve under the tree of knowledge of good and evil, Noah in the Ark on the waves of the flood, and the angel with the sword expelling Adam from the garden of Eden.

The north face of the shaft is divided into four panels, each with a narrow bead framing round it ; the bottom one is of interlaced work, the next above of two figures, which have not yet been identified ; and two more panels above of interlaced work.

The east face of the shaft is—like that of the west—not divided into panels ; it is occupied by five tiers of figures all much the same in character. At the bottom are four small squarish brackets, or pedestals, on which stand the first group of three figures. These are clothed to the knees like all the other figures that are distinguishable on the cross, and they are of unequal height, the smallest figure being that on the south or left hand, and the largest that on the north. Above them is another precisely similar group.

The position occupied by the third row of these figures is where I have come to the conclusion that the blow was struck that broke the stone in two. These figures are much injured, but I think they are the wise men from the East, because the fourth row is of two figures with one much smaller between them, this I take to be a representation of the Nativity—the Blessed Virgin Mary, with the Holy Child Jesus, and Joseph. One of these figures bears in its right hand a palm branch.

The top or fifth row on this face is of three figures with the central one the tallest.

On the south face there are three panels, the bottom one being much the smallest, and representing King David with his harp, above which are two panels of interlaced work.

The three-inch bead is wrought round the top of the shaft, and projects, like the portion next the base, one inch beyond the main portion.

The head of the cross measures four feet across the arms, and three feet from the top moulding of the shaft, just described, to its apex. The arms are connected by a ring or collar, the enclosed space being perforated, leaving a knob on each segment of the ring. These knobs in many other crosses are formed in the angles of the cross itself. The top ends in the usual representation of a shrine or church with a steep projecting roof. One bit of the top on the north-east is broken off, but this has been done at some very distant date. There was a story told to the rector that the fragment was in a well on the east slope of the churchyard, and, though the supposed site was pointed out, a man whom we had at work could find no trace of it after two days excavating. Some persons wished to have this defect made good with cement, but my advice was taken to leave it alone.

The stone out of which this head was cut was not of as durable a nature as that which was wrought into the shaft, for the weathering has been much greater on it. But from several examinations that I made of the head while it was on the ground, I could see that originally it was everywhere carved with either figures or ornamental patterns. On the west face it is possible with the aid of the photograph now in the Club's album to make out a representation of the crucifixion.

This west face has traces of eight other figures, about which I cannot speak particularly. In the uppermost part of the top, just under the little eave of the apex, are two spirals intended to represent the clouds of heaven, or merely to fill a vacant space.

On the end of the north arm is a figure in full dress, about which I can say nothing.

On the east face the weathering has been so severe that

nothing can be made out, except that there are traces of figures all over it. On the south, under the arm, is a well-preserved bit of ornamental work. The pattern is a double row of spirals separated by a small double bead. This is the place in which, on many other crosses throughout Ireland, the carving is best preserved, as it has been protected by the overhanging arms.

Discussion on the paper followed, in which Messrs. F. W. Lockwood, Edward Allworthy, and F. J. Bigger took part.

NOTE.—The illustrations of the cross have been drawn by Mr. F. W. Lockwood, from photographs apecially taken by Mr. R. Welch for the Club's antiquarian photographic survey of Ireland.

Mr. Francis Joseph Bigger, junior secretary, then exhibited and described the ancient Celtic shrine which was recently obtained in Lough Erne by Mr. Thomas Plunkett, M.R.I.A. He said that the shrine was dredged up accidentally by fishermen last April from the bottom of a secluded bay on the southern shore of Lower Lough Erne, half-way between Enniskillen and Belleek. It got entangled in a night-line on which hooks were placed, and was brought to the surface of the water from a depth of 24 feet. The inside is formed out of one piece of wood, the outer covering is bronze. It contained a small inner bronze shrine in which the relic had been kept; but this inner shrine was not perfect, and must have been broken open before it was thrown into the lake.

This interesting reliquary no doubt belonged to an ancient abbey, the foundation and foss of which are at present clearly traceable on a point of land that juts out into the bay where the shrine was found. This tongue of land is marked on the old maps " Abbey Point," but the history of the abbey is unknown, and it is evidently one of the oldest remains of the kind on Lough Erne. There are frequent references to shrines or reliquaries such as this one in the *Annals of Ulster* between the fifth and tenth centuries, and Dr. Petrie says from the number of references to shrines in the Irish annals that previously to the irruptions of the Northmen in the eighth and ninth centuries there were few, if any, of the distinguished churches

in Ireland that had not costly shrines. In Dr. Oscar Mont-
clin's work, *The Civilisation of Sweden in Heathen Times*,
there is an illustration of an interlaced pattern exactly the
same as may be seen on the end of the shrine. The date he
assigns is between the fifth and sixth centuries. In the *Annals
of Ulster* for the year A.D. 836 it is recorded that the Gentiles
destroyed all the churches on Lough Erne, and probably this
was the time that the shrine was thrown into the lake.

It will be observed that the shrine is shaped similar to an ancient Celtic cill, and the interlaced ornament along the upper
ridge is very beautiful, and is divided into panels, each one bearing
a distinct pattern. The roof-shaped lid is detached from the
body, and on one side is a beautifully carved boss with a
minute interlaced design, the centre being an amber bead. Its
diameter is $1\frac{3}{10}$ inches. The body of the shrine is composed of
one piece of yew wood hollowed out, and is covered with a
bronze sheeting with round moulded angles. On one end is
the remains of a handle with Celtic design, the other being lost.
The shrine is 7 inches long by 3 inches wide. The front side
bears the marks where two bosses have been attached, but both
are now lost ; the other side bears two plain round rings of bronze.
The lid is made in the same way as the body, and is at the base
7 inches long by 3 inches wide, and $3\frac{3}{4}$ inches from ridge to
base. The ridge is five inches in length, and $\frac{3}{4}$ of an inch in
depth at the centre or either end. The bronze coating of the
inner shrine alone remains, and would form a coffer of the same
shape as the outer shrine ; its dimensions are $4\frac{1}{5}$ inches long
and $1\frac{1}{2}$ inches deep, whilst the sloping lid is $1\frac{1}{2}$ inches from
ridge to edge. The breadth is $1\frac{1}{4}$ inches, and both ends show
the remains of handles. The wood composing the sides is $\frac{9}{10}$ of
an inch thick, and is in good preservation.

The shrine is now in the Royal Irish Academy.

Mr. Robert Patterson, M.B.O.U., then drew attention to two
birds which he exhibited, and which, he stated, were new to
Ireland. The first was a good specimen of Wilson's petrel
(*Oceanites oceanicus*), which was captured alive in a field near

Dunmurry on October 2nd, and was sent to Belfast for preservation by the owner, Mr. Charley, of Seymour Hill. This bird was sent to London a week or so before by Mr. Patterson and exhibited before the Linnean Society. A second specimen was shot on Lough Erne at the same time. In England it is very rare, only about eight having been obtained up to the present, while there is no record of it from Scotland. The other bird was a pink-footed goose (*Anser brachyrhynchus*), the first recorded Irish specimen. It was sent to Mr. Patterson for identification by Mr. D. C. Campbell, of Londonderry, who states it was shot on Lough Swilly, County Donegal, about the 19th October last. The pink-footed goose is fairly common in some parts of England and Scotland, and it is remarkable it has not been obtained in Ireland until now. Mr. Campbell has, with praiseworthy generosity, presented this unique specimen to the Belfast Museum.

Mr. R. Lloyd Praeger, B.E., said the Natural History and Philosophical Society were to be congratulated on having secured this unique Irish specimen of the pink-footed goose. It was some years, he believed, since any Irish naturalist had had the pleasure of exhibiting at the same time two birds new to Ireland, and the present interesting communication showed that the Ulster Fauna Committee were collecting local zoological information with energy and success.

The company then gathered round the table to examine the shrine and rare birds, and subsequently dispersed.

The third meeting of the Winter Session was held on Tuesday evening, December 15th, the President in the chair.

On the motion of Mr. Wm. Gray, M.R.I.A., seconded by Mr. Lavens M. Ewart, J.P., M.R.I A., the following resolution was passed unanimously:—"That we, the members of the Belfast Naturalists' Field Club, deeply regret the death of our old and valued member, the Rev. Canon Grainger, D.D., M.R.I.A., and we desire the secretaries to prepare and publish in the Club's

Proceedings a permanent record of the services rendered by our deceased friend in furthering the operations of the Club, and promoting the objects of its organisation."

Mr. Wm. Swanston, F.G.S., then proposed a resolution to the effect that the honorary membership of the Club be conferred upon Mr. Robert J. Welch for his very valuable contribution of photographs to the Club's Albums of Antiquities. He dwelt on the valuable assistance which Mr. Welch had always been ready to bestow both on the Club and on individual members in everything connected with photography, and on the great value of the splendid series of 120 full-plate platinotype photographs of local antiquities which he had recently presented to the Club to form part of their photographic archæological survey of the district. In recognition of his valuable services the Committee now wished to bestow upon him the only honour in their power, and in accordance with a unanimous resolution passed at last Committee meeting, he now moved that the honorary membership of the Club be conferred on Mr. Welch.

Mr. John Hamilton said he had much pleasure in seconding the resolution, and considered the honour well earned by Mr. Welch.

Mr. William Gray, M.R.I.A., opposed the motion on the ground that the honorary membership of the Club was intended for bestowal on very distinguished men or eminent scientists who had given assistance to the Club. He also considered that the fact of Mr. Welch being a professional photographer seriously detracted from the value of his gift as a bona-fide present to the Club, and from its meriting such a high recognition as it was proposed to give. There were members who had rendered more valuable services to the Club, and on whom no honorary membership or other recognition had been bestowed.

Mr. John Brown said he would certainly support the action of the Committee, though he considered there was a good deal in what Mr. Gray had said.

Mr. F. A. Porter considered the resolution a most suitable one, and the proposed honour well merited by Mr. Welch.

Mr. F. J. Bigger, junior secretary, doubted the advisability of Mr. Gray's opposing the unanimous action of the Committee. He altogether differed from Mr. Gray in the idea that honorary membership should only be conferred on big-wigs who had done little for the Club, while hard-working members who had conferred considerable benefit should go unhonoured. He would wish to give credit where credit was due, and would vote for the motion.

On the resolution being put to the meeting by the President it was carried *nem. con.*

Mr. Arthur J. Collins then read a paper on "Falconry." The reader, after introducing his subject, spoke of the origin of this ancient sport, and stated that it was impossible to trace the commencement of the pastime. From the earliest times that history takes notice of, the peoples of most nations, but especially those of Eastern origin, had practised the art of falconry. Some idea of its antiquity may be formed from the discovery of Sir A. H. Layard of a bas-relief among the ruins of Korsabad, in which a falconer is depicted carrying a hawk on his wrist. From this it may be inferred that hawking was practised there some 1,700 years B.C. In China, falconry was known at a still earlier date, for in an old Japanese work, a French translation of which appeared at the beginning of the present century, it is stated that hawks were among the presents made to princes in the reign of the Hia dynasty, which commenced in the year 2205 B.C. The records of King Wen Wang, who reigned over the province of Hunan between 689 and 675 B.C., show that in his day falconry was much in vogue. In Japan it seems to have been known many centuries before the Christian era, and probably at an equally early date in India, Persia, Arabia, and Syria. The date of its introduction from the East into Europe is not known, but from the brief mention made of it by Aristotle, Pliny, Martial, and Oppian, it may be inferred that it was known if not practised in Europe at least three centuries before the Christian era. John of Salisbury, who died in 1182 A.D., discussing the question of

the origin of falconry, came to the conclusion that it was intro-
duced by Ulysses after the siege of Troy—an opinion endorsed
by several subsequent writers. According to Von Hammer, the
Turks were the first masters of the art, and imparted it to the
Persians, who in turn instructed the Greeks and Arabs. This
view receives some. confirmation from a recently published
French translation of an Arabic MS. of the tenth century on
"Hunting and Hawking," by Mahomet ben Mangali. In this
work it is stated that " the first falconer was a King of Persia."
During one of his excursions he was greatly interested in
watching the movements of a wild falcon. He saw it perch on
a bough " with the air of a sovereign on his throne," where it
waited an opportunity to seize a passing bird. He saw it at
length seize one, and, having made a meal of it, fly down to
the river, drink, and bathe, and again return to the tree.
Struck with admiration of its majestic appearance, patience, and
power over other birds, the king was seized with a desire to
possess it. His fowlers gratified his wish by snaring it. He
caused it to be tied to a perch near him, and succeeded in
taming it, learning lessons from its many good qualities. This
king was said to have been of a violent temperament, but,
through watching this bird, to have become a wiser and better
sovereign. The reader then drew attention to the introduction
of the sport into the British Islands. About the middle of the
eighth century, in a letter written by King Ethelbert of Kent to
Saint Boniface of Mayence, the Sovereign asks him "to send
over two falcons to fly at the crane," for, said he, "there are
very few birds of use for this flight in this country." King
Alfred the Great was remarkable at a very early age for his
proficiency in hawking, as well as in other fashionable amuse-
ments. He is even said to have written a treatise on the
subject, although there is no such work in existence now that
can with any degree of certainty be attributed to him. Asser,
in his life of this King, writes—" His felicity in hunting and
hawking, as in all the other gifts of God, was incomparable, as
I myself have seen." His grandson, Athelstan, was also much

attached to this sport. After he defeated Constantine, King of
the Welsh, at Brunanburg, he imposed upon him an annual
tribute of gold, silver, and cattle, to which were added a certain
number of hawks and sharp-scented dogs. His successor,
Edgar, cancelled the monetary part of the tribute upon condition
of receiving annually the skins of 300 wolves ; but it is not
likely that he annulled that part of the contract dealing with
the hawks, as he was notable for his enthusiasm in all field
sports. Hawking does not appear to have suffered any check
during the short Danish reign, for after the restoration of the
Saxon rule the pastime of hawking continued to be carried on
as formerly. Edward the Confessor, though said to have been
better fitted for the Church than for the Throne, made hunting
and hawking his one outdoor pastime. It was his chiefest
delight to follow on horseback a pack of swift hounds in pursuit
of their quarry, or to attend the flight of hawks taught to
pursue and catch birds. In Saxon times so general was the
pastime that the monks of Abingdon had to procure a charter
to restrain the practice of flying hawks, in order to preserve
their lands from being trampled upon. Harold, who succeeded
Edgar, was so fond of his hawks and hounds that he rarely
travelled without them. He is represented on the famous
tapestry of Bayeaux with his hawk on his wrist and his hounds
by his side when brought before William of Normandy. At
this period it was part of the education of every young man of
position to be instructed in hawking, and people of rank carried
with them on special occasions falcons suited to their rank.
Hawking was pursued with great enthusiasm by all the Norman
princes. From the time of Henry I., and during subsequent
reigns, offences against the Crown were often punished by a fine
of so many hawks. Prisoners were ransomed on similar terms,
and lands leased from the Crown by finding annually one or
more falcons, or providing for their keep, the leasing of the
Isle of Man to a family on such terms being a notable instance.
King John was very partial to field sports, and his love of fine
horses, hounds, and hawks was remarkable. Amongst other

places he used to send for his hawks to Carrickfergus. Mr. Collins then proceeded to trace the continuance of hawking through subsequent reigns down to George II., relating some suitable anecdotes. James I. was an enthusiastic sportsman, and especially delighted in hawking, spending large sums in its perfection and furtherance ; also in cormorant fishing, which he practiced at the same time. A sketch of a cormorant establishment was then given, and the mode of training and fishing with cormorants described, illustrated by specimens. James I. had large ponds constructed on the banks of the Thames for the accommodation of his cormorants, this being the origin of the first Westminster Aquarium, on the site of which the Houses of Parliament now stand. The last member of the Royal family said to have sent for or received hawks from abroad was Frederick Prince of Wales, son of George II. This Prince used to occupy the Palace of Durdans, at Epsom, now the residence of the Earl of Rosebery, and hawked on the Downs. The reader then spoke of some old customs, laws, &c., that originated with falconry. He then proceeded to describe the species of birds used in hawking, their chief characteristics, and mode of training ; also giving a sketch of the method of capturing falcons, as annually practiced by professional falconers in Holland. Mr. Collins described some flights with falcons about Belfast by the late Mr. Wm. Sinclair and Mr. Langtry. The paper was illustrated by specimens of mounted birds, drawings, and articles used in falconry.

Mr. Wm. Swanston, F.G.S., who was then called upon, stated that he had been asked to say a few words about a nodule containing plant remains that was upon the table. The nodule had been found in the Boulder Clay during the progress of the excavations at the Water Commissioners' works at Stoneyford, Co. Antrim, by Mr. R. Lloyd Praeger. The leaves, &c., in the nodule are so crushed together that unfortunately no single species can be identified. There is no doubt, however, that it is similar to the nodules so frequently met with along the southern shores of Lough Neagh, and was like them derived from a bed of plastic clays and lignites, laid down on the Geological Survey Maps as of Pliocene age. In a paper by Mr. J. Starkie Gardner, F.G.S., read before the Club in March, 1884, the supposed Pliocene age of these beds is questioned, and the probability of their being older is pointed out. Mr. Swanston also remarked that the silicified wood found in the same neighbourhood was derived from the same source, a statement which he had made before the Club in December 1884. A later incident in the history of these interesting plant remains seems to be that during some of the epochs of the Glacial Period these so-called Pliocene beds were much denuded, the softer parts being swept away, while the solid nodules and the silicified wood were scattered in a southern direction, which accounts for their presence in the Boulder Clay at Stoneyford and elsewhere as derived fossils.

The fourth meeting of the Winter Session was held on Tuesday evening, January 19th, the President in the chair, when a paper was read by the Rev. W. F. Johnson, A.M., F.E.S., on " The Beetles of the Belfast District." The reader said—In dealing with the *Coleoptera* of the Belfast district I shall not attempt to indicate all the species which have been found within it, but shall touch upon those which are most interesting, and endeavour to select examples from each of the great divisions of the *Coleoptera*. My information as to the species occurring here has been derived from the lists of the collections of the late A. H. Haliday and R. Patterson, F.R.S., published by the Belfast Naturalists' Field Club ; from some notes on local *Coleoptera* in the latter gentleman's book *Insects mentioned in Shakspere,* and from the list compiled by myself from the collection of the Belfast Natural History and Philosophical Society, a large number of which were taken in the immediate neighbourhood of the city. The family first in order among the *Coleoptera* is that of the *Geodephaga* or predacious land beetles. Among the largest and most conspicuous of these are the *Carabi*. The two commonest are *C. nemoralis* and *C. granulatus*, both frequently found in gardens. I have often dug up the former in my own garden, and I think there is a sort of prejudice against these beetles from their presence in such a locality, arising from an idea that they injure plants. As a matter of fact they are there in search of other insects, and are consequently very useful, and in no way injurious. *C. clathratus* is a very large and handsome beetle, mentioned by Mr. Patterson in his book as occurring with another handsome species, *C. nitens*, at Birkie Bog, and there is a specimen in the Museum collection taken by the late Mr. R. Templeton at Cranmore. Mr. Patterson mentions *Anchomenus angusticollis (junceus)* as occurring in the cellar of his house, a curious locality, for this beetle, like its congeners, is mostly found in tufts of grass, or in moss at the roots of trees, under bark, &c. It is one of the largest of our native *Anchomeni*, but black, while many of its allies are brightly coloured. The *Bembidia* are small beetles of various colours, black, bronze, greenish, black with yellow markings, or straw-coloured with black markings. Several have been recorded from this district. They are found in moss, or under stones, and are fond of moisture, a favourite locality for them being the bank of a lake or river, especially if it is gravelly. The *Hydradephaga* form the next division. These beetles live in the water for the most part, but are furnished with ample wings, and fly in the bright sunshine or at night. Many of them are very voracious, especially the large *Dytiscidœ*. *Cœlambus versicolor* is a small beetle of short oval shape, ferruginous with black stripes on the elytra. The only Irish specimen of this beetle that I have seen is in the Museum collection, its captor being Mr. Hyndman. It is also recorded from this district by Mr. Haliday and from the Dublin district by Professor M'Nab. I have, however, been unable to find it in the Armagh district, though its close ally, *C. 5-lineatus*, abounds there. Probably the best known of this family is *Dytiscus marginalis*. It is a common beetle, and its great size makes it conspicuous. A smaller species, and one not quite so common, *D. punctulatus*, has been found by Mr. Haliday and Mr. Templeton. Both in the larvæ and perfect state these beetles are very fierce, and, being large and powerful, are formidable enemies to the weaker inhabitants of the waters. The genus *Gyrinus* is familiar to most people under its English title of Whirligigs, so called from the habit of whirling about on the surface of the water in a kind of mazy dance. There are three species in the Belfast list —*G. minutus*, *G. natator*, and *G. marinus*. A close ally to the *Gyrini* is *Orechtochilus villosus*, the chief difference being that the latter is dull and pubescent, while the former are glabrous and shining. The *Hydrophilidæ* are not well represented on the Belfast list. They are subaquatic in their habits, but cannot swim like the *Hydradephaga*, instead of which they crawl up and down the stems of water plants. The rarest is *Helophorus dorsalis*, recorded by Mr. Haliday. It is a small, oblong beetle, with head and thorax iridescent, and the elytra dark bronze with testaceous markings. We now come to the *Staphylinidæ*, one of the largest divisions of the *Coleoptera*. They are all of much the same shape, being long and narrow, with short, truncate elytra. Mr. Haliday records *Callicerus obscurus* as having occurred plentifully at Holywood under the shelter of furze bushes on the fresh grass of sunny banks in spring. It is a small beetle, $2\frac{2}{3}$mm. in length, dull black or pitchy brown, with lighter-coloured elytra. *Bryoporus cernuus* is a small beetle about $4\frac{1}{2}$mm. in length, shining black, with the elytra and apical margins of the hind body red, legs reddish testaceous. Canon Fowler, in his work on the *Coleoptera* of the British Islands, says of this insect, " Recorded by Stephens as found near London, and in the New Forest ; also mentioned by Haliday as from near Belfast. I know of no recent captures. It occurs in several parts of France on both forest and mountainous localities under moss, refuse, &c." The rediscovery of this beetle would consequently be exceedingly interesting. *Pœderus riparius* is a very pretty insect, head black, thorax red, elytra blue, hind body red, with the apex black. This makes it a very conspicuous insect, and attracts the notice of the casual observer. The specimen I exhibit was taken by Rev. J. Bristow in this neighbourhood. The *Bledii* are curious little beetles. They burrow in sand or mud, and throw up little casts, by which their presence is often detected. As they do not often come to the surface unless disturbed, they are frequently passed over. There is only one species in the Belfast list, *B. opacus*, but a search in suitable localities would probably produce others. I must now call your attention to another of the great divisions of the *Coleoptera.* viz., the *Clavicornia,* which are so called from their antennæ forming a more or less pronounced club at the apex. Among them are our smallest native beetles, some of the genus *Ptilium* being only a ½mm. in length. The first species I shall mention is *Clambus armadillo,* a small black insect, with the margins of the thorax, the legs, and the antennæ reddish. It is found in vegetable refuse, hotbeds, &c., and has the power, like many of its allies, of rolling itself into a ball, and thus eluding notice by its resemblance to a minute seed. Several of the *Coccinellidæ* are recorded from this district. I may mention *Hippodamia* 13-*punctata,* *Coccinella* 10-*punctata* (*variabilis*), and *C.* 7-*punctata.* The first mentioned is not a very common species. Mr. Templeton took it at Cranmore, and it is in Mr. Haliday's list. It occurs usually in marshy places on reeds and water plants. The second, *C.* 10-*punctata,* is very common, but very puzzling to the novice on account of variation in the markings of the elytra. The third, *C.* 7-*punctata,* is the common lady bird, which is be found everywhere. All three species are most useful, as both the larvæ and the perfect insects devour *Aphides* and play an important part in checking these pests. *Heterocerus marginatus* was taken by the late Mr. R. Patterson in this district, and the specimen is in the Museum collection. This is the only record of its occurrence in Ireland. These beetles live in galleries which they excavate in mud on the margins of lakes or pools and on banks of muddy streams. The *Lamellicornia* form the next division. Several of the species are large, and from their habits well-known—*e.g.*, *Geotrupes stercorarius*, the Dor beetle, and *Melolontha vulgaris*, the Cockchafer. Probably the handsomest is *Centonia aurata*, the Rose beetle, a beautiful golden-green insect. It has been taken here by Rev. J. Bristow and Mr. Haliday, and there is a specimen in the Museum labelled "Whitehouse." In Mr. Haliday's list is recorded *Aromia moschata*, one of the *Longicornia*. It is a large and handsome beetle, and, like most of its family, feeds on wood. It is noticeable also for the odour which it emits, which has caused it to be called the "Musk beetle." Canon Fowler, however, considers that the odour is much sharper and more pleasant than musk. Among the *Halticæ* are to be found some of the worst pests of the farmer. Mr. Templeton took *Longitarsus luridus* and *L. lœvis*, the latter being by no means a common insect. Mr. Haliday records *Phyllotreta undulata* and *P. nemorum*, which are the much dreaded Turnip-flies, and the Rev. J. Bristow found the pretty *Crepidodera rufipes*, with its red head and thorax and dark blue elytra. Among the *Heteromera* recorded from this district is *Meloë proscarabœus*, a remarkable insect from its habit of emitting a drop of oil from every joint when touched, also from the history of its larvæ. The parent beetle lays its eggs in little holes in the ground. When the young larvæ emerge they climb up on flowers and attach themselves to the hairy covering of certain bees. When carried to the bees' nest they devour the eggs of the bee and the food intended by the bee for its young. They then pass into what is called a false pupa, and remain torpid for a time ; after that they become active again, and probably pass into a true pupa state, but this last stage has not been observed. The curious thing is that the perfect beetle is, as a rule, found far from any bees. The *Rhyncophora*, the last of the great divisions of the *Coleoptera*, may be recognised by the prolongation of their head into what is called a rostrum. The genus *Apion*, or the Pear weevils, so called from their shape, contains a great number of species, but owing to their small size they are seldom noticed. Mr. Haliday records *A.*

craccæ, A. viciæ, and *A. hydrolapathi.* The first two are found
in various species of vetch ; the last on the common dock. *A.
frumentarium,* which is entirely red, and frequents *Rumex
acetosella,* was found here by Messrs. Hyndman and Templeton.
Otiorhynchus sulcatus, a large black species, is only too well
known to owners of gardens and hot-houses. It attacks vines,
wall fruit, and raspberries—in fact, I do not think it is at all
particular what it eats. What makes it more troublesome is
that it works at night and hides through the day. The best
way to deal with it seems to be to spread a sheet under the
affected trees, and to come at night with a lantern and tap the
branches, when the beetles fall down, and can be captured and
destroyed. Some of our species are very beautiful, *e.g., Poly-
drusus pterygomalis* and *Phyllobius argentatus,* being covered
with golden-green or coppery scales which shine like gems in
the sunlight. Concerning *Mesites Tardyi* an interesting note
occurs in Mr. Patterson's catalogue :—" Cranmore. Found
during the entire month of June by turning up the under side
of an alder which lay in the farmyard, and from which the
bark had been stripped. Generally found in clusters of three
or four ranged side by side. They were not found in any other
situation, though the adjoining trees were carefully examined
by R. T." (Mr. Templeton). It is usually found in old holly
trees, but sometimes in beech or willow. Of the Abnormal
Coleoptera, one specimen is recorded from Belfast, *Elenchus
tenuicornis.* It was taken by Mr. Templeton, and the specimen
is now in the University Museum, Oxford. It is extremely
rare, and is parasitic on *Bombus,* and perhaps on *Andrena* and
Halictus. In conclusion, Mr. Johnson specially dwelt on the
wide and interesting field for research provided by the beetles
of the neighbourhood, and strongly recommended some of the
members to take up this branch of study, which they would
find most interesting and attractive.

At the conclusion of the paper Messrs. J. Hamilton, William
Gray, M.R.I.A., R. Lloyd Praeger, and Rev. C. H. Waddell,
M.A., spoke on the subject, and asked questions regarding the
paper, to which Mr. Johnson replied.

Mr. Wm. Gray, M.R.I.A., referred to the loss which the Club had recently sustained in the death of their distinguished fellow-member, the Bishop of the diocese. He moved—" That the Belfast Naturalists' Field Club desire to record their deep sense of the loss that Irish history and archæology had sustained in the death of the Right Rev. Dr. Reeves, Lord Bishop of Down and Connor and Dromore, and President of the Royal Irish Academy, who has done such valuable work in preserving our local antiquities from oblivion." The resolution was seconded in suitable terms by Mr. Alex. Tate, C.E., and passed unanimously by all present standing up in their places.

Mr. R. Lloyd Praeger, M.R.I.A., senior secretary, briefly announced that a scheme was on foot for the establishment of an Irish Natural History Monthly Magazine. A prospectus would be issued in a few weeks, which would be sent to all members of the Club. Meanwhile he might say that the following resolution had been passed at a committee meeting of the Club held that evening :—" That the Committee of the B.N.F.C. are glad to learn of the movement on foot for the establishment of an Irish Natural History Journal, and will have pleasure in giving the new venture all the support in their power. They will be glad to recognise the *Irish Naturalist* as the official organ of the Club, and they trust that all members will render assistance as far as possible by becoming contributors and subscribers to the journal." Several members spoke in terms of high satisfaction of the scheme, and expressed their sense of the want of such a magazine in Ireland, and of the welcome which it would receive from naturalists all over the country.

The election of new members concluded the business of the evening.

The fifth meeting of the Winter Session was held on Tuesday evening, February 16th, the President in the chair, when four communications were brought forward.

The first paper was by the Rev. C. H. Waddell, M.A., on the subject of the late Mr. John Templeton, of Belfast, and his ornithological researches. The reader spoke of Mr. Templeton's work as a naturalist, and said that his name did not occupy the position to which it was entitled as that of one of the great leaders of the natural history of our country. Perhaps this was to be accounted for by the fact that he did not publish any work of importance. He had intended to write a book on the natural history of Ireland, but the plan was never carried out, and thus his researches had gone to enrich the works of others. A list of the *Vertebrata* was published by his son after his death, and his lists of the local flora have been consulted by succeeding botanists. Mr. Waddell stated that he had been unable to obtain any information about Mr. Templeton's journal of observations on natural history extending from 1805 to 1825, which is often referred to by him. If this were still extant, it would no doubt be of great value and interest ; he was such a keen observer, and had such an extended knowledge of every branch of the fauna and flora of the district. A passage was quoted from Mackay's *Flora Hibernica*, in which the author thus spoke of Templeton :—" I believe that thirty years ago his acquirements in the natural history of organised beings rivalled that of any individual in Europe. These were by no means limited to diagnostic marks, but extended to all the laws and modifications of the living force." Mr. Templeton was the father of natural history in the North of Ireland, and led the way in which others soon followed. The reader then referred to a copy of Montagu's *Ornithological Dictionary*, now in his possession, which had belonged to Mr. Templeton, and contained pencil notes on the margins in his handwriting, a selection from which was read. In one of these he laments the destruction of rare visitants to our shores which might possibly be encouraged to stay and breed in the country, and says :—" But a few years ago, an

ornithological friend mentioned to me that a specimen of the
European bee-eater, whose wonderful combination of the most
splendid colours might almost place it as a competitor for
beauty with the justly-famed birds of paradise, and the wall-
creeper were killed in the South of Ireland, and this spring a
male and female of the golden oriole had no sooner made their
appearance at Donaghadee than the male was shot." Fortunately
this bird was obtained from Mr. Joseph Russell, of Dundonald,
on 11th May, 1824, and preserved in Mr. Montgomery's
collection. A passage was quoted from Montagu on account of
its local interest. It referred to the white-tailed sea-eagle :—
" John Maxwell, Esq., of Ardbraccan, in Ireland, favoured us
with two young birds of this species alive, taken the preceding
year on a mountainous precipice or craggy cliff called Slieve
Donald, impending the sea in the County of Down." Among
others, Templeton records the glossy ibis from the Bog Meadows,
the goshawk and hobby as nesting in Ulster (but this must be
a mistake for the peregrine), and records a nest of the woodlark
with four eggs, the female hatching, found October 10th, 1824.
No mention was made of the grasshopper warbler, but the
reader stated that this bird was frequent in the district between
Carnmoney and the shore, and seemed to be increasing with
the increase of meadow land in the country.

Several members spoke of the interest of these original
manuscript notes, and of the high position which Mr. Templeton
occupied as a naturalist.

The President then called on Mr. W. J. Knowles, M.R.I.A.,
for his notice of the occurrence of flint flakes in the Glacial
gravels of Ballyrudder, near Larne, Co. Antrim.

Mr. Knowles said :—A few years ago there was a very good
section of these gravels exposed, which I examined, and, seeing
a large quantity of flints chipped and broken in the face of the
section, I excavated in various places and found a number of
objects *in situ*, which, if they occurred in other situations, I
should have no hesitation in describing as artificially-formed
flakes ; but, being found in a Glacial formation, I feel it right

to be cautious and wait for further evidence before speaking of them as worked flints. I prefer at present to call them flint flakes. These flakes are not of the finest quality, but they have the bulb of percussion and some other characteristics of artificially-produced flakes. Two are of good size, about 3 in. long by about 2½ in. broad. One of these is an outside flake—that is, it shows on one side the outside crust of the pebble from which it was struck ; the other shows only part of the original crust. These two are only slightly weathered. A third one, scarcely so large, is also an outside flake, whitened by weathering on the face, which has the bulb of percussion. There are six other small flakes, from an inch to an inch and half long by about three-quarters of an inch broad, some of which show dressing as if they had been used as scrapers. The tenth flake is one of those three-sided flakes which have a bulb on the front or broadest face and depressions on the other faces. It has had a whitened or weathered crust all over, which has scaled off almost entirely from the two back facets, just sufficient remaining on one side to show the depression, which, like the bulb, is considered to be an indication of artificial character.

In addition to the flakes I found several core-like objects which are very similar to cores produced by human agency. It seems to be a sort of doctrine that we need not look for worked flints or implements of stone in Ireland older than the neolithic age, because that Ireland, Scotland, and the North of England were covered by glaciers when palæolithic man lived in the South of England and made the flint weapons which we find there associated with the remains of extinct animals. But I think it has been proved that man was of Glacial age in Europe, and that we have had interglacial periods when he could have lived in this country. Dr. James Geikie says in *Pre-historic Europe*, pp. 347 and 348, that " When the last interglacial epoch was attained a climate approximating to that of Pliocene times characterised our continent." If this interpretation is correct, and I believe Dr. Geikie has interpreted Glacial phenomena more correctly than some English geologists, we might hope to find evidence of man's handiwork in an interglacial formation in Ireland. As regards the formation, then, I believe there is no reason why it should not produce worked flints, but what reason is there for regarding a bulb on a flake as a sign of its artificial origin ? Well, I would answer that the bulb is not a necessary accompaniment of the natural fracture of flint. If a flint stone, after long exposure to the weather, splits naturally, it will be found that it breaks up like any other rock into pieces of irregular form without bulbs, while any smooth-grained rock as well as flint will show a bulb if the fracture is caused by a blow. The reason of this is that a blow sets up a series of waves in the stone, radiating from the point of impact, and when the fracture takes place it has the circular form of the waves. Even stones of a pretty coarse texture show a bulb at the place where a hammer struck. But it may be said that man is not the only agent which can produce a blow. A stone dropping from a high cliff has been given as an example. It might fall on another stone and fracture it, producing a bulb, or the waves of the sea may dash one stone against another, and produce a flake with a bulb. I think we may dismiss the cliff theory as not likely to produce a very large supply, and if anyone makes careful observation round our shores where flint stones are abundant, he will, I believe, find very few fresh flakes knocked off by the agency of the waves. Even after a storm, I question if he could produce one newly-formed flake after the most diligent search, though that some are knocked off I am perfectly aware, as I have some stones which show the marks where small flakes or chips have been separated. But these are very few, the tendency of the waves of the sea being not to knock off large chips, but very minute ones, and, by rolling the stones against each other, round them into somewhat globular forms. It may be remarked that the rudeness of the objects I have exhibited is against their artificial character, but I have seen many undoubted artificial flakes and cores as rude as these. It must also be remembered that the palæolithic implement, which is generally recognised as man's earliest handiwork, is an object of very perfect workmanship, and evidently could not be the first implement produced by man. I believe that, if we wish to find the rude tools of which the palæolithic implements show the developed products, we must go very far back indeed. I cannot therefore on any grounds see that further search will be a useless labour, and I would urge on the Belfast Naturalists' Field Club to let the examination of the Ballyrudder gravels be part of their programme for the ensuing year.

After some remarks from Mr. Mann Harbison, in which he spoke of the interesting geological and archæological questions raised by Mr. Knowles.

Mr. F. W. Lockwood said he had always had an open mind on the subject of the occurrence of human traces in the Boulder Clay and other Glacial and post-glacial deposits in our district. At the same time, he thought the Club would require some further information and further evidence before they would be satisfied that flint implements were found in the Ballyrudder gravels. If that bed could be proved to be of inter-glacial origin, he considered there was more likelihood of articles of human workmanship occurring in it. He wished further information regarding the nature and geological position of the gravel bed in question, and the number and position in the bed of the flints which were now exhibited by Mr. Knowles, and which for his part he could not consider very satisfactory specimens.

Mr. S. A. Stewart, in reply to a call from the Chair, said, in his opinion the flints found by Mr. Knowles in these gravels, and which he had just examined, did not show any undoubted evidence of human workmanship.

Mr. R. Lloyd Praeger agreed with Mr. Stewart that the specimens were not satisfactory. At the same time, the question raised was one of high interest to local geologists, and should be thoroughly investigated. The meeting was, he was sure, much indebted to Mr. Knowles for having placed the matter before them in such a lucid manner. As regarded the contention that the beds were of inter-glacial origin, he held that this could not be sustained. The gravels yielded a somewhat extensive fauna of marine shells, which had been investigated by a number of geologists, chiefly members of the Field Club. This fauna was of a more rigidly Arctic character than that of any other post-tertiary deposit in Ireland, and yielded a larger number of species which are characteristic of high northern seas than even the Boulder Clay itself, 35 per cent. of the shells of the gravels being species which are not now to be found in Britain, but inhabit the Arctic and sub-Arctic Seas. By no stretch of imagination could a deposit which contained such a fauna be called inter-glacial, which term implied a cessation, temporary at least, of Glacial conditions. After some remarks on the flint specimens which Mr. Knowles had brought to illustrate his paper, Mr. Praeger said the gravels were well worth further investigation, and he heartily backed up Mr. Knowles's suggestion that the Club should undertake researches in this direction. Even if no result as regards the existence of man could be arrived at, the extension of our knowledge of the fauna of this interesting bed would alone be a sufficient plea for a systematic examination.

On the motion of the President, the meeting sent forward a recommendation to the Committee that a further search should be organised, and that members should be afforded an opportunity during the coming summer of examining that important deposit.

Mr. Knowles having replied to the points raised by the various speakers,

Mr. Francis Joseph Bigger, junior secretary, next exhibited and described a curious and ancient jar. He said that the curious vessel or *amphora* now exhibited was lately brought to Belfast by his friend Mr. James Young, of the steamship Horn Head, having been purchased by him for a few dollars from sponge divers who were carrying on their operations in the Bay of Ekanjik, about forty miles from the Island of Rhodes, in Asia Minor. The sponge diving was being performed by the divers at distance of about three miles from the shore, in the centre of the bay, in a depth of twenty fathoms of water. The sponges were plentiful at the spot, and he exhibited a few specimens of them just as they were brought to the surface by the divers, and attached to rocky substances in their natural position. No person was more surprised than the poor Mussulman diver in his unexpected find of this curious vessel at such a depth of water, and entirely apart from any other evidence of civilisation. Its total height is three feet ten inches, and its circumference at its widest part is twenty-two inches. Its shape is extremely graceful, and much more beautiful than either of the two *amphoræ* in this Museum, which are both clumsy compared to it, yet one of them was found in the ruins of Pompeii and the other came from Italy. This leads to the conclusion that the present exhibit is Grecian, and probably of considerable antiquity. The Bay of Ekanjik, where it was found, lies quite in the track of vessels passing between Greece and Rhodes or the Holy Land, or even Ephesus, and it is quite likely that it was thrown over (with other things) to lighten the ship, as St. Paul so graphically describes on a certain memorable occasion ; or it may have been lost in a general shipwreck. The two handles are firmly fixed to the sides, and are grooved by way of ornament. The body is so covered by marine growths that it cannot be ascertained whether the same is ornamented or inscribed. The base tapers to a point in a truly Eastern manner, which rendered a stand necessary for holding the vessel, or else, as was sometimes the case, the base was dropped heavily into the soft ground. The composition is a red clay or terra-cotta finely ground, and differs very little from a modern well-burnt flower-pot. The uses of these *amphoræ* in ancient times were manifold. Being cool, they were principally used for keeping water in, or wine, and in the latter case were covered tightly over with parchment, and a label of the same material attached, upon which was endorsed the full particulars of the contents. It will be observed that the *amphora* itself is entirely concealed from view by the curious and beautiful marine incrustations which completely cover its surface. These may have been the work of only a few years, or, as is more probably the case, the work of centuries. The animal remains which encrust the surface include two species of corals (*Astroides* and *Caryophyllia*), several sponges, and a variety of *Serpulœ*, *Polyzoa*, and nullipores. Mr. Bigger wished now to publicly thank Mr. Young for his kindness in sending down these exhibits and allowing him to describe them to the Field Club.

Mr. R. Lloyd Praeger, M.R.I.A., senior secretary, then drew attention to a skull of the Irish elk (*Cervus giganieus*) which he exhibited. It was found in December last by the workmen engaged in excavating for the east wall of the new branch floating dock which opens off Spencer Basin, in the centre of a bed of peat 3 feet thick, and at a depth of 34 feet below ordinary high-water mark. Above the peat was a deposit some 30 feet deep of blue marine clay. The skull is broken across at the orbits, the lower front portion being absent ; the fracture is evidently an old one. Both antlers are broken off at the base, one of the fractures, however, being recent. The skull is of large dimensions. In spite of diligent search, no other remains were found in the vicinity, nor were the missing portions of the skull discovered. Mr. Praeger then briefly drew attention to the series of strata occurring underneath the lower portions of Belfast, and the changes of conditions which they speak of. The peat represents an old land surface. It extends under a considerable portion of the city ; at Sydenham, Holywood, Bangor, and Kilroot its level is higher, and it may be seen on the shore between tide-marks. It is full of remains of Scotch firs, hazel, willows, and marsh plants. At Alexandra Dock bones of the red deer and wild boar were found in it. At the time of its formation the land must have stood from 10 to 40 feet higher than at present. Resting on the peat is a bed of clay full of shells which live on muddy shores between tides, showing a subsidence of the land and the breaking in of the sea over the former surface. Above this littoral clay is a deposit of very fine blue clay containing numbers of shells which live in from five to ten fathoms of water. This bed furnishes proof of a much greater subsidence, which submerged the former land surface and the present site of Belfast to a depth of at least 50 and perhaps 70 or 80 feet. Subsequently an era of elevation set in, which gradually raised the sea-bottom to its present condition of dry land. Considering the extremely slow rate at which geographical elevation or depression is known to take place, some idea may be formed of the immense period which has elapsed since this bed was formed, and which is nevertheless but a brief moment in the centuries of geological time.

After some discussion, the election of several new members brought the meeting to a close, and the audience gathered round the table to examine the various interesting objects which were on exhibition.

The sixth meeting of the Winter Session was held on March 15th, the President in the chair. The evening was devoted to microscopical work, and the receiving of the first annual report of the Microscopical Section of the Club, which was formed just a year ago. There was a crowded attendance of members and visitors. The President, in taking the chair, expressed his pleasure at the success of this new section of the Club, which was started only a year ago, as evinced by the large turn-out of members, and by the excellent and varied display of microscopical objects and apparatus. Size, he said, is not the primary essential element of the great and the sublime. Such terms are but relative. How small is our world compared to the immensity of the universe; can we draw the line where greatness begins and littleness ends? The dog is small compared to the ox, but how gigantic is he compared to the little field mouse? A poet wag has told us—

> E'en little fleas have smaller fleas
> Upon their backs to bite 'em,
> And smaller fleas have lesser fleas,
> And so ad infinitum.

When Alexander sighed for other worlds to conquer he overlooked one-half of the earth, and left to later times the discovery of countries greater and more important than any his conquering footsteps had ever reached. Africa has been rediscovered, and its immense territory now forms the subject of contention between great nations. The enterprise of explorers and scientists has been directed to investigate its unknown heart, its climate, the course of its mountain chains and rivers, and its limitless plains. To these pioneers of our ever-increasing race, the fauna and flora of a primitive country must be a source of exceeding interest. To us here at home there are still left great unknown worlds to explore, worlds within worlds, with their myriad forms of life, which the microscope reveals to our gaze. Here we see forms more strange and wonderful than those of fabled antiquity, creatures whose forms and functions upset all our preconceived ideas of animal existence. Poets never feigned anything so wonderful, so curious, so beautiful, creatures so grotesquely hideous, so remorselessly savage, as some of those we can bring within the field of our observation. But it is not alone in the study of minute animal life that the microscope reveals its marvellous power. In the examination of the structures of vegetable and animal life, and for a multitude of other purposes now indispensable, it is the great instrument of observation in investigating nature, for as Linnæus truly says, "*Natura maxima est in minima*"—nature is greatest in her smallest works. He would now call on Mr. Alexander Tate, C.E., Chairman of the Microscopical Section, for the annual report of the Section.

Mr. Tate, in some suitable remarks, spoke of the success that had attended the formation by the Naturalists' Field Club of a Section devoted to microscopical work only, and of the great field of research that lay before them. He then called on

Mr. H. M'Cleery, secretary of the Section, to read the annual report, which was as follows :—" The Microscopical Committee have much pleasure in submitting their first annual report, especially as they have every reason to believe that the formation of this Section has filled what has been a want in the Club

The special excursions were interesting and instructive, and the meetings held during the winter have been well attended. The membership of the Section now numbers 58, it having risen almost double since the first meeting, and it is a matter of congratulation that many new members of the Club have joined in order to become members of this Section. There were two excursions held during the summer; the first was to the Lagan, and the second to Donaghadee. They were both held on Saturday afternoons, and both were productive of many interesting specimens. The lagoons beside the Lagan produced a number of species of the lower forms both of animal and vegetable life; while from Donaghadee material for making many interesting slides was obtained. One beautiful minute specimen of *Asterina gibbosa*, measuring about ·05in., was obtained, as well as a number of larger specimens. The brittle stars (*Ophiocoma*) were also laid under contribution, as well as the palates of different molluscs, many sponges, a number of barnacles, and a quantity of *Foraminifera*. The first of the winter meetings, on October 28th, was taken up with a discussion on the merits of the different microscopes exhibited and explained by members, followed by a demonstration of mounting by Messrs. Gray and Firth. At the second meeting, held on December 9th, Mr. Joseph Wright, F.G.S., gave a most interesting account of ' *Foraminifera* ; what they are, and where to get and how to prepare them for microscopical slides,' and illustrated his remarks by beautiful diagrams and splendidly-mounted slides, and, with the assistance of Messrs. Donaldson and Welch, showed how they were selected and mounted. Mr. William Hanna, B.A., was to the front at the third meeting, held on Wednesday, 3rd February, giving a most interesting account of the way to stain and section animal tissues, practically illustrated. After all these meetings there was a show of slides in illustration of the different subjects brought forward."

On the motion of Mr. William Swanston, F.G.S., seconded by Mr. John Brown, the report of the Section was adopted. After some announcements by the secretaries, the President declared the meeting open, and the members were not slow in gathering round the microscopes, which, to the number of some five-and-twenty, stood ready at the tables. The exhibits represented a systematic survey of the animal kingdom, the exhibition being designed to be an illustration of the course of lectures on zoology which is being at present delivered by Professor A. C. Haddon, M.A., under the auspices of the Society for the Extension of University Teaching. At the head of the first table Mr. Joseph Wright, F.G.S., illustrated with his usual success the subject of *Foraminifera*. Mr. Alexander Tate, C.E., exhibited fine specimens of the slipper animalcule, *Paramœcium*, which were much admired. Other primitive forms, such as *Stentor* and *Vorticella*, were shown by Miss Boyd and Mr. P. F. Guibransen. Mr. Wm. Gray, M.R.I.A., undertook the demonstration of the beauties and wonders of the group of sponges. Mr. James Murdock exhibited the *Hydra*, or fresh water polyp, an old favourite of microscopical workers, and the movements of which as revealed by the microscope were watched with interest, as well as the more active, not to say lively, motions of many of the animals mentioned above and subsequently. The fixed marine *Polyzoa*, such as *Sertularia* and *Flustra*, were under the superintendence of Mr. Wm. Swanston, F.G.S. Messrs. James Stelfox and W. S. M'Kee showed a number of beautiful living objects, including fresh water *Polyzoa* and rotifers. The perhaps unpopular but highly important and interesting group of worms was illustrated by Mr. W. D. Donnan. Miss S. M. Thompson showed spines and other portions of sea-urchins, brittle-stars, &c., representing the great group of the *Echinodermata*. Mr. I. W. Ward exhibited the dental apparatus of limpets, snails, &c. The interesting class of spiders was undertaken by Mr. John Donaldson. The insects were well represented, beetles being shown by Mr. G. W. Ferguson ; flies, by Mr. John Jacques ; butterflies and moths, by Miss Clara Patterson ; and bees and wasps, by Mr. W. D. M'Murtry. Among the vertebrate animals, the beauties of fish scales and reptile skins were demonstrated by Mr. S. Cunningham.

At nine o'clock the President procured attention while a little necessary formal business was transacted. On his calling for nomination of new members of the Club, nine names were submitted to the meeting and duly elected. The secretaries having made some announcements, the meeting again became general, and it was only at a late hour that the members dispersed.

ANNUAL MEETING.

The twenty-ninth Annual Meeting of the Club was held on Wednesday evening, April 27th, in the Belfast Museum —the President (Mr. John Vinycomb, F.R.S.A.) in the chair.

The Chairman, after some introductory remarks, called on the senior secretary (Mr. R. Lloyd Praeger, M.R.I.A.) for the annual report, and subsequently on the treasurer (Mr. W. H. Phillips, F.R.H.S.) for the statement of accounts. These will be found in full in the earlier pages of the present report.

Mr. Wm. Swanston, F.G.S., in moving the adoption of the report and statement of accounts, considered they were both of a highly satisfactory nature. The income and the membership of the Society had both materially increased, and were larger this year than they had ever previously been since the foundation of the Club. The attendance of members at both summer and winter meetings also showed a large increase. There could be no doubt that the Club was not only prospering, but pushing rapidly forward in its appointed course.

Mr. Joseph Wright, F.G.S., seconded the motion, which was passed unanimously.

The election of office-bearers for the coming year was then taken up.

Mr. F. W. Lockwood moved, and Mr. C. W. Watts, F.I.C., seconded a resolution that Mr. J. Vinycomb, F.R.S.A., be re-elected President. The motion was carried by acclamation. On the motion of Mr. John Donaldson, seconded by Mr. John Hamilton, Mr. W. Swanston. F.G.S., was re-elected Vice-

President. The Treasurer (Mr. W. H. Phillips) and the Secretaries (Mr. R. Lloyd Praeger and Mr. Francis Joseph Bigger) also resumed office. One vacancy occurred on the Committee, and the selection of a lady member to fill the vacant place, for the first time in the history of the Club, was greeted with loud applause.

Discussion followed on the suggestion to amend the rule (Rule IV.) relating to the qualifications of Honorary Members, by the omission of the clause requiring that the usual residence of such should be at least 20 miles from Belfast. The point arose out of the fact that at the election of an Honorary Member at a meeting of the Club held on December 15th, this clause had been accidentally overlooked. Mr. Praeger having introduced the subject, considerable discussion ensued, in which Messrs. R. Welch, W. Gray, M.R.I.A.; F. W. Lockwood, Joseph Wright, F.G.S. ; J. Hamilton, and Francis J. Bigger took part. Ultimately it was decided, by a large majority, that the rule as at present in force should remain.

The junior secretary (Mr. Francis Joseph Bigger) brought under the notice of the Club some archæological subjects that had been engaging the attention of the Secretaries. Repeated efforts had been made to get together the various portions of the town cross of Downpatrick, but on account of the unfortunate refusal of one landowner to hand over a portion which was in his possession, the proposed restoration of the cross has had to be temporarily abandoned. A vote of thanks was passed to Major Maxwell, D.L., on the motion of Mr. W. Swanston, seconded by Mr. W. Gray, for his exertions in conserving the beautiful ruins of Inch Abbey, near Downpatrick, as advocated by the Club during the past year. It was also reported that the Belfast and County Down Railway Company would undertake the conservation of the interesting souterrain at Artole, near Ardglass, owing to the efforts of members of the Club, and that it was in contemplation to do some restorative work at the ancient church of Raholp.

Mr. R. Lloyd Praeger then drew attention to a number of

bones belonging to the Irish elk which were on exhibition. They were found in the excavations for the wall of the new branch floating dock opening off Spencer Basin, Belfast, in a bed of gravel and sand immediately underlying a stratum of peat, at a depth of some thirty-six feet below high water mark. The spot was close to where the skull was found which he had recently had the pleasure of exhibiting to the Club, but these bones all belonged to an older horizon, being just below the peat in which the skull was embedded, and being apparently washed fragments. A right and left cannon-bone were shown, which evidently belonged to two different animals ; also a number of fragments of antlers. It was very satisfactory that the efforts of the Harbour Commissioners' and contractors' employés had led to the preservation of these interesting remains.

Mr. John Hamilton exhibited cocoons of the fox moth (*Bombyx rubi*), of which he had received larvæ from Scotland last autumn. He also exhibited some beetles and locusts, showing the under-wing.

Suggestions were then received as to localities to be visited during the summer session, and the election of five new members, and an examination of the prize collections, brought the proceedings to a close.

Obituary Notice of the late
REV. CANON JOHN GRAINGER, D.D., M.R.I.A.

EX-PRESIDENT.

By the Secretaries.

THE eldest of a family of nine, John Grainger was born at Queen Street, Belfast, on 19th March, 1830. His father was David Grainger, a ship-owner, and a member of the Belfast Corporation. His mother's maiden name was Maria Belinda Parke; she was a daughter of Lieut. James Parke, of the Desertcreight Yeomanry, in Co. Tyrone, whose sword and gorget are still preserved in the Canon's collection.

The Graingers came to Belfast from Lisburn, in which district they had been long established, the name of one of the family appearing as churchwarden in Jeremy Taylor's episcopate in 1667.

Shortly after John's birth, the family removed to Vine Lodge, in Henry Street, where they lived for some 16 years. When the boy was nine years old, the reading of Peter Parley's *Wonders of Earth, Sea, and Sky*, with descriptions of strange fossils found embedded in the earth, aroused his juvenile enthusiasm, and armed with a spade he sallied forth into the garden to discover some of these marvels. A large portion of Belfast is built on slob-land, the clay composing which teems with marine shells of many species. The young scientist had, therefore, not excavated far before he struck a rich vein of *Turritella, Aporrhais*, and other beautiful shells, with which he returned to the house, radiant and triumphant. Thus his first scientific expedition turned out successful, and trivial as the incident appears, it bore abundant fruit, for in after years he continued his exploration of the beds underlying the slob-lands of Belfast with zeal and success, and it is by his papers before the British Association and elsewhere on these post-tertiary deposits that his name is best known to geologists.

At the age of ten, the boy was sent to the Belfast Academy, then located in Donegall Street and Academy Street. The head-master was Rev. Reuben John Bryce, LL.D., who undertook the classical department; his brother, James Bryce, F.G.S., had charge of the mathematical and science classes. In James Bryce young Grainger met a teacher entirely to his taste—a man devoted to science in all its branches, and an excellent geologist. Twice each week the half-hour geography lesson was superseded by a lecture on some natural history subject, and the master soon discovered that in John Grainger he had a most attentive and promising pupil. In consequence of his pupil's aptitude and love of science, Mr. Bryce soon allowed him to remain after hours with him to assist in arranging the school museum, which, in the master's skillful hands, had become a very instructive and somewhat valuable collection. On half-holidays the master would take his class to the Cave Hill, where, armed with pick and hammer, the budding geologists expended their youthful zeal on tough blocks of white Chalk and Hibernian Greensand. Twice in each half-year a longer excursion was undertaken, and raids were made under the able generalship of Mr. Bryce on the treasures of Whitehead, Woodburn, and Colin Glen, the party returning laden with gypsum and selenite, sea-urchins and fish-teeth, corals and sponges.

Meanwhile, with his companions, John and Alexander Montgomery, A. O'D. and Robert Taylor, and Samuel Ewing, all holidays were spent in country rambles ; and flowering plants, seaweeds, beetles, butterflies, birds' eggs, and rock specimens were equally welcome to the young collectors.

Under the presidency of Mr. Bryce, the "Academy Natural History Society" met monthly in the evenings, when the boys read papers, and had discussions thereon. The future Canon's contributions to the literature of this period were three in number : —" The Elephant " was his earliest effort, and the size and strength of the animal chosen for his first natural history lecture were worthy of the magnitude of the occasion, and of the force with which he expounded the leading zoological characteristics of this modern descendant of *Elephas primigenius* ; " Organic Remains " showed the direction which, since the episode of the garden at Vine Lodge, his thoughts had constantly followed ; and "Fixed Stars " afforded fine scope for the active mind and discursive eloquence of the young lecturer.

James Bryce was at this time secretary of the Belfast Natural History Society, which had been founded in 1821 by a number of local scientists for the encouragement of biological pursuits in Belfast, and was now flourishing exceedingly under the able guidance of such well-known naturalists as William Thompson, George C. Hyndman, Robert Patterson, and James MacAdam. To young Grainger, James Bryce frequently entrusted the task of writing out the reports of the Society's meetings in the minute book from his rough notes, much to the delight of the former, who thus gained valuable information, and at the same time became thoroughly acquainted with the working of the Society. In the summer vacation of 1844, Grainger had the pleasure of a trip to Edinburgh with his master, under whose guidance he made his first acquaintance with Scottish geology. In the same year, at the age of 14, he left the Academy, and began a course of private study. His tutor was Elijah Aiken, an excellent teacher, whom the young scientist soon infected with his own love of natural history pursuits, till teacher and pupil were equally enthusiastic students of science ; and it is to be suspected that Greek roots sometimes gave way to phanerogamic stems and flowers, and that etymology occasionally had to yield place to entomology.

His schoolboy friendships were not broken off by his leaving the Academy. Under the somewhat ambitious title of "The Belfast Literary and Scientific Society," weekly meetings were held at Vine Lodge, in a wing that Mr. Grainger had handed over to his son for the accommodation of his collections, which had already attained considerable dimensions. There, surrounded by fossils, butterflies, and plants, the members of this Society, under a dozen in number met weekly, including the two Taylors, the Montgomerys, James and Archie Lemon, Samuel Ewing, and young Hincks (son of Rev. Archdeacon Hincks, of Culfeightrim). Here papers were read on various scientific subjects, the more abstruse and debatable the better, and many a hot discussion and bloodless battle raged over the relics of bygone ages and the preserved remains of existing botany and zoology. Of this Society young Grainger was the life and soul, and held the high office of permanent President.

In 1846 the removal of the family residence to Marino, near Holywood, on the County Down shore of Belfast Lough, broke off some of the old connections, and brought our friend into new surroundings, and among new acquaintances. Mr. Robert Patterson then lived during the summer months at the Crescent, Holywood, and his eldest boys, William and Robert, were not far from young Grainger's age, and, like him, devoted to natural history, so they were speedily drawn together by their common interests. John Bristow, now Rev. John Bristow, M.A., had already shown the love for the study of entomology that he has maintained through life; with him our young scientist dug pupæ at the roots of the Marino trees, and raced over the Holywood meadows in pursuit of some gay butterfly or moth. With the Patterson boys he climbed trees after birds' nests, collected shells on the seashore, and flowers in the woods and glens, and hammered the Carboniferous and Permian rocks at Cultra for fish scales and brachiopods; and with David Steen, till recently head of the Classical Department at the R.A. Institution, he turned over stones and rotten trees in the search for rare beetles. A short stay at Portrush furnished an opportunity for the inspection of the remarkable raised beach there, and the collection of a representative series of its abundant fossils.

' Being now 17 years of age, his boyish love of collecting had developed into a deep scientific taste for natural history, and he had acquired an excellent knowledge of many branches of zoology and geology. In his scientific studies he derived much assistance from several gentlemen, much his seniors both in years and knowledge, but ever ready to aid whenever required—Thompson, Hyndman, Haliday, and Patterson—a band of naturalists who have left indelible marks in the annals of science, and of whom Belfast may well be proud.

William Thompson lived in Donegall Square, where he was diligently collecting material for his *Natural History of Ireland*; George C. Hyndman in Howard Street, his time being fully occupied by business pursuits; but as both gentlemen were constant visitors at Mr. Patterson's, young Grainger had the advantage of frequently coming in contact with them. A. H. Haliday,

F.L.S., resided at Tillysburn, and after Grainger's first introduction to him, he became a constant visitor at his house, and an ardent student of *Coleoptera*, in the knowledge of which Mr. Haliday was the first Irish authority.

One day in 1845 William Thompson, meeting young Grainger in Belfast, brought him into Hodson's, in High Street, then the leading book-shop of the town, to show him the first part of a magnificent new work on British *Mollusca*, which was being brought out by Edward Forbes and Sylvanus Hanley, and, on Mr. Thompson's recommendation, Grainger became a subscriber to the work, and during the four years occupied in publication, he read every part, and pored over the illustrations with the greatest delight and interest, and there acquired the intimate and critical knowledge of British shells that was so useful to him in his geological studies in after years.

Meanwhile, during all the period that had elapsed since he first began collecting, his museum had been constantly enriched by presents which he obtained from the captains of his father's vessels on their return from foreign ports. The ships traded with Charlestown, Quebec, New Orleans, Buenos Ayres, Chincha Islands, Zanzibar, Bombay, and Calcutta, and from these widely-separated spots came shells, corals, fishes, skulls and horns, snakes, nuts and seeds, native weapons and utensils ; and many of the specimens thus obtained are among the finest objects that now enrich his collections.

The year 1849 brought with it another change of scene. John Grainger passed the entrance Examination of Dublin University, taking 7th place in order of merit, and entered Trinity College. Here his natural history tastes at once made themselves felt, and with the assistance of Edward Perceval Wright and Edward Hogan, then students like himself, the "Dublin University Zoological Association" was formed, Grainger holding the office of President, and Hogan and Wright being joint Secretaries, for the first session, at the end of which time Grainger resigned his post to Robert Ball, Curator of the University Museum, and as an Irish naturalist second only to Thompson. It was in connection with this Society that the *Natural History Review* was founded, edited by E. P. Wright, and others. This Society held monthly meetings, at which papers were read and discussed, their Proceedings appearing quarterly in the *Natural History Review*. Among the leading members were Thomas Warren, well-known as a conchologist ; Harvey, afterwards the first British authority on seaweeds ; and A. H. Haliday, who had recently come from Belfast and taken up his residence in Dublin, and who took a lively interest in the welfare of the Society and the scientific work of its members.

Such time as the young student could spare for recreation were spent in collecting. The classic ground of Portmarnock and Malahide yielded to him many of their molluscan treasures. The quarries at Howth were ransacked for Carboniferous fossils, and, in company with Mr. Haliday, delightful days were spent in searching for beetles and capturing rare moths and butterflies.

Vacations were spent at home, where the naturalist's time was fully occupied.

Hyndman, Thompson, Patterson, and Getty were busily engaged in dredging operations in and around Belfast Lough ; and on many of their expeditions young Grainger accompanied the party, and his collections were enriched by numerous examples of *Mollusca*, urchins and starfishes, sponges, *Polyzoa* and *Crustacea* ; and many a delightful hour was spent in examining the material brought up by the trawls and dredges, and spread out on the deck of the " Gannet," a small yacht belonging to Edmund Getty, in which the dredging operations were carried on.

In 1848 he had joined the Belfast Natural History Society, and in 1849, at the request of William Thompson, he became a life member by the purchase of three shares, and was elected on the Council, a high honour for a lad of 19 years. This brought him into still closer connection with the leading Belfast naturalists, and strongly stimulated his scientific tastes. The Council held their meetings at the private houses of the members, and their deliberations appear to have occasionally been somewhat thirsty work, as the Canon, long afterwards, delighted to tell of a meeting of Council, held at the MacAdams' residence, when the worthy lady of the house protested against having to send 72 cups of tea to the twelve men esconced in the drawing-room !

Grainger's first paper was read before the Belfast N.H. Society on his favourite subject of the local post-tertiary beds, the title being " The Shells found in the Alluvial Deposits of Belfast Lough." This paper was read on Wednesday, November 15th, 1848.

In 1851 the family residence was changed from Marino to Whiteabbey.

In 1852 the meeting of the British Association at Belfast was an important event among local scientists. Grainger gave a further contribution to the knowledge of the post-tertiary beds in a paper read before the Zoological Section, of which his friend, Wm. Thompson, was chairman; and at the request of the chairman of the Geological Section, spoke at one of its meetings on the same subject.

In the same year, in company with some English friends, he made an extensive tour round the Irish coasts, visiting Wicklow, Cork, Kerry, the Shannon, Galway and Connemara, Donegal and Derry, the Giant's Causeway, and finishing up with Belfast. Each stopping place furnished its quota of specimens, zoological, botanical, or geological.

May, 1854, saw him on a visit to Folkstone, whence he returned with some rare butterflies and a collection of the fine fossils of the Gault.

Later in the year he visited Paris, and spent many hours in the splendid museums, and among the botanical treasures of the *Jardin des Plantes*.

Meanwhile his college studies had been proceeding steadily. In 1853 he gained Archbishop King's special prize. In the following year he took his B.A. degree, with a silver medal, and then turned his attention to divinity, and finished his course in 1855, when he returned to Whiteabbey. The degree of M.A. was conferred on him two years later.

The next three years were passed at home, where all spare time was spent as usual in collecting. The marriage of a sister in the summer of 1856 furnished occasion for a trip to the English lake district, where flowering plants and lichens, butterflies and minerals, were assiduously collected.

The succeeding summer saw him on a tour up the Rhine, where he again had scope to indulge his entomological tastes, returning with a number of species of butterflies and fireflies wherewith to enrich his collection.

In the autumn of 1858, business connected with the death of his father, which occurred at this time, took him to America, where he sojourned during the beautiful Indian summer. Time did not permit of extensive travelling, but New York, Niagara, Montreal, and Quebec were visited. The shores of the great lakes were searched for fresh-water shells, and the forests for butterflies and specimens of the various native woods. The Palæozoic rocks in the neighbourhood of Quebec yielded fossils, and the raised beach near Montreal, corresponding with that at Uddevalla in Norway, was carefully examined. A number of minerals were also acquired.

In 1856 Mr. Hyndman and his dredging party received a grant from the British Association for the purpose of systematically exploring and reporting on the marine fauna of Belfast Lough and neighbourhood, and this grant was renewed in the two following years. Thus stimulated in their work, extensive dredgings were carried out during these three years, with successful results, as may be seen from Hyndman's "Reports of the Belfast Dredging Committee" in the Association reports for the years 1857, '58, and '59. Of these expeditions Grainger was frequently a member, and he added abundantly to his marine collections from the material obtained, which included such rarities as *Emarginula crassa, Terebratula and Argiope, Lyonsia and Pandora*. The successful and interesting results of these dredgings, especially those made in the neighbourhood of the Turbot Bank, attracted several eminent conchologists to the spot, and Grainger had the pleasure of meeting and working with Dr. Gwyn Jeffreys and Edward Waller. With the former he became intimately acquainted, and derived much assistance from him in subsequent conchological work.

During the interval between his return from America and his ordination in 1863, he lived at home with his mother at Whiteabbey, engaged with business connected with the family, and diligently pursuing his scientific bent. A portion of his leisure time was devoted to obtaining a knowledge of foreign shells, for which he had a good opportunity. Richard Davison, M.P. for Belfast, of Whiteabbey, had a fine series of Ceylon shells, which he had obtained from his friend, Sir J. Emerson Tennant ; and Lieutenant-General Smythe, of Carnmoney, when acting as special Commissioner for H.M. Government in the Fiji Islands, had diligently collected the local *Mollusca*. At these collections Grainger spent many hours of study.

Wyville Thomson, afterwards Sir Wyville Thomson, and chief naturalist on board H.M.S. "Challenger," was then Professor of Zoology and Geology in

Queen's College, Belfast. In company with him and other Belfast naturalists, Grainger spent many pleasant days in dredging for starfishes and other echinoderms, in which Order Thomson was specially interested.

At this time Grainger contributed an interesting paper to the *Ulster Journal of Archæology*, Vol. 9, 1861 and 1862, entitled—"Results of Excavations in High Street, Belfast." This paper contained much local information on old coins, Belfast tokens, &c., found during the re-building of the culvert over the Farset River in High Street, and was the author's first published paper on archæology.

In 1861 Ralph Tate came to Belfast, and opened classes under the South Kensington Department, in geology, mineralogy, and botany. These classes stirred up local geologists to much fresh activity, and were highly successful; and in the examination on the subject of geology, held at various centres over the United Kingdom, in May, 1862, Tate's pupils carried off eleven first-class Queen's prizes out of a total of 13 awarded to the students who presented themselves for examination. Grainger had the honour of carrying off first place, but was disqualified from obtaining the gold medal, which would otherwise have been awarded to him, on the ground that he paid income-tax, and was consequently ineligible under the rules of the Department.

In the summer of the same year he had a pleasant walking tour through Switzerland with the Rev. Robert Carmichael, Fellow of Trinity College, who was married to his sister Belinda, and this trip furnished its quota of additions to his museum.

About this year operations undertaken by the Board of Works towards improving the navigation at Toome, where the Lower Bann leaves Lough Neagh, resulted in the discovery of an extraordinary number of stone implements, chiefly polished celts, in the bed of the river. Large quantities of these found their way into museums and private collections, and Grainger acquired a representative series, purchasing about 100 examples from a dealer for the modest price of fourpence each.

In the same year he was in London on business for a few months, and the construction of waterworks near Dulwich College presented a good opportunity for the study of the Eocene beds, and the interesting fossils which characterise these deposits were diligently sought and preserved.

A walking tour through Wales, from Chepstow to Bangor, with Thomas Valentine, brought our naturalist among a vastly older fauna. The Palæozoic rocks of Portmaddock, with their fine assemblage of Trilobites—*Angelina, Æglina, Asephus*, &c.—furnished him with material for his hammer, during the time at his disposal.

In March, 1863, the Belfast Naturalists' Field Club was founded, being an outcome of the impetus which Professor Tate's classes had given to local science, and Grainger was selected to fill the post of Chairman of Committee during its first year.

On 21st December, 1863, he was ordained in St. Anne's Church, Belfast, by

Bishop Knox (now the Lord Primate), and, after a couple of months spent at Belfast and Coleraine, he went to Dublin, as curate of Christ Church, Carysfort, Blackrock. A member of his congregation here was G. V. Du Noyer, formerly of the English, and lately of the Irish Geological Survey—an excellent draughtsman and a distinguished antiquarian. From him Grainger acquired a knowledge of the various forms of rude stone implements. J. Hellier Baily, palæontologist to the Irish Geological Survey, with whom Grainger now became intimately acquainted, was an invaluable ally in the study of the Carboniferous fossils. From Dr. Carte, of the Royal Dublin Society, an expert conchologist, assistance was obtained, as also from Professor M'Alister, of Trinity College, a highly-accomplished anatomist.

After a year and a half at Blackrock, the scene of his clerical labours was changed to the parish of St. Thomas', Dublin, where three and a half years were spent, during which St. Barnabas' Church and schools were built by his exertions.

Captain Bennett, an old Indian officer, formerly of the 86th Regiment (Royal Co. Down), an excellent mineralogist and chemist, and the young clergyman always spent a day in the week geologising in the neighbourhood—a welcome relaxation for the latter from the arduous duties of parish work among the poor.

The quarries at Lucan, Sutton, Malahide, Milltown, and Castleknock, were explored, and here the greater part of the Canon's fine set of Irish Carboniferous fossils were obtained. The limestone brought from Co. Kildare by the canal, continued, as in college days, to yield its molluscs and cephalopods, and sometimes a two-day trip would be made to Slane, Co. Kildare ; Rathkeel, Co. Limerick ; or other suitable geological locality.

On other occasions the shores of Malahide and Portmarnock would be explored for shells, or the cliffs of Howth for wild-flowers, insects, and butterflies.

In 1869 he left Dublin, and came to Broughshane, near Ballymena, as rector, where he resided until his lamented death last autumn. Archæology now began largely to engage his attention, and implements and utensils of wood, stone, iron, and bronze ; beads and pottery, were all eagerly sought after. In company with W. J. Knowles, M.R.I.A., a local archæological Society, afterwards the Ballymena Naturalists' Field Club, was founded ; and monthly meetings were held, at which papers were read, and specimens examined. The Canon now renewed his connection with the Belfast Natural History and Philosophical Society and the Belfast Naturalists' Field Club, and became a frequent attender of the meetings of both Societies.

During the visit of the British Association to Belfast in 1869, Grainger contributed a paper " On the Fossils of the Post-Tertiary Deposits of Ireland."

The summers brought a few weeks' holiday, which was usually spent in geologizing, and the collections were enriched with instalments of Oolitic fossils from Cheltenham, Dundry near Bristol, and Scarboro' ; Liassic fossils from

Barrow-on-Soar, Cheltenham, and Whitby ; Carboniferous fossils from Bristol and the Peak of Derbyshire.

With his friend, Captain Bennett, who frequently came down from Dublin to pay him a visit, many shorter trips were made. Raids were made on the Carboniferous sandstone of Cookstown and Dungannon for corals ; to Pomeroy for Silurian trilobites ; to the Causeway for zeolites and rock specimens ; to Armagh for the celebrated teeth and spines of fish that the crystalline limestones there yielded ; to Dungiven, Magilligan, Portrush, Glenarm, and other spots, and the two friends never returned to Broughshane without some geological souvenirs of the places visited.

On other occasions archæological explorations would occupy his time. The raised beaches of Kilroot, Holywood, Larne, &c., were carefully and repeatedly inspected for the rude flint implements which they yield. The sand-dunes of White Park Bay, Portrush, Portstewart, Grangemore, yielded implements of flint, pieces of pottery, glass beads, and other objects ; and no opportunity was ever lost of securing objects from dealers or others which would enrich his collections. Indeed, Canon Grainger more than once remarked to us that he made a point of never making an excursion or paying a visit without bringing something home with him.

Thus, in constant collecting and exploring, which occupied all the time he could spare from his parish work, the years passed away, until the handsome house at Broughshane became a museum, filled from top to bottom with antiquities and natural history objects, and many other illustrations of the science and art of past and present times. The savage dress and weapons of a South Sea Islander were surveyed by the glassy stare of tropical birds. The variously coloured corals stood side by side with polished jades and stone implements. The rude altar-stone of Connor, inscribed with five crosses, representing the five wounds of Christ, as was the custom in the Irish Church, and upon which the Blessed Sacrament had been dispensed for centuries, was carefully protected by glass, after having seen many vicissitudes, and having been rescued from the menial office of holding a poor woman's water-bucket. It is now rightly regarded as a great treasure, and only equalled in interest by an inscribed stone once belonging to Petrie, and brought from one of the western islands, the inscription on which no one has yet been able to decipher. A curiously-shaped altar vessel of enamel work, accurately described in the *Ulster Journal of Archæology*, stood beside a quaint old hand-bell used in an ancient Irish church, whilst many broken crosses and saintly representations were ranged around. The Celtic bronze swords and spears made a formidable array, the collecting of each specimen being an experience in itself. Many of them have been accurately described in word and pencil by W. F. Wakeman in the *Proceedings* of the Royal Irish Academy and the Royal Society of Antiquaries. The flint arrow heads number over a thousand, and the stone implements for variety of formation are extremely interesting, whilst the use of many can now be only a matter of conjecture. Space does not permit us to tell of the toils and troubles, not to speak of the expense, borne by the Canon whilst he was forming his collection, nor the mild stratagems he had often to invent to procure specimens, nor the many times he was robbed by pedlars; suffice it to say that every opportunity his avocation allowed was devoted to his favourite pursuit, and a long and busy life has resulted in an almost unequalled collection of antiquities and natural history objects.

In the latter part of the year 1890 appeared the first symptoms of the terrible disease that was destined to prematurely cut short his career. Operations by the highest surgical skill were of no avail, and in the following summer he knew that his days were numbered, and with the quiet resignation of a true Christian, he set about the disposal of his worldly goods. His first intention was to bequeath the whole of his museum and library to the Church of Ireland ; but on account of legal objections to this course, his valuable collections were destined to enrich the public rather than the Church, and a deed of gift was executed between himself and the Belfast City Council, by which the latter undertook the permanent charge of the Canon's treasures, and their proper arrangement and display at the Belfast Free Public Library. Anxious to see the work of his lifetime safely housed in its new abode before the end which he knew was approaching, he insisted that the transfer of the collections to Belfast should be commenced immediately, and no time was lost in beginning the work—a work of no small magnitude and difficulty, for the collection numbers some 60,000 specimens, and the frailty of many of the most precious antiquarian relics rendered their removal by no means easy. By a special stipulation of Canon Grainger, this work was done under the superintendence of our Secretary, Mr. R. Lloyd Praeger, B.E., M.R.I A., with the assistance of Mr. J. F. Johnston, Curator of the Free Library Museum, and the entire collection was safely transferred to Belfast. During its removal, in spite of the deadly weakness that told of the approaching end, Canon Grainger was ever cheerful, giving information as to the various treasures, with quaint stories of their acquisition, and continually assisting the work. The removal of the collections was completed in October, 1891, and on November 25th, shortly after the first portion of his museum was opened to the public in Belfast, the good Canon passed peacefully away.

Always more of a collector than a writer, Canon Grainger left comparatively few records of his wide and varied knowledge, and in his latter days especially he preferred leaving the describing and recording of his treasures to literary friends, being himself happy in their possession. Among his own papers, three dealing with the Post-tertiary deposits of Belfast Lough, written in early life, at once gave him a prominent place among local geologists. The first of these was read before the Belfast Natural History Society in 1848 ; the second before the British Association in 1852 ; and the final one before the Dublin University Zoological and Botanical Association in 1858. To the Belfast Natural History and Philosophical Society and the Belfast Naturalists' Field Club he contributed various papers, on different subjects—archæological, geological, or zoological—and contributions from his pen will be found in the *Ulster Journal of Archæology* aad several other publications.

Well-known Irish scientists have described many of the more interesting of his local finds, notably W. H. Baily in palæontology, and W. F. Wakeman in arc hæology—the three papers by the latter, in the *Journal of the Royal Society of Antiquaries of Ireland*, dealing with the wonderful find at the crannog of Lisnacroghera near Broughshane, forming a most valuable addition to our knowledge of the civilization and art of Ireland in early times.

Canon Grainger was an ex-President of the Belfast Naturalists' Field Club, and of the Dublin University Zoological and Botanical Association ; a Vice-President of the Royal Society of Antiquaries, and a member of the Royal Irish Academy and Belfast Natural History and Philosophical Society, and his cheerful presence will long be missed at the meetings of these scientific bodies, and by the large circle of scientific and non-scientific friends that his kindness and genuine enthusiasm had drawn to him.

METEOROLOGICAL SUMMARY

FOR 1892.

WE have again to thank the Council of Queen's College, Belfast, for granting access to the records kept at that Institution, from which the following summary is compiled.

The station at which the records are made is situated in the Lagan Valley, at an elevation of about sixty feet above mean sea-level. The Belfast Hills, which attain a maximum elevation of 1,567 feet, lie to the west and north, stretching in a N.E. and S.W. line, and passing within three miles of the Observatory. Southward and eastward stretch the low undulating lands of Co. Down. Lough Neagh is situated some 14 miles to the westward. Belfast Lough approaches to within two miles on the N.E., and the open sea lies some 16 miles east of the observing station.

REVIEW OF THE WEATHER FOR 1891.

Meteorological Observations taken at Queen's College, Belfast, at 9 a.m. each day.
Latitude, 54° 35′ N.; Longitude, 5° 56′ W.

1891.	BAROMETER 70 Feet above Sea Level.—Actual Readings.									SELF-REGISTERING THERMOMETERS in shade, in stand outside window, 21 feet above ground.								HYGROMETER	
	Highest of the Month.			Lowest of the Month.			Mean.		Range.	Highest of the Month		Lowest of the Month		Mean Maximum	Mean Minimum	Mean of two preceding	Monthly Range	Mean of dry Bulb	Mean of wet Bulb
	Inches.	Att. Ther.	Date	Inches	Att. Ther.	Date	Inches	Att. Ther.	Inches	Deg. F.	Date	Deg. F.	Date	Deg. F.	Deg. F.	Deg. F.	Deg F.		
January..	30·770	48·0	14	29·200	48·0	23	29·995	41·2	1·570	53·0	29	23·0	6	43·6	32·4	38·0	30·0	38·0	37·4
February..	30·650	47·0	5	29·866	48·0	26	30·006	46·3	·784	54·0	4	25·0	9	50·1	36·0	43·0	29·0	42·5	40·9
March....	30·200	44·0	3	29·350	42·0	16	29·811	42·3	·850	55·0	1	22·0	13	46·3	34·2	40·3	33·0	41·5	39·2
April......	30·334	48·0	20	29·472	50·0	30	29·970	46·0	·862	56·0	8	30·0	26	50·4	38·0	44·2	26·0	44·7	41·4
May........	30·272	59·0	12	29·180	54·0	1	29·778	52·6	1·092	72·0	13	33·0	21	56·4	42·2	49·3	39·0	47·8	46·0
June	30·350	68·0	20	29·550	62·0	29	29·987	61·2	·800	76·0	20	41·0	11	67·5	50·9	59·2	35·0	59·7	55·1
July.......	30·380	64·0	14	29·536	59·0	7	29·926	62·7	·844	73·0	21	48·0	14	64·3	52·4	58·3	25·0	60·9	55·6
August....	30·126	60·0	6	29·150	60·0	25	29·702	60·4	·976	70·0	1	44·0	31	64·6	51·3	57·9	26·0	59·6	53·3
ptember	30·180	64·8	12	29·500	57·0	26	29·870	58·8	·680	73·6	13	41·0	7	64·0	49·3	56·7	32·6	58·7	54·8
ctober...	30·650	42·0	31	28·900	48·0	16	29·600	49·7	1·750	61·0	5	31·0	25	55·2	40·9	48·0	30·0	49·0	46·5
ovember	30·676	49·0	5	29·100	42·0	12	29·780	43·6	1·570	55·0	19	28·0	23	48·9	37·6	43·3	27·0	43·5	41·9
ecember	30·550	38·0	21	29·150	46·0	3	29·731	42·6	1·400	56·0	4	24·0	23	47·4	35·0	41·2	32·0	40·6	39·3
Totals...	365·138	631·8		351·954	610·0		358·156		13·178	754·6		390·0		658·7	500·2	579·4	364·6	586·5	551·4
Means...	30·428	52·6		29·329	50·8		29·846		1·098	62·9		32·5		54·9	41·7	48·3	30·4	48·9	45·9

Review of the Weather for 1891.—Continued.

WIND.

Direction and Amount of Wind, as indicated by Casella's Self-Recording Anemometer.

1891	| Average Daily Direction (Days)									| Daily Amount					
	N.	N.E.	E.	S.E.	S.	S.W.	W.	N.W.	Var.	Greatest in one day (Miles)	Date	Least in one day (Miles)	Date	Mean Daily Am'nt (Miles)
January	2	4	2	1	8	7	1	3	3	342	14th	24	6th	159
February	—	1	—	3	5	11	6	—	2	300	2nd	35	16th	121
March	8	1	7	—	2	—	5	6	2	460	2nd	46	12th	261
April	2	2	9	9	3	1	1	1	2	425	2nd	55	14th	194
May	6	6	6	1	4	2	1	3	1	465	15th	43	27th	208
June	2	1	6	6	6	2	3	10	—	432	3rd	54	19th	197
July	8	—	4	1	2	1	2	7	3	370	7th	65	16th	175
August	3	2	—	1	2	6	6	4	4	425	18th	53	9th	193
September	1	1	1	2	3	9	8	2	1	383	1st	56	11th	192
October	—	1	2	3	4	10	7	2	2	465	5th	47	24th	201
November	2	3	3	4	2	9	3	3	3	348	11th	15	13th	138
December	—	—	—	2	10	10	3	3	3	462	15th	8	21st	171
Totals	34	22	40	33	51	68	46	44	27	4877		501		2210
Means										406		42		192

RAINFALL.

GAUGE—Diameter of Receiver, 11in.; height of top above ground, 7ft. 1in.; height above sea level, 6oft.

1891	Total Depth (Inches)	Greatest fall in one day (Inches)	Date	No. of days on which ·10 or more fell (Days)
January	1·188	·196	21st	16
February	·118	·060	21st	3
March	1·494	·348	14th	13
April	2·606	·964	1st	12
May	3·274	·694	7th	20
June	2·480	1·382	25th	12
July	1·793	·538	21st	12
August	4·640	·952	17th	20
September	2·521	·630	5th	18
October	4·316	1·234	13th	13
November	3·100	·990	12th	15
December	4·446	·763	12th	22
Totals	31·976			176

RULES

OF THE

Belfast Naturalists' Field Club.

———✠———

I.

That the Society be called "THE BELFAST NATURALISTS' FIELD CLUB."

II.

That the objects of the Society be the practical study of Natural Science and Archæology in Ireland.

III.

That the Club shall consist of Ordinary, Corresponding, and Honorary Members. The Ordinary Members to pay annually a subscription of Five Shillings, and that candidates for such Membership shall be proposed and seconded at any Meeting of the Club, by Members present, and elected by a majority of the votes of the Members present.

IV.

That the Honorary and Corresponding Members shall consist of persons of eminence in Natural Science, or who shall have done some special service to the Club ; and whose usual residence is not less than twenty miles from Belfast. That such Members may be nominated by any Member of the Club, and on being approved of by the Committee, may be elected at any subsequent Meeting of the Club by a majority of the votes of the Members present. That Corresponding Members be expected to communicate a Paper once within every two years.

V.

That the Officers of the Club be annually elected, and consist of a President, Vice-President, Treasurer, and two Secretaries, and ten Members, who form the Committee. Five to form a quorum. No Member of Committee to be eligible for re-election who has not attended at least one-fourth of the Committee Meetings during his year of office. That the office of President, or that of Vice-President, shall not be held by the same person for more than two years in succession.

VI.

That the Members of the Club shall hold at least Six Field Meetings during the year, in the most interesting localities, for investigating the Natural History and Archæology of Ireland. That the place of meeting be fixed by the Committee, and that five days' notice of each Excursion be communicated to Members by the Secretaries.

VII.

That Meetings be held Fortnightly or Monthly, at the discretion of the Committee, for the purpose of reading papers ; such papers, as far as possible, to treat of the Natural History and Archæology of the district. These Meetings to be held during the months from November to April inclusive.

VIII.

That the Committee shall, if they find it advisable, offer for competition Prizes for the best collections of scientific objects of the district ; and the Committee may order the purchase of maps. or other scientific apparatus, and may carry on geological and archæological searches or excavations, if deemed advisable, provided that the entire amount expended under this rule does not exceed the sum of £10 in any one year.

IX.

That the Annual Meeting be held during the month of April, when the Report of the Committee for the past year, and the Treasurer's Financial Statement shall be presented, the Committee and Officers elected, Bye-laws made and altered, and any proposed alteration in the general laws, of which a fortnight's notice shall have been given, in writing, to the Secretary or Secretaries, considered and decided upon. The Secretaries to give the Members due notice of such intended alteration.

X.

That, on the written requisition of twenty-five Members, delivered to the Secretaries, an Extraordinary General Meeting may be called, to consider and decide upon the subject mentioned in such written requisition.

XI.

That the Committee may be empowered to exchange publications and reports, and to extend the privilege of attending the Meetings and Excursions of the Belfast Naturalists' Field Club to members of kindred societies, on similar privileges being accorded to its members by such other societies.

*The following Rules for the Conducting of the Excursions have
been arranged by the Committee.*

I. The Excursion to be open to all members ; each one to have the privilege of introducing two friends.

II. A Chairman to be elected as at ordinary meetings.

III. One of the Secretaries to act as conductor, or in the absence of both, a member to be elected for that purpose.

IV. No change to be made in the programme, or extra expense incurred, except by the consent of the majority of the members present.

V. No fees, gratuities, or other expenses to be paid except through the conductor.

VI. Every member or visitor to have the accommodation assigned by the conductor. Where accommodation is limited, consideration will be given to priority of application.

VII. Accommodation cannot be promised unless tickets are obtained before the time mentioned in the special circular.

VIII. Those who attend an excursion without previous notice will be iable to extra charge, if extra cost be incurred thereby.

IX. No intoxicating liquors to be provided at the expense of the Club.

BELFAST NATURALISTS' FIELD CLUB.

——·:·——

THIRTIETH YEAR.

——·:·——

THE Committee offer the following Prizes to be competed for during the Session ending March 31st, 1893 :—

			£	s	d
I. Best Herbarium of Flowering Plants, representing not less than 250 species,		...	£1	o	o
II. Best Herbarium of Flowering Plants, representing not less than 150 species,		...	o	10	o
III. Best Collection of Mosses,	...	...	o	10	o
IV. .. ,,	Lichens,	...	o	10	o
V. ,,	Seaweeds, ...	...	o	10	o
VI. ,,	Ferns, Equiseta, and Lycopods,	...	o	10	o
VII. ,,	Tertiary and Post-tertiary Fossils, ...	...	o	10	o
VIII. ,, ,,	Cretaceous Fossils,	...	o	10	o
IX. ,,	Liassic Fossils, ...	...	o	10	o
X. ,,	Permian and Carboniferous Fossils, ...	...	o	10	o
XI. ,,	Older Palæozoic Fossils,		o	10	o
XII. ,, ,,	Marine Shells, ...	...	o	10	o
XIII. ,, ,,	Land and Freshwater Shells,		o	10	o
XIV. ,, ,,	Lepidoptera, ...	...	o	10	o
XV. ,,	Hymenoptera, ...	...	o	10	o
XVI. ,, ,,	Coleoptera, ...	...	o	10	o
XVII. ,, ,,	Crustacea and Echinodermata, ...	...	o	10	o

XVIII. Best Collection of Fungi; names of species not necessary. Collectors may send (post

paid, from time to time during the season)
their specimens to Rev. H. W. Lett, M.A.,
T.C.D., Aghaderg Glebe, Loughbrickland,
who will record them to their credit,   ... £0 10 0
XIX. Best Collection of Fossil Sponges,   ... 0 10 0
XX. Best Collection of 24 Microscopic Slides,
    illustrating some special branch of Natural
    History, ... 0 10 0
XXI. Best Collection of 24 Microscopic Slides,
    shewing general excellence, ... 0 10 0
XXII. Best Set of 12 Photo-micrographs, illustrating some
    some special branch of Natural History .. 0 10 0
XXIII. Best set of 6 Field Sketches appertaining to
    Geology, Archæology, or Zoology,   ... 0 10 0
XXIV. Best set of 12 Photographs, illustrative of
    Irish Archæology, ... 0 10 0

SPECIAL PRIZES.

XXV. The President offers a prize of £1 1s. for the Best Set
of three or more Original Sketches, to be placed in
the Album of the Club. These may be executed in
pen and ink, or water colour, and must illustrate
one or more ancient monuments somewhere in
Ireland. In determining the relative merits of the
sketches, accuracy in representing the subjects and
their details will have chief place. This Prize is
open to the Members of the Belfast Art Society,
and to the Students of the School of Art.
XXVI. Mr. William Swanston, F.G.S., offers a Prize of 10s. 6d.
for Six Photographs from Nature, illustrative of
Geology, contributed to the Club's Album.
XXVII. Mr. Francis Joseph Bigger, Solicitor, Belfast, offers a
Prize of £1 1s. for the Best Set of Twelve Photographs (not less than cabinet size) of Ecclesiastical
Structures mentioned in Reeves' *Ecclesiastical*

Antiquities of Down and Connor, contributed to the Club's Album. The set of Photographs taking this Prize cannot be admitted in competition for Prize XXIV.

XXVIII. The Secretaries of the Ulster Fauna Committee offer a Prize of 10s. for the Best Collection of Bats, Rodents, Insectivora, and Carnivora (names of species not necessary) collected in Ulster during the year. Specimens to be sent in a fresh state to the Museum, Belfast.

CONDITIONS.

No competitor to obtain more than two Prizes in one year.

No competitor to be awarded the same Prize twice within three years.

A member to whom Prize I. has been awarded shall be ineligible to compete for Prize II., unless the plants are additions to those in previous collection.

In every case where three or more persons compete for a Prize, a second one, of half its value, will be awarded if the conditions are otherwise complied with.

All collections to be made personally during the Session in Ireland, except those for Prize XXI., which need not necessarily be Irish, nor competitors' own collecting. The species to be classified according to a recognised system, to be correctly named, and localities stated, and a list to accompany each collection. The Flowering Plants to be collected when in flower, and classified according to the Natural System. The Microscopic Slides to be competitors' own preparation and mounting. The Sketches and Photographs to be competitors' own work, executed during the Session ; and those sets for which Prizes are awarded, to become the property of the Club.

No Prizes will be awarded except to such collections as shall, in the opinion of the Judges, possess positive merit.

The Prizes to be in books, or suitable scientific objects, at the desire of the successful competitor.

℧OTICE.

EXCHANGES OF PROCEEDINGS.

Belfast—Natural History and Philosophical Society.
Report and Proceedings, 1890.91.

Berwickshire—Naturalists' Field Club.
Prodeedings, Vol. XII., No. 3.

Brighton and Sussex—Natural History and Philosophical Society.
Annual Report, 1891.

Bristol—Naturalists' Society.
Proceedings, N.S., Vol. VI., Part III.

Cardiff—Naturalists' Society.
Report and Transactions, Vol. XXII., Part II., and Vol. XXIII., Part I.

Dublin—Royal Irish Academy.
Transactions, Vol. XXIX., Part XVI.
Proceedings, Vol. I., No. 5, Vol. II., No. 1.

Dulwich—College Science Society.
Report, 1890-91.

Dumfries and Galloway—Natural History and Antiquarian Society.
Transactions, Session 1890.91.

Eastbourne—Natural History Society.
Transactions, Vol. II., Parts IV. and V.

Edinburgh—Botanical Society of.
Transactions and Proceedings, Vols. XVIII. and XIX.

Frankfort—Helois.
Jahrgang IX., Nos. 1-12.

,,　　Sociatum Litterae.
Jahrgang V., Nos. 1-12 ; Jahrgang VI., Nos. 1-3.

Glasgow—Geological Society.
Transactions, Vol. IX., Part I.

,,   Philosophical Society.
Proceedings, Vol. XXII.

Halifax, N.S.—Nova Scotian Institute of Natural Science.
Proceedings and Transactions, Vol. VII., Part IV.

Leeds—Philosophical and Literary Society.
Annual Report, 1890.91.

Liverpool—Geological Society.
Proceedings, Vol. VI., Part III.

London—British Association for the Advancement of Science.
Annual Report, Leeds Meeting, 1890.
,,   Cardiff   ,,   1891.

Manchester—Field Naturalists' and Archæologists' Society.
Annual Report, 1891.

,,   Microscopical Society.
Transactions and Annual Report, 1890.

Plymouth—Institution.
Annual Report and Transactions, Vol. XI., Part I.

Rome—Rassegna Delle Scienze Geologiche in Italia.
Fasc I., Part II.

Stavanger—Museum.
Aarsberetning for 1890.

Toronto—The Canadian Institute.
Transactions, Vol. I., Part II., Vol. II., Part I.
Annual Report, 1890.91.

Wiltshire—Archæological and Natural History Society.
Magazine, Vols. XXV. and XXVI.

Yorkshire—Naturalists' Union.
Transactions, Parts X.-XVI.

U.S.A.—Boston—Society of Natural History.
Proceedings, Vol. XXV., Parts I. and II.

,,   Cambridge—Washington University Eclipse Party.
Report, January, 1889.

U.S.A.—Hamilton—Association.
>> Journal and Proceedings, Part VII.

,, California—Academy of Sciences.
>> Proceedings, Vol. III., Part I.

,, Meriden—Scientific Association.
>> Transactions, Vol. IV.

,, Minnesota—Geological and Natural History Survey.
>> 18th Annual Report.
>> Bulletin, No. 6 (The Iron Ores of Minnesota).

,, New York—American Museum of Natural History.
>> Annual Report, 1890-91.

>> Academy of Sciences.
>> Transactions, Vol. X., Nos. IV.-VI.

,, Philadelphia—Academy of Natural Sciences.
>> Proceedings, 1890, Part III.; 1891, Parts I.-III.
>> Reprints—Tuberculosis.

,, Raleigh—Elisha Mitchell Scientific Society.
>> Journal, 8th Year.

,, Salem—American Association for the Advancement of Science.
>> Proceedings, 1890.

,, Essex Institute.
>> Bulletin, Vol. XXI., Parts VII.-XII., Vol. XXII., Parts I.-XII.

,, Saint Louis—Academy of Sciences.
>> Report, 1890.

,, Trenton—New Jersey Natural History Society.
>> Journal, Vol. II., No. II.

,: Washington—United States Geological Survey.
>> 10th Annual Report, Part I., Geology.
>> ,, ,, II., Irrigation.

>> Smithsonian Institution.
>> Annual Report, 1889.

,, Wisconsin—Natural History Survey.
>> Papers, Vol. I., No. III.

The following received from the Authors :—

Antiquity of Man, by Samuel Lang; Brighton, 1890.

Our Trees, by John Robinson ; Salem, U.S.A., 1890.

Time Reckoning for the Twentieth Century, by Sanford Fleming ; Washington, U.S.A., 1889.

Phenological Observations, by Edward Mawley ; Hertford, 1891.

Ancient Marbles at Leeds, by E. L. Hicks ; Leeds, 1891.

BELFAST NATURALISTS' FIELD CLUB.

————✦————

THIRTIETH YEAR, 1892-93.

————✦————

LIST OF OFFICERS AND MEMBERS.

————✦————

President:

JOHN VINYCOMB, F.R.S.A.

Vice-President:

WILLIAM SWANSTON, F.G.S.

Treasurer:

W. H. PHILLIPS, F.R.H.S.,
8 CHICHESTER STREET.

Librarian:

WILLIAM SWANSTON, F.G.S.,
QUEEN STREET.

Secretaries:

R. LLOYD PRAEGER, B.E., M.R.I.A.
HOLYWOOD.

FRANCIS JOSEPH BIGGER
REA'S BUILDINGS, BELFAST.

Committee:

JOHN J. ANDREW, L.D.S.

GEORGE DONALDSON.

JOHN DONALDSON.

WILLIAM GRAY, M.R.I.A.

JOHN HAMILTON.

F. W. LOCKWOOD.

S. A. STEWART, F.B.S.Edin.

MISS S. M. THOMPSON.

ROBERT J. WELCH

JOSEPH WRIGHT, F.G.S.

Members.

Adams, John J., M.D., Ashville, Antrim.
Agnew, A. W., Dunedin, Belfast.
Allen, Hugh, 71 York Street.
Allworthy, Edward, Mosaphir.
Anderson, John, J.P., F.G.S., East Hillbrook, Holywood.
Anderson, Robert, Donegall Place.
Andrew, J. J., L.D.S., R.C.S. Eng., Belgravia.
Andrews, Miss Mary K., College Gardens.
Aston, Miss Annie, South Parade.

Barkley, James M., Larne.
Barklie, Robert, M.R.I.A., Working Men's Institute.
Barr, James, Beechleigh, Windsor Park.
Barr, John, Belmont Park.
Batt, William, Sorrento, Windsor.
Beattie, Rev. A. Hamilton, Portglenone.
Beck, Miss Emma, Old Lodge Road.
Beggs, D. C., Ballyclare.
Begley, George R , Wolfhill Lodge.
Best, James, Clarence Place.
Bigger, Francis Joseph, Ardrie, Antrim Road.
Bingham, Edward, Ponsonby Avenue
Blair, E., Camberwell Terrace.
Blair, Mrs., Camberwell Terrace.
Boyd, Miss, Beechcroft, Strandtown
Braddell, Edward, St. Ives, Malone Park.
Brandon, Hugh B., Atlantic Avenue.
Brenan, Rev. Samuel Arthur, B.A., Knocknacarry, Co. Antrim.
Brett, Chas. H., Gretton Villa South.
Bristow, Rev. John, St. James's Parsonage.
Brown, John, Belair, Windsor Av.
Brown, Thomas, Donegall Street.
Brown, R. N., Great Victoria Street.
Brown, William, Chichester Street.
Browne, W. J., M.A., M.R.I.A., Highfield, Omagh.
Bulla, Charles, Wellington Park Ter.
Burden, Henry, M.D., M.R.I.A., Alfred Street.
Burnett, John R., Rostellan, Malone Road.

Calwell, William, M.D., College Square North.
Campbell, J. O., 10 Clifton Street.
Capper, George Montgomery, Botanic Avenue.
Capper, John Malcomson, Botanic Av.
Carruthers, Miss, Claremont Street.
Carson, Robert, Talbot Street.
Carter, W., Chichester Park.
Carter, Mrs., Chichester Park.
Chancellor, William, B.A., Cromwell House, Cromwell Road
Cleland, James A , Wellington Park.
Coates, Stanley B , L.R.C.P. Edin., Shaftsbury Square.
Colbeck, James, Shaw's Bridge.
Collins, Arthur J., 3 Windsor Crescent.
Connell, Rev. John, B.A., Holywood
Corry, W. F. C. S., Chatsworth, Malone Road.
Coulson, Gerald, College St. South.
Coulson, J. P., Somerset Terrace.
Coulter, George B., 21 University Square.
Coulter, Mrs., 21 University Sqr.
Crawford, F. H., Chlorine.
Creeth, James, Knock.
Crozier, David, Mill Street.
Culbert, Robert, Distillery Street.
Cunningham, Samuel, Glencairn.
Curley, Francis, Dunedin, Antrim Rd.
Curley, Mrs., Dunedin, Antrim Rd.

Dufferin and Ava, Marquis of, Clandeboye (Hon. Mem.).
Davies, John Henry, Glenmore Cottage, Lisburn.
Davis, Henry, Holywood.
Day, Robert, J.P., F.S.A., M.R.I.A. Cork.
D'Evelyn, Alexander M., M.D., Ballymena.
Dickson, John, Hillbrook, Holywood
Dickson, J. Hill, Ballygowan.
Dixon, Wakefield H., Dunowen.
Donaldson, George, Bloomfield.
Donaldson, John, Thorndale Terrace.
Donnan, William D., Ardmore Terrace, Holywood.
Douglas, Allan E., M.D., J.P., Warrenpoint.

Duffin, Miss, Strandtown Lodge.
Dunlop, W. J., Bryson Street.

Elliott, David, Albert Bridge Road.
Elliott, George, Royal Avenue.
Elliott, George H., Holywood.
Ewart, Lavens M., J.P., M.R I.A.,
  Glenbank House.

Ferguson, Godfrey W., Murray's
  Terrace.
Ferguson, Miss, Murray's Terrace.
Ferguson, Miss Mary, Murray's
  Terrace.
Ferguson, Henry, Murray's Terrace.
Ferguson, J. H., Belgrave, Knock.
Firth, Joseph, Whiterock.
Firth, Wm. A., Glenview Terrace,
  Springfield Road.
Flynn, T. M. H., Sunnyside, Bess-
  brook.
Frame, John, 6 Lawrence Street.

Galloway, Peter, University Street.
Galloway, Joseph, 83 Eglantine
  Avenue.
Gardner, J. Starkie, F.G.S., Damer
  Terrace, Chelsea (Hon. Mem).
Gibson, Henry, Glencairn.
Gilliland, John, Prospect Street.
Gilmore, R. M, Upper Salt Hill,
  Galway.
Gilmore, W. J., Camberwell Villas.
Glenn, George J., Hartington Street.
Godwin, William, Queen Street.
Gordon, Rev. David, Downpatrick.
Goskar, James J., Carlisle Circus.
Gourley, James, J.P., Derryboy,
  Killyleagh.
Gracey, Robert, Minerva House,
  Brookfield Avenue.
Gray, Wm., M.R.I.A, Mountcharles.
Gray, Miss, Mountcharles.
Greenfield, Charles, Marino, Holy-
  wood.
Greer, Mrs., Dulce Domo, Strand-
  town.
Gulbransen, P. F., 17 Queen's
  Arcade.
Gulbransen, Ahavos, 7 Ratcliffe St.

Hamilton, James H., Eden Terrace,
  Shankill Road.
Hamilton, John, Mount Street.
Hamilton, Thomas, Queen Street.
Hanford, Ernest, Melrose Terrace.

Hanna, Richard, Charleville Street.
Hanna, William, B.A., Lisanore
  Villa, Antrim Road.
Hanna, John, jun., Lisanore Villa,
  Antrim Road.
Harbison, Mann, Ravenhill Terrace
Harris, W. D., St. Mary's Terrace.
Hartrick, Rev. Canon, M.A., The
  Rectory, Ballynure.
Haslett, Sir James, J.P., Princess
  Gardens.
Hassan, Thomas, Strangemore House
Heron, F. A., Cultra, Holywood.
Holden, J. S., M.D., F.G S., Sudbury,
  Suffolk (Cor. Mem.).
Hollis, Matthew, R.E., Victoria
  Barracks.

Imrie, James, Rugby Road.
Inglis. Wm., Riverston Terrace,
  Holywood.

Jackson, A. T., 5, Corn Market.
Jacques, John, Parkview Terrace.
Jefferson, Hugh Smith, Rosnakill,
  Strandtown.
Johnson, Rev. W. F, M.A., Armagh
Johnston, James F., Holywood.
Johnston, Wm. J., J.P., Dunesk,
  Strandmillis.
Jones, Professor T. Rupert, F.R.S.,
  Chelsea, London (Hon. Mem.).

Keay, David, 22, College Green.
Keith, Hutchinson, Glenravel Street
Kelly, W. Redfern, M. Inst. C.E,
  Elgin Terrace.
Kennedy, R. M., 41 Waring Street.
Kernaghan, Wm., Wellington Park.
Kidd, George, Lisnatore, Dunmurry.
Kirkpatrick, F., Ann Street.
Knowles, Wm. J., M.R.I.A., Bally-
  mena.
Knowles, Miss Matilda, Ballymena.
Kyle, Robert A., Cliftonville.

Lamb, Wm. W., Salisbury Avenue.
Lapworth, Professor Charles, F.G.S.,
  Mason College, Birmingham
  (Hon. Mem.)
Lawther, Stanley, Mount Vernon.
Leighton, Samuel, Cooke Terrace.
Lepper, F. R., Elsinore, Crawfords-
  burn.
Leslie, James, Eglantine Avenue.

Lett, Rev. H. W., M.A., T.C.D.,
  .. Aghaderg Glebe, Loughbrick-
  land.
Letts, Professor E. A , Ph.D., F C.S.,
  Dunavon, Craigavad.
Lewers, Hugh, M.D., Shankill Rd.
Lockwood, Frederick W., Wellington
  Park Terrace.
Logan, James, Donegall Street.
Lowson, W. B., Chichester Park.
Luther, H. W., M.D, Chlorine House

Macdonald, Miss, Bantry.
Macdonald, William, Carlisle Circus.
Mackenzie, John, C.E., Myrtlefield.
Major, Rev. J. J., Belvoir Hall.
Malcolmson, Greer, Granville
  Gardens.
Malcolmson, Harold, Holywood.
Malcolmson, James, Cairnburn,
  Strandtown.
Malcolmson, Mrs., Cairnburn,
  Strandtown.
Mann, James S., Ballyholme, Bangor.
Marsh, Mrs., Glenlyon, Holywood.
Marsh, Joseph C., Castleton Terrace.
Marshall, Hamilton, Shrigley, Killy-
  leagh.
Mathers, A. C., M.D., Coleraine.
Millen, Samuel, 44 Ulsterville
  Avenue.
Milligan, Seaton Forrest, M.R.I.A.,
  Royal Terrace.
Mollan, W. S., Helen's Bay.
Mollan, Miss, Helen's Bay.
Moore, John, Shaftesbury Square.
Morgan, C. E., 29 Atlantic Avenue.
Morrison, Thomas, Great George's
  Street.
Morrison, William J., Lower
  Crescent.
Morrow, David, Church Hill, Holy-
  wood.
Morrow, John L., Ardigon, Killy-
  leagh.
Morton, John, Clifton Park Avenue.
Moss, William, Camberwell Terrace.
Mull, Henry, Glendore, Crawfords-
  burn.
Murdoch, James, Denmark Street.
Murphy, Joseph John, Osborne Park.
Musgrave, J. R., J.P., Drumglass
  House, Malone Road.
Myles, Rev. Edward A., St. Anne's
  Vestry, Belfast.

M'Alister, Thomas, Eglinton Street.
M'Cance, J. Stouppe, Dunmurry.
M'Chesney, Joseph, Holywood.
M'Clean, Francis P., Huntly Villas.
M'Cleery, H., Clifton Park Avenue.
M'Cleery, William, General Post
  Office.
M'Clure, Rev. Ed., M.A., M.R.I A.,
  Onslow Place, South Kensing-
  ton (Cor. Mem.).
M'Clure, Sir Thomas, Bart., Belmont
M'Clure, Wm. J., Elizabeth Street.
M'Connell, James, Annadale Hall.
M'Connell, Robert, 100 York Street.
M'Cormick, H. M'Neile, Craigavad.
M'Cullough, John, Martello Terrace,
  Holywood
M'Elheran, W. F., College Gardens.
M'Caw, Miss, Wellington Park
  Terrace.
M'Ilwaine, John H., Brandon Villa,
  Strandtown
MacIlwaine, Mrs., Brandon Villa,
  Strandtown.
M'Kee, Miss, Adela Place.
M'Kee, Robert, M.A., Harlesden
  College, Bramshill Road, Lon-
  don, N.W.
M'Kee, W. S., Fleetwood Street.
M'Kinney, W. J., Ballyvesey,
  Carnmoney.
MacLaine, Alexander, J.P., Queen's
  Elms.
M'Leish, John, Ballyhackamore.
M'Mordie, Jas., Belgravia Avenue.
M'Murtry, W. D., Helen's View,
  Antrim Road, Belfast.
M'Neill, Miss J., 4 Princess Gardens.

Nelson, Miss, Wandsworth Villa,
  Strandtown.
Nepveu, Lucien, Courtney Terrace.
Nesbitt, W. Courtney, Kinnaird
  Terrace.
Nicholl, Wm., Donegall Square
  North.
Nicholson, H. J., Windsor Gardens.

O'Neill, Henry, M.D., College Square
  East.
O'Neill, James, M.A., College
  Square East.
Orr, H. Lamont, Garfield Street.
Owens, John S., St. James' Street.

Patterson, David C., Clanbrassil Terrace, Holywood.
Patterson, R. Lloyd, J.P., F.L.S., Croft House, Holywood
Patterson, Robert, M.B.O.U., Windsor Park Terrace, Lisburn Road.
Patterson, R. L., jun., Clanbrassil Terrace, Holywood.
Patterson, W. Hartley, Clanbrassil Terrace, Holywood.
Patterson, Richard, J.P., Kilmore, Holywood.
Patterson, Miss Clara, Kilmore, Holywood.
Patterson, William H., M.R.I.A., Garranard, Strandtown.
Paul, Thomas, Redcot, Knock.
Payne, H. W., Beechcroft, Holywood.
Phillips, James J., 61 Royal Avenue
Phillips, William H., F.R.H.S., Lemonfield, Holywood.
Pike, Rev. J. Kirk, Rosetta Terrace.
Pim, John, J.P., Bonaven, Antrim Road.
Pim, John William, Moyallen.
Pim, Joshua, Slieve-na-Failthe, Whiteabbey.
Pim, Thomas W., The Lodge, Strandtown.
Pinion, James, University Road.
Polley, Wm. Thomas, 52 Fitzroy Avenue.
Porter, Miss, Pakenham Terrace.
Porter, F. A., Queen's Square.
Porter, William, Eagle Chambers.
Praeger, E. A., Holywood.
Praeger, Robert Lloyd, B.A., B.E., M.R.I.A., Holywood.
Purser, William, M.A., 25 India Street.

Quail, Rev. Patrick, Dunmore, Ballynahinch.

Radley, Joseph, Prospect Hill, Lisburn.
Rea, Miss, Churchfield, Holywood.
Redmond, David, Saintfield.
Reid, Robert, King Street.
Ridings, Richard, Hampton Terrace.
Ringland, Samuel B., Ballytrim House, Killyleagh.

Robinson, Rev. George, M.A., Beech Hill House, Armagh.
Robinson, George, Woodview, Holywood.
Robinson, Jas. R., George's Terrace.
Robinson, William A., J P.,Culloden, Cultra.
Ross, John, Cliftonville.
Ross, Richard, M.D., Wellington Place.
Ross, Wm. A., Iva-Craig, Craigavad.
Rowan, J. C., Eglantine Avenue.
Russell, John, C.E., The Eyries, Newcastle.

Sefton, John R., Bangor.
Shanks, James, Ballyfounder, Portaferry.
Sheldon, Chas., M.A., B.Sc., D.Lit., Royal Academical Institution.
Skillen, Joseph, 6 Springfield Road.
Smith, Henry, C.E, Eastern Villa, Newcastle.
Smith, Rev. W. S., The Manse, Antrim.
Smyth, George I., Linen Hall Library.
Smyth, Walter, Woodview, Holywood.
Smyth, Wilson, Virginia Street.
Smyth, Rev. Canon, M.A., Coole Glebe, Carnmoney.
Speers, Adam, B.Sc., Holywood.
Stannus, A. C., Holywood.
Staples, Sir N. A., Bart., Lissan, (Life Mem.).
Stelfox, James, Oakleigh, Ormeau Park.
Stevenson, John, Coolavin, Malone Road.
Stevenson, J. M'N., Carrickfergus.
Stewart, Rev. J. A., M.A., Pond Park, Lisburn.
Stewart, S. A., F.B.S. Edin., The Museum.
Swanston, William, F.G.S., Cliftonville Avenue.
Swanston, Mrs., Cliftonville Avenue.
Symington, Samuel, Ballyoran Ho.

Tate, Alexander, C.E., Longwood.
Tate, Miss A. H., Longwood.
Tate, Prof. Ralph, F.G.S., F.L.S., Adelaide, South Australia (Hon. Mem.)

Taylor, Ernest E., Melrose Terrace.
Thomas, S. G., Limestone Road.
Todd, John, Clonaven.
Thompson, Miss S. M., Macedon.
Thompson, Mrs. Henry, Crosshill, Windsor.
Thomson, George, Broadway Factory
Todd, W. A., Elgin Terrace.
Trelford, W. J., 23 Lincoln Avenue
Turner, James, Mountain Bush.
Turtle, Jas. C., Cambridge Terrace.

Vinycomb, John, F R.S.A , Holywood.

Waddell, Rev. C. Herbert, M.A., The Rectory, Saintfield.
Wakeman, W. F., M.R.I.A., Dublin (Cor. Mem.).
Walker, Thomas R., Rugby Road.
Walkington, Thos. R., Edenvale.
Ward, George G., Eversleigh, Strandtown.
Ward, Isaac W., Salisbury Terrace.
Wardell, Miss, Cavehill Road.
Watson, Thomas, Shipquay Gate, Londonderry.

Watts, Charles W., F.I.C., Holborn Terrace.
Waugh, Isaac, Clifton Park Avenue.
Welch, Robert J., Lonsdale Street.
White, Benoni, Royal Ulster Works.
Whitla, Prof., M.D., J.P., College Square North.
Wilson, James, Oldforge, Dunmurry.
Wilson, Jas., Ballybundon, Killinchy
Wilson, Alexander G., Strandmillis.
Wilson, Walter H., Strandmillis.
Wise, Berkley D., C.E., Waterside, Greenisland.
Workman, Rev. Robert, M.A., Rubane, Glastry.
Workman, Thomas, J.P., Craigdarragh.
Wright, Joseph, F.G.S., Alfred Street.
Wright, Mrs., Alfred Street.
Wright, W. C., Lauriston, Derrievolgie Avenue.
Wylie, William, Mountpleasant.

Young, Robert, C.E., Rathvarna.

ANNUAL REPORT AND PROCEEDINGS

OF THE

BELFAST

NATURALISTS'

FIELD CLUB

For the Year ending the 31st March, 1893.

(THIRTIETH YEAR.)

SERIES II.

VOLUME III.

PART VI.

1892-93.

Belfast:

PRINTED FOR THE CLUB
BY ALEXANDER MAYNE & BOYD, 2 CORPORATION STREET,
PRINTERS TO QUEEN'S COLLEGE, BELFAST.

1893.

REPORT.

The Committee of the Belfast Naturalists' Field Club have pleasure in laying before the Society their thirtieth Annual Report, which records its continued success, and an increase both of the membership, and of the work done under the Club's auspices. The membership, which last year stood at 323, being the largest ever attained since the foundation of the Society, now numbers 404, 92 new members having been elected during the year which has just closed, while 11 names have to be struck off the list owing to death or resignation.

The summer programme was the most extensive ever held in the history of the Club, embracing as it did one three-day excursion, one two-day excursion, five whole-day excursions, and two half-day excursions. The summer work also included an investigation of the gravel-beds at Ballyrudder, Co. Antrim, when members were given an opportunity for examining these interesting deposits. The only excursion on the programme which was not carried out was a half-day trip to Cave Hill, for which was substituted the whole day Gobbins excursion, which could not be held on the appointed date owing to severity of weather. The localities visited and dates of the excursions were as follow :—

1. White Park Bay	...	...	...	May 21st.
2. Gobbins	...	...	...	June 18th.
3. Mourne Mountains	...	...	...	June 24th & 25th.
4. Lough Erne, Bundoran, and Sligo		...		July 11th, 12th, & 13th.
5. Benevenagh ...	...	...	...	July 30th.
6. Drumbo and Giant's Ring		...	...	August 13th.
7. Lagan Canal	...	...	...	August 27th.
8. Knockagh ...	...	...	...	September 10th.
9. Ardglass	...	...	...	September 17th.

The attendance of members and visitors at these excursions was large, the average attendance being 54, the largest being 120 at Lagan Canal, the smallest 11 at Mourne Mountains. The excursion to the Sligo district, when a party of 50 members spent three days of perfect summer weather in exploring the natural beauties and the fauna, flora, and antiquities of Lower

Lough Erne, Bundoran, Ben Bulben, Sligo, and Lough Gill, was voted by those present to have excelled in interest any excursion previously held under the Club's auspices; while the few members who took part in the two-day mountain-climbing trip to the Mourne Mountains brought back with them, in addition to many geological and natural history specimens of interest and rarity, a knowledge of the more inaccessible part of the Mourne Range, and of the magnificent mountain scenery that it affords—a district which is not half as well known to, or appreciated by our naturalists and artists as it merits. In connection with the summer excursions, the best thanks of your Committee are due to a number of gentlemen for kind assistance rendered: to Thomas Plunkett, M.R.I.A., and several other local gentlemen, for much assistance in connection with the arrangements for the Sligo excursion; to Sir Frederick Heygate, Bart., for permission to enter his beautiful grounds at Benevenagh; and to the Directors of the Lagan Navigation Company, for placing at the disposal of the Club their flotilla of boats, and otherwise assisting the party, on the occasion of the Lagan Canal excursion.

A resolution having been passed at one of the Winter Meetings last session appointing a sub-committee to investigate and report on the Glacial gravels of Ballyrudder, Co. Antrim, with special reference to the suggested occurrence in them of worked flints; this investigation was carried out early in the month of July, and the report of the sub-committee will be found in full in the Proceedings for the year now completed, which will shortly be in the hands of members.

The Winter Session was opened with a Social Meeting in the Exhibition Hall, Botanic Avenue, on October 28th. On the occasion of the last Social Meeting the accommodation at the Belfast Museum proved, for the first time in the history of the Club, inadequate for the company who assembled, and the engagement of more commodious premises on the present occasion was fully justified, as the fine hall at the Botanic Gardens was filled to overflowing, the attendance numbering close upon 600 members and visitors. The dates of the winter business meetings, and the subjects brought forward, are as follow :—

22nd Nov.   1. Presidential Address.
              2. Report of the Sub-Committee appointed to investigate the Glacial gravels of Ballyrudder, County Antrim.—R. Lloyd Praeger, M.R.I.A., hon. secretary.
              3. Report of the Club's Delegate to the Meeting of the British Association, 1892.—William Gray, M.R.I.A., delegate.
              4. " Rare Foraminifera obtained on the Club's last Dredging Excursion." —Joseph Wright, F.G.S.
20th Dec.   1. " Notes on New Zealand Geology."—Edward M'Connell (communicated).
              2. " Denudation at Cultra, County Down."—Miss Mary K. Andrews (communicated).
              3. Local Botanical Notes, 1891 and 1892.—R. Lloyd Praeger, M.R.I.A., hon. secretary.
17th Jan.   1. " The Aran Islands : a Study in Irish Ethnography."—Prof. Alfred C. Haddon, M.A., M.R.I.A.
21st Feb.   1. " Some Local Folk-Lore."—Francis Joseph Bigger, hon. secretary.
              2. " Worked Flints, Ancient and Modern."—William Gray, M.R.I.A.
21st March   Microscopical Evening.
11th April   Irish Folk-Lore.
              1. " Pishogues from Tipperary."—Miss Lily S. Mollan (communicated).
              2. " A Notice of Irish Fairies."—W. H. Patterson, M.R.I.A.
              3. " Notes from County Down."—Mrs. Blair (communicated).
26th April   Annual Meeting.

The average attendance at the winter meetings was 101, the largest being 300 at Professor Haddon's lecture on January 17th, the smallest 60 at December meeting. On January 18th, Professor Haddon kindly continued his lecture on Irish Ethnography, and explained the steps now being taken by the British Association for the carrying out of an ethnographical survey of the United Kingdom. A local committee, of which W. H. Patterson, M.R.I.A., was elected secretary, was appointed to carry out the work in Ulster, under direction of the central committee in Dublin, and your Committee trust that all members and others willing to assist the work of this committee by studying or collecting local folk-lore, physical measurements, language, or antiquities will communicate with Mr. Patterson ; the work offers a field of wide and varied interest, and is of very high scientific importance.

In order to increase the social usefulness of the Club, and for the convenience of members residing at a distance, your Committee have during the Winter Session, with the valuable assistance of two lady members, Mrs. Coulter and Mrs. Leslie, provided tea before each meeting at the Museum, the moderate charge of sixpence being made in order to meet expenses. This institution has proved a decided success, to judge from the number of members who have availed themselves of it, and the Committee place considerable importance on the opportunity thus afforded to members for the exchange of views on matters in which they are interested, and the examination of specimens, and answering of enquiries on scientific points.

The Microscopical Section continues its labours, but its operations during the present session have been considerably hampered owing to a vacancy in the post of secretary, Mr. H. M'Cleery having reluctantly been compelled to resign owing to a press of other engagements. No member has as yet accepted the duties of secretary to this section of the Club.

The Photographic Committee continues to receive valuable instalments of antiquarian and geological photographs from members; these are being properly classified and mounted in suitable albums, and already form a collection of high interest, nnmbering over 200 views. It is hoped that members will continue to carry on this very important branch of the Club's work, and will favour the secretaries with platinotype prints of any photographs of objects of antiquarian, biological, or geological interest that they may have an opportunity of securing.

The following are the reports of the judges appointed by your Committee to examine the collections sent in by members in competition for the Club's and special prizes :—

" Prize II. In competition for this prize Miss Jeanie Rea has sent in a collection amounting to 152 plants. These are well-selected, characteristic specimens, mounted and displayed in the very best manner. They are correctly named, and localities stated, as required, and we have much pleasure in adjudging the prize in question to Miss Rea.

Prize XVI. For this competition W. D. Donnan sent in a very large collection of Coleoptera. The specimens forming this collection are excellent. They are mounted in the most approved manner, and properly named and localised. They represent much scientific work in this difficult group, and well deserve the prize which we now award to Mr. Donnan.

Prizes XX. and XXI. There are two collections of micro-slides by ladies, both are of superior merit. Miss S. M. Thompson, of Macedon, submits a varied collection ; and Miss Patterson, of Holywood, a very excellent series of chick embryo sections. Both are very well prepared and mounted, displaying no small amount of practical skill. Miss Thompson's collection is a very considerable advance upon former efforts, and merits the highest commendation. It is difficult to distin-guish between the relative merits of the two collections. For-tunately it is not necessary to place them in the order of merit, as the collections were submitted for different prizes, and we award Prize XX. to Miss Patterson, and Prize XXI. to Miss Thompson."

(Signed)　　S. A. STEWART.
WILLIAM GRAY.

Prize XVIII. In competition for this prize, for best collection of Fungi, Rev. H. W. Lett, M.A., reports that two series have been submitted to him by members in accordance with the conditions. That of Miss Boyd numbered 46 species, that of Mr. J. J. Andrew 54 species. Your Committee do not consider either collection sufficiently extensive to merit the prize, but trust that the members named will continue their mycological studies during the coming year with better results.

Under the superintendence of P. J. O'Shea, a new member of the Club, a class has been started for the study of the Irish language. Twenty members have joined the class, and at the first meeting there was an attendance of 14. It is hoped this new effort will be successful in promoting an interest in our native tongue, and also, in a secondary sense, in increasing our general membership.

In conclusion, your Committee would again return thanks to the public bodies and kindred societies who have favoured them with their publications during the past year.

R. LLOYD PRAEGER,　⎱
FRANCIS JOSEPH BIGGER,　⎰ Hon. Secretaries.

Dr. TREASURER IN ACCOUNT WITH THE BELFAST NATURALISTS' FIELD CLUB **Cr.**

FOR THE YEAR ENDING 31ST MARCH, 1893.

Dr.	£	s	d
To Balance from last Account ...	£12	10	2
,, Subscriptions ...	93	5	0
,, Tickets for Social Meeting ...	18	12	0
,, Tickets, Professor Haddon's Lecture ...	0	14	6
,, Profit on Teas ...	1	9	0
,, Sales of Guide ...	0	8	3
,, ,, Proceedings ...	0	3	0
,, ,, Flora ...	0	8	5
	£127	10	4

Cr.		£	s	d
By Expenses of Social Meeting ...		£31	15	
,, Printing Proceedings ...		16	17	
,, Stationery, Printing, and Advertising ...		27	12	
,, Meteorological Report ...		1	0	
,, Expenses, Professor Haddon's Lecture ...		1	0	
,, Rent of Museum ...		6	6	
,, Commission to Collector ...		4	15	
,, Expenses of Micro. Section ...		2	5	
,, Investigation at Ballyrudder ...		4	9	
,, General Expenses, viz.:—				
Postages ...	£8 0 3			
Insurance ...	0 17 6			
Incidentals ...	1 15 11	22	2	
,, Prizes ...		2	0	
,, Balance ...		18	15	
		£127	1	

Audited and found correct,   S. A. STEWART.

PROCEEDINGS.

---◆---

SUMMER SESSION.

---◆---

WHITE PARK BAY.

The first excursion was held on Saturday, May 21st, White Park Bay, on the north coast of Antrim, being the place visited. A party of some five-and-thirty members assembled at the terminus of the Northern Counties Railway in time to start by the 8.15 train for Ballymoney. Arrived there, the narrow-guage railway was taken, and, proceeding at lower speed through a fertile country, interspersed with extensive peat bogs, a steep descent along the picturesque slopes of Knocklayd brought the party to the little town of Ballycastle. There wagonettes were in readiness, and no time was lost in getting under weigh, and the inland road to Bushmills was taken. The road rises steadily for several miles, and presently beautiful views opened out of Ballycastle nestling among trees, with the huge dome of Knocklayd rising behind ; and further off, the majestic front of Benmore or Fair Head impending over the sea, with the blue mountains of Cantire beyond. Turning northward now, the road ran through low heathery hills, blazing with gorse, and a sharp descent brought the party to White Park Bay, a broad sweep of white shining sand, backed by low Chalk cliffs, and shut in at one end by the black basaltic precipice of Bengore Head, and on the other by the fantastic rock-masses which fringe the shore near Ballintoy. The party were not slow in dismounting, and in making their descent over slopes and swards covered with bluebells and primroses to the strand, where the green foam-capped breakers were roaring in under the influence of a brisk northerly wind. The secretaries had announced that prizes would be given for the best collections respectively of shells and of antiquarian specimens, and the members hastened to scatter themselves over the sand in the search for objects of interest. White Park Bay is well known to archæologists for the abundant pre-historic objects which it yields, and which show that it was an important settlement of the early races. The remains consist chiefly of rude flint implements, bones, fragments of pottery, and ashes ; and occur in certain definite layers which represent the ancient land surface, though now often buried below many feet of blown sand. The constant shifting of the sand, under the influence of the wind, exposes the old surface, and thus these traces of former habitation are found on the surface, as was amply testified on the present occasion. The shell collectors had comparatively poor fortune. On the sand great quantities of three species of snails (*H. aspersa*, *H. nemoralis*, *H. virgata*) were found, and a limited supply of a number of other species ; but the strand was almost devoid of marine shells, contrary to general expectation. The extreme lateness of the season told against the botanists, but they noted the great abundance of the beautiful meadow cranesbill, locally designated the Flower of Dunluce (*Geranium pratense*), and also the wood vetch (*Vicia sylvatica*), but neither was yet in blossom. On the road from Ballycastle they had found the three-nerved sandwort (*Arenaria trinervia*) and the mare's-tail (*Hippuris vulgaris*), and later in the day, on the rocks at the east end of the bay, the senior secretary pointed out the sea-beet (*Beta maritima*), still growing in a spot where he had found it some years ago. Beetle-hunting and seaweed-collecting meanwhile engaged the attention of other members of the party. The best beetles found were *Broscus cephalotes* at Ballintoy ; and *Calathus fuscus*, *Bradycellus verbasci*, *Philonthus laurinatus, P. succula, Ægialia arenaria, Otiorrhynchus atroapterus, O. ligneus*, and *Philopedon gemminatus* at White Park Bay. An interesting find of another kind was the nest, or rather the eggs, of the ringed plover (*Ægialitis hiaticula*), four pale brown eggs, specked with black, laid in a slight hollow on the bare sand. The party was now joined by

Father Malcahy, P.P., and by Mr. Dickson, one of the local
gentry, and by several members who had come to Ballycastle
overnight, and had had a busy forenoon's photographing of the
choicest bits of scenery of this lovely spot. Passing below cliffs
of white Chalk, the curious arched rocks at the east end of the
bay were visited, and a return made to Ballintoy, where the
machines were in waiting, and brought the party by the
picturesque but very hilly old road back to Ballycastle, where
an excellent tea was ready, supplied by Mr. Hunter, and to
which the members did full justice. At the conclusion of the
repast, the President of the Club (Mr. John Vinycomb, F.R.S.A.)
congratulated the members on having had their usual good
fortune in regard to weather. He appointed Mr. William Gray,
M.R.I.A., judge of the archæological collections, and Mr. R.
Lloyd Praeger, M.R.I.A., judge for the shell prize. He referred
in suitable terms to the recent death of Professor James
Thompson, of Glasgow, an ex-President of the Club.

Mr. William Gray moved, and Mr. J. J. Andrew seconded, a
resolution of sympathy with the relatives of Professor Thompson, which was carried in silence. The election of new members was then proceeded with, and the following ladies and
gentlemen were declared duly elected :—Miss Gamble, Mrs.
Logan, Mrs. M'Coll, Miss M'Coll, Messrs. J. Dunville Coates,
Jas. Maxton, M.I.M.E., R. S. M'Dade.

The judging of the collections then took place. Mr. F. J.
Bigger carried off the archæology prize, his collection including
some large fragments of a cinerary urn and a number of bones
and flint implements. The shell prize fell to Mrs. Leslie ; a
second prize was awarded to Miss Turtle, a juvenile member of
the party, who was a good second. Road was then taken for the
railway station, and Belfast was reached at nine o'clock.

THE GOBBINS AND ISLANDMAGEE.

The second summer excursion was held on Saturday, June

18th, the Gobbins and Islandmagee being the locality visited. A party of nearly fifty members and friends assembled at the Northern Counties terminus in time to start for Ballycarry by the 9.25 train. Arrived there, cars were mounted, and a pleasant drive through a fertile country was followed by a walk along a rough country lane, which brought the party to the summit of a grassy hill, where a beautiful prospect opened out. Below lay the sea, stirred by a brisk northerly breeze, and chafing on a picturesque shore, strewn with blocks of chalk and basalt. Southward stretched the low shores of County Down and the Copeland Isles ; further eastward, seen dimly through summer haze, the hills of the Isle of Man. Right opposite lay the Mull of Galloway and the Ayrshire coast ; then Ailsa Craig, towering high out of the water ; and further northward the mountains of Arran and Cantire.

Before the party made the steep descent to the sea, the secretaries announced that a prize would be given for the best collection of flowering plants made during the day. Baskets, handkerchiefs, and umbrellas were promptly converted into botanical collecting cases, and a vigorous search for wild flowers began, the ladies of the party being conspicuous by their energy and perseverance in the search for rarities. While the majority of the party spent an hour in exploring the steep slopes and rocky sea-shore, a section started southward, and visited the outcrop of Chalk and Greensand which occurs on the coast at that point. A few fossils were obtained, and also some photographs of geological subjects, which will go presently to enrich the Club's photographic collection.

When the party had reunited, a start was made northward, along the summit of the cliffs towards Port Muck. The rocks and banks were gay with wild flowers, among which the bladder campion, milkwort, seapink, lady's fingers, and burnet rose were conspicuous. The botanists noticed the great abundance of Venus' comb (*Scandix pecten-veneris*) in the cultivated fields, and the pretty wood vetch (*Vicia sylvatica*) festooning the rocks. The steep cliffs, which descend sheer into the water for

several hundred feet, were tenanted by large colonies of herring
gulls, all now busy administering to the wants of their young,
which could be seen perched on the ledges of the cliffs, like little
balls of brown and grey down.

Presently a fine peregrine falcon, darting with a shriek from
the cliffs, betrayed the whereabouts of its eyrie, which was
detected securely placed beneath an overhanging ledge of rock,
and further search discovered two of the young falcons, now
nearly fledged, perched on a grassy ledge further down the cliff.

The wreck of the luckless s.s. Black Diamond was next
passed, her bows wedged among the rocks at the base of the
cliff, with the foremast still standing, and her sunken hull
plainly visible through the clear blue water.

Still wending their way northward, the party passed along a
less precipitous coast, where the great willow-herb (*Epilobium
angustifolium*) was observed growing on a steep slope, an addition to the flora of the Gobbins. The photographers meanwhile tried their skill in securing photographs of the nest of a
lark and a meadow pipit—the first built among the short grass
on the summit of a cliff, the second in a recess in a grassy bank.

Presently Port Muck, with its shelving beach, ancient castle,
and whitewashed coastguard station, was reached, and the party
was charmed with the extreme picturesqueness of the spot, and
the rocky islet that rose out of the water to the eastward. No
time could be spared to secure sketches or photographs here,
though several hours might have been so spent with advantage,
and the shortest way was taken for Larne. Surmounting a
high hill, new beauties opened out to the northward, where
stretched the Antrim Coast—Ballygalley Head, Garron Point,
and Runabay Head standing out in bold succession, with
heathery hills rising behind them. The road now dropped
down into Brown's Bay, where the well-known rocking-stone
was seen at the eastern end, but time did not permit of a visit.
The flower collectors picked up the fool's parsley (*Æthusa
cynapium*), greater celandine (*Chelidonium majus*), and black
horehound (*Ballota fœtida*) on roadsides as they passed along.

A walk along the firm sands of Ferris' Bay brought the party to the ferry, and they were quickly transported across the deep and narrow entrance of the lough to Larne Harbour, where wagonettes were in waiting, and a few minutes later the party was busy discussing an excellent tea at the King's Arms Hotel.

A hurried business meeting was held, the chair being taken by Mr. William Gray, M.R.I.A., in the absence of the President, and Messrs. John M'Kee, George M'Lean, and S. M. Reid were elected members of the Club. Those of the party who wished to catch the early train to Belfast were then driven to the railway station, and returned to town by the 6.5 train, while a large section elected to remain in Larne for a couple of hours longer. The judging of the collections of flowers made during the day was undertaken by Mr. S. A. Stewart, F.B.S.E. Six collections were submitted in competition, and when they had been examined, the secretaries announced the result as follows :—Miss Rea, 111 species ; Mrs. Wise, 88 ; Mrs. Ferguson, 69 ; Mrs. Blair, 50 ; Mrs. Greer, 49 ; Mr. M'Lean, 40. Miss Rea was therefore declared the winner, amid applause.

The party then scattered for a stroll around the environs of Larne, and returned to Belfast by the 8.20 train.

THE MOURNE MOUNTAINS.

On Friday and Saturday, June 24th and 25th, a special mountain-climbing excursion to the Mourne Mountains took place. The Field Club party assembled at the County Down Railway at 7.30, in time to take the first train for Newcastle, under the leadership of their senior secretary. Belfast was left in a torrent of rain, but pocket aneroids showed but an inappreciable depression, so the spirits of the naturalists were by no means damped ; and fortune indeed favoured them, for, while heavy rain fell in the city during a great portion of the day, among the mountains the weather was magnificent. The time occupied by the railway journey was turned to good account.

Maps were exhibited of the Mourne district, showing the route to be traversed by the party. Geological maps were also produced, and the construction and age of the mountains discussed, and the relation of the Mourne Mountain granites to the dolerites, syenites, and porphyries of the Carlingford hills and the granites of the adjoining highlands of Slieve Croob. Specimens of some of the rarer plants of the district were passed round also, that they might be the more easily recognised if met with by any of the party. Newcastle was reached at 9.20, and here a view of the mountains was obtained which alone would have been a recompense for the journey. Slieve Donard towered up, its lofty summit swathed in great broken patches of snow-white vapour. Below all was clear, but half way down, encircling the huge mountain as with a girdle, was a narrow horizontal belt of grey cloud, stretching far out over the sea on the one hand, and on the other merging into the masses of dazzling cloud which were rolling over the inland mountains. Breakfast next occupied the attention of the party, and, after an excellent meal at Mr. Lawrence's comfortable rooms, the party drove off rapidly. The pretty village of Bryansford was soon passed, and then the road skirted the rich woods of Tollymore Park. Rising above them, grand views of the mountains opened out, and now the destination of the party—Slieve Bearnagh— became visible, rising steeply at the head of the deep valley of the Trassey Burn, and crowned with huge masses of bare rugged granite. At Trassey Bridge the coach halted, and the day's work began ; and, taking with them only such *impedimenta* as were required in the pursuit of their scientific bents and for the preservation of specimens, the party proceeded up a rough turf road which led up the valley and into the mountains. On one side rose Slieve-na-Glough, on the other towered Slieve Meelmore, its eastern shoulder terminating in a huge cliff called the Spellick, which overhangs the glen. A steep ascent now brought the party to the Hare's Gap, where an entomologist pointed out that the granite boulders were dotted over with a pretty little moth (*Eupithecia pumilata*), which so closely resembled the colour of the rocks as to be almost indiscernible except to the experienced eye. A short climb along the southern slope of Slieve-na-Glough brought the party to the Diamond Rocks, where the geologists, who were well represented, were entirely in their element. The granite at this place is full of cavities, often several inches in diameter, which by infiltration during the gradual cooling of the molten rock-mass, and by slow crystallisation, have become lined with beautiful crystals of smoky quartz, felspar, mica, and, more rarely, topaz, beryl, and other precious stones. This remote place was now in possession of several quarrymen, who had tramped across the mountains with their tools from Annalong in the early morning to make things ready for the Visit of the Field Club, and had by this time a number of holes bored in the hard rock. The secretary's harmless-looking botanical case turned out to be full of blasting powder and fuse, with which the holes were charged, and when the party had retired to a safe distance they were fired off, producing fine echoes among the surrounding mountains. Sledges and smaller hammers were then brought to bear on the spoil, and a number of excellent specimens of the various minerals were obtained, the brown and black hexagonal pyramids of the quartz crystals being especially admired. A return was then made down the mountain to the Hare's Gap, and the ascent of Slieve Bearnagh—the *piece de resistance* of the day—commenced. The botanists now came to the front, and announced the discovery of a rare and minute orchid, the lesser twayblade (*Listera cordata*). The juniper (*Juniperus nana*) was observed in some quantity, and near the summit of the mountain abundance of the alpine club-moss (*Lycopodium alpinum*) and its congener, the fir club-moss (*L. selago*). After a stiff climb the summit of the mountain (2,394 feet) was reached, and the whole party, ladies included, scrambled up to the top of the huge masses of weather-worn granite that crown the highest peak, to gaze on the magnificent panorama of mountain, sea, and plain that opened out on every hand. To the westward stretched a sea of mountains, ridge on ridge, to where rose Slieve Gullion in

Armagh, and Carlingford Mountain in Louth. Eastward towered the higher peaks of the Mourne range, with the huge cone of Slieve Donard dominating them all. Southward the broad blue expanse of the Irish Sea, and the low shores of Louth and Meath. Northward the whole fertile plain of County Down, with the Antrim hills and Lough Neagh, behind which lay the dim hills of Londonderry and Tyrone. Luncheon next engaged the attention of the members, and a regal banquet was made of sandwiches, washed down by draughts of cool water from rock-pools in the granite. The botanists noted, flourishing among the topmost crags, the dwarf willow (*Salix herbacea*), crowberry (*Empetrum nigrum*), and cowberry (*Vaccinium vitis-idæa*), the last named having its pretty pink bells in full blossom. Then, after taking another look at the magnificent and varied prospect, the descent of the western face of the mountain was effected, and, traversing a very steep decline of a thousand feet, the saddle between Bearnagh and Meelmore was crossed, a pause being made to note the great ice-worn slopes of bare granite which characterise the western base of Slieve Bearnagh. Another steep climb was next undertaken, which brought the party to a spot near the summit of Slieve Meelmore, where there is an interesting vein of amethyst, undescribed in the memoirs of the Geological Survey, and known only to a few local geologists. With the aid of hammers, good examples of the bright purple mineral were secured, and the party then pushed on along the rough, boulder-strewn side of Slieve Meelbeg, till Lough Shannagh came full in view, embosomed in brown heather, and backed by steep hills. After a pause here to rest and to admire the splendid mountain view, way was made for the gap north of Carn Mountain, for the afternoon was flying fast, and the lengthening shadows and thoughts of dinner both inspired the members to renewed exertions. On the boggy flat behind Ott Mountain the lesser twayblade was again observed in quantity. A descent was then made into the Deer's Meadow, down the edge of the Bann River, here a mere trickling streamlet. On the mountain road the coach was waiting at the place appointed, and a rapid and most enjoyable drive past the cliffs of Pigeon Rock and the rugged slopes of Slieve Muck, and away down the southern slopes of the mountains, brought the party to Kilkeel at eight o'clock, where they were hospitably received at the Kilmorey Arms Hotel. An evening stroll down to the harbour brought to a close a highly successful and enjoyable day, and resulted in some additions to the botanists' collections, and the capture of two somewhat rare moths—*Acidalia margine-punctata* and *Eupithecia constrictata*. Another rarity, *Mixodia Schulziana*, had been captured on the mountains earlier in the day ; and of beetles, *Carabus catenulatus* was taken at Hare's Gap, and *C. arvensis* near the summit of Slieve Bearnagh.

Next morning a number of the members turned out at 6.30 for a bathe, and at eight o'clock all were assembled at breakfast. The early morning was beautifully fine, but the sky rapidly clouded over, and ere a start was made at nine o'clock it was raining. However, the barometer had fallen but little, so, hoping for the best and prepared as far as possible for the worst, the party started for Slieve Bingian. A five-mile drive brought them to Colligan Bridge, at the foot of the mountain. The wind and rain had steadily increased, and the hills were completely enshrouded in driving mist, and the prospect was as bleak and cheerless as possible. A council of war was held, at which it was decided to send the coach on to Newcastle with those of the party who did not care to face a bad day among the mountains, it being arranged that they should ascend the valley of the Annalong River and meet the rest of the party, should the weather clear in time. Only three volunteers were found for the mountain walk, who started off into the rain and mist, while the rest turned and drove towards Newcastle. The mountaineers traversed a rough turf road for some distance, and then, crossing a high bank of gravel and sand—the terminal moraine of the glacier that once filled the glen—found themselves in the Happy Valley, the most beautiful of the mountain glens of the district. Before them stretched a narrow, level, alluvial tract, extending into the mountains for several miles. On the right Slieve Bingian rose two thousand feet in one steep slope, its summit buried in mist. On the left the cliffs of Slieve-na-glogh could be seen now and then through a rift in the clouds, and straight in front Bencrom, wreathed in cloud, reared its rugged form at the head of the valley. Walking here was easy, for the wind was blowing right up the glen, but the rain still increased, and now came down in torrents. But naturalists are generally philosophically inclined, so a halt was made at some pools under Slieve Bingian, where several rare plants were known to grow, and specimens were leisurely secured of the long-leaved sundew (*Drosera intermedia*), water lobelia (*Lobelia Dortmanna*), and *Rhynchospora alba*. The party then pushed on up the glen till opposite the cliffs of Bencrom, where they turned to the right up the slope, and a steep climb brought them to the gap between Slieve Lamagan and Slieve Bingian. On the ascent some butterflies were obtained in spite of the storm, three species of Eupithecia —*E. pumilata*, *E. minutata*, and *E. satyrata* var. *callunaria*— and the larva of *Oparabia filigrammaria*. Some large specimens of felspar were also obtained. The weather had become still worse, and it was now blowing a gale, with torrents of rain, and so thick that it was impossible to see more than twenty yards ahead, so the majority of the party decided to push down the valley to Annalong, the secretary alone expressing his intention of carrying out the programme by ascending Slieve Bingian, remarking that it would be impossible to get any wetter. So two members started down the slope for the valley, while the third turned southward up the mountain. A climb up a boulder-strewn slope brought him to the summit of the cliffs which overlook the Blue Lough, and here the lesser twayblade was found growing in luxuriance. Battling on against the storm and rain, the northern peak of the mountain was reached, where the dwarf willow was growing in great quantity in the fissures of the crags of granite. A steep climb of half a mile more and the summit was attained. Here the full force of the gale made itself felt, and when a gust came roaring up the slope it was necessary to cling to the granite rocks for support, while the rain stung as if charged with gravel or sand. Under the shelter of the huge crags that form the highest point of the mountain (2,449 feet) there was comparative shelter, but the roar of the wind and rain was such that a shout could not have been heard a few yards away. Here again grew the dwarf willow and the cowberry and crowberry. The descent of the mountain was more difficult than the ascent, for the mist was so thick as to obscure everything beyond a few yards' distance, and care had to be taken to avoid several dangerous cliff-ranges in the vicinity ; but, steering by compass, Lough Bingian was soon passed, and a steep descent by the side of a roaring torrent brought the solitary representative of the Field Club into a calmer atmosphere below the cliffs. Here he fell in with one of the greatest botanical rarities of the Mourne Mountains—the parsley fern (*Cryptogramme crispa*), growing in a sheltered nook, where he had observed it just ten years ago. A short visit was then paid to the Blue Lough, and the water lobelia and curious quill-wort (*Isoetes lacustris*) were found in quantity, washed ashore by the force of the storm. A rapid descent of the valley was then made, and the eleven miles to Newcastle were covered in good time ; and as Newcastle was approached the clouds broke, and the sun shone out gloriously, giving beautiful effects of light and shade on the mountains. Presently the whole party was reunited, none the worse for their thorough soaking, and a pleasant afternoon was spent in the woods of Donard Lodge. A number of mountain plants were collected, and, among lepidoptera, the bordered white moth (*Bupalus piniarius*) was observed in large numbers among the fir trees. One specimen was obtained of the rare *Scodionia Belgiaria*, which is the second record for this species in our district ; and the barred red, *Ellopia fasciaria*, was also found. Some beetles were also obtained, of which the best were *Dascillus cervinus*, *Telephorus pellucidus*, and *Rhagium inquisitor*. A final hour was devoted to the sandhills, which yielded a large number of local maritime plants, and then the party returned to the railway refreshment rooms, where a sumptuous tea was provided by Mr. Lawrence.   Subsequently a short meeting was held, at which a little formal business was transacted, and Dr. J. St. Clair Boyd elected a member of the Club, after which the evening express brought the members quickly back to town, well pleased with their trip, which, in spite of the rain of the second day, was voted to have been highly successful and enjoyable.

LOUGH ERNE AND SLIGO.

The annual long excursion took place on Monday, Tuesday, and Wednesday, July 11th, 12th, and 13th, when a party of fifty members spent three delightful days in exploring Lough Erne, Bundoran, Ben Bulben, Sligo, and Lough Gill.

The Field Club party left Belfast at 8 o'clock on Monday morning, in a carriage specially reserved for the party, and which, by the arrangements of the obliging manager of the Great Northern Railway, accompanied them throughout their various railway journeys both going and returning.   Enniskillen was reached at 11-45, where the party was met by Mr. Thomas Plunkett, M R.I.A., chairman Enniskillen Town Commissioners, and Mr. Humphreys, manager of the Sligo and Leitrim Railway.   No time was lost in dismounting, and a half-mile walk through the neat streets of the thriving island town, crowded with country folk who were busily engaged in the many duties pertaining to a monthly fair day, brought the Belfast visitors to the river bank, where the steamer "Belturbet" lay in readiness, and in a few minutes her shrill whistle sounded a farewell to Enniskillen as she glided out on the broad, calm river, past the loop-holed barrack-walls, and left behind the ancient four-turretted castle-gateway of the Maguires, and the tall spire of the parish church, and the lofty column of Cole's monument on the Fort Hill.   The wooded narrows of Portora

were soon passed, with Portora castle frowning in picturesque
decay at their entrance. Next, Devenish Island came in
view, surmounted by its interesting abbey ruins, behind which
rose the lofty form of the finest round tower in Ireland.
This spot, celebrated in archæological literature, was fully
inspected by the Club on their Visit to Lough Erne last year,
so no halt was now made, and the steamer sped onwards among
the thickly-wooded islands around Ely Lodge. The secretaries
pointed out on one of the islands, the site of their camp, beneath
a group of tall Scotch firs close to the lake shore, where the
arrangements for the present expedition had been made a
fortnight before.

Inishmacsaint next appeared in View, with its ancient church
and cross, and then, when the fine ruin of Tully Castle was
passed, the broad expanse of the lower portion of the lake
opened out. The course lay close along the southern shore,
where limestone hills lowered over the lake in long cliff-ranges
to a height of over a thousand feet, while on the distant
northern shore the low Feimanagh meadows were backed by
the dim blue hills of Donegal. Gradually the lake narrowed
again, till it once more assumed a river-like aspect, and at
length the steamer's shrill whistle warned the peaceful
inhabitants of Belleek to prepare for an invasion of the
Northerners. Regret was expressed that time did not permit
of a Visit to the celebrated pottery, but the train had
already waited for the party fifteen minutes beyond its usual
time. A glimpse was obtained of the river Erne, foaming amid
rocks on its rapid descent to the sea, and soon Ballyshannon
was passed, and the sandhills of Bundoran rose into View ; and
a short walk through the whitewashed village street brought
the party to Sweeny's Hotel, where dinner was served in excellent style. This important part of the day's work completed,
the party started off to explore the neighbourhood. The tide
was unfortunately just full, and the strand and rockpools consequently covered, which prevented search being made for the
interesting sea-urchin *Echinus lividus*, or the extremely rare

shell *Trochus Duminyi;* but as regards the former, scientific enterprise triumphed over natural difficulties, as will appear subsequently. The members therefore strolled along the headlands in the direction of the extensive sand-dunes that stretch northward to the mouth of the Erne. The Carboniferous Limestone of which the rocks are composed, teeming with many species of fossils, offered irresistible attractions to the geologists, who were soon busy with hammer and chisel extracting encrinites, corals, and brachiopods, and it is to be feared that the loose stone walls of the enterprising Bundoran Beach Committee were not altogether safe from the ravages of the scientists. Arrived at the sandhills, the party scattered, the various members indulging in their favourite pursuits. They presently met again at tea, when notes were compared. The botanists reported a very poor flora on the sandhills, *Euphorbia portlandica* being the only noteworthy plant collected. The entomologists likewise had poor luck, but obtained *Melanippe galiata, Plutilla annulatella,* and some good species of microlepidoptera, and a few beetles. Another member secured a quantity of flood-rubbish near the mouth of the Erne, very rich in small land-shells, and reported having observed a flock of a dozen fine Sheldrake (*Tadorna cornuta*) swimming inside the bar ; the marine shells collected offered nothing of special interest. An ornithologist of the party exhibited a specimen in the flesh of the Storm Petrel, which had been cast up dead on the shore the day before. Tea was served at nine o'clock, and shortly after ten an enterprising member of the party proposed that a search should now be made for the *Echinus lividus,* which is so characteristic of the Bundoran rockpools, as the tide would by this time be low. The idea was warmly taken up, and a party of a dozen of the younger members started off for the shore, armed with a supply of candles. They safely reached the base of the cliffs south of the village, and with the aid of lights the sea-urchins was found lining the pretty rockpools in profusion, and a large number of excellent specimens were obtained, as well as examples of the local shell *Trochus lineatus.* Meanwhile others of the party had discovered an extensive sea-cave which they explored, occasionally drawing forth the echoes of the vaulted cavern with wild whoops—it is to be hoped that no solitary wayfarer of a superstitious turn of mind, wending his way home towards midnight, saw the mysterious dancing lights on the water's edge, or heard the muffled shrieks that disturbed the calm night air.

The party was early astir next morning, and while a large section of the male members had a pleasant bathe in the strong Atlantic water, others found in sketching and photography a more congenial occupation. An eight o'clock breakfast was immediately followed by a start on cars for Ben Bulben and Sligo. The morning was as the previous day had been—hazy, but quite fine—allowing dim views of the precipitous range of mountains that face the ocean. The party rattled through the streets of Bundoran, and out into the country, between hedges fragrant with wild roses and honeysuckle. The botanists noted the great abundance of three plants which are rare in the Belfast district—a thistle (*Carduus pratensis*), a willow (*Salix pentandra*), and a rush (*Juncus glaucus*). A halt was made at Bundroose to inspect and photograph the old cross by the roadside; two uncommon plants, the dwarf elder (*Sambucus ebulus*) and a grass (*Trisetum flavescens*), were found at this place. The route then lay through Cliffony and Grange to the base of Ben Bulben, whose huge limestone cliffs towered up to a height of over 1700 feet. A contingent from Sligo having joined the party, and lunch having been disposed of, the ascent of the mountain was commenced. The party passed over a boggy stretch of land, then up a talus of stony debris, past the northern extremity of the cliffs, and then right up the extremely steep slope of the mountain. The ascent was accomplished in good time, some of the ladies of the party proving themselves most expert mountaineers. A number of rare plants were collected, including the cushion pink (*Silene acaulis*), mountain sorrel (*Oxyria reniformis*), yellow saxifrage (*Saxifraga aizoides*), green spleenwort (*Asplenium viride*), and others. On the top of the mountain the force of the wind was very great, and the haze unfortunately obscured the more distant portions of the glorious panorama of sea and land that spread out on all sides, so that the descent of the southern side was commenced. Near the base of the mountain the botanists obtained the pretty grass of Parnassus (*Parnassia palustris*) and the water figwort (*Scrophularia aquatica*). The party all collected at Drumcliff, where stands a round tower, now sadly the worse for the ravages of time, and two ancient crosses. These were duly honoured by the photographers, after which a rapid drive brought the party to Sligo, where the appearance of a procession ol eleven machines, coming on the eve of a parliamentary election, produced no little sensation. Dinner was in readiness at the Imperial Hotel, and the members subsequently dispersed for a stroll through the streets, where they gathered a favourable impression of Sligo, which is a neat and flourishing town, with handsome public buildings which may well vie with any town of its size in the north-east, and shows no sign of the stagnation and decay that one sometimes hears of as characterising the western Irish towns. The beautiful ruins of the Dominican Abbey of the Holy Cross were especially the centre of attraction to the Club members, and darkness had set in ere the last of them returned to the hotel. Several members had elected to take a more extended walk than was offered by Ben Bulben alone, and were enthusiastic over the beauties of Glencar, while a member who visited the King's Mountain returned with a good supply of the extremely rare plant *Arenaria ciliata*, which he described as plentiful there.

The third morning dawned even finer than the two preceding. Probably the earliest party astir were a number of young members, who, failing to get accommodation at the Imperial Hotel, elected to sleep in a tent kindly lent by Mr. Plunkett, which was pitched in a grassy field above the town. They were off at five o'clock to visit the celebrated stone monuments of Carrowmore, three miles south-west of Sligo, whence they returned, having seen as many cromleacs and stone circles in an hour spent at this extraordinary place as any of them had seen in all the previous part of their lives ; and bringing away, as souvenirs, abundance of two fine orchids, the pyramidal (*O. pyramidalis*) and sweet-scented (*Gymnadenia conopsea*), which grew plentifully in the meadows around. At the hotel the members had been early astir also, and the old abbey had been photographed from all points of view, and visits paid to the handsome Roman Catholic cathedral. All did full justice to the sumptuous breakfast that Mr. O'Donnell provided at eight o'clock, and then the party embarked in five boats to row up the river and across Lough Gill. The sun shone brightly, while a fresh easterly breeze kept the air deliciously cool, and a more perfect day for the lake could not be imagined. The row up the Garravogue is beautiful in the extreme. The banks are wooded thickly, and above the luxuriant foliage the blue mountains stand out, and every turn brings fresh beauties to view. A halt was made to gather white and yellow water-lilies, which grew abundantly in the calm water. Further on a great crested grebe was seen paddling up the river in a state of great consternation with her brood of young behind her. Then a narrow passage was passed, and the whole lake came into view, studded with islands, and enclosed among rugged hills, wooded on their lower slopes, a sight that drew from every one's lips expressions of admiration and delight. A course was shaped for Church Island, and a landing was duly effected at the eastern end of the island. The ruined church, now conserved by the Board of Works, was inspected, and subsequently lunch engaged attention for a short time. Then, after a short stroll through the woods of the island, the secretary's whistle sounded the advance, and, re-embarkation being safely completed, the boats proceeded across the lake to the mouth of the Bonet River, which was admitted by all to be one of the loveliest spots visited on the trip, offering a charming combination of lake and river, low meadows bright with the pink flowers of the valerian, woods of larch and fir, high ivy covered rocks, and beyond the lake the high limestone mountains. The boats ascended the river's numerous windings, past the fragmentary ruin of O'Rouarke's Castle to Drumahaire Quay, where the party landed and walked to the railway station, visiting on their way the fine old banqueting hall of the O'Rouarkes, and regretting that time did not permit of a visit to the extensive abbey ruins on the opposite side of the stream. The botanists were pleased to find at Drumahaire quantities of the scale fern or scaly harts-tongue (*Ceterach officinarum*) of which plenty of roots were obtained. A member, who had visited the wooded hills of Rockwood on foot in preference to the lake trip, brought specimens of the broom-rape (*Orobanche Hederæ*), and reported the occurence of the following lepidoptera :—*Fœnonympha Davus*, *Argynnis Paphia*, *Melanippe hastata*, *Emmalesia tœniata*, and *Eupithecia debiliata*. At the station a special train was standing in readiness, and it moved off amid hearty cheers for the manager of the line (Mr. Humphreys), for Mr. Plunkett of Enniskillen, and Mr. MacArthur and Mr. White, of Sligo, all of whom had been untiring in their care and attention to the members during the trip. At Enniskillen the special carriage was hitched on to the 4.15 train, and the party proceeded to Clones, where a wait of an hour was taken advantage of to have tea, which was provided by Mrs. Robinson in good style. At the conclusion of the repast a short business meeting was held, the President in the chair, and Messrs. Alfred M'Kisack and James Doherty were elected members of the Club. Then the journey was resumed, and the train sped rapidly towards Belfast.

Two prizes had been offered the previous morning for the best collection of plants made on Ben Bulben and neighbourhood. The senior secretary now at length found time to examine the plants sent in, and he declared Mr. W. D. Donnan and Miss Stelfox to be the winners of the first and second prizes respectively. Mr. Donnan's set were as follows :—*Thalictrum minus, Draba incana, Silene acaulis, Sedum Rhodiola, Saxifraga aizoides, S. hypnoides, Scrophularia aquatica, Gymnadenia conopsea, Trisetum flavescens, Cystopteris fragilis, Asplenium viride.* Belfast was once more reached at nine o'clock, where the members dispersed, taking away with them the most pleasant of impressions of their trip through Fermanagh and Sligo, and of the genuine Irish hospitality and kindness which they met with on every hand.

BENEVENAGH.

The fourth regular excursion was held on Saturday, July 30th, when the members visited the fine basaltic mountain of Benevenagh, near Limavady. Rising abruptly from the fertile alluvial plain that lies behind the sands of Magilligan Point, this mountain towers up to a height of over 1,200 feet, its lower slopes clothed in pine woods, above which the high cliffs rise in serried ranges to the lofty summit. The Field Club party left Belfast by the 8.15 train in a saloon carriage which the manager, with his usual and well-known courtesy, had specially reserved. At Ballymena the English mails, which had come by the narrow-guage railway from Larne, were taken aboard. Coleraine and the Bann were soon left behind, and the express flew through the tunnels of Downhill and under the magnificent range of cliffs that faces the Atlantic, and by the kindness of the manager of the line was specially stopped at Bellarena Station to allow the party to alight. A short walk brought the members to the foot of the mountain, and by the permission of the owner, Sir Frederick W. Heygate, his estate was thrown open to them, and an easy ascent was made by a broad avenue through woods of fir, with a dense undergrowth of ferns and grasses. Here the botanists made the first record, a number of specimens of the curious bird's-nest orchid (*Listera nidus-avis*) being obtained. A short halt was called while the announcement was made that two prizes would be offered for competition during the day— one for the largest collection of flowering plants, the other for the rarest twelve flowering plants obtained. Mr. R. Lloyd Praeger, M.R.I.A., made a few remarks on the botany of the mountain, and exhibited dried specimens of the very rare group of plants that have long been known to grow on the basaltic cliffs of Benevenagh. He pointed out that these plants are all northern species, and that the Benevenagh flora is a lingering vestige of an arctic vegetation that long ago flourished in the country—probably during the glacial epoch.

The pine woods were soon left behind, and heathy hillocks bright with purple heather succeeded, and beyond them the dark cliffs towered up for several hundred feet. An easy ascent was made at the western end of the range, and a walk over the short turf brought the party to the summit, whence they viewed the broad fertile plain of Magilligan, chequered like patchwork with fields of all shades of green, and fringed with sand dunes and the long yellow sweep of beach.

> Yonder lay Lough Foyle,
> Which a storm was whipping,
> Covering with mist
> Lake and shores and shipping.

So wrote Thackeray some forty years ago, but on the present occasion the description did not apply, for, though a light mountain shower had just passed, the lough lay blue and calm, with the blue hills of Donegal stretching in picturesque undulations from the white lighthouse of Innishowen on the east to Londonderry on the west ; while further westward the winding River Roe lay close by, and far beyond it the cloud-tipped domes of the Sperrin Mountains. However, a short time sufficed for viewing the varied prospect, for competition for the two prizes was keen and eager, and the dangerous edges of the cliffs were closely examined for the botanical rarities that here find a congenial home. The cushion pink (*Silene acaulis*) was found in abundance along the cliffs ; the pretty mountain avens (*Dryas octopetala*) occurred more sparingly. The minute dwarf willow (*Salix herbacea*) was also gathered, and two members obtained specimens of the rare *Draba incana*, and of the extremely rare large-flowered milkwort (*Polygala vulgaris* var. *grandiflora*). Other interesting plants noted were the storksbill (*Erodium cicutarium*), a seaside plant, which was found at several spots at the base and on the summit of the cliffs ; the juniper (*Juniperus nana*) in several spots ; the wall rue (*Asplenium ruta-muraria*) growing on trap-rock ; and abundance of the mossy saxifrage (*S. hypnoides*). The main portion of the members walked along the cliffs to the eastern extremity, and returned along the base. On the descent the field gentian (*G. campestris*) and an orchid (*Habenaria viridis*) were obtained.

The whole party reassembled at Sir F. W. Heygate's pretty summerhouse on the hill at four o'clock, when tea was provided by Messrs. Inglis & Co.

Mr. William Gray. M.R.I.A., was then called to the chair, and in a few happy remarks expressed the pleasure which all had derived from the present excursion. He also said a few words extending a welcome to a member of a kindred society in Scotland who was present. Mr. John Howatt, member of the Geological Society of Glasgow, acknowledged the chairman's remarks, and spoke of the pleasure with which he always looked forward to attending the meetings of the Belfast Naturalists' Field Club. On the motion of Mr. B. D. Wise, M.I.C.E., seconded by Mr. Charles Bulla, a hearty vote of thanks was passed to Sir F. W. Heygate for his kindness to the Club. The election of two new members (Messrs. Lancelot Shaw and J. C. C. Payne), and the appointment of Mr. S. A. Stewart, F.B.S.E., as judge of the botanical collections, brought the formal business to a close, and the members, on their return to the railway, scattered through the woods to complete their collections. Near the railway station a rare thistle (*Carduus acanthoides*) was collected ; also two of the cudweeds (*Gnaphalium sylvaticum* and *Filago germanica*).

At 6.10 the train was taken for Belfast, and the saloon carriage was temporarily converted into a floral arbour by the large collections of flowers that were spread out for examination by the judge. At Ballymena the result of the competition was announced as follows :—For the largest collection of flowering

plants—Mr. J. J Andrew, 190 species ; Miss N. Coulson, 128 ;
Mr. R Hanna, 127 ; Mrs. Wise, 104 ; Miss Knowles, 102 ; and
Mr. H. Malcolmson, 77. For the rarest twelve plants—1, Mr.
Praeger ; 2, Miss M. Knowles ; 3, Mr. Bigger. The winner
retired from the competition, as he had assisted in the judging
of the collections. His set were :—*Draba incana, Sisymbrium
thalianam, Polygala grandiflora, Silene acaulis, Erodium
cicutarium* (from summit), *Dryas octopela, Carduus acanthoides,
Hieracium anglicum, Salix herbacea, Juniperus nana, Listera
nidus-avis, Agrostis pumila*. Miss Knowles was accordingly
declared winner, and Miss Coulson was awarded the prize in the
first competition, as Mr. Andrew retired in her favour.

An entomologist of the party noted the following butterflies
on the mountain :—Black rustic (*Agrestis lucernea*), antler
moth (*Charœas graminis*), and *Crambus tristillus*.

Belfast was reached shortly after nine o'clock, and the members separated, well satisfied with their visit to Benevenagh.

DRUMBO AND GIANT'S RING.

A half-day excursion to Drumbo and Giant's Ring was held
on Saturday, 3rd August. A party of over 60 left Donegall
Square at 2.30 on wagonettes and cars, and during the afternoon
the Club's usual good luck was dominant, no rain falling on the
members, although heavy thunder showers were observed
around Belfast. The pretty cottages of Newtownbreda, covered
with purple *Clematis Jackmani*, and yellow *Tropæolum
canariensis*, were much admired, whilst the over-arching trees
on the road to Purdysburn afforded a pleasing shade from the
bright sunshine.

After passing Ballylesson and approaching Drumbo magnificent views were obtained—the Lagan Valley in one direction
and Belfast in the other, Cave Hill and Black Mountain standing
out most distinct and clear, whilst the shadows of the heavy
thunder-clouds chased each other across the vista.

A halt was made at Drumbo church to inspect the ancient clochteac in the graveyard. Mr. Lockwood, C.E., gave an interesting sketch of this very early round tower. Drumbo—meaning in Irish "The Ridge of the Cow"—was a religious settlement early in the sixth century, and had for abbot St. Mochumma, brother of St. Domangart, after whom Slieve Donard gets its name. The round tower now measures about 32 feet 6 inches in height, 50 feet in circumference, and 8 feet 6 inches in the interior diameter. This remnant has been well conserved at the expense of Mr. Robert Young, C.E., a former President of the Club. Miss Stokes, in her "Ecclesiastical Antiquities of Ireland," places this bell tower amongst the very earliest erected in the country—probably the eighth century saw it built with the rude field stones dug out by the toilers of an early Christian settlement. The flat-arched doorway faces east, and is some distance from the ground ; it is 5 feet 6 inches high, 22 inches wide at the base, and 19 inches at the top. Whilst the photographers were busy with the bell tower, others of the party viewed the neat church adjoining, and the interesting old clock in the vestry.

After a short walk down the hill, vehicles were mounted, and way made towards the Giant's Ring. The fine cromleac is in the centre of a huge lis 193 yards in diameter, whose enclosing rath of considerable height is about 80 feet wide at the base. The whole is enclosed by a modern wall, and at the gate the following inscription is cut :—"This wall for the protection of the Giant's Ring was erected A.D. 1812 by Arthur, third Viscount of Dungannon, on whose estate this singular relique of antiquity is situated, and who earnestly recommends it to the care of his successors." The tomb of Viscount Dungannon is in the old churchyard at Belvoir Park. Mr. Lockwood again made a few remarks, clearly explaining the historic facts connected with these evidences of the past. He considered these cyclopean remains to be the places of burial of important personages, and in nowise connected with druids or druid worship ; he gave instances and facts to support this theory.

Much adverse comment was made on the tradesman who has vulgarly printed his advertisement upon the monument, and it was thought steps should be taken to make him remove the same.

A short business meeting was held, at which Miss Emma Boyd was elected a member of the Club, after which a pleasant drive by Shaw's Bridge brought the party to the city.

LAGAN CANAL.

The valley of the Lagan was the place chosen for the fifth excursion for the season, and well pleased indeed was the large party that assembled with the route selected. Over one hundred members and friends assembled at the Great Northern Railway on Saturday morning, 27th August, where, through the usual courtesy of the management, special carriages were reserved, and a start was made for Moira. On arrival there the numerous boats in the adjoining canal, that had been kindly put at the service of the Club by the Lagan Navigation Company, including their fine inspection boat, were soon filled with an enthusiastic gathering of ladies and gentlemen, bent upon the examination and study of natural life in its every phase. Some considerable ingenuity was required on the part of the secretaries in stowing away so many in the flotilla at their disposal, but after a short interval all was successfully accomplished, and, the tow-boys having mounted horse, and the helmsmen being duly cautioned, the aquatic procession floated gaily down the canal. The steerers at first strove to keep the centre, but this was not at all pleasing to the botanists, who were only satisfied when the boats hugged the bank, or even stuck in the reeds, for the worse the steering the greater their pleasure, as thus ample opportunities were afforded to gather into the boats all sorts of water plants. The unusual spectacle of such a large water-party wending its way between luxuriant meadows and rich corn-lands was watched with interest by little clusters of the peasantry at all the vantage points, and many pleasantries passed between the visitors and the visited. At noon the sky was clouded for a short time, but soon the weather became glorious, when the views of the distant hills were most beautiful. The contour of the White Mountain, Collin, Black Mountain, and Divis to the left was much admired, whilst the cultivated rising ground to the right lent an air of comfort and quiet pastoral beauty that readily pleased the fancy. The towers of the different churches enhanced the scene and acted as landmarks in denoting the different parishes passed through. The first stoppage was made at the Union Locks. Here the secretaries announced that a prize would be given for the best collection of aquatic plants made on the excursion. A number of good specimens were obtained during the day in the waters of the canal and the pools and ditches adjoining. The sweet sedge (*Acorus calamus*) was noticed growing along the canal banks all the way from Moira to Lambeg, attaining a maximum profusion a little above Lisburn. This curious plant is not an original native, but was introduced by Sir John Rawdon into his gardens at Moira over a century ago, whence it has spread through the waters of the district. The pretty flowering rush (*Butomus umbellatus*) grew in profusion all along the canal, and in less quantity the arrow-head (*Sagittaria sagittifolia*). The water-radish (*Armoracia amphibium*), gipsy-wort (*Lycopus europæus*), and purple loosestrife (*Lythrum salicaria*) were abundant on the damp margins, and below the water, which was, unfortunately for the collectors, rather high, flourished numerous pond-weeds, among which the fennel-leaved (*P. pectinatus*) was conspicuous. Above Lisburn a single large plant of the horse-bane (*Cicuta virosa*) was observed. Although most of the party preferred the pleasant towing in the boats, yet a goodly number took advantage of the walk along the banks, the different stoppages at the locks giving them ample time to botanise along the edges of the water and the marshes adjoining. The town of Lisburn having been passed, the banks of the river became more deeply wooded, but as time

was pressing regret was expressed that a visit could not be paid
to the only spot in the district where the lesser burnet
(*Poterium Sanguisorba*) was lately discovered by a member
Mr. J. H. Davies, of Glenmore, who joined the party at that
point, having assisted some of the members to gather another
rare plant, the bitter cress (*Cardamine amara*). The square-
stalked St. John's-wort (*Hypericum dubium*) was also found at
Glenmore. A few more windings between the banks brought
the members to Drum Bridge and tea. Rarely if ever was tea
more heartily enjoyed or more pleasantly arranged than on this
occasion. On a bank in a meadow, between the two waters,
surrounded by charming scenery, under the shadow of the cross
on Drum church, a plentiful repast was spread, to which ample
justice was done by the wearied naturalists. Advantage was
taken of the picturesque group in the evening shadows by the
photographers present, and many records were made for albums
and friends.

A short formal meeting was then held, when, after a few
pleasant remarks from the President, Mr. John Vinycomb,
F.R.S.A., Mr. R. Lloyd Praeger was appointed to judge specimens collected in competition for the prize, which was awarded
to Mr. R. Hanna. The following new members were elected:—
Mrs. M'Kean, Mrs. Proctor Smythe, Miss Crawley, Rev. John E.
Armstrong, Messrs. George Allibon, W. T. Clements, W. Costigan, Gardner Hardy, Wm. M'Candless, and W. G. MacKenzie,
M.D. After a short time spent in inspecting the beautiful
church of Drum, and photographing the handsome lytch gate,
which makes such a pretty picture when crossing the double
bridge, boats were again boarded and the journey towards home
resumed. The evening light, with the rising moon, will leave
pictures of the valley of the Lagan in the minds of those who
were present that will not be readily effaced, and will add more
to the list of those who, since the days of Ptolemy, in the
beginning of the second century, have known the beauties of the
Logia or Lagan River. Shaw's Bridge, Edenderry, and Belvoir
Park, each rivalling the other in interest and beauty, were

quickly passed, and the collecting of specimens had ceased save at Edenderry, where the find of the day was made by Mr. Praeger in the Dutch rush (*Equisetum hyemale*), which was discovered growing plentifully on the Down side.

Such a pleasant and profitable day spent in our own district must endear our land and its associations to all of us, and lead us to say—

> Oh ! the green land, the old land,
> Far dearer than the gold land,
> With all its landscape glory, and unchanging summer skies ;
> Let others seek their pleasures
> In the chase of golden treasures,
> Be mine a dream of Erin where the pleasant Lagan lies.

THE KNOCKAGH.

On Saturday afternoon, September 10th, a party of about 26 left Belfast by the 2.30 train for Carrick Junction. On arrival there the party at once proceeded up the bluffs of the Knockagh, tarrying here and there on the upward way to survey the fine views of Belfast, and the Lough spread out below, studded with the white sails of pleasure boats. On arrival at the base of the cliffs a halt was called, whilst Mr. Mann Harbison gave a lucid descriptive sketch of the geological formation of the district, pointing out the distinctive basaltic nature of the hill. Afterwards the party broke up into groups and scattered themselves over the different portions of the hill, some traversing the base of the cliffs on botanical pursuits, whilst others wandered along the brow of the hill seeking for picturesque effects, and others again crossed the summit and walked to the verge of the reservoirs of the Belfast Water Commissioners. Although it was late in the season, the botanists of the party collected some interesting plants, among which were fine specimens of the stone bramble (*Rubus saxatilis*) with clusters of ripe bright-red fruit. A brief formal meeting was held, at which Mr. James

MacDonald was elected a member of the Club. After a pleasant afternoon the party assembled again at 6.30 at the Junction Station, and returned to Belfast.

KILLOUGH AND ARDGLASS.

The tenth and last excursion took place on Saturday, 17th September, when the interesting neighbourhood of Ardglass, recently opened up by the enterprise of the County Down Railway Company, was visited. A party of seventy-five, which swelled to ninety ere their destination was reached, assembled at the railway shortly after ten o'clock, and were soon speeding through the golden harvest fields of County Down, the journey being agreeably varied by the inspection of numerous photos. taken by members on former excursions. Leaving Downpatrick, the new portion of the line was entered upon, and a steep gradient of 1 in 50 brought the train to the summit level, when Bright Castle was seen perched high on a hilltop, and near by, on a lower eminence, a fine earthen rath or fort. An equally steep descent followed, then a mile or two of level, and the train drew up at its destination, and the party lost no time in getting under weigh. Killough Bay was first visited, and its eastern shores explored. Here, in spite of the lateness of the season, the botanists of the party found ample scope for investigation. Several fields were observed gay with the brilliant flowers of the common red poppy (*Papaver rhœas*), a plant which, though abundant further southward, is extremely rare in the North-East. On a gravelly bank the pretty rest-harrow (*Ononis arvensis*) was obtained, and in fields adjoining abundance of the field convolvulus (*C. arvensis*) and two dead nettles (*Lamium intermedium* and *L. amplexicaule*). The best finds, however, fell to Mr. Praeger, who obtained the round prickly-headed poppy (*P. hybridum*) on a roadside, and on walls by the sea the rigid fescue-grass (*Festuca rigida*), both of these plants being of extreme rarity in the North of Ireland.

On the shore several other good plants were obtained—a rare drop-wort (*Œnanthe lachenalii*), the sea-beet (*Beta maritima*), the brookweed (*Samolus valerandi*), and a sedge (*Carex distans*). Presently a high projecting bank of Boulder Clay was reached, and the party were called together while the senior secretary drew attention to several interesting geological phenomena in the immediate neighbourhood. These consisted of vertically uptilted Silurian rocks, beautifully rounded, grooved, and polished by glacial action ; overlying them a bed of bluish Boulder Clay, capped by thirty or forty feet of Post-glacial gravelly beds, the lower layers of which have, by the infiltration of some cementing material, become consolidated into a hard conglomerate. When these geological features had been thoroughly examined the party again proceeded, and made their way along the picturesque shore towards Ardglass, where glorious views of the Mourne Mountains were obtained to the south. On the downs the rest-harrow was found growing in several large patches, and specimens of the centaury (*Erythræa centaurium*) with white flowers were obtained. Upon reaching Ardglass the picturesque ruins of Margaret's Castle and Catherine's Castle were examined with interest, and speculation was rife as to their origin : whether they were intended as the strongholds for some of the marauding followers of John de Courcy, or whether they were simply fortified trading stores the same as numerous others in the vicinity of Dublin; for Ardglass, we are told, was in the olden times second only in importance to Carrickfergus as a trading centre, Belfast not being even mentioned at that time. It is quite probable that the new railway will restore Ardglass to its ancient prestige. Jordan's Castle was, however, the chief rallying point, and nearly all the party ascended up its winding stairs to the breeze-swept turrets that afford such a magnificent prospect of the beautiful harbour and surrounding district. Much admiration was expended on the still perfect columbarium that occupies one angular tower of the castle, and which must have afforded ample breeding space for the pigeons used for the Baron's table, or perhaps in those times the "homer" was taken advantage of, as their services would be very useful in the time of war. This castle was conferred by Henry III. on Jordan de Sankville in the year 1217. After the photographers had made careful records of the different subjects of interest, the Castle of Ardglass, the former residence of the Beauclercs, was inspected. The site and surroundings are very beautiful, but the castle, which is modern, is poor and dilapidated. The broken remains of a rather fine sculpture representing the Virgin and Child lie close to the yard gate, and are worthy of a better fate. Something should be done for the permanent preservation of this interesting statue. After a short visit to the modern King's Castle, where the party were agreeably received by Mrs. Russell, the present owner, the party adjourned to the Castle Hotel, where an excellent tea was provided by Mr. Moore. After tea the business meeting of the Club was held, Mr. W. H. Phillips, F.R.H.S., in the chair. The following were elected members of the Club :—Mrs. J. C. C. Payne, Rev. E. A. Cooper, Messrs. George Fullerton, J. S. Mitchell, and Pakenham Stewart. The secretary took advantage of this the closing excursion to make a few remarks relative to the season's work, pointing out the unusually large average of attendance at the various excursions. A short walk was then taken round by the pier to the ruins of Ardtole Church, the ancient parish church of Ardglass, which was used as such till the woodkern of Macartan's country came down and slew the inhabitants whilst attending mass there. The ruin is picturesque, and the view through the east window is very beautiful. In the field to the west is a fine souterrain 100 feet long, now unfortunately closed. About Ardglass some good plants were collected ; the rigid fescue-grass was again found, growing in some quantity on walls by the sea, in company with another uncommon species (*Schlerochloa loliacea*). The black horehound (*Ballota alba*), white mustard (*Sinapis alba*), and a sedge (*Carex vulpina*) were obtained close to the town. Some commotion was caused amongst the botanists by the discovery of a vase full of another rare plant, the musky storksbill (*Erodium moschatum*), in a shop in the town, and exhaustive enquiries and search after its habitat were made without result ; at the last moment it was stated that the plant grew in a garden about a mile from the town. At half-past six the return journey was commenced. A momentary stoppage at Ballyknowe enabled the botanists to note two more plants. the toad-flax (*Linaria vulgaris*) and a rather rare spurge (*Euphorbia exigua*). At Downpatrick the Club's carriages were hitched on the main line train, and Belfast was duly reached at 8.30.

WINTER SESSION.

NOTE.—The authors of the various Papers, of which abstracts are here appended, are alone responsible for the views expressed in them.

SOCIAL MEETING.

THE Winter Session was opened on 28th October with a Social Meeting in the Exhibition Hall, Botanic Avenue. On the occasion of the Social Meeting last year, the accommodation at the Belfast Museum in College Square proved, for the first time in the Club's history, inadequate for the large attendance of members and their friends, and on the present occasion the spacious hall in Botanic Avenue was filled to overflowing, the numbers far exceeding those of any meeting since the foundation of the society. From seven to eight o'clock tea was dispensed by an active body of lady members. Immediately after tea, the chair was taken by the President, who, in his opening remarks, drew attention to the steady progress and growth of the Club, and to its present very satisfactory condition, as shown by the large attendance of members and visitors, and the valuable and interesting collections, mainly the work of members, that were on view. After some announcements by the secretaries, the meeting became general, and the company spent a busy and profitable time in examining the works of nature and art that crowded the tables and walls. The specialité of the evening was an extensive collection illustrating the past condition and history of the City of Belfast and district.

On a centre screen was arranged one of the best collections of maps ever shown in Belfast illustrative of local and general

Irish subjects, kindly exhibited by Mr. Lavens M. Ewart, J.P.,
M.R.I A., who also exhibited many other views of Belfast and
neighbourhood. Mrs. Moore lent several very clever sketches by
her late husband, Dr. James Moore, representing old corners and
entries of Belfast long since removed. The President was well
represented in two panoramic views, one of Belfast from Castlereagh, the other of Larne Harbour; also in the historical painting
of the fight between the Clan Savage and the MacGilmore on Ben-
Madighan. Several paintings by the late A. Nicholl, R.H.A., were
shown by his kinsman, Mr. Wm. Nicholl. A unique view of the
old paper mill was shown by Mr. John Kane, LL.D., also a view
of Castleton. A very clever and comprehensive series of the old
entries of Belfast was shown by Mr. Ernest Hanford. The well-
known sea-fight between the "Paul Jones" and H.M.S. Ranger
in Belfast Lough was cleverly painted and shown by Mr. Joseph
Carey. Two very fine old engravings illustrating the sea-fight
between Francois Thurot and the English, and the subsequent
defeat of the former in 1760, were lent by Mr. Francis Joseph
Bigger, together with some other views of local interest. Miss
Carruthers lent some clever sketches of old houses, particularly
of the now removed Castle of Ormeau. Mr. S. Ramsey's sketches
in oils of views now passed away from our city were very
interesting; the premier place, however, was given to Mr.
Clarke's Old High Street in 1791. A fine View of Donegall
Quay from Queen's Bridge was shown by Mr. Lyttle; whilst
perhaps the finest set of modern views of the city ever brought
together were shown by Marcus Ward & Co., Limited. Mr.
Robert Young, C.E., lent the original of a very clever drawing
by George Petrie of the Long Bridge, and also some other
valuable pictures. Mr. William Harper's picture of "A Fair
Client," representing a young widow and the late Attorney
Joy, was much admired, as was also his general view of Belfast.
Mr. William Swanston, F.G.S., exhibited a set of fine maps and
engravings, some modern and some old. The other exhibitors
were Messrs. James Magill, J. Douglas, Wm. Gray, M.R.I.A.;
J. J. Phillips, J. Malcolm, J. Simms, E. W. White, Miss Clarke,

and the Belfast Water Commissioners. One of the most interesting and valuable exhibits was a sketch-book of the late A. Nicholl, R.H.A., lent by Mrs. Andrews, which was quite a treasure-house of local scenes. Mr. J. Simms' list of old Belfast merchants, dated 1803, who formed our first Insurance Company, attracted considerable attention, as did also his plan of the Volunteer Review held in the Bog Meadows about 1782. A most valuable and representative collection of Belfast-printed books was displayed by Mr. Ewart ; whilst Mr. Swanston and Mr. Malcolm showed the manuscript records of the Belfast Yeomanry Corps.

The Club's new albums, containing over three hundred platinotype photographs of local antiquities and geological subjects, were much admired, their arrangement by the secretaries having been just completed in time for the meeting. The walls were also enhanced by the fine geological prize set of sketches by Miss S. M. Thompson, the geological prize photos. of Miss Tate, and photos. of the Ballyrudder gravels by Mr. George Donaldson. Some fine photos. of rude stone monuments near Warrenpoint were shown by Dr. Douglas ; whilst the Club's photographic benefactor, Mr. R. Welch, contributed a series of Views, taken on excursions, unsurpassable for beauty and excellence of workmanship, and at the same time presented a set of his Sligo antiquities to the Club's albums, to augment his previous gifts made on the starting of these local records.

In the section devoted to Natural History a number of highly interesting exhibits were on view. Conspicuous among these were two handsome cases illustrative of native wild life, the work of Mr. J. Sheals, taxidermist, Belfast, and deserving of high praise from both a zoological and an artistic point of View. The one consisted of a pair of corn-crakes (*Crex pratensis*), with their infant brood, seeking for food amid the congenial shelter of tall grass; the other of a pine marten (*Martes abietinum*), which is very cleverly set up as standing on a large branch, holding in its teeth a squirrel which it has just captured : both

of these handsome groups have been obtained for the Belfast
Natural History and Philosophical Society through the exertions of the Ulster Fauna Committee, the former having been
presented to the Society by Mr. James Thompson, J.P.,
Macedon, and the latter by Major Percival Maxwell, D.L.,
Finnebrogue, Downpatrick, on whose estate the marten was
captured. There were also on exhibition an excellent set of
beetles from County Armagh, for which the Rev. W. F. Johnson,. M.A., obtained a Club's prize last year ; a fine set of local
lepidoptera, exhibited by Mr. Isaac Waugh ; and a number of
aquaria, and glass jars containing various strange live animals,
which were under the superintendence of Mr. John Hamilton.
There were shown the well-known but seldom seen chameleon,
the curious little green tree-frog, the large American bull-frog,
and a beautiful green lizard ; while the glass jars swarmed with
newts, water-scorpions, water-beetles, cray-fish, and many
smaller forms of aquatic life. In the department of botany, Mr.
R. Lloyd Praeger, M.R.I.A., showed a series of very rare plants
from County Armagh, the result of a few weeks botanising in
that neighbourhood ; several of these have not been previously
found in Ireland, and none of them are recorded from the
north-central district of Ireland. The same exhibitor showed a
series of plants illustrating the additions to the flora of the
North-east of Ireland since the publication of Messrs. Stewart
and Corry's work on the subject, and also a number of the
rarest plants obtained on the Club's excursions of the past
season. A beautiful stand of exotic ferns and foliage plants,
artistically grouped, were shown by Mr. Charles M'Kimm, curator of the Belfast Botanic Gardens ; this collection included
over sixty different varieties of the maiden-hair fern (*Adiantum*).
At the lower end of the room a magnificent series of dried and
mounted specimens of species and varieties of British ferns were
exhibited by an "old hand" at this subject, Mr. W. H. Phillips,
F.R.H.S. ; the same gentleman, in company with Mr. Praeger,
was responsible for a collection of several hundreds of fresh-
cut fronds of choice varieties of British ferns, which were

placed at the disposal of the company at the close of the evening, who eagerly availed themselves of the permission to select such as they fancied, with the result that the table was soon completely cleared. The science of geology was represented by some fine coloured photographs of Swiss glaciers, kindly lent by Mr. Robert Brownlie ; interesting specimens of small basaltic columns from a quarry at Killead, shown by Mr. W. F. M'Kinney ; and a good series of fossils from the local Carboniferous beds, for which Miss S. M. Thompson gained a Club's prize last year. On another table were an excellent series of geodes from Iowa, U.S.A., which have been recently presented to the Natural History and Philosophical Society by Mr. W. E. Praeger ; these curious concretionary masses, which have the form of hollow spheres of rock filled with a variety of beautiful crystals, are found in the State of Iowa in a bed of impure limestone which lies at the base of the Carboniferous formation. A large suspended label, " Microscopical Section," showed where a number of adepts were displaying the wonders of that unseen world, teeming with animal and vegetable life in the myriad different forms that pervade the air and water, and, indeed, every object around us. The exhibitors were Messrs. James Stelfox, W. S. M'Kee, W. D. Donnan, Joseph Wright, F.G.S.; Wm. Hanna, B.A.; W. Gray, M.R.I.A.; E. M'Connell, S. Cunningham, and H. M'Cleery. Among the subjects illustrated were pond life, living organisms, Foraminifera, phosphorescent animalculæ, and potato-disease fungus.

Other exhibits which were on view were flint implements from various foreign countries, showing their likeness and unlikeness to Irish forms, by Mr. S. F. Milligan, M.R.I.A. ; while fine stereoscopes with glacier and other views were lent by Mr. James Wilson, M.E., and Mr. James O'Neill, M.A.

At nine o'clock silence was called, while the senior secretary read the nominations of new members which had been handed in ; they were as follow :—Miss E. Bruce, Mrs. Isaac Green, Mrs. White-Spunner, Messrs. Samuel E. Acheson, S. D. Bell, Hamilton Carse, Henry Cosgrove, George G. Crymble, Adam

Duffin, Alexander Hamilton, James A. Hanna, Robert Hill, Samuel F. Keith, John A. Kirkwood, Joseph Lewis, John C. M'Cullough, Hugh M'Williams, F. H. O'Flaherty, J Finlay Peddie, C.E.; John C. W. Reid, Fred. W. Rew, James Ritchie, Samuel Robinson, E. C. Stacke, M.D.; David Steel, Robert J. Steel, and William Watson. The names were formally submitted to the meeting, and the new members declared duly elected. A half-hour's display with the oxy-hydrogen lantern was then given by Mr. William Nicholl, the subjects illustrated being principally views taken on the Club's last year's excursions, the three-day trip to the beautiful Sligo district being especially conspicuous. Aquatic life was also shown by means of a narrow trough of water, filled with various forms of animal life, used as a slide ; and ants and spiders were shown in the same manner. The conversazione was then resumed, and the company did not separate until a late hour.

—————————

The first business meeting of the Winter Session was held on Tuesday evening, November 22nd, the President (Mr. John Vinycomb, M.R.I.A.) in the chair. The first business was to receive the President's opening address, which consisted of a discourse on the subject of the origin and significance of our national emblems.

The President said that on the first night of meeting of the Winter Session last year it had been his privilege to give some discursive remarks upon the subject of " Symbolism," and the important part it has played in the history of our race. This night he proposed to be more special, and devote the time at his disposal to placing before them some information bearing upon our national emblems, remarking upon their history, their meanings, and the changes that have taken place from time to time in the armorial ensigns of our country owing to wars, changes of dynasty, &c. Every nation of ancient or modern times seems to have found it necessary to possess some distinguishing mark or marks by which the national existence is symbolised and its authority represented. The uses of national insignia are, however, as imperative to-day as at any previous period. The national insignia of the United Kingdom possess a most interesting story, of which it is the epitome, the changes that have taken place from time to time serving as links in the chain of momentous events in our national history. These changes which have taken place on the Royal Shield, from William the Conqueror to the present time, too tedious to describe in detail, he had for greater clearness represented in a series of diagrams.

THE ROYAL ARMS.

In describing the national insignia, the Royal achievement is the first and most important thing to consider. It is a combination of the armorial devices or honourable emblems borne by the three sister kingdoms. Under the term "Royal Arms" is embraced :—

(a) *The Arms* of ENGLAND, SCOTLAND, and IRELAND, quartered upon one shield.

(b) *Crest*—upon a Royal Crown a lion statant, guardant, or, imperially crowned.

(c) *Supporters*—a gold lion and a silver unicorn.

(d) *The Motto*—DIEU ET MON DROIT, adopted as a *cri de guerre* by our Plantagenet kings in their expeditions into France.

(*e*) The ribbon and motto of the most noble Order of the Garter encircling the shield ; and, as symbolic and decorative adjuncts, the helmet of the sovereign with its appropriate mantling surmount the shield, while underneath, the floral emblems of the three countries are displayed.

NATIONAL FLAGS—THE ROYAL STANDARD AND THE UNION JACK.

The Royal Standard is a banner of large dimensions, the quartered arms of England, Scotland, and Ireland occupying the entire field.

While the Royal Arms and the Royal Standard are the special emblems of Imperial sovereignty, and indicate the Royal presence or deputed authority, the national ensign of the country is the Union Jack, the second in rank of the flag family.

THE QUARTERINGS ON THE ROYAL SHIELD.

1st and 4th Quarterings—"Gules three lions passant guardant, in pale, or," for England.

It is remarkable that, with the exception of the eagle, the lion is the only living creature figured in the early coats of arms. Lions are said to have been so borne by the sovereigns of England from the time of the Norman William. Planche, who fully discusses the subject in his " Pursuivant of Arms," says that the earliest intimation we receive of anything like a heraldic decoration in England is in the time of Henry I., A.D. 1127 ; and that the earliest undoubted representation of a Royal achievement occurs on the seal of Prince John, afterwards King of England, on which he is represented bearing a shield with two lions upon it. Writers seem to be agreed that the Royal Arms of England were two lions from the time of the Conquest till the marriage of Henry II. with Eleanor of Aquitaine, when the lion borne in the arms of that province was added to the English shield, completing the number still seen in the Royal achievement ; be this as it may, Richard Cœur-de-Leon, during the lifetime of his father, certainly bore two lions (as seen on his first great seal), which may be blazoned as *two lions combattant.* On the great seal of Richard, after his return from the Holy Land and his captivity in Germany, A.D. 1194, we have the first representation of the three lions, or leopards as they were at this time sometimes designated. Lions were depicted only in the act of combat (that is, rampant) ; in a walking position they were heraldically leopards, a practice which has continued as late as the fifteenth century, and which has given rise to many mistakes in the description of the English shield. " Lion Leopards" was a term afterwards applied to all lions not rampant.

It is a remarkable fact that all these lions are the insignia of territories which have long been separated from the crown of England ; the first is said to denote Normandy, the second Poictou, and the third, as stated, Aquitaine. About the same period (that is, during the eleventh century), the monarchs of England, the kings of Scotland, Norway, Denmark, Leon, Bohemia, Hungary, the native Princes of Wales, the Dukes of Normandy, the Counts of Flanders, Holland, Hainault, &c., appear as with one accord to have adopted the lion as a device or heraldic bearing, illustrating in a remarkable manner the popularity of the emblem, and the readiness of each of these heroes to " assume a virtue if they had it not."

It may be mentioned here that Dickens commits a curious anachronism in placing three lions upon the Norman standard at the Battle of Hastings. The following passage from " The Child's History " is one in which it is attempted to be shown that some of the great novelist's prose writings are virtually blank verse :—

> Soldiers with torches going to and fro
> Sought the corpse of Harold 'mongst the dead.
> The warrior, worked with stones and golden thread,
> Lay low, all torn and soiled with English blood,
> And *the three lions* kept watch o'er the field.

THE LION IN HERALDRY.

The lion plays such an important part in our national insignia that a few words must here be devoted to his majesty.

" Chiefest of all terrestrial animals," according to old Guillam, the lion occupies the foremost place in the heraldry of every land that has beheld his majestic form and heard the sound of his mighty voice. It may be interesting to enquire in what light he has been represented in past times by his contemporary—man. From the earliest times the lion appears to have been a favourite allegorical device   By universal consent he has been assigned the dignity of the " king of beasts," and endowed by tradition with powerful physical and also mental qualities, such as courage and generosity, and made almost equal to man himself. His whole appearance, with his noble human-like expression, has in it something truly magnificent, and seems to be almost a too powerful adversary of man, and however far back we trace the history of mankind we find him represented on the monuments of every epoch. In Egypt, Africa, Persia, and Greece we have abundant traces of the terror inspired by his name. A golden lion was the emblem of the tribe of Judah, a silver lion was the badge of the Macedonian conqueror. Lions, not tigers, were, we are told in Pocock's " India in Greece," the insignia of many early Indian dynasties. " The head of the lion," says Maurice (Oriental Trinities, p. 232), " both in Persia and Tartary was in a peculiar manner sacred to the solar light : the superior strength, nobility, and grandeur of that animal, and from his being a distinguishing constellation of the Zodiac, the sun shining forth in his greatest splendour from that sign, rendered him a proper type of the sun. In their allegorical fancy the majestic orb of his countenance, his glowing eyeballs and shaggy mane spreading in glory around like rays or clustering sparks of fire, would suggest, better than any other in the animal kingdom, that luminary to the Oriental mind."

As an emblem of power and sovereignty the lion has been assigned the highest place, and we find abundant use made of him in this respect by early nations, both in their writings and art representations. Heroes thought it an honour to be compared to him. The lion hunt was a Royal amusement. In another point of view he became the emblem of solitude. Mark, the Evangelist, opens his Gospel with the mission of John the Baptist, " The voice of one crying in the wilderness," hence his symbol—a lion—which like John is a denizen of the desert. He also sets forth the Royal dignity of Christ, and dwells upon his power manifested in his resurrection from the dead. The lion was accepted in ancient times as a symbol of the resurrection because the young lion was awakened to vitality by the breath, the tongue, and the roaring of its sire. This mightiest of animals became figuratively the guardian of places held sacred by man, watching before the graves of departed heroes and the temples of the gods. There are twenty-four lions around the tomb erected by Artemisia, 353 B.C., to her hero husband Mausoleus. We find the lion represented as "the watcher" over the gateway of Mycenæ, as they were before the Trojan War, fitting emblem of the courage and virtue of the patriot or of the whole nation, as in the lions on the base of Nelson's Monument in London.

The physiognomy of the lion bears an unmistakable resemblance to the human countenance in its noblest aspects ; this fact was noticed in very early times, and is alluded to in 2 Samuel xxiii. 20, and 1 Chronicles xi. 22 in the description of Benaiah, the son of Jehoiada, who " slew two lion-like men of Moab," from their noble leonine appearance and valiant bearing ; and men, not content to assume the likeness and high qualities of the king of beasts, have in every age called themselves by his name, as if emulous of his virtues. *Leo, Leonidas, Leopold, Leon,* and various other forms of the name in different languages were favourite appellations. Many of the Emperors of Constantinople adopted the cognomen on their accession to the throne of the Cæsars, and of the two hundred and fifty-two popes who have guided the destinies of the Latin church, the present Sovereign Pontiff is the thirteenth who has assumed the grandly sounding name of Leo.

The symbolic use of the lion's name is not confined to western nations. In the great East, warlike potentates blazon him upon their standards and armour as emblems of themselves and the valour of their people. The imperial standard of the great Mogul pictured in Tavernier Terry's Voyage to India represents the sun rising in glory behind the body of a recumbent lion ; the ensign of Persia is a lion passant guardant holding a sword, the sun in splendour rising behind—all emblems of the highest kind. A writer in " Nature and Art," referring to the lion in the East, says. "The present inhabitants of the Punjaub, the Sikhs, were so named from the Hindustanee verb Sikna, to teach, and they claimed to be men of peace from being taught; but the cruelties of the Mahommedans of Northern India caused them to become men of war, and they called themselves LIONS, which in their language is SINGH. Every SIKH now calls himself by this name ; DUNLEEP SINGH is the *Lion Dunleep*, and his father in like manner, RUNJEET SINGH, the *Lion Runjeet*."

The name of the lion in Welsh, Gaelic, and the Scandinavian dialects appears to indicate that the cognomen, and probably the idea of this animal, was from a Latin source.

Through the whole course of our national literature he is represented in the noblest light ; our greatest writers compared their heroes to him, his courage and magnanimity affording the highest type of these qualities. Shakespeare, in his historical plays, has numberless allusions to the English lions—

> " Your brother kings and monarchs of the earth
> Do all expect that you should rouse yourself
> As did the former lions of your blood."—(H. V., 1., 2.)

> " The awless lion could not wage the fight
> Nor keep his princely heart from Richard's hand."—(K. J., 1, 1.)

Richard Cœur-de-Leon fitly embodied the mediæval conception of the valorous chief and leader capable of every daring.

> " The man that once did sell the lion's skin
> Whilst the beast lived, was killed in hunting him."—(H. V., 4, 3.)

The figurative personification of the lion overcoming his

enemies (also typified by the armorial bearings) is finely introduced in Lord Macaulay's " Armada "—

> " Look how the lion of the sea lifts up his ancient crown,
> And underneath his deadly paws treads the gay lilies down ;
> So stalked he when he turned to flight on that famed Picard field,
> Bohemia's plume, Genoa's bow, and Cæsar's eagle shield ;
> So glared he when at Agincourt in wrath he turned to bay,
> And crushed and torn beneath his claws the princely hunters lay."

The introduction of the French lilies on the English shield
by Edward III. in 1340, when prosecuting his claim to the
French throne, and the various changes in form and position
until finally expunged in 1801 were dwelt on in detail. The
successive changes in the different reigns were illustrated by a
series of heraldic shields cleverly sketched out in diagram form.

THE SUPPORTERS OF THE ROYAL SHIELD.

Until the reign of King James I. there was no settled understanding concerning the use of supporters, each sovereign
adopting what pleased him best. We find angels, antelopes,
white harts, white lions, &c. Richard III. had a lion and a
boar ; Henry VII., a lion and a greyhound ; his son, Henry
VIII., first of the Tudor sovereigns, a golden lion and a red
dragon, the latter as indicating his descent from Owen Tudor
and the Princes of Wales ; Edward VI., Mary, and Elizabeth
had the same. On legislative union with Scotland in 1603,
one of the Scottish supporters, the UNICORN, was substituted
for the Welsh dragon. From this time to the present, the Lion
and Unicorn have remained as sovereign emblems of power and
majesty.

The legendary history of the mythical unicorn must be
passed over in a few words. The oldest author who describes
it is Etesias (B.C. 400). Aristotle, Pliny, and other ancient
writers also speak of it. It is several times referred to in Scripture. During the middle ages it was a favourite emblem of
Christ. Its horn was considered a certain test for poison, and
rendered a poisoned chalice harmless. The one horn symbolizes
the great Gospel doctrine that Christ is one with God.

THE SCOTTISH ARMS.

2nd Quarter—Or, within a double-tressure flory counter flory,
a lion rampant gules.

On the accession of James VI. of Scotland to the English
throne as James I., the Scottish arms were quartered for the
first time with those of England and Ireland.

Though we may not, like some Scottish antiquarians, be
prepared to refer the origin of the " ruddy lion rampant " of
Scotland to the mythical King Fergus, it can unquestionably
lay claim to great antiquity. The earliest representation of it
appears distinctly upon the seal of William King of Scotland,
who died in 1214. It is probably from this circumstance that
he received the title of " the Lion." After describing at length
the peculiar features of the Royal Shield of Scotland, with
some special reference to the origin of the " double-tressure
flory counter flory," Mr. Vinycomb added that, as a matter of
fact, the double tressure first appears upon the seal of Alexander
III., 1251—1286. Lyon King of Arms is the title of the chief
herald for Scotland, and the establishment over which he
presides is styled the " Lyon Office."

Sir Walter Scott, who had the most intimate acquaintance
with the gentle science of armorie and all heraldic lore, frequently introduces such allusions and descriptions in his
writings in the happiest manner. Witness his description of
the old Scottish poet, Sir David Lindsay, of the Mount, as
Lyon King of Arms :—

> " From his steed's shoulder, loin, and breast
> Silk housings swept the ground,
> With Scotland's arms, device, and crest
> Embroidered round and round.
> The double tressure might you see
> First by Achaius borne ;
> The thistle and the fleur-de-lis,
> And gallant unicorn.
> So bright the King's armorial coat
> That scarce one dazzled eye could note,
> In living colours blazoned brave
> The lion which his title gave."

In a similar heroic strain Professor Ayton, in his " Lays of the Scottish Cavaliers," describes the raising of the standard of the Pretender :—

> " The noble Tullibardine stood beneath its weltering fold
> With the ruddy lion ramping in its field of tressur'd gold."

Ariosti (1510) thus refers to the Arms of Scotland :—

> " Yon lion placed two unicorns between,
> That rampant with a silver sword is seen,
> Is for the King of Scotland's banner known."—(Hoole's tr.)

THE HERALDY OF IRELAND.

3rd Quarter—Azure, a harp or, stringed argent.

It does not appear that the native Irish knew anything of the science of heraldry before the advent of the Anglo-Norman settlers. They were not sufficiently methodical, says an eminent authority, to accept it or abide by the laws of arms. Even their shields, at least such of them as remain, were of a form and structure little adapted to blazonry. Ireland never at any time possessed a native coinage, nor had any recognised national emblems. The Danish settlers, under their kings, in the South of Ireland, assumed the prerogative of issuing money stamped with their own devices. From the time of Henry II. the English-coined money was brought into use.

THE HARP IN THE ARMS OF IRELAND.

Three crowns in pale (found on the Irish coinage of Edward IV., Richard III., and Henry VII.) were the armorial bearings of Ireland from the time of Richard II. to that of Henry VIII., in 1530. It has been suggested that Henry VIII., on being presented by the Pope with the harp of Brian Boru, was induced to change the arms of Ireland to a representation of the relic of her most celebrated native king.

It is stated by Sir Bernard Burke that the three crowns were relinquished for the harp as the arms of Ireland by Henry VIII. from an apprehension, it is said, lest they might be taken for the Papal tiara, to which, from being in pale (*i.e.*, one above the other), the resemblance was somewhat close.

With the accession of James I. to the English throne, a new arrangement of the national insignia was made, and a gold harp with silver strings for Ireland was for the first time quartered in the Royal Arms. At that time Sir William Segar relates that the Earl of Northampton, then Deputy Earl Marshal, observed that " he had no affection for the change ; that for the adoption of the harp the best reason he could assign was that it resembled Ireland in being such an instrument that it required more cost to keep it in tune than it was worth."

Sir Arthur Chichester was re-appointed to the government of Ireland as Lord Deputy, July, 1613; it is stated that it was at his instigation the *Harp of Ireland* was first marshalled with the arms of the sister kingdoms upon the Irish currency, and in one form or another it has ever since continued to be impressed

CARRICKFERGUS.

upon the coin of the realm. Some of the copper coins of Henry VIII. and Queen Elizabeth have, it is said, the three harps for Ireland upon the shield, as if undetermined whether to follow the triple or single representation of the device. A curious old seal of the port of Carrickfergus, dated 1605, has upon the shield *three harps* of the Brian Boru type. After tracing the history and development of the various types of harps on the great seals of the sovereigns, we find the symbolic angel gradually became the regulation pattern on the coinage and all heraldic representations ; modern taste, however, tends towards the older form.

THE COLOUR OF THE NATIONAL SHIELD OF IRELAND.

According to the evidence afforded by Sir Bernard Burke, Ulster King-at-Arms, there was, previous to the Anglo Norman invasion, no colour or standard for Ireland at large. Brian Boru's banner at Clontarf was red. The favourite colours of those days were crimson, saffron, and blue ; green was not in favour. Sir Bernard's conclusion is that none of the Celtic records or authorities show that any one colour or banner was adopted in the earlier times for Ireland, while he is equally certain that " since the introduction of the English rule the national colour established by and derived from the national arms has been invariably blue." While on this subject, Mr. Vinycomb referred to the peculiar badge of the baronetcy.

THE RED HAND.

Arms of Ulster.

Sir Bernard Burke, Ulster King-at-Arms, than whom there is no greater authority, in several of his published works on heraldry refers to the arms of the province of Ulster. In his "General Armory" he blazons the arms of Ulster as, *Or, on a cross gules an inescutcheon argent charged with a dexter hand of the second (i.e.,* red). This it will be perceived is a dexter or right hand.

One of the most beautiful seals, the only approach to heraldry in Ireland in early times, is that of Hugh O'Neill (*circa* 1335), King of Ulster, a distinguished soldier. His death is recorded in the "Annals of the Four Masters;" Hugh O'Neill, the best man of the Irish of his time, died in 1364, having gained the palm for humanity, hospitality, valour, and renown. The legend upon the seal is " *Sigillum Odonis O'Neill Regis Hybernicorum Ultoniae.*" " It will be observed," says Sir Bernard Burke, " that the hand, as in other early seals of the family of O'Neill, is a *dexter hand.*" This exquisite seal found its way into the possession of Horace Walpole in the course of last century, having come to him

from the neighbourhood of Belfast.   In his own description of
Strawberry Hill, printed there in 1784, he describes the relic as
a silver seal, extremely ancient, of Hugh O'Neill, King of
Ulster, brought out of Ulster by Mr. William Bristowe.   It was
sold at the Strawberry Hill sale, passed into the hands of Mr.
Otway Cave, and is now among the treasures which have
descended to his nephew, Lord Braye.

At the institution of the Order of Baronetcy by James I., it
was declared that they " should, for their distinction, bear in
their coat of arms, either in a canton or in an escutcheon, *in a
field argent, a hand gules,* being the arms of the ancient kings
of Ulster."   "It is a curious circumstance, however," says Sir
Bernard Burke, "that at the present day the baronets do not
adhere to the O'Neill arms, but bear the badge of the red hand
sinister, which is clearly shown by the O'Neill seals to be
incorrect.   This inaccuracy dates only from modern times.   In
the funeral entries in Ulster's office of the Irish baronets who
died in the XVII. century the hand is properly *dexter,* as one may
see on the funeral banners of Sir Thomas Alen, Bart., of St.
Wolstan's, who died 7th March, 1626 ; Sir Valentine Brown,
Bart., Nolahiffe, 7th September, 1633 ; Sir George Rawdon,
Bart., and Sir Richard Bulkely, Bart., who both died in 1684.
Still more recently, so late as 1740, Sir John Denny Vesey,
Bart., when created Baron Knapton, had his arms and supporters
registered with the baronet's hand *dexter* as it should be."

So we may with confidence accept the dictum of Sir
Bernard Burke, that "the red hand of Ulster now used as the
badge of the baronets of England and Ireland is 'sinister' ;
but a *dexter hand* was used by the O'Neills, and is registered in
this office as the cognizance of the Province of Ulster.   In
neither case should there be drops of blood," and in his "General
Armory" he gives the arms as I have already described, *i.e., a
red cross on a gold field with a dexter hand on a small white
shield placed upon the centre of the cross.*

The legend of the cutting off of the left hand and throwing
it ashore from a boat is a pure myth of very uncertain origin.

There are innumerable legends of the red hand in every part of the world, but these we must pass by for the present.

THE UNION JACK.

Known all the world over as the national ensign of the United Kingdom of Great Britain and Ireland. The Union Jack has a history, and an interesting one. It symbolises the union of the three kingdoms by the combined crosses of the three patron saints—SS. George, Andrew, and Patrick.

CROSS OF ST. GEORGE—ARGENT A CROSS GULES.

" Saint George for merrie England "—(Cri-de-guerre of the middle ages).

First in order in English heraldry is the simple form of the cross. A red cross upon a white field, the peculiar ensign of St. George, the patron saint of England, has been the distinguishing badge of England, at least from the time of Edward III.

CROSS OF ST. ANDREW—AZURE A SALTIRE ARGENT.

And cry " Saint Andrew and our right."—(The Scottish Slogan)—Scott's " Marmion."

The cross of St. Andrew is a white diagonal cross upon a blue field. Upon a cross of this form it is related that the saint

516   [Proc. B.N.F.C.,

suffered martyrdom in Greece. Its adoption in Scotland dates
back to very remote times. It was the blue banner of the
Covenant, and has played part in the eventful history of that
country.

CROSS OF ST. PATRICK—ARGENT A SALTIRE GULES.

The third cross of the Union Jack is the red saltire (or diagonal
cross) of St. Patrick, adopted as the national ensign, and named
after the patron saint of Ireland, as those of England and
Scotland had been. It does not appear as having been in any
way associated with the life and labours of St. Patrick. Its
adoption, the lecturer thought, dates from the institution of the
Knightly Order of St. Patrick, in 1783, when it became the badge
of the Order. The Royal Irish Academy in 1785 adopted the
same cross, with a royal crown in the centre, as the arms of the
Society. A red saltire is the arms of the noble family of
Fitzgerald, Duke of Leinster, and it may have been adopted from
this ancient house.

1st Union Jack, 1606

2nd Union Jack 1801.

THE FIRST UNION JACK was formed in 1606 by proclamation
of James I., so as to put an end to disputes as to precedence of
the respective banners of St. George and St. Andrew, by providing a common flag for the nation as a single kingdom. THE
SECOND or PRESENT UNION JACK was adopted on the legislative
union with Ireland in 1801. The peculiar arrangement of the

crosses in combination was fully explained, by which the red saltire of St. Patrick and the white saltire of St. Andrew are conjoined, with equal precedence, side by side, and along with the cross of St. George—a matter, as he pointed out, very rarely to be seen correctly done. The name *Jack* is said to take its name from King James, the original author of the Union flag, whose name in French would be *Jacques;* in Latin is *Jacobus;* and his followers were *Jacobites.*

In the army, each regiment has a distinctive flag; while in the navy, flags are of supreme importance as marks of distinction. The anchor of hope on a red ground denotes the admiralty ; a pennant indicates a ship of war ; whilst the ensign on the mast-head denotes the ship's nationality. In the British navy there used to be three ensigns, RED, WHITE, and BLUE, respectively named from the colour of the field. THE WHITE ENSIGN is now alone used by the navy. It is a white flag with a St. George's cross extending over the field, a small Union Jack occupying the upper corner next the flag staff. THE RED ENSIGN is carried by the merchant service, and the BLUE ENSIGN by the naval reserve ; each ensign bearing on its respective colour a small Union Jack in the canton or upper corner.

The address, which was listened to with much interest, was illustrated by a fine series of the various flags and standards, kindly lent by Mr. S. Wilson, of Corporation Square, and by a large number of drawings of armorial shields of the various sovereigns, &c.

———————

The next business was the receiving of the Report of the Sub-Committe appointed to investigate the glacial gravels of Ballyrudder, County Antrim, which was read by Mr. R. Lloyd Praeger, M.R.I.A., senior secretary, and which is here given *in extenso:*

REPORT

OF THE SUB-COMMITTEE APPOINTED TO INVESTIGATE THE GRAVELS OF BALLYRUDDER, COUNTY ANTRIM.

Compiled by R. Lloyd Praeger, Hon. Secretary.

I. *Preliminary.*—On 16th February, 1892, Mr. W. J. Knowles, in a paper read before the Club (*Proc.* 1891-92, p. 410-4), called attention to a number of rough flakes and core-like objects of flint which he had obtained in the gravel bed at Ballyrudder, on the coast half-way between Larne and Glenarm, and which he considered to closely resemble flakes of human manufacture, and to be possibly of artificial origin. As a result of the discussion on the paper, a resolution was passed by the meeting recommending the Committee to undertake the investigation of these beds with a view of settling the point raised by Mr. Knowles. The Committee accordingly appointed Messrs. Knowles, Gray, G. Donaldson, Stewart, and the secretaries a Sub-Committee to investigate and report on the deposit in question.

II. *The Investigation.*—The investigation, of which notice was given to all members of the Club, commenced on July 5th, when Messrs. Donaldson and Praeger went to Ballyrudder, and remained there during the period occupied by the enquiry. Messrs. Gray and Bulla were also present for a short time on the first day, and in the evening the excavations were visited by Messrs. Bigger and J. Hanna. The removal of the heavy bank of talus that obscured the section, which had been proceeding for some days back under the superintendence of Mr. John Dale, was completed. The Boulder Clay which overlies the gravels was carefully examined, and some general measurements taken. The next day was devoted to a careful examination of the gravel bed from top to base, many cubic yards of material being spread out by the workmen employed, and closely crutinized for flints, shells, &c., which were preserved in labelled boxes. Mr. Knowles assisted the investigation during the greater part of the day. On July 7th the examination of the gravels was completed, and the beds were traced as far as possible northward and southward. Mr. Stewart assisted the work during the afternoon.

III. *Description of Beds.*—The gravels to which the present report refers are seen in the face of the steep bluff impending over the Antrim Coast Road at the townland of Ballyrudder. They underlie a thick bed of Boulder Clay, which rises above them to a height of about 100 feet above high water mark, the top of the gravels being 40 to 50 feet above the same level. The base of the gravels is nowhere visible, but the underlying Keuper marls crop out on the sea-shore below, and, further south, in the face of the bluff. This gravel bed was first observed by Messrs. Gwyn Jeffreys and G. C. Hyndman in 1859,[1] and further inspection has since been made by Messrs. Grainger,[2] T. Mellard Reade,[3] and Stewart.[4] Your Sub-Committee selected for the examination of the beds the gravel-pit by the roadside about 300 yards south of Milltown stream. Here, when the talus was removed, the section seen was as follows :—

	Feet.	Inches.
Boulder Clay	36	0
Fine hard Clay	4	0
Coarse gravel, finer below ...	20	0
Fine clay	0	6
Fine gravel	1	0
Brownish sand	2	0
Gravel, overlying Undetermined beds }	12	0
New Red Sandstone	8	0
Highwater mark		
Total	83	6

[1] Report of British Association, 1859.

[2] Report of British Association, 1874.

[3] Quarterly Journal of the Geological Society of London, Vol. XXXV., 1879.

[4] Proc. B.N.F.C., 1879-80, Appendix.

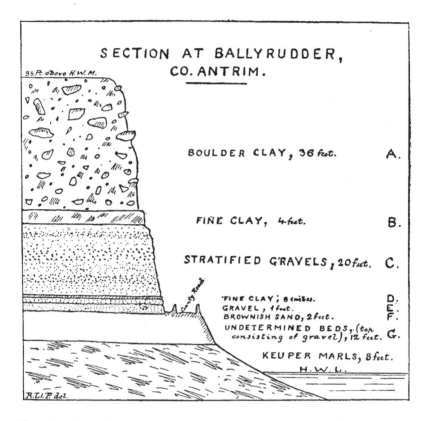

SECTION AT BALLYRUDDER, CO. ANTRIM.

95 ft. above H.W.M.

BOULDER CLAY, 36 feet.   A.

FINE CLAY, 4 feet.   B.

STRATIFIED GRAVELS, 20 feet.   C.

FINE CLAY; 6 inches.   D.
GRAVEL, 1 foot.   E.
BROWNISH SAND, 2 feet.   F.
UNDETERMINED BEDS, (top
  consisting of gravel), 12 feet. G.

KEUPER MARLS, 8 feet.
H.W.L.

R.Ll.P. del.

The Boulder Clay is such as commonly occurs in Co. Antrim. In its upper portion it contains numerous large blocks of chalk and basalt, many of them much glaciated. Throughout its depth a very large proportion of the pebbles are of these two rocks ; a few fragments of mica schist and quartz were also observed, and a number of flints derived from the Chalk. The clay varies in colour, being dark red or blackish, and exhibits no trace of stratification. A hundred yards southward its surface rises 15 or 20 feet higher than at the spot where our section was taken. No shells were obtained in this bed.

The coarse clay passed downward into very fine hard red clay, with fewer pebbles, some 4 feet in thickness ; this bed, however, is only a local development. A few shells were found in it, the species being *Astarte sulcata* var. *elliptica*, *A. cómpressa* var. *striata*, and *Tellina balthica*.

Below the clay is 20 feet of gravel. In its upper portion the deposit is coarse, somewhat reddish in colour, and with a slight admixture of clay ; the lower portion is very fine and clean, with layers of clean grey sand. The bed is stratified somewhat irregularly, but more or less horizontally. At one spot, beside a waterfall, a bed of fine red clay, 5 feet in thickness, is suddenly intercalated with the gravels. The pebbles in the gravel are mostly of trap, chalk, quartz, and flint. The larger flints are often more or less broken, having chips and flakes knocked off them, which also occur in the gravels, still looking quite fresh. The larger flints frequently show two fractures—an older series, the faces of which are now thickly encrusted ; and a newer series with uncoated faces, perhaps formed at the time of the deposition of the gravel. Some of the flint chips are encrusted, others quite free from crust. Shells, generally fragmentary, are abundant in the gravels, and they are rarer and more fragile in the upper portions of the bed, probably on account of its coarser and more open nature, which affords less protection from the influences of air and water ; but in the fine lower gravel also the strongest shells, such as *Astarte*, are very frequently fragmentary, and appear to have been broken prior to, or during deposition. Single valves only were observed, and the whole aspect of the bed and of its fauna is that it is an ancient seabeach. The layers of sand appeared devoid of shells. The species observed in the gravels were as follow :—

Puncturella noachina, vr.	*Astarte sulcata* var. *elliptica*, vc.
Buccinum undatum, f.	*A. compressa* var. *striata*, vc.
Trophon truncatus, vr.	*A. borealis*, vr.
T. clathratus, vr.	*Tellina balthica*, c.
T. clathratus var. *gunneri*, vr.	*Mactra subtruncata*, c.
Pleurotoma trevelyana, vr.	*Mya truncata*, vr.
Mytilus edulis, r.	*Saxicava rugosa*, vr.
Leda pernula, f.	*Balanus tulipa-alba*, c.

The layers of clay, sand, and gravel which underlie the thick gravel bed are of the same age, and yield a similar fauna. Without a good deal of further excavation, which your Sub-Committee was unable to undertake, no determination could be made as to the nature of the beds intervening between the base of the section explored (road level) and the New Red Sandstone, which crops out on the shore 12 feet lower, this portion of the deposit being effectually hidden by the heavily pitched slope that extends from the road to the beach. The gravel-bed is traceable along the face of the bluff for about 100 yards southward, where its surface has risen to 50 feet above high water mark. 200 yards further south the Keuper marls crop out 40 feet above high water. Northward some 300 yards the gravels may be seen on the southern side of the glen formed by the stream which passes Milltown ; here, as occasionally elsewhere, natural cement has consolidated the bed into a hard conglomerate, especially in its upper layer.

Conclusions of the Committee.—The deposits at Ballyrudder consist of a bed of stratified gravels underlying a thick layer of unstratified Boulder Clay. There is no clear line of demarcation between the two beds, the one merging gradually into the other. The fauna of the gravels shows that they were deposited during a period of intensely arctic conditions : the gravels represent a former shore-line, which a subsequent submergence has covered with marine Boulder Clay. The clay and all the zones of the gravels yield flints derived from the Chalk. These are frequently broken, and core-like objects and rude flakes are the result. The flakes are usually quite shapeless, and only one was found by the Sub-Committee bearing a bulb of percussion. None of the flints found bore any characters which might lead your Sub-Committee to suppose that they were formed by human hands.

The best thanks of your Sub-Committee are due to Mr. John Dale, of Ballyrudder, for assistance rendered during the investigation ; to Mr. J. T. Marshall, of Torquay, who gave them the benefit of his conchological knowledge in the determination of the species of shells ; and to our fellow-member, Mr. Joseph Wright, F.G.S., who has examined samples of the various beds for Foraminifera.

(Signed),   GEO. DONALDSON.
                         W. J. KNOWLES.
                         R. LLOYD PRAEGER.

Mr. Wright, in reply to a call from the chair, said that, as the result of a careful examination, he had found Foraminifera in all the Ballyrudder clays and gravels, many of them being forms which are now most abundant in shallow water around our coast. They were invariably small, starved specimens, and, with the exception of one bed, from which twenty-three different species were obtained, these microzoa were very rare in the deposits. *Nonionina depressula* was the most abundant fora-minifer in the clays. *Cassidulina crassa* was also frequent, and these two species differed less in size than the others.

It was instructive to compare the relative sizes of these glacial microzoa with the average size of the same species as they are now found living in British waters. The following are the relative sizes (bulk) of six of the commoner species of the clays as compared with recent British examples :—

Globigerina bulloides, $\frac{1}{25}$.   *Rotalia beccarii*, $\frac{1}{65}$.
Orbulina universa, $\frac{1}{10}$.   *Nonionina depressula*, $\frac{1}{4}$.
Truncatulina lobatula, $\frac{1}{125}$.   *Polystomella crispa*, $\frac{1}{65}$.

Mr. Wright stated that a short time ago he received from Mr. S. A. Stewart a sample of Glacial clay from St. John's, New Brunswick, containing a number of bivalve shells. On exa-mining it microscopically, it yielded four species of Foraminifera, viz. :—*Nonionina depressula*, very common; *Cassidulina crassa*, frequent ; *Polystomella striato-punctata*, frequent ; and *Milio-lina seminulum*, very rare. These forms have all been met with in the Ballyrudder clays, but the New Brunswick specimens were of normal size, and not depauperated as in the latter beds.

Mr. Wright submitted the following table showing the

distribution of Foraminifera in the Ballyrudder deposits, as determined by his examination of samples selected by the Sub-Committee :—

	Bed A.—Common Boulder Clay.	Bed B.—Fine Boulder Clay.	Bed C.—Gravel.	Bed F.—Brownish sand.	Bed G.	
					Sand.	Gravel.
Miliolina seminulum (Linné), ...	...	f	...	...	vr	...
,, *subrotunda* (Mont.), ...	...	f	...	...	...	...
Textularia gramen (D'Orb.), ...	...	vr	...	...	...	...
Bulimina pupoiaes (D'Orb.), ...	vr	r	...	...	...	...
,, *elegantissima* (D'Orb.),	...	r	...	...	...	...
,, *fusiformis* (Will.), ...	...	vr	...	...	...	...
Bolivina plicata (D'Orb.) ...	...	f	...	...	...	..
,, *punctata* (D'Orb.), ...	...	f	...	...	...	...
,, *lœvigata* (Will.) ...	...	vr	...	...	...	...
Cassidulina lœvigata (D'Orb.) ...	...	vr	...	..	...	...
,, *crassa* (D'Orb.) ...	r	c	...	...	vr	r
Lagena lœvigata (Rss.), ...	vr	...	...	...	...	...
,, *marginata* (W. & B.), ...	...	f	...	...	...	...
Uvigerina angulosa (Will.), ...	...	...	...	...	...	vr
Globigerina bulloides (D'Orb.), ...	...	f	...	...	...	...
Orbulina universa (D'Orb.), ...	vr	r	...	...	...	vr
Discorbina rosacea (D'Orb.), ...	...	r	...	...	...	...
,, *globularis* (D'Orb.), ...	...	vr	...	...	...	...
Pulvinulina patagonica (D'Orb.),	...	vr	...	...	...	...
Rotalia beccarii (Linné), ..	vr	c	...	...	...	...
Truncatulina lobatula (W. & J.),	...	r	...	vr	vr	r
Nonionina depressula (W. & J.),	c	c	r	...	r	c
Polystomella crispa (Linné), ..	...	vr	...	...	...	...
,, *striato-punctata* (F. & M.),	r	r	...	...	vr	...

Mr. Wright showed diagrams to illustrate the extremely small size of many of the species when compared with recent British and abyssal specimens, and stated that in several instances it was only with the greatest difficulty that he was able to definitely assign a name, so minute and depauperated were the specimens.

Messrs. W. Gray, M.R.I.A., W. H. Patterson, M.R.I.A., and F. W. Lockwood spoke on the subject of these interesting beds and their fauna, and some discussion ensued, which elicited the fact that, while the Foraminifera were so few and starved, the mollusca of the beds were tolerably abundant, and attained fully the size of recent specimens.

The President then called on Mr. W. Gray, the Club's delegate to the last meeting of the British Association, for his report as to the subjects brought before the meetings of delegates of Corresponding Societies. Mr. Gray said that the Conference meetings were held on the 4th and 9th of August under the chairmanship of Professor R. Meldola, President, and forty-one Corresponding Societies were represented by their respective delegates, among them being the delegate from the Belfast Natural History Society and the Club's representative.

The main object of the organisation was to utilise as far as possible the services of local scientific societies in promoting the investigation of such subjects as engage the attention of the several sections of the Association, so far as such subjects come within the scope of local societies' operations, and at the Conference the work done in this direction during the year is discussed, and the result is formulated into a report to the General Committee of the Association. The nature of the subjects thus referred to the delegates for their consideration will be best understood if they are considered in the order in which they are dealt with by the several sections of the Association. The latter are eight in number, each being distinguished by a letter of the alphabet from A to H.

In section A (Mathematical and Physical Science) the only subject connected with this section that co-operation is solicited is the work undertaken by the Sub-Committee on the applica-

tion of photography to the elucidation of meteorological phenomenon.

In section B (Chemistry and Mineralogy) nothing of special
interest was brought forward.

In section C (Geology) local societies have done good work,
and none have done better work than has been done by members of the Belfast Naturalists' Field Club, a service well
appreciated by the Association.

In connection with the investigation of underground waters
the members of the Club could render most valuable aid by
keeping a record of the result of well-sinking in and around
Belfast, and also the temperature and the variations in the depth
of water in wells. Perhaps the most successful and useful work
done by the local Society under this section is their contribution
to the committee on geological photography. Already seven
hundred excellent photographs, illustrative of geological phenomena, have been obtained, of which one hundred and twenty-three
are from Ireland, and by far the larger number of these are by
members of the Belfast Naturalists' Field Club. It is earnestly
hoped that the members will continue their valuable services
in this direction, for there is a vast amount of work yet required
towards the completion of the scheme the Committee have in
view.

Section D (Biology)—Discussing the subjects under this
section, a very animated debate took place at the Conference
upon the disappearance of native wild plants, and the mischief
done to the local flora owing to many causes, avoidable and
otherwise ; and the delegates were earnestly requested to bring
the subject before their respective Societies, and do all they
could to prevent the wilful destruction of our native plants.
A similar discussion took place on the means of preserving
wild birds' eggs ; not in the cabinet, but in the nest. After a
very exhaustive debate and a unanimous condemnation of the
destruction of wild birds' eggs, the following resolution was
agreed to :—" The Conference of delegates having heard of the
threatened extermination of certain birds of British breeding

species, through the destruction of their eggs, deprecates the encouragement given to dealers by collectors, through their demands for British-taken eggs, and trust that the Corresponding Societies will do all that lies in their power to interest and influence naturalists, landowners, and others in the preservation of such birds and their eggs."

In the following sections—E (Geography), F (Economic Science and Statistics), and G (Mechanical Science) there was little that called for the special services of the members of local societies.

The last and youngest section of the British Association, Section H, devoted to Anthropology, is one of the most active and popular sections during the annual meetings, and, as such, calls for assistance in promoting an ethnographical survey of the United Kingdom.

The President said he was sure that the members were deeply indebted to Mr. Gray for attending the British Association meeting on their behalf, and bringing the leading subjects before them in such a lucid manner.

Mr. Francis Joseph Bigger, junior secretary, was glad to say that the Committee of the Club had already had under their consideration the subject of local ethnography, and with a view of encouraging this work had arranged with Professor Haddon, of Dublin, a member of the British Association Ethnographical Committee, to lecture before the Club on this subject in January next, when it was hoped a local ethnographical committee would be formed.

Mr. Joseph Wright, F.G.S., then made some remarks on rare local Foraminifera recently found, of which he exhibited diagrams. He said that on the dredging cruise which the Club had some years ago in the steam-tug Protector one of the hauls was taken in deep water, 100 fathoms, about midway between Belfast and Portpatrick. This material, which has only recently been examined microscopically, has yielded a large number of foraminifera, several of them being rare and interesting species; the most noteworthy are *Technitella legumen, Hyperammina arborescens, H. elongata*, very large in size, *Webbina clavata*, and *W. hemisphærica*. The last of these is a very simple organism, of great rarity, and hitherto only known from three specimens—one fossil from the Sutton Crag, the other two from dredgings taken by Messrs. Norman and Robertson off the Durham coast. In a dredging recently taken by their fellow-member, Mr. Hamilton M'Cleery, in shallow water, Strangford Lough, no fewer than 85 different species of Foraminifera were obtained, two of them, *Ammodiscus shoneanus* and *Discorbina parisiensis*, being very rare forms.

The following new members were elected :—Miss F. Whitaker, Messrs. David Fulton, John Hungerford, Benjamin Hobson, Henry Barnes, and James Megahy.

The second business meeting was held on Tuesday evening, December 20th. Before the commencement of the meeting a new departure was made in the providing of tea in the lower room for members and visitors, and, to judge from the number that availed themselves of the excellent repast provided by the Committee of lady members in charge, there can be little doubt that the new institution will be both of convenience and of social value to the members and their friends. When tea had been disposed of, the President took the chair at 7.30.

The first communication brought forward was a paper by Mr. Edward M'Connell entitled " Notes on the Geology of New Zealand," which was read by the senior secretary. The general characteristics of the island were first discussed—its climate, agriculture, and physical features. The geological formations of New Zealand are varied, almost all the periods being represented, from Azoic to Recent. Metamorphic schists are represented in Westland, Nelson, and Otago. They contain deposits of magnetic iron ore, from which much gold has been derived. Nuggets have been found valued at from £25 to £60. Silver, antimony, and pyrites are found in large quantities in the

Thames district. In Stafford township and elsewhere gold is found embedded in a morainic argillaceous clay, with intersecting quartz reefs. Other alluvial goldfields are situated at Blue Spur, Kumara, and elsewhere. The theory of the formation of auriferous veins was next discussed, and it was pointed out that the gold must have been injected into the rock-fissures during periods of intense heat and pressure. The coal-beds of New Zealand belong to the Cretaceous and Eocene periods, and are therefore immensely more recent than those of Britain. The price of coal varies from 18s. to 36s. per ton according to quality. The deposits of antimony, bog iron-ore, and sulphur were also mentioned, and the paper closed with a description of the building stones most used in the colony. A number of interesting specimens were shown in illustration of the paper.

The next paper was by Miss M. K. Andrews, on the subject of "Denudation at Cultra, County Down," and was read by the junior secretary. The writer stated that tradition, history, and geological evidence all bear testimony to the continued interchange, within certain limits, of land and water. Although the deep depressions of the ocean and the main trends of the land seem from the very earliest geological periods to have preserved the same general positions on the globe, yet a careful comparison of the upheaved stratified formations, with the layers of gravel, shells, sand, and mud deposited in the comparatively shallow seas around our coasts, leaves little doubt that the greater part of our land areas was at one period or another laid down upon the floor of the sea. From the raised beaches of our own coasts to the great terraces of Patagonia, rising like mighty steps, one behind the other, we see the effects of the same co-operating actions—erosion, deposition, and upheaval. So also in the present, we know that some regions of the earth are relatively rising, others are gradually sinking. The sea is making encroachments on certain coasts, it is receding on others. As a general rule, where the rocks are hard, erosion is slow ; where they are soft and more easily disintegrated, it is rapid. Striking illustrations of marine erosion might be drawn

from the tunnelled caves and imposing sea-stacks of our Irish
coast, but the encroachment of the sea at Cultra Bay, on the
southern side of Belfast Lough, to which I wish to draw attention in the present paper, has left no such impressive features.
Much land has been washed away, of which no trace would
have remained, had it not been for one insignificant landmark,
and before it, too, disappears, I have made a few notes of the
encroachment of the sea to which it testifies, which I hope may
not be devoid of interest. The landmark to which I refer is a
shaft of crown Memel pine, about 23 feet high, standing on the
beach opposite Cultra Point, a mile north-east of Holywood.
It formed part of a windmill pump, erected, I am informed by
Mr. John Lennox, in 1824 or 1825 to remove the water from an
old quarry. The upright standard above the much-decayed
suction-pipe of the pump still remains, with a loose iron rod
attached to a small handle at the top. Although 50 feet distant
from present high water mark, and surrounded by the sea to a
depth of three feet at high tide, this old pump marks the
centre of a sandstone quarry, opened on what was formerly
known as the " point field." An inhabitant of Holywood, Mr.
William Nimick, who remembers the locality since 1829,
informs me that the sea was at that time fifty feet distant
from the centre of the quarry, and that the fields, through
which a broad carriage drive passed to Cultra Quay, and in
which he saw numerous tents pitched, and large crowds of
spectators assembled to watch one of the celebrated regattas
of the Northern Yacht Club, have now completely disappeared.
He estimates that at least four acres of land have since been
washed away between Cultra Point and Cultra Pier. Disintegrated by the action of rain, frost, and other subaërial agents,
portion after portion of the low cliffs has slipped down, an
easy prey to the warfare of wave and current ; the destruction of the land still further aided by the removal of sand and
gravel from the beach below. And now, at ebb tide, instead of
the vanished fields, we see low denuded reefs that carry us back
through vistas of time immeasurably vast. Here in this one

THE OLD PUMP, CULTRA, CO. DOWN.

small bay we find represented each great division of the geological record. Shales that carry us back to the Palæozoic era, and recall the gradual submergence of the Devonian continent beneath the waters of the Carboniferous ocean ; sandstones that bring us to the Mesozoic era, and restore for us the vast Triassic lakes ; dykes that link us with the great basaltic sheets of Tertiary time, and, covering the low surrounding cliffs, drift deposits that bring us to post-Tertiary periods and gradually forward to the time we are considering.

Encroachments of the sea similar to those described have taken place on the adjacent coast. Although no landmark survives, it is estimated that within living memory the sea has advanced more than 150 feet at Cooper's Bay, near Holywood ; and Cooper's Green, once a favourite resort for rural games, has now, with part of an inner adjoining field, completely disappeared. In confirmation of the foregoing notes it is interesting to trace the changes recorded on successive maps of the Ordnance Survey. On the six-inch map, surveyed and engraved in 1834, we find both the quarry at Cultra Point and the road leading to Cultra Quay, while on the same map, revised in 1858, and engraved in 1860, Cultra Point has a more smoothed and rounded appearance, the quarry is no longer marked, and all traces of the road are gone. A comparison of successive Admiralty charts gives indications of somewhat similar interesting changes in Belfast Lough. In the chart for 1883, corrected up to 1891, the three-fathom line (close to the end of the new cut recently opened in continuation of the Victoria Channel) is more than 800 feet nearer to Belfast than in the chart for 1841, corrected up to 1856. Within the same period the three-fathom line has also approached more closely to Holywood and to Carrickfergus.

After an accurate description of the various geological formations at Cultra, the long and interesting record that they show us, and the part that their varying hardness has borne in their own recent erosion by the sea, the writer concluded—We have glanced at the apparent destruction of a small land surface, we have seen its materials loosened, disintegrated, falling a prey to the energy of waves and currents, but the destruction is not ultimate. The sea not only grinds down ; it sorts and arranges the fragments, and lays them down to form new strata on its floor. Consolidation and ultimate upheaval will surely follow, but the processes by which these stages in the earth's architecture are effected remain obscure. We await further light, satisfied if we have illustrated one small link in that marvellous cycle of order and change traceable throughout the whole geological record.

Messrs. F. W. Lockwood, Alexander Tate, C.E. ; William Gray, M.R.I.A. ; W. H. Patterson, M.R.I.A. ; and R. Lloyd Praeger criticised the paper, and spoke of the high scientific interest of such authentic and detailed accounts of coast erosion.

The third item on the programme consisted of some remarks by Mr. R. Lloyd Praeger, M.R.I.A., senior secretary, on rare plants found in the district during 1891 and 1892, of which he exhibited specimens. These notes being a continuation of his supplemental notes to the "Flora of the North-East of Ireland," a systematic abstract of them is here given.

Mr. Praeger said that two years ago he had had the pleasure of laying before the Club some notes on the rarest species found in the twelfth botanical district of Ireland (Down, Antrim, and Derry) since the publication of Stewart and Corry's "Flora of the North-East of Ireland" (1888) ; he now wished to draw attention to the more important discoveries made in that district during 1891 and 1892. He regretted that the small number of workers caused his own name to appear with undue frequency.

Ranunculus circinatus, Sibth. In the Lagan Canal, close to its junction with Lough Neagh, Co. Down, R.Ll.P., 1892 (*fide* A. Bennett). It also grows close by, inside the Armagh boundary, and is extremely abundant in Derryadd Bay in Lough Neagh, some three miles to the west ; the latter station is also in Armagh. Not previously recorded from any part of Ulster.

Papaver hybridum, Linn. Roadside half-way between Killough and Ardglass, sparingly, September 1892, R.Ll.P. *P.*

rhœas is plentiful in fields at the same place. Only previously recorded habitat in Ulster is along the Down shore of Belfast Lough, where it has been known for nearly a century.

‡*Barbarea præcox*, R. Br.   Cultivated ground at Struell Wells, near Downpatrick, R.Ll.P., 1891 (*fide* A. Bennett). New to District 12, the plants recorded under this name in "Flora Belfastiensis" being referable to *B. intermedia*.

Lavatera arborea, Linn.   Growing in some abundance near the summit of Stackaniskan, an isolated sea-stack, rising about 100 feet above the water at the western end of Rathlin Island ; R.Ll.P., June, 1892. Stackaniskan stands about 100 yards from the shore, and can only be approached by boat in calm weather ; the habitat of the tree-mallow is quite inaccessible, and I do not see how the plant can have been possibly introduced here. It grows sparingly on the cliffs of the mainland further northward, but I did not observe it in any cottage garden on the island. (See *Irish Naturalist*, 1893, p. 53.)

Hypericum quadrangulum, Linn., var. *maculatum*, Bab.   Side of the lane leading from Marino Station to Cultra Garden, Co. Down, R.Ll.P., August, 1892. Only previous record in district 12 is in Co. Antrim, by the Lagan, a few miles above Belfast. Mr. J. H. Davies has recently found it at Glenmore, near Lisburn, further up the same river.

Geranium pyrenaicum, Linn.   Roadside, near Whitewell Quarries on Cave Hill, W. D. Donnan. Not hitherto recorded from Co. Antrim.

Erodium cicutarium, L'Herit.   Observed on the Field Club Excursion to Binevenagh, Co. Derry, July 30th, 1892, in several spots along the base and summit of the cliffs (800— 1,200 feet *circa*) growing among *Silene acaulis*, *S. maritima*, *Dryas octopetala*, *Salix herbacea*, and other alpines.

†*Prunus cerasus*, Linn.   Not uncommon in Down and Antrim, but often in suspicious situations. Near Crossgar and Downpatrick in Down, Cushendun and Ballycastle in Antrim, and Draperstown in Derry, R.Ll.P.

Poterium sanguisorba, Linn.   In some abundance in a meadow at Glenmore, near Lisburn, Co. Antrim, J. H. Davies, June, 1892 (*Irish Naturalist,* 1892, p. 81).   The plant grows luxuriantly here, but is apparently confined to one meadow. The geological formation is New Red Sandstone, but the Chalk is not far away.   An addition to the flora of District 12.

Agrimonia odorata, Mill.   Roadside near the steamboat quay, Downpatrick, R.Ll.P.

Rubus chamæmorus, Linn.   The rediscovery by Messrs. H. C. Hart and R. M. Barrington of this rare alpine bramble in Ireland, on the Sperrin Mountains, whence Admiral Jones recorded it 63 years ago, is recorded in *Journal of Botany,* 1892, p. 279.   One small patch was found on the Tyrone side of the county boundary, and a smaller one on the Derry side.   An addition to the flora of District 12.

Sium angustifolium, Linn.   Very rare in District 12, but frequent in the neighbourhood of Downpatrick.   Not recently seen at the recorded station, "roadside between Downpatrick and the sluice" (Dickie, *Flor. Ulst.*), but found by Mr. Stewart at a spot by the Clough Road, a mile from Downpatrick ; and by the reader at Ballydugan Lake and marshes S.W. of it ; at a pool near the "Bull's Eye ;" in ditches near Inch Abbey ; at the north end of Money Lake ; and in Carrigullion Lake, near Killinchy.

Ligustucum scoticum, Linn.   Rocks on the shore at Bushfoot, Antrim, R.Ll.P.   Recently refound in Dr. Moore's Garron Point station by Rev. S. A. Brenan.

Torilis nodosa, Huds.   Side of the road leading inland from the quay, Rathlin Island, R.Ll.P., June, 1892.

Peucedanum ostruthium, Koch.   The Cave Hill station of *Flor. N.E.I.* turns out to be an error, the plant being a luxuriant state of *Ægopodium podagraria.*   Stoneyford, Co. Antrim, R. Ll. P.

Galium mollugo, Linn.   Near Eglinton, Co. Derry, Mrs. Leebody (H. C. Hart in *Journ. Bot.,* 1892, p. 281).   New to Co. Derry.

Leontodon hirtus, Linn. Fields by the sea at Dalchoolin, near Craigavad, Co. Down, abundant over a limited area, R.Ll.P., September, 1892. Though recorded from two stations in Down and two in Antrim, Macedon Point, on the opposite (Antrim) shore of Belfast Lough, is the only habitat in which the plant has been seen for the last thirty years. *L. hispidum* is rarer still, if, indeed, it occurs at all in the district ; neither Mr. S. A. Stewart nor the reader has ever seen a specimen from the North of Ireland.

Hieracium flocculosum, Backhouse. Sallagh Braes, Co. Antrim, S. A. Stewart (*fide* F. J. Hanbury). The only other Irish station is in the Mourne Mountains, Co. Down.

H. euprepes, Hanb. This plant was gathered on Cave Hill, near Belfast, by Dr. Matier, in 1845 (spec. in Boswell herbarium, *fide* F. J. Hanbury). Since 1879 it has been well known to Mr. S. A. Stewart, who repeatedly gathered it at this station, and also at Sallagh Braes, Co. Antrim, and Binevenagh, Co. Derry, and submitted it on various occasions to Mr. Backhouse and Mr. Hanbury without their assigning a satisfactory name to it, but Mr. Hanbury now refers Mr. Stewart's large series of specimens unhesitatingly to his *H. euprepes*, which has not previously been recorded from Ireland.

H. rubicundum, Hanb. Sallagh Braes, Co. Antrim, S. A. Stewart, 1890 (*fide* F. J. Hanbury). Only previous Irish station is Innishowen, Co. Donegal, where it has been found by Mr. H. C. Hart.

H. Farrense, Hanb. Collected by Mr. Stewart at Sallagh Braes, Co. Antrim, July, 1890 (*fide* F. J. Hanbury). Another addition to the list of Irish hawkweeds.

H. auratum, Fries. This hawkweed, first recorded as Irish by Mr. Stewart and the reader (*Proc. R.I.A.*, 3rd Ser., Vol. II., No. 2) from the Mourne Mountains, where it is widely distributed, is probably of frequent occurence in Antrim. Specimens gathered on the Lough Neagh shore at Cranfield by Mr. Stewart, and on sea-cliffs at Cushendun by R.Ll.P., have been confirmed by Mr. Hanbury.

Vaccinium oxycoccos, Linn.   Marsh at Saul Camp near Down-patrick ; by a lakelet N.W. of Carnlough, Co. Antrim, at about 1,000 feet elevation ; and in bog on shores of Lough Ouske, in the Sperrin Mountains, on the borders of Derry and Tyrone, R Ll.P.   Rare in District 12, and not pre-viously recorded from Antrim.

**Orobanche minor*, Linn.   Abundant in a field by the sea at Craigavad, Co. Down, H. C. Marshall, July, 1892.   No doubt introduced with seed, and probably will not be per-manent.   *Medicago sativa*, another alien, is abundant in the same field.

**Erinus alpinus*, Linn.   Growing freely on the wall of the goal at Downpatrick, Co. Down, R.Ll.P., 1890 and 1892.   A South European plant, that has become established in the North of England, but has apparently not been previously noticed in Ireland.

‡*Verbena officinalis*, Linn.   Roadside, about a mile from Pointz-pass on the way to Loughbrickland, Co. Down, Rev. H. W. Lett.   Doubtfully native in many of its Irish stations, and not known as indigenous in the North of Ireland.   If per-manent here, it should, however, rank at least as a colonist.

Myosotis collina, Hoffm.   Gravelly banks at the mouth of the Six-mile River, Lough Neagh, Co. Antrim, R.Ll.P.   Very rare in the North-east, and I do not know of any other inland locality in Ireland.

Galeopsis speciosa, Mill.   In fields below Glenariff waterfalls, and at Ardclinis on Garron Point, and at Cushendun, R.Ll.P.   Large flowered forms of *G. tetrahit* have been often mistaken for this species, but the splendid yellow-spotted flowers of *G. speciosa* when once seen will not again be mistaken.

Atriplex farinosa, Dum.   Sandy shores at Redbay, Cushendun, and Bushfoot, R.Ll.P.

Hydrocharis morsus-ranæ, Linn.   In bog-holes at Gawley's Gate, one and a half miles west of its Portmore habitat, R.Ll.P.

Orchis pyramidalis, Linn. The exclusion of this plant from Co. Derry (*Flor. N.E.I.* and R.Ll.P. in *Proc. B.N.F.C.*, 1890-91, p. 290) turns out to be incorrect, as the plant has been since found in some abundance at the eastern end of Magilligan Strand by Mrs. Leebody.

Typha angustifolia, Linn. In Lough Neagh at the mouth of the Lagan Canal, R.Ll.P., August, 1892. This station is on the borders of Antrim and Armagh ; the plant grows here in both counties.

Carex aquatilis, Wahlb. As recorded in *Journal of Botany* (1892, p. 153) this plant was obtained in a ditch by the River Main in Shane's Castle Park, Co. Antrim, R.Ll.P., June, 1891. It may be expected on the Lough Neagh shores. New to District 12.

C. limosa, Linn. Plentiful in a wet marsh on Saul Camp ground, Downpatrick, Co. Down ; more sparingly on the margins of Lough Ouske, on the borders of Derry and Tyrone, and growing in both counties, R.Ll.P. A very rare sedge in the North of Ireland, and not hitherto observed in Derry nor in District 10.

Schlerochloa rigida, Linn. Walls by the sea at Ardglass and Killough, Co. Down, R.Ll.P., September, 1892. In District 12 is apparently confined to South Down.

Equisetum hyemale, Linn. Plentiful by the side of the Lagan, just below Edenderry factory, Co. Down, R.Ll.P., Sept., 1892. In Down only known previously in the Mourne Mountains. By the Glenarm River above Park Mill, and at two spots in northern branch of Glenariff, Co. Antrim, R.Ll.P. Recorded by Dr. Moore in "Cybele Hibernica" as " in many of the glens of Antrim."

Chara contraria, Kuetz. Clandeboye Lake, R.Ll.P., 1891 (*fide* H. and J. Groves). Only previous record in District 12 was in the reader's previous paper before the Club.

Some further additions to the flora of District 12, and stations for a number of the rarer species, will be found in the " Report on the Botany of the Mourne Mountains" (Proc. Royal Irish Academy, 3rd Series, Vol. II., No. 2, 1892), by Messrs. Stewart and Praeger, the additions to the flora there recorded being *Drosera intermedia, Rubus ammobius, R. nitidus, Rosa involuta* (type), *Saussurea alpina, Hieracium argenteum,* and *H. auratum.*

At the close of the proceedings the following new members were elected :—Mrs. Leslie, Mr. J. Campbell Carson, and Mr. William Bryson.

The third meeting was held on January 17th, the President in the chair, when Professor A. C. Haddon, M.A , M.R.I.A., delivered a lecture on "The Aran Islands ; a study in Irish Ethnography." There was a very large attendance of members and visitors. The President briefly introduced the lecturer, remarking that Professor Haddon needed little introduction to any audience assembled in that hall.

Professor Haddon said that there is even in Ireland considerable ignorance respecting its western isles. People have a hazy notion that they are extremely interesting, and that their scenery is fine ; but few have any definite knowledge about them. He had been invited by the Belfast Naturalists' Field Club to give an account, so far as he was able, by word and picture, of the Aran Islands, Co. Galway. He gladly embraced the opportunity thus afforded of suggesting to that energetic Club a new kind of field work. Of late years the study of Irish Natural History has received a fresh impetus, but the natural history of the Irish man is as yet unworked, and owing to various causes it is increasingly becoming more difficult to study, hence the necessity for prompt action in the matter. He proposed, then, illustrating the methods of this new study by limiting his remarks to a description of a very circumscribed area. This would necessitate the grouping of his facts into a more academic form than is customary in popular lectures.

His remarks would be arranged under the following heads :—
ENVIRONMENT, THE PEOPLE THEMSELVES, MODE OF LIFE,
FOLK-LORE, ARCHÆOLOGY, and HISTORY. In other words, in
order to find out who people are and how they have become
what they are, we must first study what they are, what they do,
what they think, and what they have done. Analysis must
precede synthesis.

(1) ENVIRONMENT :—The three main islands of Aran lie
N.W.—S.E. at the mouth of Galway Bay. Aranmore, or
Inishmore, the largest of them, is about 9 miles long and
averages 1½ broad, and had in 1891 a population of 1996.
Inishmaan is about the third of the size of the north island,
with a population of about 456. Inishsheer, the south island,
is somewhat smaller, and has a population of about 455. The
climate is mild and uniform, it rarely freezes, but there is any
amount of rain. The geological formation is Carboniferous
Limestone, and the conformation of the land is such that
towards the Atlantic there are vertical cliffs which range up to
250 feet in height. The hills decrease in height by numerous
terraces towards the north-east. By far the greater portion of
the island (he was practically confining himself now to Aranmore) is covered with bare rock intersected in all directions by
deep crevasses, which are choked with maiden-hair and other
ferns, beautiful and rare flowers, and sweet grass. In places the
naked rock forms large slabs. Scattered all over the island are
large erratic boulders from the Connemara mountains. There
are some arable and pasturage fields, but some of them, at least,
are artificial and not natural, for the people bring up sea-sand
and sea-weed and strew them on the live rock, when there is
sufficient depth of soil they plant potatoes, and after several
crops of these they can make a grass meadow, and later they
can grow rye. Only in two sheltered spots are there any trees
growing.

(2) PEOPLE :—The people are well-made, of moderate stature,
and good-looking, with fresh complexion, brown hair, and blue-
grey eyes. Their heads are rather long and narrow, their faces,

too, are rather long, the cheek bones are not prominent. On the occasion of my last visit, Dr. C. R. Browne, of Dublin, and myself made numerous careful measurements of 27 men. To a visitor the people appear pleasant and courteous, but they are said to be cunning, untrustworthy, and very boastful when in liquor. They are also said to occasionally treat the old people badly. Love-making is practically unknown. The people are subject to very few diseases, and they are long lived. A considerable number of the young people emigrate.

(3) MODE OF LIFE :—A well-to-do man will have what is locally called a " crogarry," or 11 to 14 acres of land, or more correctly speaking of rocks and stones, for probably about one-fourth only of the land is fit for pasturage or tillage. He will have a mare, one or two cows, sheep and pigs. Enough potatoes are grown for home consumption, but all the meal is imported from Galway. The rye is grown for the straw for thatching. Most of the better-off men own a curragh. The men of the north island do very little fishing, but spend most of their energies in making kelp. £40 a year can be made in this way ; but half this sum, or even less, is a more usual amount. All their peat has to be imported from Connemara ; in the early spring, cow-dung is dried and used as fuel. Even now most of their clothing is entirely home-made. The women spin the wool of their own sheep. There are several weavers on the islands, and the yarn or the flannel is dyed at home. The men usually wear white frieze, or may have grey or brown waistcoats; a Tam-o'-Shanter cap is in very general wear. The women wear white or red flannel petticoats ; they never wear caps or bonnets. Most wear red tartan shawls, which they buy in Galway. Both sexes wear sandals made of raw cowhide, the hair being outside. The edges of the hide are caught up with string, with which they are tied on over the instep. There is nothing very special in the dwellings ; the kitchen always has a front and a back door opposite to one another, and the pigs have comfortable quarters by the fire.

(4) FOLK-LORE :—A wide-spread folk-custom is praying and

making offerings at holy wells—these abound at Aran. At one
prayers for the sick are efficacious ; the water of this well won't
boil, and dead fish put into it come to life again. At St.
Eaney's well the women pray for children, and the men at the
rag well close by the church of the Four Comely Ones ; this
well contains numerous buttons, fish-hooks, bits of crockery,
nails, etc. There are numerous unlucky days—Mondays, the
Cross day, and the day of the week on which the Feast of the
Holy Innocents falls. On none of these days will a grave be
dug. The evil-eye is firmly believed in.

(5) ARCHÆOLOGY :—Besides the holy wells already mentioned there are numerous other " blessed places," and several
broken carved crosses occur in different places, the most
interesting of which is a holed stone on which a cross is incised.
Aran was formerly famous for its saints, and this is borne out
by the numerous early Christian churches which occur, many
of which are of the highest interest. The pagan antiquities are
also of extreme interest. Only one cromleac was known to
the lecturer ; as usual it is called "Diarmad and Grania's bed."
There are several cloghauns or bee-hive stone huts ; but the
most unique feature is the number of stone forts which are to
be found in these islands. Four, at least, occur in Aranmore,
two in Inishmaan, and one in Inishsheer. They are built of
stones, but without cement ; the walls towards the interior
present three tiers with numerous steps, and inside some of
them are remains of stone huts. The finest one, Dun Ængus,
is further protected on the landward side by three defence walls
and an almost impenetrable *chevaux de frise.* The fort itself
is semi-circular, and perched on the edge of the cliffs, which go
sheer down nearly 300 feet. This stray fortress is a silent
memento of one of the fierce race-struggles in Ireland, but the
page of its history is unwritten.

We have now gained some conception of *what* the "Aranites"
are, how they live, what they do and believe, and what monuments they have left us from the past ; but we cannot at present
say *who* they are. In order to speak with assurance on this

point, it is essential to have data for comparison from all parts
of Ireland, and it was to be hoped that the Belfast Field Club
would take up this work and record the remnants of a vanishing
past before it is too late. When we have a combined study of
the present inhabitants of Ireland, of their folk-lore, and of
Irish archæology, then we shall be able to decipher the real
history of the Irish people.

Mr. Robert Young, C.E., in moving a vote of thanks to
Professor Haddon, dwelt on the interest of the study of these
ancient types, and spoke of the work already accomplished in
Ireland, especially in the department of folk-lore.

Mr. William Gray, M.R.I.A., had much pleasure in seconding
the resolution. He pointed out what an excellent field our own
district offers for the study of ethnography and archæology,
and strongly supported Professor Haddon's appeal for local
work in these departments.

The secretaries announced that Professor Haddon had kindly
consented to give a further communication on the subject, with
special reference to the collecting of information and material
for an ethnographical enquiry, and the meeting accordingly
stood adjourned until the following afternoon.

The adjourned meeting was held in the Museum, on Wednesday afternoon, 18th inst., Mr. W. H. Patterson, M.R.I.A.,
in the chair. On being called upon by the Chairman, Professor
Haddon said that he did not propose on the present occasion to
give them a lecture, but to explain in a conversational way the
organization and programme of work of the British Association
Ethnographical Committee, and point out to them the ways in
which they could assist its operations. He dwelt on the pressing
importance of the subject of British and Irish Ethnography.
In this age of progress the relics of the pre-historic past were
passing away with alarming rapidity, and if not studied and
gathered together with all speed they would be lost to us for
ever. In the endeavour to determine the ancient origin of the
present races, we had to study them on a systematic scientific
basis : he specially dwelt on the importance of beliefs and

customs as affording important evidence on this point. Owing to the representations of scientists who recognised the necessity for immediate action in the direction of an ethnographical survey, the British Association was acting in concert with the Folk-Lore Society, the Anthropological Institute, and the Society of Antiquaries of London, as well as other kindred societies ; and a committee, of which he had the honour of being a member, had been appointed for the purpose of carrying out this work. A committee had now been formed in Dublin to carry out the survey in Ireland, under direction of the central committee in London, and he now suggested that the Belfast Naturalists' Field Club should appoint a committee to undertake ethnographical work in Ulster, their results to pass through the Dublin committee to the central institution. Professor Haddon then explained at length the lines on which work should be carried on, dealing especially with physical measurements, folk-lore, and dialect. He stated that the central committee would shortly issue schedules and instructions, which would be passed to the local committee for distribution among individuals interested in the subject and willing to aid in this important work.

Mr. Seaton F. Milligan, M.R.I.A., said that Mr. R. M. Young, M.R.I.A., hon. secretary of the Belfast Natural History and Philosophial Society, who had to leave early, would suggest that the proposed local ethnographical committee should be a joint one, composed of members both of the Society which he represented and of the Field Club.

Mr. Wm. Gray, M.R.I.A., thought that a joint committee was not advisable ; each Society was a Corresponding Society of the British Association, and the interests of science would be best met by each reporting independently to that body on the local ethnographical work accomplished.

Mr. R. Lloyd Praeger, M.R.I.A., senior secretary, thought that as the Field Club had initiated matters, they might fairly carry it on without recourse to a joint committee, which would only complicate the work. Professor Haddon and the secretaries had had the appointment of a local committee under consideration for some time, and the committee which they would recommend would include the leading archæologists of both Societies. The names suggested were as follows :—Messrs. Wm. Gray, W. H. Patterson, Miss S. M. Thompson, Rev. S. A. Brenan, and Mr. R. Welch, and the President and secretaries of the Club *ex officio ;* with power to add to their number.

Professor Haddon considered that to have two committees working in the same district at this subject would be a most unfortunate waste of energy. He wanted the Belfast committee to be entirely responsible for the whole of Ulster, and to report to the central committee in Dublin, who would in turn report to the committee for the British Islands in London. He urged the importance of preparing local maps with all pre-historic remains carefully mapped upon them.

The Chairman said Professor Haddon would be glad to hear that Mr. Gray had in his possession such maps of Counties Antrim and Down, which he had prepared for the British Association.

Professor Haddon suggested that these valuable maps should be placed at the disposal of the committee.

Mr. Gray had much pleasure in placing the maps in the hands of the committee. He explained the method employed in marking on them the various classes of remains, and in describing their position.

The names of Messrs. S. F. Milligan, M.R.I.A., F. W. Lockwood, and J. Brown having been added to the committee, on the motion of Mr. Lockwood, seconded by Mr. Milligan, the committee were elected.

On the motion of Professor Haddon, seconded by Mr. Gray, Mr. W. H. Patterson was appointed secretary to the committee.

After further discussion, the Chairman announced that the committee would be shortly called together to consider their *modus operandi ;* and the Chairman having expressed the deep obligation of the Club to Professor Haddon for coming so far to lecture to them, and giving them so much information and assistance in starting their local committee,

The proceedings terminated.

The fourth meeting was held on February 21st, the President in the chair, when two papers were read. The first was by Mr. Francis Joseph Bigger, junior secretary, his subject being " Local Folk-Lore."

Mr. Bigger said that he did not intend to bring before the Club any lengthened paper on this subject, nor to occupy their time, save for a few minutes only. His remarks would be short and simple, and would be entirely culled from his own recollection, being a chronicle of mythical fairy stories learned at his mother's knee—none had been adapted from books nor derived from any outside source. He had adopted this course to show in a slight manner what valuable services might be rendered to the study of ethnology by many of our members simply recording the primitive fancies which float about the winter hearth, or circle round the family table. This is the sort of material our Ethnographical Committee is anxious to have recorded ; and we as a Society should strive to carry out their aims as far as possible. It was his good fortune to have a mother who had still a lingering fancy for the " good people " —to whom good luck and bad luck were expressions that meant something definite ; who was always pleased to see the curious fairy circle (made by that strange fungus growth we have all observed). A fairy thorn would not be injured by her for anything, for had she not heard of the calamities that befell those who interfered with them ? In passing, he might remark that he had always found the belief in the supernatural to be much more common in County Down than in County Antrim, for in the latter county the hard-headed Scotchmen are much more unbelieving and incredulous—in fact, he knew a sturdy cattle-dealer in the parish of Templepatrick who, but a few years ago, had no belief whatever in the sanctity of an old fort upon his farm, and even scouted the idea that on midsummer nights the fairies held mad revelry around its charmed circle. This matter-of-fact Presbyterian even discovered that the soil of the fort would make excellent top-dressing for his land, and forthwith he commenced to utilise the haunt of the " denee shee " ;

carts, horses, and men were busily employed all one day, carting the fort for manure, never dreading for a moment that for this interference the good people might turn out bad people. Strange to say, that night in the byre, where all had been well, a cow died. Still the work went on with vigour the second day, but that night three cows died. Now this gave food for reflection, and caused a shaking of heads at a family council duly assembled. Still it was absurd for a sturdy farmer to believe in any such nonsense as fairies, and on went the work of demolition during the third day, and that settled the matter; for that night five cows died, and the stubborn old tiller of the soil gave way. He not only gave way, he made restitution by carting back to the fort all the soil he had removed. The fairies were satisfied, and no more deaths ensued amongst the cattle. This astonishing coincidence saved a pleasant feature of the landscape, and vindicated the character of the slooa-shee amongst an unbelieving peasantry.

And now let us go to the Bann-side. Some unlucky people had an " evil eye," for if any animal did not thrive, it was said it had been blinked—that is, some person with an evil eye had looked at it. I remember my old nurse threatening to leave, and using dreadful language, because a clutch of chickens had died off mysteriously, and some one had said she had blinked them, thus causing the calamity. This same nurse had a lame foot that there was always a mystery about, until her aged mother told its history to my mother. It appeared that when Mary Murphy (for that was her name) was a child about three or four years of age, her father took her to the field where he was working and lapped her in his coat, putting her to sleep under an aged thorn ; when she awoke her foot was twisted, and she was unable to walk. From her birth till then her mother stated that she had been a perfect child without any physical defect. Mr. Bigger said he was not much of a stickler for forms or ceremonies, but he always religiously observed one —that was, to turn his money when he saw the new moon, for he was told if you do that you will never want cash. You should first see the new moon in the open air, and not through glass, as that is unlucky. You should never turn back if you have started on a journey, for if you do, your errand will be fruitless or unfortunate. A crowing hen should be made into broth as quickly as possible ; she should never be allowed to crow twice. A dog howling at a door earnestly but without any apparent object, is as sure a sign of death as the cry of a banshee. It is very unlucky to weigh a new-born baby, nor should it be taken down any stairs until it has first been taken up-stairs. When a child sneezes the nurse should piously say "God bless the child." If your ear is warm, some person is talking about you. If your elbow is itchy, you are going to sleep away from home. If you find a straw on the floor, you are going to have a visitor, and the same applies to a cinder jumping out of the fire. A hen should be set with an odd number of eggs, either eleven or thirteen, and as the chickens come out, the empty shells should all be kept together until the chickens grow up. It is a great calamity to strike any one with a broom plant. You should not kill a spider nor brush one off your coat, as the worthy insect is weaving you a new one. It is lucky if by accident you should get into your sleeping garment inside out ; you should not change it. Evergreens put up at Christmas should not be allowed to remain over New Year's Day. A bed should never be placed with the foot of it to the east, for that is the way the dead are buried. A graveyard should not be entered at night, nor should a mirror be left uncovered in a room with the dead. If a stranger enters while churning is going on, he should always give the churn a brash or two, otherwise the butter might be prevented from coming and the churn spoiled.

The fairies used sometimes to steal children away and leave ill-favoured brats in their places ; my old nurse used to state that my grandfather was found just in time as the fairies were taking him away, for when a few months old he had been placed in bed, and was subsequently found under it. A little cousin of Mary Murphy's was often sent to the field of the fairy thorn with her clothes carefully pinned on, but she always came back with the pins extracted by the fairies. At Bellevy on the Bann, one evening, a little woman came at milking-time to the door of a cottage, and asked for some meal, which she was refused, when, to requite the insult, the Sheoque said she would be revenged. Very shortly afterwards the byre and cows were burned, with two children of the house. Young girls used to gather yarrow upon May Eve, and put it under their pillows that night, to induce dreams about their future husbands. Similar freaks for similar objects were performed at All Hallows' Eve. Sometimes the looms in a cottage would be heard working all night, and the owner would be quite certain that all the ends would be broken in the morning, but it was always found the deenee shee had done no harm. At Lis-la-ard on moonlight nights, the midnight traveller has often heard the gentry singing and dancing around the old rath there. On Midsummer Eve they were at their gayest, and could be heard some distance off.

> By the craggy hill-side,
> Through the mosses bare,
> They have planted thorn-trees,
> For pleasure here and there.

> Up the airy mountain,
> Down the rushy glen,
> We daren't go a hunting
> For fear of little men ;
> Wee folk, good folk,
> Trooping all together,
> Green jacket, red cap,
> And white owl's feather.

Several members spoke of the value of such contributions to local folk-lore, and expressed the hope that more communications of the kind would be forthcoming to aid the work of the new Ethnographical Committee.

The second paper was by Mr. William Gray, M.R.I.A., and was entitled " Worked Flints : Ancient and Modern." Mr. Gray said:—Primitive man was a Naturalist—a Field Naturalist—pure and simple, for he studied nature in the field. The phenomena of nature, physical and organic, were to him subjects of the closest observation and study, not as a matter of choice merely, but as a matter of downright necessity. His study of the fauna and flora of the country he dwelt in, was not to fill cabinets with curious or rare specimens of minerals or fossils, animals or plants ; his sole and only aim was, like the animals he lived with, to procure food and shelter from the weather, and to protect himself from the attacks of the wild beasts.

The very earliest evidence of his existence that we have discovered, are worked flints—rudely worked flints, of the most unattractive appearance ; and yet from their ethnological interest, they are of the very highest value, and mark one of the most important steps in the progress of the development of species in the animal world. Looking back through the entire record of geological time we have no similar fossil remains of any other animal.

The lowly forms of the Cambrian and Silurian periods, the strange fishes of the Devonian and Carboniferous deposits, the saurians and cephalopods of the Oolitic, and the mammals of the Tertiaries, have all left unquestioned remains of their bodily structure, sufficient to unable us to realize their forms, dimensions, and modes of life.

No other animal but man has left for our contemplation any kind of object to be compared with a rude worked flint, which, by its form, number, distribution, and modes of occurrence, demonstrates that a new agency had come into operation, and that that agent was man. No other animal but man is, or ever was, capable of making or using an implement, weapon, or tool as a secondary agent for the purpose of adapting his surroundings to his requirements, and hence man may be called the toolmaking animal.

Throughout the animal world there are many creatures capable of providing themselves with protective coverings, or places for retreat : many of the results of such efforts are of the highest interest, as the cocoon of insects, the shells of the Mollusca, the cases of the Crustacea, and the tubes of *Serpulæ* and many other kinds of worms, the wonderful web of the spider, and the arborescent products of corals,—all such may, however, be considered instinctive secretions of the body, more or less independent of volition.

Another group of animals appropriate for their use external materials within their reach, as the marine worms, like the *Terebella* of our sandy beaches, which build their tubes by selecting and bringing together grains of sand, fragments of shells, or the cases of dead Foraminifera. Larvæ of flies, such as the various forms of caddis-worm, will construct their cases or tubes of glass beads, fragments of wood, or any similar materials supplied them for the purpose. Birds will collect sticks, mud, hair, feathers, wool, leaves and moss, with which to construct their nests, according to their species. Thrushes will even use a stone on which to break and remove the shells of snails on which they feed. And some crows will carry shell-fish up into the air, and then drop them on the rocks to be broken, so that they may feed on the flesh thus exposed. A rook will break off a branch with which to build its nest, or an elephant may even whisk itself with a detached branch ; or a monkey may use a stone with which to break a nut :—But no other animal except man makes for itself an implement or tool to be used as a secondary agent in fashioning or adapting other materials or objects for their intended purposes in the operations of life. Hence man may be called a tool-making animal. Such a tool or implement, in the shape of a somewhat rudely-worked flint, is the earliest evidence we have yet discovered of the existence of man. With reference to his origin, or to his condition prior to the manufacture of this flint, we have no physical evidence. The question of his origin is not at present relevant to our subject, but we may fairly speculate as to his condition immediately antecedent to the finding of this worked flint.

It is manifest that he must have existed for a very long— literally an indefinite—period before he left the worked flint at, or near, the spot where it is now found. This is evident from the consideration that he had sufficient time to spread over a very extended area, embracing many countries, and far from the

central point of dispersion, wherever that may have been. He
had also time to develop that amount of manipulative skill
sufficient to enable him to fabricate tools of a material so hard
and intractable as flint. We may fairly assume that this was
not his first-formed implement or weapon ; and, doubtless, many
others were, from time to time, formed from other materials,
such as wood, or bone, that perished by the lapse of time ; and
the worked flints, even of the most ancient and rudest forms,
mark a comparatively advanced stage in the culture of the
human race—the capacity for this culture indicating a distinct
difference between man and his companions, the lower animals.

Was this culture the result of developed instinct, such as is
found amongst many of the lower animals ? or, was it the result
of a superior intelligence bestowed on man, and not possessed
by any other creature in the animal world ? The worked flint
demonstrates that its maker, man, differed from the brute, and
it is the first evidence, and a fitting emblem, of those impressions of the Deity—the creative skill, and intellectual
power—that in man has grown with the ages, and culminates
in the highest achievements of literature, science, and art.

In the infancy of mankind, as with individuals, the development of intellectual culture was very slow, and the progressive
steps of human experience were weak and faltering, because of
the absence of that stimulating influence, the struggle for
existence. Man's wants were then few, and were readily
satisfied by the abounding rich provisions of nature. As the
family increased and spread over large areas, the struggle for
existence became more acute. In the competition between man
and man, as well as between man and the beasts of the forest,
new wants were created, and new difficulties arose, to tax the
ingenuity, and develop the skill of the increasing human family.

It was this struggle that brought man into closer contact
with nature, and induced, if not compelled him to study and
become acquainted with its varied phenomena, that he might
gather from its exhaustless resources the materials required to
satisfy his increasing wants. As a hunter after fish, flesh, and

fowl, to supply the cravings of his appetite, he became familiar with the home, the habits, and the life-history of the animals required for food. He had not only to hunt down the animals for food, but he had to protect himself against the attacks of wild beasts that shared in the same pursuit.

Man, in common with all other animals, was instinctively prompted to the necessity for self-preservation, and his reason guided him in the selection of those methods best adapted to secure this end, and to the necessity for weapons of defence in dealing with the natural propensities of the various, numerous, and often ferocious animals with which he was surrounded, and with which he had to compete during the earliest ages. It was by the exercise of his reason, and by the experience obtained after many years of conference with his fellows, that he was at length led to select flint as a suitable material for his purpose ; and no doubt for ages those strange and distinctive nodules of flint, common to the Cretaceous rocks, were, to primitive man, objects of no less interest than they are still to the modern naturalist.

Primitive man being a field naturalist, who observed all that was strange and distinctive in natural phenomena, we can easily imagine that his attention and interest were aroused when, as a wandering nomad, he first beheld a Chalk cliff, such as the "White Rocks" along the northern coast of Antrim, or an inland section of pure white Cretaceous rocks, with its well-marked bands of dark flints standing out from the weathered surface ; or, having fallen, lying broken up into suggestive implements at the base, such as is common in the Chalk quarries and cliffs of Antrim ; and the adoption of this suggestion was to him, and his race, equivalent to our discovery of coal, or the magnet.

This was the commencement of that indefinite period known as the Stone Age,—a period that has never closed since then. We employ at the present day, as primitive man did then, stone for a great variety of purposes, and the application of stone for such purposes has been continuous from the earliest ages. As a means of attack and defence, our modern gun-flints superseded the flint arrow-heads. We grind our corn with stone as the ancients did : and like them use stone as sharpening implements : the finger-ring, the breast-pin, and the pendant of diamonds, amethyst, agates, and other forms of stone, are but the survivals of those personal ornamental embellishments that, with other-wise scanty apparel, were supposed to add dignity and grace to the charms of primitive man, attractions which, no doubt, were largely availed of by the ladies of the period.

In a general sense, what is known as the Stone Period is divided into the earlier or Palæolithic, and the later or Neolithic ages. Such terms are, however, indefinite ; we should therefore rather divide the Stone Period into three *stages*—the Palæolithic or earliest stage ; the Neolithic or pre-historic stage, and the Modern or historic stage. These three culture stages will embrace the entire Stone Age, or Ages, during which stone was used for implements, weapons, personal ornaments, or any other article complete in itself. Accepting this as the most correct subdivision, we will consider the Palæolithic, the Pre-historic, and the Modern stages respectively.

THE PALÆOLITHIC STAGE.

The Palæolithic implements are peculiar in many respects—they are almost exclusively formed from flint nodules, and are invariably rudely chipped into form, and never artificially polished. They do not include anything like the variety of forms that subsequently came into use in Pre-historic times. They are rude, lumpy, and weathered, and often rounded and glazed by friction. They are found in river-gravels, and so distributed through the gravels as to indicate that they existed before the formation of the deposits, and in many instances prior to the excavation of the valleys in which the gravels are now found. Such flints are the only evidence of the existence of man at the period when the physical changes which originated the gravels took place, and they are the first evidence of man's manipulative skill as a manufacturer.

These gravels occur along the sides of the valleys through which the originating rivers flowed, such as the Seine and the Somme in France, and the Thames and the Ouse in England, and they appear to have been deposited when the respective rivers flowed at a much higher level than they do at present. The worked flints from the drift include oval or almond-shaped implements, varying into the shoe-, the pear-, and the heart-shaped, pointed weapons, the ends being formed of the undressed flint.* Flint flakes occur, but by no means commonly,—the scraper, also, which is still rarer.

With such flints are frequently found the remains of the great Mammalia of the Quaternary period ; there are no osseous remains of any animal so small as man. The remains found are chiefly the mammoth, woolly rhinoceros, rein-deer, and musk ox, indicating climatic conditions partaking more of an arctic character, and altogether different from what prevailed during Pre-historic and modern times.† It is probable, also, that at that time Great Britain was united with the Continent, and that glaciers were the active agents in moulding the surface of the land.

Other sources from which the rudely-worked flints of the Palæolithic type are obtained, are the ossiferous caverns of Great Britain and the Continent ; many of them have been systematically explored in France, Germany, Belgium, Italy, Poland, and England, and they have yielded a much more varied assortment of worked flints than are found in the drift gravels, indicating an advance in culture.‡

Caverns occur in all parts of the world, and in all limestone districts, no matter what the geological formation may be. We have in County Antrim some very interesting examples still used by our fishermen as shelters for boats, nets, fish, &c., as for example at Ballintoy. Caverns are formed by marine denudation

* "Ancient Stone Implements of Great Britain," by John Evans, F.S.A.
† See Sir John Lubbock's "Pre-historic Times"; Geikie's "Ice Age"; Croll's "Climate and Time."
‡ See Pengelly's Report of the Exploration of Kruts Cave.

in the chalk rocks all round our shore in Antrim. We have also caves in the trap rocks at Ballycastle and Ballintoy, and at Torr Head we have extensive caves in the Primary rocks. The caves at Cushendun are in red conglomerate. Many caves in various parts of the world are very extensive, and have become places of special interest to travellers and tourists because of their strange position, great extent, and often fantastic natural embellishments. Primitive man, no doubt, resorted to many of them as places of retreat and shelter, which he shared with the wild animals, whose remains are now found so abundantly in the cavern deposits, and demonstrate that man and the now extinct mammalia were contemporary, and that the earlier cavern contents were accumulated under climatic conditions similar to what prevailed during the formation of the river-drift. But because of their more gradual accumulation, and because man must have occupied the caves for long periods, such caves yield a much greater variety of worked flints, and a greater variety of animal remains, than the river-gravels, indicating step by step the slow development of human culture. We have in the cavern deposits the accumulation of the very earliest times, and a continuance of them to within the Historic period ; we are thereby furnished with a connection between the Palæolithic and the Neolithic stages of flint manufacture, although some scientific observers maintain that there was a distinct break between the former and the later stages.*

In Ireland, we have no deposits or remains equivalent to the true Palæolithic stage, although the worked flints found in the raised beaches, and marine gravels of Antrim and Down, approximate in some cases to the forms which in England and on the continent are unquestionably attributed to the Palæolithic stage. The worked flints of such gravels as Ballyholme, Cultra, Holywood, Kilroot, Larne, Carnlough, and Cushendun, are all rudely chipped and unpolished, and so far conform to the characteristics of the true Palæolithic type,† but the absence of

* See " Reliquiæ Aquitanicæ," edited by T. Rupert Jones, F.R.S.
† See a paper by J. H. Staple in Report B.N.F.C. for 1869.

remains of extinct Mammalia, the geological character of the deposits themselves, and the fact that similar implements are found in abundance associated with Pre-historic or Neolithic worked flints, justify the opinion that the worked flints of our gravels are not attributable to the Palæolithic stage.*

In the North of Ireland, the absence of the older Mammalia of the caves, the hippopotamus, rhinoceros, hyena, and rein-deer, only shews that they had not migrated so far westward in Palæolithic times. It is probable that the hippopotamus never visited the shores of Lough Neagh, and that the rhinoceros never traversed the banks of the Bann or Blackstaff, Connswater or the Lagan. It is probable that the hyena never took refuge in the caves of Ballintoy, and that the lion never prowled in the gorges of Glendun. The bear may not have visited our northern area, although it is not beyond the bounds of the possible, for the remains of the bear have been found elsewhere in Ireland, and it is demonstrated that in Great Britain the bear survived until within historic times.†

In the North of Ireland we are not quite destitute of the remains of extinct Mammalia. The teeth of the mammoth have been found at Ballyrudder and Larne.‡ The remains of the great Irish elk have been found in abundance, and distributed over an extended area, including the lacustrine deposits of Antrim and Down, at present obliterated by our peat-bogs; but we have no physical evidence of man's existence cotemporary with the mammoth, or even with the Irish elk, one of the last of the ancient Mammalia that became extinct in Ireland, and the remains of which have been found near Banbridge, Dromore, and at Islandmagee. We may be assured, however, that the mammoth browsed along the slopes of Slieve Dhu and Bally-

---

* Report on the Larne Gravels, in Proceedings of B.N.F.C., 1889-90.

† Thompson's "Natural History of Ireland," Vol. IV ,: Prof. Boyd Dawkins' "Cave Hunting," p. 75 ; J. E. Harting's "Extinct British Animals."

‡ J. Grainger in Report of Belfast Meeting of British Association, 1874 ; Dr. Moran in Proceedings of Belfast Nat. Hist. Society, 1888-89 ; Professor Adams' Journal of the Royal Geological Society of Ireland, 1877, Vol. IV., new series.

gilbert, and crushed through the underwood of Glenoe, Glen-wherry, and Glenarm, and that the Irish elk often inhaled the fresh breezes from the summits of Trostan and Divis, the Knockagh and Black Mountain, herded with the red deer and long-faced ox in the alluvial plains of the Lagan valley, roamed freely in the woods of Derryaghy, and by their magnificent antlers cleared a pathway through the oak forests of Ballinderry, and slaked their thirst by the waters of Lough Neagh.*

PRE-HISTORIC STAGE.

With the *Megaceros hibernicus*, or Irish elk, we must leave the Palæolithic stage, and deal with that long, progressive, but remote stage known as the Neolithic or Pre-historic stage, during which the working of flint attained its highest development in the North of Ireland, as indicated by the numerous, varied, and in many cases, beautiful examples of worked flints scattered over the country, and which were undoubtedly manufactured in, or around, the County of Antrim. Indeed, there is every reason to believe that the ancient flint factories of Antrim supplied all Ireland, if not Great Britain itself, with implements and weapons of flint.

The ability to do so was due, mainly, to the fact that we have in the northern counties of Antrim, Derry, and Down a most excellent and unique development of the Cretaceous or Chalk rocks, popularly recognised as "the white limestone," which supply an abundance of flints, such as may be seen when the white limestone is exposed on the face of the magnificent cliffs that form the boundary of the northern and eastern coast of Antrim, and are equally abundant on the slopes and precipitous escarpments that look westward on the valley of the Roe, and southward towards Armagh, Lough Neagh, and the valley of the Lagan. Indeed, wherever the Chalk crops out from below the great northern sheet of dark basaltic rocks, there may be

---

* Several heads and horns of the red deer were found when excavating for foundation of Gamble & Shillington's Mills, Upper Falls. A portion of the horn of the Irish elk was found in the foundation of the new Albert Bridge over the Lagan.

found an abundant supply of flints—some inter-bedded *in situ*, and some weathered out and exposed, ready to the hand of the flint manufacturer, as at Glenarm and the headland of Garron Pont.

As already stated, the flints were, no doubt, objects of interest to primitive man, as they continue to be with the modern naturalist, who finds it difficult to account for such quantities of flints inter-bedded with purely limestone rocks, that are otherwise so free from any silicious material.

Our white limestone, or Chalk, originated as a marine deposit, laid down in a remote period of geological time, as its fossils and microscopic structure testify, and yet we have no flints in our modern sea-bottom, or anything that may be considered equivalent to the flints of the Chalk.

The voyage of the "Challenger" has thrown some light on this question, and Sir Wyville Thomson has shewn that silica, to the extent of from 30 to 40 per cent., occurs in the deep-sea mud, or ooze, to which the *spiculæ* of sponges and radiolarians, and the frustules of diatoms largely contribute. And while he recognises the difficulty of giving a satisfactory explanation of the origin of flints, he suggests that "the organic silica distributed in the shape of sponge *spiculæ*, and other silicious organisms of the Chalk, had been dissolved, and reduced to a colloid state, and accumulated in moulds formed by the cells, or outer walls, of embedded animals of various classes." In this manner ventriculites, sponges, and similar organisms would become the receptacles of the silicious material, and thereby assume the form and property of what we now know as flints.

This material, so abundant in the white limestone of the counties Antrim and Derry, as already described, was the stock-in-trade of the primitive Irish manufacturers, and from this they fabricated the worked flints that are considered such interesting, and, indeed, necessary additions to the collections in the museums of Europe and America, from the simple flake, scraper, and arrow-head, to the elaborately chipped, polished, and systematically formed spear-head.

Sir William Wilde seems to think that the flake "was the first attempt at a weapon, or tool of stone."* This is scarcely consistent with the fact that they are so rare in the river-gravels of the Palæolithic age. They are, it is true, comparatively abundant in the cavern deposits, but their full development is within Pre-historic times.

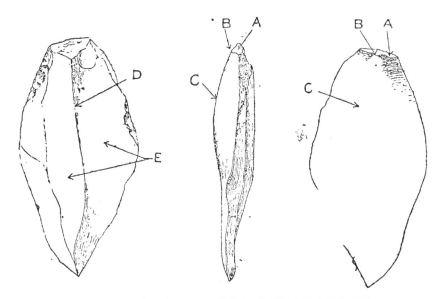

A SIMPLE FLAKE WITHOUT SECONDARY CHIPPING.

A. The flat face of the original core.   B. The bulb of percussion, at the point where the blow that dislodged the flake was struck.   C. The conchoidal or shell-like fracture of the face of the flake.   D. The central ridge at the back of the flake ; sometimes there are several ridges.   E. The facets or planes at the back of the flake divided by the ridge D.

Simple as the flake is, in form and construction, it, no doubt, marked a distinct advance in the manufacture of worked flints ; and it is possible that ages passed before its applicability to the variety of purposes to which it was subsequently applied was appreciated by primitive man.   It was, so to speak, the bye-product, or refuse, of the earlier manufacture of the clumsy Palæolithic tools and weapons ; but, when its capabilities were

* Wilde's Catalogue of Irish Antiquities.

duly recognized, it continued as an important element in the
manufacture of worked flints, down to our own day.

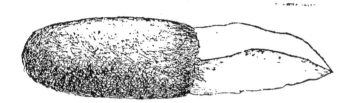

A MOUNTED FLAKE FROM AUSTRALIA.

This implement, used at present by the natives of the interior of Australia, is simply
an unchipped flake mounted in a handle.   Probably some of our Antrim flakes
were intended to be mounted in a similar way.

The sites of the early factories of the North of Ireland, such
as at Ormeau, Annadale, Larne, Glenarm, &c., yield vast quantities of flakes.   They occur also on the present sites of ancient
settlements, such as at Ballyholme, Dundrum, Kilroot, Larne,
Ballygally, Carnlough, Portrush, Portballintrae, Portstewart,
and Castlerock.   At the sites of such factories all the appliances
and refuse of the workers are found.*   In the sand-dunes they
are very abundant, particularly at both sides of the Bannmouth.   Here the primitive Irish flint manufacturers wrought
to the music of "the waves of Tuagh" as they rolled heavily
over the sands of "Invir Glais."   Flakes are scattered freely
all over the ground of the County Antrim, on the heather-clad
hill-tops, on the cultivated slopes, on the meadows in the valleys,
and on the sites of former lakes now almost obliterated by the
accumulation of peat.   Wherever they are found, they are
known to the expert by certain characteristics of form and
fracture that distinguish them from mere natural fragments
of flint.

The sites of the early factories of the North of Ireland, such
Their dimensions, shape, and necessarily their lithological
character, correspond with the worked flint-flakes found the
wide world over.   Indeed, the same may be said of nearly all

* Our northern sand-dunes have been described in several valuable communications
   published in the Transactions of the R.I.A. and the Journal of the R.S.A.I.
   The papers from the pen of Mr. W. J. Knowles are of special interest.

our forms of worked flints. The flakes are interesting as Ireland's earliest tools or weapons, but they are still more so, as typical of the earliest weapons of all other countries in the Old and New Worlds. The flint-flakes collected from the plains about Ormeau, Belfast, are undistinguishable from the flakes picked up on the plains of Marathon, quarried from the stalagmitic floors of French caverns, or dug from the lake dwellings of Switzerland, and the kitchen-middens of Denmark.* The flint scraper, so abundant in the sand-dunes of Dundrum, Portrush, and Ballintoy, and indeed, wherever the flakes are numerous in County Antrim, is in every respect a facsimile of what may be found among the antiquarian remains of China, America, Egypt, India, and the older countries of Europe, and there are no varieties of this flint scraper from any of the pre-historic stations of Europe that could not be matched by similar forms from the ancient settlements of Antrim.†

A simple flake, being the result of a single blow, with or without preparation, must assume an indefinite variety of forms, as various as the purposes to which it was applied,—what such purposes were it is vain to speculate. Many of the rudest and most shapeless flakes show such an amount of careful secondary chipping as would indicate that the fabricators aimed at adapting each to some special definite purpose. Many flakes were struck off by a single blow, perfectly formed without any secondary chipping or dressing, and were adapted to useful purposes, as the Australian flake already referred to. Others again only required a very slight additional dressing to convert them into the required implement. As the most unskilful workman labours hardest to accomplish his object, so we find that the most awkward or irregular forms of worked flints show the greatest amount of secondary chipping. There are several leading forms, such as scrapers, knives, borers, and particularly the well-known arrow-heads, towards the manufacture of

* See " Reliquiæ Aquitanicæ," edited by T. Rupert Jones, F.R.S.

† See the author's paper on " The character and distribution of rudely-worked flints of the North of Ireland "—Proceedings of the Royal Historical and Archæological Society of Ireland, Vol. V., fourth series.

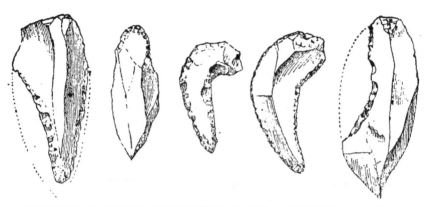

IRREGULAR FORMS OF WORKED FLINTS, SHOWING LABOURED
CHIPPINGS.

which a suitable flint flake was the first step. Such forms
vary much in size and in the amount of workmanship they
display ; we have both the rounded and the hollow scrapers,
the former being by far the most abundant, and similar to the
forms characteristic of the ancient worked flints of France,
Belgium, Denmark, &c. The hollow scraper is not nearly so
abundant, yet it occurs much more frequently in Ireland than
elsewhere ; a few specimens only have been recorded from
Yorkshire, and similar forms occur in Scotland.*

Like the scraper, or thumb-flint, the flint arrow-heads are
found throughout the northern counties in large numbers, and
of a great variety of forms ; some are very rude indeed, some
elaborately wrought ; some are comparatively large, others are
extremely small. The forms they assume include very distinct
differences, which pass one into the other by almost impercep-
tible degrees, all apparently emanating from the typical leaf-shape
of the original perfect flake, from which the greatest departure
is the long, flat, polished, and pointed spear-head.

Next to the arrow-heads in importance are the celts, picks,
and chisels, the distinction between them being often very slight,
the respective terms applied to them are intended more to assist in
their classification than to determine the uses to which they were

* Evans on " Ancient Stone Implements of Great Britain,"

applied.   They vary in dimensions from 1 in. or 2 in. long to
8 in. or 10 in.—sometimes even more.   They exhibit several
degrees of finish ; sometimes they are very rudely chipped, such
as those found in the raised beaches and sand-dunes, at river
fords, such as Toome Bridge and Coleraine, and even on the
sites of settlements, such as Mount Sandal on the Bann.   Many
are so roughly chipped they appear as if roughed out for more
skilful finish subsequently.   Others pass from such rude forms
up to the well-formed and highly-polished weapons or tools more
sparingly distributed over our northern area.   In each case we
have fairly typical examples for comparison with similar worked
flints in other countries ; yet the varieties from the types are
almost endless, as indeed is the case with any form of implement
or tool in modern use.

Suppose we take a collection of knives, scissors, walking sticks,
or umbrellas, what a puzzle it would be to Lord Macaulay's New
Zealander to determine how to arrange and classify them in
illustration of a communication, we will suppose, he is to prepare
for reading before a scientific body some few thousand years
hence.   The difficulty is no less in dealing with our Antrim
worked flints, although to the expert it is not quite insur-
mountable.

The general character of the finely-worked flint arrowheads of
this stage indicate a considerable advance in the social condition
of primitive man, who, as a hunter and a warrior, used in the
chase or in war many of the worked flints we now find on the
surface of the ground.   Their abundance and distribution may to
some extent be accounted for by supposing that the ancient
Irishmen, like the modern Bushmen, never used a second time
an arrow that once missed its mark.

With flint implements of this kind, no doubt, the dwellers in
the hill-forts of Lurig and Drummaul hunted the long-faced ox
in the valley of Glenariff, and the holders of the fort on Cave
Hill, or the residents in the settlements of Ormeau followed the
red deer to the woods of Derryaghy, as the American Indian
hunted the buffalo on the western prairies, or the wolf in the
forests of Indiana.

Could we have stood on the summit of Little Collin, County Antrim, on some favourable occasion in the long past, we might have, perhaps, witnessed the chase of the wild boar, accompanied by the boisterous uproar of our wild Irish forefathers, or, looking northward towards Slemish, we might have seen in the hollow of Glenwherry a pack of wolves panting on the run for the woods of Crebilly, and we might have heard the yelp of following wolf-dogs as they were urged forward in the chase by the shouts of the warriors from Rathmore.

No doubt many of the animals now extinct, or that have migrated from the North, were common during that prolonged period of Pre-historic time during which worked flints constituted the principal weapons of the chase and of war.

THE HISTORIC, OR MODERN STAGE.

Notwithstanding the abundance and perfection of our ancient flint arrow-heads, it is very strange that we have not more distinct reference to them in the ancient annals. This, coupled with the fact that the arrow or elf-stone is looked upon with very great superstition by the country people, would go to show that they are of extreme antiquity, the theory as to their reputed virtues and healing properties having grown up long after they ceased to be used for any practical purposes.

In the pages of Irish history we have some references to the use of what were probably worked flints. The Book of Lismore records a battle with the Danes near Limerick, in the year A.D. 920, and, describing the persons engaged in the battle, says that "their youths and their champions, and their proud, haughty veterans came to the front of the battle to cast their stones, and their small arrows, and their smooth spears, on all sides."

There are repeated references to the use of sling-stones, and the Irish warrior was armed with the *Lia Miledh* to cast at his adversary, and he did so with effect, even when his adversary was a woman. An ancient Irish tract tells how one of the Princes of Ulster threw a stone and struck a hag or druidess in the fore part of the head, which it passed through, and carried out its own size of the brains at the poll. In modern times women's brains are, happily, more usefully applied. The Dinnseanchus records the fact of a poetess, Dubh, having been slain by a stone cast from a sling, when she fell into the Linn, or dark pool of the Liffey, and hence the place was said to have been called from her Dubhlinn.*

In later times, on the introduction of cannon, stone shot were used, and there is a record of an attack made by the Irish upon a certain castle, when the Irish, who made the attack, provided a cannon, constructed out of staves like a barrel : this was charged with powder and a stone shot, which, having been fired, gave a puff behind and before, and left the shot in the middle.

Later still, worked flints formed an important item in the munitions of war, and flints were used for the purpose of discharging cannon, as well as the smaller fire-arms.

The dressed flake, assuming the form of a scraper, as has been shewn, was a distinct and well recognised form, widely distributed over the world, and of extreme antiquity. For whatever purpose it was originally formed, we know that in process of time it was adapted for the dressing of skins by the modern Esquimaux, but, no doubt, it was used for a great variety of purposes,—one of the most interesting and important being its use for producing fire ; the property of eliciting a spark when struck, was a discovery of the highest importance to primitive man, and its practical use for this purpose has survived until our own time. Flint strike-a-lights superseded the tedious, wooden fire-drill of the Finns and Laps, and the Bow-drill of the Sioux and the Dacota Indians, and was in use long before the employment of steel implements for striking the spark.

The worked flint strike-a-lights were first used with prepared nodules of iron pyrites, of which a flat surface was formed, and the violent friction of the flint against the surface produced the spark. Implements of this kind—iron pyrites and flint scrapers— were found by Canon Greenwell, of Durham, in some ancient

* See Sir W. Wilde's " Catalogue of Irish Antiquities."

British barrows explored by him.* Similar implements have been found in the French and Belgium ossiferous caves, where they occur in connection with extinct Mammalia.†

After the discovery of iron, the pyrites was superseded by strikers of iron or steel, yet the scraper-like shape of the worked flint was retained, and thus flint and steel became an established fire-producing apparatus. Even this method of producing fire is of very considerable antiquity. In Pliny's "Natural History" there is a reference to the importance of worked flint as part of the equipment of a camp, and the translator thus expresses the reason,—"for if they strike them either with an iron spike or another stone they will cast forth sparks of fire, which lighting upon matches dipt in brimstone, dried puffs, or leaves, will cause them to catch fire sooner than a man can say the word."

The use of the flint and steel was probably known to the Romans, as it was to the early Britons, and since then it has survived till our day. In many countries the fire was kindled by a spark struck from the flint on dried fungus or moss ; in this country, prepared cotton was used in a tinder-box ; this was an essential apparatus in the production of fire for domestic purposes. Touch-paper, or what is called in the South of Ireland "spunk," was used with the flint and steel in lighting the workman's pipe ; this was the chief method of producing a light previous to the introduction of matches, and the form of match now used originated with the sulphur match necessary to produce a flame from the spark kindled in the tinder-box by the flint and steel, such as is referred to by Pliny, and was in use in the younger days of the present generation.

Flint strike-a-lights for domestic purposes became an important article of commerce, and flint factories were established almost wherever the flint-bearing Chalk rocks occur, as they do so extensively in the North of Ireland. England, France, and Belgium carried on the trade, and the form of the strike-a-lights varied somewhat with the country that produced them.

* " British Barrows," by Greenwell and Rolleston.
† " Reliquiæ Aquitanicæ."

The scraper-like, or ancient form was called an " Englishman," because that form was retained in England as in ancient times, whereas another form more like a square gun-flint was called a " Frenchman " because it was introduced from France.*

After the discovery of gunpowder, pyrites and matches were used to "fire" the powder in the pan of the lock, and an improvement was subsequently made by the introduction of the flint-lock, which had the effect of considerably extending the trade in worked flints, chiefly for the supply of the army—for pistols, muskets, and cannon were now fitted with a flint-lock. In England, the trade was carried on at Brandon, in Suffolk, where it still survives, the methods of procuring and working the fiints being extremely primitive. From Brandon, worked flints as strike-a-lights are sent to Spain, Italy, and many other places ; even gun-flints are still produced and exported in quantities.

In ancient times there were numerous factories for worked flints in the north of Ireland, and, no doubt, an extensive trade was carried on with other parts of the kingdom. Although the trade was pre-historic, we have positive evidence of the existence of former flint factories on the sites of many ancient settlements in Antrim and Down, where we find, in large quantities, the remains of worked flints, the cores from which the flakes were struck, the hammers of various forms and sizes, by which the flakes were dislodged, the refuse splinters, or spoilbank, of the manufactory, as well as many of the more highly-finished forms of flint, and the perfected arrow-head, scraper, and celt, which it was the aim of the manipulator to produce.

No better, and scarcely a more prolific factory, could be mentioned than the one which existed near Ormeau Bridge, Belfast, on the site lately allotted to the workshops of some of our chief contracting builders, who had to clear away the debris of the ancient factory to make way for the modern innovation. Similar ancient factories have been discovered in Antrim, and have yielded a vast quantity of worked flints of various kinds.

* See Stevens' " Flint Chips," p. 578.

At Larne, and elsewhere in the north, there are indications of a survival of the art of working flints to supply the demand for gun-flints and strike-a-lights. Possibly no settled factory of importance existed, and the trade in gun-flints and strike-a-lights was carried on by travelling workmen, who removed from place to place as the supply of materials and the requirements of trade demanded.

In still later times, a new and profitable industry has been created in reproductions, counterfeits, imitations, or models of ancient worked flints, such as are vulgarly called "forgeries." This active trade has originated in the extravagant demand for Irish antiquities that has grown up within the last quarter of the century.

Antrim, and indeed the north of Ireland generally, has been ransacked for every form of ancient stone and bronze object that could be found. Bagmen and ragmen, hawkers of note-paper and Provident Insurance agents have been employed for that purpose, and the greater proportion of the finds have been transferred to the antique departments of public museums and private collections throughout Great Britain. Fortunately we have in the North some judicious collectors, who have rescued fairly good examples of the most typical objects. The rage for collecting specimens, without caring for the record of the particulars under which they were found, has affected so many tourists and visitors, that the demand is in advance of the supply, and the absurdly high prices too often paid for indifferent specimens, have called for the manufacture of spurious examples, which are now produced and distributed by the hundred. The manipulative skill thereby displayed is well worthy of primitive man himself, and highly calculated to mislead any who are not experts in determining the true character of ancient worked flints.

The practice of using flints in their natural condition, or squared for paving, or for the facing of buildings, has not been adopted in Ireland as it has been in England, with the most satisfactory results. Our architects have yet to learn how to apply this material in the carrying out of their designs.

Although not used for strictly architectural or decorative purposes, our North of Ireland flints have been utilised in the potteries of Staffordshire and Belleek, and large quantities are now prepared at Glenarm, and shipped to the other side of the channel, where they are used in the manufacture of an excellent quality of furnace brick, highly appreciated by the trade. As this trade is not quite within the scope of the present paper, we must leave it, with the expression of an earnest hope that this and every other enterprise calculated to develop the industrial resources of Ireland, may prosper.

Mr. Gray illustrated his lecture by lantern views, which were shown by Mr. R. Welch, and by a large collection of ancient worked flints, which were supplemented by a selection of special forms kindly lent by Mr. Robert Day, J.P., High Sheriff of Cork, and flint celts lent by Mr. W. H. Patterson and Mr. F. W. Lockwood.

On the motion of Mr. W. H. Patterson, M.R.I.A., seconded by Mr. F. W. Lockwood, C.E., the Committee of the Club were requested to print the paper *in extenso* in the Club's proceedings. The paper was also commented upon by Mr. R. M. Young, M.R.I.A.; Mr. Joseph Wright, F.G.S.; and the President. The following new members were then elected :—Mrs. Otto Jaffé, Rev. H. N. Creeny, Messrs. Wm. Graham, Solicitor; J. B. M'Crea, C.E.; Allan P. Swan, David Simms, C.E.; W. B. Munce, and P. J. O'Shea.

The fifth meeting of the Winter Session was held on March 21st in the Museum, the President in the chair, and was devoted to a display of microscopical objects and apparatus. This being the second annual meeting of the Microscopical Section of the Club, the report of the Section, which ran as follows, was read by the secretary, Mr. H. M'Cleery, and was, on the motion of

Mr. W. H. Patterson, M.R.I.A., seconded by Mr. Lockwood, unanimously adopted :—

"Your Committee regret that owing to different circumstances the progress of the Section has not been so successful during the past session as had been anticipated. Four excursions had been arranged for, but owing to the severity of the weather, only the first was carried through. The Section was well represented at the annual conversazione of the Club, and contributed in no small degree to the success of that meeting. During the winter there was only one meeting held, when a communication was given by the secretary on the structure of the Honey Bee, illustrated by lime-light by Mr. John Brown, and another communication and practical demonstration on Photo-micrography was given at the same meeting by Mr. John Donaldson. Owing to business engagements, the secretary, Mr. M'Cleery, has been obliged to resign the position, so that the post is now vacant, and we hope some gentleman will soon be found who will be able to carry on the work of the section in a thorough manner."

On the motion of Mr. R. Lloyd Praeger, seconded by Mr. W. D. Donnan, the Committee of the Section was re-appointed. The chairman of the Section, Mr. Alexander Tate, C.E., then in a few brief pointed remarks introduced the business of the evening, and in doing so said that it was evident, both here and at the conversazione of the Club, as had been already referred to, that the interest in microscopical research in our city had become greater, and he hoped that this interest would still further increase. He referred to the investigations into the beginning of life by Professor Virchow, and showed how these could not have been made without the aid of the microscope. After referring to the extent and variety of the exhibits before them, he asked the audience to go carefully round the different instruments and examine the beauties they unfolded. The following exhibited :—Mr. J. J. Andrew, L.D.S., section of eyebrow ; Mr. S. Cunningham, Ostracoda and other forms of minute pond-life ; Mr. Henry Davis, lichens in section and otherwise, showing spores, etc. ; Mr. W. D. Donnan, marine life ; Mr. William Gray, M.R.I.A., *Hydra;* Mr. P. F. Gulbransen, Infusoria ; Mr. William Hanna, B.A., structure of sponges ; Mr. John Jacques, crystals under polarised light ; Mr. H. M'Cleery, insect eggs, skin of sole, and other opaque objects ; Mr. W. S. M'Kee, eggs of molluscs, etc. ; Miss C. M. Patterson, embryology of chick, illustrated with drawings ; Mr. Adam Speers, B.Sc., vegetable sections and section-cutting ; Mr. Alex. Tate, C.E., diatoms; Mr. Robert Welch, marine Algæ ; Mr. Joseph Wright, F.G.S., Foraminifera, showing the variation in size according to their habitat, some deep-sea specimens being one thousand times larger than the same species taken near shore.

At nine o'clock a short business meeting was called, at which the following new members were elected :—Mrs. Lancelot Shaw, Rev. John MacDermott, Messrs. Andrew Adams, W. Aird, Richard Brownlie, Nathaniel Carruthers, Arthur P. Hoskins, F.I.C., Edward J. Morissey. After some announcements by the secretaries, the work of the evening was resumed, after which the company by degrees separated.

The sixth meeting of the Winter Session was held in the Museum, on April 11th, the President in the chair, when the evening was devoted to Irish Folk-lore.

The first paper was " Pishogues from Tipperary," by Miss Lily S. Mollan, and was read by the junior secretary. The following is an abstract :—

Some misfortune will befall the person who strikes a horse with a hazel switch.

If some salt is not thrown outside the door before churning, no butter will come.

When entering a house always say "God bless your work," or some misfortune will come upon the inmates.

A marriage will never take place out of a house in which there is a black teapot.

If a child has whooping-cough it will be cured by putting it three times over and three times under an ass.

Anyone suffering from erysipelas will be cured by getting one drop of blood from the tail of a black cat and rubbing it on the infected part.

Never rock an empty cradle, for it will bring misfortune on the baby.

Never invite three persons having the same name to your house, or one of them will die before the year is out.

If a child goes into a decline it is said to be a changeling. To prove this it is put sitting on a hot shovel outside the door for about three minutes ; if it does not move during that time it is not a changeling.

If a person has warts, he must take a stone for every wart he has, tie them up in a bag, and throw them out on a public road ; a snail must then be rubbed on each wart, and afterwards stuck on a blackthorn bush to wither ; as the snail withers the warts disappear, and go to the person who picks up the bag of stones.

To the foregoing, Miss Mollan added the following " Freets " from Co. Monaghan :—

A bride should always wear on her wedding day for luck—

" Something old, something new,
Something borrowed, and something blue."

If your nose itches, it means you are going to drink tea with strangers.

It is very unlucky for a weasel to cross your path.

If a girl finds nine peas in a pod she should put the pod over the door, and the first person who enters will have the same Christian name as her future husband.

When you lose your way at night turn your coat inside out, and you will then see your way distinctly.

A man was going home one dark night, and as he was passing a rath he suddenly lost his way, and kept moving round in a circle.   At last he took off his coat, turned it inside out, put it on again, and found his way home immediately.

Several stories were quoted to show the prevailing belief in the danger of interfering with or injuring a fairy ring or a rath.

The second paper on the programme was by Mr. William H. Patterson, M.R.I.A., on the subjects of "Irish Fairies."   The reader said that among all nations and races of men, especially in their earlier and more primitive days, beliefs were held in things that were beyond the objects and events of every-day life, and many of these beliefs have come down to our own days.   In the old times life was hard enough ; the struggle for bare existence took all the time that people had, and when serious hurts or sickness came, death generally followed soon. Some simple remedies gathered from the ground or the trees were tried, but help was also sought from charms and strange practices.   It was well for these unlearned forefathers of ours that they had something wherewith they could hope to meet the hostile influences which they believed were all around them.

They believed that fairies were on the watch, as soon as dusk or darkness had set in, to steal them away, or to smite them with pains in every limb, with blindness, or with madness ; to carry off their infants, and leave a grinning, peevish imp in the cradle where the chubby, smiling baby had lain an hour before ; to kill their cattle, or with their impish tricks to steal away their milk, which in early days was a matter of far more consequence than we can now understand ; even still in many parts of this country the flint arrow-heads, which can be seen in many museums, are called elf-shots or elf-stones, and the belief is that these are made by the fairies and shot at cows by the fairies, and in many places when a cow takes ill, the people send for the fairy-doctor, who not at once, but after certain charms are made, pretends to find and take out the elf-shot from some part of the animal's body.   Flint arrow-heads and stone hatchets are kept in farm houses to use as charms against the evil doings of the fairy race.

The fairies were fond of stealing the butter from the churn, while the good woman of the house was toiling away with the churn-staff, and no butter came for all her pains. One cure for this was to nail a horse-shoe on the bottom of the churn. Sometimes the mischief came from some greedy neighbour who practised witchcraft to rob her neighbour. A horse-shoe was always looked upon as a good thing to keep away fairies, and so we often see one hung over the door of a house or nailed upon the stable-lintel : this latter was to prevent fairies or witches taking the horses out, and riding them over hill and dale the livelong night, bringing them back before the dawn all trembling and exhausted. A horse-shoe was also nailed inside a fishing-boat or to the mast of a vessel, because fairies worked mischief to fishermen and hindered them in their toilsome work. Fairies were supposed to lurk in fishing-boats when they were drawn up on the beach during the night, and therefore a little fire of sticks was lighted in the bottom of the boat in the morning to drive out these unseen but mischievous little pests. Anything of iron, if red with rust all the better, or anything of a red colour, such as a bunch of rowan-berries, was a good thing to keep fairies away ; a cross of rowan-tree twigs was also used.

It was thought the fairies did not like to be called by this name, so, as they might be listening about, perched perhaps like fowls on the rafters of the kitchen roof, they were always spoken of as "the good people," "the little people," or "the gentry." The places they frequented were let alone, so as not to anger them, especially ancient forts or raths, or high earthern mounds, of which so many are found in Ireland; while old thorn-trees, usually called "fairy thorns" or "gentle bushes," were never injured or meddled with, because the fairies met and danced in these places on moonlight nights. If any person was so rash as to harm or meddle with these favourite meeting places, some harm overtook him or his family or his cattle in a short time, and his neighbours considered he was rightly served, and that he had brought his trouble upon himself by his own foolish act. When fairies wished to go upon a long journey at night, rushes and rag-weeds served as flying horses, and bore them high in the air over land and sea. In Ireland the fairy race was spoken of as the *Sidhe*, pronounced Shee ; this was a general term applied to all sorts of elves and fairies.

But these were not the only creatures, the belief in which, the terrors which these beliefs caused, made life harder to the people of this country. Demons were about, with power to kill, or to transform persons into beasts. One demon, which had concealed himself in an apple, went down the throat of a king of Connaught, and caused him such a terrible hunger that in three half-years he had eaten so much that a famine came to his kingdom. In order to feed this monster, the king took for his breakfast a pig, a fat cow, and an ordinary cow, sixty cakes of pure wheat, a tub of new ale, and thirty eggs ; then followed lunch. As regards his dinner, it is said that it exceeded all counting ; his supper was as great, and was more troublesome, because he added to it three things—a sack of nuts, a sack of apples, and a sack of biscuits. When the famine grew in the land, the poor king was only able to eat these meals by travelling about his country with a body of his guards, and visiting from house to house among his well-to-do subjects ; every one of whom was eaten out of house and home before the king moved on to the next house.

These demons had also the power of taking the forms of people, so that sometimes when a man thought he was safe in the company of his wife, his child, or his trusted comrade, the companion would change into some frightful shape, and the poor man might be dashed down a cliff of the mountains, thrown into a burning house, or torn to pieces. Some families in Ireland had the strange gift of taking the form of wolves for two or three years, and then becoming people again. The woods were peopled by little hairy creatures called Loughrey men ; but these did not harm people, and sometimes even helped them in their work.

The earliest settlers in Ireland, of whom we have any know-

ledge, were the Tuatha-de-Denaans. These people are believed
to have been very small, but clever in all sorts of magic, spells,
and witchcraft ; they are believed to have used stone weapons
only, and were utterly overcome and destroyed by a race of
invaders, the Milesians, who afterwards landed in Ireland ; but
the Irish people believe that, instead of being killed, the De
Denaans took refuge under ground, entering the earth at old
forts or raths, or through caves, or under green mounds, and
that these people are the fairies of Ireland, and that these same
places are the gateways by which they come out when they wish
to visit the upper world again. As it is believed they were
conquered by a race using weapons of metal, the fairies hate
metal, especially iron or steel, to this day.

This underground country is called Tir-na-oge, or the Land
of Youth, because the fairies do not grow old or die. There
are many stories of persons being carried off by the good people,
and escaping after a longer or shorter stay in Tir-na-oge. Music
was often heard beside these green hills, or raths, but it was
dangerous to linger, for although the melodies were most
charming and the airs easily remembered, some mischief—such
as lameness, deformity, or sickness—often fell upon the listener.
On the other hand, the fairies sometimes acted kindly towards
people, by curing their ailments and removing their deformities
or misfortunes.

During moonlight nights fairies are seen by mortals flitting in
shadowy troops between the eye and the newly-risen moon ;
many of these seemed to be finely dressed lords and ladies. The
summer or autumn nights were chosen as favourite times for
having their dances in lonely vales or on green hill-sides ; sometimes they sport near old ivied castles, beside a lake or river, or
sometimes in a gloomy churchyard, under the walls of its ruined
church, or over lonely tombs of the dead ; but they are very
jealous of mortal intruders, and usually punish them severely.
Although elfin sports may continue during night, the first glow
of morning is a signal for instant departure to their deep caves,
rocky crevices, or their favourite hollows under green mounds.

On alighting at, or departing from, a particular spot, their rapid motion through the air creates a noise somewhat resembling the loud humming of bees when swarming from a hive. Sometimes what is called a *Shee gaoithe*, in English a whirlwind, is supposed to have been raised by the passing of the fairy host. Sometimes they go out hunting, and in the calm summer evenings may be heard the sound of horns, cry of dogs, tramp of horses, cracking of whips, and " tally-ho " of huntsmen.

It is only at a distance that fairies appear graceful in figure or handsome in countenance, but their clothes are always of rich and fine material. Frequently they change their shapes ; they suddenly appear, and as suddenly vanish. These elves are found on a near inspection to be old, withered, bent, and having very ugly features, especially the men, though the female fairies are often lovely. Fairies are generally supposed by the country people to have a mixed nature, partly human and partly spiritual, but at the same time to have no solid substance, unless they assume this for a time to enable them to carry out some plan or trick against mortals. Although invisible to men, at least during the day, they hear and see all that takes place among them, especially any things that seem to concern themselves : hence the peasantry are always anxious to have their good opinion and kind offices, and try to turn away their anger by civil doings and kind acts. It is considered unfriendly and wicked to strain potatoes, or spill hot water over the threshold of a door, as thousands of invisible little creatures are supposed sometimes to gather at such a spot and to suffer from such doings.

The fairies appear, like human beings in Ireland, to belong to certain districts, for although we hear of the king and queen of the Irish fairies, we also know by many a tale of the king and queen of the Ulster fairies, or the Munster or Connaught ones. They are sufficiently quarrelsome among themselves, and sometimes desperate battles with opposing bands hostile to each other are waged ; some are like knights in complete armour. The air bristles with their spears and flashing swords, their helmets and red coats gleam in the moonlight, while the battle rages.

No opinion was more prevalent among country people, than that relating to the carrying away of people by the elfin tribe. Young and lovely children were the special objects of desire, and often, when these had been carried away from the parents' home, old, ugly, and starved fairies were left in their stead. These latter are called changelings. To guard against such accidents, nurses were accustomed to give a small spoonful of whisky mixed with earth to newly-born infants as their first food. This was supposed to protect them from some spell. Young children should be carefully watched until after their christening is over, lest they should be carried away or changed. To sneeze was very dangerous, and was supposed to put a child at the mercy of the fairies, to harm or carry away, unless some one present at once said " bless him " or " God bless him."

Lovely children were in greater danger than plainer ones. But children were not the only persons who were sometimes carried away to fairy-land ; young mothers were carried off to nurse fairy-born children, or mortal children that had been stolen ; and doctors, male and female, were sent for at midnight, and borne off by a mysterious messenger, who came in a coach drawn by coal-black horses, to take charge of some urgent case in the country underground. After receiving a handful of guineas as a fee, the doctor was driven back to his home, and the guineas, put safely into a drawer, were found to have turned to withered leaves when daylight came. Fairy changelings could be known by their spiteful, tricky nature, and by their constant complaining and crying for food. The changeling, if he could, would get a set of bag-pipes, and would then sit up in the cradle and play a variety of fine airs with great enjoyment and many strange grimaces. When he plays reels, jigs, and other lively airs the people in the cottage feel themselves forced to dance till they sink with fatigue. For a long time the mother cannot believe that her baby has been really carried away, and she will not consent to do the hard and cruel things that the neighbours say should be done to prove the child a changeling. One plan was to throw the child across the hearth fire, when he would vanish up the chimney with shrieks, calling out all sorts of bad wishes against the family that had harboured him so unwillingly. Another plan was to carry the changeling on a shovel from the cottage to the dunghill, and leave him upon the top of it. This operation was under the charge of a so-called fairy-man or fairy-woman, who, after performing a number of charms with the help of the family, got the mother to repeat a rhyming address to the fairies.

Fairies sometimes take a fancy to famous pipers or fiddlers, and carry them off to their underground houses : if these unfortunates eat or drink of the good things offered to them, they never return to their homes on earth. When the friends of a person who has been carried away venture into the country underground to try to bring back their friend they must bring with them a bible and a dagger ; the latter is stuck in the threshold of the door—this prevents the fairies from pursuing the rescue party when they have found and borne off their friend. It is said that the splendid halls, the grand feasts, and the lovely appearance of the finely dressed little people are mere illusions. There is a story of a nurse who was carried away to wash and dress a newly-born fairy child ; she was given a box of fairy ointment with which to anoint the infant, and, without intending it, she touched one of her eyes with her finger on which some of the ointment remained. In a moment she saw everything with this eye as it really was ; all the splendour gone, dull earthen floors and halls, squalid food and furniture, and the fine lords and ladies had become wizened and deformed imps. When she shut that eye all was fairy-land again. This same woman some time after attended a fair, when she saw the fairy-man who had brought her to dress the baby, she addressed him and asked him how the baby was doing. " Which eye do you see me with ? " he asked her. " This one," she replied, pointing to the one which had been touched with the ointment. " Then take that," he cried out, and struck her eye with his switch, blinding her for life in that eye.

Fairies keep a watch over buried treasures, and although persons may sometimes have the treasure within their grasp, yet they can never really get it. Generally a person dreams three nights running that he has found a crock of gold in some particular spot—at an old rath, or among the walls of some ruined castle, or under a fairy thorn. He goes to the spot and digs a hole, and after a time comes to the crock, or pot, or chest, and on removing the cover sees as many gleaming guineas as will make him and all his family rich for their lives ; at this moment a voice cries out " Do you see the mountain there on fire," or anything else which makes the gold-digger turn round for a moment, and so take his eyes off the treasure ; when he looks back again the hole is filled up, and no matter how he digs and searches, he never sees the treasure again. There are various classes of fairies, such as the Fear-shee, or man fairy, and the Ban-shee, or woman fairy. The Ban-shee wails in the darkness to foretell a death in the family to which she is particularly attached. Sometimes these fairies have names ; for instance, the Banshee of the O'Neills of Shane's Castle is called Mave-roe, that is, Red Mary or Maud. The Phooka is a demon in the form of a horse, who tempts people to mount him ; he then spreads a pair of wings which were hidden before, and springs up into the air, careering wildly through the sky till day-break, when the unfortunate rider is tossed off into an old churchyard or some other unpleasant place, almost dead with terror and fatigue. Sometimes when a person is bending over a well or stepping across a little stream, the Phooka suddenly rises beneath him, and in one moment he is borne off astride this fearful demon. Sometimes the Phooka takes the form of a bull.

The Leprauhauns are supposed to be the artizans of the fairy kingdom—the tailors, shoemakers, smiths, and coachbuilders—and are acquainted with all the hidden treasures of the earth. Still they are of an inferior grade, and have more of solid matter in their bodies than most of the other fairies. They are generally seen in the evening in some lonely wooded place working at their trade of brogue-making or tailoring, and when caught, have not the power of escaping as long as you keep your eye steadily fixed upon them. Keep one in this manner if you can catch him, and you can command treasures to whatever extent you may ask. The little creature will use every wile he knows to induce you to loosen your hold or to take your eyes off him even for a second, and if you do he vanishes at once, and is almost certain to outwit you and to get safely away without leaving you a penny the richer. Sometimes a person is lucky enough to catch a Leprauhaun several times, and at last succeeds in forcing him to give enough gold to make him rich for life.

The mermen and mermaids belonged to another branch of the fairy kingdom. Sometimes a fisherman succeeded in catching a mermaid asleep on the beach, and if he could obtain possession of her little cap, she not only could not take to the water, but lost all wish to do so. Usually the fisherman and the mermaid fall in love and are married ; they live happily together and have many children, till one unlucky day, when the husband is away, the wife goes rummaging about the house and finds the little cap that her husband has kept hidden all these years. She tries it on, and in a moment is seized with a desire to visit her own people under the sea ; she runs down to the rocks, plunges in, and is never seen again.

In connection with lakes, and rivers, and pools in Ireland, there is a wide-spread belief in certain enchanted monsters that haunt their waters, and endeavour to drag in persons or animals which venture too near the edge at certain times. Sometimes this beast is described as like a grey-hound, but with a black and shiny skin like that of an eel. More generally the lake is haunted by a serpent or dragon of immense size. Near Dun-given, in County Derry, there is a deep glen called Lig-na-peisthe, because they say a great snake, called in Irish a piast or peisthe, wriggled its way up from the sea and formed the glen as it went ; at the head of the glen the snake made a deep hole for itself beneath a waterfall, and went in head downwards ; but he still claims one out of every three living creatures that come to the edge of this bottomless hole.

Will o' the Wisp, or Jack o' Lantern as he is called in some places, and in parts of Ireland the Water Sherrie, is a kind of malicious fairy, who, by showing a light in marshes and dangerous bogs, lures benighted travellers into danger, and sometimes to death. According to another account, he is the spirit of a man who was very wicked on earth, and also managed to trick and outwit the devil ; and, in fact, made himself so feared by the prince of darkness, that after death he could not enter heaven, nor was even allowed into the other place, so afraid of him were the authorities there, and he must, therefore, wander about with his torch over dreary bogs and wastes for ever.

Another kind of fairy known in Ireland is the Cluricaune. He is a good-natured imp, and finds his pleasure in drinking whisky or anything of that nature, and in attending horse-races; in these respects not unlike a good many people we have heard of. As the Cluricaune are not bigger than one's finger, and are invisible to all who do not possess the fairy sight, they can indulge their taste for horse-racing by perching, three or four of them at once, on the saddles before the jockeys, and thus enjoying all the excitement of the race.

There is a kind of fairy called a Linnaun or Lennan-Shee. This means a fairy companion, or fairy sweetheart ; both men and women are supposed to have had these companions, who are very jealous of any interference with them. It is not told how the friendship is formed in the first place. The Linnaun is generally invisible to all except the person concerned, and sooner or later the affair ends badly for the person ; generally a violent death is the end of it, or madness. In one case, a family who lived near Oban had, as they supposed, a delicate child ; it was advancing in years, but not growing a bit. At length a visitor from Ireland came to the castle, and recognised her as the fairy sweetheart of an Irish gentleman of his acquaintance ; he addressed her in Irish, saying : " There thou art, little fairy sweetheart of Brian Mac Broadh." So offended was the elf at being exposed, that she ran out of the castle and leaped into the sea from the point called Ruadh-na-Sirach, the Fairy's Point, to this day.

The more a belief in the actual existence of fairies and their doings finds a home in the minds of persons, the more these little creatures are disliked and feared. It is perhaps because we have but little belief in their existence that we like to hear fairy tales; and how true some of them seem to be. The doings of the elfin race have greatly enriched our literature, and there is hardly a writer of imagination and poetic feeling who has not entered into fairy-land himself, or who does not offer to carry with him all those who will come.

In conclusion, Mr. Patterson acknowledged his indebtedness to Rev. John O'Hanlon, and other students of Irish Folk-lore, for much of the matter contained in the foregoing paper.

The next communication was "Items of Folk-lore, principally from County Down," by Mrs. Blair, and was read by the junior secretary. The writer stated that a great number of the following items of Irish Folk-lore had been familiar to her since childhood, and that she had at that time and for many years a considerable amount of faith in them.

If the fire burns up at one side there is going to be a difference of opinion in the family, and if the centre burns away some person is going to leave the house.

A spark appearing on the side of the wick of a tallow candle betokened a letter on its way to the person who was sitting opposite to it. To find when the letter would arrive, a slight knock was given to the candlestick; if it went off at the first knock the letter would arrive that day, but if not, then for every knock required to displace the spark a day was counted

A similar belief was mentioned in regard to soot hanging to the bars of a grate having a connection with the visits of strangers.

When putting on feet-wear be sure not to put a stocking and shoe on one foot before you put any on the other; but put on a stocking on one, and then the stocking on the other, and so with the shoes; if this is not attended to, you will surely walk into mischief that day.

If you use a pair of bellows, take care that you do not lay them down on a table, or there is sure to be a row in the house. If any other person than yourself lift them, the quarrel will be between you two.

Occasionally a white spot appears on the nails of the hand. On the thumb it signifies a gift, on the first finger a friend, the second a foe, the third a sweetheart, the fourth a journey ; and the nearer to the top of the nail, the sooner may you expect the gift, &c.

Peacocks' feathers are considered very unlucky to have in your possession. Several stories were quoted in illustration of the prevalence of this belief.

The majority of the houses occupied by the poorer class of farmers have two entrances, front and back. It is a commonly received opinion that a stranger entering by one and departing by the other takes away the luck of the fowls.

A horse-shoe put underneath the churn is said to be a great help towards obtaining a large quantity of good butter. If you see a pin on the ground in the morning with its point towards you, do not on any account lift it, as bad luck will surely follow ; but if the head is next you, pick it up at once, for in that case some luck is on its way to you which you would miss if you did not secure it. It is a great calamity to break a looking-glass, as that scares luck away for seven years.

Many items have reference to particular days. As for instance days of birth :—

> Monday's child is fair of face,
> Tuesday's child is full of grace ;
> Wednesday's child is full of woe,
> Thursday's child has far to go ;
> Friday's child is loving and giving,
> Saturday's child works hard for its living ;
> A child that is born on the Sabbath day, is blythe and
>   bonnie and good and gay.

All persons intending to marry should be very careful with

regard to the choice of the day, as the following shows:—Monday for health, Tuesday for wealth, Wednesday the best day of all ; Thursday for losses, Friday for crosses, and Saturday no luck at all.

Days to do washing :—

> Monday's wash is a dainty dame,
> Tuesday's wash is much the same ;
> Wednesday's wash is next door by, ·
> Thursday's wash just in time to dry ;
> Friday's wash is one of need,
> Saturday's wash is a slut indeed.

If you purpose removing to another residence, be sure to avoid Saturday, as " Saturday's flit is a short sit." Saturday is also considered an unlucky day for a farmer to commence the putting in of his crop.

Other items have reference to animals. Magpies are great indicators of future events, lucky or unlucky according to the number in view at one time. " One sorrow, two mirth, three a wedding, four a birth, five silver, six gold, seven a secret never told."

A crowing hen is not a good thing to have about a house. A young person told me of a white hen they once had, which one day flew up on the yard wall and crowed loudly. After that her mother died. " But," she said with great earnestness, " we did not let her live long after she crowed."

If the cat sits down with her back to the fire, a storm is brewing ; and when she scratches the leg of a chair or table, that is a sign a stranger is coming.

When a donkey brays, that's a sure sign of rain.

If you deliberately kill a cricket, its companions will avenge its death by cutting stockings and other garments.

When a cock comes to the door of a house and crows in, that indicates news coming. But when it crows in the night, that is a sign of a death.

You should never cut with scissors a baby's nails, or you are in danger of making it one of the light-fingered gentry.

If knives get accidentally across each other, that is a sure sign of a sharp quarrel.

When your right eye twitches you are going to see a stranger, but if the left a lover. If you have a singing in your ears, you will hear soon of the death of one you know. The sole of your foot itching shows you are going to walk on strange ground. If the itching is on the palm of the right hand you are going to shake hands with a stranger, but if it be the left you will soon receive money. A person who habitually sneezes loudly is destined to be a long liver. If the outside of your elbow itches, that shows you are likely to sleep away from home, but the inside signifies some one is coming to sleep in your home.

A branch of a rowan-tree should be put over the door on May eve to keep the witches from entering. For the purpose of keeping these undesirable visitors away from the byre, salt is to be kept there. A newly-calved cow should be milked the first three times on silver.

An old aunt of Mrs. Blair's frequently told about her intercourse with fairies. On one occasion she opened a drawer where linen was kept. To her surprise she found a tenpenny (a coin then in use) in it, which she took out. She went several times to the same drawer, and each time was rewarded by finding the same kind of coin. She at last told the circumstance, after which the fairy's donation ceased. I was told of a man who had several cows that died most unaccountably. By some means he was given to understand that his byre was situated in a way displeasing to the little people. Of course he at once rectified this, and no further deaths occurred.

The papers were criticised by several members, and satisfaction was expressed that the formation of an Ethnographical Section of the Club was already beginning to bear fruit.

Miss Dora Bain and Mr. P. F. Townsend were subsequently elected members of the Club.

ANNUAL MEETING.

The thirtieth Annual Meeting of the Club was held in the Belfast Museum on Wednesday evening, April 27th, the President in the chair.

The Chairman read a letter of apology for non-attendance from the senior secretary (Mr. R. Lloyd Praeger) who was absent in London, and called on the junior secretary (Mr. Francis Joseph Bigger) to read the Annual Report. This, together with the statement of accounts, which was next submitted by the treasurer (Mr. W. H. Phillips), will be found in the earlier pages of the present part of the Proceedings of the Club.

On the motion of Mr. W. H. Patterson, M.R.I.A., seconded by Mr. F. A. Porter, the report was adopted ; and the statement of accounts was adopted on the motion of Mr. Joseph Wright, F.G.S., seconded by Mr. Hugh Allen.

The President (Mr. John Vinycomb, M.R I.A.) next moved that Mr. William Swanston, F.G.S., should be elected President for the coming year. He referred in suitable terms to Mr. Swanston's long official connection with the Club, and to the prosperous condition that the Society maintained during his fifteen years secretaryship. The motion was seconded by Mr. J. J. Andrew, L.D.S., and carried unanimously.

Mr. F. W. Lockwood, C.E., was elected Vice-President, on the motion of Mr. John Vinycomb, M.R.I.A., seconded by Mr. W. D. Donnan.

The Secretaries were re-elected on the motion of Mr. John Vinycomb, M.R.I.A., seconded by Mr. W. Gray, M.R.I.A. ; and the Treasurer on the motion of Mr. W. S. M'Kee, seconded by Dr. St. Clair Boyd. Two vacancies occurred on the Committee, which were filled by Mr. John Vinycomb, M.R.I.A., and Mr. L. M. Ewart, J.P., M.R.I.A., and the Committee as thus constituted were elected on the motion of Mr. W. H. Phillips, F.R.H.S., seconded by Mr. J. O. Campbell.

The Ex-President moved, and Mr. R. Welch seconded, a

hearty vote of thanks to the lady members who, at considerable labour, had so successfully carried out the tea arrangements during the Winter Session; the motion was carried amid applause.

A discussion ensued as to the improvement and extension of the Club's work, which was taken part in by Messrs. Lockwood, Welch, Bigger, Gray, and others. Subsequently suggestions were received for the summer excursions. The following new members were then elected :—Miss Andrews, Messrs. James Stirling, Charles Murdock, Adam Martin. An inspection of the collections to which prizes had been awarded brought the proceedings to a close.

METEOROLOGICAL SUMMARY
FOR 1892.

WE have again to thank the Council of Queen's College, Belfast, for granting access to the records kept at that Institution, from which the following summary is compiled.

The station at which the records are made is situated in the Lagan Valley, at an elevation of about sixty feet above mean sea-level. The Belfast Hills, which attain a maximum elevation of 1,567 feet, lie to the west and north, stretching in a N.E. and S.W. line, and passing within three miles of the Observatory. Southward and eastward stretch the low undulating lands of Co. Down. Lough Neagh is situated some 14 miles to the westward. Belfast Lough approaches to within two miles on the N.E., and the open sea lies some 16 miles east of the observing station.

REVIEW OF THE WEATHER FOR 1892.

Meteorological Observations taken at Queen's College, Belfast, at 9 a.m. each day.
Latitude, 54° 35' N.; Longitude, 5° 56' W.

	BAROMETER 70 Feet above Sea Level.—Actual Readings.									SELF-REGISTERING THERMOMETERS in shade, in stand outside window, 21 feet above ground.								HYGROMETER	
	Highest of the Month			Lowest of the Month			Mean		Range	Highest of the Month		Lowest of the Month		Mean Maximum	Mean Minimum	Mean of two preceding	Monthly Range	Mean of dry Bulb	Mean of wet Bulb
	Inches	Att. Ther.	Date	Inches	Att. Ther.	Date	Inches	Att. Ther.	Inches	Deg. F	Date	Deg. F	Date	Deg. F	Deg. F	Deg. F	Deg. F		
	30·370	49·5	25	29·230	35·0	16	29·755	45·0	1·140	55·0	30	22·0	15	42·8	31·7	37·2	33·0	37·4	36·5
	30·610	51·0	13	28·980	36·0	1	29·795	43·5	1·630	55·0	11	29·0	18	46·3	36·3	41·3	26·0	41·0	39·4
	30·620	49·0	22	29·250	36·0	15	29·930	42·5	1·370	56·0	18	22·0	11	45·4	32·1	38·7	34·0	38·8	36·5
	30·470	55·0	1	29·550	40·0	27	30·010	47·0	·920	63·0	2	25·0	16	54·0	37·2	45·6	38·0	46·4	42·4
	30·360	64·0	11	29·462	45·0	16	29·911	54·5	·898	68·0	28	36·0	5	60·6	44·2	52·4	32·0	55·0	49·7
	30·370	67·0	8	29·226	54·0	7	29·798	60·5	1·144	77·0	10	39·0	14	64·0	47·5	55·7	38·0	57·9	52·3
	30·360	65·0	24	29·500	58·0	12	29·930	61·5	·860	70·0	1	46·0	25	64·8	50·7	57·7	24·0	60·2	55·0
	30·240	63·8	10	29·000	56·0	30	29·620	59·9	1·240	73·0	22	43·8	10	66·2	51·1	58·6	29·2	59·9	55·4
	30·290	59·0	22	29·280	52·0	29	29·785	55·5	1·010	65·0	7	40·0	28	60·2	46·6	53·4	25·0	55·0	50·4
	30·350	52·0	18	29·000	36·0	14	29·675	44·0	1·350	59·0	29	23·0	26	54·7	39·0	46·8	36·0	46·3	43·4
	30·300	53·0	22	29·400	40·0		29·850	46·5	·900	56·0	6	32·0	2	51·9	38·9	45·4	23·0	45·7	44·6
	30·186	52·0	8	29·450	32·0	3	29·818	42·0	·736	53·0	18	18·0	27	45·0	33·0	39·0	35·0	38·5	37·3
	364·526	680·3		351·328	520·0		357·871		13·198	749·0		375·8		655·9	488·3	571·8	373·2	582·1	542·9
	30·377	56·7		29·277	43·3		29·823		1·091	62·4		31·3		54·6	40·7	47·6	31·1	48·5	45·2

REVIEW OF THE WEATHER FOR 1892.—*Continued.*

Direction and Amount of Wind, as indicated by Casella's Self-Recording Anemometer.

GAUGE.—Diameter of Receiver, 1 1in.; height of top above ground, 7ft. 1in.; height above sea level, 6oft.

1892.	N.	N.E.	E.	S.E.	S.	S.W.	W.	N.W.	Var.	Greatest in one day (Miles)	Date	Least in one day (Miles)	Date	Mean Daily Am'nt (Miles)	Total Depth (Inches)	Greatest fall in one day (Inches)	Date	No. of days ·01 or more (Days)
	Days	Days	Days	Days	Days	Days	Days	Days	Days									
January	2	1	2	3	2	7	9	3	2	435	29th	35	18th	216	3·102	·583	7th	20
February	2	3	3	6	2	—	6	6	3	555	20th	65	18th	239	1·143	·278	7th	11
March	6	3	2	6	—	4	1	4	4	365	9th	38	29th	140	·728	·250	9th	4
April	4	5	4	1	2	4	5	4	2	535	27th	40	1st	179	1·107	·206	26th	15
May	—	8	1	8	1	4	5	2	3	645	3rd	90	25th	232	3·727	·530	22nd	17
June	3	4	1	5	5	2	3	7	2	350	17th	53	20th	192	3·626	·926	10th	14
July	3	7	5	1	1	3	6	6	3	525	19th	30	14th	187	2·547	·730	9th	10
August	2	3	—	5	—	9	6	6	2	310	21st	82	11th	184	5·011	1·100	7th	16
September	1	2	—	—	4	1	7	4	1	350	3rd	65	6th	227	2·060	·628	1st	18
October	5	6	—	1	5	7	7	8	1	643	14th	40	24th	212	2·962	·793	14th	17
November	—	—	3	8	2	—	5	1	1	530	29th	35	23rd	214	3·056	·522	25th	20
December	2	—	4	6	5	6	7	2	3	485	5th	10	26th	204	2·138	·343	13th	15
Totals	30	37	26	49	28	51	65	53	27	5728		583		2426	31·207			177
Means										477		49		202				

RULES

OF THE

Belfast Naturalists' Field Club.

——— ✠ ———

I.

That the Society be called "THE BELFAST NATURALISTS' FIELD CLUB."

II.

That the objects of the Society be the practical study of Natural Science and Archæology in Ireland.

III.

That the Club shall consist of Ordinary, Corresponding, and Honorary Members. The Ordinary Members to pay annually a subscription of Five Shillings, and that candidates for such Membership shall be proposed and seconded at any Meeting of the Club, by Members present, and elected by a majority of the votes of the Members present.

IV.

That the Honorary and Corresponding Members shall consist of persons of eminence in Natural Science, or who shall have done some special service to the Club ; and whose usual residence is not less than twenty miles from Belfast. That such Members may be nominated by any Member of the Club, and on being approved of by the Committee, may be elected at any subsequent Meeting of the Club by a majority of the votes of the Members present. That Corresponding Members be expected to communicate a Paper once within every two years.

V.

That the Officers of the Club be annually elected, and consist of a President, Vice-President, Treasurer, and two Secretaries, and ten Members, who form the Committee. Five to form a quorum. No member of Committee to be eligible for re-election who has not attended at least one-fourth of the Committee Meetings during his year of office. That the office of President, or that of Vice-President, shall not be held by the same person for more than two years in succession.

VI.

That the Members of the Club shall hold at least ₎Six Field Meetings during the year, in the most interesting localities, for investigating the Natural History and Archæology of Ireland. That the place of meeting be fixed by the Committee, and that five days' notice of each Excursion be communicated to Members by the Secretaries.

VII.

That Meetings be held Fortnightly or Monthly, at the discretion of the Committee, for the purpose of reading papers ; such papers, as far as possible, to treat of the Natural History and Archæology of the district. These Meetings to be held during the months from November to April inclusive.

VIII.

That the Committee shall, if they find it advisable, offer for competition Prizes for the best collections of scientific objects of the district ; and the Committee may order the purchase of maps, or other scientific apparatus, and may carry on geological and archæological searches or excavations, if deemed advisable, provided that the entire amount expended under this rule does not exceed the sum of £10 in any one year.

IX.

That the Annual Meeting be held during the month of April, when the Report of the Committee for the past year, and the Treasurer's Financial State-ment shall be presented, the Committee and Officers elected, Bye-laws made and altered, and any proposed alteration in the general laws, of which a fortnight's notice shall have been given, in writing, to the Secretary or Secretaries, con-sidered and decided upon. The Secretaries to give the Members due notice of such intended alteration.

X.

That, on the written requisition of twenty-five Members, delivered to the Secretaries, an Extraordinary General Meeting may be called, to consider and decide upon the subject mentioned in such written requisition.

XI.

That the Committee may be empowered to exchange publications and reports, and to extend the privilege of attending the Meetings and Excursions of the Belfast Naturalists' Field Club to members of kindred societies, on similar privileges being accorded to its members by such other societies.

The following Rules for the Conducting of the Excursions have been arranged by the Committee.

I. The Excursion to be open to all members ; each one to have the privilege of introducing two friends.

II. A Chairman to be elected as at ordinary meetings.

III. One of the Secretaries to act as conductor, or in the absence of both, a member to be elected for that purpose.

IV. No change to be made in the programme, or extra expense incurred, except by the consent of the majority of the members present.

V No fees, gratuities, or other expenses to be paid except through the conductor.

VI. Every member or visitor to have the accommodation assigned by the conductor. Where accommodation is limited, consideration will be given to priority of application.

VII. Accommodation cannot be promised unless tickets are obtained before the time mentioned in the special circular.

VIII. Those who attend an Excursion without previous notice will be liable to extra charge, if extra cost be incurred thereby.

IX. No intoxicating liquors to be provided at the expense of the Club.

BELFAST NATURALISTS' FIELD CLUB.

————·:·————

THIRTY-FIRST YEAR.

————·:·————

THE Committee offer the following Prizes to be competed for during the Session ending March 31st, 1894 :—

I. Best Herbarium of Flowering Plants, representing not less than 250 species, ...£1			0	0
II. Best Herbarium of Flowering Plants, representing not less than 150 species, ...			0	10	0
III. Best Collection of Mosses, ...			0	10	0
IV. .. ,, Lichens ...			0	10	0
V. ,, Seaweeds			0	10	0
VI. ,, Ferns, Equiseta, and Lycopods, ...			0	10	0
VII. ,, Tertiary and Post-tertiary Fossils, ...			0	10	0
VIII. ,, ,, Cretaceous Fossils, ...			0	10	0
IX. ,, Liassic Fossils, ...			0	10	0
X. ,, Permian and Carboniferous Fossils, ...			0	10	0
XI. ,, ,, Older Palæozoic Fossils,			0	10	0
XII. ,, ,, Marine Shells, ...			0	10	0
XIII. , ,, Land and Freshwater Shells,			0	10	0
XIV. ,, ,, Lepidoptera, ...			0	10	0
XV. ,, Hymenoptera, ...			0	10	0
XVI. ,, ,, Coleoptera, ...			0	10	0
XVII. ,, ,, Crustacea and Echinodermata, ...			0	10	0

XVIII. Best Collection of Fungi ; names of species
not necessary. Collectors may send (post
païd, from time to time during the season)
their specimens to Rev. H. W. Lett, M.A.,
Loughbrickland, Co. Down, who will record
them to their credit, ...£0 10 0
XIX. Best Collection of Fossil Sponges, ... 0 10 0
XX. Best Collection of 24 Microscopic Slides,
illustrating some special branch of Natural
History, ... 0 10 0
XXI. Best Collection of 24 Microscopic Slides,
shewing general excellence, ... 0 10 0
XXII. Best Set of 12 Photo-micrographs, illustrating
some special branch of Natural History, ... 0 10 0
XXIII. Best Set of 6 Field Sketches appertaining to
Geology, Àrchæology, or Zoology, ... 0 10 0
XXIV. Best Set of 12 Photographs, illustrative of
Irish Archæology, ... 0 10 0

SPECIAL PRIZES.

XXV. The President offers a prize of £1 1s. for the Best Set
of three or more Original Sketches, to be placed in
the Album of the Club. These may be executed in
pen and ink, or water-colour, and must illustrate
one or more ancient monuments somewhere in
Ireland. In determining the relative merits of the
sketches, accuracy in representing the subjects and
their details will have chief place. This Prize is
open to the Members of the Belfast Art Society,
and to the Students of the School of Art.
XXVI. The President offers a Prize of 10s. 6d. for Six Photographs from Nature, illustrative of Geology, contributed to the Club's Album.

XXVII. Mr. Francis Joseph Bigger, Solicitor, Belfast, offers a Prize of £1 1s. for the Best Set of Twelve Photographs (not less than cabinet size) of Ecclesiastical Structures mentioned in Reeves' *Ecclesiastical Antiquities of Down and Connor*, contributed to the Club's Album. The set of Photographs taking this Prize cannot be admitted in competition for Prize XXIV.

XXVIII. W. H. Patterson, M.R.I.A., offers a Prize of £1 1s. for the best collection of Flowering Plants, species not to exceed 50 in number, and 20 of these at least to be plants of considerable rarity ; to be personally collected in Ulster during the year, to be named, with localities and dates attached. Judges—S. A. Stewart and R. L. Praeger, or either.

XXIX. The Secretaries of the Ulster Fauna Committee offer a Prize of 10s. for the Best Collection of Bats, Rodents, Insectivora, and Carnivora (names of species not necessary) collected in Ulster during the year. Specimens to be sent in a fresh state to the Museum, Belfast.

CONDITIONS.

No competitor to obtain more than two Prizes in one year.

No competitor to be awarded the same Prize twice within three years.

A member to whom Prize I. has been awarded shall be ineligible to compete for Prize II., unless the plants are additions to those in previous collection.

In every case where three or more persons compete for a Prize, a second one, of half its value, will be awarded if the conditions are otherwise complied with.

All collections to be made personally during the Session in Ireland, except those for Prize XXI., which need not necessarily be Irish, nor competitors' own collecting. The species to be classified according to a recognised system, to be correctly named, and localities stated, and a list to accompany each collection. The Flowering Plants to be collected when in flower, and classified according to the Natural System. The Microscopic Slides to be competitors' own preparation and mounting. The Sketches and Photographs to be competitors' own work, executed during the Session ; and those sets for which Prizes are awarded, to become the property of the Club.

No Prizes will be awarded except to such collections as shall, in the opinion of the Judges, possess positive merit.

The Prizes to be in books, or suitable scientific objects, at the desire of the successful competitor.

ΩOTICE.

EXCHANGES OF PROCEEDINGS.

Amiens—Societé Linnéenne de Nord de la France.
Bulletin, Nos. 223 to 234.
Memoirs 1889-91.

Belfast—Natural History and Philosophical Society.
Report and Proceedings, 1891-92.

Bath—Natural History and Antiquarian Field Club.
Proceedings, Vol. III., No. 3.

Berwickshire—Naturalists' Field Club.
Proceedings, Vol. XIII., Nos. 1 and 2.

Brighton and Sussex—Natural History and Philosophical
Society.
Annual Report, 1892.

Bristol—Naturalists' Society.
Proceedings, Vol. VII., Part I.

Cardiff—Naturalists' Society.
Report and Transactions, Vol. XXIV., Part I.

Cornwall—Royal Institution of.
Journal, Vol. XI., Part I.

Costa Rica—Instituto Fisico-Geographico Y. del Musco Nacional.
Anàles, Tomo III., 1890.

Dublin—Royal Irish Academy.
Proceedings, Vol. II., No. 2.
Transactions, Vol. XXIX., Parts 18 and 19; Vol. XXX.,
Parts 1 to 4.
Cunningham Memoirs, No. VII.

Dumfries and Galloway—Natural History and Antiquarian
   Society.
   Transactions and Journal, No. 8.

Edinburgh—Geological Society.
   Transactions, Vol. VI., Part III.

Frankfort—Helios.
   Jahrgang X., Nos. 1 to 12.

,,   Societatum Litteræ.
   Jahrgang VI., Nos. 4 to 8.

,,   Katalog der Batrichier-Sammlung im Museum der
   Senckenbergischen naturforchenden Gesell·
   schaft.

,,   Bericht fiber die Senckenbergische naturforchende
   Gesellschaft, 1892.

Glasgow—Philosophical Society of.
   Index to Proceedings, Vol. I. to XX.

,,   Natural History Society of.
   Proceedings and Transactions, Vol. III., Parts 2 and 3.

Halifax, N.S.—Nova Scotian Institute of Science.
   Proceedings and Transactions, Vol. I., Part I.

Hamilton (Canada)—Hamilton Association.
   Journal and Transactions, No. VII.

Hertfordshire—Natural History Society and Field Club.
   Transactions, Vol. VI., Parts 4 to 8 ; Vol. VII., Parts 1 to 4.

Leeds—Philosophical and Literary Society.
   Annual Report, 1891-92.

Liverpool—Naturalists' Field Club.
   Proceedings, 1892.

,,   Geological Association.
   Journal, Vols. XI. and XII.

,,   Geological Society.
   Proceedings, Vol. VI., Part 4.

London—Geologists' Association.
   Proceedings, Vol. XII., Parts 7 to 10.
   List of Members.

,,   Royal Microscopical Society.
   Journal, April, 1893.

London—British Association for the Advancement of Science.
Annual Report, Edinburgh Meeting, 1892.

,,   Society of Antiquaries.

Manchester—Field Naturalists' and Archæologists' Society.
Report and Proceedings, 1891.

Marlborough—College Natural History Society.
Reports, Nos. 40 and 41.

Penzance—Natural History and Antiquarian Society.
Report and Transactions, 1891-92.

Plymouth—Institution.
Annual Report and Transactions, Vol. XI., Part 2.

Rome—Rassegna delle Scienze Geologiche in Italia.
Fasc. 1, 2, 3, 1892.

,,   Societa Botanica Italiana.
Bulletins, 1891-92.

St. John, N.B.—Natural History Society of New Brunswick.
Bulletin, No. X.

Stavanger—Museum.
Aarsberetning for 1891.

Toronto—Canadian Institute.
Transactions, Nos. 4 and 5.
Annual Archæological Report, 1891.
An Appeal to the Institute.

Wiltshire—Archæological and Natural History Society
Magazine, Vol. XXVI, Nos. 77 and 78.

Yorkshire—Naturalists' Union.
Transactions, Part 17.

U S.A.—Boston—Society of Natural History.
Proceedings, Vol. XXV., Parts 3 and 4.

,,   Bridgeport—Scientific Society.
List of Birds.

,,   Minnesota—Geological and Natural History Survey.
Annual Report (Nineteenth), 1890.
Bulletin, No. 7 (Mammals of Minnesota).

,,   New York—American Museum of Natural History.
Annual Report, 1891.
Bulletin, Vol. III., No. 2; and Vol. IV., 1892.

U.S.A.—New York—Academy of Sciences.
Transactions, Vol. X., Nos. 7 and 8; Vol. XI, Nos. 1 to 6.

,,   Philadelphia—Academy of Natural Sciences.
Proceedings, 1892, Parts 1 and 2.
American Naturalist, Vol. XXVI., No. 311.

,,   Raleigh, N.C.—Elisha Mitchell Scientific Society.
Journal, Vol. VIII., Part 2; Vol. IX., Part 1.

,,   Rochester—Academy of Sciences.
Proceedings, Vols. 1 and 2.

,,   Salem—American Association for the Advancement of Science.
Proceedings Washington Meeting, 1891.
,,   ,,   ,,   1892.

,,   Smithsonian Institution.
Annual Report, 1889.
,,   1890.

,,   St. Louis—Academy of Sciences.
Transactions, Vol. V., Nos. 3 and 4; Vol. VI., No. 1.

,,   Washington—University Eclipse Party.
Report and Observations, 1891.

BELFAST NATURALISTS' FIELD CLUB.

THIRTY-FIRST YEAR, 1893-94.

LIST OF OFFICERS AND MEMBERS.

President:
WILLIAM SWANSTON, F.G.S.

Vice-President:
F. W. LOCKWOOD.

Treasurer:
W. H. PHILLIPS, F.R.H.S.,
8 CHICHESTER STREET.

Librarian:
WILLIAM SWANSTON, F.G.S.,
QUEEN STREET.

Secretary:
FRANCIS JOSEPH BIGGER,
REA'S BUILDINGS, BELFAST.

Committee:

JOHN J. ANDREW, L.D.S.	S. A. STEWART, F.B.S.Edin.
GEORGE DONALDSON.	MISS S. M. THOMPSON.
L. M. EWART, J.P., M.R.I.A.	JOHN VINYCOMB, M.R.I.A.
WILLIAM GRAY, M.R.I.A.	ROBERT J. WELCH.
JOHN HAMILTON.	JOSEPH WRIGHT, F.G.S.

Members.

Any changes in the Addresses of Members should be notified to the Secretaries.

Adams, Andrew, 25 Atlantic Avenue
Adams, John J., M.D., Ashville, Antrim.
Acheson, Samuel E. A., 42 Cromac Street
Agnew, A. W., Dunedin, Belfast.
Aird, M. W., 46 Royal Avenue.
Allen, Hugh, 71 York Street.
Allibon, George, 30 Donegall Place.
Allworthy, Edward, Mosaphir.
Anderson, John, J P., F.G.S., East Hillbrook, Holywood.
Anderson, Robert, Donegall Place.
Andrew, J. J., L.D.S., R.C.S.Eng., Belgravia.
Andrews, Miss, 12 College Gardens.
Andrews, Miss Mary K., College Gardens.
Armstrong, Rev. John E., 22 Belgravia Avenue.
Aston, Miss Annie, South Parade.

Bain, Miss Dora, Downshire Road, Holywood.
Barkley, James M., Queen's Square, Belfast.
Barklie, Robert, M.R.I.A., Working Men's Institute.
Barnes, Henry, 7 Skipper Street.
Barr, James, Beechleigh, Windsor Park.
Barr, John, Belmont Park.
Batt, William, Sorrento, Windsor.
Beattie, Rev. A. Hamilton, Portglenone.
Beck, Miss Emma, Old Lodge Road.
Beggs, D. C., Ballyclare.
Begley, George R., Kenbella Avenue, Belfast.
Bell, S. D., 41 Fitzwilliam Street.
Best, James, Clarence Place.
Bigger, Francis Joseph. Ardrie, Antrim Road.
Bingham, Edward, Ponsonby Avenue
Blair, E., 130 Elgin Terrace.
Blair, Mrs., 130 Elgin Terrace.
Boyd, J. St. Clair, M.D., 27 Great Victoria Street.
Boyd, Miss, Beechcroft, Strandtown
Boyd, Miss, Cultra House, Holywood.

Braddell, Edward, St. Ives, Malone Park.
Brandon, Hugh B., Atlantic Avenue
Brenan, Rev. Samuel Arthur, B.A., Knocknacarry, Co. Antrim.
Brett, Chas. H., Gretton Villa South
Bristow, Rev. John, St. James's Parsonage.
Brown, John, Edenderry House, Shaw's Bridge, Belfast.
Brown, Thomas, Donegall Street.
Brown, R. N., Monaghan.
Brown, William, Chichester Street.
Browne, W. J., M.A., M.R.I.A., Highfield, Omagh.
Brownlie, Richard, Victoria Street.
Bruce, Miss E., The Farm.
Bryson, Wm. H., Skipper Street.
Bulla, Charles, Wellington Park Ter.
Burnett, John R., Rostellan, Malone Road.

Calwell, William, M.D., College Square North
Campbell, J. O., 10 Clifton Street.
Carrothers, Nathaniel, 47 Strandmillis Road.
Carruthers, Miss, Claremont Street.
Carse, Hamilton, Kensington Villa, Knock.
Carson, J. Campbell, 73 Victoria Street.
Carson, Robert, Talbot Street.
Carter, W., Chichester Park.
Carter, Mrs., Chichester Park.
Chancellor, William, B.A., Cromwell House, Cromwell Road.
Cleland, James A., Wellington Park.
Clements, W. T., 1 Agincourt Avenue.
Coates, J. Dunville, Chichester St.
Coates, Stanley B., L.R.C.P.Edin., Shaftesbury Square
Colbeck, James, Shaw's Bridge.
Collins, Arthur J., 3 Windsor Cres.
Connell, Rev John, B.A., Holywood
Cooper, Rev. E. A., Carrowdore Rectory, Donaghadee.
Corry, W. F. C. S., Chatsworth, Malone Road.
Cosgrove, Henry, 35 Rugby Road.
Costigan, W., Great Victoria Street.

Coulson, Gerald, College St. South.
Coulson, J. P., Somerset Terrace.
Coulter, George B., 21 University
   Square.
Coulter, Mrs., 21 University Square
Crawford, F. H., Chlorine.
Crawley, Miss Anna, 67 High Street
Creeny, Rev. H. N., Edenderry
   House, Lisburn.
Creeth, James, Knock.
Crozier. David, Mill Street.
Crymble, George G., Gordon House,
   Annadale.
Culbert, Robert, Distillery Street.
Cunningham, Samuel, Glencairn.
Curley, Francis, Dunedin, Antrim
   Road.
Curley, Mrs., Dunedin, Antrim Road

Dufferin and Ava, Marquis of,
   Clandeboye (Hon. Mem.).
Davies, John Henry, Glenmore Cot-
   tage, Lisburn.
Davis, Henry, Holywood.
Day, Robert, J.P., F.S.A., M R.I.A.,
   Cork.
D'Evelyn, Alexander M., M.D.,
   Ballymena.
Dickson, John, Hillbrook, Holywood
Dixon, Wakefield H., Dunowen.
Doherty, James, Queen's College.
Donaldson, George, 88 North Street.
Donaldson, John, 5 West-end Terrace
   Dufferin Avenue, Bangor
Donnan, Wm. D., Ardmore Terrace,
   Holywood.
Douglas, Allan E., M.D., J.P.,
   Warrenpoint.
Duffin, Adam. University Square.
Duffin, Miss, Strandtown Lodge.
Dunlop, W. J., Bryson Street.

Elliott, David, Albert Bridge R ad.
Elliott, George, Royal Avenue
Elliott, George H., Holywood.
Ellison, Rev. Allan, Hillsborough.
Ewart, Lavens M., J.P., M.R.I.A.,
   Glenbank House.

Ferguson, Godfrey W., Donegall
   Park, Antrim Road.
Ferguson, Henry, Donegall Park.
Ferguson, J. H., 2 Wellesley Av.
Firth, Joseph, Whiterock.
Firth, Wm. A., Glenview Terrace,
   Springfield Road.

Flynn, T. M. H., Sunnyside, Bess-
   brook.
Frame, John, 6 Lawrence Street.
Fullerton, Geo., Croaghbeg, Bush-
   mills.
Fulton, David, Glenbrook, Cregagh.

Galloway, Peter, University Street
Galloway, Joseph, 83 Églantine
   Avenue.
Gamble, Miss, Royal Terrace.
Gardner, J. Starkie, F.G S., 29
   Albert Embankment, S.E. (Hon.
   Mem.)
Gibson, Henry, Glencairn.
Gilliland, John, Prospect Street.
Gilmore, R. M., Upper Salt Hill,
   Galway.
Gilmore, W. J., Camberwell Villas.
Glenn, George J., Hartington Street.
Godwin, William, Queen Street.
Gordon, Rev. David, Downpatrick.
Gourley, James, J.P., Derryboy,
   Killyleagh.
Gracey, Robert, Minerva House,
   Brookhill Avenue.
Graham, Wm., Lombard Street.
Gray, Wm., M R.I A , Mountcharles
Gray, Miss, Mountcharles.
Green, Mrs. Isaac, Bloomfield.
Greenfield, Charles, Marino, Holy-
   wood.
Greer, Mrs., Dulce Domo, Strand-
   town.
Gulbransen, P. F., 17 Queen's
   Arcade.
Gulbransen, Ahavos, 7 Ratcliffe St.

Hamilton, Alex., 20 Atlantic Av.
Hamilton, James H., Eden Terrace,
   Shankill Road
Hamilton, John, Church Avenue,
   Holywood.
Hamilton, Thomas, Queen Street.
Hanford, Ernest, Melrose Terrace.
Hanna, Jas. A., 5 Old Park Road.
Hanna, Richard, Charleville Street.
Hanna, William, B.A., Lisanore
   Villa, Antrim Road.
Hanna, John, jun., Lisanore Villa,
   Antrim Road.
Harbison, Mann, Ravenhill Terrace.
Hardy, Gardner, 5 Wellington Park.
Harris, W. D., St. Mary's Terrace.
Hartrick, Rev. Canon, M.A., The
   Rectory, Ballynure.

Haslett, Sir James, J.P., Princess Gardens.
Hassan, Thomas, Strangemore House
Heron, F. A., Cultra, Holywood.
Hill, Robert, 28 Ponsonby Avenue.
Hobson, Ben., F. Green & Co.
Holden, J. S., M.D., F.G.S., Sudbury, Suffolk (Cor. Mem.).
Holland, Wm., Osborne Park.
Hoskins, Arthur P., F.I.C., F.C.S., 25 Blenheim Terrace, Cromwell Road.
Hungerford, John, Royal Ulster Works.

Imrie, James, Rugby Road.
Inglis, Wm., Riverston Terrace, Holywood.

Jackson, A. T., 5 Corn Market.
Jacques, John, Parkview Terrace.
Jaffé, Mrs. Otto, Kinedar, Strandtown.
Jefferson, Hugh Smith, Rosnakill, Strandtown.
Johnson, Rev. W. F., M.A., Armagh.
Johnson, Mrs., Armagh.
Johnston, Wm. J., J.P., Dunesk, Stranmillis.
Johnston, James, 19 Waring Street.
Jones, Professor T. Rupert, F.R.S., Chelsea, London (Hon. Mem.).

Keay, David, 22 College Green.
Keith, Hutchinson, Glenravel Street.
Keith, Samuel F, 7 Glenravel St.
Kelly, W. Redfern, M. Inst. C.E., Elgin Terrace.
Kennedy, R. M., 41 Waring Street.
Kernaghan, Wm., Wellington Park.
Kidd, George, Lisnatore, Dunmurry.
Kirkpatrick, F., Ann Street
Kirkwood, John A., Dundonald Cottage.
Knowles, Wm. J., M.R.I.A., Ballymena.
Knowles, Miss Matilda, Skelwith Fold, Ambleside, Westmoreland.
Kyle, Robert A., 31 Donegall Place

Lamb, Wm. W., Salisbury Avenue.
Lapworth, Professor Charles, F.G S., Mason College, Birmingham (Hon. Mem.)
Lawther, Stanley, Mount Vernon.
Leighton, Samuel, Cooke Terrace.

Lepper, F. R., Elsinore, Crawfordsburn.
Leslie, James, Eglantine Avenue.
Leslie, Mrs., Eglantine Avenue.
Lett, Rev. H. W., M.A., T.C.D., Aghaderg Glebe, Loughbrickland.
Letts, Professor E. A., Ph.D., F.C.S., Dunavon, Craigavad.
Lewers, Hugh, M.D., Shankill Rd.
Lewis, Joseph, 13 Pakenham Street.
Lockwood, Frederick W., Wellington Park Terrace.
Logan, James, Donegall Street.
Logan, Mrs. James, Bangor.
Lowson, W. B., Chichester Park.
Luther, H. W., M.D., Chlorine House

Macdonald, Miss, Bantry, Co. Cork.
Macdonald, William, Carlisle Circus.
Mackenzie, John, C E., Malone.
Major, Rev. J. J., Belvoir Hall.
Malcolmson, Greer, Granville Gardens.
Malcolmson, Harold, Holywood.
Malcolmson, James, Cairnburn, Strandtown.
Malcolmson, Mrs., Cairnburn, Strandtown.
Mann, James S , Ballyholme, Bangor.
Marsh, Mrs., Glenlyon, Holywood.
Martin, Adam, Knock.
Marsh, Joseph C., Castleton Terrace.
Marshall, Hamilton, 15 Rockmount, Castlereagh Place, Mountpottinger.
Maxton, James, M.I.M.E., 26 Waring Street.
Megahy, Jas., 27 University Road.
Millen, Samuel, B.A., 44 Ulsterville Avenue.
Milligan, Seaton Forrest, M.R.I.A., Chelsea, Antrim Road.
Mitchell, J. S., 47 Magdala Street.
Mollan, W. S., Helen's Bay.
Mollan, Miss, Helen's Bay.
Moore, John, Shaftesbury Square.
Morrisey, Edward J., 14 Lavinia St.
Morrow, David, Church Hill, Holywood.
Morrow, John L., Ardigon, Killyleagh.
Morton, John, Clifton Park Avenue.
Moss, William, Camberwell Terrace.
Mull, Henry, Glendore, Crawfordsburn.

Munce, W. B., Rosemary Street.
Murdoch, Charles, 230 Grosvenor St.
Murdoch, James, Denmark Street.
Murphy, Joseph John, Osborne Park.
Musgrave, J. R., J.P., Drumglass
House, Malone Road.
Myles, Rev. Edward A., St. Anne's
Vestry, Belfast.
M'Alister, Thomas, Eglinton Street.
M'Cance, J. Stouppe, Dunmurry.
M'Candless, Wm., 3 Finvoy Terrace,
Fitzroy Avenue.
M'Gaw, Miss, Wellington Park
Terrace.
M'Chesney, Joseph, Holywood.
M'Clean, Francis P., Huntly Villas.
M'Cleery, H., Clifton Park Avenue.
M'Cleery, Wm. Henry, 5 St. James
Street.
M'Clure, Rev. Ed., M.A., M.R.I.A.,
Onslow Place, South Kensing-
ton (Cor. Mem.)
M'Clure, Wm. J., Elizabeth Street.
MacColl, Mrs., Saxonia, Strandtown.
MacColl, Miss.   ,,   ,,
M'Connell, James, Annadale Hall.
M'Connell, Edward, 100 York St.
M'Cormick, H. M'Neile, Craigavad.
M'Crea, J. B., C E., Hesseville,
Ballynafeigh.
M'Cullough, John, Martello Terrace,
Holywood.
M'Cullough, John C., Holywood.
M'Dade, R. S., 148 Donegall Pass.
M'Dermott, Rev John, Belmont.
M'Donald, James, 37 Donegall St
M'Elheran, W. F., College Gardens.
MacIlwaine, John H., Ravensdale,
Strandtown.
MacIlwaine, Mrs., Ravensdale,
Strandtown.
M'Kean, Mrs. Wm , 17 University
Square.
M'Kee, John, Newtownards.
M'Kee, Miss, Harlesden College,
Bramshill Road, London, N.W.
M'Kee, Robert, M.A., Harlesden
College. Bramshill Road, Lon-
don, N W.
M'Kee, W. S., Fleetweod Street.
M'Kenzie, W. G., M.D , Gt. Victoria
Street.
M'Kinney, W. F., Ballyvesey,
Carnmoney.
M'Kisack, Alfred, Mountcharles.
M'Lean, George, 8 Pottinger Street.

MacLaine, Alexander, J.P., Queen's
Elms.
M'Leish, John, Ballyhackamore.
M'Mordie, Jas., Belgravia Avenue.
M'Neill, Miss J., 4 Princess Gardens.
M'William, Hugh, Knocknagoney
Holywood.

Nelson, Miss, Wandsworth Villa,
Strandtown.
Nepveu, Lucien, Courtney Terrace.
Nesbitt, W. Courtney, Kinnaird
Terrace.
Nicholl, Wm., Donegall Square
North.
Nicholson, H. J., Windsor Gardens.

O'Flaherty, F. H., Cultra.
O'Neill, Henry, M.D., College Square
East
O'Neill, James, M.A., College Square
East.
O'Shea, P. J., 3 Woodvale Avenue,
Belfast.
Orr, H. Lamont, Garfield Street.
Owens, John S., St. James' Street.

Patterson, David C., C.anbrassil
Terrace, Holywood.
Patterson, R. Lloyd, J. P., F.L S.,
Croft House, Holywood
Patterson, Robert, M.B O.U.,
Windsor Park Terrace, Lisburn
Road.
Patterson, R. L., jun , Clanbrassil
Torraoc, Holywood
Patterson, W. Hartley, Clanbrassil
I eriace, Holywood
Patterson, Richard, J.P., Kilmore,
Holywood.
Patterson, Miss Clara, Kilmore,
Holywood.
Patterson, William H., M.R.I.A.,
Garranard, Strandtown.
Paul, Thomas, Redcot, Knock.
Payne, H. W., Beechcroft, Holy-
wood
Payne, J. C. C., Oxford Buildings.
Payne, Mrs., Botanic Avenue.
Peddie, J. Finlay, C.E., 83 Royal
Avenue.
Phillips, James J , 61 Royal Avenue.
Phillips, William H., F.R.H.S.,
Lemonfield, Holywood.
Pike, Rev. J. Kirk, Wynnstay,
Rosetta Terrace.

Pim, John, J.P., Bonaven, Antrim Road.
Pim, John William, 21 Victoria St.
Pim, Joshua, Slieve-na-Failthe, Whiteabbey.
Pim, Thomas W., 21 Victoria St.
Pinion, James, Co. Down Railway.
Polley, Wm. Thomas, 52 Fitzroy Avenue.
Porter, Miss, 27 Belgravia Avenue.
Porter. F. A., Queen's Square.
Porter, William. Eagle Chambers.
Praeger, E. A., Holywood.
Praeger, Robert Lloyd, B.A., B.E., M.R.I.A., National Library of Ireland, Dublin.

Quail, Rev. Patrick, Dunmore, Ballynahinch.

Radley, Joseph, Prospect Hill, Lisburn.
Rea, Miss, Churchfield, Holywood.
Redmond, David, Saintfield.
Reid, J. C. W., Montalto, South Parade.
Reid, Robert, King Street.
Reid, S. M., 80 Albert Bridge Road
Rew, Fred. W., 49 Atlantic Avenue.
Ridings, Richard, Hampton Terrace
Ringland, Samuel B., Ballytrim House, Killyleagh.
Ritchie, James (Miller, Boyd, & Reid), Calendar Street.
Robinson, Rev. George, M.A., Beech Hill House, Armagh.
Robinson, George, Woodview, Holywood.
Robinson. Jas. R , George's Terrace
Robinson, Samuel, Helen's Pay.
Robinson, William A., J.P., Culloden, Cultra.
Ross, John, Cliftonville.
Ross. Richard, M.D., Wellington Place.
Ross, Wm. A., Iva-Craig, Craigavad
Rowan, J. C., Eglantine Avenue.
Russell, John, C.E., 16 Waring St.

Sefton, John R., Bangor.
Shanks, James, Ballyfounder, Portaferry.
Shaw, Lancelot. Brooklyn, Knock.
Shaw, Mrs. Lancelot, Brooklyn, Knock.
Sheldon, Chas., M.A., B.Sc., D.Lit.,

Simms, David, C.E., Cromwell Rd., Botanic Avenue.
Skillen, Joseph, 34 Beverley Street.
Smith, Rev. W. S., The Manse, Antrim.
Smyth, George I., Linen Hall Library.
Smyth, Walter, Woodview, Holywood.
Smyth, Rev. Canon, M.A., Coole Glebe, Carmoney.
Smythe, Mrs. Proctor, Antrim Road
Speers, Adam, B.Sc., Holywood.
Stacke, Dr. E. C., 15 Gt. Victoria Street.
Staples, Sir N. A., Bart., Lissan, Dungannon (Life Mem.).
Steele, David, 5 Maryville Crescent, Bangor.
Steele, Robert J., 113 Royal Avenue
Stelfox, James, Oakleigh. Ormeau Park.
Stevenson, John, Coolavin, Malone Road.
Stevenson, J. M'N., Carrickfergus.
Stewart, Rev. J. A., M A., Pond Park, Lisburn.
Stewart, Pakenham, Knockbreda Rectory, Belfast.
Stewart, S. A., F.B.S. Edin., The Museum.
Stirling, J., 14 Rugby Road
Swan. Allan P., Bushmills.
Swanston, William, F.G.S., Cliftonville Avenue.
Swanston, Mrs., Cliftonville Avenue
Symington, Samuel, Ballyoran Ho., Dundonald.

Tate, Alexander, C.E., Longwood.
Tate, Miss A. H., Longwood.
Tate, Prof. Ralph, F.G.S., F.L.S., Adelaide, South Australia (Hon. Mem)
Taylor, Ernest E., 4 Cromwell Rd.
Thomas, S. G., Limestone Road.
Thompson, Miss S. M., Macedon.
Thompson, Mrs. Henry, Crosshill, Windsor.
Thomson, George, Broadway Factory
Todd, John, Fortwilliam Park.
Todd, W. A., 24 Victoria Street.
Townsend, P. F., 1 Holborn Terrace, University Street.
Traill, W. A., B.E, M.A.I., Bushmills.

Turner, James, Mountain Bush.
Turtle, Jas. C., Claremont, Strandtown.

Vinycomb, John, M.R.I.A., Holywood.

Waddell, Rev. C. Herbert, M.A.,
The Rectory, Saintfield.
Wakeman, W. F., M.R.I.A.,
Knightsville, Blackrock, Dub-
lin (Cor. Mem.)
Walker, Thomas R., Rugby Road.
Walkington, Thos. R., Edenvale.
Ward, George G., Eversleigh,
Strandtown.
Ward, Isaac W., Ulster Terrace.
Wardell, Miss. 63 Botanic View,
University Road.
Watson, Thomas, Shipquay Gate,
Londonderry.
Watson, Wm., Rosslyn, Knock.
Watts, Charles W., F.I.C., Holborn
Terrace.

Waugh, Isaac, 17 Wilmont Terrace.
Welch, Robert J., Lonsdale Street.
Whitaker, Miss F., Cliftonville.
White, Benoni, Royal Ulster Works
White-Spunner, Mrs., Greenisland.
Whitla, Prof., M.D., J.P., College
Square North.
Wilson, James, Oldforge, Dunmurry
Wilson, Jas,. Ballybundon, Killinchy
Wilson, Alexander G., Strandmillis.
Wilson, Walter H., Strandmillis.
Wise, Berkley D., C.E., Waterside,
Greenisland.
Workman, Rev. Robert, M.A.,
Rubane, Glastry.
Workman, Thomas, J.P., Craig-
darragh.
Wright, Joseph, F G.S., Alfred
Street
Wright, Miss, Alfred Street.
Wright, W. C., Lauriston, Derrie-
volgie Avenue.
Wylie, William, Mountpleasant.

Young, Robert, C.E., Rathvarna.

GRAY—WORKED FLINTS.

PLATES AND DESCRIPTIONS.

FIG. I.—RAISED BEACH GRAVELS, LARNE.

The raised beach gravels constitute deposits of marine origin laid down during certain variation of coast line levels that took place at the close of the Tertiary period.

The gravels occur at Carrickfergus and Kilroot at one side, and at Holywood, Cultra, and Ballyholme at the other side of Belfast Harbour.

They are very well represented at Carnlough ; the Curran or Corran of Larne is made up of such raised beach gravels. All the above gravels contain worked flints, of various forms, showing that man occupied the locality during the deposition of the gravels.

The section at Larne demonstrates that the period of accumulation was of long duration and of remote antiquity. Our plate shows the beds A, B, and C resting upon the tilted-up edges of a series of beds marked D. Worked flints have been found in all the beds, forming a face of about 20 feet deep.— *See B.N.F.C. Report for* 1889-90, *p.* 198.

FIG. 2.—SAND-DUNES, BANNMOUTH.

Sand-dunes are accumulations of sand, chiefly collected on the sea shore, at or near the mouth of rivers. Such collections are not permanent, being of eolian origin, and subject to constant alteration by the wind. The effect of the wind produces deep basin-like hollows between the undulating heaps of sand, and on exposed sections the old surfaces are indicated by bands of carbonised vegetable matter.

The hollows between the sand-heaps formed capital shelter-places, and were used as such by primitive man, who established settlements on the sand-dunes, from which he went forth to hunt and fish. Here he manufactured his implements and weapons of flint, and here he left the refuse of his workshop and his dwellings in such abundance and variety as to furnish a very fair indication of his habits and mode of life. Sand-dunes of the kind occur at each side of the Bann mouth, also at Portrush, in Co. Antrim, and Dundrum, in Co. Down. The illustration shows the bands of old surfaces, and in the hollow of the basin the gravel in which the worked flints are usually found,

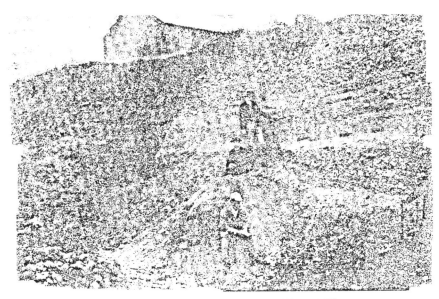

FIG. I.—RAISED BEACH GRAVELS, LARNE.

FIG. 2.—SAND DUNES, BANNMOUTH.

PLATE 2.

FIG. 3.—PALÆOLITHIC TYPES.

$\frac{1}{4}$ *Full Size.*

Fig. 3 shows two examples of the river gravel Palæolithic implements, one from Suffolk and one from Devonshire ; and below them two worked flints from the Larne Gravels.   No. 3 is formed from a flint nodule pointed at one end, and the other end is left with the rounded natural surface of the flint.   No. 4, also from Larne, is flat on one side and chipped with a tongue-shaped surface on the other.   Like Nos. 1 and 2, Nos. 3 and 4 are very rough.

NOTE.—The above and all the other illustrations, except Fig. 1, 2, and 16 are shown one-fourth full size, and are from photographs of the objects.

FIG. 4.—ROUGH CELTS FROM RAISED BEACHES.

$\frac{1}{4}$ *Full Size.*

Fig. 4 illustrate 10 rough celts, chiefly from the raised beach gravels.   The central celts, Nos. 3 and 8, are from the Larne gravels.   No. 3 was found at a depth of 11 ft. from the surface by the B.N.F.C.'s exploring committee.   No. 8 was found by R. Young, Esq., C.E.   No. 5 was found at Holywood.   No. 6 at Islandmagee ; and all the others were found by W. H. Patterson, Esq., at Cultra and Ballyholme, Co. Down.   Similar rough flint celts are found with surface finds all over the north-east of Ireland.

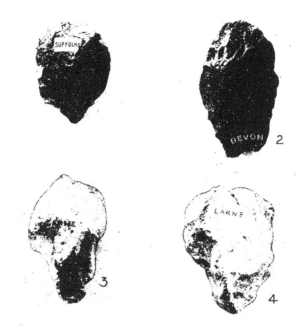

FIG. 3.—PALÆOLITHIC TYPES.

PLATE 3.

FIG. 5.—SAND-DUNE FINDS.

¼ *Full Size.*

This illustration shows the nature of the objects commonly found on the sites of settlements on sand-dunes. The group of objects is composed of fragments of pottery, bones, shells, flint chips, worked flints, flint cores, and hammers. The fragments of pottery are probably the remains of food vessels. The flints were probably worked on the spot, and the tools are found as they were left by the primitive flint manufacturer. A single hollow in the dunes has, in many cases, yielded several dozen hammers, scrapers, and hundreds of flakes.

FIG. 6.—SPECIAL FORMS OF WORKED FLINTS.

¼ *Full Size.*

In a large collection of ordinary flakes, no matter how rough they may be, certain forms frequently occur of the same general shape. For example, a number will be found narrow at one end and very thick at the other, as the upper four in the illustration. Others will be found with a hook or bend, as the lower six in the illustration. Such and many other forms are due to the peculiarity of the flint fracture and not to the intention of the fabricator ; but primitive man observed this quality of the flint, and often adopted such forms to answer his purpose.

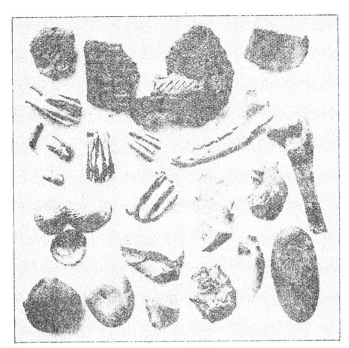

FIG. 5.—SAND-DUNE FINDS.

FIG. 7.—HAMMERS.

$\frac{1}{4}$ *Full Size.*

The tools supposed to have been employed in the manufacture of worked flint in ancient times are chiefly in the form of hammers. They occur on the sites of ancient settlements, and assume definite typical forms. The simplest forms are ordinary water-worn pebbles, chiefly those of quartzite, such as are weathered out of the Boulder Clay. They were selected and used by primitive man as hammers ; their continued use as such is demonstrated by the manner in which their ends are crushed and broken. Many of these pebbles are more or less ground into form, others have hollows sunk in the sides, and in some cases the holes are pierced through, as shown in the centre of the illustration. Others are oval or round in form, and are distinguished by a long indention at both sides, as if used for sharping a hard metal point. They are represented in the finds from each of the sand-dune stations. The variety of forms that occur among the hammer-stones, suggests the probability that they were also used for many other purposes.

FIG. 8.—CORES, FROM GRAVELS, ETC.

$\frac{1}{4}$ *Full Size.*

On the sites of all the ancient flint-factories, a large number of flint cores occur. Many of them are so weathered and round that only an expert can detect them. But the greater number are so well and clearly marked as to satisfy any ordinary observer that they formed the original block of flint from which the flakes were struck. They are of various sizes, some very large, and some very small, indeed, not more than $\frac{3}{4}$ inch long, yet they all show the scars or depressions from which the flakes were struck off. Usually the rough core shows the outside crust of the flint nodule at one side, but many show that the manipulator struck off flakes all round, such as is done by the flint workers at Brandon, &c., where modern gunflints are now manufactured.

FIG. 7.—HAMMERS.

PLATE 5.

FIG. 9.—PLAIN FLAKES.

$\frac{1}{4}$ *Full Size.*

County Antrim has yielded a large number of simple flakes, perfect and uniform in shape and character, although struck off by a single blow. Such flakes generally assume the typical form described in the text, and illustrated by Fig. 9. The skilled worker formed a central ridge by striking off a flake from each side, and then by a dexterous blow behind the ridge, the flake is struck off, well shaped, sharp, and clean on the edges.

FIG. 10.—FLAKES WITH SECONDARY CHIPPING.

$\frac{1}{4}$ *Full Size.*

The great bulk of the flakes are more or less chipped into form by a process of secondary chipping, which is used to enable the fabricator to adapt the flake to its intended purpose. Obviously the badly-formed flake required the most chipping, but many of the otherwise well-formed flakes require to be mounted for use, and the preparation for this required a tang or handle to be formed at the thick end, next the bulb of percussion. This tang is common among the chipped flakes, and is formed by chipping away a portion of the blade at each side, as shown by the illustration.

FIG. 9.—PLAIN FLAKES.

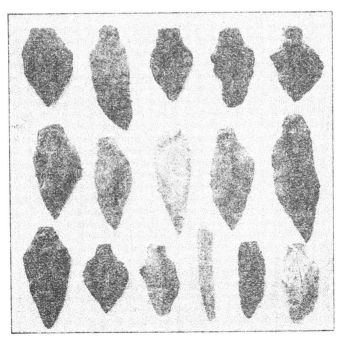

FIG. 10.—FLAKES WITH SECONDARY CHIPPING.

PLATE 6.

FIG. 11.—SCRAPERS, ETC.

¼ *Full Size.*

The flint implements known as scrapers are very common, chiefly in Antrim. They are found on the sites of ancient settlements, and are distributed over the surface of the ground. They are formed by chipping away the pointed end of the flake, which forms a more or less circular end. Sometimes the scraper is carefully chipped into a disc-shaped implement, sometimes into a spoon-shaped, with every variety of form between the two. The chipped edge is sometimes extremely blunt, but generally the scraper has a bevelled edge all round.

The lower row of implements in the illustration shows some of the variety of forms into which flakes are converted by a system of secondary chipping.

FIG. 12.—FINELY-CHIPPED ARROW-HEADS.

¼ *Full Size.*

The most beautifully-formed and elaborately-chipped flints found in the North of Ireland are the arrow-heads. They assume an endless variety of forms, all developed from the original simple leaf-shaped flint-flake. In the arrow-heads, all the characteristic points of the simple flake are obliterated by an elaboration of surface-chipping, and the ultimate forms assumed are the result of development in two lines : one in the direction of hollowing out the base of the leaf-shaped flake, and the other in the direction of forming a definite stem or tang at the base of the flake. All the forms are distinguished by careful surface-chipping, and they occur from $\frac{3}{8}$ of an inch long, to 4 and 5 inches. The spear-heads are very much larger and are commonly ground on the flat surface. The illustration is

FIG. II.—SCRAPERS, ETC.

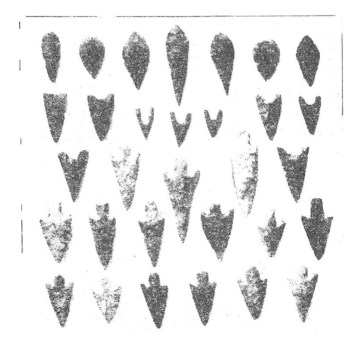

PLATE 7.

FIG. 13.—SMALL ROUGHLY CHIPPED CELTS.

$\frac{1}{4}$ *Full Size.*

A large number of roughly-chipped flint celts have been found in Co. Antrim, and the type is tolerably uniform, whether the specimens are collected from the raised beach gravels, the sites of settlements, river fords, or the general surface of the ground. The celts are from 3 to 4 inches long, and from 1 to $1\frac{1}{2}$ inches wide. The illustration gives an idea of the range of forms. It is taken from a photograph of specimens found in the river Bann, the sand-dunes at Portrush, and the hill-fort of Mount Sandal overlooking the salmon leap on the Bann, above Coleraine. Similar forms have been found at Toombridge, the gravels of Carnlough, Larne, Holywood, Cultra, and Ballyholme. See a communication from the author in the *Journal* of the Royal Historical and Archæological Association of Ireland, Vol. VIII., Ninth Series, 1887-8, p. 505.

FIG. 14.—FLINT PICKS AND POLISHED CELTS.

$\frac{1}{4}$ *Full Size.*

Among the various forms of worked flints collected in Antrim there is occasionally found a form that is more like a pick than a celt, being rudely pointed at one end, and it may have been used as an agricultural implement. It is quite distinct, and is shown by the upper central example on Fig. 14. On each side is one of the larger forms of flint celt. At the bottom are shown four celts polished at the lower or cutting edge. Rarely, flint celts are found with all the surface polished. No doubt many of the roughly-chipped celts found were intended by the maker to be polished more or less. In this, and all other classes of worked flints, the rudeness of the chipping is not necessarily an indication of antiquity.

FIG. 13.—SMALL ROUGHLY-CHIPPED CELTS.

PLATE 8.

FIG. 15.—MODERN REPRODUCTIONS.

$\frac{1}{4}$ *Full Size.*

This illustration is from a collection of recent reproductions of the ancient forms of arrow-heads and flint celts. As explained in the text, they are now made to meet the demand for Irish antiquities. This trade may be justified so long as the manufactured article is sold as a reproduction, and not as a genuine ancient Irish weapon ; but, unfortunately, the ignorance of collectors is such that they are left too often under the impression that the reproduction they have secured by purchase is really a genuine ancient weapon.

FIG. 16.—A MANUFACTURER OF REPRODUCTIONS IN FLINT.

This illustration shows how the modern maker of flint arrow-heads manipulates his material. Very much depends upon the character of the flint selected for manipulation. As the finished article must have an aged look, a fresh unaltered flint would not answer the maker's purpose ; therefore he carefully selects some of the indurated flints that occur where the Chalk is in contact with the Trap ; such flints are discoloured, and may be found of every shade from white to red, and objects made from them have the looked-for " patina " of age. If an ancient flint implement is broken, the " patina " will be found to coat the implement in lines parallel with the surface, but if a reproduction is broken, the colour of the material is the same all through. The modern maker of arrow-heads selects a suitable flake of indurated flint, and holds it in a fold of cloth, his coat-collar or any other cloth, and with a sharp rough splinter of hard trap he presses against the edge of the flint and skilfully removes the material chip by chip, first from one side, then the other, until he forms his outline, and thus with marvellous rapidity he can

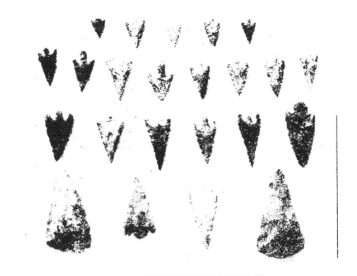

FIG. 15.—MODERN REPRODUCTIONS.

FIG. 16.—A MANUFACTURER OF REPRODUCTIONS IN FLINT.

CPSIA information can be obtained
at www.ICGtesting.com
Printed in the USA
BVHW04*0744011018
528775BV00026B/296/P